WEBSTER'S NEW WORLD™

POCKET SPANISH DICTIONARY

Spanish-English

English-Spanish

Series Editor:
Michael W. Keathley

Editors/Redactores:
Alicia de Benito Harland
Fernando León Solis
Hugh O'Donnell

Consulting Editor:
Michael Cunningham

MACMILLAN • USA

© Chambers Harrap Publishers Ltd. 1998

First published in Great Britain
as Harrap's Spanish Micro Dictionary, 1995
by Chambers Harrap Publishers Ltd
7 Hopetoun Crescent, Edinburgh EH7 4AY

MACMILLAN is a registered trademark of
Macmillan, Inc.

ISBN: 0-02-862383-5

Macmillan General Reference
A Simon & Schuster Macmillan Company
1633 Broadway
New York, NY 10019-6785

First published in the United States in 1995.

Manufactured in the United States of America

  4 5 6 7 8 9 10   99 00 01 02

Contents/Materias

Trademarks/Marcas Registradas

Preface

Based on the text of Harrap's *Micro Spanish Dictionary,* this handy dictionary provides a concise, up-to-date, reliable guide to the language that is particularly helpful for beginning and occasional learners. It provides a core vocabulary of over 25,000 of the most useful English and Spanish words and expressions with a focus on American forms. The dictionary is designed to be easily read and used, with bold headwords and a compact, time-saving format.

The dictionary's clear text gives maximum guidance in pinpointing exact language equivalents. The new system for Spanish alphabetical order has been adopted. In this system, **ch** and **ll** are no longer considered as separate letters of the alphabet, but each is incorporated at its respective position under **c** and **l**. Phrasal verbs are indicated by a bullet point • and are listed after the verb on which they are based (e.g., see entry for **get**). Numbers are used to divide grammatical categories of headwords with a solid block ▪ denoting meaning categories within longer entries (e.g., see entry for **do**). A number code (1–7) against a Spanish verb means that the verb is irregular. Model verbs for these irregular forms are displayed on page (**viii**). Patterns for other important irregular verbs are given along with regular verb conjugations on pages (**i–vii**). An asterisk against an English verb denotes that it is irregular. Forms for these verbs are located on pages (**xi**). A double asterisk against a Spanish noun, however, means that the feminine noun takes the masculine definite article **el** (e.g., **el agua**). The plural form is **las**. Finally, context indicators and labels are presented in Spanish in the Spanish section and in English in the English section. All labeling has been kept to a minimum so as not to distract the reader.

Guide to the pronunciation of Spanish

Letter	Phonetic symbol	Examples	Approximate English equivalent
Vowels:			
a	[a]	gato, amar, mesa	as in father, but shorter
e	[e]	estrella, vez, firme	as in labor
i	[i]	inicuo, iris	as in see, but shorter
o	[o]	bolo, cómodo, oso	between lot and taught
u	[u]	turuta, puro, tribu	as in food, but shorter, but u in -que- or -qui- and -gue- or -gui- is silent (unless -güe- or -güi-)
y	[i]	y	as in see, but shorter
Diphthongs:			
ai, ay	[ai]	baile, hay	as in life, aisle
au	[au]	fauna	as in fowl, house
ei, ey	[ei]	peine, ley	as in hate, feign
eu	[eu]	feudo	pronounce each vowel separately
oi, oy	[oi]	boina, hoy	as in boy
Semi-consonants:			
u	[w]	buey, cuando, fuiste	as in wait
i	[j]	viernes, vicio, ciudad, ciar	as in yes
y	[j]	yermo, ayer, rey	as in yes
Consonants:			
b	[b]	boda, burro, ambos	as in be
	[β]	haba, traba	a very light b
c	[k]	cabeza, cuco, acoso, frac	as in car, keep
	[θ]	cecina, cielo	as in thing, but in

			Andalusia and all of Latin America as s as in silly
ch	[tʃ]	**ch**epa, o**ch**o	as in *ch*amber
d	[d]	**d**edo, an**d**ar	as in *d*ay
	[ð]	**d**edo, ána**d**e, aba**d**	as in *th*is (often omitted in spoken Spanish when at the end of a word)
f	[f]	**f**iesta, a**f**ición	as in *f*or
g	[g]	**g**as, ran**g**o, **g**ula	as in *g*et
	[ɣ]	a**g**ua, a**g**osto, la**g**ar	a very light g
g	[x]	**g**enio, le**g**ión	similar to Scottish [x] in lo*ch*
h	—	**h**ambre, a**h**íto	Spanish h is silent
j	[x]	**j**abón, a**j**o, carca**j**	similar to Scottish [x] in lo*ch*
k	[k]	**k**ilo, **k**imono	as in *c*ar, *k*eep
l	[l]	**l**abio, hábi**l**, e**l**egante	as in *l*aw
ll	[ʎ]	**ll**uvia, ca**ll**e	similar to the sound in mi*lli*on
m	[m]	**m**ano, a**m**igo, ha**m**bre	as in *m*an
n	[n]	**n**ata, rató**n**, a**n**tes, e**n**emigo	as in *n*ight
ñ	[ŋ]	a**ñ**o, **ñ**o**ñ**o	similar to the sound in o*ni*on
p	[p]	**p**i**p**a, **p**elo	as in *p*oint
q	[k]	**q**uiosco, **q**uerer, alambi**q**ue	as in *c*ar
r(r)	[r]	pe**r**o, corre**r**, pad**r**e	always pronounced, rolled as in Scots
	[rr]	reí**r**, hon**r**ado, pe**rr**o	rr is a lengthened r sound
s	[s]	**s**auna, a**s**ado, corté**s**	similar to the s in hissing
t	[t]	**t**eja, es**t**én, a**t**raco	as in *t*ime
v	[b]	**v**erbena, **v**ena	as in *b*e
	[β]	a**v**e, vi**v**o	a very light b

w	[b]	**w**agón, **w**aterpolo	as in *be*
x	[ks]	é**x**ito, e**x**amen	as in e*x*ercise
	[s]	e**x**tensión	as in e*s*tate
z	[θ]	**z**orro, a**z**ul, ca**z**a, soe**z**	as in *th*ing, but in Andalusia and in all of Latin America as *s* in *s*illy

Stress rules

If a word ends in a vowel, **-n** or **-s**, the stress falls on the second last syllable:

mano, e**xa**men, boca**di**llos

If a word has any other ending, the stress falls on the last syllable:

ha**blar**, Ma**drid**, a**yer**

Exceptions to these rules carry a written accent on the stressed syllable:

cómodo, le**gió**n, **há**bil

Abbreviations

Abreviaturas

adjective	*a*	adjetivo
abbreviation	*abbr, abr*	abreviatura
adverb	*adv*	adverbio
somebody, someone	*algn*	alguien
Latin American	*Am*	hispano americano
article	*art*	artículo
conjunction	*conj*	conjunción
definite	*def*	definido
demonstrative	*dem*	demostrativo
feminine	*f*	femenino
familiar	*fam*	familiar
figurative use	*fig*	uso figurado
feminine plural	*fpl*	plural femenino
future	*fut*	futuro
impersonal	*impers*	impersonal
indefinite	*indef*	indefinido
indeterminate	*indet*	indeterminado
indicative	*indic*	indicativo
infinitive	*infin*	infinitivo
interjection	*interj*	interjección
interrogative	*interr*	interrogativo
invariable	*inv*	invariable
irregular	*irreg*	irregular
masculine	*m*	masculino
masculine plural	*mpl*	plural masculino
noun	*n*	nombre
personal	*pers*	personal
plural	*pl*	plural
possessive	*poss, pos*	posesivo
past participle	*pp*	participio pasado
preposition	*prep*	preposición
present	*pres*	presente
preterite	*pret*	pretérito

pronoun	*pron*	pronombre
past tense	*pt*	pretérito
relative	*rel*	relativo
somebody, someone	*sb*	alguien
singular	*sing*	singular
something	*sth*	algo
subjunctive	*subj*	subjuntivo
auxiliary verb	*v aux*	verbo auxiliar
intransitive verb	*vi*	verbo intransitivo
impersonal verb	*v impers*	verbo impersonal
reflexive verb	*vr*	verbo reflexivo
transitive verb	*vt*	verbo transitivo
cultural equivalent	≈	equivalencia cultural

A

a *prep* (*dirección*) to; **llegar a Valencia** to arrive in Valencia; **subir al tren** to get on the train. ▪ (*lugar*) at, on; **a la derecha** on the right; **a lo lejos** in the distance; **a mi lado** next to me; **al sol** in the sun. ▪ (*tiempo*) at; **a las doce** at twelve o'clock; **a los tres meses/la media hora** three months/half an hour later; **al final** in the end; **al principio** at first. ▪ (*distancia*) **a cien kilómetros de aquí** a hundred kilometers from here. ▪ (*manera*) **a mano** by hand. ▪ (*proporción*) **a 90 kilómetros por hora** at 90 kilometers an hour; **a 300 pesetas el kilo** three hundred pesetas a kilo; **tres veces a la semana** three times a week. ▪ **ganar cuatro a dos** to win four (to) two. ▪ (*complemento*) to; (*procedencia*) from; **díselo a Javier** tell Javier; **te lo di a ti** I gave it to you; **comprarle algo a algn** to buy sth from sb; (*para algn*) to buy sth for sb; **saludé a tu tía** I said hello to your aunt. ▪ *fam* **ir a por algn/algo** to go and get sb/sth. ▪ (*verbo + a + infinitivo*) to; **aprender a nadar** to learn (how) to swim. ▪ **a decir verdad** to tell (you) the truth; **a no ser que** unless; **a ver** let's see; **¡a comer!** food's ready!; **¡a dormir!** bedtime!; **¿a que no lo haces?** (*desafío*) I bet you don't do it!

abajo **1** *adv* (*en una casa*) downstairs; (*dirección*) down; **el piso de a.** the apartment downstairs; **aquí a.** down there/here; **la parte de a.** the bottom (part); **más a.** further down; **hacia a.** down; **venirse a.** (*edificio*) to fall down. **2** *interj* **¡a. la censura!** down with censorship!

abalanzarse [4] *vr* **a. sobre/contra** to rush towards.

abalear *vt Am* to shoot at.

abandonar *vt* (*lugar*) to leave; (*persona, cosa*) to abandon; (*proyecto, plan*) to give up.

abanico *m* fan; (*gama*) range.

abarcar [1] *vt* to embrace; *Am* (*acaparar*) to monopolize.

abarrotado,-a *a* crammed (**de** with).

abarrotes *mpl Am* groceries.

abastecer **1** *vt* to supply. **2 abastecerse** *vr* to stock up (**de** o **con** with).

abatible *a* folding; **asiento a.** folding seat.

abatir **1** *vt* (*derribar*) to knock down; (*desanimar*) to depress. **2 abatirse** *vr* (*desanimarse*) to become depressed.

abdicar [1] *vti* to abdicate.

abdominales *mpl* sit-ups.

abecedario *m* alphabet.

abedul *m* birch.

abeja *f* bee; **a. reina** queen bee.

abejorro *m* bumblebee.

abertura *f* (*hueco*) opening; (*grieta*) crack.

abeto *m* fir (tree).

abierto,-a *a* open; (*grifo*) (turned) on; (*persona*) open-minded.

abismo *m* abyss.

ablandar **1** *vt* to soften. **2 ablandarse** *vr* to go soft; *fig* (*persona*) to mellow.

abnegado,-a *a* selfless.

abogado,-a *mf* lawyer; (*en tribunal supremo*) attorney; **a. defensor** counsel for the defense.

abolir *vt defectivo* to abolish.

abollar *vt* to dent.

abonado,-a *mf* subscriber.

abono *m* (*producto*) fertilizer; (*estiércol*) manure; (*pago*) payment; (*billete*) season ticket.

aborrecer *vt* to detest.

aborto *m* miscarriage; (*provocado*) abortion.

abrasar **1** *vti* to scorch. **2 abrasarse** *vr* to burn.

abrazadera *f* clamp.

abrazar [4] **1** *vt* to embrace. **2 abrazarse** *vr* **abrazarse a algn** to embrace sb; **se abrazaron** they embraced each other.

abrazo *m* hug.

abrelatas *m inv* can opener.

abreviar 1 *vt* to shorten; (*texto*) to abridge; (*palabra*) to abbreviate. **2** *vi* to be quick *o* brief; **para a.** to cut a long story short.

abreviatura *f* abbreviation.

abridor *m* (*de latas, botellas*) opener.

abrigado,-a *a* wrapped up.

abrigar [7] **1** *vt* to keep warm; (*esperanza*) to cherish; (*duda*) to harbor. **2** *vi* **esta chaqueta abriga mucho** this cardigan is very warm.

abrigo *m* (*prenda*) coat; **ropa de a.** warm clothes *pl*.

abril *m* April.

abrir¹ *m* **en un a. y cerrar de ojos** in the twinkling of an eye.

abrir² (*pp* **abierto**) **1** *vi* to open. **2** *vt* to open; (*cremallera*) to undo; (*gas, grifo*) to turn on. **3 abrirse** *vr* to open; **abrirse paso** to make one's way.

abrochar *vt*, **abrocharse** *vr* (*botones*) to do up; (*camisa*) to button (up); (*cinturón*) to fasten; (*zapatos*) to tie up; (*cremallera*) to do up.

abrumar *vt* to overwhelm.

abrupto,-a *a* (*terreno*) steep.

absceso *m* abscess.

absolutamente *adv* absolutely.

absoluto,-a *a* absolute; **en a.** not at all.

absolver [4] (*pp* **absuelto**) *vt* to acquit.

absorbente *a* (*papel*) absorbent; (*fascinante*) engrossing.

absorber *vt* to absorb.

absorto,-a *a* engrossed (**en** in).

abstenerse *vr* to abstain (**de** from); (*privarse*) refrain (**de** from).

abstracto,-a *a* abstract.

abstraído,-a *a* (*ensimismado*) engrossed (**en** in).

absuelto,-a *a pp de* **absolver.**

absurdo,-a *a* absurd.

abuchear *vt* to boo.

abuela *f* grandmother; *fam* grandma, granny.

abuelo *m* grandfather; *fam* gran-

dad, grandpa; **abuelos** grandparents.

abultado,-a *a* bulky.

abundancia *f* abundance; . . . **en a.** plenty of . . .

abundante *a* abundant.

aburrido,-a *a* (*ser*) to be boring; **estar a.** to be bored; (*harto*) to be tired (**de** of).

aburrimiento *m* boredom; **¡qué a.!** what a bore!.

aburrir 1 *vt* to bore. **2 aburrirse** *vr* to get bored.

abusar *vi* (*propasarse*) to go too far; **a. de** (*situación, persona*) to take (unfair) advantage of; (*poder, amabilidad*) to abuse; **a. de la bebida/del tabaco** to drink/smoke too much *o* to excess.

abuso *m* abuse.

a. C. *abr de* **antes de Cristo** before Christ, BC.

acá *adv* (*lugar*) over here; **más a.** nearer; **¡ven a.!** come here!

acabar 1 *vt* to finish (off); (*completar*) to complete. **2** *vi* to finish; **a. de . . .** to have just . . .; **acaba de entrar** he has just come in; **acabaron casándose** *o* **por casarse** they ended up getting married. **3 acabarse** *vr* to finish; **se nos acabó la gasolina** we ran out of gas.

acacia *f* acacia.

academia *f* academy.

académico,-a *a & mf* academic.

acalorado,-a *a* hot; (*debate etc*) heated.

acampar *vi* to camp.

acantilado *m* cliff.

acaparar *vt* (*productos*) to hoard; (*mercado*) to corner.

acariciar *vt* to caress; (*pelo, animal*) to stroke.

acarrear *vt* (*transportar*) to transport; (*conllevar*) to entail.

acaso *adv* perhaps, maybe; **por si a.** just in case; **si a. viene . . .** if he should come . . .

acatar *vt* to comply with.

acatarrado,-a *a* **estar a.** to have a cold.

acceder *vi* **a. a** (*consentir*) to consent to.

accesible *a* accessible; (*persona*) approachable.

acceso *m* (*entrada*) access; (*en carretera*) approach.

accesorio,-a *a* & *m* accessory.

accidentado,-a 1 *a* (*terreno*) uneven; (*viaje, vida*) eventful. **2** *mf* casualty.

accidental *a* accidental; **un encuentro a.** a chance meeting.

accidente *m* accident; **a. laboral** industrial accident.

acción *f* action; (*acto*) act; (*en la bolsa*) share; **poner en a.** to put into action; **película de a.** adventure film.

accionar *vt* to drive.

accionista *mf* shareholder.

acechar *vt* to lie in wait for.

aceite *m* oil; **a. de girasol/maíz/oliva** sunflower/corn/olive oil.

aceituna *f* olive; **a. rellena** stuffed olive.

acelerador *m* accelerator.

acelerar *vti* to accelerate.

acento *m* accent; (*énfasis*) stress.

acentuar 1 *vt* to stress. **2 acentuarse** *vr* to become more pronounced.

aceptar *vt* to accept.

acequia *f* irrigation ditch *o* channel.

acera *f* sidewalk.

acerca *adv* **a. de** about.

acercar [1] **1** *vt* to bring (over). **2 acercarse** *vr* to approach (**a -**); (*ir*) to go; (*venir*) to come.

acero *m* steel; **a. inoxidable** stainless steel.

acérrimo,-a *a* (*partidario*) staunch; (*enemigo*) bitter.

acertado,-a *a* (*solución*) correct; (*decisión*) wise.

acertar [1] **1** *vt* (*pregunta*) to get right; (*adivinar*) to guess correctly. **2** *vi* to be right.

acertijo *m* riddle.

achacar [1] *vt* (*atribuir*) to attribute.

achaque *m* ailment.

achicharrar *vt* to burn to a crisp.

acholado,-a *a Am* mixed.

achuchar *vt* (*empujar*) to shove.

aciago,-a *a* ill-fated.

acicalarse *vr* to dress up.

acidez *f* (*de sabor*) sharpness; **a. de estómago** heartburn.

ácido,-a 1 *a* (*sabor*) sharp. **2** *m* acid.

acierto *m* (*buena decisión*) good choice.

aclamar *vt* to acclaim.

aclarado *m* rinse.

aclarar 1 *vt* (*explicar*) to clarify; (*color*) to make lighter; (*enjuagar*) to rinse. **2** *v impers* (*tiempo*) to clear (up). **3 aclararse** *vr* **aclararse la voz** to clear one's throat.

aclimatarse *vr* **a. a algo** to get used to sth.

acné *m* acne.

acogedor,-a *a* (*habitación*) cozy.

acoger [5] **1** *vt* (*recibir*) to receive; (*persona desvalida*) to take in. **2 acogerse** *vr* **acogerse a** to take refuge in; **acogerse a la ley** to have recourse to the law.

acometer *vt* (*emprender*) to undertake; (*atacar*) to attack.

acomodado,-a *a* well-off.

acomodador,-a *mf* usher.

acomodar 1 *vt* (*alojar*) to accommodate; (*en cine etc*) to find a place for. **2 acomodarse** *vr* (*instalarse*) to make oneself comfortable; (*adaptarse*) to adapt.

acompañante 1 *mf* companion. **2** *a* accompanying.

acompañar *vt* to accompany; **¿te acompaño a casa?** can I walk you home?; (*en funeral*) **le acompaño en el sentimiento** my condolences.

acomplejar 1 *vt* to give a complex. **2 acomplejarse** *vr* **acomplejarse por** to develop a complex about.

acondicionado,-a *a* **aire a.** air conditioning.

acondicionador *m* conditioner.

aconsejar *vt* to advise.

acontecimiento *m* event.

acopio *m* **hacer a. de** to store.

acordar [2] **1** *vt* to agree; (*decidir*) to decide. **2 acordarse** *vr* to remember.

acordeón *m* accordion.

acordonar *vt* (*zona*) to cordon off.

acorralar *vt* to corner.

acortar *vt* to shorten.

acoso *m* harassment; **a. sexual** sexual harassment.

acostar [2] **1** *vt* to put to bed. **2 acostarse** *vr* to go to bed.

acostumbrado,-a *a* usual; **es lo a.** it is the custom; **a. al frío/calor** used to the cold/heat.

acostumbrar 1 *vi* **a. a** (*soler*) to be in the habit of. **2** *vt* **a. a algn a algo** (*habituar*) to get sb used to sth. **3 acostumbrarse** *vr* (*habituarse*) to get used (**a** to).

acotejar *vt Am* to arrange.

acre *m* (*medida*) acre.

acreditar *vt* to be a credit to; (*probar*) to prove.

acreedor,-a *mf* creditor.

acrílico,-a *a* acrylic.

acriollarse *vr Am* to adopt local customs.

acrobacia *f* acrobatics *sing*.

acta *f* (*de reunión*) minutes *pl*; (*certificado*) certificate.

actitud *f* attitude.

actividad *f* activity.

activo,-a *a* active.

acto *m* act; (*ceremonia*) ceremony; (*de teatro*) act; **en el a.** at once; **a. seguido** immediately afterwards.

actor *m* actor.

actriz *f* actress.

actuación *f* performance; (*intervención*) intervention.

actual *a* current, present.

actualidad *f* present time; (*hechos*) current affairs *pl*; **en la a.** at present.

actualmente *adv* (*hoy en día*) nowadays.

actuar *vi* to act.

acuarela *f* watercolor.

acuario *m* aquarium.

acuciante *a* urgent.

acudir *vi* (*ir*) to go; (*venir*) to come.

acuerdo *m* agreement; **¡de a.!** all right!, OK!; **de a. con** in accordance with; **ponerse de a.** to agree.

acumular *vt*, **acumularse** *vr* to accumulate.

acuñar *vt* (*moneda*) to mint; (*frase*) to coin.

acurrucarse [1] *vr* to curl up.

acusación *f* accusation; (*en juicio*) charge.

acusado,-a 1 *mf* accused. **2** *a* (*marcado*) marked.

acusar 1 *vt* to accuse (**de** of); (*en juicio*) to charge (**de** with). **2 acusarse** *vr* (*acentuarse*) to become more pronounced.

acústica *f* acoustics *sing*.

acústico,-a *a* acoustic.

adaptador *m* adapter.

adaptar 1 *vt* to adapt; (*ajustar*) to adjust. **2 adaptarse** *vr* to adapt (oneself) (**a** to).

adecuado,-a *a* appropriate.

a. de J. C. *abr de* **antes de Jesucristo** before Christ, BC.

adelantado,-a *a* advanced; (*desarrollado*) developed; (*reloj*) fast; **pagar por a.** to pay in advance.

adelantamiento *m* overtaking.

adelantar 1 *vt* to move forward; (*reloj*) to put forward; (*en carretera*) to overtake; (*fecha*) to move forward. **2** *vi* to advance; (*progresar*) to make progress; (*reloj*) to be fast. **3 adelantarse** *vr* (*ir delante*) to go ahead; (*reloj*) to be fast.

adelante 1 *adv* forward; **más a.** (*lugar*) further on; (*tiempo*) later. **2** *interj* **¡a!** (*pase*) come in!

adelanto *m* advance; (*progreso*) progress; **el reloj lleva diez minutos de a.** the watch is ten minutes fast.

adelgazar [4] *vi* to slim.

ademán *m* gesture.

además *adv* moreover, furthermore; **a. de él** besides him.

adherir [5] **1** vt to stick on. **2 adherirse** vr **adherirse a** to adhere to.

adhesión f adhesion.

adicción f addiction.

adicto,-a 1 mf addict. **2** a addicted (**a** to).

adiestrar vt to train.

adinerado,-a a wealthy.

adiós (pl **adioses**) interj goodbye; fam bye-bye; (al cruzarse) hello.

aditivo,-a a & m additive.

adivinanza f riddle.

adivinar vt to guess.

adjetivo m adjective.

adjudicar 1 vt (premio, contrato) to award; (en subasta) to sell. **2 adjudicarse** vr to appropriate.

adjuntar vt to enclose.

adjunto,-a 1 a enclosed, attached. **2** mf (profesor) assistant teacher.

administración f (gobierno) authorities pl; (de empresa) management; (oficina) (branch) office; **a. central** (gobierno) central government; **a. pública** civil service.

administrador,-a 1 mf administrator. **2** a administrating.

administrar vt to administer; (dirigir) to run.

administrativo,-a 1 a administrative. **2** mf (funcionario) official.

admiración f admiration; (ortográfica) exclamation mark.

admirar 1 vt to admire; (sorprender) to amaze. **2 admirarse** vr to be amazed.

admisión f admission.

admitir vt to let in; (aceptar) to accept; (permitir) to allow; (reconocer) to acknowledge.

ADN m abr de **ácido desoxirribonucleico** deoxyribonucleic acid, DNA.

adobe m adobe.

adobo m marinade.

adolescencia f adolescence.

adolescente a & mf adolescent.

adónde adv where (to)?

adonde adv where.

adondequiera adv wherever.

adopción f adoption.

adoptar vt to adopt.

adoptivo,-a a (hijo) adopted; (padres) adoptive.

adorar vt to worship.

adormecer 1 vt to make sleepy. **2 adormecerse** vr (dormirse) to doze off; (brazo etc) to go numb.

adornar vt to adorn.

adorno m decoration; **de a.** decorative.

adosado,-a a adjacent; (casa) semidetached.

adquirir vt to acquire; (comprar) to purchase.

adquisición f acquisition; (compra) purchase.

adrede adv deliberately, on purpose.

aduana f customs pl.

aduanero,-a mf customs officer.

aducir vt to adduce.

adueñarse vr a. **de** to take over.

aduje pt indef de **aducir**.

adular vt to adulate.

adulterar vt to adulterate.

adulterio m adultery.

adulto,-a a & mf adult.

aduzco indic pres de **aducir**.

adverbio m adverb.

adversario,-a 1 mf opponent. **2** a opposing.

adversidad f adversity; (revés) setback.

adverso,-a a adverse.

advertencia f warning.

advertir [5] vt to warn; (informar) to advise; (notar) to notice.

adviento m Advent.

adyacente a adjacent.

aéreo,-a a aerial; (correo, transporte) air; **por vía aerea** by air.

aerodinámico,-a a aerodynamic; **de línea aerodinámica** streamlined.

aeromoza f Am flight attendant.

aeronáutico,-a a **la industria aeronáutica** the aeronautics industry.

aeroplano m light airplane.

aeropuerto m airport.

aerosol m aerosol.

afable *a* affable.

afán *m* (*pl* **afanes**) (*esfuerzo*) effort; (*celo*) zeal.

afanarse *vr* **a. por conseguir algo** to do one's best to achieve sth.

afección *f* disease.

afectar *vt.* **a** to affect; **le afectó mucho** she was deeply affected.

afecto *m* affection; **tomarle a. a algn** to become fond of sb.

afectuoso,-a *a* affectionate.

afeitar *vt*, **afeitarse** *vr* to shave.

afeminado,-a *a* effeminate.

aferrarse *vr* to cling (**a** to).

afianzar [4] *vt* to strengthen.

afición *f* liking; **tiene a. por la música** he is fond of music; (*de deporte*) **la a.** the fans *pl*.

aficionado,-a 1 *mf* enthusiast; (*no profesional*) amateur. **2** *a* keen; (*no profesional*) amateur; **ser a. a algo** to be fond of sth.

aficionarse *vr* to take a liking (**a** to).

afilado,-a *a* sharp.

afiliarse *vr* **a. a** to join, to become a member of.

afinar *vt* (*puntería*) to sharpen; (*instrumento*) to tune.

afinidad *f* affinity.

afirmación *f* statement.

afirmar *vt* (*aseverar*) to state; (*afianzar*) to strengthen.

afligir [6] **1** *vt* to afflict. **2 afligirse** *vr* to be distressed.

aflojar 1 *vt* to loosen. **2 aflojarse** *vr* (*rueda*) to work loose.

afluencia *f* influx; **gran a. de público** great numbers of people.

afluente *a* tributary.

afónico,-a *a* **estar a.** to have lost one's voice.

afortunado,-a *a* lucky, fortunate.

afrontar *vt* to confront; **a. las consecuencias** to face the consequences.

afuera 1 *adv* outside; **la parte de a.** the outside; **más a.** further out. **2 afueras** *fpl* outskirts.

agachar 1 *vt* to lower. **2 agacharse** *vr* to duck.

agarrar 1 *vt* to grasp; *Am* to take; **agárralo fuerte** hold it tight. **2 agarrarse** *vr* to hold on.

agasajar *vt* to smother with attentions.

agazaparse *vr* to crouch (down).

agencia *f* agency; (*sucursal*) branch; **a. de viajes** travel agency; **a. de seguros** insurance agency; **a. inmobiliaria** estate agency.

agenda *f* diary.

agente *mf* agent; **a. de policía** (*hombre*) policeman; (*mujer*) policewoman; **a. de seguros** insurance broker.

ágil *a* agile.

agilidad *f* agility.

agilizar [4] *vt* (*trámites*) to speed up.

agitación *f* agitation; (*inquietud*) restlessness.

agitado,-a *a* agitated; (*persona*) anxious; (*mar*) rough.

agitar 1 *vt* (*botella*) to shake. **2 agitarse** *vr* (*persona*) to become agitated.

aglomeración *f* (*de gente*) crowd.

agobiante *a* (*trabajo*) overwhelming; (*lugar*) claustrophobic; (*calor*) oppressive; (*persona*) tiresome.

agobiar 1 *vt* to overwhelm. **2 agobiarse** *vr* (*angustiarse*) to worry too much.

agobio *m* (*angustia*) anxiety; (*sofoco*) suffocation.

agolparse *vr* to crowd.

agonía *f* agony, last days.

agonizar [4] *vi* to be dying.

agosto *m* August.

agotado,-a *a* (*cansado*) exhausted; (*existencias*) sold out; (*provisiones*) exhausted; (*libro*) out of print.

agotador,-a *a* exhausting.

agotamiento *m* exhaustion.

agotar 1 *vt* (*cansar*) to exhaust; (*acabar*) to use up (completely). **2 agotarse** *vr* (*acabarse*) to run out; (*producto*) to be sold out; (*persona*) to become exhausted *o* tired out.

agradable *a* pleasant.

agradar *vi* to please; **no me agrada** I don't like it.

agradecer *vt* (*dar las gracias*) to thank for; (*estar agradecido*) to be grateful to; **te lo agradezco mucho** thank you very much.

agradecimiento *m* gratitude.

agrandar 1 *vt* to enlarge. 2 **agrandarse** *vr* to become larger.

agrario,-a *a* agrarian.

agravar 1 *vt* to aggravate. 2 **agravarse** *vr* to get worse.

agredir *vt defectivo* to assault.

agregado,-a *a* **profesor a.** (*de escuela*) secondary school teacher; (*de universidad*) teaching assistant.

agregar [7] *vt* (*añadir*) to add.

agresión *f* aggression.

agresivo,-a *a* aggressive.

agrícola *a* agricultural.

agricultor,-a *mf* farmer.

agricultura *f* agriculture.

agrietar 1 *vt* to crack; (*piel, labios*) to chap. 2 **agrietarse** *vr* to crack; (*piel*) to get chapped.

agringarse [7] *vr Am* to behave like a gringo.

agrio,-a *a* sour.

agropecuario,-a *a* agricultural.

agrupación *f* association.

agua** *f* water; **a. potable** drinking water; **a. corriente/del grifo** running/tap water; **a. dulce/salada** fresh/salt water; **a. mineral sin/con gas** still/fizzy mineral water.

aguacate *m* (*fruto*) avocado (pear).

aguacero *m* downpour.

aguanieve *f* sleet.

aguantar 1 *vt* (*soportar*) to tolerate; (*sostener*) to support; **no lo aguanto más** I can't stand it any longer; **aguanta la respiración** hold your breath. 2 **aguantarse** *vr* (*contenerse*) to keep back; (*resignarse*) to resign oneself; **no pude aguantarme la risa** I couldn't help laughing.

aguardar 1 *vt* to await. 2 *vi* to wait.

aguardiente *m* brandy.

aguarrás *m* turpentine.

aguatero,-a *mf Am* water-carrier o seller.

agudizar [4] *vt*, **agudizarse** *vr* to intensify.

agudo,-a *a* (*dolor*) acute; (*voz*) high-pitched; (*sonido*) high.

aguijón *m* sting.

águila** *f* eagle.

aguja *f* needle; (*de reloj*) hand; (*de tocadiscos*) stylus.

agujerear *vt* to make holes in.

agujero *m* hole; **a. negro** black hole.

agujetas *fpl* **tener a.** to be stiff.

aguzar [4] *vt* **a. el oído** to prick up one's ears; **a. la vista** to look attentively.

ahí *adv* there; **a. está** there he/she/ it is; **por a.** (*en esa dirección*) that way; (*aproximadamente*) over there.

ahínco *m* **con a.** eagerly.

ahogado,-a 1 *a* (*en líquido*) drowned; (*asfixiado*) suffocated; **morir a.** to drown. 2 *mf* drowned person.

ahogar [7] *vt*, **ahogarse** *vr* (*en líquido*) to drown; (*asfixiar*) to suffocate; (*motor*) to flood.

ahora 1 *adv* now; **a. mismo** right now; **de a. en adelante** from now on; **por a.** for the time being; **a. voy** I'm coming; **hasta a.** (*hasta el momento*) until now, so far; (*hasta luego*) see you later. 2 *conj* **a. bien** (*sin embargo*) however.

ahorcar [1] 1 *vt* to hang. 2 **ahorcarse** *vr* to hang oneself.

ahorita *adv Am* right now.

ahorrar *vt* to save.

ahorros *mpl* savings; **caja de a.** savings bank.

ahuevado,-a *a Am* stupid.

ahumado,-a *a* smoked; (*bacon*) smoky.

ahuyentar *vt* to scare away.

aindiado,-a *a Am* Indian-like.

airado,-a *a* angry.

aire *m* air; (*de automóvil*) choke; (*viento*) wind; (*aspecto*) appearance; **a. acondicionado** air conditioning; **al a.** (*al descubierto*) uncovered; **a la libre** in the open air; **en el a.** (*pendiente*) in the air; **tomar el a.** to get some fresh air; **cambiar de aires** to change one's surroundings; **darse aires** to put on airs.

aislado,-a *a* isolated; (*cable*) insulated.

aislante 1 *a* **cinta a.** insulating tape. **2** *m* insulator.

aislar *vt* to isolate; (*cable*) to insulate.

ajedrez *m* (*juego*) chess; (*piezas y tablero*) chess set.

ajeno,-a *a* belonging to other people; **por causas ajenas a nuestra voluntad** for reasons beyond our control.

ajetreado,-a *a* hectic.

ajo *m* garlic; **cabeza/diente de a.** head/clove of garlic.

ajustado,-a *a* tight.

ajustar *vt* to adjust; (*apretar*) to tighten.

ajuste *m* adjustment; (*de precio*) fixing; (*de cuenta*) settlement; **a. de cuentas** settling of scores.

ajusticiar *vt* to execute.

al (*contracción de* **a** & **el**) *ver* **a**; (**al** + *infinitivo*) **al salir** on leaving.

ala *f* wing; (*de sombrero*) brim.

alabar *vt* to praise.

alabastro *m* alabaster.

alambrada *f*, **alambrado** *m* barbed wire fence.

alambre *m* wire; **a. de púas** barbed wire.

álamo *m* poplar.

alarde *m* (*ostentación*) bragging; **hacer a. de** to show off.

alardear *vi* to brag.

alargadera *f* (*cable*) extension.

alargado,-a *a* elongated.

alargar [7] **1** *vt* to lengthen; (*estirar*) to stretch; (*prolongar*) to prolong; (*dar*) to pass. **2 alargarse** *vr* to get longer; (*prolongarse*) to go on.

alarido *m* shriek; **dar una a.** to howl.

alarma *f* alarm; **falsa a.** false alarm; **señal de a.** alarm (signal).

alarmar 1 *vt* to alarm. **2 alarmarse** *vr* to be alarmed.

alba** *f* dawn.

albañil *m* bricklayer; (*obrero*) building worker.

albaricoque *m* (*fruta*) apricot; (*árbol*) apricot tree.

alberca *f* (*poza*) (small) reservoir.

albergar [7] **1** *vt* (*alojar*) to house. **2 albergarse** *vr* to stay.

albergue *m* (*lugar*) hostel; (*refugio*) refuge; **a. juvenil** youth hostel.

albino,-a *a* & *mf* albino.

albóndiga *f* meatball.

albornoz *m* bathrobe.

alborotar 1 *vt* (*desordenar*) to turn upside down. **2** *vi* to make a racket. **3 alborotarse** *vr* to get excited; (*mar*) to get rough.

albufera *f* lagoon.

álbum *m* album.

alcachofa *f* artichoke.

alcalde *m* mayor.

alcaldesa *f* mayoress.

alcance *m* reach; **dar a. a** to catch up with; **fuera del a. de los niños** out of the reach of children.

alcantarilla *f* sewer; (*boca*) drain.

alcanzar [4] **1** *vt* to reach; (*persona*) to catch up with; (*conseguir*) to achieve. **2** *vi* (*ser suficiente*) to be sufficient.

alcaparra *f* (*fruto*) caper.

alcayata *f* hook.

alcazaba *f* citadel.

alcázar *m* (*fortaleza*) fortress; (*castillo*) castle.

alcoba *f* bedroom.

alcohol *m* alcohol.

alcoholemia *f* **prueba de a.** breath test.

alcohólico,-a *a* & *mf* alcoholic.

alcoholímetro *m* Breathalyzer®.

alcornoque *m* cork oak.

alcurnia *f* ancestry.

aldea *f* village.

aleccionador,-a *a* (*ejemplar*) exemplary.

alegar [7] *vt* (*aducir*) to claim.

alegrar 1 *vt* (*complacer*) to make glad; **me alegra que se lo hayas dicho 1** am glad you told her. **2 alegrarse** *vr* to be glad; **me alegro de verte** I am pleased to see you.

alegre *a* (*contento*) glad; (*color*) bright; (*música*) lively.

alegría *f* happiness.

alejado,-a *a* remote.

alejar 1 *vt* to move further away. **2 alejarse** *vr* to go away.

alemán,-ana 1 *a* & *mf* German. **2** *m* (*idioma*) German.

alentar [1] *vt* to encourage.

alergia *f* allergy.

alérgico,-a *a* allergic.

alerta *f* & *a* alert.

aleta *f* (*de pez*) fin; (*de foca, de nadador*) flipper.

aletargar [7] **1** *vt* to make lethargic. **2 aletargarse** *vr* to become lethargic.

aletear *vi* to flutter *o* flap its wings.

alfabetización *f* **campaña de a.** literacy campaign.

alfabeto *m* alphabet.

alfalfa *f* alfalfa grass.

alfarería *f* pottery.

alféizar *m* windowsill.

alférez *m* second lieutenant.

alfil *m* (*en ajedrez*) bishop.

alfiler *m* pin.

alfombra *f* rug; (*moqueta*) carpet.

alga *f* (*marina*) seaweed.

álgebra** *f* algebra.

álgido,-a *a* **el punto a.** the climax.

algo 1 *pron indef* (*afirmativo*) something; (*interrogativo*) anything; (*cantidad indeterminada*) some; **a. así** something like that; **¿a. más?** anything else?; **¿queda a. de pastel?** is there any cake left? **2** *adv* (*un poco*) somewhat; **está a. mejor** she's feeling a bit better.

algodón *m* cotton.

alguacil *m* bailiff.

alguien *pron indef* (*afirmativo*) somebody, someone; (*interrogativo*) anybody, anyone.

algún *a* (*delante de nombres masculinos en singular*) *ver* **alguno,-a.**

alguno,-a 1 *a* (*delante de nombre*) (*afirmativo*) some; (*interrogativo*) any; **alguna que otra vez** now and then; **¿le has visto alguna vez?** have you ever seen him?; **no vino persona alguna** nobody came. **2** *pron indef* (*afirmativo*) someone, somebody; (*interrogativo*) anyone, anybody; **algunos,-as** some (people).

alhaja *f* jewel.

alhelí *m* (*pl* alhelíes) wallflower.

aliado,-a *a* allied.

alianza *f* (*pacto*) alliance; (*anillo*) wedding ring.

aliarse *vr* to ally, to become allies.

alicates *mpl* pliers *pl*.

aliciente *m* (*atractivo*) charm; (*incentivo*) incentive.

aliento *m* breath; **sin a.** breathless.

aligerar 1 *vt* (*carga*) to lighten; (*acelerar*) to speed up; **a. el paso** to quicken one's pace. **2** *vi fam* **¡aligera!** hurry up!

alijo *m* haul; **un a. de drogas** a consignment of drugs.

alimaña *f* vermin.

alimentación *f* (*comida*) food; (*acción*) feeding.

alimentar 1 *vt* (*dar alimento*) to feed; (*ser nutritivo para*) to be nutritious for. **2 alimentarse** *vr* **alimentarse con** *o* **de** to live on.

alimenticio,-a *a* nutritious; **valor a.** nutritional value.

alimento *m* food.

alinear 1 *vt* to align. **2 alinearse** *vr* to line up.

aliñar *vt* to season; (*ensalada*) to dress.

alistar *vt*, **alistarse** *vr* (*en el ejército*) to enlist.

aliviar 1 *vt* (*dolor*) to relieve; (*carga*) to lighten. **2 aliviarse** *vr* (*dolor*) to diminish.

allá *adv* (*lugar alejado*) over there; **a. abajo/arriba** down/up there; **más a.** further on; **más a. de** beyond; **a. tú** that's your problem.

allí *adv* there; **a. abajo/arriba** down/up there; **por a.** (*movimiento*) that way; (*posición*) over there.

alma** *f* soul.

almacén *m* (*local*) warehouse; **grandes almacenes** department store.

almacenar *vt* to store.

almanaque *m* calendar.

almeja *f* clam.

almendra *f* almond.

almendro *m* almond tree.

almíbar *m* syrup.

almirante *m* admiral.

almizcle *m* musk.

almohada *f* pillow.

almohadón *m* large pillow.

almorrana *f* *fam* pile.

almorzar [2] 1 *vi* to have lunch. 2 *vt* to have for lunch.

almuerzo *m* lunch.

aló *interj Am* hello.

alojar 1 *vt* to accommodate. 2 **alojarse** *vr* to stay.

alojamiento *m* accommodations; **dar a.** to accommodate.

alondra *f* lark.

alpargata *f* canvas sandal.

alpinismo *m* mountaineering.

alpinista *mf* mountaineer.

alquilar *vt* to hire; (*pisos, casas*) to rent; **'se alquila'** 'to let', 'for rent'.

alquiler *m* (*acción*) hiring; (*de pisos, casas*) letting; (*precio*) rental; (*de pisos, casas*) rent; **a. de coches** car rental; **de a.** (*pisos, casas*) to let; (*coche*) for hire; **en una casa de a.** in a rented house.

alquitrán *m* tar.

alrededor 1 *adv* (*lugar*) round. 2 *prep* **a. de** round; **a. de quince** about fifteen. 3 **alrededores** *mpl* surrounding area *sing*.

alta *f* **dar de** o **el a.** (*a un enfermo*) to discharge from hospital.

altamente *adv* extremely.

altanero,-a *a* arrogant.

altar *m* altar.

altavoz *m* loudspeaker.

alteración *f* (*cambio*) alteration; (*alboroto*) quarrel; (*excitación*) agitation.

alterar 1 *vt* to alter. 2 **alterarse** *vr* (*inquietarse*) to be upset.

altercado *m* argument.

alternar 1 *vt* to alternate. 2 *vi* (*relacionarse*) to socialize. 3 **alternarse** *vr* to alternate.

alternativa *f* alternative.

alterno,-a *a* alternate.

altibajos *mpl* ups and downs.

altitud *f* altitude.

altivez *f* arrogance.

alto¹ *m* (*interrupción*) stop; **dar el a. a algn** to tell sb to stop; **un a. el fuego** a cease-fire.

alto,-a² 1 *a* (*persona, árbol, edificio*) tall; (*montaña, techo, presión*) high; (*sonido*) loud; (*precio, tecnología*) high; (*agudo*) high; **en lo a.** at the top; **clase alta** upper class; **en voz alta** aloud; **a altas horas de la noche** late at night. 2 *adv* high; (*fuerte*) loud; **¡habla más a.!** speak up. 3 *m* (*altura*) height; **¿cuánto tiene de a.?** how tall/high is it?

altoparlante *m* *Am* loudspeaker.

altura *f* height; (*nivel*) level; **de diez metros de a.** ten meters high; **estar a la a. de las circunstancias** to meet the challenge; *fig* **a estas alturas** by now.

alubia *f* bean.

alud *m* avalanche.

aludir *vi* to allude.

alumbrar *vt* (*iluminar*) to illuminate; (*parir*) to give birth to.

aluminio *m* aluminum.

alumno,-a *mf* (*de colegio*) pupil; (*de Universidad*) student.

alusión *f* allusion.

alverjana *f* *Am* pea.

alza** *f* rise; **en a.** rising.

alzamiento *m* (*rebelión*) uprising.

alzar [4] 1 *vt* to raise; **a. los ojos/la vista** to look up. 2 **alzarse** *vr* (*levantarse*) to rise; (*rebelarse*) to rebel.

ama *f* (*dueña*) owner; **a. de casa** housewife.

amabilidad *f* kindness; **tenga la a. de esperar** would you be so kind as to wait.

amable *a* kind, nice.

amaestrar *vt* (*animal*) to train; (*domar*) to tame.

amainar vi (viento etc) to die down.

amamantar vt to breast-feed; (entre animales) to suckle.

amanecer 1 v impers **¿a qué hora amanece?** when does it get light?; **amaneció lluvioso** it was rainy at daybreak. **2** vi **amanecimos en Finlandia** we were in Finland at daybreak; **amaneció muy enfermo** he woke up feeling very ill. **3** m dawn; **al a.** at dawn.

amanerado,-a a affected.

amante mf lover.

amapola f poppy.

amar 1 vt to love. **2 amarse** vr to love each other.

amargar [7] **1** vt to make bitter; (relación) to embitter. **2 amargarse** vr to become embittered.

amargo,-a a bitter.

amargor m, **amargura** f bitterness.

amarillo,-a a & m yellow.

amarilloso,-a a Am yellowish.

amarrar vt (atar) to tie (up).

amasar vt to knead.

amateur a & mf amateur.

ámbar m amber.

ambición f ambition.

ambicioso,-a 1 a ambitious. **2** mf ambitious person.

ambiental a environmental.

ambiente 1 m environment. **2** a environmental; **temperatura a.** room temperature.

ambiguo,-a a ambiguous.

ámbito m field.

ambos,-as a & pron pl both.

ambulancia f ambulance.

ambulatorio m surgery.

amedrentar vt to frighten.

amenaza f threat.

amenazador,-a, amenazante a threatening.

amenazar [4] vt to threaten.

ameno,-a a entertaining.

americana f (prenda) jacket.

americano,-a a & mf American.

ametralladora f machine gun.

amígdala f tonsil.

amigdalitis f tonsillitis.

amigo,-a mf friend; **hacerse amigos** to become friends; **son muy amigos** they are very good friends.

aminorar vt to reduce; **a. el paso** to slow down.

amistad f friendship; **amistades** friends.

amnistía f amnesty.

amo m (dueño) owner.

amodorrarse vr to become sleepy.

amoldar vt, **amoldarse** vr to adapt.

amonestación f reprimand.

amontonar 1 vt to pile up. **2 amontonarse** vr to pile up; (gente) to crowd together.

amor m love; **hacer el a.** to make love; **a. propio** self-esteem.

amoratado,-a a (de frío) blue with cold; (de un golpe) black and blue.

amordazar [4] vt (a una persona) to gag.

amoroso,-a a loving.

amortiguador m (de vehículo) shock absorber.

amortiguar vt (golpe) to cushion; (ruido) to muffle.

amortizar [4] vt to pay off.

amotinar 1 vt to incite to riot. **2 amotinarse** vr to rise up.

amparar 1 vt to protect. **2 ampararse** vr to seek refuge.

ampliación f enlargement; (de plazo, casa) extension.

ampliar vt to enlarge; (casa, plazo) to extend.

amplificador m amplifier.

amplio,-a a large; (ancho) broad.

ampolla f (vejiga) blister; (de medicina) ampule.

amputar vt to amputate.

amueblar vt to furnish.

amuleto m amulet.

anaconda f anaconda.

anacronismo m anachronism.

anales mpl annals.

analfabeto,-a mf illiterate.

analgésico,-a a & m analgesic.

análisis m inv analysis; **a. de sangre** blood test.

analizar [4] vt to analyze.

analogía f analogy.

análogo,-a a analogous.

ananá *m* (*pl* **ananaes**), **ananás** *m* (*pl* **ananases**) *Am* pineapple.

anarquista *a* & *mf* anarchist.

andaluz,-a *a* & *mf* Andalusian.

antártico,-a 1 *a* Antarctic. **2** *m* **el A.** the Antarctic.

anatomía *f* anatomy.

ancho,-a 1 *a* wide, broad; **a lo a.** breadthwise; **te está muy a.** it's too big for you. **2** *m* (*anchura*) width, breadth; **dos metros de a.** two meters wide; **¿qué a. tiene?** how wide is it?

anchoa *f* anchovy.

anchura *f* width, breadth.

anciano,-a 1 *a* very old. **2** *mf* old person.

ancla** *f* anchor.

andamiaje *m* scaffolding.

andamio *m* scaffold.

andar *m*, **andares** *mpl* gait *sing*.

andar 1 *vi* to walk; (*coche etc*) to move; (*funcionar*) to work; *fam* **anda por los cuarenta** he's about forty; **¿cómo andamos de tiempo?** how are we on time?; **tu bolso debe de a. por ahí** your bag must be over there somewhere. **2** *vt* (*recorrer*) to walk.

andariego,-a *a* fond of walking.

andén *m* platform.

andinismo *m* *Am* mountaineering.

andino,-a *a* & *mf* Andean.

andrajo *m* rag.

anécdota *f* anecdote.

anegar *vt*, **anegarse** *vr* [7] to flood.

anejo,-a *a* attached (**a** to).

anemia *f* anemia.

anestesia *f* anesthesia.

anexión *f* annexation.

anexionar *vt* to annex.

anexo,-a 1 *a* attached (**a** to). **2** *m* appendix.

anfitrión,-ona 1 *m* host. **2** *f* hostess.

ángel *m* angel; *Am* (*micrófono*) hand microphone.

angina *f* **tener anginas** to have tonsillitis; **a. de pecho** angina pectoris.

anglosajón,-ona *a* & *mf* Anglo-Saxon.

angosto,-a *a* narrow.

anguila *f* eel.

angula *f* elver.

ángulo *m* angle.

angustia *f* anguish.

anhídrido *m* **a. carbónico** carbon dioxide.

anilla *f* ring.

anillo *m* ring.

animado,-a *a* (*fiesta etc*) lively.

animadversión *f* animosity.

animal 1 *m* animal; *fig* (*basto*) brute. **2** *a* animal.

animar 1 *vt* (*alentar*) to encourage; (*alegrar*) (*persona*) to cheer up; (*fiesta, bar*) to liven up. **2 animarse** *vr* (*persona*) to cheer up; (*fiesta, reunión*) to brighten up.

ánimo *m* (*valor, coraje*) courage; **estado de á.** state of mind; **con á. de** with the intention of; **¡á.!** cheer up!

aniquilar *vt* to annihilate.

anís *m* (*bebida*) anisette.

aniversario *m* anniversary.

anoche *adv* last night; (*por la tarde*) yesterday evening; **antes de a.** the night before last.

anochecer 1 *v impers* to get dark. **2** *m* nightfall.

anodino,-a *a* (*insustancial*) insubstantial; (*soso*) insipid.

anómalo,-a *a* anomalous.

anónimo,-a 1 *a* (*desconocido*) anonymous; **sociedad anónima** corporation. **2** *m* (*carta*) anonymous letter.

anorak *m* (*pl* **anoraks**) anorak.

anormal *a* abnormal; (*inusual*) unusual.

anotar *vt* (*apuntar*) to note.

anquilosarse *vr* to stagnate.

ansiar *vt* to long for.

ansiedad *f* anxiety; **con a.** anxiously.

antagonismo *m* antagonism.

antaño *adv* in the past.

ante[1] *m* (*piel*) suede.

ante[2] *prep* (*delante de*) in the presence of; (*en vista de*) faced with; **a. todo** most of all.

anteanoche *adv* the night before last.

anteayer *adv* the day before yesterday.

antecedente 1 *a* previous. **2 antecedentes** *mpl* (*historial*) record *sing;* **antecedentes penales** criminal record *sing.*

antecesor,-a *mf* (*en un cargo*) predecessor.

antelación *f* **con un mes de a.** a month beforehand.

antemano *adv* **de a.** beforehand, in advance.

antena *f* (*de radio, television, animal*) antenna; **a. parabólica** satellite dish; **en a.** on the air.

anteojo *m* telescope; **anteojos** (*binoculares*) binoculars; *Am* (*gafas*) glasses, spectacles.

antepecho *m* (*de ventana*) sill.

antepenúltimo,-a *a* **el capítulo a.** the last chapter but two.

anteproyecto *m* draft; **a. de ley** draft bill.

antepuesto,-a *pp de* **anteponer.**

antepuse *pt indef de* **anteponer.**

anterior *a* previous; (*delantero*) front.

anteriormente *adv* previously.

antes 1 *adv* before; (*antaño*) in the past; **mucho a.** long before; **cuanto a.** as soon as possible; **a. prefiero hacerlo yo** I'd rather do it myself; **a. (bien)** on the contrary. **2** *prep* **a. de** before.

antiadherente *a* nonstick.

antibiótico,-a *a & m* antibiotic.

anticaspa *a* anti-dandruff.

anticipar 1 *vt* (*acontecimiento*) to bring forward; (*dinero*) to pay in advance. **2** **anticiparse** *vr* (*llegar pronto*) to arrive early; **él se me anticipó** he beat me to it.

anticonceptivo,-a *a & m* contraceptive.

anticongelante *a & m* (*de radiador*) antifreeze; (*de parabrisas*) de-icer.

anticonstitucional *a* unconstitutional.

anticuado,-a *a* antiquated.

anticuario,-a *mf* antique dealer.

anticuerpo *m* antibody.

antídoto *m* antidote.

antifaz *m* mask.

antigüedad *f* (*período histórico*) antiquity; (*en cargo*) seniority; **tienda de antigüedades** antique shop.

antiguo,-a *a* old; (*pasado de moda*) old-fashioned; (*anterior*) former.

antihistamínico *m* antihistamine.

antiniebla *a inv* **luces a.** foglights.

antipático,-a *a* unpleasant.

antirrobo 1 *a inv* **alarma a.** burglar alarm; (*para coche*) car alarm. **2** *m* burglar alarm; (*para coche*) car alarm.

antiséptico,-a *a & m* antiseptic.

antojarse *vr* **cuando se me antoja** when I feel like it; **se le antojó un helado** he wanted an ice-cream.

antojo *m* (*capricho*) whim; (*de embarazada*) craving.

antorcha *f* torch.

antropología *f* anthropology.

anual *a* annual.

anudar *vt* (*atar*) to knot.

anular *vt* (*matrimonio*) to annul; (*ley*) to repeal.

anunciar *vt* (*producto etc*) to advertise; (*avisar*) to announce.

anuncio *m* (*comercial*) advertisement; (*aviso*) announcement; (*cartel*) notice.

anzuelo *m* (fish) hook.

añadir *vt* to add (**a** to).

añejo,-a *a* (*vino, queso*) mature.

año *m* year; **el a. pasado** last year; **el a. que viene** next year; **hace años** a long time ago; **los años noventa** the nineties; **todo el a.** all the year (round); **¿cuántos a. tienes?** how old are you?; **tiene seis a.** he's six years old.

añorar *vt* to long for.

apacible *a* mild.

apagar [7] *vt* (*fuego*) to put out; (*luz, tele etc*) to switch off.

apagón *m* power cut.

apaisado,-a *a* (*papel*) landscape.

aparador *m* (*mueble*) sideboard.

aparato *m* (*piece of*) apparatus; (*dispositivo*) device; (*instrumento*) instrument; **a. de radio/televisión** radio/television set; **a. digestivo** digestive system.

aparcamiento *m* (*en la calle*) parking place; (*parking*), parking lot.

aparcar [1] *vti* to park.

aparecer 1 *vi* to appear; **no aparece en mi lista** he is not on my list; (*en un sitio*) to turn up; **¿apareció el dinero?** did the money turn up?; **no apareció nadie** nobody turned up. 2 **aparecerse** *vr* to appear.

aparejador,-a *mf* quantity surveyor.

aparejo *m* (*equipo*) equipment.

aparentar 1 *vt* (*simular*) to affect; (*tener aspecto*) **no aparenta esa edad** she doesn't look that age. 2 *vi* to show off.

apariencia *f* appearance; **en a.** apparently; **guardar las apariencias** to keep up appearances.

apartamento *m* apartment.

apartar 1 *vt* (*alejar*) to remove; (*guardar*) to put aside. 2 *vi* **¡aparta!** move out of the way! 3 **apartarse** *vr* (*alejarse*) to move away.

aparte 1 *adv* aside; **modestia/bromas a.** modesty/joking apart; **eso hay que pagarlo a.** (*separadamente*) you have to pay for that separately; **punto y a.** full stop, new paragraph. 2 *prep* **a. de eso** (*además*) besides that; (*excepto*) apart from that.

apasionado,-a *a* passionate.

apasionante *a* exciting.

apasionar *vt* to excite.

apático,-a 1 *a* apathetic. 2 *mf* apathetic person.

apearse *vi* (*de un autobús, tren*) to get off; (*de un coche*) to get out.

apedrear *vt* to throw stones at.

apelar *vi* (*sentencia*) to appeal; (*recurrir*) to resort (**a** to).

apellido *m* surname; **a. de soltera** maiden name.

apenar 1 *vt* to grieve. 2 **apenarse** *vr* to be grieved; *Am* (*avergonzarse*) to be ashamed.

apenas *adv* (*casi no*) hardly, scarcely; **a. (si) hay nieve** there is hardly any snow; **a. llegó, sonó el teléfono** he hardly had arrived when the phone rang.

apéndice *m* appendix.

apendicitis *f* appendicitis.

aperitivo *m* (*bebida*) apéritif; (*comida*) appetizer.

apertura *f* (*comienzo*) opening.

apestar *vi* to stink (**a** of).

apetecer *vi* **¿qué te apetece para cenar?** what would you like for supper?; **¿te apetece ir al cine?** do you want to go to the movie theater?

apetito *m* appetite; **tengo mucho apetito** I'm really hungry.

apiadarse *vr* to take pity (**de** on).

apilar *vt*, **apilarse** *vr* to pile up.

apiñarse *vr* to crowd together.

apio *m* celery.

apisonadora *f* steamroller.

aplacar [1] *vt*, **aplacarse** *vr* to calm down.

aplanar *vt* to level.

aplastar *vt* to squash.

aplaudir *vt* to applaud.

aplauso *m* applause.

aplazamiento *m* postponement.

aplazar [4] *vt* to postpone.

aplicar [1] 1 *vt* to apply. 2 **aplicarse** *vr* (*esforzarse*) to apply oneself; (*usar*) to apply.

aplique *m* wall lamp.

aplomo *m* aplomb.

apoderado,-a *mf* representative.

apoderarse *vr* **a. de** to take possession of.

apodo *m* nickname.

apogeo *m* **estar en pleno a.** (*fama etc*) to be at its height.

apoplejía *f* apoplexy.

aporrear *vt* to beat; (*puerta*) to bang.

aportar *vt* to contribute.

aposento *m* (*cuarto*) room.

aposta *adv* on purpose.

apostar [2] *vti*, **apostarse** *vr* to bet (**por** on).

apoyar 1 *vt* to lean; (*causa*) to support. **2 apoyarse** *vr* **apoyarse en** to lean on; (*basarse*) to be based on.

apoyo *m* support.

apreciar 1 *vt* to appreciate; (*percibir*) to see. **2 apreciarse** *vr* (*notarse*) to be noticeable.

aprecio *m* regard; **tener a. a algn** to be fond of sb.

aprender *vt* to learn.

aprendiz,-a *mf* apprentice.

aprensivo,-a *a & mf* apprehensive.

apresar *vt* to capture.

apresurar 1 *vt* (*paso etc*) to speed up. **2 apresurarse** *vr* to hurry up.

apretado,-a *a* (*ropa, cordón*) tight; **íbamos todos apretados en el coche** we were all squashed together in the car.

apretar [1] **1** *vt* (*botón*) to press; (*nudo, tornillo*) to tighten; **me aprietan las botas** these boots are too tight for me. **2 apretarse** *vr* to squeeze together.

aprieto *m* tight spot; **poner a algn en un a.** to put sb in an awkward position.

aprisa *adv* quickly.

aprisionar *vt* to trap.

aprobado *m* (*nota*) pass.

aprobar [2] *vt* (*autorizar*) to approve; (*estar de acuerdo con*) to approve of; (*examen*) to pass; (*ley*) to pass.

apropiado,-a *a* suitable.

aprovechamiento *m* use.

aprovechar 1 *vt* to make good use of; (*recursos etc*) to take advantage of. **2** *vi* **¡que aproveche!** enjoy your meal! **3 aprovecharse** *vr* **aprovecharse de algo/algn** to take advantage of sth/sb.

aproximadamente *adv* approximately.

aproximado,-a *a* approximate.

aproximar 1 *vt* to bring nearer. **2 aproximarse** *vr* to approach (**a** -).

apto,-a *a* (*apropiado*) suitable; (*capacitado*) capable; (*examen*) passed.

apuesta *f* bet.

apuntador,-a *mf* (*en el teatro*) prompter.

apuntalar *vt* to prop up.

apuntar 1 *vt* (*con arma*) to aim; (*anotar*) to note; (*indicar*) to suggest. **2 apuntarse** *vr* (*en una lista*) to put one's name down; *fam* to take part (**a** in).

apuntes *mpl* notes; **tomar apuntes** to take notes.

apuñalar *vt* to stab.

apurar 1 *vt* (*terminar*) to finish off; (*preocupar*) to worry. **2 apurarse** *vr* (*preocuparse*) to worry; (*darse prisa*) to hurry.

apuro *m* (*situación difícil*) tight spot; (*escasez de dinero*) hardship; (*vergüenza*) embarrassment; **pasar apuros** to be hard up; **¡qué a.!** how embarrassing!

aquel,-ella *a dem* that; **a. niño** that boy; **aquellos,-as** those; **aquellas niñas** those girls.

aquél,-élla *pron dem mf* that one; (*el anterior*) the former; **todo a. que** anyone who; **aquéllos,-as** those; (*los anteriores*) the former.

aquella *a dem f ver* **aquel**.

aquélla *pron dem f ver* **aquél**.

aquello *pron dem neutro* that, it.

aquellos,-as *a dem pl ver* **aquel, -ella**.

aquéllos,-as *pron dem mfpl ver* **aquél.-élla**.

aquí *adv* (*lugar*) here; **a. arriba/ fuera** up/out here; **a. mismo** right here; **de a. para allá** up and down, to and fro; **hasta a.** this far; **por a., por favor** this way please; **está por a.** it's around here somewhere; (*tiempo*) **de a. en adelante** from now on.

árabe 1 a & mf Arab. **2** m (idioma) Arabic.

arado m plow.

aragonés,-esa a & mf Aragonese.

arancel m customs duty.

arandela f washer.

araña f spider.

arañazo m scratch.

arar vti to plow.

arbitrario,-a a arbitrary.

árbitro,-a mf referee; (de tenis) umpire; (mediador) arbitrator.

árbol m tree; **á. genealógico** family tree.

arbusto m bush.

arcada f (de puente) arch; (náusea) retching.

arcén m verge; (de autopista) hard shoulder.

archipiélago m archipelago.

archivador m filing cabinet.

archivar vt (documento etc) to file (away); (caso, asunto) to shelve.

archivo m file; (archivador) filing cabinet; **archivos** archives.

arcilla f clay.

arco m (de edificio etc) arch; (de violín, para flechas) bow; **a. iris** rainbow.

arder vi to burn.

ardilla f squirrel.

ardor m fervor; **a. de estómago** heartburn.

área f area; (medida) are (100 square meters).

arena f sand; (en plaza de toros) bullring; **playa de a.** sandy beach.

arenisca f sandstone.

arenque m herring.

arete m Am earring.

argelino,-a a & a Algerian.

argentino,-a a & mf Argentinian, Argentine.

argolla f (large) ring; Am (alianza) wedding ring.

argot m (popular) slang; (técnico) jargon.

argumento m (trama) plot; (razonamiento) argument.

árido,-a a arid.

arisco,-a a (persona) unfriendly; (áspero) gruff; (animal) unfriendly.

aristócrata mf aristocrat.

aritmética f arithmetic.

arma f weapon; **a. de fuego** firearm; **a. nuclear** nuclear weapon.

armada f navy.

armador,-a mf shipowner.

armadura f (armazón) frame.

armamento m (armas) armaments; **a. nuclear** nuclear weapons.

armar 1 vt (tropa, soldado) to arm; (montar) to assemble. **2 armarse** vr to arm oneself; **armarse de paciencia** to summon up one's patience; **armarse de valor** to pluck up courage.

armario m (para ropa) wardrobe; (de cocina) cupboard; **a. empotrado** built-in wardrobe/cupboard.

armazón m frame; (de madera) timberwork.

armisticio m armistice.

armonioso,-a a harmonious.

aro m hoop; (servilletero) napkin ring.

aroma m aroma; (de vino) bouquet.

arpa** f harp.

arpón m harpoon.

arqueología f archaeology.

arquitecto,-a mf architect.

arquitectura f architecture.

arrabales mpl slums.

arraigado,-a a deeply rooted.

arrancar [1] **1** vt (planta) to uproot; (diente, pelo) to pull out; (coche, motor) to start; **a. de raíz** to uproot. **2** vi (coche, motor) to start; (empezar) to begin.

arrasar vt to devastate.

arrastrar 1 vt to drag (along); **lo arrastró la corriente** he was swept away by the current. **2 arrastrarse** vr to drag oneself.

arrebatar 1 vt (coger) to seize. **2 arrebatarse** vr (enfurecerse) to become furious; (*exaltarse*) to get carried away.

arrebato *m* outburst.

arreciar *vi* (*viento, tormenta*) to get worse.

arrecife *m* reef.

arreglado,-a *a* (*reparado*) repaired; (*solucionado*) settled; (*habitación*) tidy; (*persona*) smart.

arreglar 1 *vt* to arrange; (*problema*) to sort out; (*habitación*) to tidy; (*papeles*) to put in order; (*reparar*) to repair. **2 arreglarse** *vr* (*vestirse*) to get ready; *fam* **arreglárselas** to manage.

arreglo *m* arrangement; (*acuerdo*) compromise; (*reparación*) repair; **no tiene a.** it is beyond repair; **con a. a** in accordance with.

arremangarse [7] *vr* to roll one's sleeves/trousers up.

arrendar [1] *vt* (*piso*) to rent; (*dar en arriendo*) to lease; (*tomar en arriendo*) to take on a lease.

arrepentirse [5] *vr* **a. de** to regret; (*en confesión*) to repent.

arrestar *vt* to arrest; (*encarcelar*) to put in prison.

arriba 1 *adv* up; (*encima*) on the top; (*en casa*) upstairs; **ahí a.** up there; **de a. abajo** from top to bottom; **mirar a algn de a. abajo** to look sb up and down; **desde a.** from above; **hacia a.** upwards; **más a.** further up; **la parte de a.** the top (part); **vive a.** he lives upstairs; **véase más a.** see above. **2** *interj* up you go!; **¡a. la República!** long live the Republic!; **¡a. las manos!** hands up! **3** *prep Am* **a. de** on top of.

arribeño,-a *Am* **1** *a* highland. **2** *mf* highlander.

arriendo *m* lease.

arriesgado,-a *a* (*peligroso*) risky; (*persona*) daring.

arriesgar [7] *vt*, **arriesgarse** *vr* to risk.

arrimar 1 *vt* to move closer; *fam* **a. el hombro** to lend a hand. **2 arrimarse** *vr* to move nearer.

arrinconar *vt* (*poner en un rincón*)

to put in a corner; (*acorralar*) to corner.

arrodillarse *vr* to kneel down.

arrogante *a* arrogant.

arrojar 1 *vt* (*tirar*) to throw. **2 arrojarse** *vr* to throw oneself.

arrollador,-a *a* overwhelming; (*éxito*) resounding; (*personalidad*) captivating.

arropar 1 *vt* to wrap up; (*en cama*) to tuck in. **2 arroparse** *vr* to wrap oneself up.

arroyo *m* stream.

arroz *m* rice; **a. con leche** rice pudding.

arruga *f* (*en piel*) wrinkle; (*en ropa*) crease.

arrugar [7] **1** *vt* (*piel*) to wrinkle; (*ropa*) to crease; (*papel*) to crumple (up). **2 arrugarse** *vr* (*piel*) to wrinkle; (*ropa*) to crease.

arruinar 1 *vt* to ruin. **2 arruinarse** *vr* to be ruined.

arsenal *m* arsenal.

arte *m & f* art; (*habilidad*) skill; **bellas artes** fine arts.

artefacto *m* device.

arteria *f* artery.

artesanía *f* craftsmanship; (*objetos*) crafts *pl*.

ártico,-a 1 *a* arctic; **el océano a.** the Arctic Ocean. **2** *m* **el A.** the Arctic.

articulación *f* (*de huesos*) joint.

artículo *m* article.

artificial *a* artificial; (*sintético*) man-made, synthetic.

artillería *f* artillery.

artista *mf* artist; **a. de cine** film star.

artritis *f* arthritis.

arveja *f Am* pea.

as *m* ace.

asa** *f* handle.

asado,-a *a* roast; **pollo a.** roast chicken. **2** *m* roast.

asaltar *vt* to attack; (*banco*) to rob.

asamblea *f* meeting; **a. general** general meeting.

asar 1 *vt* to roast. **2 asarse** *vr fig* to be roasting.

ascender [3] **1** *vt* (*en un cargo*) to promote. **2** *vi* move upward; (*temperatura etc*) to rise; **a. de categoría** to be promoted; **la factura asciende a . . .** the bill adds up to . . .

ascenso *m* promotion; (*subida*) rise.

ascensor *m* elevator.

asco *m* disgust; **me da a.** it makes me (feel) sick; **¡qué a.!** how disgusting!

ascua** *f* live coal, ember.

asear 1 *vt* to tidy up. **2 asearse** *vr* to wash.

asedio *m* siege.

asegurar 1 *vt* to insure; (*garantizar*) to assure; (*cuerda*) to fasten. **2 asegurarse** *vr* to insure oneself; **asegurarse de que . . .** to make sure that . . .

asemejarse *vr* **a.** to look like.

asentamiento *m* settlement.

asentir [5] *vi* to agree; **a. con la cabeza** to nod.

aseo *m* (*limpieza*) tidiness; (*cuarto de baño*) toilet.

asequible *a* affordable; (*alcanzable*) attainable.

aserrín *m* sawdust.

asesinar *vt* to murder; (*rey, ministro*) to assassinate.

asesinato *m* murder; (*de rey, ministro*) assassination.

asesino,-a 1 *a* murderous. **2** *mf* (*hombre*) murderer; (*mujer*) murderess; (*de político*) assassin.

asesorar *vt* to advise.

asesoría *f* consultancy.

asfalto *m* asphalt.

asfixiar *vt*, **asfixiarse** *vr* to asphyxiate.

así 1 *adv* (*de esta manera*) like this o that, this way; **ponlo a.** put it this way; **a. de grande/alto** this big/tall; **algo a.** something like this o that; **¿no es a.?** isn't that so o right?; **a las seis o a.** around six o'clock; **a. como** as well as; **aun a.** and despite that. **2** *conj* **a. pues . . .** so. . .; **a. que . . .** so . . .

asiático,-a *a* & *mf* Asian.

asiduo,-a 1 *a* assiduous. **2** *mf* regular customer.

asiento *m* seat; **a. trasero/delantero** front/back seat; **tome a.** take a seat.

asignar *vt* to allocate; (*nombrar*) to appoint.

asignatura *f* subject.

asilo *m* asylum; **a. de ancianos** old people's home.

asimismo *adv* also, as well.

asistencia *f* (*presencia*) attendance; (*público*) audience; **falta de a.** absence; **a. médica/técnica** medical/technical assistance.

asistenta *f* cleaning lady.

asistente 1 *a* **el público a.** the audience; (*en estadio*) spectators *pl.* **2** *mf* (*ayudante*) assistant; **a. social** social worker; **los asistentes** the audience; (*en estadio*) the spectators.

asistir 1 *vt* to assist. **2** *vi* to attend (**a -**).

asma *f* asthma.

asno *m* donkey.

asociación *f* association.

asociar 1 *vt* to associate. **2 asociarse** *vr* to be associated.

asomar 1 *vt* to stick out; **asomó la cabeza por la ventana** he put his head out the window. **2** *vi* to appear. **3 asomarse** *vr* to lean out; **asomarse a la ventana** to lean out of the window.

asombrar 1 *vt* to astonish. **2 asombrarse** *vr* to be astonished; **asombrarse de algo** to be amazed at sth.

asombro *m* astonishment.

asorocharse *vr Am* to suffer from altitude sickness.

aspa *f* (*de molino*) arm; (*de ventilador*) blade; (*cruz*) cross.

aspecto *m* look; (*de un asunto*) aspect.

áspero,-a *a* rough; (*carácter*) surly.

aspersor *m* sprinkler.

aspiradora *f* vacuum cleaner.

aspirante *mf* candidate.

aspirar *vt* (*respirar*) to inhale.

aspirina *f* aspirin.

asqueroso,-a 1 *a* (*sucio*) filthy; (*desagradable*) disgusting. **2** *mf* filthy o revolting person.

asterisco *m* asterisk.

astilla *f* splinter.

astillero *m* shipyard.

astringente *a* & *m* astringent.

astro *m* star.

astrología *f* astrology.

astronauta *mf* astronaut.

astronave *f* spaceship.

astronomía *f* astronomy.

asturiano,-a *a* & *mf* Asturian.

astuto,-a *a* astute.

asunto *m* subject; **no es a. tuyo** it's none of your business.

asustar 1 *vt* to frighten. **2 asustarse** *vr* to be frightened.

atacar [1] *vt* to attack.

atajo *m* shortcut.

atañer *vi* to concern.

ataque *m* attack; (*de nervios, tos*) fit; **a. cardíaco** *o* **al corazón** heart attack.

atar 1 *vt* (*ligar*) to tie; **a. cabos** to put two and two together; *fam* **loco de a.** as mad as a hatter. **2 atarse** *vr fig* to get tied up; **átate los zapatos** do your shoes up.

atardecer 1 *v impers* to get dark. **2** *m* evening.

atareado,-a *a* busy.

atascar [1] **1** *vt* (*bloquear*) to block. **2 atascarse** *vr* (*bloquearse*) to become blocked.

atasco *m* traffic jam.

ataúd *m* coffin.

atemorizar [4] *vt* to frighten.

atención 1 *f* attention; **llamar la a.** to attract attention; **prestar/poner a.** to pay attention (**a** to). **2** *interj* attention!; (*cuidado*) watch out!

atender [3] **1** *vt* to attend to. **2** *vi* (*alumno*) to pay attention (**a** to).

atentado *m* attack.

atentamente *adv* (*con atención*) attentively; **le saluda a.** (*en carta*) yours sincerely.

atento,-a *a* attentive; (*amable*) thoughtful; **estar a. a** to be aware of.

aterrador,-a *a* terrifying.

aterrar 1 *vt* to terrify. **2 aterrarse** *vr* to be terrified.

aterrizaje *m* landing.

aterrizar [4] *vi* to land.

aterrorizar [4] **1** *vt* to terrify. **2 aterrorizarse** *vr* to be terrified.

ático *m* attic; (*vivienda*) attic apartment.

atingencia *f Am* connection.

atizar [4] *vt* (*fuego*) to poke.

atlas *m inv* atlas.

atleta *mf* athlete.

atletismo *m* athletics *sing.*

atmósfera *f* atmosphere.

atolondrado,-a *a* stunned; (*atontado*) stupid.

atómico,-a *a* atomic.

átomo *m* atom.

atónito,-a *a* astonished.

atontado,-a *a* (*tonto*) silly; (*aturdido*) bewildered.

atorarse *vr* to get stuck.

atormentar 1 *vt* to torment. **2 atormentarse** *vr* to torment oneself.

atornillar *vt* to screw on.

atracar [1] **1** *vt* to hold up; (*persona*) to rob. **2** *vi* (*barco*) to come alongside. **3 atracarse** *vr* (*de comida*) to stuff oneself (**de** with).

atracción *f* attraction; **parque de atracciones** amusement park.

atraco *m* hold-up; **a. a mano armada** armed robbery.

atracón *m fam* binge.

atractivo,-a 1 *a* attractive. **2** *m* attraction.

atraer *vt* to attract.

atragantarse *vr* to choke (**con** on).

atraigo *indic pres de* **atraer.**

atraje *pt indef de* **atraer.**

atrancar [1] **1** *vt* (*puerta*) to bolt. **2 atrancarse** *vr* to get stuck.

atrapar *vt* to catch.

atrás *adv* (*lugar*) at the back, behind; **hacia/para a.** backwards; **puerta de a.** back *o* rear door; **echarse a.** to back out; **venir de muy a.** to go back a long time.

atrasado,-a a late; (*pago*) over-due; (*reloj*) slow; (*país*) backward.
atrasar 1 vt to put back. **2** vi (*reloj*) to be slow. **3 atrasarse** vr to lag behind; (*tren*) to be late.
atravesar [1] **1** vt (*cruzar*) to cross; (*traspasar*) to go through; (*poner a través*) to put across. **2 atravesarse** vr to get in the way.
atreverse vr to dare; **a. a hacer algo** to dare to do sth.
atrevido,-a a (*osado*) daring; (*insolente*) insolent; (*ropa etc*) daring.
atropellar vt to knock down.
atroz a (*bárbaro*) atrocious; *fam* (*hambre, frío*) tremendous.
ATS mf abr de **ayudante técnico sanitario** nurse.
atuendo m attire.
atún m tuna.
aturdido,-a a stunned.
aturdir vt (*con un golpe*) to stun; (*confundir*) to bewilder.
audaz a audacious.
audición f hearing; (*en el teatro*) audition.
audiencia f (*público*) audience; (*entrevista*) audience; (*tribunal*) high court.
audiovisual a audio-visual.
auditor,-a mf auditor.
auge m peak; (*económico*) boom; **estar en a.** to be booming.
aula** f (*en colegio*) classroom; (*en universidad*) lecture room.
aulaga f gorse.
aullido m howl.
aumentar 1 vt to increase; (*precios*) to put up; (*producción*) to step up; (*imagen*) to magnify. **2** vi (*precios*) to go up; (*valor*) to appreciate.
aumento m increase; (*de imagen*) magnification; **ir en a.** to be on the increase.
aun adv even; **a. así** even so.
aún adv still; (*en negativas*) yet; **a. está aquí** he's still here; **ella no ha venido a.** she hasn't come yet; **a. más** even more.
aunque conj although, though; (*enfático*) even if, even though.

aureola f halo.
auricular m (*del teléfono*) receiver; **auriculares** headphones.
aurora f dawn.
auscultar vt to sound (with a stethoscope).
ausencia f absence.
ausentarse vr (*irse*) to go away.
ausente 1 a absent. **2** mf absentee.
austero,-a a austere.
australiano,-a a & mf Australian.
austríaco,-a a & mf Austrian.
auténtico,-a a authentic.
autista 1 a autistic. **2** mf autistic person.
auto[1] m Am car.
auto[2] m (*sentencia*) writ; **autos** (*pleito*) documents.
autobiografía f autobiography.
autobiográfico,-a a autobiographical.
autobús m bus.
autocar m coach.
autóctono,-a a indigenous.
autodefensa f self-defense.
autoescuela f driving school.
autógrafo m autograph.
automático,-a a automatic.
automotor m diesel train.
automóvil m car.
automovilista mf motorist.
automovilístico,-a a car.
autonomía f autonomy; (*región*) autonomous region.
autonómico,-a a autonomous.
autopista f highway.
autopsia f autopsy.
autor,-a mf author; (*de crimen*) perpetrator.
autoridad f authority.
autoritario,-a a authoritarian.
autorizar [4] vt to authorize.
autoservicio m self-service; (*tienda*) supermarket.
autostop m hitch-hiking; **hacer a.** to hitch-hike.
autostopista mf hitch-hiker.
autosuficiencia f self-sufficiency.
auxiliar 1 a & mf auxiliary. **2** vt to assist.
auxilio m assistance; **primeros auxilios** first aid *sing*.

avalancha *f* avalanche.
avance *m* advance.
avanzado,-a *a* advanced; **de avanzada edad** advanced in years.
avanzar [4] *vt* to advance.
avaricia *f* avarice.
avaro,-a 1 *a* miserly. 2 *mf* miser.
ave** *f* bird.
avellana *f* hazelnut.
avellano *m* hazelnut tree.
avena *f* oats *pl*.
avenida *f* avenue.
avenido,-a *a* **bien/mal avenidos** on good/bad terms.
aventajar *vt* (*ir por delante de*) to be ahead, be in front (**a** of); (*superar*) to outdo.
aventura *f* adventure; (*amorosa*) (love) affair.
aventurarse *vr* to venture.
aventurero,-a 1 *a* adventurous. 2 *mf* adventurous person.
avergonzar [2] 1 *vt* to shame. 2 **avergonzarse** *vr* to be ashamed (**de** of).
avería *f* breakdown.
averiar 1 *vt* to break. 2 **averiarse** *vr* (*estropearse*) to malfunction; (*coche*) to break down.
averiguar *vt* to find out.
aversión *f* aversion.
avestruz *m* ostrich.
aviación *f* aviation; (*militar*) air force; **accidente de a.** plane crash.
aviador,-a *mf* aviator; (*piloto militar*) air force pilot.
ávido,-a *a* avid; **a. de** eager for.
avión *m* airplane; **por a.** (*en carta*) airmail.
avioneta *f* light aircraft.
avisar *vt* (*informar*) to inform; (*advertir*) to warn; (*llamar*) to call for.
aviso *m* notice; (*advertencia*) warning; (*nota*) note; **sin previo a.** without notice.
avispa *f* wasp.
avivar *vt* (*fuego*) to stoke (up); (*paso*) to quicken.
axila *f* armpit.
ay *interj* (*dolor*) ouch!

ayer *adv* yesterday; **a. por la mañana/por la tarde** yesterday morning/afternoon; **a. por la noche** last night; **antes de a.** the day before yesterday.
ayuda *f* help.
ayudante *mf* assistant.
ayudar 1 *vt* to help. 2 **ayudarse** *vr* (*unos a otros*) to help; **ayudarse de** to make use of.
ayunas en a. without having eaten breakfast.
ayuntamiento *m* (*institución*) town council; (*edificio*) town hall.
azafata *f* (*de avión*) flight attendant; (*de congresos*) stewardess; (*de concurso*) hostess.
azafrán *m* saffron.
azahar *m* (*del naranjo*) orange blossom.
azar *m* chance; **al a.** at random.
azorado,-a *a* embarrassed.
azorar 1 *vt* to embarrass. 2 **azorarse** *vr* to be embarrassed.
azotar *vt* to beat; (*lluvia*) to beat down on; (*con látigo*) to whip.
azotea *f* flat roof.
azteca *a* & *mf* Aztec.
azúcar *m* & *f* sugar; **a. blanco** refined sugar; **a. moreno** brown sugar.
azucarero,-a 1 *m* sugar bowl. 2 *a* sugar.
azucena *f* lily.
azul *a* & *m* blue; **a. celeste** sky blue; **a. marino** navy blue.
azulejo *m* (glazed) tile.

B

baba *f* dribble.
babero *m* bib.
babor *m* port.
babosa *f* slug.
baboso,-a *a* *fam* slimy; *Am* stupid.
baca *f* roof rack.
bacalao *m* cod.
bache *m* (*en carretera*) pot hole; (*mal momento*) bad patch.
bachillerato *m* high school diploma.

bacon m bacon.
bacteriológico,-a a bacteriológical; **guerra b.** germ warfare.
badén m (en carretera) bump.
bádminton m badminton.
bafle m loudspeaker.
bahía f bay.
bailar vti to dance.
bailarín,-ina mf dancer.
baile m (danza) dance; (formal) ball.
baja f (disminución) drop; (en batalla) loss; **dar de b. a algn** (despedir) to lay sb off; **darse de b.** (por enfermedad) to take sick leave.
bajada f (descenso) descent; (señal) way down; (cuesta) slope.
bajar 1 vt to come/go down; (descender) to get down; (volumen) to turn down; (voz, telón) to lower; (precios etc) to cut; (cabeza) to lower; **b. la escalera** to come/go downstairs. **2** vi to go/come down; (apearse) to get off; (de un coche) to get out (**de** of); (disminuir) to fall. **3 bajarse** vr to come/go down; (apearse) to get off; (de un coche) to get out (**de** of).
bajío m Am lowland.
bajo,-a 1 a low; (persona) short; (sonido) faint; **en voz baja** in a low voice; **planta baja** ground floor; **de baja calidad** of poor quality. **2** adv low; **hablar b.** to speak quietly. **3** prep (lugar) under, underneath; **b. tierra** underground; **b. cero** below zero; **b. juramento** under oath; **b. fianza** on bail.
bajón m (bajada) sharp fall.
bala f bullet; **como una b.** like a shot.
balance m balance; (declaración) balance sheet.
balanza f scales pl ; **b. comercial** balance of trade; **b. de pagos** balance of payments.
balbucear vi (adulto) to stutter, stammer; (niño) to babble.
balbucir vi defectivo ver **balbucear.**
balcón m balcony.

balde m **de b.** free; **en b.** in vain.
baldosa f (ceramic) floor tile.
baliza f (boya) buoy; (en aviación) beacon.
ballena f whale.
ballet m ballet.
balneario m health resort.
balón m ball.
baloncesto m basketball.
balonmano m handball.
balonvolea m volleyball.
balsa f raft.
bálsamo m balm.
bambú m (pl **bambúes**) bamboo.
banana f banana.
banca f (asiento) bench; **la b.** (the) banks.
bancarrota f bankruptcy.
banco m bank; (asiento) bench.
banda f (de música) band; (cinta) sash; **b. sonora** sound track; (línea de) **b.** touchline; **saque de b.** throw-in.
bandada f flock.
bandeja f tray.
bandera f flag.
bandido m bandit.
bando m side.
bandolero m bandit.
banquero,-a mf banker.
banqueta f stool.
banquete m banquet; **b. de bodas** wedding reception.
bañador m (de mujer) swimming suit; (de hombre) swimming trunks pl.
bañar 1 vt to bath. **2 bañarse** vr (en baño) to have a bath; (en mar, piscina) to go for a swim.
bañera f bath.
bañista mf swimmer.
baño m bath; (de chocolate etc) coating; (cuarto de baño) bathroom; (lavabo) toilet; **tomar un b.** to take a bath.
bar m bar, pub.
baraja f pack, deck.
baranda, barandilla f (de escalera) banister; (de balcón) handrail.
baratija f knick-knack.
barato,-a 1 a cheap. **2** adv cheaply.

barba f (pelo) beard.
barbacoa f barbecue.
barbaridad f atrocity; (disparate) piece of nonsense; **una b.** a lot.
barbería f barber's (shop).
barbilla f chin.
barbo m barbel.
barbudo,-a a with a heavy beard.
barca f small boat.
barcaza f lighter.
barco m ship; **b. de vapor** steamer.
barlovento m windward.
barman m barman.
barniz m (en madera) varnish; (en cerámica) glaze.
barómetro m barometer.
barquillo m wafer.
barra f bar; **b. de pan** French loaf; **b. de labios** lipstick.
barraca f (caseta) hut; (en Valencia y Murcia) thatched farmhouse.
barranco m (despeñadero) cliff; (torrentera) ravine.
barrendero,-a mf (street) sweeper.
barreno m (taladro) large drill; (explosivo) charge.
barreño m tub.
barrer vt to sweep.
barrera f barrier.
barricada f barricade.
barriga f belly, fam tummy.
barril m barrel; **cerveza de b.** draft beer.
barrio m district; **del b.** local; **b. chino** red-light district; **barrios bajos** slums.
barro m (lodo) mud; (arcilla) clay; **objetos de b.** earthenware sing.
bártulos mpl fam bits and pieces.
barullo m (alboroto) row; (confusión) confusion.
basar 1 vt to base (**en** on). **2 basarse** vr (teoría, película) to be based (**en** on).
báscula f scales pl.
base f base; (de argumento, teoría) basis; (de partido) grass roots; **sueldo b.** minimum wage; **b. de datos** database; **a b. de estudiar** by

studying; **a b. de productos naturales** using natural products.
básico,-a a basic.
básquet m basketball.
bastante 1 a (suficiente) enough; **b. tiempo/comida** enough time/food; (abundante) quite a lot of; **hace b. calor/frío** it's quite hot/cold; **bastantes amigos** quite a lot of friends. **2** adv (suficiente) enough; (considerablemente) fairly, quite; **con esto hay b.** that is enough; **no soy lo b. rico (como) para . . .** I am not rich enough to . . .; **me gusta b.** I quite like it; **vamos b. al cine** we go to the cinema quite often.
bastar vi to be sufficient o enough; **basta con tres** three will be enough; **¡basta (ya)!** that's enough!
basto,-a a (cosa) rough; (persona) coarse.
bastos m (in Spanish pack of cards) ≈ clubs.
bastón m stick.
basura f trash.
basurero m (persona) garbage collector; (lugar) garbage dump.
bata f (para casa) dressing gown; (de médico etc) white coat.
batalla f battle.
bate m (de béisbol) bat.
batería 1 f battery; (percusión) drums pl; **b. de cocina** set of pans. **2** mf drummer.
batida f (de la policía) raid.
batido,-a 1 a (huevo, crema) whipped. **2** m milk shake.
batidora f mixer.
batir vt to beat; (huevo) to beat; (nata) to whip; (récord) to break.
baudio m baud.
baúl m trunk; Am (de coche) trunk.
bautizar vt to baptize, christen.
bautizo m baptism.
baya f berry.
bayeta f floorcloth.
bazar m bazaar.
bazo m spleen.
bazofia f fam garbage.
beato,-a a peyorativo sanctimonious.
bebé m baby.

beber *vti* to drink.

bebida *f* drink.

beca *f* grant.

becario,-a *mf* grant holder.

becerro *m* calf.

bechamel *f* bechamel; **salsa b.**
white sauce.

bedel *m* janitor.

beige *a & m inv* beige.

béisbol *m* baseball.

belga *a & mf* Belgian.

bélico,-a *a* warlike; (*preparativos
etc*) war.

belleza *f* beauty.

bello,-a *a* beautiful.

bellota *f* acorn.

bencina *f Am* gas.

bendición *f* blessing.

bendito,-a *a* blessed.

beneficencia *f* charity.

beneficiar 1 *vt* to benefit. 2 **beneficiarse** *vr* **beneficiarse de** *o* **con
algo** to profit from sth.

beneficio *m* profit; (*bien*) benefit;
en b. propio in one's own interest;
un concierto a b. de . . . a concert
in aid of . . .

beneficioso,-a *a* beneficial.

benevolencia *f* benevolence.

bengala *f* flare.

benigno,-a *a* (*persona*) gentle.

benjamín,-ina *mf* youngest child.

berberecho *m* (*common*) cockle.

berbiquí *m* drill.

berenjena *f* eggplant.

Bermudas 1 *fpl* **las (Islas) B.** Bermuda *sing*. 2 *mpl o fpl* **bermudas**
(*prenda*) Bermuda shorts.

berrear *vi* to bellow.

berrinche *m fam* tantrum.

berro *m* watercress.

berza *f* cabbage.

besar *vt*, **besarse** *vr* to kiss.

beso *m* kiss.

best-seller *m* best-seller.

bestia 1 *f* beast. 2 *mf fam* brute. 3 *a
fig* brutish.

besugo *m* (*pez*) sea bream.

betún *m* (*para el calzado*) shoe
polish.

biberón *m* baby's bottle.

Biblia *f* Bible.

bibliografía *f* bibliography.

biblioteca *f* (*edificio*) library; (*estantería*) bookcase.

bicarbonato *m* bicarbonate; **b.
sódico** bicarbonate of soda.

bíceps *m inv* biceps.

bicho *m* bug.

bici *f* fam bike.

bicicleta *f* bicycle; **montar en b.** to
ride a bicycle.

bidón *m* drum.

bien[1] *adv* (*correctamente*) well;
responder b. to answer correctly;
hiciste b. en decírmelo you were
right to tell me; **las cosas le van b.**
things are going well for him; **¡b.!**
good!, great!; **¡muy b.!** excellent!;
¡qué b.! great!; **vivir b.** to live com-
fortably; **¡está b.!** (*¡de acuerdo!*)
fine!, all right!; **¡ya está b.!** that's
(quite) enough!; **esta falda te está
b.** this skirt suits you; **ese libro
está muy b.** that book is very
good. ▪ (*intensificador*) very; **b.
temprano** nice and early; **b.
caliente** pretty hot; **más b.** rather.
2 *conj* **o b.** or else; **b. . . . o b. . . .**
either . . . or . . .; **no b. llegó . . .**
no sooner had she arrived than
. . .; **si b.** although.

bien[2] *m* (*bondad*) good; **el b. y el
mal** good and evil; **por el b. de** for
the good of; **lo hace por tu b.** he
does it for your sake; **bienes** goods;
bienes inmuebles real estate;
bienes de consumo consumer
goods.

bienestar *m* well-being.

bienvenida *f* welcome; **dar la b. a
algn** to welcome sb.

bienvenido,-a *a* welcome.

bifurcación *f* (*de la carretera*)
fork.

bigote *m* (*de persona*) mustache;
bigotes (*de animal*) whiskers *pl*.

bilateral *a* bilateral.

bilingüe *a* bilingual.

bilis *f* bile.

billar *m* (*juego*) billiards *sing*;
(*mesa*) billiard table; **b. americano**
pool; **b. ruso** snooker.

billete *m* ticket; (*de banco*) bill;

b. de ida y vuelta round-trip ticket; **b. sencillo** o **de ida** one-way (ticket); **un b. de mil pesetas** a thousand peseta note.

billetera f, **billetero** m wallet.

billón m thousand billion.

bingo m (juego) bingo; (sala) bingo hall.

biografía f biography.

biología f biology.

biombo m (folding) screen.

biopsia f biopsy.

bioquímica f biochemistry.

bióxido m **b. de carbono** carbon dioxide.

biquini m bikini.

birria f fam garbage.

bisabuela f great-grandmother.

bisabuelo m great-grandfather; **bisabuelos** great-grandparents.

bisagra f hinge.

bisiesto a **año b.** leap year.

bisonte m bison.

bisté, bistec m steak.

bisturí m scalpel.

bisutería f imitation jewelry.

bizco,-a 1 a cross-eyed. **2** mf cross-eyed person.

bizcocho m sponge cake.

blanco,-a¹ 1 a white; (tez) fair. **2** mf (hombre) white man; (mujer) white woman; **los blancos** whites.

blanco² ** m (color) white; (hueco) blank; (diana) target; **pasar la noche en b. to have a sleepless night; **me quedé en b.** my mind went blank; **ser el b. de todas las miradas** to be the center of attention.

blancura f whiteness.

blando,-a a soft.

blanquear vt (encalar) to whitewash.

blasfemar vi to blaspheme (**contra** against).

blindado,-a a (carro) armoured; (antibalas) bullet-proof; **coche b.** bullet-proof car; **puerta blindada** reinforced door.

bloc m pad; **b. de notas** notepad.

bloque m block; **b. de pisos** block (of apartments).

bloquear vt to block; (sitiar) to blockade.

blusa f blouse.

blusón m loose blouse.

bobada f nonsense; **decir bobadas** to talk nonsense.

bobina f reel.

bobo,-a 1 a (tonto) stupid, silly; (ingenuo) naïve. **2** mf fool.

boca f mouth; **b. abajo** face downward; **b. arriba** face upward; fam **¡cierra la b!** shut up!; **con la b. abierta** open-mouthed; **se le hizo la b. agua** his mouth watered; **la b. del metro** the entrance to the subway station.

bocacalle f entrance to a street.

bocadillo m sandwich; **un b. de jamón/tortilla** a ham/omelette sandwich.

bocado m bite.

bocanada f (de humo) puff; **una b. de viento** a gust of wind.

bocata m fam sandwich.

bocazas mf inv fam bigmouth.

boceto m (de cuadro etc) sketch; (esquema) outline.

bochorno m (tiempo) sultry weather; (calor sofocante) stifling heat; (vergüenza) embarrassment.

bocina f horn; **tocar la b.** to sound one's horn.

boda f marriage; **bodas de plata** silver wedding sing.

bodega f (en casa) wine cellar; (tienda) wine shop; Am grocery store, grocer's.

body m bodystocking.

bofetada f, **bofetón** m slap on the face; **dar una b./un b. a algn** to slap sb's face.

bohío m Am hut.

boicotear vt to boycott.

boina f beret.

bola f ball; (canica) marble; Am (rumor) rumor; **b. de nieve** snowball; **no dar pie con b.** to be unable to do anything right.

bolera f bowling alley.

boletería f Am (de estadio, estación) ticket office; (de teatro) box office.

boletín m bulletin.

boleto m Am ticket.

boli m biro®.

bólido m (coche) racing car.

bolígrafo m ballpoint (pen).

boliviano,-a a & mf Bolivian.

bollo m (de pan) roll; (abolladura) dent.

bolo m skittle; **bolos** (juego) skittles.

bolsa[1] f bag; **b. de deportes** sports bag; **b. de la compra** shopping bag; **b. de viaje** travel bag.

bolsa[2] f (de valores) Stock Exchange.

bolsillo m (prenda) pocket; **de b.** pocket; **libro de b.** paperback.

bolso m purse.

bomba[1] f pump; **b. de incendios** fire engine.

bomba[2] f (explosivo) bomb; **b. atómica/de hidrógeno/de neutrones** atom/hydrogen/neutron bomb; **b. de relojería** time bomb; fam **pasarlo b.** to have a great time.

bombardear vt to bomb.

bombero,-a mf (hombre) fireman; (mujer) firewoman; (ambos sexos) firefighter; **cuerpo de bomberos** fire brigade; **parque de bomberos** fire station.

bombilla f (light) bulb.

bombín m bowler hat.

bombo m (de percusión) bass drum; (de sorteo) lottery drum; (de lavadora) drum.

bombón m chocolate.

bombona f cylinder.

bonachón,-ona a good-natured.

bonanza f (tiempo) fair weather; (prosperidad) prosperity.

bondadoso,-a a good-natured.

boniato m sweet potato.

bonificación f bonus.

bonito,-a[1] a pretty, nice.

bonito[2] m tuna.

bono m (vale) voucher; (título) bond.

bono-bus m bus pass.

boquerón m anchovy.

boquete m hole.

boquiabierto,-a a openmouthed; **se quedó b.** he was flabbergasted.

boquilla f (de cigarro) tip; (de pipa) mouthpiece.

borda f gunwale; **arrojar** o **echar por la b.** to throw overboard; **fuera b.** (motor) outboard motor.

bordado,-a 1 a embroidered. 2 m embroidery.

bordar vt to embroider.

borde m (de mesa, camino) edge; (de prenda) hem; (de vasija) rim; **al b. del mar** at the seaside.

bordear vt to skirt.

bordillo m curb.

bordo m **a b.** on board; **subir a b.** to go on board.

borrachera f (embriaguez) drunkenness; (curda) binge; **coger** o **pillar una b.** to get drunk.

borracho,-a 1 a (bebido) drunk; (bizcocho) with rum; **estar b.** to be drunk. 2 mf drunk.

borrador m (escrito) rough copy; (de pizarra) duster.

borrar vt (con goma) to rub out; (pizarra) to clean; (en pantalla) to delete.

borrasca f area of low pressure.

borrego,-a mf yearling lamb; (persona) sheep.

borroso,-a a blurred; **veo b.** I can't see clearly.

bosque m wood.

bosquejo m (de dibujo) sketch; (de plan) draft.

bostezar [4] vi to yawn.

bota f boot; (de vino) wineskin.

botana f Am snack.

botánico,-a a botanic; **jardín b.** botanic gardens pl.

botar 1 vi (saltar) to jump; (pelota) to bounce. 2 vt (barco) to launch; (pelota) to bounce; Am (arrojar) to throw out.

bote[1] m jump; (de pelota) bounce.

bote[2] m (lata) can, tin; (para propinas) jar o box for tips.

bote³ m (*lancha*) boat; **b. salvavidas** lifeboat.

botella f bottle.

botellín m small bottle.

botijo m earthenware pitcher (with spout and handle).

botín m (*de un robo*) loot.

botiquín m medicine cabinet; (*portátil*) first aid kit; (*enfermería*) first aid post.

botón m button.

botones m inv (*en hotel*) bellboy, bellhop; (*recadero*) errand boy.

boutique f boutique.

boxeador m boxer.

boxeo m boxing.

boya f (*baliza*) buoy; (*corcho*) float.

boy-scout m boy scout.

bozal m muzzle.

bracear vi (*nadar*) to swim.

bragas fpl panties pl, knickers pl.

bragueta f (*de pantalón etc*) fly, flies pl.

braille m Braille.

bramido m bellowing.

brandy m brandy.

brasa f ember; **chuletas a la b.** barbecued chops.

brasero m brazier.

brasileño,-a, Am **brasilero,-a** a & mf Brazilian.

bravo,-a 1 a (*valiente*) brave; **un toro b.** a fighting bull. **2** interj **¡b.!** well done!

braza f breast stroke; **nadar a b.** to do the breast stroke.

brazada f stroke.

brazalete m (*pulsera*) bracelet; (*insignia*) armband.

brazo m arm; **en brazos** in one's arms; **ir del b.** to walk arm in arm; **con los brazos abiertos** with open arms.

brecha f (*en muro*) gap; (*herida*) wound.

brécol m broccoli.

breva f (*higo*) early fig; fam **¡no caerá esa b.!** no such luck!

breve a brief; **en b., en breves momentos** shortly, soon.

brezo m heather.

bribón,-ona 1 a roguish. **2** mf rogue.

bricolaje m do-it-yourself, DIY.

bridge m bridge.

brigada f brigade; (*de policías*) squad.

brillante 1 a brilliant. **2** m diamond.

brillantina f brilliantine.

brillar vi (*resplandecer*) to shine; (*ojos, joyas*) to sparkle; (*lentejuelas etc*) to glitter.

brillo m (*resplandor*) shine; (*del sol, de la luna*) brightness; (*de lentejuelas etc*) glittering; (*del cabello, tela*) sheen; (*de zapatos*) shine; **sacar b. a** to polish.

brincar [1] vi to skip.

brindar 1 vi to drink a toast; **b. por algn/algo** drink to sb/sth. **2 brindarse** vr to volunteer (**a** to).

brindis m toast.

brío m energy.

brisa f breeze; **b. marina** sea breeze.

británico,-a 1 a British; **las Islas Británicas** the British Isles. **2** mf Briton; **los británicos** the British.

brocha f (*para pintar*) paintbrush; (*de afeitar*) shaving brush.

broche m (*joya*) brooch; (*de vestido*) fastener.

bróculi m broccoli.

broma f (*chiste*) joke; **en b.** as a joke; **¡ni en b.!** not on your life!; **b. pesada** practical joke; **gastar una b.** to play a joke.

bronca f (*riña*) row; **echar una b. a algn** to bawl sb out.

bronce m bronze.

bronceado,-a 1 a (sun)tanned. **2** m (sun)tan.

bronceador,-a 1 a **leche bronceadora** suntan lotion. **2** m suntan lotion.

bronquitis f inv bronchitis.

brotar vi (*planta*) to sprout; (*agua*) to gush; (*epidemia*) to break out.

bruces de b. face downwards; **se cayó de b.** he fell flat on his face.

bruja f witch.

brújula f compass.

bruma f mist.

brusco,-a a (persona) brusque; (repentino) sudden.

bruto,-a 1 a (necio) stupid; (grosero) coarse; (no neto) gross; **un diamante en b.** an uncut diamond. **2** mf blockhead.

bucear vi to swim under water.

bucle m curl.

budín m pudding.

budista a Buddhist.

buen a (delante de un nombre masculino singular) good; **¡b. viaje!** have a good trip!; ver **bueno, -a.**

buenamente adv **haz lo que b. puedas** just do what you can; **si b. puedes** if you possibly can.

bueno,-a 1 a good; (amable) (con ser) good, kind; (sano) (con estar) well, in good health; **un alumno muy b.** a very good pupil; **lo b.** the good thing; **hoy hace buen tiempo** it's fine today; **un buen número de** a good number of; **una buena cantidad** a considerable amount; **un buen trozo de pastel** a nice o good big piece of cake; **¡en buen lío te has metido!** that's a fine mess you've got yourself into!; **¡buenas!** (saludos) hello!; **buenas tardes** (desde mediodía hasta las cinco) good afternoon; (desde las cinco) good evening; **buenas noches** (al llegar) good evening; (al irse) good night; **buenos días** good morning; **de buenas a primeras** all at once; **por las buenas** willingly; **por las buenas o por las malas** willy-nilly; **¡buena la has hecho!** that's done it!; **¡estaría b.!** I should hope not!; **librarse de una buena** to get off scot free. **2** interj **¡b.!** (vale) all right, OK.

buey m ox.

búfalo,-a mf buffalo.

bufanda f scarf.

bufete m (despacho de abogado) lawyer's office.

buhardilla f attic.

búho m owl.

buitre m vulture.

bujía f (de coche) spark plug.

bulbo m bulb.

bulla f (ruido) noise; **armar b.** to make a lot of noise.

bullicio m noise.

bulto m (cosa indistinta) shape; (maleta, caja) piece of luggage; (hinchazón) lump; **hacer mucho b.** to be very bulky.

búnker m bunker.

buñuelo m doughnut.

buque m ship; **b. de guerra** warship; **b. de pasajeros** passenger ship.

burbuja f bubble.

burdel m brothel.

burguesía f bourgeoisie.

burladero m refuge in bullring.

burlarse vr to make fun (de of).

burlón,-ona a mocking.

burocracia f bureaucracy.

burocrático,-a a bureaucratic.

burro,-a 1 a (necio) stupid; (obstinado) stubborn.

bursátil a stock market.

busca f search; **ir en b. de** to go in search of.

buscar [1] **1** vt to look o search for; **ir a b. algo** to go and get sth; **fue a buscarme a la estación** she picked me up at the station. **2** buscarse vr fam **buscarse la vida** to try and earn one's living; **se busca** wanted.

búsqueda f search.

busto m bust.

butaca f (sillón) armchair; (de teatro, cine) seat; **b. de platea** o **patio** seat in the stalls.

butano m (gas) **b.** butane gas.

buzo m diver.

buzón m mailbox; **echar una carta al b.** to mail a letter.

C

cabalgar [7] vti to ride.

caballa f mackerel.

caballería *f* (*cuerpo*) cavalry; (*cabalgadura*) mount, steed.

caballero *m* gentleman; **ropa de c.** menswear; **caballeros** (*en letrero*) gents.

caballo *m* horse; (*de ajedrez*) knight; (*de naipes*) queen; **a c.** on horseback; **montar a c.** to ride; *fig* **a c. entre . . .** halfway between . . .

cabaña *f* (*choza*) cabin.

cabaret *m* (*pl* **cabarets**) cabaret.

cabecera *f* top, head.

cabecilla *mf* leader.

cabello *m* hair.

caber *vi* to fit; **cabe en el maletero** it fits in the boot; **en este coche/ jarro caben . . .** this car/jug holds . . .; **no cabe duda** there is no doubt; **cabe la posibilidad de que . . .** there is a possibility that . . .; **no está mal dentro de lo que cabe** it isn't bad, under the circumstances.

cabestrillo *m* sling.

cabeza 1 *f* head; **en c.** in the lead; **por c.** a head, per person; **a la c. de** at the head of; **estar mal de la c.** to be a mental case. **2** *mf* **el** o **la c. de familia** the head of the family.

cabida *f* capacity.

cabina *f* cabin; **c. telefónica** telephone booth.

cable *m* cable.

cabo *m* (*extremo*) end; (*rango*) corporal; (*policía*) sergeant; (*de barco*) rope, cable; (*geográfico*) cape; **al c. de** after; **atar cabos** to put two and two together.

cabra *f* goat.

cabré *indic fut de* **caber.**

cabriola *f* skip.

cacahuete *m* peanut.

cacao *m* cacao; (*polvo, bebida*) cocoa.

cacatúa *f* cockatoo.

cacerola *f* saucepan.

cacharro *m* earthenware pot *o* jar; *fam* (*cosa*) thing, piece of junk; **cacharros** (*de cocina*) pots and pans.

cachear *vt* to frisk, search.

cachetada *f* *Am* slap.

cachete *m* (*bofetada*) slap; *Am* (*mejilla*) cheek.

cachimba *f* pipe.

cachivache *m* *fam* thing, knick-knack.

cacho¹ *m* *fam* (*pedazo*) bit, piece.

cacho² *m* *Am* (*cuerno*) horn.

cachondeo *m* *fam* laugh; **tomar algo a c.** to take sth as a joke.

cachorro,-a *mf* (*de perro*) pup, puppy; (*de gato*) kitten; (*de otros animales*) cub, baby.

cacique *m* (*jefe*) local boss.

caco *m* *fam* thief.

cacto *m*, **cactus** *m inv* cactus.

cada *a* (*de dos*) each; (*de varios*) each, every; **c. día** every day; **c. dos días** every second day; **c. vez más** more and more; **¿c. cuánto?** how often?; **cuatro de c. diez** four out of (every) ten.

cadáver *m* (*de persona*) corpse, body; (*de animal*) body, carcass.

cadena *f* chain; (*correa de perro*) lead, leash; (*canal*) channel; (*de montañas*) range; **trabajo en c.** assembly line work; **c. perpetua** life imprisonment; (*para ruedas*) **cadenas** tire chains.

cadera *f* hip.

caducar [1] *vi* to expire.

caducidad *f* expiration; **fecha de c.** (*en alimentos*) ≈ sell-by date; (*en medicinas*) to be used before.

caer 1 *vi* to fall; (*entender*) to understand, see; (*hallarse*) to be; **dejar c.** to drop; **ya caigo** I get it; **cae por Granada** it is somewhere near Granada; **me cae bien/mal** I like/ don't like her. **2 caerse** *vr* to fall (down); **me caí de la moto** I fell off the motorbike; **se le cayó el pañuelo** she dropped her handkerchief.

café *m* coffee; (*cafetería*) café; **c. solo/con leche** black/white coffee.

cafeína *f* caffeine.

cafetera *f* (*para hacerlo*) coffee-maker; (*para servirlo*) coffeepot.

cafetería f snack bar, coffee bar; (en tren) buffet car.

caída f fall; (de pelo, diente) loss; (de gobierno) downfall, collapse.

caigo indic pres de **caer**.

caimán m cayman, alligator.

caja f (de embalaje) crate, case; (en tienda) cash desk; (en banco) cashier's desk; (féretro) coffin, casket; **c. fuerte** safe; **c. de cerveza** case of beer; **c. de cambios** gearbox; **c. de ahorros** o **de pensiones** savings bank.

cajero,-a mf cashier; **c. automático** automatic teller machine (ATM).

cajón m (en un mueble) drawer; (caja grande) crate, chest.

cal f lime; **a c. y canto** hermetically.

calabacín m (pequeño) zucchini; (grande) squash.

calabaza f pumpkin, gourd.

calabozo m (prisión) jail, prison; (celda) cell.

calado,-a a (mojado) soaked.

calamar m squid inv; **calamares a la romana** squid fried in batter.

calambre m (descarga) electric shock; (en músculo) cramp; **ese cable da c.** that wire is live.

calamidad f calamity.

calar 1 vt (mojar) to soak, drench. **2** vi (prenda) to let in water. **3 calarse** vr (prenda, techo) to let in water; (mojarse) to get soaked; (coche) to stall; **calarse el sombrero** to pull one's hat down.

calavera f skull.

calcar [1] vt (dibujo) to trace; (imitar) to copy, imitate.

calcetín m sock.

calcio m calcium.

calco m tracing; **papel de c.** carbon paper.

calculadora f calculator.

calcular vt to calculate; (evaluar) to (make an) estimate; (suponer) to guess.

cálculo m calculation; (matemático) calculus.

caldera f boiler.

caldo m stock, broth; **c. de cultivo** breeding ground.

calefacción f heating; **c. central** central heating.

calendario m calendar.

calentador m heater.

calentar [1] **1** vt (agua, horno) to heat; (comida, habitación) to warm up. **2 calentarse** vr to get hot, heat up.

calentura f fever, temperature.

calidad f quality; **de primera c.** first-class; **vino de c.** good-quality wine.

cálido,-a a warm.

caliente a hot; (debate) heated.

calificar [1] vt to describe (de, as); (examen) to mark, grade.

caligrafía f calligraphy; (modo de escribir) handwriting.

caliza f limestone.

callar 1 vi (dejar de hablar) to stop talking; (no hablar) to keep quiet, say nothing; **¡calla!** be quiet!, shut up! **2** vt (noticia) to not mention, keep to oneself. **3 callarse** vr to be quiet, shut up; **¡cállate!** shut up!

calle f street, road; (de piscina, pista) lane; **c. de dirección única** one-way street.

callejón m back alley, back street; **c. sin salida** cul-de-sac, dead end.

callista mf chiropodist.

callo m callus, corn; **callos** tripe sing.

calma f calm; **¡c.!** calm down!; **en c.** calm; **tómatelo con c.** take it easy.

calmante m painkiller; (relajante) tranquillizer.

calmar 1 vt (persona) to calm (down); (dolor) to soothe, relieve. **2 calmarse** vr (persona) to calm down; (dolor, viento) to ease off.

calor m heat; (entusiamo) warm; **hace c.** it's hot; **tengo c.** I'm hot; **entrar en c.** to warm up.

caloría f calorie.

calumnia f slander.

caluroso,-a a hot; (acogida etc) warm.

calvicie f baldness.
calvo,-a 1 a bald. **2** m bald man.
calzada f road.
calzado m shoes pl.
calzador m shoehorn.
calzar [4] **1** vt (poner calzado) to put shoes on; (mueble) to wedge; **¿qué número calzas?** what size shoe do you wear? **2 calzarse** vr **calzarse los zapatos** to put on one's shoes.
calzones nmpl trousers.
calzoncillos nmpl underpants, pants.
cama f bed; **estar en** o **guardar c.** to be confined to bed; **hacer la c.** to make the bed; **irse a la c.** to go to bed; **c. doble/sencilla** double/single bed.
cámara 1 f (aparato) camera; (de rueda) inner tube; **a c. lenta** in slow motion; **c. frigorífica** cold-storage room. **2** mf (hombre) cam-eraman; (mujer) camerawoman.
camarada mf comrade.
camarera f (de hotel) (chamber)-maid.
camarero,-a mf (de restaurante) (hombre) waiter; (mujer) waitress; (tras la barra) bartender.
camarón m prawn.
camarote m cabin.
cambiar 1 vt to change; (intercam-biar) to swap, exchange; **c. algo de sitio** to move sth. **2** vi to change; **c. de casa** to move (house); **c. de idea** to change one's mind. **3 cambiarse** vr (de ropa) to change (clothes); (de casa) to move (house).
cambio m change; (de impre-siones) exchange; (de divisas) ex-change; **c. de marcha** gear change; **a c. de** in exchange for; **en c.** on the other hand; **¿tienes c. de mil pese-tas?** have you got change for a thousand pesetas?
camello,-a mf camel.
camilla f stretcher.
caminar 1 vi to walk. **2** vt to walk; **caminaron diez kilómetros** they walked (for) ten kilometres.

camino m (ruta) route, way; (vía) path, track; **ponerse en c.** to set off; **abrirse c.** to break through; **a medio c.** half-way; **estar en c.** to be on the way; **nos coge** o **pilla de c.** it is on the way.
camión m truck; **c. cisterna** tanker; **c. de la basura** garbage truck; **c. frigorífico** refrigerated truck.
camionero,-a mf truck driver.
camioneta f van.
camisa f shirt; **en mangas de c.** in one's shirtsleeves; **c. de fuerza** straightjacket.
camiseta f (de uso interior) under-shirt; (de uso exterior) T-shirt; (de deporte) shirt.
camisón m nightgown.
camote m Am sweet potato.
campamento m camp.
campana f bell.
campanada f peal of a bell.
campanilla f small bell.
campaña f campaign; **c. electoral** election campaign; **c. publicitaria** advertising campaign.
campeón,-ona mf champion; **c. mundial** world champion.
campeonato m championship.
campesino,-a mf (hombre) coun-tryman; (mujer) countrywoman.
camping m campsite; **hacer** o **ir de c.** to go camping.
campista mf camper.
campo m country, countryside; (de fútbol) pitch; (de tenis) court; (de golf) course; (parcela, ámbito) field; **a c. traviesa** o **través** cross-country; **c. de batalla** battlefield; **c. de concentración** concentra-tion camp; **c. de trabajo** work camp.
camposanto m cemetery.
cana f (gris) grey hair; (blanco) white hair; **tener canas** to have grey hair.
canal m (artificial) canal; (natural, de televisión) channel; **C. de la Mancha** English Channel.
canalla mf swine, rotter.

canalón *m* gutter.

canapé *m* canapé; (*sofá*) couch, sofa.

canario,-a 1 *a* & *mf* Canarian; **Islas Canarias** Canary Islands, Canaries. **2** *m* (*pájaro*) canary.

canasta *f* basket.

cancela *f* wrought-iron gate.

cancelar *vt* to cancel; (*deuda*) to pay off.

cáncer *m* cancer; **c. de pulmón/ mama** lung/breast cancer.

cancerígeno,-a *a* carcinogenic.

canceroso,-a *a* cancerous.

cancha *f* ground; (*de tenis, baloncesto*) court.

canciller *mf* chancellor.

canción *f* song.

candado *m* padlock.

candelabro *m* candelabra.

candidato,-a *mf* candidate; (*a un puesto*) applicant.

candidatura *f* (*lista*) list of candidates.

cándido,-a *a* candid.

candoroso,-a *a* innocent, pure.

canela *f* cinnamon.

canelones *mpl* (*pasta*) cannelloni.

cangrejo *m* (*de mar*) crab; (*de río*) freshwater crayfish.

canguro 1 *m* kangaroo. **2** *mf fam* baby-sitter.

caníbal *a* & *mf* cannibal.

canica *f* marble.

canícula *f* dog days, midsummer heat.

caniche *m* poodle.

canillera *f Am* (*cobardía*) cowardice; (*miedo*) fear.

canillita *m Am* newspaper boy.

canino,-a 1 *a* canine. **2** *m* (*colmillo*) canine.

canoa *f* canoe.

canoso,-a *a* (*de pelo blanco*) white-haired; (*de pelo gris*) grayhaired; (*pelo*) white; gray.

cansado,-a *a* (*agotado*) tired, weary.

cansancio *m* tiredness, weariness.

cansar 1 *vt* to tire. **2** *vi* to be tiring. **3 cansarse** *vr* to get tired; **se cansó de esperar** he got tired of waiting, he got fed up (with) waiting.

cantante 1 *mf* singer. **2** *a* singing.

cantaor,-a *mf* flamenco singer.

cantar *vti* to sing.

cántaro *m* pitcher; **llover a cántaros** to rain cats and dogs.

cante *m* (*canto*) singing; **c. hondo, c. jondo** flamenco.

cantera *f* (*de piedra*) quarry; (*de equipo*) young players *pl*.

cantidad *f* quantity; (*de dinero*) sum; *fam* **c. de gente** thousands of people.

cantina *f* canteen.

canto[1] *m* (*arte*) singing; (*canción*) song.

canto[2] *m* (*borde*) edge; **de c.** on its side.

canturrear *vi* to hum, croon.

caña *f* (*de cerveza*) draft beer; (*tallo*) cane, stem; (*de pescar*) rod; **c. de azúcar** sugar cane.

cañada *f* (*barranco*) gully, ravine.

cañería *f* (piece of) piping; **cañerías** plumbing *sing*.

caño *m* (*tubería*) pipe; (*tubo*) tube; (*chorro*) spout.

cañón *m* cannon; (*de fusil*) barrel; (*garganta*) canyon.

cañonazo *m* gunshot.

caoba *f* mahogany.

caos *m* chaos.

caótico,-a *a* chaotic.

capa *f* (*prenda*) cloak, cape; (*de pintura*) layer, coat.

capacidad *f* capacity.

caparazón *m* shell.

capataz *mf* (*hombre*) foreman; (*mujer*) forewoman.

capaz *a* capable, able; **ser c. de hacer algo** (*tener la habilidad de*) to be able to do sth; (*atreverse a*) to dare to do sth; *Am* **es c. que** it is likely that.

capicúa *a* **número c.** reversible number; **palabra c.** palindrome.

capilla *f* chapel.

capital 1 f capital. **2** m (dinero) capital. **3** a capital, main; **pena c.** capital punishment.

capitalismo m capitalism.

capitalista a & mf capitalist.

capitán,-ana mf captain.

capitulación f agreement; (pacto) capitulation.

capítulo m (de libro) chapter; (tema) subject.

capó m (de coche) hood.

capota f (de coche) convertible.

capote m (de torero) cape.

capricho m (antojo) whim, caprice.

caprichoso,-a a whimsical.

cápsula f capsule.

captar vt (ondas) to receive, pick up; (comprender) to understand, grasp; (interés etc) to attract.

captura f capture.

capturar vt (criminal) to capture; (cazar, pescar) to catch.

capucha f hood.

capullo m (de insecto) cocoon; (de flor) bud.

caqui 1 a (color) khaki. **2** m (fruto) persimmon.

cara 1 f face; (lado) side; (de moneda) right side; fam (desfachatez) cheek, nerve; **c. a c.** face to face; **tener buena/mala c.** to look good/bad; **(de) c. a** with a view to; **echarle a algn algo en c.** to reproach sb for sth; **¿c. o cruz?** heads or tails?; **echar algo a c. o cruz** to flip (a coin) for sth; **¡qué c. (más dura) tienes!** you've got a lot of nerve! **2** m fam (desvergonzado) bold person.

caracol m (de tierra) snail; Am shell.

caracola f conch.

carácter m (pl **caracteres**) character; (índole) nature; **tener buen/mal c.** to be good-natured/bad-tempered.

característica f characteristic.

característico,-a a characteristic.

caramba interj (sorpresa) good grief!; (enfado) damn it!

carámbano m icicle.

caramelo m (dulce) candy; (azúcar quemado) caramel.

caravana f caravan; (cola) hatchback.

carbón m coal; **c. vegetal** charcoal; **c. mineral** coal.

carbonizar [4] vt, **carbonizarse** vr to char.

carbono m carbon.

carburador m carburetor.

carburante m fuel.

carcajada f guffaw.

cárcel f prison, jail.

carcelero,-a mf warden.

cardenal m cardinal; (en la piel) bruise.

cardiaco,-a, cardíaco,-a a cardiac, heart; **ataque c.** heart attack.

cardinal a cardinal; **punto/número c.** cardinal point/number.

cardiólogo,-a mf cardiologist.

cardo m (con espinas) thistle.

carecer vi **c. de** to lack.

carencia f lack (**de**, of).

careta f mask; **c. antigás** gas mask.

carezco indic pres de **carecer**.

carga f (acción) loading; (cosa cargada) load; (de avión, barco) cargo, freight; (explosiva, eléctrica) charge; (obligación) burden.

cargado,-a a loaded; (bebida) strong; **un café c.** a strong coffee; **atmósfera cargada** stuffy atmosphere; **c. de deudas** full of debt.

cargamento m (carga) load; (mercancías) cargo, freight.

cargar [7] **1** vt to load; (mechero, pluma) to fill; (batería) to charge; **cárguelo a mi cuenta** charge it to my account. **2** vi **c. con** (llevar) to carry; **c. con las consecuencias** to suffer the consequences. **3 cargarse** vr to load oneself with; fam (estropear) to smash, ruin; fam (matar) to kill, bump off.

cargo m (puesto) post, position; (persona) top person; (débito) charge, debit; (acusación) charge, accusation; **alto c.** (puesto) top job; **estar al c. de** to be in charge of; **co-**

rrer a c. de (*gastos*) to be met by; **hacerse c. de** to take charge of; **hazte c. de mi situación** please try to understand my situation; **con c. a mi cuenta** charged to my account.

caricatura f caricature.

caricia f caress, stroke.

caridad f charity.

caries f inv decay, caries.

cariño m (*amor*) affection; (*querido*) darling; **coger/tener c. a algo/algn** to grow/to be fond of sth/sb; **con c.** (*en carta*) love.

cariñoso,-a a loving, affectionate.

cariz m look.

carmín m (de color) c. carmine; **c. (de labios)** lipstick.

carnaval m carnival.

carne f flesh; (*alimento*) meat; **ser de c. y hueso** to be only flesh and blood; **c. de gallina** goose pimples; **c. de cerdo/cordero/ternera/vaca** pork/lamb/veal/beef.

carné, carnet m card; **c. de conducir** driver's license; **c. de identidad** identity card.

carnero m ram; (*carne*) mutton.

carnicería f butcher's (shop).

caro,-a a (*precios*) expensive; (*querido*) dear. **2** adv **salir c.** to cost a lot; **te costará c.** (*amenaza*) you'll pay dearly for this.

carpa f (*pez*) carp; (de circo) big top, marquee; Am (de camping) tent.

carpeta f folder.

carpintería f (oficio) carpentry; (taller) carpenter's (shop).

carpintero,-a mf carpenter.

carraspear vi to clear one's throat.

carrera f run; (de media) run, ladder; (competición) race; (estudios) degree; (profesión) career, profession; **c. de coches** rally, meeting; **echar una c. a algn** to race sb.

carrerilla f **tomar c.** to take a run; **de c.** parrot fashion.

carrete m (de hilo) reel; (de película) spool.

carretera f road; **c. de circunvala-**

ción bypass; **c. de acceso** access road.

carretilla f wheelbarrow.

carril m (de trenes) rail; (de carretera) lane.

carrillo m cheek.

carro m (carreta) cart; (de máquina de escribir) carriage; Am car; **c. de combate** tank.

carrocería f bodywork.

carta f letter; (menú) menu; (baraja) card; **c. certificada/urgente** registered/express letter; **a la c.** à la carte; **c. de vinos** wine list; **tomar cartas en un asunto** to take part in an affair.

cartel m poster.

cartera f (de bolsillo) wallet; (de mano) handbag; (para documentos etc) briefcase; (de colegial) satchel, schoolbag; Am (bolso) handbag, purse.

cartero,-a mf (hombre) postman; (mujer) postwoman.

cartilla f (libreta) book; (para leer) first reader; **c. de ahorros** savings book.

cartón m (material) card, cardboard; (de cigarrillos) carton.

cartucho m cartridge; (de papel) cone.

cartulina f card.

casa f (edificio) house; (hogar) home; (empresa) company, firm; **c. de huéspedes** boarding house; **c. de socorro** first aid post.

casado,-a 1 a married. **2** mf married person; **los recién casados** the newlyweds.

casar 1 vt to marry. **2 casarse** vr to marry, get married.

cascabel m bell.

cascada f waterfall, cascade.

cascar [1] vt, **cascarse** vr to crack.

cáscara f shell; (de fruta) skin, peel; (de grano) husk.

casco m helmet; (de caballo) hoof; (envase) empty bottle; (de barco) hull; **c. urbano** city center; **cascos** (auriculares) headphones.

casero,-a 1 a (hecho en casa) home-made; (persona) home-loving. **2** *mf* (*dueño*) (*hombre*) landlord; (*mujer*) landlady.

caseta *f* hut, booth; (*de feria*, *exposición*) stand, stall.

casete 1 *m* (*magnetófono*) cassette player *o* recorder. **2** *f* (*cinta*) cassette (tape).

casi *adv* almost, nearly; **c. nunca** hardly ever; **c. nadie** hardly anyone; **c. me caigo** I almost fell.

casino *m* casino.

caso *m* case; **el c. es que . . .** the thing is that . . .; **el c. Mattei** the Mattei affair; **(en) c. contrario** otherwise; **en c. de necesidad** if need be; **en cualquier c.** in any case; **en el mejor/peor de los casos** at best/ worst; **en ese c.** in such a case; **en todo c.** in any case; **hacer c.** a *o* de **algn** to pay attention to sb; **no venir al c.** to be beside the point; **pongamos por c.** let's say.

caspa *f* dandruff.

cassette *m & f* = **casete.**

castaña *f* chestnut.

castaño,-a 1 *a* chestnut-brown; (*pelo, ojos*) brown, dark. **2** *m* (*árbol*) chestnut.

castigar [7] *vt* to punish; (*penalizar*) to penalize.

castigo *m* punishment; (*pena*) penalty.

castillo *m* castle.

casual *a* accidental, chance.

casualidad *f* chance, coincidence; **de** *o* **por c.** by chance; **dio la c. de que . . .** it so happened that . . .; **¿tienes un lápiz, por c.?** do you happen to have a pencil?; **¡que c.!** what a coincidence!

casualmente *adv* by chance.

cataclismo *m* cataclysm.

catalejo *m* telescope.

catalogar [7] *vt* catalog; (*clasificar*) to classify.

catálogo *m* catalog.

catapulta *f* catapult.

catarata *f* waterfall; (*enfermedad*) cataract.

catarro *m* (common) cold.

catástrofe *f* catastrophe.

cátedra *f* (*universidad*) chair.

catedral *f* cathedral.

catedrático,-a *mf* (*de universidad*) professor; (*de instituto*) head of department.

categoría *f* category; **de c.** (*persona*) important.

cateto,-a *mf* (*paleto*) yokel, bumpkin.

católico,-a *a* & *mf* Catholic.

catorce *a* & *m inv* fourteen.

cauce *m* (*de un río*) bed; *fig* channel.

caucho *m* rubber; *Am* (*cubierta*) tire.

caudal *m* (*de un río*) flow; (*riqueza*) wealth.

caudillo *m* leader, head.

causa *f* cause; **a** *o* **por c. de** because of.

causante 1 *a* causal. **2** *mf* **el c. del incendio** the person who caused the fire.

causar *vt* to cause; **c. buena/mala impresión** to make a good/bad impression.

cautela *f* caution.

cautivar *vt* to capture, take prisoner.

cautiverio *m*, **cautividad** *f* captivity.

cautivo,-a *a* & *mf* captive.

cava 1 *f* (*bodega*) wine cellar. **2** *m* (*vino espumoso*) champagne.

cavar *vt* to dig.

caverna *f* cave.

caviar *m* caviar.

cavidad *f* cavity.

cavilar *vt* to ponder.

cayado *m* (*de pastor*) crook.

caza *f* hunting; (*animales*) game; (*persecución*) hunt; **ir de c.** to go hunting; **c. furtiva** poaching; **c. mayor/menor** big/small game.

cazador,-a *mf* hunter.

cazadora *f* (waist-length) jacket.

cazar [4] *vt* to hunt.

cazo *m* (*cacerola*) saucepan; (*cucharón*) ladle.

cazuela *f* saucepan; (*guiso*) casserole, stew; **a la c.** stewed.

cebada f barley.

cebo m bait.

cebolla f onion.

cebolleta f spring onion.

cebra f zebra; **paso de c.** crosswalk.

ceder 1 vt to give, hand over; **c. el paso** to give way. **2** vi (cuerda, cable) to give way; (consentir) to give in.

cédula f document, certificate; **c. de identidad** identity card.

cegar [1] vt to blind; (puerta, ventana) to wall up.

ceguera f blindness.

ceja f eyebrow.

celador,-a mf attendant; (de cárcel) warder.

celda f cell.

celebración f (festejo) celebration; (de juicio etc) holding.

celebrar 1 vt to celebrate; (reunión, juicio, elecciones) to hold. **2 celebrarse** vr to take place, be held.

célebre a famous, well-known.

celeste 1 a (de cielo) celestial; (color) sky-blue. **2** m sky blue.

celibato m celibacy.

celo m zeal; **en c.** (macho) in rut; (hembra) in heat; **celos** jealousy sing; **tener celos (de algn)** to be jealous (of sb).

celo® m Scotch tape®.

celofán m cellophane.

celoso,-a a jealous.

célula f cell.

celulitis f inv cellulite.

cementerio m cemetery.

cemento m cement; (hormigón) concrete.

cena f dinner.

cenar 1 vi to have dinner. **2** vt to have for dinner.

cenicero m ashtray.

cenit m zenith.

censo m census; **c. electoral** electoral roll.

censura f censorship; **moción de c.** vote of no confidence.

censurar vt (libro, película) to censor.

centavo m Am cent.

centellear vi to flash, sparkle.

centena f, **centenar** m hundred.

centenario m centenary.

centeno m rye.

centésimo,-a a & mf hundredth.

centígrado,-a a centigrade.

centilitro m centiliter.

centímetro m centimeter.

céntimo m cent.

centinela m sentry.

centollo m spider crab.

central 1 a central. **2** f (oficina principal) head office; **c. nuclear/térmica** nuclear/coal-fired power station.

centralismo m centralism.

centralita f switchboard.

centralizar [4] vt to centralize.

céntrico,-a a centrally situated.

centrifugar [7] vt (ropa) to spin-dry.

centro m center; **c. de la ciudad** city center; **c. comercial** shopping center, mall.

ceñido,-a a tight-fitting, clinging.

cepillar vt, **cepillarse** vr to brush.

cepillo m brush; (en carpintería) plane; **c. de dientes** toothbrush; **c. del pelo** hairbrush.

cera f wax; (de abeja) beeswax.

cerámica f ceramics sing.

cerca¹ 1 adv near, close; **de c.** closely. **2** prep **c. de** (al lado de) near, close to; (casi) nearly, around; **el colegio está c. de mi casa** the school is near my house; **c. de cien personas** about one hundred people.

cerca² f enclosure.

cercano,-a a nearby; **el C. Oriente** the Near East.

cercar [1] vt (tapiar) to fence, enclose; (rodear) to surround.

cerdo m pig; (carne) pork.

cereal m cereal.

cerebro m brain; (inteligencia) brains pl.

ceremonia f ceremony.

cereza f cherry.

cerezo *m* cherry tree.

cerilla *f* match.

cero *m* zero; (*en resultado*) nil; **ser un c. a la izquierda** to be useless.

cerrado,-a *a* closed, shut; (*intransigente*) uncompromising; (*acento*) broad; (*curva*) sharp.

cerradura *f* lock.

cerrar [1] **1** *vt* to shut, close; (*grifo, gas*) to turn off; (*cremallera*) to do up; (*negocio*) to close down; (*cuenta*) to close; (*sobre*) to seal; **c. con llave** to lock; **c. el paso a algn** to block sb's way. **2** *vi* to close, shut. **3 cerrarse** *vr* to close, shut.

cerril *a* (*obstinado*) pig-headed, headstrong.

cerro *m* hill.

cerrojo *m* bolt; **echar el c. (de una puerta)** to bolt (a door).

certamen *m* competition, contest.

certeza, certidumbre *f* certainty; **tener la c. de que . . .** to be certain that . . .

certificado,-a **1** *a* certified; (*correo*) registered. **2** *m* certificate; **c. médico** medical certificate.

cervecería *f* (*bar*) pub, bar; (*fábrica*) brewery.

cerveza *f* beer; **c. de barril** draft beer; **c. negra** stout.

cesar **1** *vi* to stop, cease (**de** -); **sin c.** incessantly. **2** *vt* (*empleado*) to dismiss.

césped *m* lawn, grass.

cesta *f* basket.

cesto *m* basket.

chabola *f* shack.

chacinería *f* pork butcher's shop.

chacra *f Am* small farm.

chafar *vt fam* (*plan etc*) to ruin; (*aplastar*) to squash.

chal *m* shawl.

chalado,-a *a fam* crazy, nuts (**por** about).

chalé *m* (*pl* **chalés**) villa.

chaleco *m* vest; (*de punto*) sleeveless pullover; **c. salvavidas** life jacket.

chalet *m* villa.

champán, champaña *m* champagne.

champiñón *m* mushroom.

champú *m* shampoo.

chamuscar [1] *vt* to singe, scorch.

chancaca *f Am* syrup cake.

chance *m Am* opportunity.

chancear *vi* to joke, horse around.

chanchada *f Am fam* dirty trick.

chancho,-a *m f Am* pig.

chancla *f* flipflop.

chándal *m* track suit, jogging suit.

chantaje *m* blackmail; **hacer c. a algn** to blackmail sb.

chantajear *vt* to blackmail.

chapa *f* (*tapón*) bottle top, cap; (*de adorno*) badge; *Am* lock.

chapado,-a *a* (*metal*) plated; **c. en oro** gold-plated.

chaparrón *m* downpour, heavy shower.

chapotear *vi* to splash about, paddle.

chapurrear *vt* (*idioma*) to speak badly.

chapuza *f* (*trabajo mal hecho*) shoddy piece of work; (*trabajo ocasional*) odd job.

chapuzón *m* (*baño corto*) dip; **darse un c.** to have a dip.

chaqueta *f* jacket.

charca *f* pond, pool.

charco *m* puddle.

charcutería *f* delicatessen.

charla *f* (*conversación*) talk, chat; (*conferencia*) informal lecture.

charlar *vi* to talk, chat.

charlatán,-ana **1** *a* (*parlanchín*) talkative. **2** *mf* (*parlanchín*) chatterbox; (*embaucador*) charlatan.

charol *m* patent leather.

chárter *a inv* **vuelo c.** charter flight.

chasca *f Am* (*cabellera revuelta*) mop of hair, tangled hair.

chasco *m fam* (*decepción*) disappointment; **llevarse un c.** to be disappointed.

chasis *m inv* chassis.

chasqui *m Am* messenger, courier.

chasquido *m* (*de la lengua*) click;

(de los dedos) snap; (de látigo, madera) crack.

chatarra f scrap (metal), scrap iron; (cosa inservible) junk.

chato,-a a (nariz) snub; (persona) snub-nosed.

chauvinista a & mf chauvinist.

chaval,-a mf (chico) boy, lad; (chica) girl, lass.

chepa f hump.

cheque m check; **c. de viaje** traveler's check.

chequeo m checkup.

chicano,-a a a & mf chicano.

chicha f Am maize liquor.

chícharo m Am (guisante) pea.

chicharra f cicada.

chichón m bump, lump.

chicle m chewing gum.

chico,-a 1 mf (muchacho) boy, lad; (muchacha) girl, lass. **2** a (pequeño) small, little.

chicote m Am whip.

chiflado,-a a fam mad, crazy (por about).

chillar vi (persona) to scream, shriek.

chillido m (de persona) scream, shriek.

chillón,-ona a (voz) shrill, high-pitched; (sonido) harsh; (color) loud.

chimenea f fireplace, hearth; (conducto) chimney.

chincheta f thumbtack.

chingana f Am bar.

chip m (pl **chips**) chip.

chipirón m baby squid.

chiquillo,-a mf kid, youngster.

chiringuito m (en playa etc) refreshment stall; (en carretera) roadside snack bar.

chirriar vi (puerta) to creak; (frenos) to screech.

chirrido m (de puerta) creak, creaking; (de frenos) screech.

chisme m (habladuría) piece of gossip; fam (trasto) knick-knack; (cosa) thing.

chismear vi to gossip.

chismoso,-a 1 a (murmurador) gossipy. **2** mf gossip.

chispa f spark.

chispear vi to spark; (lloviznar) to spit.

chiste m joke; **contar un c.** to tell a joke.

chivatazo m fam (soplo) tip-off; **dar el c.** to squeal.

chivato,-a mf fam (acusica) tell-tale; (delator) grass.

chocante a (sorprendente) surprising; (raro) strange.

chocar [1] **1** vi (topar) to crash, collide; (pelota) to hit, strike; **c. con o contra** to run into, collide with. **2** vt to knock; (sorprender) to surprise.

chochear vi (viejo) to be senile.

chocolate m chocolate.

chocolatina f bar of chocolate, chocolate bar.

chófer m (pl **chóferes**), Am **chofer** m (pl **choferes**) driver; (particular) chauffeur.

chomba f Am jumper, pullover.

chonta f Am palm tree.

chopo m poplar.

choque m impact; (de coches etc) crash, collision.

chorizo m highly-seasoned pork sausage.

chorrear vi to gush, spurt; (gotear) to drip, trickle; fam **estoy chorreando** I am soaking wet.

chorro m (de agua etc) spurt; (muy fino) trickle; **salir a chorros** to gush forth.

chovinista 1 a chauvinistic. **2** mf chauvinist.

choza f hut, shack.

chubasco m heavy shower, downpour.

chubasquero m raincoat.

chuleta f chop, cutlet; **c. de cerdo** pork chop.

chulo,-a fam **1** mf show-off. **2** a (bonito) smashing.

chupachup® m lollipop.

chupar 1 vt to suck; (lamer) to lick; (absorber) to soak up, absorb. **2** vi to suck. **3 chuparse** vr **está para chuparse los dedos** it's really mouthwatering.

chupete m pacifier.

churrete *m* dirty mark, grease spot.

churro *m* cruller.

chutar *vi* (*a gol*) to shoot.

cicatriz *f* scar.

cicatrizar [4] *vti* to heal.

ciclismo *m* cycling.

ciclista 1 *a* cycling. 2 *mf* cyclist.

ciclo *m* cycle; (*de conferencias etc*) series.

ciclomotor *m* moped.

ciclón *m* cyclone.

ciego,-a 1 *a* blind; **a ciegas** blindly. 2 *mf* blind person; **los ciegos** the blind *pl*.

cielo *m* sky; (*gloria*) heaven; (*de la boca*) roof.

ciempiés *m inv* centipede.

cien *a & m inv* hundred; **c. libras** *a* *o* one hundred pounds; **c. por c.** one hundred per cent.

ciencia *f* science; **saber algo a c. cierta** to know something for certain; **c. ficción** science fiction.

cieno *m* mud.

científico,-a 1 *a* scientific. 2 *mf* scientist.

ciento *a* hundred; **c. tres** one hundred and three; **por c.** per cent.

cierre *m* (*acción*) closing, shutting; (*de fábrica*) shutdown; (*de emisión*) close-down; (*de bolso*) clasp; (*de puerta*) catch.

cierto,-a 1 *a* certain; (*verdadero*) true; **lo c. es que . . .** the fact is that . . .; **por c.** by the way. 2 *adv* certainly.

ciervo,-a *mf* deer; (*macho*) stag; (*hembra*) doe, hind.

cifra *f* (*número*) figure, number; (*suma*) amount.

cigala *f* Norway lobster.

cigarra *f* cicada.

cigarrillo *m* cigarette.

cigarro *m* (*cigarrillo*) cigarette; (*puro*) cigar.

cigüeña *f* stork.

cilindro *m* cylinder.

cima *f* summit.

cimientos *nmpl* foundations.

cinco *a & m inv* five.

cincuenta *a & m inv* fifty.

cine *m* movie theater; (*arte*) cinema.

cinematográfico,-a *a* cinematographic; **la industria cinematográfica** movie industry.

cínico,-a 1 *a* cynical. 2 *mf* cynic.

cinta *f* (*tira*) band, strip; (*para adornar*) ribbon; (*película*) film; **c. adhesiva/aislante** adhesive/insulating tape; **c. de vídeo** video tape; **c. transportadora** conveyor belt.

cintura *f* waist.

cinturón *m* belt; **c. de seguridad** safety belt.

ciprés *m* cypress.

circo *m* circus.

circuito *m* circuit.

circulación *f* circulation; (*tráfico*) traffic.

circular 1 *a & f* circular. 2 *vi* (*moverse*) to circulate; (*líquido*) to flow; (*tren, autobús*) to run; (*rumor*) to go round.

círculo *m* circle.

circuncisión *f* circumcision.

circundante *a* surrounding.

circunferencia *f* circumference.

circunscripción *f* district.

circunstancia *f* circumstance.

cirio *m* wax candle.

ciruela *f* plum; **c. claudia** greengage; **c. pasa** prune.

ciruelo *m* plum tree.

cirugía *f* surgery; **c. estética** *o* **plástica** plastic surgery.

cirujano,-a *mf* surgeon.

cisne *m* swan.

cisterna *f* cistern, tank.

cita *f* appointment; (*amorosa*) date; (*mención*) quotation.

citar *vt* (*mencionar*) to quote; **me ha citado el dentista** I have an appointment with the dentist.

cítrico,-a 1 *a* citric, citrus. 2 *nmpl* **cítricos** citrus fruits.

ciudad *f* town; (*grande*) city.

ciudadano,-a 1 *mf* citizen. 2 *a* civic.

cívico,-a *a* civic.

civil *a* civil; (*no militar*) civilian; **matrimonio c.** civil marriage.

civilización *f* civilization.

civilizado,-a *a* civilized.

civismo *m* civility.

clamoroso,-a *a* resounding.

clan *m* clan.

clandestino,-a *a* clandestine.

clara *f (de huevo)* white.

claraboya *f* skylight.

clarear *vi (amanecer)* to dawn; *(despejar)* to clear up.

clarete *a & m* claret.

claridad *f (luz)* brightness; *(inteligibilidad)* clarity; **con c.** clearly.

clarificar [1] *vt* to clarify.

clarinete *m* clarinet.

claro,-a 1 *a* clear; *(líquido, salsa)* thin; *(color)* light. **2** *interj* of course!; **¡c. que no!** of course not!; **¡c. que sí!** certainly! **3** *m (en un bosque)* clearing; *(tiempo despejado)* bright spell. **4** *adv* clearly.

clase *f* class; *(tipo)* kind, sort; *(curso)* class; *(aula)* classroom; **c. alta/media** upper/middle class; **primera/segunda c.** first/second class; **toda c. de . . .** all kinds of . . .

clásico,-a 1 *a* classical; *(típico, en el vestir)* classic. **2** *m* classic.

clasificación *f* classification; *(para campeonato, concurso)* qualification.

clasificar [1] **1** *vt* to classify, class. **2 clasificarse** *vr* to qualify.

claustrofobia *f* claustrophobia.

cláusula *f* clause.

clausura *f (cierre)* closure.

clavar 1 *vt* to nail; *(clavo)* to hammer in; *(estaca)* to drive in. **2 clavarse** *vr* **clavarse una astilla** to get a splinter.

clave *f* key; **la palabra c.** the key word.

clavel *m* carnation.

clavícula *f* collarbone.

clavo *m* nail; *fig* **dar en el c.** to hit the nail on the head; *(especia)* clove.

claxon *m (pl* **cláxones)** horn; **tocar el c.** to sound the horn.

clemencia *f* mercy, clemency.

clementina *f* clementine.

clérigo *m* priest.

clero *m* clergy.

cliché *m (tópico)* cliché; *(negativo)* negative.

cliente *mf* customer, client.

clima *m* climate.

climatizado,-a *a* air-conditioned.

clínica *f* clinic.

clip *m (para papel)* clip.

cloaca *f* sewer, drain.

cloro *m* chlorine.

cloroformo *m* chloroform.

club *m (pl* **clubs** *o* **clubes)** club; **c. náutico** yacht club.

coacción *f* coercion.

coalición *f* coalition.

coartada *f* alibi.

cobarde 1 *a* cowardly. **2** *mf* coward.

cobaya *f* guinea pig.

cobertizo *m* shed, shack.

cobertor *m* bedspread.

cobija *f Am* blanket.

cobijar *vt,* **cobijarse** *vr* to shelter.

cobra *f* cobra.

cobrador,-a *mf (de autobús) (hombre)* conductor; *(mujer)* conductress; *(de luz, agua etc)* collector.

cobrar *vt (dinero)* to charge; *(cheque)* to cash; *(salario)* to earn; **c. importancia** to become important.

cobre *m* copper; *Am (moneda)* copper cent.

cobro *m (pago)* collecting; *(de cheque)* cashing; **llamada a c. revertido** collect call.

coca *f* coca.

cocaína *f* cocaine.

cocción *f* cooking; *(en agua)* boiling; *(en horno)* baking.

cocer [4] *vt,* **cocerse** *vr (comida)* to cook; *(hervir)* to boil; *(en horno)* to bake.

coche *m* car; **en c.** by car; **c. de bomberos** fire engine; *(vagón)* carriage, coach; **c. cama** sleeper.

cochecito *m (de niño)* baby carriage.

cochera *f* garage; *(de autobuses)* depot.

cochino,-a 1 *mf (macho)* pig;

(*hembra*) sow; *fam* (*persona*) pig. **2** *a* (*sucio*) filthy.

cocido *m* stew.

cocina *f* kitchen; (*aparato*) cooker; (*arte*) cooking; **c. eléctrica/de gas** electric/gas cooker; **c. casera** home cooking.

cocinar *vti* to cook.

cocinero,-a *mf* cook.

coco *m* coconut.

cocodrilo *m* crocodile.

cocotero *m* coconut palm.

cóctel *m* cocktail.

codazo *m* (*señal*) nudge with one's elbow; (*golpe*) blow with one's elbow.

codicia *f* greed.

codicioso,-a **1** *a* covetous. **2** *mf* greedy person.

código *m* code.

codo *m* elbow; *fam* **hablar por los codos** to talk nonstop.

coeficiente *m* **c. intelectual** IQ.

coetáneo,-a *a & mf* contemporary.

coexistir *vi* to coexist.

cofre *m* trunk, chest.

coger [5] **1** *vt* to take; (*del suelo*) to pick (up); (*fruta, flores*) to pick; (*asir*) to seize, take hold of; (*coche, bus*) to take, catch; (*pelota, ladrón, resfriado*) to catch; (*atropellar*) to run over. **2 cogerse** *vr* (*agarrarse*) to hold on.

cogote *m* back of the neck.

cohabitar *vi* to live together, cohabit.

coherente *a* coherent.

cohete *m* rocket.

cohibir **1** *vt* to inhibit. **2 cohibirse** *vr* to feel inhibited.

coincidencia *f* coincidence.

coincidir *vi* to coincide; (*concordar*) to agree; (*encontrarse*) to meet by chance.

cojear *vi* (*persona*) to limp; (*mesa etc*) to wobble.

cojín *m* cushion.

cojinete *m* bearing.

cojo,-a **1** *a* (*persona*) lame; (*mueble*) rickety. **2** *mf* lame person.

col *f* cabbage; **c. de Bruselas** Brussels sprout.

cola[1] *f* tail; (*de vestido*) train; (*de pelo*) ponytail; (*fila*) line; **a la c.** at the back; **hacer c.** to stand in line.

cola[2] *f* glue.

colaboración *f* collaboration.

colaborador,-a **1** *mf* collaborator. **2** *a* collaborating.

colaborar *vi* to collaborate.

colada *f* wash, laundry; **hacer la c.** to do the washing.

colador *m* colander, sieve; (*de té, café*) strainer.

colapso *m* collapse; **c. circulatorio** traffic jam.

colar [2] **1** *vt* (*líquido*) to strain. **2 colarse** *vr* to slip in; (*a fiesta*) to gatecrash; (*en una cola*) to cut in line.

colcha *f* bedspread.

colchón *m* mattress.

colchoneta *f* air bed.

colección *f* collection.

coleccionar *vt* to collect.

colecta *f* collection.

colectivo,-a **1** *a* collective. **2** *m* (*asociación*) association; *Am* long-distance taxi.

colega *mf* colleague.

colegial,-a **1** *a* (*escolar*) school. **2** *mf* (*alumno*) schoolboy; (*alumna*) schoolgirl; **los colegiales** the schoolchildren.

colegio *m* (*escuela*) school; **c. mayor** *o* **universitario** (*residencia*) residence hall.

cólera[1] *f* anger, rage.

cólera[2] *m* (*enfermedad*) cholera.

colesterol *m* cholesterol.

colgante **1** *m* (*joya*) pendant. **2** *a* hanging.

colgar [2] **1** *vt* to hang (up); (*colada*) to hang (out); (*ahorcar*) to hang. **2** *vi* to hang (**de** from); (*teléfono*) to hang up. **3 colgarse** *vr* (*ahorcarse*) to hang oneself.

cólico *m* colic.

coliflor *f* cauliflower.

colilla *f* cigarette end.

colina *f* hill.

colirio *m* eyedrops.

colisión f collision, crash.

collar m (adorno) necklace; (de perro) collar.

colmado,-a a full, filled; (cucharada) heaped.

colmena f beehive.

colmillo m eye tooth; (de carnívoro) fang; (de jabalí, elefante) tusk.

colmo m ¡eso es el c.! that's the last straw!; **para c.** to top it all off.

colocación f (acto) positioning; (situación) situation; (empleo) job.

colocar [1] **1** vt to place, put; (emplear) to give work to. **2 colocarse** vr (situarse) to put oneself; (emplearse) to take a job (**de** as).

Colón n Columbus.

colonia¹ f colony; (campamento) summer camp.

colonia² f (agua de colonia) cologne.

colonial a colonial.

colonizar [4] vt to colonize.

coloquio m discussion.

color m color; **de colores** multicolored.

colorado,-a **1** a red; **ponerse c.** to blush. **2** m red.

colorante m coloring.

colorear vt to color.

colorete m rouge.

colorido m color.

columna f column; **c. vertebral** spinal column.

columpio m swing.

coma¹ f (ortográfica) comma.

coma² m (estado) coma.

comadrona f midwife.

comandante m commander, commanding officer; (de avión) captain.

comarca f region.

combate m combat; (de boxeo) fight; (batalla) battle; **fuera de c.** out for the count.

combatir vti to fight.

combinación f combination; (prenda) slip.

combinar vt, **combinarse** vr to combine.

combustible **1** m fuel. **2** a combustible.

comedia f comedy.

comedor m dining room.

comentar vt (escribir) to comment on; (discutir) to discuss.

comentario m comment; **sin c.** no comment.

comenzar [1] vti to begin, start; **comenzó a llover** it started raining o to rain; **comenzó diciendo que . . .** he started by saying that . . .

comer **1** vti to eat; **dar de c. a algn** to feed sb. **2 comerse** vr to eat.

comercial a commercial.

comercializar [4] vt to market.

comerciante mf merchant.

comercio m commerce, trade; (tienda) shop.

comestible **1** a edible. **2** nmpl **comestibles** food sing.

cometa **1** m comet. **2** f (juguete) kite.

cometer vt (error, falta) to make; (delito, crimen) to commit.

comezón m itch.

comicios nmpl elections.

cómico,-a **1** a (divertido) comical, funny; **actor c.** comic. **2** mf comic; (hombre) comedian; (mujer) comedienne.

comida f (alimento) food; (almuerzo, cena) meal.

comienzo m beginning, start; **dar c. (a algo)** to start (sth).

comillas nfpl inverted commas; **entre c.** in inverted commas.

comisaría f police station.

comisión f (retribución) commission; (comité) committee.

comité m committee.

como **1** adv (manera) as; **hazlo c. quieras** do it however you like. ▪ (comparación) as; **blanco c. la nieve** as white as snow; **habla c. su padre** he talks like his father. ▪ (según) as; **c. decíamos ayer** as we were saying yesterday. ▪ (en calidad de) as; **lo compré c. recuerdo** I bought it as a souvenir. ▪ (aproxi *madamente*) about; **c. unos diez** about ten. **2** *conj* **c. + *subj* (*si*)** if; **c. no estudies vas a suspender** if you don't study hard, you'll fail. ■ (*porque*) as, since; **c. no venías me marché** as you didn't come I left. ■ **c. si as** if; **c. si nada** *o* **tal cosa** as if nothing had happened.

cómo *adv* **¿c.?** (*¿perdón?*) what? ■ (*interrogativo*) how; **¿c. estás?** how are you?; **¿a c. están los tomates?** (*a cuánto*) how much are the tomatoes?; (*por qué*) **¿c. es eso?** how come?; **¿c. fue que no viniste a la fiesta?** how come you didn't come to the party? ■ (*exclamativo*) how; **¡c. has crecido!** you've really grown a lot!; **¡c. no!** but of course!

cómoda *f* chest of drawers.

comodidad *f* comfort; (*conveniencia*) convenience.

comodín *m* joker.

cómodo,-a *a* comfortable; (*útil*) handy, convenient.

compacto,-a *a* compact; **disco c.** compact disc.

compadecer 1 *vt* to feel sorry for, pity. **2 compadecerse** *vr* to take pity (**de** on).

compañero,-a *mf* companion; **c. de piso** roommate.

compañía *f* company; **hacer c. a algn** to keep sb company.

comparación *f* comparison; **en c.** comparatively; **en c. con** compared to; **sin c.** beyond compare.

comparar *vt* to compare (**con** with).

compartimento, compartimiento *m* compartment.

compartir *vt* to share.

compás *m* (pair of) compasses; (*brújula*) compass; (*ritmo*) rhythm; **al c. de** in time to.

compasión *f* compassion, pity; **tener c. de algn** to feel sorry for sb.

compatible *a* compatible.

compatriota *mf* compatriot; (*hombre*) fellow countryman; (*mujer*) fellow countrywoman.

compensar 1 *vt* (*pérdida, error*) to make up for; (*indemnizar*) to compensate (for). **2** *vi* to be worthwhile.

competencia *f* (*rivalidad, empresas rivales*) competition; (*capacidad*) competence; (*incumbencia*) field.

competición *f* competition.

competir [6] *vi* to compete.

competitivo,-a *a* competitive.

compinche *mf* (*cómplice*) accomplice.

complacer *vt* to please.

complejo,-a *a* & *m* complex.

complemento *m* complement; (*objeto*) object.

completar *vt* to complete.

completo,-a *a* (*terminado*) complete; (*lleno*) full; **por c.** completely.

completamente *adv* completely.

complicado,-a *a* (*complejo*) complicated; (*implicado*) involved.

complicar [1] **1** *vt* to complicate; (*involucrar*) to involve (**en** in). **2 complicarse** *vr* to get complicated.

cómplice *mf* accomplice.

complot *m* (*pl* **complots**) conspiracy, plot.

componer (*pp* **compuesto**) **1** *vt* to compose; (*reparar*) to mend, repair. **2 componerse** *vr* (*consistir*) to be made up (**de** of), consist (**de** of).

comportamiento *m* behavior.

composición *f* composition.

compra *f* (*acción*) buying; (*cosa comprada*) purchase, buy; **ir de compras** to go shopping.

comprar *vt* to buy.

comprender *vt* (*entender*) to understand; (*contener*) to comprise, include.

comprensión *f* understanding.

comprensivo,-a *a* understanding.

compresa *f* (*para mujer*) sanitary napkin.

comprimido,-a 1 *m* tablet. **2** *a* compressed.

comprobar [2] *vt* to check.

comprometer 1 *vt* (*arriesgar*) to compromise; (*obligar*) to compel. **2 comprometerse** *vr* (*involucrarse*) to involve oneself; (*novios*) to become engaged; **comprometerse a hacer algo** to undertake to do sth.

compromiso *m* (*obligación*) obligation, commitment; (*acuerdo*) agreement; **por c.** out of a sense of duty; **poner a algn en un c.** to put sb in a difficult situation.

compuesto,-a *a* compound; **c. de** composed of. **2** *m* compound.

compuse *pt indef de* **componer.**

computadora *f* computer.

común *a* common; (*compartido*) shared; **poco c.** unusual; **por lo c.** generally.

comunicación *f* communication; (*oficial*) communiqué; (*telefónica*) connection; (*unión*) link, connection.

comunicar [1] **1** *vt* to communicate; **comuníquenoslo lo antes posible** let us know as soon as possible. **2** *vi* to communicate; (*teléfono*) to be engaged. **3 comunicarse** *vr* to communicate.

comunidad *f* community; **C. Europea** European Community.

comunión *f* communion.

con *prep* with; **c. ese frío/niebla** in that cold/fog; **estar c. (la) gripe** to have the flu; **una bolsa c. dinero** a bag (full) of money; **habló c. todos** he spoke to everybody. ▪ (*con infinitivo*) **c. llamar será suficiente** it will be enough just to phone. ▪ (*con subj* + **que**) **bastará c. que lo esboces** a general idea will do; **c. tal (de) que . . .** provided that . . .

concebir [6] **1** *vt* (*plan, hijo*) to conceive; (*entender*) to understand. **2** *vi* (*mujer*) to conceive.

conceder *vt* to grant; (*premio*) to award; (*admitir*) to concede.

concejal,-a *mf* town councilor.

concentración *f* concentration; (*de manifestantes*) gathering.

concentrar *vt,* **concentrarse** *vr* to concentrate (**en** on).

concepción *f* conception.

concepto *m* concept; **bajo/por ningún c.** under no circumstances.

concernir [5] *v impers* (*afectar*) to concern; (*corresponder*) to be up to; **en lo que a mí concierne** as far as I am concerned; **en lo que concierne a** with regard to/respect to.

concesión *f* concession; (*de premio, contrato*) awarding.

concha *f* (*caparazón*) shell; (*carey*) tortoiseshell.

conciencia *f* conscience; (*conocimiento*) consciousness, awareness; **a c.** conscientiously.

concienzudo,-a *a* conscientious.

concierto *m* concert; (*composición*) concerto; (*acuerdo*) agreement.

concluir *vt* to conclude.

conclusión *f* conclusion; **sacar una c.** to draw a conclusion.

concreto,-a 1 *a* (*preciso, real*) concrete; (*particular*) specific; **en c.** specifically. **2** *m Am* concrete.

concretamente *adv* specifically.

concurrido,-a *a* crowded, busy.

concursante *mf* contestant, competitor.

concurso *m* (*competición*) competition; (*de belleza etc*) contest; (*televisivo*) quiz show.

condena *f* sentence; (*desaprobación*) condemnation, disapproval.

condenado,-a 1 *a* convicted; **c. a muerte** condemned to death. **2** *mf* convicted person; (*a muerte*) condemned person.

condenar *vt* to convict, find guilty; (*desaprobar*) to condemn.

condensado,-a *a* condensed; **leche condensada** condensed milk.

condensar *vt,* **condensarse** *vr* to condense.

condición *f* condition; **en buenas/ malas condiciones** in good/bad condition; **con la c. de que . . .** on condition that . . .

condimento *m* seasoning, flavoring.

condón *m* condom.

conducir 1 *vt* (*coche*) to drive; (*electricidad*) to conduct. **2** *vi* to drive; (*llevar*) to lead; **permiso de c.** driver's license.

conducta *f* behavior, conduct.

conducto *m* (*tubería*) pipe.

conductor,-a *mf* driver.

conectar *vt* to connect up; (*enchufar*) to plug in, switch on.

conejillo *m* **c. de Indias** guinea pig.

conejo *m* rabbit.

conexión *f* connection.

confección *f* dressmaking; (*de ropa masculina*) tailoring; (*de plan*) making.

conferencia *f* lecture; (*telefónica*) long-distance call.

confesar [1] **1** *vti* to confess. **2 confesarse** *vr* to confess; (*de pecados*) to go to confession; **confesarse culpable** to admit one's guilt.

confianza *f* (*seguridad*) confidence; **tener c. en uno mismo** to be self-confident; **de c.** reliable; **tener c. con algn** to be on intimate terms with sb.

confiar 1 *vt* (*entregar*) to entrust; (*información, secreto*) to confide. **2** *vi* **c. en** to trust; **no confíes en su ayuda** don't count on his help. **3 confiarse** *vr* to confide (**en, a** in).

confidencial *a* confidential.

confirmar *vt* to confirm.

confiscar [1] *vt* to confiscate.

confitería *f* candy store; *Am* café.

confitura *f* preserve, jam.

conflicto *m* conflict.

conformarse *vr* **tendrás que conformarte (con esto)** you will have to be content with that.

conforme 1 *a* (*satisfecho*) satisfied; **no estoy c.** I don't agree. **2** *conj* as. **3** *prep* **c. a** in accordance with.

confort *m* (*pl* **conforts**) comfort.

confortable *a* comfortable.

confrontación *f* confrontation.

confundir 1 *vt* to confuse (**con** with); (*engañar*) to mislead; **c. a una persona con otra** to mistake somebody for somebody else. **2 confundirse** *vr* (*equivocarse*) to be mistaken; (*mezclarse*) to mingle; (*colores, formas*) to blend.

confusión *f* confusion.

confuso,-a *a* confused; (*formas, recuerdo*) vague.

congelado,-a 1 *a* frozen. **2** *nmpl* **congelados** frozen food *sing.*

congelador *m* freezer.

congelar 1 *vt* to freeze. **2 congelarse** *vr* to freeze.

congoja *f* sorrow, grief.

congreso *m* congress, conference; **c. de los Diputados** ≈ Congress.

congrio *m* conger eel.

conjugación *f* conjugation.

conjunción *f* conjunction.

conjunto,-a 1 *m* (*grupo*) collection, group; (*todo*) whole; (*pop*) group, band; (*prenda*) outfit; **de c.** overall; **en c.** on the whole. **2** *a* joint.

conmemoración *f* commemoration.

conmigo *pron pers* with me; **él habló c.** he talked to me.

conmoción *f* commotion, shock; **c. cerebral** concussion.

conmovedor,-a *a* touching.

conmover [4] *vt* to touch, move.

conmutador *m* switch; *Am* switchboard.

cono *m* cone.

conocedor,-a *a* & *mf* expert; (*de vino, arte etc*) connoisseur.

conocer 1 *vt* to know; (*por primera vez*) to meet; (*reconocer*) to recognize; **dar (algo/algn) a c.** to make (sth/sb) known. **2 conocerse** *vr* (*dos personas*) to know each other; (*por primera vez*) to meet.

conocido,-a 1 *a* known; (*famoso*) well-known. **2** *mf* acquaintance.

conocimiento *m* knowledge; (*conciencia*) consciousness; **perder/recobrar el c.** to lose/regain consciousness; **conocimientos** knowledge.

conquistador,-a *mf* conqueror.

conquistar *vt* (*país, ciudad*) to conquer; **c. a algn** to make a conquest of sb.

consabido,-a *a* (*bien conocido*) well-known; (*usual*) familiar, usual.

consagrar 1 *vt* (*artista*) to establish; (*vida, tiempo*) to devote. **2 consagrarse** *vr* (*dedicarse*) to devote oneself (**a** to); (*lograr fama*) to establish oneself.

consciente *a* conscious.

consecuencia *f* consequence; (*coherencia*) consistency; **a** o **como c. de** as a consequence of; **en c.** therefore.

consecuente *a* consistent.

consecutivo,-a *a* consecutive; **tres días consecutivos** three days in a row.

conseguir [6] *vt* to get, obtain; (*objetivo*) to achieve; (*lograr*) to manage.

consejero,-a *mf* (*asesor*) adviser; (*ministro*) regional minister.

consejo *m* (*recomendación*) advice; (*junta*) council; (*reunión*) cabinet meeting; **un c.** a piece of advice; **c. de ministros** cabinet; **c. de administración** board of directors.

consentido,-a *a* spoiled.

consentimiento *m* consent.

consentir [5] **1** *vt* (*tolerar*) to allow, permit; (*mimar*) to spoil; **no consientas que haga eso** don't allow him to do that. **2** *vi* to consent; **c. en** to agree to.

conserje *m* (*bedel*) janitor.

conserva *f* tinned *o* canned food.

conservador,-a *a & mf* conservative; (*derechista*) Conservative.

conservante *m* preservative.

conservar 1 *vt* to conserve, preserve; (*mantener*) to keep; (*alimentos*) to preserve. **2 conservarse** *vr* (*tradición etc*) to survive.

conservatorio *m* conservatory.

considerado,-a *a* (*atento*) considerate, thoughtful.

considerar *vt* to consider; **lo considero imposible** I think it's impossible.

consigna *f* (*para maletas*) checkroom.

consigo[1] *pron pers* (*tercera persona*) (*hombre*) with him; (*mujer*) with her; (*cosa, animal*) with it; (*plural*) with them; (*usted*) with you; **hablar c. mismo** to speak to oneself.

consigo[2] *indic pres de* **conseguir.**

consiguiente *a* consequent; **por c.** therefore, consequently.

consistente *a* (*firme*) firm, solid.

consistir *vi* to consist (**en** of).

consola *f* console.

consolar [2] **1** *vt* to console, comfort. **2 consolarse** *vr* to console oneself.

consomé *m* clear soup, consommé.

consonante *a & f* consonant.

consorte *mf* (*cónyuge*) partner, spouse.

conspiración *f* conspiracy, plot.

conspirar *vi* to conspire, plot.

constancia *f* perseverance; (*testimonio*) proof, evidence.

constante 1 *a* constant; (*persona*) steadfast. **2** *f* constant feature.

constantemente *adv* constantly.

constar *vi* (*figurar*) to figure in, be included (in); **me consta que ...** I am absolutely certain that ...; **c. de** (*consistir*) to consist of.

constatar *vt* to state; (*comprobar*) to check.

constipado,-a 1 estar c. to have a cold. **2** *m* cold.

constiparse *vr* to catch a cold.

constitución *f* constitution.

constituir **1** *vt* (*formar*) to constitute; (*suponer*) to represent; (*fundar*) to constitute, set up; **estar constituido por** to consist of. **2 constituirse** *vr* to set oneself up (**en** as).

construcción *f* construction; (*sector*) building industry.

constructor,-a 1 *mf* builder. **2** *a*

empresa constructora builders *pl*, construction company.

construir *vt* to construct, build.

consuelo *m* consolation.

cónsul *mf* consul.

consulado *m* consulate.

consulta *f* consultation; (*médica*) surgery; (*despacho*) consulting room; **horas de c.** surgery hours.

consultar *vt* to consult.

consultivo,-a *a* consultative, advisory.

consultorio *m* (*médico*) medical center.

consumidor,-a **1** *mf* consumer. **2** *a* consuming.

consumir **1** *vt* to consume. **2 consumirse** *vr* (*agua, jugo*) to boil away.

consumo *m* consumption; **bienes de c.** consumer goods; **sociedad de c.** consumer society.

contabilidad *f* (*profesión*) accountancy; (*de empresa, sociedad*) accounting.

contable *mf* accountant.

contactar *vi* **c. con** to contact.

contacto *m* contact; (*en coche*) ignition; **ponerse en c.** to get in touch.

contado,-a 1 *a* (*pocos*) few and far between; **contadas veces** very seldom. **2** *m* **pagar al c.** to pay cash.

contador *m* meter.

contagiar **1** *vt* (*enfermedad*) to pass on. **2 contagiarse** *vr* (*enfermar*) to get infected; (*transmitirse*) to be contagious.

contagioso,-a *a* contagious; (*risa*) infectious.

contaminación *f* contamination; (*del aire*) pollution.

contar [2] **1** *vt* (*sumar*) to count; (*narrar*) to tell. **2** *vi* to count; **c. con** (*confiar en*) to count on; (*tener*) to have.

contemplar *vt* to contemplate; (*considerar*) to consider.

contemporáneo,-a *a & mf* contemporary.

contenedor *m* container.

contener **1** *vt* to contain; (*reprimir*) to restrain, hold back. **2 contenerse** *vr* to control oneself, hold (oneself) back.

contenido *m* content, contents *pl*.

contentar **1** *vt* (*satisfacer*) to please; (*alegrar*) to cheer up. **2 contentarse** *vr* (*conformarse*) to make do, be satisfied (**con** with).

contento,-a *a* happy, pleased (**con** with).

contestador *m* **c. automático** answering machine.

contestación *f* answer.

contestar *vt* to answer.

contienda *f* struggle.

contigo *pron pers* with you.

contiguo,-a *a* adjoining.

continente *m* continent.

continuación *f* continuation; **a c.** next.

continuar *vti* to continue.

continuo,-a *a* continuous; (*reiterado*) continual, constant.

continuamente *adv* continuously.

contra **1** *prep* against; **en c. de** against. **2** *nmpl* **los pros y los contras** the pros and cons.

contrabajo *m* double bass.

contrabando *m* smuggling; **pasar algo de c.** to smuggle sth in.

contracción *f* contraction.

contracepción *f* contraception.

contradecir (*pp* **contradicho**) *vt* to contradict.

contradicción *f* contradiction.

contraer **1** *vt* to contract; **c. matrimonio** to get married. **2 contraerse** *vr* to contract.

contraigo *indic pres de* **contraer.**

contraje *pt indef de* **contraer.**

contrapeso *m* counterweight.

contraproducente *a* counterproductive.

contrariedad *f* (*contratiempo*) obstacle, setback; (*decepción*) annoyance.

contrario,-a **1** *a* opposite; **en el lado/sentido c.** on the other side/

in the other direction; **al c., por el c.** on the contrary; **de lo c.** otherwise; **todo lo c.** quite the opposite. **2** *mf* opponent, rival. **3** *f* **llevar la contraria** to be contrary.

contrariamente *adv* **c. a . . .** contrary to . . .

contrarrestar *vt* to offset, counteract.

contrastar *vt* to contrast (**con** with).

contraste *m* contrast.

contratar *vt* (*empleado*) to hire, engage.

contratiempo *m* setback, hitch.

contratista *mf* contractor.

contrato *m* contract.

contribución *f* contribution; (*impuesto*) tax.

contribuir *vti* to contribute (**a** to).

contribuyente *mf* taxpayer.

contrincante *mf* rival, opponent.

control *m* control; (*inspección*) check; (*de policía etc*) checkpoint; **c. remoto** remote control.

controlador,-a *mf* **c. (aéreo)** air traffic controller.

controlar 1 *vt* to control. **2 controlarse** *vr* to control oneself.

controversia *f* controversy.

convalecencia *f* convalescence.

convalidar *vt* to validate; (*documento*) to ratify.

convencer [2] *vt* to convince; **c. a algn de algo** to convince sb about sth.

convencional *a* conventional.

convenio *m* agreement.

convenir *vti* (*acordar*) to agree; (*ser oportuno*) to suit, be good for; **c. en** to agree on; **conviene recordar que . . .** it's as well to remember that . . .

convento *m* (*de monjas*) convent.

conversación *f* conversation.

conversión *f* conversion.

convertir [5] **1** *vt* to change, convert. **2 convertirse** *vr* **convertirse en** to turn into, become.

convicción *f* conviction.

convidado,-a *a & mf* guest.

convidar *vt* to invite.

convivencia *f* life together.

convivir *vi* to live together.

convocar [1] *vt* to summon; (*reunión, elecciones*) to call.

convocatoria *f* (*a huelga etc*) call.

convulsión *f* convulsion.

conyugal *a* conjugal; **vida c.** married life.

cónyuge *mf* spouse; **cónyuges** married couple *sing*, husband and wife.

coñac *m* brandy, cognac.

cooperación *f* co-operation.

cooperar *vi* to co-operate (**a, en** in; **con** with).

cooperativa *f* co-operative.

coordenada *f* co-ordinate.

coordinar *vt* to co-ordinate.

copa *f* glass; (*de árbol*) top; (*premio*) cup; **tomar una c.** to have a drink.

copia *f* copy.

copiar *vt* to copy.

copla *f* verse, couplet.

copo *m* flake; **c. de nieve** snowflake; **copos de maíz** cornflakes.

coquetear *vi* to flirt.

coqueto,-a *a* coquettish.

coraje *m* (*valor*) courage; (*ira*) anger, annoyance.

coral[1] *m* coral.

coral[2] *f* (*composición*) choral, chorale.

Corán *m* Koran.

coraza *f* armor.

corazón *m* heart; (*de fruta*) core; **tener buen c.** to be kind-hearted.

corbata *f* necktie.

corcho *m* cork; (*de pesca*) float.

cordel *m* rope, cord.

cordero,-a *mf* lamb.

cordial *a* cordial, warm.

cordillera *f* mountain range.

cordón *m* string; (*de zapatos*) shoelace.

cornada *f* (*de toro*) goring.

córner *m* corner (kick).

corneta *f* bugle.

cornisa f cornice.

coro m (musical) choir; (en tragedia) chorus; **a c.** all together.

corona f crown; (de flores etc) wreath, garland.

coronación f coronation.

coronel m colonel.

coronilla f crown of the head; fam **estar hasta la c.** to be fed up (de with).

corporación f corporation.

corporal a corporal; **olor c.** body odor, BO.

corpulento,-a a corpulent, stout.

corral m corral.

correa f (tira) strap; (de pantalón) belt; (de perro) lead, leash; (de motor) belt.

corrección f (rectificación) correction; (educación) courtesy, politeness.

correcto,-a a (sin errores) correct; (educado) polite, courteous (con to); (conducta) proper.

corredizo,-a a (puerta etc) sliding; **nudo c.** slipknot.

corredor,-a mf (deportista) runner; (balconada) gallery.

corregir [6] **1** vt to correct. **2 corregirse** vr (persona) to mend one's ways.

correo m post, mail; **echar al c.** to post; **por c.** by post; **c. aéreo** airmail; **c. certificado** registered post; **correos** (edificio) post office sing.

correr 1 vi to run; (coche) to go fast; (conductor) to drive fast; (viento) to blow; **c. prisa** to be urgent. **2** vt (cortina) to draw; (cerrojo) to close; (mover) to pull up, draw up; **c. el riesgo** to run the risk. **3 correrse** vr (moverse) to move over.

correspondencia f correspondence.

corresponder 1 vi to correspond (a to; con with); (ajustarse) to go (con with); (incumbir) to concern; (pertenecer) to be one's due; **me dieron lo que me correspondía**

they gave me my share. **2 corresponderse** vr (ajustarse) to correspond; (dos cosas) to tally; **no se corresponde con la descripción** it does not match the description.

correspondiente a corresponding (a to).

corresponsal mf correspondent.

corrida f **c. (de toros)** bullfight.

corriente 1 a (común) common; (agua) running; (mes, año) current, present; (cuenta) current; **estar al c.** to be up to date. **2** f current, stream; (de aire) draft; (tendencia) trend, current; fam **seguirle** o **llevarle la c. a algn** to humor sb; **c. (eléctrica)** (electric) current.

corrijo indic pres de **corregir**.

corro m circle, ring; (juego) ring-a-ring-a-roses.

corromper vt, **corromperse** vr to go bad, rot.

corrupción f corruption.

corrupto,-a a corrupt.

cortacésped m & f lawnmower.

cortar 1 vt to cut; (carne) to carve; (árbol) to cut down; (piel) to chap, crack; (luz, teléfono) to cut off; (paso, carretera) to block. **2 cortarse** vr (herirse) to cut oneself; (leche etc) to curdle; **cortarse el pelo** to have one's hair cut; **se cortó la comunicación** we were cut off.

corte m cut; (sección) section; **c. de pelo** haircut.

cortés a courteous, polite.

corteza f (de árbol) bark; (de queso) rind; (de pan) crust.

cortijo m Andalusian farmhouse.

cortina f curtain.

corto,-a a (distancia, tiempo) short; **c. de vista** short-sighted; **luz corta** dipped headlights pl; **quedarse c.** (calcular mal) to underestimate.

cortocircuito m short circuit.

cosa f thing; (asunto) matter, business; **eso es c. tuya** that's your business; **eso es otra c.** that's different; **hace c. de una hora** about an hour ago.

coscorrón *m* knock on the head.

cosecha *f* harvest, crop; (*año del vino*) vintage.

coser *vt* to sew.

cosmético,-a *a* & *m* cosmetic.

cosmonauta *mf* cosmonaut.

coso *m* (*taurino*) bullring.

cosquillas *fpl* **hacer c. a algn** to tickle sb; **tener c.** to be ticklish.

costa *f* coast; (*litoral*) coastline; (*playa*) beach, seaside.

costado *m* (*lado*) side; **de c.** sideways.

costar [2] *vi* to cost; **¿cuánto cuesta?** how much is it?; **c. barato/caro** to be cheap/expensive; **c. trabajo** *o* **mucho** to be hard; **me cuesta hablar francés** I find it hard to speak French.

coste *m* cost; **c. de la vida** cost of living.

costear 1 *vt* to afford, pay for. **2 costearse** *vr* to pay for.

costilla *f* (*hueso*) rib; (*chuleta*) cutlet.

costo *m* cost.

costra *f* crust; (*de herida*) scab.

costumbre *f* (*hábito*) habit; (*tradición*) custom; **como de c.** as usual; **tengo la c. de levantarme temprano** I usually get up early; **tenía la c. de . . .** he used to . . .

costura *f* sewing; (*confección*) dressmaking; (*línea de puntadas*) seam; **alta c.** haute couture.

costurero *m* sewing basket.

cotidiano,-a *a* daily.

cotilla *mf fam* busybody, gossip.

cotilleo *m fam* gossip.

cotización *f* (market) price, quotation.

coto *m* enclosure; **c. de caza** game reserve.

cotorra *f* parrot; (*persona*) chatterbox.

coz *f* kick.

cráneo *m* cranium, skull.

cráter *m* crater.

creación *f* creation.

crear *vt* to create.

creativo,-a *a* creative.

crecer *vi* to grow.

crecimiento *m* growth.

credencial *a* credential; **cartas credenciales** credentials.

crédito *m* credit; **dar c. a** to believe.

creer 1 *vt* to believe; (*pensar*) to think; **creo que no** I don't think so; **creo que sí** I think so; **ya lo creo** I should think so. **2** *vi* to believe. **3 creerse** *vr* **se cree guapo** he thinks he's good-looking.

crema *f* cream.

cremallera *f* zipper.

crematorio *m* crematory.

cremoso,-a *a* creamy.

crepe *f* pancake.

crepúsculo *m* twilight.

cresta *f* crest; (*de gallo*) comb.

crezco *indic pres de* **crecer.**

cría *f* (*cachorro*) young; (*crianza*) breeding.

criada *f* maid.

criado,-a 1 *a* **mal c.** spoiled. **2** *mf* servant.

criar *vt* (*animales*) to breed; (*niños*) to bring up.

criatura *f* (living) creature; (*crío*) baby, child.

criba *f* sieve.

crimen *m* (*pl* **crímenes**) crime.

criminal *mf* & *a* criminal.

crin *f*, **crines** *fpl* mane *sing*.

crío,-a *mf* kid.

criollo,-a *a* & *mf* Creole.

crisis *f inv* crisis; **c. nerviosa** nervous breakdown.

crispar *vt* to make tense; **me crispa los nervios** it makes me nervous.

cristal *m* crystal; (*vidrio*) glass; (*de gafas*) lens; (*de ventana*) (window) pane.

cristiano,-a *a* & *mf* Christian.

Cristo *m* Christ.

criterio *m* (*pauta*) criterion; (*opinión*) opinion.

crítica *f* criticism; (*reseña*) review.

criticar [1] **1** *vt* to criticize. **2** *vi* (*murmurar*) to gossip.

crítico,-a 1 *a* critical. **2** *mf* critic.

croissant *m* croissant.

crol *m* (*en natación*) crawl.

cromo *m* (*metal*) chromium, chrome; (*estampa*) picture card.

cromosoma *m* chromosome.

crónica *f* feature.

crónico,-a *a* chronic.

cronológico,-a *a* chronological.

cronometrar *vt* to time.

cronómetro *m* stopwatch.

croqueta *f* croquette.

croquis *m inv* sketch.

cruce *m* crossing; (*de carreteras*) crossroads.

crucero *m* (*viaje*) cruise; (*barco*) cruiser.

crucifijo *m* crucifix.

crucigrama *m* crossword (puzzle).

crudo,-a 1 *a* (*natural*) raw; (*comida*) underdone; (*color*) cream. **2** *m* (*petróleo*) crude.

cruel *a* cruel.

crueldad *f* cruelty.

crujiente *a* crunchy.

crujir *vi* (*madera*) to creak; (*comida*) to crunch; (*hueso*) to crack.

cruz *f* cross; **C. Roja** Red Cross; **¿cara o c.?** ≈ heads or tails?

cruzado,-a *a* crossed; (*atravesado*) lying across; **con los brazos cruzados** arms folded.

cruzar [4] **1** *vt* to cross; (*palabra, mirada*) to exchange. **2** *vi* (*atravesar*) to cross. **3 cruzarse** *vr* to cross; **cruzarse con algn** to pass sb.

cuaderno *m* notebook.

cuadra *f* (*establo*) stable; *Am* block (of houses).

cuadrado,-a *a & m* square; **elevar (un número) al c.** to square (a number).

cuadriculado,-a *a* **papel c.** squared paper.

cuadro *m* square; (*gráfico*) chart, graph; (*pintura*) painting, picture; **tela a cuadros** checked cloth; **c. de mandos** control panel.

cual *pron rel* **el/la c.** (*persona*) who; (*cosa*) which; **con el/la c.** with whom/which; **lo c.** which.

cuál 1 *pron interr* which (one)?; **¡c. quieres?** which one do you want? **2** *a interr* which.

cualidad *f* quality.

cualquier *a indef* any; **c. cosa** anything; **en c. momento** at any moment.

cualquiera (*pl* **cualesquiera**) **1** *a indef* (*indefinido*) any; (*corriente*) ordinary. **2** *pron indef* (*persona*) anybody, anyone; (*cosa, animal*) any one; **c. que sea** whatever it is.

cuando 1 *adv & conj* when; **de c. en c., de vez en c.** from time to time; **c. quieras** whenever you want; **c. vengas** when you come; (**aun**) **c.** even if.

cuándo *adv interr* when; **¿desde c.?** since when; **¿para c. lo quieres?** when do you want it for?

cuanto,-a 1 *a* **toma cuantos caramelos quieras** take all the sweets you want; **unas cuantas niñas** a few girls. **2** *pron rel* as much as; **coma (todo) c. quiera** eat as much as you want. **3** *pron indef pl* **unos cuantos** a few. **4** *adv* (*tiempo*) **c. antes** as soon as possible; **en c.** as soon as; **c. más . . . más** the more . . . the more; **en c. a** with respect to, regarding.

cuánto,-a 1 *a & pron interr* how much; **¿cuántos?** how many; **¿cuántas veces?** how many times; **¿c. es?** how much is it? **2** *adv* how, how much; **¡cuánta gente hay!** what a lot of people there are!

cuarenta *a & m inv* forty.

cuartel *m* (*militar*) barracks *pl*; **c. general** headquarters.

cuartilla *f* sheet of paper.

cuarto,-a 1 *m* (*habitación*) room; (*cuarta parte*) quarter; **c. de baño** bathroom; **c. de estar** living room; **c. de hora** quarter of an hour. **2** *a & mf* fourth.

cuatro *a & m inv* four.

cuatrocientos,-as *a & mf* four hundred.

cubano,-a *a & mf* Cuban.

cubata *m fam* cubalibre.

cubierta f cover; (de rueda) tire; (de barco) deck.

cubierto,-a 1 a covered; (piscina etc) indoor; (cielo) overcast. 2 mpl **cubiertos** cutlery sing.

cubo m bucket; (en matemática) cube; **c. de la basura** trash bin.

cubrir (pp **cubierto**) 1 vt to cover. 2 **cubrirse** vr (cielo) to become overcast.

cucaracha f cockroach.

cuchara f spoon.

cucharada f spoonful.

cucharilla f teaspoon; **c. de café** coffee spoon.

cucharón m ladle.

cuchichear vi to whisper.

cuchilla f blade; **c. de afeitar** razor blade.

cuchillo m knife.

cuco m cuckoo.

cucurucho m (de helado) cornet; (envoltorio) paper cone.

cuello m neck; (de camisa etc) collar.

cuenco m bowl.

cuenta f (factura) check; (de banco) account; (cálculo) count; (de collar) bead; **c. corriente** current account; **caer en la c., darse c.** to realize; **tener en c.** to take into account; **traer c.** to be worthwhile; **en resumidas cuentas** in short; **trabajar por c. propia** to be self-employed.

cuentakilómetros m inv (distancia) ≈ milometer; (velocidad) speedometer.

cuento m story; **contar un c.** to tell a story; **c. de hadas** fairy story.

cuerda f (cordel) rope; (de instrumento) string; (del reloj) spring; **dar c. al reloj** to wind up a watch.

cuerdo,-a a sane.

cuerno m horn; (de ciervo) antler; fam **¡vete al c.!** get lost!

cuero m leather; **chaqueta de c.** leather jacket; **c. cabelludo** scalp.

cuerpo m body; (cadáver) corpse; **c. de bomberos** fire brigade; **c.**

diplomático diplomatic corps; **c. de policía** police force.

cuesta f slope; **c. abajo** downhill; **c. arriba** uphill. 2 adv **a cuestas** on one's back.

cuestión f (asunto) matter, question; (pregunta) question; **en c. de unas horas** in just a few hours.

cuestionario m questionnaire.

cueva f cave.

cuezo indic pres de **cocer**.

cuidado,-a 1 a careful. 2 m care; **con c.** carefully; **tener c.** to be careful; **estar al c. de** to be in charge of; (persona) to look after; **me trae sin c.** I couldn't care less; **cuidados intensivos** intensive care sing. 3 interj **¡c.!** look out!

cuidadoso,-a a careful.

cuidar 1 vt to care for, look after. 2 **cuidarse** vr **cuídate** take care of yourself.

culebra f snake.

culebrón m soap opera.

culo m fam (trasero) backside; (de recipiente) bottom.

culpa f blame; (culpabilidad) guilt; **echar la c. a algn** to put the blame on sb; **fue c. mía** it was my fault; **por tu c.** because of you.

culpable 1 mf offender, culprit. 2 a guilty; **declararse c.** to plead guilty.

cultivar vt to cultivate.

culto,-a 1 a educated; (palabra) learned. 2 m cult; (devoción) worship.

cultura f culture.

culturismo m body building.

cumbre f (de montaña) summit, top; **(conferencia) c.** summit conference.

cumpleaños m inv birthday; **¡feliz c.!** happy birthday!

cumplir 1 vt to carry out; (deseo) to fulfill; (promesa) to keep; **ayer cumplí veinte años** I was twenty (years old) yesterday. 2 vi (plazo) to expire, end; **c. con el deber** to do one's duty. 3 **cumplirse** vr (deseo) to come true; (plazo) to expire.

cuna f cot.

cuneta f (de la carretera) gutter.

cuñado,-a mf (hombre) brother-in-law; (mujer) sister-in-law.

cuota f (de club etc) membership fees pl; (porción) quota, share; Am **carretera de c.** toll road.

cupe pt indef de **caber.**

cupiera subj imperfecto de **caber.**

cupón m coupon, voucher.

cura 1 m (religioso) priest. **2** f (de enfermedad) cure.

curación f cure, treatment.

curar 1 vt to cure; (herida) to dress; (enfermedad) to treat. **2** vi & vr **curar(se)** (sanar) to recover, get well; (herida) to heal up.

curiosidad f curiosity.

curioso,-a 1 a (extraño) strange, odd; (indiscreto) curious, inquisitive. **2** mf (mirón) onlooker.

currículum m **c. vitae** curriculum vitae.

cursi a posh.

cursillo m short course; **c. de reciclaje** refresher course.

curso m (año académico) year; (clase) class; (de acontecimientos, río) course; **en el c. de** in the course of; **moneda de c. legal** legal tender.

cursor m cursor.

curtir vt (cuero) to tan; (endurecer) to harden.

curva f curve; (en carretera) bend; **c. cerrada** sharp bend.

cutis m complexion.

cuyo,-a pron rel & pos (persona) whose; (de cosa) of which; **en c. caso** in which case.

D

D. abr de **don** Mister, Mr.

D.ª abr de **doña** Mrs; (señorita) Miss.

dado m dice.

dálmata mf Dalmatian.

dama f (señora) lady; **damas** (juego) checkers.

danés,-esa 1 a Danish. **2** mf (persona) Dane. **3** m (idiom) Danish; **gran d.** (perro) Great Dane.

danza f dancing; (baile) dance.

daño m (a cosa) damage; (a persona) (físico) hurt; (perjuicio) harm.

dar 1 vt to give; (noticia) to tell; (mano de pintura, cera) to apply; (fruto, flores) to bear; (beneficio, interés) to yield; (hora) to strike; **dale a la luz** switch the light on; **d. la mano a algn** (saludo) to shake hands with sb; **d. los buenos días/las buenas noches a algn** to say good morning/good evening to sb; **me da lo mismo** or **me da igual** it's all the same to me; **¿qué más da?** what difference does it make?; **d. de comer a** to feed; **d. a conocer** (noticia) to release; **d. a entender que. . .** to imply that. . .; **d. por** (considerar) to consider; **d. por descontado/sabido** to take for granted. **2** vi **me dio un ataque de tos/risa** I had a coughing fit/an attack of the giggles; **d. a** (ventana, habitación) to overlook; (puerta) to open onto; **d. con la solución** to hit upon the solution; **d. de sí** (ropa) to stretch; **el presupuesto no da para más** the budget will not stretch any further; **d. que hablar** to get people talking. **3** darse vr **se dio la circunstancia de que** it happened that; **se dio a la bebida** he started drinking; **darse con** o **contra** to bump into; **darse por satisfecho** to feel satisfied; **darse por vencido** to give in; **se le da bien/mal el francés** she's good/bad at French.

dardo m dart.

dársena f dock.

dátil m date.

dato m piece of information; **datos** (de ordenador) data.

d.C. abr de **después de Cristo** Anno Domini, AD.

dcha. abr de **derecha** right.

de prep (pertenencia) of; **el título de la novela** the title of the novel;

el coche/hermano de Sofía Sofía's car/brother. ▪ (*procedencia*) from; **vino de Madrid** he came from Madrid. ▪ (*descripción*) **el niño de ojos azules** the boy with blue eyes; **una avenida de quince kilómetros** an avenue fifteen kilometers long; **una botella de litro** a liter bottle; **el señor de la chaqueta** the man in the jacket; **un reloj de oro** a gold watch. ▪ (*contenido*) of; **un saco de patatas** a sack of potatoes. ▪ (*oficio*) by, as; **trabaja de secretaria** she's working as a secretary. ▪ (*acerca de*) about; **curso de informática** computer course. ▪ (*tiempo*) **a las tres de la tarde** at three in the afternoon; **de día** by day; **de noche** at night; **de lunes a jueves** from Monday to Thursday; **de pequeño** as a child. ▪ (*con superlativo*) in; **el más largo de España** the longest in Spain. ▪ (*causa*) with, because of; **llorar de alegría** to cry with joy; **morir de hambre** to die of hunger. ▪ **de cuatro en cuatro** four at a time; **de semana en semana** every week.

debajo 1 *adv* underneath, below. **2** *prep* **de** under(neath); **por d. de lo normal** below normal

debate *m* debate.

debatir 1 *vt* to debate. **2 debatirse** *vr* to struggle.

deber[1] *m* duty; (*en el colegio*) **deberes** homework *sing.*

deber[2] **1** *vt* (*dinero, explicación*) to owe. **2** *vi* **debe irse ahora** she has to leave now; **la factura debe pagarse mañana** the bill must be paid tomorrow; **deberías visitar a tus padres** you ought to visit your parents; **debería haber ido ayer** I should have gone yesterday; **no debiste hacerlo** you shouldn't have done it; **deben de estar fuera** they must be out. **3 deberse** *vr* **deberse a** to be due to.

debidamente *adv* duly.

debido,-a *a* **d. a** due to.

débil *a* weak; (*luz*) dim; **punto d.** weak spot.

debutar *vi* to make one's debut.

década *f* **en la d. de los noventa** during the nineties.

decadencia *f* decadence.

decano,-a *mf* dean.

decena *f* (about) ten; **una d. de veces** (about) ten times; **por decenas** in tens.

decenio *m* decade.

decente *a* decent; (*decoroso*) modest.

decepción *f* disappointment.

decidido,-a *a* determined.

decidir 1 *vti* to decide. **2 decidirse** *vr* **decidirse (a hacer algo)** to make up one's mind (to do sth); **decidirse por algo** to decide on sth.

décima *f* tenth.

decimal *a & m* decimal.

décimo,-a 1 *a & mf* tenth. **2** *m* (*parte*) tenth.

decir (*pp* **dicho**) **1** *vt* to say; **d. una mentira/la verdad** to tell a lie/the truth; **dígame** (*al teléfono*) hello; **esta película no me dice nada** this film doesn't appeal to me; **querer d.** to mean; (*locuciones*) **es d.** that is (to say); **por así decirlo** so to speak; **digamos** let's say; **digo yo** in my opinion; **ni que d. tiene** needless to say; **¡no me digas!** really! **2 decirse** *vr* **¿cómo se dice 'mesa' en inglés?** how do you say 'mesa' in English?; **se dice que . . .** they say that . . .

decisión *f* decision; (*resolución*) determination; **tomar una d.** to make a decision; **con d.** decisively.

declaración *f* declaration; **d. de (la) renta** tax return; (*afirmación*) statement; **hacer declaraciones** to comment.

declarar 1 *vt* to declare; (*afirmar*) to state; **d. la guerra a** to declare war on. **2** *vi* (*en juicio*) to testify. **3 declararse** *vr* (*guerra, incendio*) to break out; **declararse a favor/en contra de** to declare oneself in favor of/against; **declararse en huelga** to go on strike; **declararse a algn** to declare one's love for sb.

decoración *f* decoration.

decorar vt to decorate.

decreto m decree.

decorativo,-a a decorative.

decreto-ley m decree.

dedal m thimble.

dedicar [1] 1 vt to dedicate; (tiempo, esfuerzos) to devote (**a** to). 2 **dedicarse** vr ¿**a qué se dedica Vd.?** what do you do for a living?; **los fines de semana ella se dedica a pescar** on weekends she spends her time fishing.

dedo m (de la mano) finger; (del pie) toe; **d. anular/corazón/índice/meñique** ring/middle/index/little finger; **d. pulgar, d. gordo** thumb.

deducir 1 vt to deduce. 2 **deducirse** vr **de aquí se deduce que . . .** from this it follows that . . .

defecar [1] vi to defecate.

defecto m defect.

defectuoso,-a a defective.

defender [3] 1 vt to defend (**contra** against; **de** from). 2 **defenderse** vr to defend oneself.

defensa 1 f defense; **en d. propia, en legítima d.** in self-defense. 2 m (en equipo) defender.

deficiente 1 a deficient. 2 m (nota) fail.

definición f definition.

definir vt to define.

deformar 1 vt to deform; (cara) to disfigure; (la verdad, una imagen) to distort. 2 **deformarse** vr to become distorted.

defraudar vt to disappoint; **d. a Hacienda** to evade taxes.

defunción f demise.

degenerado,-a a & mf degenerate.

degollar [2] vt to behead.

degradante a degrading.

degustación f tasting.

dejar 1 vt to leave; (prestar) to lend; (abandonar) to give up; (permitir) to let, allow; **déjame en paz** leave me alone; **dejé el tabaco y la bebida** I gave up smoking and drinking; **d. caer** to drop; **d. entrar/salir** to let in/out; **d. triste** to make sad; **d. preocupado/sorprendido** to worry/surprise. 2 v aux **d. de** + inf to stop; (renunciar) give up; **no deja de llamarme** she's always calling me. 3 **dejarse** vr **me he dejado las llaves dentro** I've left the keys inside; **dejarse barba** to grow a beard; **dejarse llevar por** to be influenced by.

del (contracción de **de** + **el**) ver **de**.

delantal m apron.

delante 1 adv in front; **la entrada de d.** the front entrance; **por d.** in front; **se lo lleva todo por d.** he destroys everything in his path; **tiene toda la vida por d.** he has his whole life ahead of him. 2 prep **d. de** in front of; (en serie) ahead of.

delatar vt to inform against.

delegación f (acto, delegados) delegation; (oficina) local office.

delegado,-a mf delegate.

deletrear vt to spell (out).

delfín m dolphin.

delgado,-a a slim; (capa) fine.

deliberado,-a a deliberate.

delicadeza f (finura) daintiness; (tacto) tactfulness; **falta de d.** tactlessness.

delicado,-a a delicate.

delicioso,-a a (comida) delicious; (agradable) delightful.

delincuente a & mf delinquent.

delineante mf (hombre) draftsman; (mujer) draftswoman.

delirar vi to be delirious.

delirio m delirium.

delito m crime.

delta m delta.

demanda f (judicial) lawsuit.

demandar vt to sue.

demás 1 a **los/las d.** the rest of. 2 pron **lo/los/las d.** the rest; **por lo d.** otherwise, apart from that.

demasiado,-a 1 a (singular) too much; (plural) too many. 2 adv too (much); **es d. grande/caro** it is too big/dear; **fumas/trabajas d.** you smoke/work too much.

demencia f insanity.

democracia f democracy.

democrático,-a a democratic.

demográfico,-a a demographic;

crecimiento d. population growth.

demonio *m* devil.

demora *f* delay.

demorar 1 *vt* to delay, hold up. **2 demorarse** *vr* (*retrasarse*) to be delayed, be held up.

demostrar [2] *vt* (*mostrar*) to show; (*evidenciar*) to prove.

denegar [1] *vt* to refuse.

denigrante *a* humiliating.

denominación *f* denomination.

denominar *vt* to name.

denotar *vt* to denote.

densidad *f* density.

denso,-a *a* dense.

dentadura *f* teeth; **d. postiza** false teeth *pl*, dentures *pl*.

dental *a* dental.

dentera *f* **me da d.** it sets my teeth on edge.

dentífrico,-a 1 *a* **pasta/crema dentífrica** toothpaste. **2** *m* toothpaste.

dentista *mf* dentist.

dentro 1 *adv* (*en el interior*) inside; **aquí d.** in here; **por d.** (on the) inside. **2** *prep* **d. de** (*lugar*) inside; **d. de poco** shortly, soon; **d. de un mes** in a month's time.

denunciar *vt* (*delito*) to report (**a** to).

departamento *m* department; (*territorial*) province; *Am* (*piso*) apartment.

depender *vi* to depend (**de** on); (*económicamente*) to be dependent (**de** on).

dependienta *f* shop assistant.

dependiente 1 *a* dependent (**de** on). **2** *m* shop assistant.

depilación *f* depilation.

depilar *vt* to remove the hair from; (*cejas*) to pluck.

depilatorio,-a *a & m* depilatory; **crema depilatoria** hair-remover.

deportar *vt* to deport.

deporte *m* sport; **hacer d.** to go out for sports.

deportista 1 *mf* (*hombre*) sportsman; (*mujer*) sportswoman. **2** *a* sporty.

deportivo,-a 1 *a* sports; **club d./**

chaqueta deportiva sports club/jacket. **2** *m* (*coche*) sports car.

depositar 1 *vt* (*colocar*) to put. **2 depositarse** *vr* to settle.

depósito *m* (*dinero*) deposit; (*de agua, gasolina*) tank.

depresión *f* depression.

deprimente *a* depressing.

deprimir 1 *vt* to depress. **2 deprimirse** *vr* to get depressed.

deprisa *adv* quickly.

derecha *f* (*mano*) right hand; (*lugar*) right, right-hand side; **a la d.** on the right, on the right-hand side; (*en política*) **la d.** the right.

derecho,-a 1 *a* (*de la derecha*) right; (*recto*) straight. **2** *m* (*privilegio*) right; (*carrera*) law; **derechos civiles/humanos** civil/human rights; **tener d. a** to be entitled to; **no hay d.** it's not fair. **3** *adv* **siga todo d.** go straight ahead.

derivar 1 *vi* to drift; **d. de** to derive from. **2 derivarse** *vr* to stem (**de** from).

dermatólogo,-a *mf* dermatologist.

derramar 1 *vt* to spill; (*lágrimas*) to shed. **2 derramarse** *vr* to spill.

derrapar *vi* to skid.

derretir [6] *vt*, **derretirse** *vr* to melt; (*hielo, nieve*) to thaw.

derribar *vt* (*demoler*) to knock down; (*gobierno*) to bring down.

derrochar *vt* to waste.

derroche *m* waste.

derrota *f* defeat.

derrotar *vt* to defeat.

derruir *vt* to demolish.

derrumbar 1 *vt* (*edificio*) to knock down. **2 derrumbarse** *vr* to collapse; (*techo*) to fall in.

desabrido,-a *a* (*tono*) harsh; (*persona*) irritable.

desabrochar 1 *vt* to undo. **2 desabrocharse** *vr* (*prenda*) to come undone; **desabróchate la camisa** undo your shirt.

desacato *m* lack of respect (**a** for).

desacertado,-a *a* unwise.

desacreditar *vt* (*desprestigiar*) to discredit; (*criticar*) to disparage.

desactivar vt (bomba) to defuse.
desacuerdo m disagreement.
desafiante a defiant.
desafiar vt to challenge.
desafinar 1 vi to sing out of tune; (instrumento) to play out of tune. **2 desafinarse** vr to go out of tune.
desafío m challenge.
desafortunado,-a a unfortunate.
desagradable a unpleasant.
desagradar vi to displease.
desagradecido,-a 1 a ungrateful. **2** mf ungrateful person.
desagrado m displeasure.
desagüe m (cañería) drainpipe; (vaciado) drain.
desaguisado m mess.
desahogado,-a a (acomodado) well-off; (espacioso) spacious.
desahogarse [7] vr to let off steam.
desahuciar vt (desalojar) to evict; (enfermo) to deprive of all hope.
desairar vt to slight.
desajuste m disorder, imbalance.
desalentar [1] **1** vt to dishearten. **2 desalentarse** vr to get discouraged.
desaliento m discouragement.
desaliñado,-a a untidy.
desalmado,-a a heartless.
desalojar vt (inquilino) to evict; (público) to move on; (lugar) to evacuate; (abandonar) to abandon.
desamparado,-a a (persona) helpless.
desangrarse vr to lose (a lot of) blood.
desanimado,-a a (persona) downhearted; (fiesta etc) dull.
desanimar 1 vt to dishearten. **2 desanimarse** vr to lose heart.
desánimo m dejection.
desapacible a unpleasant.
desaparecer vi to disappear.
desaparición f disappearance.
desapercibido,-a a pasar d. to go unnoticed.
desaprovechar vt (dinero, tiempo) to waste.

desarmar vt (desmontar) to dismantle; (ejército) to disarm.
desarme m disarmament; **d. nuclear** nuclear disarmament.
desarraigado,-a a rootless.
desarreglar vt to mess up.
desarrollado,-a a developed.
desarrollar 1 vt to develop. **2 desarrollarse** vr (persona, enfermedad) to develop; (tener lugar) to take place.
desarrollo m development; **países en vías de d.** developing countries.
desarticular vt to dismantle.
desasir 1 vt to release. **2 desasirse** vr to get loose; **desasirse de** to free oneself of.
desasosiego m uneasiness.
desastrado,-a a scruffy.
desastre m disaster.
desastroso,-a a disastrous.
desatar 1 vt to untie, undo. **2 desatarse** vr (zapato, cordón) to come undone.
desatascar [1] vt to clear.
desatornillar vt to unscrew.
desatrancar [1] vt to unblock; (puerta) to unbolt.
desautorizar [4] vt to disallow; (huelga etc) to ban.
desavenencia f disagreement.
desayunar 1 vi to have breakfast. **2** vt to have for breakfast.
desayuno m breakfast.
desbarajuste m confusion.
desbaratar vt to ruin.
desbordar 1 vt to overflow. **2** vi to overflow (**de** with). **3 desbordarse** vr to overflow.
descabellado,-a a crazy.
descafeinado,-a a decaffeinated.
descalabro m misfortune.
descalificar [1] vt to disqualify.
descalzarse [4] vr to take one's shoes off.
descalzo,-a a barefoot.
descampado m garbage dump.
descansado,-a a (persona) rested; (vida, trabajo) restful.
descansar vi to rest, have a rest; (poco tiempo) to take a break.
descansillo m landing.

descanso *m* rest; (*en teatro, cine*) interval; (*en deporte*) half-time; **un día de d.** a day off.

descapotable *a* & *m* convertible.

descarado,-a 1 *a* (*insolente*) rude; (*desvergonzado*) shameless. **2** *mf* rude person.

descarga *f* unloading; (*eléctrica, explosiva*) discharge.

descargar [7] **1** *vt* to unload; (*golpe*) to deal. **2** *vi* (*tormenta*) to burst. **3 descargarse** *vr* to go flat.

descaro *m* cheek.

descarrilar *vi* to be derailed.

descartar *vt* to rule out.

descender [3] **1** *vi* (*temperatura, nivel*) to fall; **d. de** to descend from. **2** *vt* to lower.

descendiente *mf* descendant.

descenso *m* descent; (*de temperatura*) fall.

descifrar *vt* to decipher; (*mensaje*) decode; (*misterio*) to solve.

descolgar [2] *vt* (*el teléfono*) to pick up; (*cuadro, cortinas*) to take down.

descolorido,-a *a* faded.

descomponer (*pp* **descompuesto**) **1** *vt* to break down; (*corromper*) to decompose. **2 descomponerse** *vi* (*corromperse*) to decompose; (*ponerse nervioso*) to lose one's cool.

descomposición *f* (*de carne*) decomposition.

descompuse *pt indef de* **descomponer.**

descomunal *a* massive.

desconcertar [1] **1** *vt* to disconcert. **2 desconcertarse** *vr* to be bewildered.

desconectar *vt* to disconnect.

desconfiado,-a *a* distrustful.

desconfiar *vi* to distrust (**de** -).

descongelar *vt* to defrost.

desconocer *vt* not to know.

desconocido,-a 1 *a* unknown; (*irreconocible*) unrecognizable. **2** *m* **lo d.** the unknown. **3** *mf* stranger.

desconsolado,-a *a* disconsolate.

descontar [2] *vt* to deduct.

descontento,-a 1 *a* unhappy. **2** *m* dissatisfaction.

descorchar *vt* to uncork.

descorrer *vt* to draw back.

descoser *vt* to unpick.

descoyuntar *vt* to dislocate.

descrédito *m* disrepute.

descremado,-a *a* skimmed.

describir (*pp* **descrito**) *vt* to describe.

descripción *f* description.

descuartizar [4] *vt* to cut into pieces.

descubierto,-a 1 *a* open. **2** *m* **al d.** in the open; **poner al d.** to bring out into the open.

descubrimiento *m* discovery.

descubrir (*pp* **descubierto**) *vt* to discover; (*conspiración*) to uncover; (*placa*) to unveil.

descuento *m* discount.

descuidado,-a *a* (*negligente*) careless; (*desaseado*) untidy; (*desprevenido*) off one's guard.

descuido *m* oversight; (*negligencia*) carelessness; **por d.** inadvertently.

desde *adv* (*tiempo*) since; (*lugar*) from; **no lo he visto d. hace un año** I haven't seen him for a year; **d. siempre** always; **d. luego** of course; **d. que** ever since.

desdén *m* disdain.

desdeñar *vt* to disdain.

desdichado,-a 1 *a* unfortunate. **2** *mf* poor devil.

desdoblar *vt* to unfold.

desear *vt* to desire; (*querer*) to want; **¿qué desea?** can I help you?; **estoy deseando que vengas** I'm looking forward to your coming; **te deseo buena suerte/feliz Navidad** I wish you good luck/a Merry Christmas.

desechable *a* disposable.

desechar *vt* (*tirar*) to discard; (*idea, proyecto*) to drop.

desembarcar [1] **1** *vt* (*mercancías*) to unload; (*personas*) to disembark. **2** *vi* to disembark.

desembarco, desembarque *m* (*de mercancías*) unloading; (*de personas*) disembarkation.

desembocar [1] *vi* (*río*) to flow (**en** into); (*calle, situación*) to lead (**en,** to).

desembolsar *vt* to pay out.

desempaquetar *vt* to unpack.

desempate *m* play-off.

desempeñar *vt* (*cargo*) to hold; (*función*) to fulfill; (*papel*) to play.

desempleado,-a 1 *a* unemployed, out of work. **2** *mf* unemployed person; **los desempleados** the unemployed.

desempleo *m* unemployment; **cobrar el d.** to be on welfare.

desencadenar 1 *vt* (*provocar*) to unleash. **2 desencadenarse** *vr* (*viento, pasión*) to rage; (*conflicto*) to break out.

desencanto *m* disillusion.

desenchufar *vt* to unplug.

desenfadado,-a *a* free and easy.

desenfocado,-a *a* out of focus.

desenganchar *vt* to unhook; (*vagón*) to uncouple.

desengaño *m* disappointment.

desengrasar *vt* to remove the grease from.

desenlace *m* outcome; (*de historia*) ending.

desenmascarar *vt* to unmask.

desenredar *vt* to disentangle.

desenrollar *vt* to unroll; (*cable*) to unwind.

desenroscar [1] *vt* to unscrew.

desentenderse [3] *vr* **se desentendió de mi problema** he didn't want to have anything to do with my problem.

desentonar *vi* to be out of tune; (*colores etc*) not to match; (*persona, comentario*) to be out of place.

desentrañar *vt* to unravel.

desentrenado,-a *a* out of training.

desenvolver [4] (*pp desenvuelto*) **1** *vt* to unwrap. **2 desenvolverse** *vr* (*persona*) to manage.

desenvuelto,-a *a* relaxed.

deseo *m* wish; (*sexual*) desire.

desequilibrado,-a 1 *a* unbalanced. **2** *mf* unbalanced person.

desértico,-a *a* desert.

desertor,-a *mf* deserter.

desesperado,-a *a* (*sin esperanza*) desperate; (*exasperado*) exasperated.

desesperante *a* exasperating.

desesperar 1 *vt* to drive to despair; (*exasperar*) to exasperate. **2 desesperarse** *vr* to despair.

desfachatez *f* cheek.

desfallecer *vi* (*debilitarse*) to feel faint; (*desmayarse*) to faint.

desfavorable *a* unfavorable.

desfigurar *vt* (*cara*) to disfigure.

desfiladero *m* narrow pass.

desfilar *vi* to march in single file; (*soldados*) to march past.

desfile *m* (*militar*) parade; **d. de modas** fashion show.

desganado,-a *a* (*apático*) apathetic; **estar d.** (*inapetente*) to have no appetite.

desgarrador,-a *a* bloodcurdling.

desgarrar *vt* to tear.

desgastar *vt,* **desgastarse** *vr* to wear out.

desgaste *m* wear.

desgracia *f* misfortune; **por d.** unfortunately.

desgraciadamente *adv* unfortunately.

desgraciado,-a 1 *a* unfortunate; (*infeliz*) unhappy. **2** *mf* unfortunate person.

desgravación *f* deduction; **d. fiscal** tax deduction.

desgravar *vt* to deduct.

deshabitado,-a *a* uninhabited.

deshacer (*pp deshecho*) **1** *vt* (*paquete*) to undo; (*maleta*) to unpack; (*destruir*) to destroy; (*disolver*) to dissolve; (*derretir*) to melt. **2 deshacerse** *vr* to come undone; **deshacerse de algn/algo** to get rid of sb/sth; (*disolverse*) to dissolve; (*derretirse*) to melt.

deshielo *m* thaw.

deshonesto,-a *a* dishonest; *(indecente)* indecent.

deshonrar *vt* to dishonor; *(a la familia etc)* to bring disgrace on.

deshora a.d. *adv* at an inconvenient time.

deshuesar *vt* *(carne)* to bone; *(fruta)* to stone.

desierto,-a 1 *m* desert. **2** *a (deshabitado)* uninhabited; *(vacío)* deserted.

designar *vt* to designate; *(fecha, lugar)* to fix.

desigual *a* uneven.

desigualdad *f* inequality; *(del terreno)* unevenness.

desilusión *f* disappointment.

desilusionar *vt* to disappoint.

desinfectante *a & m* disinfectant.

desinflar 1 *vt* to deflate; *(rueda)* to let down. **2 desinflarse** *vr* to go flat.

desintegrar *vt*, **desintegrarse** *vr* to disintegrate.

desinteresado,-a *a* selfless.

desistir *vi* to desist.

deslenguado,-a *a (insolente)* insolent.

desliz *m* slip.

deslizar [4] **1** *vi* to slide. **2 deslizarse** *vr (patinar)* to slide; *(bajar)* to slide down.

deslumbrador,-a, deslumbrante *a* dazzling; *fig* stunning.

deslumbrar *vt* to dazzle.

desmandarse *vr* to get out of hand.

desmantelar *vt* to dismantle.

desmaquillador,-a 1 *m* make-up remover. **2** *a* **leche desmaquilladora** cleansing cream.

desmaquillarse *vr* to remove one's make-up.

desmayarse *vr* to faint.

desmayo *m* fainting fit; **tener un d.** to faint.

desmedido,-a *a* out of proportion.

desmejorar(se) *vi & vr* to deteriorate.

desmemoriado,-a *a* forgetful.

desmentir [5] *vt* to deny.

desmenuzar [4] *vt* to crumble.

desmesurado,-a *a* excessive.

desmontar *vt* to dismantle.

desmoralizar [4] *vt* to demoralize.

desmoronarse *vr* to crumble.

desnatado,-a *a (leche)* skim milk.

desnivel *m* drop.

desnudar *vt*, **desnudarse** *vr* to undress.

desnudista *a & mf* nudist.

desnudo,-a *a* naked.

desnutrido,-a *a* undernourished.

desobedecer *vt* to disobey.

desobediente 1 *a* disobedient. **2** *mf* disobedient person.

desocupado,-a *a (vacío)* empty; *(ocioso)* free.

desodorante *a & m* deodorant.

desolar [2] *vt* to devastate.

desollar [2] **1** *vt* to skin. **2 desollarse** *vr* to scrape; **me desollé el brazo** I scraped my arm.

desorbitado,-a *a (precio)* exorbitant.

desorden *m* mess; **d. público** civil disorder.

desordenado,-a *a* untidy.

desordenar *vt* to make untidy, mess up.

desorientar 1 *vt* to disorientate. **2 desorientarse** *vr* to lose one's bearings.

despabilado,-a *a (sin sueño)* wide awake; *(listo)* quick.

despachar *vt (asunto)* to get through; *(en tienda)* to serve.

despacho *m (oficina)* office; *(en casa)* study.

despacio *adv (lentamente)* slowly.

desparramar *vt*, **desparramarse** *vr* to scatter; *(líquido)* to spill.

despavorido,-a *a* terrified.

despectivo,-a *a* derogatory.

despedida *f* goodbye.

despedir [6] **1** *vt (empleado)* to sack; *(decir adiós a)* to say goodbye to; *(olor, humo etc)* to give off. **2 despedirse** *vr (decir adiós)* to say goodbye (**de** to).

despegar [7] **1** *vt* to detach. **2** *vi* (*avión*) to take off. **3 despegarse** *vr* to come unstuck.

despegue *m* takeoff.

despeinado,-a *a* dishevelled.

despejar 1 *vt* to clear. **2 despejarse** *vr* (*cielo*) to clear; (*persona*) to clear one's head.

despeje *m* (*de balón*) clearance.

despensa *f* pantry.

despeñarse *vr* to go over a cliff.

desperdiciar *vt* to waste; (*oportunidad*) to throw away.

desperdicio *m* waste; **desperdicios** (*basura*) trash *sing*; (*desechos*) leftovers.

desperdigar [7] *vt*, **desperdigarse** *vr* to scatter.

desperezarse [4] *vr* to stretch (oneself).

desperfecto *m* (*defecto*) flaw; (*daño*) damage.

despertador *m* alarm clock.

despertar [1] *vt*, **despertarse** *vr* to wake (up).

despiadado,-a *a* merciless.

despido *m* dismissal.

despierto,-a *a* (*desvelado*) awake; (*listo*) quick.

despilfarrar *vt* to squander.

despistado,-a 1 *a* (*olvidadizo*) scatterbrained. **2** *mf* scatterbrain.

despistar 1 *vt* (*hacer perder la pista a*) to lose. **2 despistarse** *vr* (*perderse*) to get lost; (*distraerse*) to switch off.

desplazamiento *m* (*viaje*) journey.

desplazar [4] **1** *vt* to displace. **2 desplazarse** *vr* to travel.

despojar *vt* to strip (**de** of); *fig* to deprive (**de** of).

desposar *vt* to marry.

déspota *mf* despot, tyrant.

despreciar *vt* (*desdeñar*) to scorn; (*rechazar*) to reject.

desprender 1 *vt* (*separar*) to remove; (*olor, humo etc*) to give off. **2 desprenderse** *vr* (*soltarse*) to come off; **desprenderse de** to rid oneself (**de** of).

despreocupado,-a *a* (*tranquilo*) unconcerned; (*descuidado*) careless; (*estilo*) casual.

desprestigiar *vt* to discredit.

desprevenido,-a *a* unprepared; **coger** *o* **pillar a algn d.** to catch sb unawares.

desproporcionado,-a *a* disproportionate.

desprovisto,-a *a* lacking (**de** -).

después 1 *adv* afterwards, later; (*entonces*) then; (*seguidamente, lugar*) next; **poco d.** soon after. **2 p. de** after. **3** *conj* **d. de que** after.

destacar [1] **1** *vt* to stress. **2 destacar(se)** *vi & vr* to stand out.

destapar 1 *vt* to take the lid off; (*botella*) to open. **2 destaparse** *vr* to get uncovered.

destartalado,-a *a* rambling; (*desvencijado*) ramshackle.

destello *m* sparkle.

desteñir [6] **1** *vti* to discolor. **2 desteñirse** *vr* to fade.

desternillarse *vi* **d. (de risa)** to split one's sides laughing.

desterrar [1] *vt* to exile.

destierro *m* exile.

destilería *f* distillery.

destinar *vt* (*dinero etc*) to assign; (*empleado*) to appoint.

destino *m* (*rumbo*) destination; (*sino*) fate; (*de empleo*) post; **el avión con d. a Bilbao** the plane to Bilbao.

destituir *vt* to remove from office.

destornillador *m* screwdriver.

destreza *f* skill.

destrozar [4] *vt* (*destruir*) to destroy; (*abatir*) to shatter.

destrucción *f* destruction.

destruir *vt* to destroy.

desuso *m* disuse; **caer en d.** to fall into disuse.

desvalijar *vt* (*robar*) to rob; (*casa, tienda*) to burgle.

desván *m* loft.

desvanecerse *vr* (*disiparse*) to vanish; (*desmayarse*) to faint.

desvariar *vi* to talk nonsense.

desvelar 1 *vt* to keep awake. **2 desvelarse** *vr* to make every effort.

desvencijarse *vr* to fall apart.

desventaja *f* disadvantage; (*inconveniente*) drawback; **estar en d.** to be at a disadvantage.

desvergonzado,-a 1 *a* (*indecente*) shameless; (*descarado*) insolent. **2** *mf* (*sinvergüenza*) shameless person; (*fresco*) insolent person.

desvestir [6] *vt*, **desvestirse** *vr* to undress.

desviar 1 *vt* (*río, carretera*) to divert; (*golpe, conversación*) to deflect. **2 desviarse** *vr* to go off course; (*coche*) to turn off.

desvío *m* diversion.

detallado,-a *a* detailed.

detalle *m* detail; (*delicadeza*) nice thought.

detallista *a* perfectionist.

detectar *vt* to detect.

detective *mf* detective; **d. privado** private detective.

detener 1 *vt* to stop; (*arrestar*) to arrest. **2 detenerse** *vr* to stop.

detenidamente *adv* carefully.

detenido,-a 1 *a* (*parado*) stopped; (*arrestado*) detained; (*minucioso*) thorough. **2** *mf* detainee.

detergente *a* & *m* detergent.

deteriorar 1 *vt* to spoil. **2 deteriorarse** *vr* (*estropearse*) to get damaged.

determinado,-a *a* (*preciso*) definite; (*resuelto*) resolute.

determinar 1 *vt* (*fecha etc*) to set; (*decidir*) to decide on. **2 determinarse** *vr* **determinarse a** to make up one's mind to.

detestar *vt* to hate.

detrás 1 *adv* behind. **2** *prep* **d. de** behind.

detuve *pt indef de* **detener.**

deuda *f* debt; **d. pública** national debt.

deudor,-a *mf* debtor.

devaluar *vt* to devalue.

devastador,-a *a* devastating.

devoción *f* devoutness; (*al trabajo etc*) devotion.

devolución *f* return; (*de dinero*) refund.

devolver [4] (*pp* **devuelto**) **1** *vt* to give back; (*dinero*) to refund. **2** *vi* (*vomitar*) to vomit. **3 devolverse** *vr* *Am* to go/come back.

devorar *vt* to devour.

devoto,-a 1 *a* devout. **2** *mf* pious person; (*seguidor*) devotee.

devuelto,-a *pp de* **devolver.**

DF *m abr de* **Distrito Federal** Federal District.

di *pt indef de* **dar;** *imperativo de* **decir.**

día *m* day; **¿qué d. es hoy?** what's the date today?; **d. a d.** day by day; **de d.** by day; **durante el d.** during the daytime; **un d. sí y otro no** every other day; **pan del d.** fresh bread; **hoy (en) d.** nowadays; **el d. de mañana** in the future; **d. festivo** holiday; **d. laborable** working day; **d. libre** day off; **es de d.** it is daylight; **hace buen/mal d.** it's a nice/rotten day.

diabético,-a *a* & *mf* diabetic.

diablo *m* devil.

diadema *f* tiara.

diagnóstico *m* diagnosis.

diagonal *a* & *f* diagonal; **en d.** diagonally.

dial *m* dial.

diálogo *m* dialog.

diamante *m* diamond.

diámetro *m* diameter.

diana *f* (*blanco*) bull's eye.

diapositiva *f* slide.

diariamente *adv* daily.

diario,-a 1 *a* daily; **a d.** daily. **2** *m* (daily) newspaper; (*memorias*) diary.

diarrea *f* diarrhea.

dibujante *mf* drawer; (*de cómic*) cartoonist; (*delineante*) (*hombre*) draftsman; (*mujer*) draftswoman.

dibujar *vt* to draw.

dibujo *m* drawing; **dibujos animados** cartoons.

diccionario *m* dictionary.

dicho,-a *a* said; **mejor d.** or rather; **d. y hecho** no sooner said than done; **dicha persona** the above-mentioned person.

dichoso,-a *a* (*feliz*) happy; *fam* (*maldito*) damned.

diciembre *m* December.

dictado *m* dictation.

dictadura *f* dictatorship.

dictáfono® *m* Dictaphone®.

dictar *vt* to dictate; (*ley*) to enact.

didáctico,-a *a* didactic.

diecinueve *a & m inv* nineteen.

dieciocho *a & m inv* eighteen.

dieciséis *a & m inv* sixteen.

diecisiete *a & m inv* seventeen.

diente *m* tooth; **d. de ajo** clove of garlic; **d. de leche** milk tooth; **dientes postizos** false teeth.

diera *subj imperfecto de* dar.

diesel *a & m inv* diesel.

diestro,-a 1 *a* (*hábil*) skillful. **2** *m* bullfighter.

dieta *f* (*paga*) diet; **estar a d.** to be on a diet; **dietas** expenses.

diez *a & m inv* ten.

diferencia *f* difference; **a d. de** unlike.

diferenciar 1 *vt* to differentiate (*entre* between). **2 diferenciarse** *vr* to differ (*de* from).

diferente 1 *a* different (*de* than). **2** *adv* differently.

diferido,-a *a* **en d.** recorded.

difícil *a* difficult; **d. de creer/hacer** difficult to believe/do; **es d. que venga** it is unlikely that she'll come.

dificultad *f* difficulty; (*aprieto*) problem.

difundir *vt*, **difundirse** *vr* to spread.

difunto,-a *mf* deceased.

digestión *f* digestion.

digestivo,-a *a* easy to digest.

digital *a* digital; **huellas digitales** fingerprints.

dígito *m* digit.

digno,-a *a* (*merecedor*) worthy; (*decoroso*) decent.

digo *indic pres de* decir.

dije *pt indef de* decir.

dilatar *vt*, **dilatarse** *vr* to expand.

dilema *m* dilemma.

diluir *vt*, **diluirse** *vr* to dilute.

diluviar *v impers* to pour with rain.

diluyo *indic pres de* diluir.

dimensión *f* dimension; **de grandes dimensiones** very large.

dimisión *m* resignation; **presentar la d.** to hand in one's resignation.

dimitir *vi* to resign (*de* from).

dinamita *f* dynamite.

dinamo *f*, **dínamo** *f* dynamo.

dinero *m* money; **d. efectivo** *o* **en metálico** cash.

dinosaurio *m* dinosaur.

dios *m* god; **¡D. mío!** my God!; **¡por D.!** for goodness sake!

diploma *m* diploma.

diplomacia *f* diplomacy.

diplomarse *vr* to graduate.

diplomático,-a 1 *a* diplomatic. **2** *mf* diplomat.

diptongo *m* diphthong.

diputación *f* **d. provincial** ≈ county council.

diputado,-a *mf* & (*hombre*) Congressman; (*mujer*) Congresswoman; **Congreso de los Diputados** ≈ Congress.

dique *m* dike.

diré *fut de* decir.

dirección *f* direction; (*señas*) address; (*destino*) destination; (*de vehículo*) steering; (*dirigentes*) management; (*cargo*) directorship; (*de un partido*) leadership; **d. prohibida** no entry; **calle de d. única** one-way street.

directa *f* (*marcha*) top gear.

directiva *f* board of directors.

directamente *adv* directly.

directo,-a *a* direct; **en d.** live.

director,-a *mf* director; (*de colegio*) (*hombre*) headmaster; (*mujer*) headmistress; (*de periódico*) editor; **d. de cine** (film) director; **d. de orquesta** conductor; **d. gerente** managing director.

dirigir [6] **1** *vt* to direct; (*empresa*)

to manage; (negocio, colegio) to run; (orquesta) to conduct; (partido) to lead; (periódico) to edit; **d. la palabra a algn** to speak to sb. **2 dirigirse** vr **dirigirse a** o **hacia** (ir) to make one's way towards; (hablar) to speak to.

disciplina f discipline.

discípulo,-a mf disciple.

disco m disk; (de música) record; **d. compacto** compact disc; **d. duro** hard disk; **d. óptico** optical disk.

discoteca f discotheque.

discrepar vi (disentir) to disagree (**de** with; **en** on).

discreto,-a a discreet.

discriminación f discrimination.

disculpa f excuse; **dar disculpas** to make excuses; **pedir disculpas a algn** to apologize to sb.

disculpar 1 vt to excuse. **2 disculparse** vr to apologize (**por** for).

discurrir vi to think.

discurso m speech; **dar** o **pronunciar un d.** to make a speech.

discusión f argument.

discutir 1 vi to argue (**de** about). **2** vt to discuss.

diseñar vt to design.

diseño m design.

disfrazar [4] 1 vt to disguise. **2 disfrazarse** vr to disguise oneself.

disfrutar 1 vi (gozar) to enjoy oneself; (poseer) to enjoy (**de** -). **2** vt to enjoy.

disgustar 1 vt to upset. **2 disgustarse** vr (molestarse) to get upset; (dos amigos) to quarrel.

disgusto m (preocupación) upset; (desgracia) trouble; **llevarse un d.** to get upset; **dar un d. a algn** to upset sb; **a d.** unwillingly.

disimular vt to conceal.

disipar 1 vt (niebla) to drive away; (temor, duda) to dispel. **2 disiparse** vr (niebla, temor etc) to disappear.

dislocar [1] vt to dislocate.

disminuir 1 vt to reduce. **2** vi to diminish.

disolvente a & m solvent.

disolver [4] (pp **disuelto**) vt to dissolve.

disparar 1 vt (pistola etc) to fire; (flecha, balón) to shoot. **2 dispararse** vr (arma) to go off; (precios) to rocket.

disparate m (dicho) nonsense; **decir disparates** to talk nonsense; (acto) foolish act.

dispersar vt, **dispersarse** vr to disperse.

disponer (pp **dispuesto**) 1 vt (arreglar) to arrange; (ordenar) to order. **2** vi **d. de** to have at one's disposal. **3 disponerse** vr to get ready.

disposición f (colocación) layout; (orden) law; **a su d.** at your service.

dispositivo m device.

disputa f (discusión) argument; (contienda) contest.

disquete m diskette, floppy disk.

disquetera f disk drive.

distancia f distance.

distante a distant.

distinguir 1 vt (diferenciar) to distinguish; (reconocer) to recognize. **2** vi (diferenciar) to discriminate. **3 distinguirse** vr to distinguish oneself.

distintivo,-a 1 a distinctive. **2** m distinctive mark.

distinto,-a a different.

distracción f entertainment; (pasatiempo) pastime; (descuido) absent-mindedness.

distraer 1 vt (atención) to distract; (divertir) to entertain. **2 distraerse** vr (divertirse) to amuse oneself; (abstraerse) to let one's mind wander.

distraído,-a a entertaining; (abstraído) absent-minded.

distribuidor,-a 1 a distributing. **2** mf distributor.

distribuir vt to distribute; (trabajo) to share out.

distrito m district; **d. postal** postal district.

disturbio m riot.

disuadir vt to dissuade.

disuelto,-a pp de **disolver.**

diván m couch.

diversión f fun.

diverso,-a a different; **diversos** various.

divertido,-a a funny.

divertir [5] **1** vt to amuse. **2 divertirse** vr to enjoy oneself.

dividir vt, **dividirse** vr to divide (**en** into).

divisa f foreign currency.

división f division.

divorciado,-a 1 a divorced. **2** mf (hombre) divorcé; (mujer) divorcée.

divorciarse vr to get divorced.

divorcio m divorce.

divulgación f disclosure.

DNI m abr de **Documento Nacional de Identidad** Identity Card, ID card.

dóberman m Doberman (pinscher).

dobladillo m hem.

doblar 1 vt to double; (plegar) to fold up; (torcer) to bend; (la esquina) to go round. **2** vi (girar) to turn. **3 doblarse** vr (plegarse) to fold; (torcerse) to bend.

doble 1 a double. **2** m double; **gana el d. que tú** he earns twice as much as you do.

doce a & m inv twelve.

docena f dozen.

docente a teaching; **centro d.** educational center.

dócil a docile.

doctor,-a mf doctor.

doctorado m doctorate, PhD.

documentación f documentation; (DNI, de conducir etc) papers pl.

documental a & m documentary.

documento m document; **d. nacional de identidad** identity card.

dogo m bulldog.

dólar m dollar.

doler [4] vi to ache; **me duele la cabeza** I've got a headache.

dolor m pain; (pena) grief; **d. de cabeza** headache; **d. de muelas** toothache.

domar vt to tame; (caballo) to break in.

doméstico,-a a domestic; **animal d.** pet.

domicilio m residence; (señas) address.

dominante a dominant; (déspota) domineering.

dominar 1 vt to dominate; (situación) to control; (idioma) to speak very well. **2** vi to dominate; (resaltar) to stand out. **3 dominarse** vr to control oneself.

domingo m inv Sunday; **D. de Resurrección** o **Pascua** Easter Sunday.

dominical 1 a Sunday. **2** m (suplemento) Sunday supplement.

dominicano,-a a & mf Dominican; **República Dominicana** Dominican Republic.

dominio m (poder) control; (de un idioma) command; (territorio) dominion.

dominó, dómino m dominoes pl.

don¹ m (habilidad) gift; **tener el d. de** to have a knack for.

don² m **Señor D. José García** Mr José García; **D. Fulano de Tal** Mr So-and-So.

donar vt (sangre etc) to donate.

donativo m donation.

dónde adv where (in questions); **¿por d. se va a la playa?** which way is it to the beach?

donde adv rel where; **a** o **en d.** where; **de** o **desde d.** from where.

doña f **Señora D. Leonor Benítez** Mrs Leonor Benítez.

dorada f (pez) gilthead bream.

dorado,-a a golden.

dormido,-a a asleep; **quedarse d.** to fall asleep; (no despertarse) to oversleep.

dormilón,-ona fam **1** a sleepy-headed. **2** mf sleepyhead.

dormir [7] **1** vi to sleep. **2** vt **d. la**

siesta to have an afternoon nap.
3 dormirse *vr* to fall asleep; **se me
ha dormido el brazo** my arm has
gone to sleep.

dormitorio *m* (*de una casa*) bedroom; (*de colegio, residencia*) dormitory.

dorsal 1 *a* **espina d.** spine. **2** *m* (*de
camiseta*) number.

dorso *m* back; **instrucciones al d.**
instructions over; **véase al d.** see
overleaf.

dos 1 *a* two. **2** *m inv* two; **los d.**
both; **nosotros/vosotros d.** both of
us/you.

doscientos,-as *a* & *mf* two hundred.

dosis *f inv* dose.

doy *indic pres de* **dar.**

Dr. *abr de* **doctor** doctor, Dr.

Dra. *abr de* **doctora** doctor, Dr.

dragón *m* dragon.

drama *m* drama.

dramático,-a *a* dramatic.

drástico,-a *a* drastic.

droga *f* drug; **d. blanda/dura** soft/
hard drug.

drogadicto,-a *mf* drug addict.

drogar [7] **1** *vt* to drug. **2 drogarse**
vr to take drugs.

droguería *f* hardware and household goods shop.

ducha *f* shower; **darse/tomar una
d.** to take/have a shower.

ducharse *vr* to take a shower.

duda *f* doubt; **sin d.** without a
doubt; **no cabe d.** (there is) no
doubt.

dudar 1 *vi* to doubt; (*vacilar*) to
hesitate (**en** to). **2** *vt* to doubt.

dueña *f* owner; (*de pensión*)
landlady.

dueño *m* owner; (*de casa etc*)
landlord.

dulce 1 *a* (*sabor*) sweet; (*carácter,
voz*) gentle; (*agua*) fresh. **2** *m* (*pastel*) cake; (*caramelo*) candy.

duna *f* dune.

duodécimo,-a *a* & *mf* twelfth.

duplicar [1] **1** *vt* to duplicate;

(*cifras*) to double. **2 duplicarse** *vr*
to double.

duración *f* duration.

durante *prep* during.

durar *vi* to last.

durazno *m Am* (*fruto*) peach; (*árbol*) peach tree.

dureza *f* hardness; (*severidad*) severity; (*callosidad*) corn.

duro,-a 1 *a* hard; (*resistente*)
tough. **2** *m* (*moneda*) five-peseta
coin. **3** *adv* hard.

E

e *conj* (*before words beginning with
i or* **hi**) and.

ébano *m* ebony.

ebullición *f* boiling; **punto de e.**
boiling point.

echar 1 *vt* to throw; (*carta*) to post;
(*vino, agua*) to pour; (*expulsar*) to
throw out; (*despedir*) to sack;
(*humo, olor etc*) to give off; **e. una
mano** to give a hand; **e. una mi-
rada/una ojeada** to have a look/a
quick look; **e. gasolina al coche** to
put gas in the car; **e. de menos** *o*
en falta to miss. **2** *vi* (+ **a** + *infinitivo*) (*empezar*) to begin to; **echó a
correr** he ran off. **3 echarse** *vr*
(*tumbarse*) to lie down; (*lanzarse*)
to throw oneself; (+ **a** + *infinitivo*)
(*empezar*) to begin to do; *fig* **echarse
atrás** to get cold feet; **echarse a
llorar** to burst into tears; **echarse a
perder** (*comida*) to go bad.

eclesiástico,-a 1 *a* ecclesiastical.
2 *m* clergyman.

eclipse *m* eclipse.

eco *m* echo.

ecológico,-a *a* ecological.

ecologista 1 *a* ecological. **2** *mf*
ecologist.

economía *f* economy; (*ciencia*)
economics *sing*.

económico,-a *a* economic; (*barato*) economical.

economizar [4] *vti* to economize.

ecuación *f* equation.

ecuador *m* equator.

ecuatoriano,-a *a & mf* Ecuadorian.

ecuánime *a* (*temperamento*) eventempered; (*juicio*) impartial.

ecuestre *a* equestrian.

edad *f* age; **¿qué e. tienes?** how old are you?; **E. Media** Middle Ages *pl*.

edición *f* (*publicación*) publication; (*conjunto de ejemplares*) edition.

edicto *m* edict.

edificio *m* building.

edil,-a *mf* town councilor.

editar *vt* (*libro, periódico*) to publish; (*disco*) to release; (*en ordenador*) to edit.

editor,-a 1 *a* publishing. 2 *mf* publisher. 3 *m* **e. de textos** text editor.

editorial 1 *a* publishing. 2 *f* publishing house. 3 *m* editorial.

edredón *m* duvet, eiderdown.

educación *f* education; (*formación*) upbringing; **buena/mala e.** (*modales*) good/bad manners; **falta de e.** bad manners.

educado,-a *a* polite.

educar [1] *vt* (*hijos*) to raise.

educativo,-a *a* educational.

efectivamente *adv* yes indeed!

efectivo,-a 1 *a* effective; **hacer e. un cheque** to cash a check. 2 *m* **en e.** in cash.

efecto *m* (*resultado*) effect; (*impresión*) impression; **efectos personales** personal belongings; **en e.** yes indeed!

efectuar *vt* to carry out; (*viaje*) to make; (*pedido*) to place.

eficacia *f* (*de persona*) efficiency; (*de remedio etc*) effectiveness.

eficaz *a* (*persona*) efficient; (*remedio, medida etc*) effective.

eficiente *a* efficient.

efusivo,-a *a* effusive.

EGB *f abr de* **Enseñanza General Básica** ≈ Primary School Education.

egipcio,-a *a & mf* Egyptian.

egoísmo *m* egoism.

egoísta 1 *a* selfish. 2 *mf* ego(t)ist.

egresar *vi Am* to leave school; to graduate.

ej. *abr de* **ejemplo** example.

eje *m* (*de rueda*) axle; (*de máquina*) shaft.

ejecutar *vt* (*ajusticiar*) to execute; (*sinfonía*) to perform.

ejecutiva *f* (*gobierno*) executive.

ejecutivo,-a 1 *a* executive; **el poder e.** the government. 2 *mf* executive.

ejemplar 1 *m* (*de libro*) copy; (*de revista, periódico*) specimen; (*especimen*) specimen. 2 *a* exemplary.

ejemplo *m* example; **por e.** for example; **dar e.** to set an example.

ejercer [2] *vt* (*profesión etc*) to practice; (*influencia*) to exert.

ejercicio *m* exercise; (*de profesión*) practice; **hacer e.** to take exercise.

ejercitar *vt* to practice.

ejército *m* army.

el 1 *art def* the; **el Sr. García** Mr. García. ▪ (*no se traduce*) **el hambre/destino** hunger/fate. ▪ (*con partes del cuerpo, prendas de vestir*) **me he cortado el dedo** I've cut my finger; **métetelo en el bolsillo** put it in your pocket. ▪ (*con días de la semana*) **el lunes** on Monday. 2 *pron* the one; **el de las once** the eleven o'clock one; **el que tienes en la mano** the one you've got in your hand; **el que quieras** whichever one you want; **el de tu amigo** your friend's.

él *pron pers* (*sujeto*) (*persona*) he; (*animal, cosa*) it; (*complemento*) (*persona*) him; (*animal, cosa*) it.

elaboración *f* (*de un producto*) production.

elaborar *vt* (*producto*) to produce.

elasticidad *f* elasticity; *fig* flexibility.

elástico,-a *a & m* elastic.

elección f choice; (votación) election.

electorado m electorate pl.

electoral a electoral; **campaña e.** election campaign; **colegio e.** polling station.

electricidad f electricity.

electricista mf electrician.

eléctrico,-a a electric.

electrocutar vt to electrocute.

electrodoméstico m (domestic) electrical appliance.

electrónico,-a a electronic.

elefante m elephant.

elegancia f elegance.

elegante a elegant.

elegir [6] vt to choose; (en votación) to elect.

elemental a (fundamental) basic; (simple) elementary.

elemento m element; (componente) component.

elepé m LP (record).

elevación f elevation; (de precios) rise.

elevado,-a a high; (edificio) tall.

elevalunas m inv **e. eléctrico** electric windows pl.

elevar 1 vt to raise. **2 elevarse** vr (subir) to rise; **elevarse a** (cantidad) to come to.

elijo indic pres de **elegir**.

eliminar vt to eliminate.

eliminatorio,-a a qualifying.

ella pron pers f (sujeto) she; (animal, cosa) it, she; (complemento) her; (animal, cosa) it, her.

ellas pron pers fpl (sujeto) they; (complemento) them.

ello pron pers neutro it; **por e.** for that reason.

ellos pron pers mpl (sujeto) they; (complemento) them.

elocuente a eloquent.

elogiar vt to praise.

elote m Am tender corncob.

eludir vt to avoid.

embajada f embassy.

embajador,-a mf ambassador.

embalaje m packing.

embalse m reservoir; (presa) dam.

embarazada 1 a pregnant. **2** f pregnant woman.

embarazo m (preñez) pregnancy; (turbación) embarrassment.

embarazoso,-a a embarrassing.

embarcación f boat.

embarcadero m quay.

embarcar [1] **1** vt to ship. **2** vi to go on board. **3 embarcarse** vr to go on board (**en** -); (en avión) to board (**en** -).

embarque m (de persona) boarding; (de mercancías) loading; **tarjeta de e.** boarding card.

embestida f onslaught; (de toro) charge.

embestir [6] vt (a torero) to charge; (atacar) to attack.

emblema m emblem.

embobado,-a a fascinated.

émbolo m piston.

embolsar vt, **embolsarse** vr to pocket.

emborrachar vt, **emborracharse** vr to get drunk.

emboscada f ambush.

embotellamiento m traffic jam.

embotellar vt to bottle; (tráfico) to block.

embrague m clutch.

embriagar [7] **1** vt to intoxicate. **2 embriagarse** vr to get drunk.

embriaguez f intoxication.

embrollar 1 vt to confuse. **2 embrollarse** vr to get confused.

embrujado,-a a (sitio) haunted.

embudo m funnel.

embuste m lie.

embustero,-a mf cheat.

embutido m sausage.

emergencia f emergency; **salida de e.** emergency exit; **en caso de e.** in an emergency.

emigración f emigration.

emigrante a & mf emigrant.

emigrar vi to emigrate.

emisión f emission; (de radio, TV) broadcasting.

emisora f (de radio) radio station; (de televisión) television station.

emitir *vt* to emit; *(luz, calor)* to give off; *(opinión, juicio)* to express; *(programa)* to transmit.

emoción *f* emotion; *(excitación)* excitement; **¡qué e.!** how exciting!

emocionante *a (conmovedor)* moving; *(excitante)* exciting.

emocionar 1 *vt (conmover)* to move; *(excitar)* to thrill. **2 emocionarse** *vr (conmoverse)* to be moved; *(excitarse)* to get excited.

empacar [1] *vt Am (mercancías)* to pack; to annoy.

empacho *m (de comida)* indigestion.

empalagoso,-a *a (dulce)* sickly sweet.

empalizada *f* fence.

empalmar 1 *vt (unir)* to join; *(cuerdas, cables)* to splice. **2** *vi* to converge; *(trenes)* to connect.

empanada *f* pie.

empanadilla *f* pasty.

empañar *vt*, **empañarse** *vr (cristales)* to steam up.

empapado,-a *a* soaked.

empapar 1 *vt (mojar)* to soak; *(absorber)* to soak up. **2 empaparse** *vr (persona)* to get soaked.

empapelar *vt* to wallpaper.

empaquetar *vt* to pack.

emparedado *m* sandwich.

empaste *m (de diente)* filling.

empatar *vi* to draw; *Am (unir)* to join.

empate *m* draw.

empedrado,-a 1 *a* cobbled. **2** *m (adoquines)* cobblestones *pl*.

empeine *m (de pie, de zapato)* instep.

empellón *m* shove.

empeñar 1 *vt* to pawn. **2 empeñarse** *vr (insistir)* to insist (**en** on); *(endeudarse)* to get into debt.

empeño *m (insistencia)* insistence; *(deuda)* pledge.

empeorar 1 *vi* to deteriorate. **2** *vt* to make worse. **3 empeorarse** *vr* to deteriorate.

emperador *m* emperor.

empezar [1] *vti* to begin, start (**a hacer algo** to do sth).

empinado,-a *a (cuesta)* steep.

empinar 1 *vt* to raise. **2 empinarse** *vr (persona)* to stand on tiptoe.

emplazamiento *m (colocación)* location.

empleado,-a *mf* employee; *(de oficina, banco)* clerk.

emplear *vt (usar)* to use; *(contratar)* to employ; *(dinero, tiempo)* to spend.

empleo *m* employment; *(oficio)* job; *(uso)* use; **modo de e.** instructions for use.

emplomar *vt Am (diente)* to fill.

empobrecer 1 *vi* to impoverish. **2 empobrecerse** *vr* to become impoverished.

empobrecimiento *m* impoverishment.

empollón,-ona *mf fam* grind.

emporio *m Am* department store.

empotrado,-a *a* fitted.

emprendedor,-a *a* enterprising.

empresa *f* firm; *(tarea)* undertaking.

empresarial *a (de empresa)* business; *(espíritu)* entrepreneurial; **(ciencias) empresariales** business studies.

empresario,-a *mf (hombre)* businessman; *(mujer)* businesswoman; *(patrón)* employer.

empujar *vt* to push, shove.

empujón *m* push, shove.

emulsión *f* emulsion.

en *prep (posición)* in; at; *(sobre)* on; **en Madrid/Bolivia** in Madrid/Bolivia; **en casa/el trabajo** at home/work; **en la mesa** on the table. ■ *(movimiento)* into; **entrar en la casa** to go into the house. ■ *(tiempo)* in; on; at; **en 1940** in 1940; **en la mañana** in the morning; **cae en martes** it falls on a Tuesday; **en ese momento** at that moment. ■ *(transporte)* by; **en coche/tren** by car/train. ■ *(modo)* **en español** in Spanish; **en broma** jokingly; **en serio** seriously. ■ *(reducción, aumento)* by; **los precios aumentaron en un diez por ciento** the prices went up by ten percent. ■ (*tema, materia*) at, in; **bueno en deportes** good at sports; **experto en política** expert in politics. ■ (*división, separación*) in; **lo dividió en tres partes** he divided it in three. ■ (*con infinitivo*) **fue rápido en responder** he was quick to answer.

enaguas *fpl* petticoat *sing.*

enamorado,-a 1 *a* in love. **2** *mf* person in love.

enamorar 1 *vt* to win the heart of. **2 enamorarse** *vr* to fall in love (**de** with).

enano,-a *a* & *mf* dwarf.

encabezamiento *m* (*de carta*) heading; (*de periódico*) headline.

encabezar [4] *vt* (*carta, lista*) to head; (*periódico*) to lead; (*rebelión, carrera, movimiento*) to lead.

encajar 1 *vt* (*ajustar*) to insert; **e. un golpe a algn** to land sb a blow. **2** *vi* (*ajustarse*) to fit; **e. con** to fit (in) with.

encaje *m* lace.

encallar *vi* to run aground.

encantado,-a *a* (*contento*) delighted; (*embrujado*) enchanted; **e. de conocerle** pleased to meet you;

encantador,-a *a* charming.

encantar 1 *vt* (*hechizar*) to cast a spell on; **me encanta nadar** I love swimming.

encanto *m* charm; **ser un e.** to be charming.

encapricharse *vr* to set one's mind (**con** on).

encaramarse *vr* to climb up.

encarar 1 *vt* to face. **2 encararse** *vr* **encararse con** to face up to.

encarcelar *vt* to imprison.

encarecer 1 *vt* to put up the price of. **2 encarecerse** *vr* to go up (in price).

encargado,-a 1 *mf* manager; (*responsable*) person in charge. **2** *a* in charge.

encargar [7] **1** *vt* to entrust with; (*mercancías*) to order. **2 encargarse** *vr* **encargarse de** to see to.

encargo *m* order; (*recado*) errand; (*tarea*) job.

encariñarse *vr* to become fond (**con** of).

encarnado,-a *a* (*rojo*) red.

encarnizado,-a *a* fierce.

encauzar [4] *vt* to channel.

encendedor *m* lighter.

encender [3] **1** *vt* (*luz, radio, tele*) to switch on, put on; (*cigarro, vela, fuego*) to light; (*cerilla*) to strike. **2 encenderse** *vr* (*fuego*) to catch; (*lámpara etc*) to go o come on.

encendido *m* ignition.

encerado *m* (*pizarra*) blackboard.

encerrar [1] **1** *vt* to shut in; (*con llave*) to lock in. **2 encerrarse** *vr* to shut oneself in; (*con llave*) to lock oneself in.

encharcar [1] *vt*, **encharcarse** *vr* to flood.

enchufado,-a *a fig fam* **estar e.** to have good connections. **2** *mf* (*favorito*) pet.

enchufar *vt* to plug in; (*unir*) to join.

enchufe *m* (*hembra*) socket; (*macho*) plug; *fam* contact.

encía *f* gum.

enciclopedia *f* encyclopedia.

encima 1 *adv* on top; (*arriba*) above; (*en el aire*) overhead; (*además*) besides. **2** *prep* **e. de** (*sobre*) on; (*además*) besides; **ahí e.** up there; **por e.** above; **leer un libro por e.** to skim through a book.

encina *f* holm oak.

encinta *a* pregnant.

enclenque *a* (*débil*) puny; (*enfermizo*) sickly.

encoger [5] **1** *vti* to contract; (*prenda*) to shrink. **2 encogerse** *vr* (*contraerse*) to contract; (*prenda*) to shrink; **encogerse de hombros** to shrug (one's shoulders).

encolar *vt* (*papel*) to paste; (*madera*) to glue.

encolerizar [4] **1** *vt* to infuriate. **2 encolerizarse** *vr* to become furious.

encono *m* spitefulness.

encontrar [2] **1** vt (hallar) to find; (a persona) to meet; (problema) to come up against. **2 encontrarse** vr (sentirse) to feel, be; (estar) to be; **encontrarse a gusto** to feel comfortable; **encontrarse con algn** to meet sb.

encontronazo m (choque) clash.

encorvarse vr to bend (over).

encrucijada f crossroads.

encuadernar vt to bind.

encubrir vt to conceal.

encuentro m meeting; (deportivo) match.

encuesta f (sondeo) (opinion) poll; (investigación) investigation.

encuestar vt to poll.

endeble a weak.

endémico,-a a endemic.

enderezar [4] **1** vt (poner derecho) to straighten out; (poner vertical) to set upright. **2 enderezarse** vr to straighten up.

endeudarse vr to get into debt.

endiablado,-a a mischievous.

endibia f endive.

endulzar [4] vt to sweeten.

endurecer vt, **endurecerse** vr to harden.

enemigo,-a a & mf enemy.

enemistar **1** vt to set at odds. **2 enemistarse** vr to become enemies; **enemistarse con algn** to fall out with sb.

energía f energy; **e. nuclear** nuclear power; **e. vital** vitality.

enérgico,-a a energetic; (tono) emphatic.

enero m January.

enfadado,-a a angry.

enfadar **1** vt to make angry. **2 enfadarse** vr to get angry (con with); (dos personas) to fall out.

enfado m anger.

énfasis m inv emphasis.

enfermar vi **enfermarse** vr Am to fall ill.

enfermedad f illness; (contagiosa) disease.

enfermería f infirmary.

enfermero,-a mf (mujer) nurse; (hombre) male nurse.

enfermizo,-a a unhealthy.

enfermo,-a **1** a ill. **2** mf ill person; (paciente) patient.

enfocar [1] vt (imagen) to focus; (tema) to approach; (con linterna) to shine a light on.

enfrentamiento m clash.

enfrentar **1** vt (situación, peligro) to confront; (enemistar) to set at odds. **2 enfrentarse** vr **enfrentarse con** o a (encararse) to confront.

enfrente **1** adv opposite; **la casa de e.** the house opposite. **2** prep **e. de** opposite.

enfriamiento m (proceso) cooling; (catarro) chill.

enfriar **1** vt to cool (down). **2 enfriarse** vr to get cold; (resfriarse) to catch a cold.

enfurecer **1** vt to enrage. **2 enfurecerse** vr to get furious.

enganchar **1** vt to hook. **2 engancharse** vr (ropa) to get caught; (persona) to get hooked.

engañar **1** vt to deceive; (estafar) to cheat; (mentir a) to lie to; (al marido, mujer) to be unfaithful to. **2 engañarse** vr to deceive oneself.

engaño m deceit; (estafa) fraud; (mentira) lie.

engañoso,-a a (palabras) deceitful; (apariencias) deceptive.

engarzar [4] vt (unir) to link; (engastar) to mount.

engastar vt to mount.

engendrar vt fig to engender.

englobar vt to include.

engordar **1** vt to make fat. **2** vi to put on weight; (comida, bebida) to be fattening.

engorro m nuisance.

engranaje m gearing.

engrasar vt (lubricar) to lubricate; (manchar) to make greasy.

engreído,-a a conceited.

engrudo m paste.

engullir vt to gobble up.

enhebrar vt to thread.

enhorabuena f congratulations pl; **dar la e. a algn** to congratulate sb.

enigma *m* enigma.

enjabonar *vt* to soap.

enjambre *m* swarm.

enjaular *vt* (*animal*) to cage.

enjuagar [7] *vt* to rinse.

enjugar [7] *vt*, **enjugarse** *vr* (*secar*) to mop up; (*lágrimas*) to wipe away.

enjuiciar *vt* (*criminal*) to prosecute.

enlace *m* connection; (*casamiento*) marriage.

enlatado,-a *a* canned, tinned.

enlazar [4] *vti* to connect (**con** with).

enloquecer 1 *vi* to go mad. 2 *vt* to drive mad. 3 **enloquecerse** *vr* to go mad.

enmarañar 1 *vt* (*pelo*) to tangle; (*complicar*) to complicate. 2 **enmarañarse** *vr* (*pelo*) to get tangled.

enmascarar *vt* (*problema, la verdad*) to disguise.

enmendar [1] 1 *vt* (*corregir*) to put right. 2 **enmendarse** *vr* (*persona*) to mend one's ways.

enmienda *f* correction; (*de ley*) amendment.

enmohecerse *vr* (*metal*) to rust; (*comida*) to get moldy.

enmudecer *vi* to fall silent; (*por sorpresa etc*) to be dumbstruck.

ennegrecer *vt*, **ennegrecerse** *vr* to turn black.

enojado,-a *a* angry.

enojar 1 *vt* to anger. 2 **enojarse** *vr* to get angry.

enorgullecer 1 *vt* to fill with pride. 2 **enorgullecerse** *vt* to be proud (**de** of).

enorme *a* enormous.

enraizar *vi*, **enraizarse** *vr* (*planta, costumbre*) to take root.

enrarecerse *vr* (*aire*) to become rarefied.

enredadera *f* climbing plant.

enredar 1 *vt* (*enmarañar*) to entangle; *fig* (*implicar*) to involve (**en** in). 2 **enredarse** *vr* (*enmarañarse*) to get tangled up; *fig* (*involucrarse*) to get involved, to get entangled (**con** with).

enriquecer 1 *vt* to make rich; *fig* to enrich. 2 **enriquecerse** *vr* to become rich; *fig* to become enriched.

enrojecer(se) *vi* & *vr* (*ruborizarse*) to blush.

enrollado,-a *a* rolled up.

enrollar 1 *vt* to roll up; (*cable*) to coil; (*hilo*) to wind up. 2 **enrollarse** *vr fam* (*hablar*) to go on and on.

enroscar [1] 1 *vt* to coil (round); (*tornillo*) to screw in; (*tapón*) to screw on. 2 **enroscarse** *vr* to coil.

ensaimada *f* kind of spiral pastry from Majorca.

ensalada *f* salad.

ensaladilla rusa *f* Russian salad.

ensanchar 1 *vt* to widen; (*ropa*) to let out. 2 **ensancharse** *vr* to widen.

ensangrentado,-a *a* bloodstained.

ensayar *vt* to try out; (*obra, canción*) to rehearse.

ensayo *m* trial; (*de obra*) rehearsal; **e. general** dress rehearsal.

enseguida, en seguida *adv* (*inmediatamente*) at once, straight away; (*poco después*) in a minute, soon.

ensenada *f* inlet.

enseñanza *f* (*educación*) education; (*de idioma etc*) teaching.

enseñar *vt* to teach; (*mostrar*) to show; (*señalar*) to point out; **e. a algn a hacer algo** to teach sb how to do sth.

ensimismado,-a *a* (*absorbido*) engrossed; (*abstraído*) lost in thought.

ensimismarse *vr* (*absorberse*) to become engrossed; (*abstraerse*) to be lost in thought.

ensombrecer 1 *vt* to cast a shadow over. 2 **ensombrecerse** *vr* to darken.

ensopar *vt Am* to soak.

ensordecedor,-a *a* deafening.

ensuciar *vt*, **ensuciarse** *vr* to get dirty.

ensueño *m* dream.

entablar *vt* (*conversación*) to begin; (*amistad*) to strike up.

entallado,-a *a* (*vestido*) close-fitting; (*camisa*) fitted.

entender [3] **1** *vt* (*comprender*) to understand; **dar a algn a e. que . . .** to give sb to understand that . . . **2** *vi* (*comprender*) to understand; **e. de** (*saber*) to know about. **3 entenderse** *vr* (*comprenderse*) to be understood.

entendimiento *m* understanding.

enteramente *adv* entirely.

enterarse *vr* to find out; **me he enterado de que . . .** I understand . . . ; **ni me enteré** I didn't even realize it.

entereza *f* strength of character.

enternecer 1 *vt* to move. **2 enternecerse** *vr* to be moved.

entero,-a *a* (*completo*) entire, whole.

enterrar [1] *vt* to bury.

entidad *f* organization, entity.

entierro *m* burial; (*ceremonia*) funeral.

entonar *vt* (*canción*) to intone, to sing.

entonces *adv* then; **por aquel e.** at that time.

entornar *vt* (*ojos etc*) to half-close; (*puerta*) to leave ajar.

entorpecer *vt* (*obstaculizar*) to hinder.

entrada *f* entrance; (*billete*) ticket; (*recaudación*) takings *pl*; (*plato*) entrée; **entradas** (*en la frente*) receding hairline.

entrar 1 *vi* to enter; (*venir dentro*) to come in; (*ir dentro*) go in; (*encajar*) to fit; **me entró dolor de cabeza** I got a headache; **me entraron ganas de reír** I felt like laughing. **2** *vt* (*datos*) to enter.

entre *prep* (*dos*) between; (*más de dos*) among(st).

entreabierto,-a *a* (*ojos etc*) half-open; (*puerta*) ajar.

entreacto *m* interval.

entrecejo *m* space between the eyebrows.

entrecortado,-a *a* (*voz*) faltering.

entrega *f* (*de productos*) delivery;

(*de premios*) presentation; (*devoción*) selflessness.

entregar [7] **1** *vt* (*dar*) to hand over; (*deberes etc*) to hand in; (*mercancía*) to deliver. **2 entregarse** *vr* (*rendirse*) to give in; **entregarse a** to devote oneself to.

entrelazar [4] *vt*, **entrelazarse** *vr* to entwine.

entremedias *adv* in between.

entremés *m* hors d'oeuvres.

entremeterse *vr* = **entrometerse.**

entrenador,-a *mf* trainer.

entrenamiento *m* training.

entrenar *vi*, **entrenarse** *vr* to train.

entresuelo *m* mezzanine.

entretanto *adv* meanwhile.

entretención *f* *Am* entertainment.

entretener 1 *vt* (*divertir*) to entertain; (*retrasar*) to delay; (*detener*) to detain. **2 entretenerse** *vr* (*distraerse*) to amuse oneself; (*retrasarse*) to be held up.

entretenido,-a *a* entertaining.

entretenimiento *m* entertainment.

entretiempo *a* **ropa de e.** lightweight clothing.

entrevista *f* interview.

entrevistar 1 *vt* to interview. **2 entrevistarse** *vr* **entrevistarse con algn** to have an interview with sb.

entristecer 1 *vt* to sadden. **2 entristecerse** *vr* to be sad (**por** about).

entrometerse *vr* to meddle (**en** in, with).

entumecerse *vr* to go numb.

enturbiar 1 *vt* to make cloudy. **2 enturbiarse** *vr* to become cloudy.

entusiasmar 1 *vt* to fill with enthusiasm. **2 entusiasmarse** *vr* to get enthusiastic (**con** about).

entusiasmo *m* enthusiasm; **con e.** enthusiastically.

enumerar *vt* to enumerate.

envasar *vt* (*embotellar*) to bottle; (*empaquetar*) to pack; (*enlatar*) to can, tin.

envase *m* (*recipiente*) container; (*botella vacía*) empty.

envejecer *vti* to age.

envenenar *vt* to poison.
envergadura *f* **de gran e.** large-scale.
enviar *vt* to send.
envidia *f* envy; **tener e. de algn** to envy sb.
envidiable *a* enviable.
envidiar *vt* to envy.
envidioso,-a *a* envious.
envío *m* sending; (*remesa*) consignment; (*paquete*) parcel; **gastos de e.** postage and packing.
envoltorio *m*, **envoltura** *f* wrapping.
envolver [4] (*pp* **envuelto**) **1** *vt* (*con papel*) to wrap; (*en complot etc*) to involve (**en** in). **2 envolverse** *vr* to wrap oneself up (**en** in).
enyesar *vt* to put in plaster.
epidemia *f* epidemic.
episodio *m* episode.
época *f* time; (*periodo*) period.
equilibrio *m* balance.
equilibrista *mf* tightrope walker; *Am* opportunist.
equipaje *m* luggage; **hacer el e.** to pack.
equipar *vt* to equip (**con, de** with).
equiparar *vt* to compare (**con** with).
equipo *m* (*de expertos, jugadores*) team; (*aparatos*) equipment; (*ropas*) outfit; **e. de alta fidelidad** hi-fi stereo system.
equitación *f* horseriding.
equitativo,-a *a* equitable.
equivalente *a* equivalent.
equivaler *vi* to be equivalent (**to** a).
equivocación *f* error.
equivocado,-a *a* mistaken.
equivocar [1] **1** *vt* to mix up. **2 equivocarse** *vr* to make a mistake.
equívoco,-a *a* misleading.
era *pt imperfecto de* **ser.**
eras *pt imperfecto de* **ser.**
eres *indic pres de* **ser.**
erguir [5] *vt* to erect.
erizarse [4] *vr* to stand on end.
erizo *m* hedgehog; **e. de mar, e. marino** sea urchin.

ermita *f* shrine.
erosión *f* erosion.
erótico,-a *a* erotic.
erradicar [1] *vt* to eradicate.
errante *a* wandering.
errata *f* misprint.
erróneo,-a *a* erroneous.
error *m* mistake.
eructar *vi* to belch.
eructo *m* belch, burp.
erudito,-a **1** *a* erudite. **2** *mf* scholar.
erupción *f* (*de volcán*) eruption; (*en la piel*) rash.
es *indic pres de* **ser.**
esa *a dem* that.
ésa *pron dem ver* **ése.**
esbelto,-a *a* slender.
escabeche *m* brine.
escabullirse *vr* to scurry off.
escala *f* scale; (*parada*) (*de barco*) port of call; (*escalera*) ladder; **a gran e.** on a large scale; **hacer e. en** to stop over in.
escalada *f* climb.
escalador,-a *mf* climber.
escalar *vt* to climb.
escaldar *vt* to scald.
escalera *f* stair; (*escala*) ladder; **e. de incendios** fire escape; **e. mecánica** escalator.
escalerilla *f* steps *pl*.
escalfar *vt* to poach.
escalofrío *m* shiver.
escalón *m* step; **e. lateral** (*en letrero*) ramp.
escalonar *vt* to space out.
escama *f* (*de animal*) scale; (*de jabón*) flake.
escamotear *vt* cheat out of.
escampar *vi* to clear up.
escandalizar [4] **1** *vt* to scandalize. **2 escandalizarse** *vr* to be shocked (**de** at, by).
escándalo *m* (*alboroto*) racket; (*desvergüenza*) scandal; **armar un e.** to kick up a fuss.
escanear *vt* to scan.
escáner *m* scanner.
escaño *m* (*parlamentario*) seat.
escapada *f* (*de prisión*) escape.

escapar 1 *vi* to escape. **2 escaparse**
vr to escape; (*gas etc*) to leak.

escaparate *m* shop window.

escape *m* (*huida*) escape; (*de gas
etc*) leak; **tubo de e.** exhaust (pipe).

escarabajo *m* beetle.

escarbar *vt* (*suelo*) to scratch.

escarcha *f* frost.

escarlata *a* scarlet.

escarlatina *f* scarlet fever.

escarmentar [1] *vi* to learn one's
lesson.

escarmiento *m* lesson.

escarola *f* escarole.

escarpado,-a *a* (*paisaje*) craggy.

escasear *vi* to be scarce.

escasez *f* scarcity.

escaso,-a *a* scarce; (*dinero*) tight;
(*conocimientos*) scant.

escayola *f* plaster of Paris; (*para
brazo etc*) plaster.

escayolar *vt* (*brazo etc*) to put in
plaster.

escena *f* scene; (*escenario*) stage.

escenario *m* (*en teatro*) stage; (*de
película*) setting.

escéptico,-a *a & mf* sceptic.

esclarecer *vt* to shed light on.

esclavo,-a *a & mf* slave.

esclusa *f* lock.

escoba *f* brush.

escocer [4] *vi* to sting.

escocés,-a 1 *a* Scottish, Scots;
falda escocesa kilt. **2** *mf* Scot.

escoger [5] *vt* to choose.

escolar 1 *a* (*curso, año*) school. **2** *mf*
(*niño*) schoolboy; (*niña*) school-
girl.

escollo *m* reef; (*obstáculo*) pitfall.

escolta *f* escort.

escoltar *vt* to escort.

escombros *mpl* debris *sing*.

esconder *vt*, **esconderse** *vr* to
hide (**de** from).

escondidas a e. *adv* secretly.

escondite *m* (*lugar*) hiding place;
(*juego*) hide-and-seek.

escondrijo *m* hiding place.

escopeta *f* shotgun; **e. de aire
comprimido** air gun.

escorpión *m* scorpion.

escotado,-a *a* low-cut.

escote *m* low neckline.

escotilla *f* hatch.

escozor *m* stinging.

escribir (*pp* escrito) **1** *vt* to write;
e. a máquina to type. **2 escribirse**
vr (*dos personas*) to write to each
other.

escrito,-a 1 *a* written; **por e.** in
writing. **2** *m* (*documento*) document.

escritor,-a *mf* writer.

escritorio *m* (*mueble*) writing
desk.

escritura *f* (*documento*) document.

escrúpulo *m* (*recelo*) scruple; **una
persona sin escrúpulos** an unscru-
pulous person.

escrupuloso,-a *a* squeamish; (*honesto*) scrupulous; (*meticuloso*)
painstaking.

escrutinio *m* (*de votos*) count.

escuadra *f* (*intrumento*) square;
(*militar*) squad; (*de barcos*)
squadron.

escuálido,-a *a* emaciated.

escuchar 1 *vt* to listen to; (*oír*) to
hear. **2** *vi* to listen.

escudo *m* (*arma defensiva*) shield;
(*blasón*) coat of arms.

escuela *f* school; **e. de idiomas** language school.

escueto,-a *a* plain.

escuezo *indic pres de* escocer.

esculcar [1] *vt Am* (*registrar*) to
search.

escultor,-a *mf* (*hombre*) sculptor;
(*mujer*) sculptress; (*de madera*)
woodcarver.

escultura *f* sculpture.

escupidera *f* (*recipiente*) spittoon,
cuspidor; (*orinal*) chamberpot.

escupir 1 *vi* to spit out. **2** *vt* to spit out.

escurreplatos *m inv* dish rack.

escurridizo,-a *a* slippery.

escurridor *m* colander; (*escurreplatos*) dish rack.

escurrir 1 *vt* (*plato, vaso*) to drain;
(*ropa*) to wring out; **e. el bulto** to
wriggle out. **2 escurrirse** *vr* (*resbalarse*) to slip.

ese,-a *a dem* that; **esos,-as** those.

ése,-a *pron dem mf* that one; **ésos, -as** those (ones); *fam* **¡ni por ésas!** no way!

esencia *f* essence.

esencial *a* essential; **lo e.** the main thing.

esencialmente *adv* essentially.

esfera *f* sphere; (*de reloj de pulsera*) dial; (*de reloj de pared*) face.

esforzarse [2] *vr* to endeavour (**por** to).

esfuerzo *m* effort.

esfumarse *vr fam* to beat it.

esgrima *f* fencing.

esguince *m* sprain.

eslabón *m* link.

eslogan *m* (*pl* **eslóganes**) slogan.

esmalte *m* enamel; (*de uñas*) nail polish.

esmeralda *f* emerald.

esmerarse *vr* to be careful; (*esforzarse*) to go to great lengths.

esmoquin *m* (*pl* **esmóquines**) tuxedo.

esnob (*pl* **esnobs**) **1** *a* (*persona*) snobbish; (*restaurante etc*) posh. **2** *mf* snob.

eso *pron dem neutro* that; **¡e. es!** that's it!; **por e.** that's why; **a e. de las diez** around ten.

esos,-as *a dem* those.

ésos,-as *pron dem mfpl* those.

espabilado,-a *a* (*despierto*) wide awake; (*listo*) clever.

espabilar *vt,* **espabilarse** *vr* to wake up.

espacial *a* spatial; **nave e.** spaceship.

espacio *m* space; (*de tiempo*) length; (*programa*) program.

espacioso,-a *a* spacious.

espada *f* sword; **pez e.** swordfish.

espaguetis *mpl* spaghetti *sing*.

espalda *f* back; (*en natación*) backstroke; **espaldas** back *sing*; **a espaldas de algn** behind sb's back; **por la e.** from behind; **volver la e. a algn** to turn one's back on sb.

espantajo *m* (*muñeco*) scarecrow.

espantapájaros *m inv* scarecrow.

espantar 1 *vt* (*asustar*) to frighten; (*ahuyentar*) to frighten away. **2 espantarse** *vr* to become frightened (**de** of).

espantoso,-a *a* dreadful.

español,-a 1 *a* Spanish. **2** *mf* Spaniard; **los españoles** the Spanish. **3** *m* (*idioma*) Spanish.

esparadrapo *m* sticking plaster.

esparcir [3] **1** *vt* (*papeles, semillas*) to scatter; (*rumor*) to spread. **2 esparcirse** *vr* to be scattered.

espárrago *m* asparagus.

espátula *f* spatula.

especia *f* spice.

especial *a* special; **en e.** especially.

especialidad *f* specialty.

especialista *mf* specialist.

especializarse [4] *vr* to specialize (**en** in).

especialmente *adv* (*exclusivamente*) specially; (*muy*) especially.

especie *f* species *inv*; (*clase*) kind.

específicamente *adv* specifically.

especificar [1] *vt* to specify.

específico,-a *a* a specific.

espectacular *a* spectacular.

espectáculo *m* show.

espectador,-a *mf* spectator; (*en teatro, cine*) member of the audience; **los espectadores** the audience *sing*; (*de televisión*) viewers.

especulación *f* speculation.

espejismo *m* mirage.

espejo *m* mirror; **e. retrovisor** rear-view mirror.

espeluznante *a* horrifying.

espera *f* wait; **en e. de** waiting for; **a la e. de** expecting; **sala de e.** waiting room.

esperanza *f* hope; **e. de vida** life expectancy.

esperar 1 *vi* (*aguardar*) to wait; (*tener esperanza*) to hope. **2** *vt* (*aguardar*) to wait for; (*tener esperanza*) to hope for; (*estar a la espera de, bebé*) to expect; **espero que sí** I hope so; **espero que vengas** I hope you'll come.

esperma m sperm; Am (vela) candle.

espesar vt, **espesarse** vr to thicken.

espeso,-a a (bosque, niebla) dense; (líquido) thick; (masa) stiff.

espesor m thickness; **tres metros de e.** three meters thick.

espía mf spy.

espiar 1 vi to spy. 2 vt to spy on.

espiga f (de trigo) ear.

espigado,-a a slender.

espina f (de planta) thorn; (de pescado) bone; **e. dorsal** spine.

espinaca f spinach.

espinazo m spine.

espinilla f shin; (en la piel) spot.

espionaje m spying.

espiral a & f spiral.

espirar vi to breathe out.

espíritu m spirit; (alma) soul.

espiritual a spiritual.

espléndido,-a a (magnífico) splendid; (generoso) lavish.

esplendor m splendor.

espliego m lavender.

esponja f sponge.

espontáneo,-a a spontaneous.

esposado,-a a (con esposas) handcuffed.

esposas fpl handcuffs.

esposo,-a mf spouse; (hombre) husband; (mujer) wife.

esprint m sprint.

espuela f spur.

espuma f foam; (de cerveza) head; (de jabón) lather; **e. de afeitar** shaving foam.

espumoso,-a a frothy; (vino) sparkling.

esqueleto m skeleton.

esquema m diagram.

esquemático,-a a (escueto) schematic; (con diagramas) diagrammatic.

esquí m (objeto) ski; (deporte) skiing; **e. acuático** water-skiing.

esquiador,-a mf skier.

esquiar vi to ski.

esquimal a & mf Eskimo.

esquina f corner.

esquivar vt (a una persona) to avoid; (un golpe) to dodge.

esta a dem this.

está indic pres de **estar.**

ésta pron dem f this (one).

estabilidad f stability.

estable a stable.

establecer 1 vt to establish; (récord) to set. 2 **establecerse** vr (instalarse) to settle.

establecimiento m establishment.

establo m cow shed.

estaca f stake; (de tienda de campaña) peg.

estación f station; (del año) season; **e. de servicio** service station; **e. de esquí** ski resort; **e. de trabajo** work station.

estacionamiento m (acción) parking.

estacionar vt, **estacionarse** vr to park.

estacionario,-a a stationary.

estada f, **estadía** f Am stay.

estadio m (deportivo) stadium; (fase) stage.

estadística f statistics sing; **una e.** a statistic.

estado m state; **e. civil** marital status; **e. de cuentas** statement of account.

estadounidense 1 a United States, American. 2 mf United States citizen.

estafa f swindle.

estafar vt to swindle.

estafeta f **e. de Correos** sub post office.

estallar vi to burst; (bomba) to explode; (guerra) to break out.

estallido m explosion; (de guerra) outbreak.

estampa f illustration.

estampado,-a 1 a (tela) printed. 2 m (de tela) print.

estampilla f Am (postage) stamp.

estancar [1] 1 vt (agua) hold back; (paralizar) to block; (negociaciones) to bring to a standstill. 2 **estancarse** vr to stagnate.

estancia (*permanencia*) stay; (*habitación*) room; *Am* (*hacienda*) ranch.

estanco *m* tobacconist's.

estándar (*pl* **estándares**) *a* & *m* standard.

estanque *m* pond.

estante *m* shelf; (*para libros*) bookcase.

estantería *f* shelves.

estaño *m* tin.

estar 1 *vi* to be; **¿está tu madre?** is your mother in?; **¿cómo estás?** how are you?; **está escribiendo** she is writing; **estamos a 2 de noviembre** it is the 2nd of November; **están a 100 pesetas el kilo** they're 100 pesetas a kilo. **¿estamos?** OK?; **e. de más** not to be needed. ▪ (+ **para**) **estará para las seis** it will be finished by six; **hoy no estoy para bromas** I'm in no mood for jokes today; **el tren está para salir** the train is just about to leave. ▪ (+ **por**) **está por hacer** it has still to be done; **eso está por ver** it remains to be seen. ▪ (+ **con**) to have; **e. con la gripe** to have the flu. ▪ (+ **sin**) to have no. **2 estarse** *vr* **¡estáte quieto!** keep still!

estatal *a* state.

estatua *f* statue.

estatura *f* height.

estatuto *m* statute; (*de empresa etc*) rules *pl*.

este 1 *a* eastern; (*dirección*) easterly. **2** *m* east; **al e. de** to the east of.

esté *subj pres de* **estar**.

este,-a *a dem* this; **estos,-as** these.

éste,-a *pron dem mf* this one; **aquél . . . é.** the former . . . the latter; **éstos,-as** these (ones); **aquéllos . . . éstos** the former . . . the latter.

estela *f* (*de barco*) wake; (*de avión*) vapor trail.

estepa *f* steppe.

estera *f* rush mat.

estéreo *m* & *a* stereo.

estereofónico,-a *a* stereophonic.

estereotipo *m* stereotype.

estéril *a* sterile.

esterlina *a* **libra e.** pound (sterling).

esternón *m* breastbone.

estero *m Am* marsh.

esteticienne, esteticista *f* beautician.

estético,-a *a* aesthetic; **cirugía estética** plastic surgery.

estiércol *m* manure.

estilarse *vr* to be in vogue.

estilo *m* style; (*modo*) manner; (*en natación*) stroke.

estilográfica *f* (**pluma**) **e.** fountain pen.

estima *f* esteem.

estimación *f* (*estima*) esteem; (*valoración*) evaluation; (*cálculo aproximado*) estimate.

estimado,-a *a* respected; **E. Señor** (*en carta*) Dear Sir.

estimar *vt* (*apreciar*) to esteem; (*considerar*) to think; (*valuar*) to value.

estimulante 1 *a* stimulating. **2** *m* stimulant.

estimular *vt* to stimulate.

estímulo *m* stimulus.

estirar *vt*, **estirarse** *vr* to stretch.

estival *a* summer.

esto *pron dem* (*esta cosa*) this, this thing; (*este asunto*) this matter.

estocada *f* stab.

estofado *m* stew.

estómago *m* stomach; **dolor de e.** stomach ache.

estoque *m* sword.

estorbar 1 *vt* (*dificultar*) to hinder. **2** *vi* to be in the way.

estorbo *m* (*obstáculo*) obstacle.

estornudar *vi* to sneeze.

estornudo *m* sneeze.

estos,-as *a dem pl* these.

éstos,-as *pron dem mfpl* these.

estoy *indic pres de* **estar**.

estrangular *vt* to strangle.

estraperlo *m* black market.

estratagema *f* ruse.

estratégico,-a *a* strategic.

estrechamente *adv* (*íntimamente*) closely.

estrechamiento *m* narrowing; **'e.**

de calzada' (*en letrero*) 'road narrows'.

estrechar 1 *vt* to make narrow; **e. la mano a algn** to shake sb's hand; (*lazos de amistad*) to tighten. **2 estrecharse** *vr* to narrow.

estrechez *f* narrowness; **pasar estrecheces** to be hard up.

estrecho,-a 1 *a* narrow; (*ropa, zapato*) tight; (*amistad, relación*) close. **2** *m* strait.

estrella *f* star; **e. de cine** film star; **e. de mar** starfish; **e. fugaz** shooting star.

estrellar 1 *vt fam* to smash. **2 estrellarse** *vr* (*chocar*) to crash (**contra** into).

estremecer *vt*, **estremecerse** *vr* to shake.

estrenar *vt* to use for the first time; (*ropa*) to wear for the first time; (*obra, película*) to premiere.

estreno *m* (*teatral*) first performance; (*de película*) premiere.

estreñimiento *m* constipation.

estrépito *m* din.

estrés *m* stress.

estribillo *m* (*en canción*) chorus; (*en poema*) refrain.

estribo *m* stirrup; *fig* **perder los estribos** to fly off the handle.

estribor *m* starboard.

estricto,-a *a* strict.

estropajo *m* scourer.

estropear 1 *vt* (*máquina, cosecha*) to damage; (*fiesta, plan*) to spoil; (*pelo, manos*) to ruin. **2 estropearse** *vr* to be ruined; (*máquina*) to break down.

estructura *f* structure; (*armazón*) framework.

estrujar *vt* (*limón etc*) to squeeze; (*ropa*) to wring; (*apretar*) to crush.

estuche *m* case.

estudiante *mf* student.

estudiar *vti* to study.

estudio *m* study; (*encuesta*) survey; (*sala*) studio; (*apartamento*) studio (apartment).

estudioso,-a 1 *a* studious. **2** *mf* specialist.

estufa *f* heater.

estupefaciente *m* drug.

estupefacto,-a *a* astounded.

estupendamente *adv* marvellously.

estupendo,-a *a* marvelous; **¡e.!** great!

estupidez *f* stupidity.

estúpido,-a 1 *a* stupid. **2** *mf* idiot.

estuve *pt indef de* **estar.**

ETA *f abr de* **Euzkadi Ta Askatasuna** (*Patria Vasca y Libertad*) ETA.

etapa *f* stage.

etcétera *adv* etcetera.

eterno,-a *a* eternal.

ético,-a *a* ethical.

etílico,-a *a* **alcohol e.** ethyl alcohol.

etiqueta *f* (*de producto*) label; (*ceremonia*) etiquette; **de e.** formal.

étnico,-a *a* ethnic.

eucalipto *m* eucalyptus.

eufórico,-a *a* euphoric.

europeo,-a *a & mf* European.

EU *f abr de* **Unión Europea.**

euskera *m* Basque.

eutanasia *f* euthanasia.

evacuación *f* evacuation.

evacuar *vt* to evacuate.

evadir 1 *vt* (*respuesta, peligro, impuestos*) to avoid; (*responsabilidad*) to shirk. **2 evadirse** *vr* to escape.

evaluación *f* evaluation; (*en colegio*) assessment.

evaluar *vt* to assess.

evangelio *m* gospel.

evaporación *f* evaporation.

evaporar *vt*, **evaporarse** *vr* to evaporate.

evasión *f* (*fuga*) escape; (*escapismo*) escapism; **e. de capitales** flight of capital.

evasiva *f* evasive answer.

evento *m* (*acontecimiento*) event; (*incidente*) unforeseen event.

eventual *a* (*posible*) possible; (*trabajo, obrero*) casual.

evidencia *f* obviousness; **poner a algn en e.** to show sb up.

evidente *a* obvious.

evidentemente *adv* obviously.

evitar *vt* to avoid; (*problema futuro*) to prevent; (*desastre*) to avert.

evocar [1] *vt* (*traer a la memoria*) to evoke.

evolución *f* evolution; (*desarrollo*) development.

evolucionar *vi* to develop; (*especies*) to evolve.

ex *prefijo* former, ex-; **ex alumno** former pupil; **ex marido** ex-husband; *fam* **mi ex** my ex.

exacerbar 1 *vt* (*agravar*) to exacerbate. 2 **exacerbarse** *vr* (*irritarse*) to feel exasperated.

exactamente *adv* exactly.

exactitud *f* accuracy; **con e.** precisely.

exacto,-a *a* exact; **¡e.!** precisely!

exageración *f* exaggeration.

exagerado,-a *a* exaggerated; (*excesivo*) excessive.

exagerar *vti* to exaggerate.

exaltarse *vr* (*acalorarse*) to get carried away.

examen *m* examination, exam; **e. de conducir** driving test.

examinar 1 *vt* to examine. 2 **examinarse** *vr* to sit for an examination.

exasperante *a* exasperating.

exasperar 1 *vt* to exasperate. 2 **exasperarse** *vr* to become exasperated.

excavación *f* excavation; (*en arqueología*) dig.

excavadora *f* digger.

excedencia *f* leave (of absence).

excedente *a & m* surplus.

exceder 1 *vt* to exceed 2 **excederse** *vr* to go too far.

excelencia *f* excellence.

excelente *a* excellent.

excéntrico,-a *a* eccentric.

excepción *f* exception; **a e. de** except for.

excepcional *a* exceptional.

excepto *adv* except (for).

exceptuar *vt* to except.

excesivo,-a *a* excessive.

exceso *m* excess; **e. de velocidad** speeding.

excitación *f* (*sentimiento*) excitement; (*acción*) excitation.

excitante *a* exciting.

excitar 1 *vt* to excite. 2 **excitarse** *vr* to get excited.

exclamación *f* exclamation.

exclamar *vti* to exclaim.

excluir *vt* to exclude.

exclusive *adv* (*en fechas*) exclusive.

exclusivo,-a *a* exclusive.

excremento *m* excrement.

excursión *f* excursion.

excursionista *mf* tripper; (*a pie*) hiker.

excusa *f* (*pretexto*) excuse; (*disculpa*) apology.

excusar 1 *vt* (*justificar*) to excuse; (*eximir*) to exempt (**de** from). 2 **excusarse** *vr* (*disculparse*) to apologize.

exención *f* exemption.

exento,-a *a* exempt (**de** from).

exhalar *vt* to breathe out.

exhaustivo,-a *a* exhaustive.

exhausto,-a *a* exhausted.

exhibición *f* exhibition.

exhibir 1 *vt* (*mostrar*) to exhibit; (*lucir*) to show off. 2 **exhibirse** *vr* to show off.

exigente *a* demanding.

exigir [6] *vt* to demand.

exilado,-a 1 *a* exiled. 2 *mf* exile.

exilar 1 *vt* to exile. 2 **exilarse** *vr* to go into exile.

exiliado,-a = exilado,-a.

exiliar *vt* = **exilar.**

exilio *m* exile.

existencia *f* (*vida*) existence; **existencias** stocks.

existente *a* existing.

existir *vi* to exist.

éxito *m* success; **con é.** successfully; **tener é.** to be successful.

éxodo *m* exodus.

exorbitante *a* exorbitant.

exótico,-a *a* exotic.

expandir *vt*, **expandirse** *vr* to expand.

expansión f expansion; (de noticia) spreading; (diversión) relaxation.

expectación f (interés) excitement.

expectativa f expectancy.

expedición f expedition.

expediente m (informe) record; (ficha) file; **e. académico** student's record.

expedir [6] vt (pasaporte etc) to issue.

expendeduría f tobacconist's.

expensas fpl **a e. de** at the expense of.

experiencia f experience; (experimento) experiment.

experimentado,-a a experienced.

experimental a experimental.

experimentar 1 vi to experiment. **2** vt to undergo; (aumento) to show; (pérdida) to suffer; (sensación) to experience.

experimento m experiment.

experto,-a a & mf expert.

expirar vi to expire.

explanada f esplanade.

explicación f explanation.

explicar [1] **1** vt to explain. **2** **explicarse** vr (persona) to explain (oneself); **no me lo explico** I can't understand it.

exploración f exploration.

explorador,-a mf (persona) explorer.

explorar vt to explore.

explosión f explosion; **hacer e.** to explode.

explosivo,-a a & m explosive.

explotación f exploitation.

explotar 1 vi (bomba) to explode, go off. **2** vt to exploit.

exponer (pp **expuesto**) **1** vt (mostrar) to exhibit; (presentar) to put forward; (arriesgar) to expose. **2** **exponerse** vr to expose oneself (**a** to).

exportación f export.

exportar vt to export.

exposición f exhibition.

exprés a express; **olla e.** pressure cooker; **café e.** espresso (coffee).

expresamente adv expressly.

expresar 1 vt to express; (manifestar) to state. **2** **expresarse** vr to express oneself.

expresión f expression.

expreso,-a 1 a express. **2** m express (train). **3** adv on purpose.

exprimidor m juicer.

exprimir vt (limón) to squeeze; (zumo) to squeeze out.

expulsar vt to expel; (jugador) to send off.

expuse pt indef de **exponer.**

exquisito,-a a exquisite; (comida) delicious; (gusto) refined.

extender [3] **1** vt to extend; (agrandar) to enlarge; (mantel, mapa) to spread (out); (mano, brazo) to stretch (out); (crema, mantequilla) to spread. **2** **extenderse** vr (en el tiempo) to last; (en el espacio) to stretch; (rumor, noticia) to spread.

extendido,-a a extended; (mapa, plano) open; (mano, brazo) outstretched; (costumbre, rumor) widespread.

extensión f (de libro etc) length; (de terreno) expanse.

extenso,-a a (terreno) extensive; (libro, película) long.

extenuar 1 vt to exhaust. **2** **extenuarse** vr to exhaust oneself.

exterior 1 a (de fuera) outer; (puerta) outside; (política, deuda) foreign; **Ministerio de Asuntos Exteriores** State Department. **2** m (parte de fuera) outside; (extranjero) abroad.

exteriormente adv outwardly.

exterminar vt to exterminate.

externo,-a a external.

extinguir 1 vt (fuego) to extinguish; (raza) to wipe out. **2** **extinguirse** vr (fuego) to go out; (especie) to become extinct.

extintor m fire extinguisher.

extorsionar vt to extort.

extra 1 a extra; (superior) top quality; **horas e.** overtime; **paga e.** bonus. **2** *mf* extra.

extracto *m* extract; **e. de cuenta** statement of account.

extraer *vt* to extract.

extranjero,-a 1 *a* foreign. **2** *mf* foreigner. **3** *m* abroad; **en el e.** abroad.

extrañar 1 *vt* (*sorprender*) to surprise; *Am* (*echar de menos*) to miss. **2 extrañarse** *vr* **extrañarse de** (*sorprenderse*) to be surprised at.

extrañeza *f* (*sorpresa*) surprise; (*singularidad*) strangeness.

extraño,-a **1** *a* strange. **2** *mf* stranger.

extraoficial *a* unofficial.

extraordinario,-a *a* extraordinary.

extrarradio *m* suburbs *pl*.

extraterrestre *mf* alien.

extravagante *a* outlandish.

extravertido,-a *a* = **extrovertido,-a.**

extraviar 1 *vt* to mislay. **2 extraviarse** *vr* to be missing.

extremeño,-a *a* & *mf* Estremaduran.

extremidad *f* (*extremo*) tip; (*miembro*) limb.

extremo,-a 1 *m* (*de calle, cable*) end; (*máximo*) extreme; **en último e.** as a last resort; *f* **e. derecha/izquierda** outside-right/-left. **2** *a* extreme; **E. Oriente** Far East.

extrovertido,-a *a* & *mf* extrovert.

exuberante *a* exuberant; (*vegetación*) lush.

F

fabada *f* stew of beans, pork sausage and bacon.

fábrica *f* factory.

fabricación *f* manufacture.

fabricante *mf* manufacturer.

fabricar [1] *vt* to manufacture.

fabuloso,-a *a* fabulous.

facción *f* faction; **facciones** (*rasgos*) features.

facha *f fam* look.

fachada *f* facade.

facial *a* facial.

fácil *a* easy; **es f. que . . .** it's (quite) likely that . . .

facilidad *f* (*sencillez*) easiness; (*soltura*) ease; **facilidades de pago** easy terms.

facilitar *vt* (*simplificar*) to make easy o easier; **f. algo a algn** to provide sb with sth.

fácilmente *adv* easily.

facsímil, facsímile *m* facsimile.

factoría *f* factory.

factura *f* invoice.

facturación *f* (*en aeropuerto*) check-in; (*en estación*) registration.

facturar *vt* (*en aeropuerto*) to check in; (*en estación*) to register.

facultad *f* faculty.

faena *f* (*tarea*) task; (*en corrida*) performance.

faisán *m* pheasant.

faja *f* (*corsé*) corset.

fajo *m* (*de billetes*) wad.

falda *f* (*prenda*) skirt; (*de montaña*) slope; **f. pantalón** culottes *pl*.

falla *f Am* (*defecto*) fault.

fallar 1 *vi* to fail; **le falló la puntería** he missed his target. **2** *vt* to miss.

fallecer *vi* to pass away, die.

fallo *m* (*error*) mistake; (*del corazón, de los frenos*) failure.

falsear *vt* (*hechos, la verdad*) to distort.

falsificar [1] *vt* to falsify; (*cuadro, firma, moneda*) to forge.

falso,-a *a* false; (*persona*) insincere.

falta *f* (*carencia*) lack; (*escasez*) shortage; (*ausencia*) absence; (*error*) mistake; (*defecto*) fault, defect; (*fútbol*) foul; (*tenis*) fault; **sin f.** without fail; **echar algo/a algn en f.** to miss sth/sb; **f. de ortografía** spelling mistake; **hacer f.** to be necessary; **(nos) hace f. una escalera** we need a ladder; **harán f. dos personas para mover el piano** it'll take two people to move the piano; **no hace f. que . . .** there is no need for . . .

faltar *vi* (*no estar*) to be missing;

(*escasear*) to be lacking *o* needed; (*quedar*) to be left; **¿quién falta?** who is missing?; **le falta confianza en sí mismo** he lacks confidence in himself; **¡lo que me faltaba!** that's all I needed!; **¡no faltaría *o* faltaba más!** (*por supuesto*) (but) of course!; **¿cuántos kilómetros faltan para Managua?** how many kilometers is it to Managua?; **ya falta poco para las vacaciones** it won't be long now until the holidays; **f. a la verdad** not to tell the truth.

fama *f* fame; (*reputación*) reputation.

familia *f* family.

familiar 1 *a* (*de la familia*) family; (*conocido*) familiar. **2** *mf* relation, relative.

famoso,-a *a* famous.

fan *mf* fan.

fanático,-a 1 *a* fanatical. **2** *mf* fanatic.

fanfarrón,-ona 1 *a* boastful. **2** *mf* show-off.

fango *m* (*barro*) mud.

fantasía *f* fantasy.

fantasma *m* ghost.

fantástico,-a *a* fantastic.

fardo *m* bundle.

farmacéutico,-a 1 *a* pharmaceutical. **2** *mf* pharmacist.

farmacia *f* pharmacy.

faro *m* (*torre*) lighthouse; (*de coche*) headlight.

farol *m* (*luz*) lantern; (*en la calle*) streetlight, streetlamp.

farola *f* streetlight, streetlamp.

fascículo *m* installment.

fascinar *vt* to fascinate.

fascista *a & mf* fascist.

fase *f* phase, stage.

fastidiar 1 *vt* (*molestar*) to annoy, bother. **2 fastidiarse** *vr* (*aguantarse*) to put up with it; **que se fastidie** that's his tough luck; **fastidiarse el brazo** to hurt one's arm.

fastuoso,-a *a* (*acto*) splendid, lavish.

fatal 1 *a* (*muy malo*) awful; (*mortal*) fatal. **2** *adv* awfully; **lo pasó f.** he had a rotten time.

fatiga *f* (*cansancio*) fatigue.

fatigar, [7] *vt*, **fatigarse** *vr* to tire.

fauna *f* fauna.

favor *m* favor; **¿puedes hacerme un f.?** can you do me a favor?; **estar a f. de** to be in favor of; **por f.** please; **haga el f. de sentarse** please sit down.

favorable *a* favorable.

favorecer *vt* to favor; (*sentar bien*) to flatter.

favorito,-a *a & mf* favorite.

fe *f* faith; **fe de bautismo/matrimonio** baptism/marriage certificate.

fealdad *f* ugliness.

febrero *m* February.

fecha *f* date; **f. de caducidad** sell-by date; **hasta la f.** so far.

fechar *vt* to date.

fecundación *f* fertilization.

federación *f* federation.

felicidad *f* happiness; **(muchas) felicidades** (*en cumpleaños*) many happy returns.

felicitar *vt* to congratulate (**por** on); **¡te felicito!** congratulations!

feliz *a* (*contento*) happy; **¡felices Navidades!** Merry Christmas!

felpa *f* (*tela*) plush; **oso *o* osito de f.** teddy bear.

felpudo *m* mat.

femenino,-a *a* feminine; (*equipo, ropa*) women's; **sexo f.** female sex.

feminista *a & mf* feminist.

fémur *m* femur.

fenomenal 1 *a* phenomenal; *fam* (*fantástico*) great. **2** *adv fam* wonderfully.

fenómeno,-a *m* phenomenon; (*prodigio*) genius; (*monstruo*) freak.

feo,-a *a* ugly.

féretro *m* coffin.

feria *f* fair; **f. de muestras/del libro** trade/book fair.

fermentar *vi* to ferment.

feroz *a* fierce, ferocious.

ferretería *f* hardware store.

ferrocarril *m* railroad.

ferroviario,-a *a* railway, rail.

ferry *m* ferry.

fértil a fertile.
fertilizante m fertilizer.
fertilizar [4] vt to fertilize.
festejar vt to celebrate.
festín m feast.
festival m festival.
festividad f festivity.
festivo,-a 1 a (ambiente etc) festive; **día f.** holiday. **2** m holiday.
feto m fetus.
fiable a reliable, trustworthy.
fiador,-a mf guarantor.
fiambre m cold meat.
fiambrera f lunch box.
fianza f (depósito) deposit; (jurídica) bail.
fiarse vr to trust (**de** -).
fibra f fibre.
ficción f fiction.
ficha f (de archivo) filing card; (en juegos) counter; (de ajedrez) piece.
fichaje m signing.
fichero m card index; (de ordenador) file.
ficticio,-a a fictitious.
fidelidad f faithfulness; **alta f.** high fidelity, hi-fi.
fideo m noodle.
fiebre f fever; **tener f.** to have a temperature.
fiel 1 a (leal) faithful, loyal. **2** mpl **los fieles** the congregation.
fieltro m felt.
fiera f wild animal.
fierro m Am (hierro) iron; (navaja) knife.
fiesta f (entre amigos) party; (vacaciones) holiday; (festividad) celebration.
figura f figure.
figurar 1 vi (aparecer) to figure. **2 figurarse** vr to imagine; **ya me lo figuraba** I thought as much; **¡figúrate!, ¡figúrese!** just imagine!
fijador m (gomina) gel.
fijamente adv **mirar f.** to stare.
fijar 1 vt to fix. **2 fijarse** vr (darse cuenta) to notice; (poner atención) to pay attention, watch.
fijo,-a a fixed; (trabajo) steady.
fila f file; (de cine, teatro) row; **en f. india** in single file.

filántropo,-a mf philanthropist.
filarmónico,-a a philharmonic.
filatelia f philately, stamp collecting.
filete m fillet.
filial 1 a (de hijos) filial. **2** f (empresa) subsidiary.
filmar vt to film.
film(e) m film.
filo m edge.
filosofía f philosophy.
filosófico,-a a philosophical.
filósofo,-a mf philosopher.
filtración f filtration; (de noticia) leak(ing).
filtrar 1 vt to filter; (noticia) to leak. **2 filtrarse** vr (líquido) to seep; (noticia) to leak out.
filtro m filter.
fin m (final) end; (objetivo) purpose, aim; **dar** o **poner f.** to put an end to; **en f.** anyway; **¡por** o **al f.!** at last!; **f. de semana** weekend; **al f. y al cabo** when all's said and done; **a f. de** in order to, so as to.
final 1 a final. **2** m end; **al f.** in the end; **a finales de octubre** at the end of October. **3** f (de campeonato) final.
finalizar [4] vti to end, finish.
finalmente adv finally.
financiación f financing.
financiar vt to finance.
financiero,-a a financial.
financista mf Am financier.
finanzas fpl finances.
finca f (de campo) country house.
fingir [6] 1 vt to feign. **2** vi to pretend.
fino,-a 1 a (hilo, capa) fine; (flaco) thin; (educado) refined, polite; (oído) sharp, acute. **2** m (vino) type of dry sherry.
firma f signature; (empresa) firm.
firmar vt to sign.
firme 1 a firm; **tierra f.** terra firma. **2** adv hard.
firmemente adv firmly.
fiscal 1 a fiscal, tax. **2** mf district attorney.
fisco m treasury.
física f physics sing.

físico,-a a physical.

fisioterapia f physiotherapy.

flaco,-a a (delgado) skinny.

flamenco,-a 1 a (música) flamenco; (de Flandes) Flemish. **2** m (música) flamenco.

flan m caramel custard.

flanco m flank, side.

flaquear vi (fuerzas, piernas) to weaken, give way.

flash m flash.

flauta f flute.

flecha f arrow.

flechazo m (enamoramiento) love at first sight.

fleco m fringe.

flema f phlegm.

flemático,-a a phlegmatic.

flemón m gumboil.

flequillo m bangs pl.

fletar vt to charter.

flexible a flexible.

flexión f flexion.

flexionar vt to bend; (músculo) to flex.

flexo m reading lamp.

flirtear vi to flirt.

flojera f fam weakness, faintness.

flojo,-a a (tornillo, cuerda etc) loose, slack; (perezoso) lazy, idle.

flor f flower.

flora f flora.

floreado,-a a flowery.

florecer vi (plantas) to flower; (negocio) to flourish, thrive.

floreciente a flourishing, prosperous.

florero m vase.

floristería f florist's (shop).

flota f fleet.

flotador m (para nadar) rubber ring.

flotar vi to float.

flote m a f. afloat.

flotilla f flotilla.

fluctuar vi to fluctuate.

fluido,-a 1 a fluid; (estilo etc) fluent. **2** m liquid.

fluir vi to flow.

flujo m flow; (de la marea) rising tide.

flúor m fluorine.

fluorescente a fluorescent.

fluvial a river.

FMI m abr de **Fondo Monetario Internacional** International Monetary Fund, IMF.

fobia f phobia (**a** of).

foca f seal.

foco m spotlight, floodlight; (bombilla) (electric light) bulb; (de coche) (car) headlight; (farola) street light.

fogata f bonfire.

fogón m (de cocina) ring.

folio m sheet of paper.

folklórico,-a a música f. folk music.

follaje m foliage.

folletín m (relato) newspaper serial.

folleto m leaflet; (turístico) brochure.

follón m fam (alboroto) ruckus; (enredo, confusión) mess.

fomentar vt to promote.

fomento m promotion.

fonda f inn.

fondear vi to anchor.

fondista mf (corredor) long-distance runner.

fondo¹ m (parte más baja) bottom; (de habitación) back; (de pasillo) end; (segundo término) background; **a f.** thoroughly; **al f. de la calle** at the end of the street; **en el f. es bueno** deep down he's kind; **música de f.** background music.

fondo² (dinero) fund; **cheque sin fondos** bad check.

fonético,-a a phonetic.

fontanero,-a mf plumber.

footing m jogging; **hacer f.** to go jogging.

forastero,-a mf outsider.

forcejear vi to wrestle.

forense 1 a forensic. **2** mf (médico) f. forensic surgeon.

forestal a forest; **repoblación f.** reafforestation.

forjar vt to forge.

forma f form, shape; (manera) way; **¿qué f. tiene?** what shape is it?; **de esta f.** in this way; **de f. que**

so that; **de todas formas** anyway, in any case; **estar en f.** to be in shape; **estar en baja f.** to be out of shape.

formación f formation; (*enseñanza*) training; **f. profesional** vocational training.

formal a formal; (*serio*) serious; (*fiable*) reliable.

formalizar [4] vt (*hacer formal*) to formalize; (*contrato*) to legalize.

formar 1 vt to form; **f. parte de algo** to be a part of sth; (*enseñar*) to educate, train. **2 formarse** vr to be formed, form.

formidable a (*estupendo*) terrific.

fórmula f formula.

formular vt (*quejas, peticiones*) to make; (*deseo*) to express; (*pregunta*) to ask; (*una teoría*) to formulate.

formulario m form.

forrar vt (*por dentro*) to line; (*por fuera*) to cover.

forro m (*por dentro*) lining; (*por fuera*) cover.

fortalecer vt to fortify, strengthen.

fortificar [1] vt to fortify.

fortísimo,-a a very strong.

fortuito,-a a fortuitous.

fortuna f (*suerte*) luck; (*capital*) fortune; **por f.** fortunately.

forzado,-a a forced; **trabajos forzados** hard labor.

forzar [2] vt to force.

forzosamente adv necessarily.

forzoso,-a a obligatory, compulsory.

fosa f (*sepultura*) grave; (*hoyo*) pit.

fósforo m (*cerilla*) match.

fósil a & m fossil.

foso m (*hoyo*) pit.

foto f photo.

fotocopia f photocopy.

fotocopiadora f photocopier.

fotocopiar vt to photocopy.

fotografía f photograph; **hacer fotografías** to take photographs.

fotografiar vt to photograph, take a photograph of.

fotógrafo,-a mf photographer.

FP f Educ abr de **Formación Profesional** vocational training.

frac m (pl **fracs** o **fraques**) dress coat, tails pl.

fracasar vi to fail.

fraccionar vt, **fraccionarse** vr to break up.

fractura f fracture.

fragancia f fragrance.

frágil a (*quebradizo*) fragile; (*débil*) frail.

fragmento m fragment; (*de novela etc*) passage.

fraile m friar, monk.

frambuesa f raspberry.

francamente adv frankly.

franco,-a[1] a (*persona*) frank; **puerto f.** free port.

franco[2] m (*moneda*) franc.

franela f flannel.

franja f (*de terreno*) strip; (*de bandera*) stripe.

franqueo m postage.

frasco m small bottle, flask.

frase f (*oración*) sentence; (*expresión*) phrase.

fraterno,-a a fraternal, brotherly.

fraude m fraud.

frecuencia f frequency; **con f.** frequently.

frecuentar vt to frequent.

frecuente a frequent.

frecuentemente adv frequently, often.

fregadero m (kitchen) sink.

fregar [1] vt (*lavar*) to wash; (*suelo*) to mop; Am to annoy.

fregona f mop.

freidora f (deep) fryer.

freír [5] (pp **frito**) vt to fry.

frenar vti to brake.

frenazo m sudden braking.

frenético,-a a frantic.

freno m brake; **pisar/soltar el f.** to press/release the brake; **f. de mano** handbrake.

frente 1 m front; **chocar de f.** to crash head on; **hacer f. a algo** to face up to sth. **2** f (*de la cara*) forehead; **f. a f.** face to face. **3** adv **f. a** opposite.

fresa f strawberry.

fresco,-a a (frío) cool; (comida, fruta) fresh; (descarado) rude. 2 m (frescor) fresh air; (caradura) cheek; **hace f.** it's chilly.

frescura f freshness; (desvergüenza) nerve.

fresón m (large) strawberry.

fríamente adv coolly.

fricción f friction.

frígido,-a a frigid.

frigorífico m refrigerator, fridge.

frijol, fríjol m kidney bean.

frío,-a 1 a cold; (indiferente) cold, cool. 2 m cold; **hace f.** it's cold.

friolero,-a a sensitive to the cold, chilly.

frívolo,-a a frivolous.

frontera f frontier.

frontón m pelota.

frotar 1 vt to rub. 2 **frotarse** vr **f. las manos** to rub one's hands together.

fruncir [3] vt **f. el ceño** to frown.

frustrar 1 vt to frustrate. 2 **frustrarse** vr (esperanza) to fail; (persona) to be frustrated o disappointed.

fruta f fruit; **f. del tiempo** fresh fruit.

frutería f fruit shop.

frutero m fruit dish o bowl.

fruto m fruit; **frutos secos** nuts.

fucsia f fuchsia.

fuego m fire; (lumbre) light; **fuegos artificiales** fireworks; **¿me da f., por favor?** have you got a light, please?

fuel, fuel-oil m diesel.

fuente f (artificial) fountain; (recipiente) dish; (origen) source; (de caracteres) font.

fuera[1] 1 adv outside; **desde f.** from (the) outside; **por f.** on the outside; **la puerta de f.** the outer door. 2 prep **f. de** out of; **f. de serie** extraordinary.

fuera[2] 1 subj imperfecto de **ir.** 2 subj imperfecto de **ser.**

fuerte 1 a strong; (dolor) severe;

(sonido) loud; (comida) heavy. 2 m (fortaleza) fort. 3 adv **¡abrázame f.!** hold me tight!; **¡habla más f.!** speak up!; **¡pégale f.!** hit him hard!

fuerza f (fortaleza) strength; (cuerpo) force; **a la f.** (por obligación) of necessity; (con violencia) by force; **por f.** of necessity; **Fuerzas Armadas** Armed Forces.

fuese 1 subj imperfecto de **ir.** 2 subj imperfecto de **ser.**

fuete m Am whip.

fuga f (huida) escape; (de gas etc) leak.

fugarse [7] vr to escape.

fui 1 pt indef de **ir.** 2 pt indef de **ser.**

fulminante a (muerte, enfermedad) sudden; (mirada) withering.

fumador,-a mf smoker; **los no fumadores** non-smokers.

fumar 1 vti to smoke; **no f.** (en letrero) no smoking. 2 **fumarse** vr **f. un cigarro** to smoke a cigarette.

función f function; (cargo) duties pl; (de teatro, cine) performance.

funcionamiento m operation; **poner/entrar en f.** to put/come into operation.

funcionar vi to work; **no funciona** (en letrero) out of order.

funcionario,-a mf civil servant.

funda f cover; (de gafas etc) case; **f. de almohada** pillowcase.

fundación f foundation.

fundamental a fundamental.

fundar 1 vt (crear) to found. 2 **fundarse** vr (empresa) to be founded; (teoría, afirmación) to be based.

fundir vt, **fundirse** vr (derretirse) to melt; (bombilla, plomos) to blow; (unirse) to merge.

fúnebre a (mortuorio) funeral; **coche f.** hearse.

funeral m funeral.

funeraria f funeral parlor.

fungir vi Am to act (de as).

furgoneta f van.

furia f fury.

furioso,-a a furious.

furor m fury.

furtivo,-a a furtive; **cazador/pescador f.** poacher.

furúnculo m boil.

fusible m fuse.

fusil m gun, rifle.

fusilar vt to shoot, execute.

fusión f (de metales) fusion; (del hielo) thawing, melting; (de empresas) merger.

fusionar vt, **fusionarse** vr (metales) to fuse; (empresas) to merge.

fútbol m soccer; **f. americano** football.

futbolín m table football.

futbolista mf football/soccer player.

futuro,-a 1 a future. 2 m future.

G

gabardina f (prenda) raincoat.

gabinete m (despacho) study; (de gobierno) cabinet.

gacho,-a a **con la cabeza gacha** hanging one's head.

gafas fpl glasses, spectacles; **g. de sol** sunglasses.

gafe m **ser (un) g.** to be a jinx.

gaita f bagpipes pl.

gajo m (de naranja, pomelo etc) segment.

gala f (espectáculo) gala; **de g.** dressed up; (ciudad) decked out.

galán m handsome young man; (personaje) leading man.

galante a gallant.

galápago m turtle.

galardón m prize.

galardonar vt to award a prize to.

galería f (corredor) covered balcony; (museo) art gallery.

Gales m (el país de) G. Wales.

galés,-esa 1 a Welsh. 2 mf (hombre) Welshman; (mujer) Welshwoman; **los galeses** the Welsh. 3 m (idioma) Welsh.

galgo m greyhound.

Galicia f Galicia.

galimatías m inv gibberish.

gallego,-a 1 a Galician; Am Spanish. 2 mf Galician; Am Spaniard. 3 m (idioma) Galician.

galleta f cracker.

gallina f hen.

gallinero m henhouse.

gallo m cock.

galopante a (inflación etc) galloping.

galopar vi to gallop.

gama f range.

gamba f prawn.

gamberro,-a 1 mf hooligan. 2 a uncouth.

gamo m fallow deer.

gamuza f (trapo) chamois o shammy leather.

gana f (deseo) wish (de for); (apetito) appetite; **de buena g.** willingly; **de mala g.** reluctantly; **tener ganas de (hacer) algo** to feel like (doing) sth.

ganado m livestock.

ganador,-a 1 a winning. 2 mf winner.

ganancia f profit.

ganar 1 vt (sueldo) to earn; (premio) to win; (aventajar) to beat. 2 **ganarse** vr to earn.

ganchillo m crochet work.

gancho m hook; Am (horquilla) hairpin.

ganga f bargain.

ganso,-a mf goose; (macho) gander; fam dolt.

garabato m scrawl.

garaje m garage.

garantía f guarantee.

garantizar [4] vt (cosa) to guarantee; (a persona) to assure.

garbanzo m chickpea.

garfio m hook.

garganta f throat; (desfiladero) narrow pass.

garra f claw; (de ave) talon; **tener g.** to be compelling.

garrafa f carafe.

garrapata f tick.

garrote m (porra) club.

gas m gas; (en bebida) fizz; **g. ciudad** town gas; **gases (nocivos**

fumes; **g. de escape** exhaust fumes; **agua con g.** fizzy water.
gasa f gauze.
gaseosa f lemonade.
gasoducto m gas pipeline.
gasoil, gasóleo m diesel oil.
gasolina f gasoline.
gasolinera f gas station.
gastar 1 vt (consumir) (dinero, tiempo) to spend; (gasolina, electricidad) to consume; (malgastar) to waste; (ropa) to wear; **g. una broma a algn** to play a practical joke on sb. **2 gastarse** vr (zapatos etc) to wear out.
gasto m expenditure; **gastos** expenses.
gatas a gatas adv on all fours.
gatear vi to crawl.
gatillo m (de armas) trigger.
gato m cat; (de coche) jack.
gaviota f seagull.
gay a inv & m (pl gays) gay.
gazpacho m gazpacho.
gel m gel; **g. (de ducha)** shower gel.
gelatina f (ingrediente) gelatin; (para postre) jelly.
gema f gem.
gemelo,-a 1 a & mf (identical) twin. **2** mpl **gemelos** (de camisa) cufflinks; (anteojos) binoculars.
gemido m groan.
gemir [6] vi to groan.
generación f generation.
general a general; **por lo** o **en g.** in general.
generalizar [4] **1** vt to generalize. **2 generalizarse** vr to become widespread o common.
generalmente adv generally.
generar vt to generate.
género m (clase) kind, sort; (mercancía) article; (gramatical) gender.
generoso,-a a generous (**con, para** to).
genético,-a a genetic.
genial a brilliant.
genio mf inv genius; (mal carácter) temper; **estar de mal g.** to be in a bad mood.

genocidio m genocide.
gente f people pl; Am respectable people.
gentuza f riffraff.
genuino,-a a (puro) genuine; (verdadero) authentic.
geografía f geography.
geología f geology.
geometría f geometry.
geranio m geranium.
gerente mf manager.
gérmen m germ.
gerundio m gerund.
gestación f gestation.
gesticular vi to gesticulate.
gestión f (administración) management; **gestiones** (negociaciones) negotiations; (trámites) formalities.
gesto m (mueca) face; (con las manos) gesture.
gigante,-a a & mf giant.
gigantesco,-a a gigantic.
gimnasia f gymnastics pl.
gimnasio m gymnasium.
ginecólogo,-a mf gynecologist.
gira f (musical, teatral) tour.
girar vi (dar vueltas) to spin; **g. a la derecha/izquierda** to turn right/left.
girasol m sunflower.
giratorio,-a a revolving.
giro m (vuelta) turn; (frase) turn of phrase; (libranza) draft; **g. telegráfico** giro o money order; **g. postal** postal o money order.
gitano,-a a & mf gypsy.
glaciar m glacier.
glándula f gland.
global a comprehensive.
globo m balloon; (esfera) globe.
gloria f (fama) glory; (cielo) heaven.
glorieta f (plazoleta) small square; (encrucijada de calles) roundabout, traffic circle.
glosario m glossary.
glotón,-ona 1 a greedy. **2** mf glutton.
glucosa f glucose.
gobernación f government; **Mi-**

nisterio de la Gobernación, ≈ Department of the Interior.

gobernador,-a *mf* governor.

gobernante 1 *a* ruling. **2** *mpl* **los gobernantes** the rulers.

gobernar [1] *vt* to govern; (*un país*) to rule.

gobierno *m* government; (*mando*) running.

gofio *m* (*en América y Canarias*) roasted maize meal.

gol *m* goal.

golf *m* golf; **palo de g.** golf club.

golfo,-a¹ *mf* good for nothing.

golfo² *m* gulf.

golondrina *f* swallow.

golosina *f* candy.

goloso,-a *a* sweet-toothed.

golpe *m* blow; (*llamada*) knock; (*puñetazo*) punch; (*choque*) bump; (*desgracia*) blow; **de g.** all of a sudden; **g. de estado** coup d'état.

golpear *vt* to hit; (*con el puño*) to punch; (*puerta, cabeza*) to bang.

goma *f* rubber; (*elástica*) rubber band; **g. de borrar** eraser.

gomal *m* Am rubber plantation.

gomero *m* Am gum tree; (*recolector*) rubber collector.

gordo,-a 1 *a* (*carnoso*) fat; (*grueso*) thick. **2** *mf* fat person, *fam* fatty. **3** *m* **el g.** (*de lotería*) first prize.

gorila *m* gorilla.

gorra *f* cap.

gorrión *m* sparrow.

gorro *m* cap.

gota *f* drop; **g. a g.** drop by drop; **ni g.** not a bit.

gotear *v impers* to drip; **el techo gotea** there's a leak in the ceiling.

gotera *f* leak.

gozar [4] **1** *vt* to enjoy. **2** *vi* (*disfrutar*) to enjoy (**de** -).

gozne *m* hinge.

grabación *f* recording.

grabado,-a *m* (*arte*) engraving; (*dibujo*) drawing.

grabadora *f* tape recorder.

grabar *vt* (*sonidos, imágenes*) to record; (*en ordenador*) to save.

gracia *f* (*chiste*) joke; (*indulto*) pardon; **hacer** *o* **tener g.** to be funny.

gracias *fpl* thanks; **muchas** *o* **muchísimas g.** thank you very much.

gracioso,-a *a* (*divertido*) funny. **2** *mf* (*personaje*) comic character.

grada *f* (*peldaño*) step; **gradas** (*estadio*) terracing.

grado *m* degree; **de buen g.** willingly.

gradual *a* gradual.

gradualmente *adv* gradually.

graduar [30] **1** *vt* (*regular*) to regulate. **2 graduarse** *vr* (*soldado, alumno*) to graduate; **g. la vista** to have one's eyes tested.

gráfico,-a 1 *a* graphic. **2** *mf* graph; **gráficos** (*de ordenador*) graphics.

gragea *f* pill.

gral. *abr de* **General** Gen.

gramática *f* grammar.

gramo *m* gram.

gran *a ver* **grande.**

granada *f* (*fruto*) pomegranate; (*explosivo*) grenade.

granate 1 *a inv* maroon. **2** *m* maroon.

grande *a* (before singular noun **gran** is used) (*tamaño*) big, large; *fig* (*persona*) great; (*cantidad*) large; **pasarlo en g.** to have a great time.

granel *m* **a granel** (*sin medir exactamente*) loose.

granito *m* granite.

granizada *f*, **granizado** *m* iced drink.

granizo *m* hail.

granja *f* farm.

granjear(se) *vt & vr* to gain.

granjero,-a *mf* farmer.

grano *m* grain; (*de café*) bean; (*espinilla*) spot.

granuja *m* **1** (*pilluelo*) rascal. **2** (*estafador*) con-man.

grapa *f* staple.

grapadora *f* stapler.

grasa *f* grease.

grasiento,-a *a* greasy.

graso,-a *a* (*pelo*) greasy; (*materia*) fatty.

gratis *adv* free.

gratitud f gratitude.

gratuito,-a a (de balde) free (of charge); (arbitrario) gratuitous.

grava f (guijas) gravel; (en carretera) gravel pl.

gravar vt (impuestos) to tax.

grave a (importante) serious; (muy enfermo) seriously ill; (voz, nota) low.

gravedad f seriousness; (fuerza) gravity.

gravilla f (en carretera) gravel pl.

grieta f crack; (en la piel) chap.

grifo m faucet.

grillo m cricket.

gringo,-a a & mf gringo, yankee.

gripe f flu.

gris a m gray.

grisáceo,-a a grayish.

gritar vti to shout.

grito m shout.

grosella f (fruto) redcurrant; **g. negra** blackcurrant; **g. silvestre** gooseberry.

grosería f (ordinariez) rude word o expression.

grosor m thickness.

grotesco,-a a grotesque.

grúa f (en construcción) crane; (para coches) tow truck.

grueso,-a 1 a thick; (persona) stout. **2** m (parte principal) bulk.

grumo m lump.

gruñido m grunt.

gruñón,-ona a grumpy.

grupo m group.

gruta f cave.

guacamol, guacamole m Am avocado sauce.

guachafita f Am uproar.

guacho,-a a & mf Am orphan.

guagua[1] f (en Canarias y Cuba) bus.

guagua[2] f Am baby.

guante m glove.

guantera f (en coche) glove compartment.

guapo,-a a good-looking; (mujer) beautiful, pretty; (hombre) handsome.

guaraca f Am sling.

guarango,-a a Am rude.

guarda mf guard; **g. jurado** security guard.

guardacoches mf inv parking attendant.

guardacostas m inv (persona) coastguard; (embarcación) coastguard vessel.

guardaespaldas mf inv bodyguard.

guardameta mf goalkeeper.

guardar vt (conservar, reservar) to keep; (un secreto) to keep; (poner en un sitio) to put away; (en ordenador) to save.

guardería infantil f nursery (school).

guardia 1 f (vigilancia) watch; (turno de servicio) duty; **la g. civil** the civil guard. **2** mf (hombre) policeman; (mujer) policewoman.

guardián,-ana mf (hombre) watchman; (mujer) watchwoman.

guarecerse vr to take shelter o refuge (de from).

guaso,-a a Am peasant.

guasón,-ona 1 a humorous. **2** mf joker.

guata f (relleno) padding; Am (barriga) paunch.

guayabo,-a mf Am (chica bonita) pretty young girl; (chico guapo) good-looking boy.

guerra f war; **g. civil/fría/mundial/ nuclear** civil/cold/world/nuclear war.

guerrilla f (partida armada) guerrilla force o band; (lucha) guerrilla warfare.

guía 1 mf (persona) guide. **2** f (libro) guide; **la g. de teléfonos** the telephone directory.

guiar [29] **1** vt (indicar el camino) to guide; (automóvil) to drive. **2 guiarse** vr to be guided (por by).

guijarro m pebble.

guindilla f chili.

guiñapo m (andrajo) rag.

guiñar vt to wink.

guión m (de cine, televisión) script; (ortográfico) hyphen; (esquema) sketch.

guirnalda f garland.
guisante m pea.
guisar vt to cook.
guita f rope.
guitarra 1 f guitar. **2** mf guitarist.
gula f gluttony.
gusano m worm; (oruga) cater-pillar.
gustar 1 vt **me gusta el vino** I like wine; **me gustaban los caramelos** I used to like sweets; **me gusta nadar** I like swimming; **me gustaría ir** I would like to go. **2** vi **g. de** to enjoy.
gusto m taste; **con (mucho) g.** with (great) pleasure; **tanto g.** pleased to meet you; **estar a g.** to feel comfortable o at ease; **ser de buen/mal g.** to be in good/bad taste; **tener buen/mal g.** to have good/bad taste.

H

ha indic pres de **haber**.
haba f broad bean.
habano m Havana (cigar).
haber 1 v aux (en tiempos compuestos) to have; **lo he visto** I have seen it; **ya lo había hecho** he had already done it. ■ **h. de** + infin (obligación) to have to; **has de ser bueno** you must be good. **2** v impers (special form of present tense: **hay**) (existir, estar) (singular used also with plural nouns) **hay** there is o are; **había** there was o were; **habrá una fiesta** there will be a party; **había una vez . . .** once upon a time. . .; **no hay de qué** you're welcome; **¿qué hay?** how are things? ■ **hay que** + infinitivo it is necessary to.
habichuela f kidney bean.
hábil a (diestro) skillful; **días hábiles** working days.
habitación f (cuarto) room; (dormitorio) bedroom; **h. individual/doble** single/double room.
habitante mf inhabitant.

hábito m (costumbre) habit; (de monje) habit.
habitual a usual, habitual.
habituar 1 vt to accustom (**a** to). **2 habituarse** vr to get used (**a** to), become accustomed (**a** to).
hablador,-a a (parlanchín) talkative.
hablar 1 vi to speak, talk; **h. con algn** to speak to sb; **¡ni h.!** no way!; fam **¡quién fue a h.!** look who's talking! **2** vt (idioma) to speak. **3 hablarse** vr to speak o talk to one another; **'se habla español'** 'Spanish spoken'.
habré indic fut de **haber**.
hacer 1 vt to do; (crear, fabricar) to make; **hazme un favor do me a favor; ¿qué haces?** (en este momento) what are you doing?; (para vivir) what do you do (for a living)?; **tengo mucho que h.** I have a lot to do; **lo hizo con sus propias manos** he made it with his own hands; **h. la cama** to make the bed; **h. la cena** to make dinner; **el negro le hace más delgado** black makes him look slimmer; **ya no puedo leer como solía hacerlo** I can't read as well as I used to; **¡bien hecho!** well done! **2** vi (actuar) to play; **hizo de Desdémona** she played Desdemona; **h. por o para** + infinitivo to try to; **haz por venir** try and come. **3** v impers **hace calor/frío** it's hot/cold; **hace mucho (tiempo)** a long time ago; **hace dos días que no lo veo** I haven't seen him for two days; **hace dos años que vivo en Chicago** I've been living in Chicago for two years. **4 hacerse** vr (volverse) to become, grow; (simular) to pretend; **hacerse el dormido** to pretend to be sleeping; **hacerse con** (apropiarse) to get hold of; **hacerse a** (habituarse) to get used to.
hacha f (herramienta) ax.
hachís m hashish.
hacia prep (dirección) towards, to; (aproximadamente) at about, at

around; **h. abajo** down, downwards; **h. adelante** forwards; **h. arriba** up, upwards; **h. atrás** back, backwards.

hacienda f ranch.

hada f fairy; **cuento de hadas** fairy tale.

hago indic pres de hacer.

halagar [7] vt to flatter.

halago m flattery.

halcón m falcon.

hallar 1 vt (encontrar) to find; (descubrir) to discover. **2 hallarse** vr (estar) to be, find oneself; (estar situado) to be situated.

hallazgo m (descubrimiento) discovery; (cosa encontrada) find.

hamaca f hammock.

hambre f (apetito) hunger; (inanición) starvation; (catástrofe) famine; **tener h.** to be hungry.

hamburguesa f hamburger.

han indic pres de haber.

haré indic fut de hacer.

harina f flour.

hartar 1 vt (cansar, fastidiar) to annoy; (atiborrar) to satiate. **2 hartarse** vr (saciar el apetito) to eat one's fill; (cansarse) to get fed up (de with).

harto,-a a (lleno) full; (cansado) fed up; **estoy h. de trabajar** I'm fed up with working.

has indic pres de haber.

hasta 1 prep (lugar) up to, as far as; (tiempo) until, up to; (con cantidad) up to, as many as; (incluso) even; **h. la fecha** up to now; **h. luego** see you later. **2** conj **h. que** until.

hay indic pres de haber.

haya subj pres de haber.

haz imperativo de hacer.

he indic pres de haber.

hebilla f buckle.

hebra f thread.

hebreo,-a 1 a Hebrew. **2** mf Hebrew.

hechizo m (embrujo) spell.

hecho,-a 1 a made, done; (carne) done; (ropa) ready-made. **2** m (rea-lidad) fact; (acto) act, deed; (suceso) event, incident; **de h.** in fact.

hectárea f hectare.

hedor m stink, stench.

helada f frost.

heladería f ice-cream parlor.

helado,-a 1 m ice cream. **2** a (muy frío) freezing cold; fig **quedarse h.** (atónito) to be flabbergasted.

helar [1] **1** vt (congelar) to freeze. **2** v impers to freeze; **anoche heló** there was a frost last night. **3 helarse** vr (congelarse) to freeze.

helecho m fern.

hélice f (de avión, barco) propeller.

helicóptero m helicopter.

hembra f Bot Zool female; (mujer) woman.

hemorragia f hemorrhage.

hemos indic pres de haber.

hendidura f crack.

heno m hay.

herbolario m (tienda) herbalist's (shop).

heredar vt to inherit.

heredero,-a mf (hombre) heir; (mujer) heiress.

herencia f inheritance, legacy; (biológica) heredity.

herida f (lesión) injury; (corte) wound.

herido,-a 1 a injured, hurt. **2** mf injured person.

herir [5] **1** vt (físicamente) (lesionar) to injure; (cortar) to wound. **2 herirse** vr to injure o hurt oneself.

hermana f sister.

hermano m brother; **primo h.** first cousin; **hermanos** brothers and sisters.

herméticamente adv **h. cerrado** hermetically sealed.

hermético,-a a (cierre) hermetic, airtight; fig (grupo) secretive.

hermoso,-a a beautiful, lovely; (grandioso) fine.

héroe m hero.

heroína f (mujer) heroine; (droga) heroin.

herradura f horseshoe.
herramienta f tool.
hervir [5] 1 vt (hacer bullir) to boil. 2 vi (bullir) to boil.
heterogéneo,-a a heterogeneous.
hice pt indef de hacer.
hiciste pt indef de hacer.
hidratante a moisturizing; **crema/leche h.** moisturizing cream/lotion.
hidráulico,-a a hydraulic.
hidroavión m hydroplane.
hiedra f ivy.
hielo m ice.
hiena f hyena.
hierba f grass; **mala h.** weed.
hierbabuena f mint.
hierro m iron.
hígado m liver.
higiénico,-a a hygienic; **papel h.** toilet paper.
hija f daughter.
hijo m son; **hijos** children.
hilera f line, row.
hilo m thread; (grueso) yarn; (fibra) linen; **perder el h.** to lose the thread; **h. musical** background music.
himno m hymn; **h. nacional** national anthem.
hincapié m hacer h. en (insistir) to insist on; (subrayar) to emphasize.
hincar [1] 1 vt (clavar) to drive (in). 2 hincarse vr h. de rodillas to kneel (down).
hincha 1 mf (de equipo) fan, supporter. 2 f (antipatía) grudge, dislike.
hinchado,-a a swollen.
hinchar 1 vt (inflar) to inflate, blow up. 2 hincharse vr to swell (up); (fam) (hartarse) to stuff oneself.
hindú a & mf Hindu.
hipermercado m hypermarket.
hípico,-a a horse.
hipnotizar [4] vt to hypnotize.
hipo m tener h. to have the hiccups.
hipócrita 1 a hypocritical. 2 mf hypocrite.
hipopótamo m hippopotamus.

hipoteca f mortgage.
hipótesis f inv hypothesis.
hispánico,-a a Hispanic.
hispano,-a 1 a Hispanic. 2 mf Spanish American, Hispanic.
hispanohablante 1 a Spanish-speaking. 2 mf Spanish speaker.
histérico,-a a hysterical.
historia f (estudio del pasado) history; (narración) story.
historial m record; (antecedentes) background.
histórico,-a a historical; (de gran importancia) historic, memorable.
historieta f (tira cómica) comic strip.
hizo indic indef de hacer.
hocico m (de animal) snout.
hogar m (casa) home; (de la chimenea) hearth.
hoguera f bonfire.
hoja f leaf; (de papel) sheet; (de cuchillo, espada) blade; (impreso) hand-out.
hojalata f tin.
hojaldre m puff pastry.
hojear vt to leaf through.
hola interj hello!
holgado,-a a (ropa) loose, baggy; (económicamente) comfortable; (espacio) roomy.
holgazán,-ana 1 a lazy. 2 mf lazybones inv.
hollín m soot.
hombre 1 m man; **h. de negocios** businessman. 2 interj (saludo) hey!; **¡sí h.!, ¡h. claro!** (enfático) sure! you bet!
hombrera f shoulder pad.
hombro m shoulder; **a hombros** on one's shoulders; **encogerse de hombros** to shrug one's shoulders; **mirar a algn por encima del h.** to look down one's nose at sb.
homenaje m homage, tribute.
homicida 1 mf (hombre) murderer; (mujer) murderess. 2 a homicidal.
homicidio m homicide.
homogéneo,-a a homogeneous, uniform.
homosexual a & mf homosexual.

hondo,-a *a* deep; **plato h.** soup dish.

honesto,-a *a* (*honrado*) honest; (*recatado*) modest.

hongo *m* fungus; (*sombrero*) derby (hat); **h. venenoso** toadstool.

honor *m* honor; **palabra de h.** word of honor.

honorario,-a-1 *a* honorary. **2** *mpl* **honorarios** fees.

honra *f* (*dignidad*) dignity; (*honor*) honor; **¡a mucha h.!** and proud of it!

honradez *f* honesty.

honrado,-a *a* (*de fiar*) honest.

hora *f* hour; (*cita*) appointment; **media h.** half an hour; **h. punta** rush hour; **horas extra** overtime (hours); **¿qué h. es?** what time is it?; **a última h.** at the last moment; **pedir h.** (*al médico etc*) to ask for an appointment.

horario *m* schedule.

horca *f* gallows *pl.*

horchata *f* sweet milky drink made from chufa nuts or almonds.

horizonte *m* horizon.

hormiga *f* ant.

hormigón *m* concrete.

hormiguero *m* anthill.

hormona *f* hormone.

horno *m* (*de cocina*) oven; (*para metales*) furnace; (*para cerámica etc*) kiln; **pescado al h.** baked fish.

horóscopo *m* horoscope.

horquilla *f* (*del pelo*) hair-grip.

horrible *a* horrible.

horror *m* horror; **¡qué h.!** how awful!; *fam* **tengo h. a las motos** I hate motorbikes.

horrorizar [4] *vt* to horrify; (*dar miedo*) to terrify.

horroroso,-a *a* horrifying; (*que da miedo*) terrifying; *fam* (*muy feo*) hideous; *fam* (*malísimo*) awful.

hortaliza *f* vegetable.

hortera *a fam* (*persona*) flashy; (*cosa*) tacky.

hospedar 1 *vt* to put up. **2 hospedarse** *vr* to stay (**en** at).

hospicio *m* (*para huérfanos*) orphanage.

hospital *m* hospital.

hospitalizar [4] *vt* to send into hospital, hospitalize.

hostal *m* guest house.

hostelería *f* (*negocio*) catering business; (*estudios*) hotel management.

hostería *f Am* hostel, inn.

hostil *a* hostile.

hotel *m* hotel.

hoy *adv* (*día*) today; **h. (en) día** nowadays.

hoyo *m* hole.

hube *pt indef de* **haber.**

hubiera *subj imperfecto de* **haber.**

hucha *f* piggy bank.

hueco,-a 1 *a* (*vacío*) empty, hollow; (*sonido*) resonant. **2** *m* (*cavidad*) hollow, hole; (*sitio no ocupado*) empty space.

huele *indic pres de* **oler.**

huelga *f* strike; **estar en** *o* **de h.** to be on strike; **hacer h.** to go on strike.

huella *f* (*del pie*) footprint; (*coche*) track; **h. dactilar** fingerprint; *fig* (*vestigio*) trace.

huérfano,-a *a & mf* orphan.

huerta *f* (*parcela*) truck garden; (*región*) irrigated area used for cultivation.

huerto *m* (*de verduras*) vegetable garden; (*de frutales*) orchard.

hueso *m* (*del cuerpo*) bone; (*de fruto*) pit; *Am* (*enchufe*) soft job.

huésped,-a *mf* guest; **casa de huéspedes** guesthouse.

huevo *m* egg; **h. duro** hard-boiled egg; **h. frito** fried egg; **h. pasado por agua,** *Am* **h. tibio** soft-boiled egg; **huevos revueltos** scrambled eggs.

huida *f* flight, escape.

huir *vi* (*escaparse*) to run away (**de** from), flee; (*evadirse*) to escape (**de** from).

hule *m* (*tela impermeable*) oilcloth; (*de mesa*) tablecloth; *Am* rubber.

humanitario,-a *a* humanitarian.

humano,-a 1 a (relativo al hombre) human; (compasivo) humane; **ser h.** human being. **2** m human (being).

humeante a (chimenea) smoky, smoking.

humedad f (atmosférica) humidity; (de lugar) dampness.

humedecer 1 vt to moisten, dampen. **2 humedecerse** vr to become damp o moist.

húmedo,-a a (casa, ropa) damp; (clima) humid, damp.

humildad f (de persona) humility; (de cosa) humbleness.

humilde a humble; (familia) poor.

humillar 1 vt (rebajar) to humiliate. **2 humillarse** vr **humillarse ante algn** to humble oneself before sb.

humo m smoke; (gas) fumes pl; (vapor) steam.

humor m (genio) mood; (gracia) humor; **estar de buen** o **mal h.** to be in a good o bad mood; **sentido del h.** sense of humor.

hundimiento m (de edificio) collapse; (de barco) sinking; (de tierra) subsidence; (ruina) downfall.

hundir 1 vt (barco) to sink; (derrumbar) to bring o knock down. **2 hundirse** vr (barco) to sink; (edificio, empresa) to collapse.

huracán m hurricane.

huraño,-a a unsociable.

hurgar [7] **1** vi (fisgar) to poke one's nose (**en** in). **2** vt (fuego etc) to poke.

hurto m petty theft.

huyo indic pres de **huir.**

I

ibérico,-a a Iberian.

iberoamericano,-a a & mf Latin American.

iceberg m (pl **icebergs**) iceberg.

icono m icon.

ida f **billete de i. y vuelta** round trip ticket.

idea f idea; **hacerse a la i. de** to get used to the idea of; **ni i.** no idea; **cambiar de i.** to change one's mind.

ideal a & m ideal.

idear vt (inventar) to devise; (concebir) to think up.

idéntico,-a a identical.

identidad f identity; **carnet de i.** identity card.

identificación f identification.

identificar [1] **1** vt to identify. **2 identificarse** vr to identify oneself; (simpatizar) to identify (**con** with).

idilio m (romance) romance.

idioma m language.

idiota 1 a idiotic. **2** mf idiot.

ídolo m idol.

idóneo,-a a suitable.

iglesia f (edificio) church; **la I.** the Church.

ignorante 1 a (sin instrucción) ignorant; (no informado) unaware (**de** of). **2** mf ignoramus.

ignorar 1 vt (algo) not to know; (algn) to ignore. **2 ignorarse** vr to be unknown.

igual 1 a (lo mismo) the same; (equivalente) equal; **i. que** the same as; **a partes iguales** fifty-fifty; **al i. que** just like; **por i.** equally; **6 más 7 i. a 13** 6 plus 7 equals 13. **2** m equal. **3** adv **me da i.** I don't mind; **lo haces i. que yo** you do it the same way I do; **es i.** it doesn't matter.

igualmente adv equally; (también) also, likewise; **¡gracias! — ¡i.!** thank you!—the same to you!

igualar vt to make equal; (nivelar) to level.

igualdad f equality; (identidad) sameness; **en i. de condiciones** on equal terms.

ilegal a illegal.

ilegalmente adv illegally.

ilegítimo,-a a illegitimate.

ileso,-a a unharmed.

ilícito,-a a unlawful.

ilimitado,-a a unlimited.

iluminación f (alumbrado) illumination.

iluminar vt to illuminate.

ilusión f (esperanza) hope; (esperanza vana) illusion; (emoción) excitement; **hacerse ilusiones** to build up one's hopes; **me hace i. verla** I'm looking forward to seeing her; **¡qué i.!** how exciting!

ilusionar 1 vt (esperanzar) **i. a algn** to build up sb's hopes; (entusiasmar) to excite. **2 ilusionarse** vr (esperanzarse) to build up one's hopes; (entusiasmarse) to be excited (**con** about).

ilustración f (grabado) illustration; (erudición) learning.

ilustrar vt to illustrate.

ilustre a distinguished.

imagen f image; (de televisión) picture.

imaginación f imagination.

imaginar 1 vt to imagine. **2 imaginarse** vr to imagine; **me imagino que sí** I suppose so.

imán m magnet.

imbécil 1 a stupid. **2** mf imbecile.

imitar vt to imitate; (gestos) to mimic.

impacientar 1 vt **i. a algn** to exasperate sb. **2 impacientarse** vr to get impatient (**por** at).

impaciente a (deseoso) impatient; (intranquilo) anxious.

impacto m impact.

impar a odd.

imparcial a impartial.

impasible a impassive.

impecable a impeccable.

impedimento m impediment; (obstáculo) hindrance.

impedir [6] vt (obstaculizar) to impede; (imposibilitar) to prevent, stop.

impenetrable a impenetrable.

imperante a (gobernante) ruling; (predominante) prevailing.

imperativo,-a 1 a imperative. **2** m imperative.

imperdible m safety pin.

imperfecto,-a a imperfect; (defectuoso) defective; (tiempo verbal) imperfect.

imperio m empire.

impermeable 1 a impervious; (ropa) waterproof. **2** m raincoat.

impertinente a (insolente) impertinent; (inoportuno) irrelevant.

impetuoso,-a a (violento) violent; (fogoso) impetuous.

implacable a implacable.

implicar [1] vt (involucrar) to involve (**en** in); (conllevar) to imply.

implícito,-a a implicit.

implorar vt to implore.

imponente a (impresionante) imposing; (sobrecogedor) stunning.

imponer (pp **impuesto**) **1** vt to impose; (impresionar) to be impressive; **i. respeto** to inspire respect. **2 imponerse** vr (prevalecer) to prevail; (ser necesario) to be necessary.

importación f (mercancía) import; (acción) importing; **artículos de i.** imported goods.

importancia f importance; (tamaño) size.

importante a important; (grande) significant.

importar¹ vi (tener importancia) to be important; **no importa** it doesn't matter; **eso no te importa a tí** that doesn't concern you; **¿te importa si fumo?** do you mind if I smoke? **2** vt (valer) to amount to.

importar² vt to import.

importe m amount.

imposibilitar vt (impedir) to make impossible; (incapacitar) to disable.

imposible a impossible; **me es i. hacerlo** I can't (possibly) do it.

impostor,-a mf impostor.

impotencia f powerlessness.

imprenta f (taller) printer's; (aparato) printing press.

imprescindible a essential.

impresión f (efecto, opinión) impression; (acto, de revista etc) printing; (edición) edition.

impresionante *a* impressive.

impresionar *vt* (*causar admiración*) to impress; (*sorprender*) to stun.

impresionismo *m* impressionism.

impreso,-a 1 *a* printed. **2** *m* (*papel, folleto*) printed matter; (*formulario*) form; **i. de solicitud** application form.

impresora *f* printer; **i. de chorro de tinta** ink-jet (printer); **i. láser** laser (printer); **i. matricial** dot matrix (printer).

imprevisible *a* unforeseeable.

imprevisto,-a 1 *a* unforeseen. **2** *m* unforeseen event.

imprimir (*pp* **impreso**) *vt* to print.

impropio,-a *a* (*inadecuado*) inappropriate.

improvisado,-a *a* (*espontáneo*) improvised; (*provisional*) makeshift.

improvisar *vt* to improvise.

imprudencia *f* rashness; (*indiscreción*) indiscretion.

impuesto *m* tax; **i. sobre la renta** income tax; **libre de impuestos** tax-free.

impulsar *vt* to drive.

impulso *m* impulse.

impunemente *adv* with impunity.

impureza *f* impurity.

impuse *pt indef de* **imponer**.

inacabable *a* endless.

inaccesible *a* inaccessible.

inaceptable *a* unacceptable.

inadaptado,-a 1 *a* maladjusted. **2** *mf* misfit.

inadecuado,-a *a* unsuitable.

inadmisible *a* inadmissible.

inagotable *a* (*recursos etc*) inexhaustible; (*persona*) tireless.

inaguantable *a* unbearable.

inapreciable *a* (*valioso*) invaluable; (*insignificante*) insignificant.

inasequible *a* (*producto*) unaffordable; (*meta*) unattainable; (*persona*) unapproachable.

inaudito,-a *a* unprecedented.

inauguración *f* inauguration.

inaugurar *vt* to inaugurate.

inca *a & mf* Inca.

incalculable *a* incalculable.

incandescente *a* white hot.

incansable *a* tireless.

incapacidad *f* inability; (*incompetencia*) incompetence.

incapacitar *vt* to incapacitate; (*inhabilitar*) to disqualify.

incapaz *a* incapable (**de** of).

incendiar 1 *vt* to set fire to. **2 incendiarse** *vr* to catch fire.

incendio *m* fire; **i. forestal** forest fire.

incentivo *m* incentive.

incertidumbre *f* uncertainty.

incierto,-a *a* uncertain.

incinerar *vt* (*basura*) to incinerate; (*cadáveres*) to cremate.

incipiente *a* incipient.

incitar *vt* to incite.

inclinación *f* (*de terreno*) slope; (*del cuerpo*) stoop; (*reverencia*) bow.

inclinar 1 *vt* to incline; (*cabeza*) to nod. **2 inclinarse** *vr* to lean; (*al saludar*) to bow; (*optar*) **inclinarse a** to be inclined to.

incluir *vt* to include; (*contener*) to contain; (*adjuntar*) to enclose.

inclusive *adv* (*incluido*) inclusive; (*incluso*) even; **hasta la lección ocho i.** up to and including lesson eight.

incluso *adv* even.

incógnita *f* (*misterio*) mystery.

incoherente *a* incoherent.

incoloro,-a *a* colorless.

incombustible *a* incombustible.

incomodidad *f* discomfort; (*molestia*) inconvenience.

incómodo,-a *a* uncomfortable.

incompatible *a* incompatible.

incompetencia *f* incompetence.

incompetente *a & mf* incompetent.

incompleto,-a *a* incomplete; (*inacabado*) unfinished.

incomprensible *a* incomprehensible.

incomunicado,-a *a* (*aislado*) isolated; (*en la cárcel*) in solitary con-

finement; **el pueblo se quedó i.** the town was cut off.
inconcebible *a* inconceivable.
incondicional *a* unconditional; (*apoyo*) wholehearted; (*amigo*) faithful; (*partidario*) staunch.
inconfundible *a* unmistakable.
incongruente *a* incongruous.
inconsciencia *f* unconsciousness; (*irresponsabilidad*) irresponsibility.
inconsciente 1 *a* (*con estar*) (*desmayado*) unconscious; (*con ser*) (*despreocupado*) unaware (**de** of); (*irreflexivo*) thoughtless.
inconsistente *a* (*argumento*) weak.
inconstante *a* fickle.
incontrolable *a* uncontrollable.
inconveniente 1 *a* inconvenient; (*inapropiado*) unsuitable. **2** *m* (*objeción*) objection; (*desventaja*) disadvantage; (*problema*) difficulty.
incorporación *f* incorporation.
incorporar 1 *vt* to incorporate (**en** into); (*levantar*) to help to sit up. **2 incorporarse** *vr* (*en la cama*) to sit up; **incorporarse a** (*sociedad*) to join; (*trabajo*) to start.
incorrecto,-a *a* (*equivocado*) incorrect.
incorregible *a* incorrigible.
incrédulo,-a 1 *a* incredulous. **2** *mf* disbeliever.
increíble *a* incredible.
incrementar 1 *vt* to increase. **2 incrementarse** *vr* to increase.
inculto,-a 1 *a* uneducated. **2** *mf* ignoramus.
incumplimiento *m* (*de un deber*) non-fulfillment; (*de una orden*) failure to execute.
incurrir *vi* to fall (**en** into).
indagar [7] *vt* to investigate.
indebido,-a *a* (*desconsiderado*) undue; (*ilegal*) unlawful.
indecente *a* indecent.
indeciso,-a 1 *a* hesitant. **2** *m* (*en encuesta*) don't know.
indefenso,-a *a* defenseless.

indefinidamente *adv* indefinitely.
indefinido,-a *a* (*indeterminado*) indefinite; (*impreciso*) vague; (*tiempo verbal*) indefinite.
indemnización *f* (*acto*) indemnification; (*compensación*) compensation.
indemnizar [4] *vt* to compensate (**por** for).
independencia *f* independence.
independiente *a* (*libre*) independent; (*individualista*) self-reliant.
independientemente *adv* independently (**de** of); (*aparte de*) irrespective (**de** of).
indescriptible *a* indescribable.
indeseable *a & mf* undesirable.
indeterminado,-a *a* indefinite; (*impreciso*) vague; (*artículo*) indefinite.
indicación *f* (*señal*) indication; (*instrucción*) instruction.
indicador,-a *m* indicator.
indicar [1] *vt* to indicate.
indicativo,-a *a* indicative (**de** of); (*modo*) **i.** indicative (mode).
índice *m* (*de libro*) index; (*relación*) rate; **í. de natalidad/mortalidad** birth/death rate; (*dedo*) **í.** index finger.
indicio *m* indication (**de** of).
índico,-a *adj* Indian; **Océano I.** Indian Ocean.
indiferente *a* indifferent; **me es i.** it makes no difference to me.
indígena 1 *a* indigenous (**de** to). **2** *mf* native (**de** of).
indigestión *f* indigestion.
indignación *f* indignation.
indignar 1 *vt* to infuriate. **2 indignarse** *vr* to be indignant (**por** at, about).
indio,-a *a & mf* Indian.
indirecta *f* fam insinuation.
indirecto,-a *adj* indirect.
indiscreto,-a *a* indiscreet.
indiscutible *a* indisputable.
indispensable *a* indispensable.
indisponer (*pp* **indispuesto**) **1** *vt*

to make ill. **2 indisponerse** *vr* to become ill.

indispuse *pt indef de* **indisponer**.

indistintamente *adv* **pueden escribir en inglés o en español i.** you can write in English or Spanish, it doesn't matter which.

individual *a* individual; **habitación i.** single room.

individuo *m* individual.

índole *f (carácter)* character; *(clase, tipo)* kind.

inducir *vt* to lead.

indudable *a* indubitable; **es i. que** there is no doubt that.

induje *pt indef de* **inducir**.

indultar *vt* to pardon.

indumentaria *f* clothing.

industria *f* industry.

industrial 1 *a* industrial. **2** *mf* manufacturer.

industrialización *f* industrialization.

induzco *indic pres de* **inducir**.

ineficacia *f (ineptitud)* inefficiency; *(inutilidad)* ineffectiveness.

ineficaz *adj (inepto)* inefficient; *(inefectivo)* ineffective.

ineptitud *f* ineptitude, incompetence.

inepto,-a *a* inept. **2** *mf* incompetent person.

inerte *a (inanimado)* inert; *(inmóvil)* motionless.

inesperado,-a *a (fortuito)* unexpected; *(imprevisto)* sudden.

inestabilidad *f* instability.

inevitable *a* inevitable.

inexistente *a* non-existent.

inexperiencia *f* lack of experience.

inexplicable *a* inexplicable.

infalible *a* infallible.

infancia *f* childhood.

infantería *f* infantry.

infantil *a* **literatura i.** *(para niños)* children's literature. **2** *(aniñado)* childlike; *(peyorativo)* childish.

infarto *m* **i. (de miocardio)** heart attack.

infección *f* infection.

infeliz 1 *a* unhappy; *(desdichado)* unfortunate. **2** *mf fam* simpleton.

inferior 1 *a (más bajo)* lower; *(calidad)* inferior; *(cantidad)* lower. **2** *mf (persona)* subordinate.

infestado,-a i. de infested with; **infestado de turistas** swarming with tourists.

infidelidad *f* unfaithfulness.

infierno *m* hell; *(horno)* inferno; *fam* **¡vete al i.!** go to hell!

infinidad *f* infinity; *(sinfín)* great number; **en i. de ocasiones** on countless occasions.

infinitivo,-a *a & m* infinitive.

infinito,-a 1 *a* infinite. **2** *m* infinity.

inflable *a* inflatable.

inflación *f* inflation.

inflamable *a* flammable.

inflamación *f* inflammation.

inflamar *f* infinity; *(sinfín) (encender)* to set on fire. **2 inflamarse** *vr* to become inflamed; *(incendiarse)* to catch fire.

inflar 1 *vt* to inflate. **2 inflarse** *vr* to inflate.

inflexible *a* inflexible.

influencia *f* influence; **ejercer** *o* **tener i. sobre algn** to have an influence on sb.

influir 1 *vt* to influence. **2** *vi* to have influence; **i. en** *o* **sobre** to influence.

información *f* information; *(servicio telefónico)* directory enquiries *pl*.

informal *a (reunión, cena)* informal; *(comportamiento)* casual; *(persona)* unreliable.

informar 1 *vt (enterar)* to inform *(de* of); *(dar informes)* to report. **2 informarse** *vr (procurarse noticias)* to find out *(de* about); *(enterarse)* to inquire *(de* about).

informática *f* information technology, IT.

informe *m* report; **informes** references.

infracción *f* infringement.

infraestructura f infrastructure.

infringir [6] vt **i. una ley** to break a law.

infundir vt to infuse; (idea etc) to instil.

infusión f infusion.

ingeniero,-a mf engineer; **i. de caminos** civil engineer; **i. técnico** technician.

ingenio m (talento) talent; (inventiva) inventiveness; (agudeza) wit.

ingenioso,-a a ingenious; (vivaz) witty.

ingenuo,-a 1 a naïve. **2** mf naïve person.

ingle f groin.

inglés,-esa 1 a English. **2** mf (hombre) Englishman; (mujer) Englishwoman; **los ingleses** the English. **3** m (idioma) English.

ingratitud f ingratitude.

ingrediente m ingredient.

ingresar 1 vt (dinero) to pay in; (enfermo) to admit; **la ingresaron en el hospital** she was admitted to the hospital. **2** vi to enter.

ingreso m (dinero) deposit; (entrada) entry (**en** into); (admisión) admission (**en** to); **ingresos** (sueldo, renta) income sing; (beneficios) revenue sing.

inhalador m inhaler.

inhalar vt to inhale.

inhumano,-a a inhumane; (cruel) inhuman.

inicial a & f initial.

iniciar 1 vt (empezar) to begin, start; (discusión) to initiate; (una cosa nueva) to pioneer. **2 iniciarse** vr to begin, start.

iniciativa f initiative; **por i. propia** on one's own initiative.

inicio m beginning, start.

ininterrumpido,-a a uninterrupted.

injerirse vr to interfere (**en** in).

injuria f insult.

injusticia f injustice.

injustificado,-a a unjustified.

injusto,-a a unjust.

inmaduro,-a a immature.

inmediatamente adv immediately, at once.

inmediato,-a a (en el tiempo) immediate; (en el espacio) next (**a** to); **de i.** at once.

inmejorable a (trabajo) excellent; (precio) unbeatable.

inmenso,-a a immense.

inmigración f immigration.

inmigrante a & mf immigrant.

inminente a imminent.

inmiscuirse vr to interfere (**en** in).

inmobiliaria f real estate company.

inmoral a immoral.

inmortal a & mf immortal.

inmóvil a motionless.

inmovilizar [4] vt to immobilize.

inmueble m building.

inmune a immune (**a** to).

inmunidad f immunity (**contra** to).

inmunizar [4] vt to immunize (**contra** against).

innato,-a a innate.

innecesario,-a a unnecessary.

innegable a undeniable.

innovación f innovation.

innumerable a countless.

inocencia f innocence; (ingenuidad) naïvety.

inocentada f ≈ April Fools' joke.

inocente 1 a innocent. **2** mf innocent.

inocuo,-a a innocuous.

inofensivo,-a a harmless.

inolvidable a unforgettable.

inoportuno,-a a inappropriate.

inoxidable a. **acero i.** stainless steel.

inquietante a worrying.

inquietar 1 vt to worry. **2 inquietarse** vr to worry (**por** about).

inquieto,-a a (preocupado) worried (**por** about); (intranquilo) restless.

inquietud f (preocupación) worry; (agitación) restlessness.

inquilino,-a mf tenant.

insaciable a insatiable.

insatisfecho,-a a dissatisfied.

inscribir (pp **inscrito**) **1** vt (registrar) to register; (matricular) to enroll; (grabar) to inscribe. **2 inscribirse** vr (registrarse) to register; (hacerse miembro) to join; (matricularse) to enroll; **inscribirse en un club** to join a club.

inscripción f (matriculación) enrollment; (escrito etc) inscription.

insecticida m insecticide.

insecto m insect.

inseguridad f (falta de confianza) insecurity; (duda) uncertainty; (peligro) lack of safety.

insensato,-a 1 a foolish. **2** mf fool.

insensible a (indiferente) unfeeling; (imperceptible) imperceptible; (miembro) numb.

inseparable a inseparable.

insertar vt to insert.

inservible a useless.

insignia f badge.

insignificante a insignificant.

insinuar vt to insinuate.

insistir vi to insist (**en** on).

insolación f sunstroke.

insolente a insolent.

insólito,-a a (poco usual) unusual; (extraño) strange, odd.

insomnio m insomnia.

insoportable a unbearable.

insospechado,-a a unsuspected.

inspección f inspection.

inspeccionar vt to inspect.

inspector,-a mf inspector; **i. de Hacienda** tax inspector.

inspiración f inspiration; (inhalación) inhalation.

inspirar 1 vt to inspire; (inhalar) to inhale. **2 inspirarse** vr **inspirarse en** to be inspired by.

instalación f installation; **instalaciones deportivas** sports facilities.

instalar 1 vt to install; (erigir) to set up. **2 instalarse** vr to settle (down).

instancia f (solicitud) request; **a instancia(s) de** at the request of; **en última i.** as a last resort.

instantáneamente adv instantly.

instantáneo,-a a instantaneous; **café i.** instant coffee.

instante m instant; **a cada i.** constantly; **al i.** immediately.

instaurar vt to found.

instigar [7] vt to instigate.

instintivo,-a a instinctive.

instinto m instinct; **por i.** instinctively.

institución f institution.

instituto m institute; (colegio) high school.

institutriz f governess.

instrucción f (educación) education; **instrucciones para el o de uso** instructions o directions for use.

instructivo,-a a instructive.

instruir vt to instruct; (enseñar) to educate.

instrumento m instrument.

insubordinarse vr to rebel (**contra** against).

insuficiente 1 a insufficient. **2** m (nota) fail.

insultar vt to insult.

insulto m insult.

insurrección f insurrection.

intacto,-a a intact.

integral a integral; **pan i.** wholewheat bread.

integrar 1 vt to integrate; (formar) to compose. **2 integrarse** vr to integrate (en with).

integridad f integrity.

íntegro,-a a (entero) whole; (honrado) upright; **versión íntegra** unabridged version.

intelectual a & mf intellectual.

inteligencia f intelligence.

inteligente a intelligent.

inteligible a intelligible.

intemperie f **a la i.** in the open (air).

intención f intention; **con i.** deliberately; **tener la i. de hacer algo** to intend to do sth.

intencionadamente adv on purpose.

intencionado,-a a deliberate.

intensidad *f* intensity; (*del viento*) force.

intensificar [1] *vt,* **intensificarse** *vr* to intensify; (*relación*) to strengthen.

intenso,-a *a* intense.

intentar *vt* to try.

intento *m* attempt; **i. de suicidio** attempted suicide.

intercambiar *vt* to exchange.

interceder *vi* to intercede.

interceptar *vt* (*detener*) to intercept; (*carretera*) to block; (*tráfico*) to hold up.

interés *m* interest; (*provecho personal*) self-interest; **tener i. en** *o* **por** to be interested in; **tipos de i.** interest rates.

interesante *a* interesting.

interesar 1 *vt* (*tener interés*) to interest; (*concernir*) to concern. **2** *vi* (*ser importante*) to be of interest. **3 interesarse** *vr* **interesarse por** *o* **en** to be interested in.

interferencia *f* interference; (*en radio, televisión*) jamming.

interfono *m* intercom.

interior 1 *a* inner; **ropa i.** underwear; (*política, vuelo*) domestic; (*región*) inland. **2** *m* inside; (*de un país*) interior; **Ministerio del I.** Department of the Interior.

interjección *f* interjection.

interlocutor,-a *mf* speaker.

intermediario,-a *mf* intermediary, middleman.

intermedio,-a 1 *a* intermediate. **2** *m* (*en televisión*) break.

interminable *a* endless.

intermitente 1 *a* intermittent. **2** *m* (*de automóvil*) indicator.

internacional *a* international.

internado *m* (*colegio*) boarding school.

interno,-a 1 *a* internal; (*política*) domestic. **2** *mf* (*alumno*) boarder.

interpretación *f* interpretation.

interpretar *vt* to interpret; (*papel*) to play; (*obra*) to perform; (*concierto*) to perform; (*canción*) to sing.

intérprete *mf* (*traductor*) interpreter; (*actor, músico*) performer; (*cantante*) singer.

interrogación *f* interrogation; **(signo de) i.** question mark.

interrogar [7] *vt* to question; (*testigo etc*) to interrogate.

interrogatorio *m* interrogation.

interrumpir *vt* to interrupt; (*tráfico*) to block.

interruptor *m* switch.

interurbano,-a *a* intercity; **conferencia interurbana** long-distance call.

intervalo *m* interval.

intervenir 1 *vi* (*mediar*) to intervene (**en** in); (*participar*) take part (**en** in). **2** *vt* (*teléfono*) to tap.

interviú *m* (*pl* **interviús**) interview.

intestino *m* intestine.

intimidar *vt* to intimidate.

íntimo,-a *a* intimate; (*vida*) private; (*amigo*) close.

intolerante 1 *a* intolerant. **2** *mf* intolerant person.

intoxicación *f* poisoning; **i. alimenticia** food poisoning.

intranquilizarse *vr* to get worried.

intransitivo,-a *a* intransitive.

intriga *f* intrigue; (*trama*) plot.

intrigar [7] **1** *vt* (*interesar*) to intrigue. **2** *vi* (*maquinar*) to plot.

intrínseco,-a *a* intrinsic.

introducir *vt* to introduce; (*meter*) to insert.

introvertido,-a 1 *a* introverted. **2** *mf* introvert.

intruso,-a *mf* intruder.

intuición *f* intuition.

intuir *vt* to know by intuition.

inundación *f* flood.

inusitado,-a *a* unusual.

inútil 1 *a* useless; (*esfuerzo, intento*) pointless. **2** *mf fam* good-for-nothing.

inutilizar [4] *vt* to make useless.

invadir *vt* to invade; **los estudiantes invadieron la calle** students poured out onto the street.

inválido,-a 1 a (nulo) invalid; (minusválido) disabled. **2** mf disabled person.

invariable a invariable.

invasión f invasion.

invencible a (enemigo) invincible; (obstáculo) insurmountable.

invención f (invento) invention; (mentira) fabrication.

inventar vt (crear) to invent; (excusa, mentira) to concoct.

inventario m inventory.

invento m invention.

invernadero m greenhouse.

invernal a winter.

inversión f inversion; (de dinero) investment.

inverso,-a a **en sentido i.** in the opposite direction; **en orden i.** in reverse order.

invertir [5] vt (orden) to invert; (dinero) to invest (**en** in); (tiempo) to spend (**en** on).

investigación f (policial etc) investigation; (científica) research.

investigar [7] vt (indagar) to investigate; (científicamente) to research.

invierno m winter.

invisible a invisible.

invitado,-a 1 a invited. **2** mf guest.

invitar vt to invite; **me invitó a una copa** he treated me to a drink.

involuntario,-a a involuntary; (impremeditado) unintentional.

inyección f injection; **poner una i.** to give an injection.

ir 1 vi to go; **¡vamos!** let's go!; **¡ya voy!** (I'm) coming!; **¿cómo le va el nuevo trabajo?** how is he doing in his new job?; **el negro no te va** black doesn't suit you; **ir con falda** to wear a skirt; **ir de blanco/de uniforme** to be dressed in white/in uniform; **va para abogado** he's studying to be a lawyer; **ir por la derecha** to keep to (the) right; **ve (a) por agua** go and fetch some water; **voy por la página noventa** I've got as far as page ninety; **en lo que va de año** so far this year; **ir a parar** to end up; **¡qué va!** of course not!;

va a lo suyo he looks after his own interests; **¡vamos a ver!** let's see!; **¡vaya!** fancy that; **¡vaya moto!** what a bike! **2** v aux **ir andando** to go on foot; **va mejorando** she's improving; **ya van rotos tres** three (of them) have already been broken; **iba a decir que . . .** I was going to say that . . .; **va a llover** it's going to rain. **3** irse vr (marcharse) to go away; **me voy** I'm off; **¡vámonos!** let's go!; **¡vete!** go away!; **¡vete a casa!** go home!; **¿por dónde se va a . . .?** which is the way to . . .?

ira f rage.

iraní a & mf (pl iraníes) Iranian.

iraquí a & mf (pl iraquíes) Iraqi.

irascible a irascible.

iris m inv arco i. rainbow.

irlandés,-esa 1 adj Irish. **2** mf (hombre) Irishman; (mujer) Irishwoman; **los irlandeses** the Irish. **3** m (idioma) Irish.

ironía f irony.

irónico,-a a ironic.

irracional a irrational.

irreal a unreal.

irregular a irregular.

irremediable a incurable.

irresistible a (impulso, persona) irresistible; (insoportable) unbearable.

irresponsable a irresponsible.

irritar 1 vt to irritate. **2 irritarse** vr to become irritated.

irrompible a unbreakable.

irrumpir vi to burst (**en** into).

isla f island.

islámico,-a a Islamic.

israelí a & mf (pl israelíes) Israeli.

italiano,-a 1 a Italian. **2** mf (persona) Italian. **3** m (idioma) Italian.

itinerario m itinerary.

IVA m abr de **impuesto sobre el valor añadido** value-added tax, VAT.

izda., izqdᵃ abr de **izquierda** left.

izqdo., izqdᵒ abr de **izquierda** left.

izquierda f left; (mano) left hand; **a la i.** on the left; **girar a la i.** to turn left.

izquierdo,-a a left.

J

jabalí *m* (*pl jabalíes*) wild boar.
jabalina *f* javelin.
jabón *m* soap; **j. de afeitar/tocador** shaving/toilet soap.
jabonera *f* soap dish.
jaca *f* gelding.
jacaré *m Am* caiman.
jacinto *m* hyacinth.
jactarse *vr* to boast (**de** about).
jadear *vi* to pant.
jalea *f* jelly.
jaleo *m* (*alboroto*) ruckus; (*confusión*) muddle.
jalón *m Am* lift.
jamás *adv* never; **j. he estado allí** I have never been there; **el mejor libro que j. se ha escrito** the best book ever written; **nunca j.** never again.
jamón *m* ham; **j. de York/serrano** boiled/cured ham.
japonés,-esa *a & mf* Japanese; **los japoneses** the Japanese.
jaque *m* check; **j. mate** checkmate; **j. al rey** check.
jaqueca *f* migraine.
jarabe *m* syrup; **j. para la tos** cough mixture.
jardín *m* garden; **j. botánico** botanical garden; **j. de infancia** nursery school.
jardinero,-a *mf* gardener.
jarra *f* pitcher.
jarro *m* (*recipiente*) jug; (*contenido*) jugful.
jarrón *m* vase.
jaula *f* cage.
jazmín *m* jasmine.
J.C. *abr de* **Jesucristo** Jesus Christ, J.C.
jeep *m* jeep.
jefa *f* manager.
jefatura *f* (*cargo, dirección*) leadership; (*sede*) central office.
jefe *m* head; (*de empresa*) manager; (*de partido*) leader; **J. de Estado** Head of State.
jengibre *m* ginger.

jerez *m* sherry.
jerga *f* (*técnica*) jargon; (*vulgar*) slang.
jeringa *f* syringe.
jeringuilla *f* (hypodermic) syringe.
jeroglífico *m* hieroglyphic; (*juego*) rebus.
jersey *m* (*pl jerseis*) pullover.
Jesucristo *m* Jesus Christ.
Jesús **1** *m* Jesus. **2** *interj* (*al estornudar*) bless you!
jíbaro,-a *mf Am* peasant.
jícara *f Am* gourd.
jilguero *m* goldfinch.
jinete *m* horseman, rider.
jirafa *f* giraffe.
jirón *m* (*trozo desgarrado*) strip; (*pedazo suelto*) scrap; **hecho jirones** in tatters.
JJOO *mpl abr de* **Juegos Olímpicos** Olympic Games.
jornada *f* **j. (laboral)** (*día de trabajo*) working day; **trabajo de media j./j. completa** part-time/full-time work.
jornal *m* day's wage.
jornalero,-a *mf* day laborer.
joroba *f* hump.
jorobado,-a **1** *a* hunchbacked. **2** *mf* hunchback.
joven **1** *a* young; **de aspecto j.** young-looking. **2** *mf* (*hombre*) young man; (*mujer*) young woman; **de j.** as a young man/woman; **los jóvenes** young people.
joya *f* jewel; **ser una j.** (*persona*) to be a gem.
joyería *f* (*tienda*) jewelry shop.
joyero,-a **1** *mf* jeweler. **2** *m* jewel case.
jubilado,-a **1** *a* retired. **2** *mf* retired person; **los jubilados** retired people.
judía *f* bean; **j. verde** green bean.
judío,-a **1** *a* Jewish. **2** *mf* Jew.
judo *m* judo.
juego *m* game; (*conjunto de piezas*) set; (*apuestas*) gambling; **j. de azar** game of chance; **j. de cartas** card game; **Juegos Olímpicos** Olympic Games; **terreno de j.**

field; **fuera de j.** offside; **j. de café/té** coffee/tea service; **ir a j. con** to match.

juerga f fam rave-up; **ir de j.** to go on a binge.

jueves m inv Thursday; **J. Santo** Holy Thursday.

juez,-a mf judge; **j. de línea** linesman.

jugada f move; fam dirty trick.

jugador,-a player; (apostador) gambler.

jugar 1 vi to play; **j. a(l) fútbol** to play football; **j. sucio** to play dirty. 2 vt to play; (apostar) to bet. 3 **jugarse** vr (arriesgar) to risk; (apostar) to bet.

jugo m juice.

juguete m toy; **pistola de j.** toy gun.

juicio m (facultad mental) judgement; (sensatez) reason; (opinión) opinion; (en tribunal) trial; **a j. de** in the opinion of; **a mi j.** in my opinion; **perder el j.** to go mad.

julio m July.

junco m rush.

jungla f jungle.

junio m June.

júnior a junior.

junta f (reunión) meeting; (dirección) board; (gobierno militar) junta.

juntar 1 vt (unir) to join; (piezas) to assemble; (dinero) to raise. 2 **juntarse** vr (unirse) to join; (ríos, caminos) to meet; (personas) to gather.

junto,-a 1 a together. 2 **junto** adv **j. con** together with; **j. a** next to.

jurado m jury.

juramento m oath; **bajo j.** under oath.

jurar 1 vi to swear. 2 vt to swear; **j. el cargo** to take the oath of office.

jurídico,-a a legal.

justicia f justice; **tomarse la j. por su mano** to take the law into one's own hands.

justificado,-a a justified.

justificante m written proof.

justamente adv **¡j.!** precisely! **j. detrás de.** right behind.

justo,-a 1 a just; (apretado) (ropa) tight; (exacto) accurate; **un trato j.** a fair deal; **estamos justos de tiempo** we're pressed for time; **llegamos en el momento j. en que salían** we arrived just as they were leaving; **lo j.** just enough. 2 **justo** adv (exactamente) precisely; **j. al lado de** right beside.

juvenil a young; **ropa j.** (de joven) young people's clothes; **delincuencia j.** juvenile delinquency.

juventud f (edad) youth; (jóvenes) young people.

juzgado m court.

juzgar [7] vt to judge; **a j. por . . .** judging by . . .

K

kárate m karate.

kilo m (medida) kilo.

kilogramo m kilogram.

kilometraje m ≈ mileage.

kilómetro m kilometer.

kiosco m kiosk.

kiwi m (fruto) kiwi (fruit).

kleenex® m tissue.

L

la¹ 1 art def f the. 2 pron dem the one; **la del vestido azul** the one in the blue dress.

la² pron pers f (persona) her; (usted) you; (cosa) it; **la invitaré** I'll invite her along; **ya la avisaremos, señora** we'll let you know, madam; **no la dejes abierta** don't leave it open.

labio m lip.

labor f job; (de costura) needlework.

laborable a día l. working day.

laboral a industrial; **accidente l.** industrial accident; **jornada l.** working day.

laboratorio *m* laboratory.

laca *f* hairspray; **l. de uñas** nail polish.

ladera *f* slope.

lado *m* side; **a un l.** aside; **al l.** close by, nearby; **al l. de** next to; **ponte de l.** stand sideways; **por todos lados** on all sides; **por otro l.** (*además*) moreover; **por un l. . . ., por otro l. . . .** on the one hand . ., on the other hand . . .

ladrar *vi* to bark.

ladrillo *m* brick.

ladrón,-ona *mf* thief.

lagartija *f* small lizard.

lagarto *m* lizard.

lago *m* lake.

lágrima *f* tear.

laguna *f* small lake.

lamentar 1 *vt* to regret; **lo lamento** I'm sorry. **2 lamentarse** *vr* to complain.

lamer *vt* to lick.

lámina *f* sheet.

lámpara *f* lamp; (*bombilla*) bulb.

lana *f* wool.

lancha *f* motorboat; **l. motora** speedboat; **l. neumática** rubber dinghy; **l. salvavidas** lifeboat.

langosta *f* lobster; (*insecto*) locust.

langostino *m* king prawn.

lanza *f* spear.

lanzar [4] **1** *vt* (*arrojar*) to throw; (*grito*) to let out; (*ataque, producto*) to launch. **2 lanzarse** *vr* to throw oneself.

lápiz *m* pencil; **l. de labios** lipstick; **l. de ojos** eyeliner.

largo,-a 1 *a* long; **a lo l. de** (*espacio*) along; (*tiempo*) through; **a la larga** in the long run. **2** *m* (*longitud*) length; **¿cuánto tiene de l.?** *fam* how long is it? *fam* **esto va para l.** this is going to last a long time. **3 largo** *adv fam* **¡l. (de aquí)!** clear off!

largometraje *m* feature film.

las¹ 1 *art def fpl* the. **2** *pron dem* **l. que** (*personas*) those who; (*objetos*) those that; **toma l. que quieras** take whichever ones you want.

las² *pron pers fpl* (*ellas*) them; (*ustedes*) you; **no l. rompas** don't break them; **l. llamaré mañana** (*a ustedes*) I'll call you tomorrow.

láser *m inv* laser.

lástima *f* pity; **¡qué l.!** what a pity!; **es una l. que . . .** it's a pity (that) . . .

lata¹ *f* (*envase*) tin, can; (*hojalata*) tin(plate); **en l.** tinned, canned.

lata² *f fam* drag; **dar la l.** to be a nuisance.

lateral *a* side; **escalón l.** (*en letrero*) ramp.

latido *m* beat.

látigo *m* whip.

latín *m* Latin.

latinoamericano,-a *a & mf* Latin American.

latir *vi* to beat.

latón *m* brass.

laucha *f Am* mouse.

laurel *m* bay leaf.

lava *f* lava.

lavable *a* washable.

lavabo *m* (*pila*) washbasin; (*cuarto de aseo*) washroom; (*retrete*) toilet.

lavado *m* washing; **l. en seco** dry-cleaning.

lavadora *f* washing machine.

lavanda *f* lavender.

lavandería *f* laundromat; (*atendida por personal*) laundry.

lavaplatos *m inv* dishwasher.

lavar *vt* to wash.

lavavajillas *m inv* dishwasher.

laxante *a & m* laxative.

lazo *m* (*adorno*) bow; (*nudo*) knot; **lazos** (*vínculo*) links.

le 1 *pron pers mf* (*objeto indirecto*) (*a él*) (to/for) him; (*a ella*) (to/for) her; (*a cosa*) (to/for) it; (*a usted*) (to/for) you; **lávale la cara** wash his face; **le compraré uno** I'll buy one for her; **¿qué le pasa (a usted)?** what's the matter with you? **2** *pron pers m* (*objeto directo*) (*él*) him; (*usted*) you; **no le oigo** I can't hear him; **no quiero molestarle** I don't wish to disturb you.

leal a faithful.
lección f lesson.
leche f milk; **dientes de l.** milk teeth; **l. descremada** o **desnatada** skim milk.
lechuga f lettuce.
lechuza f owl.
lector,-a mf (persona) reader; (de colegio) (language) assistant.
lectura f reading.
leer vt to read.
legal a legal.
legalizar [4] vt to legalize; (documento) to authenticate.
legislación f legislation.
legítimo,-a a legitimate; (auténtico) real; **en legítima defensa** in self-defense; **oro l.** pure gold.
legumbres fpl pulses.
lejano,-a a far-off.
lejía f bleach.
lejos adv far (away); **a lo l.** in the distance; **de l.** from a distance; fig **sin ir más l.** to take an obvious example.
lema m motto.
lencería f (prendas) lingerie; (ropa blanca) linen (goods pl).
lengua f (idioma) language; **l. materna** mother tongue.
lenguado m sole.
lenguaje m language; **l. corporal** body language.
lente mf lens; **lentes de contacto** contact lenses.
lenteja f lentil.
lentilla f contact lens.
lento,-a a slow; **a fuego l.** on a low heat.
leña f firewood.
leño m log.
león m lion.
leopardo m leopard.
leotardos mpl thick tights.
les pron pers mfpl (a ellos/ellas) them; (a ustedes) you; **dales el dinero** give them the money; **l. he comprado un regalo** I've bought you/them a present; **l. esperaré** I shall wait for you/them; **no quiero molestarles** I don't wish to disturb you/them.

lesión f (física) injury.
lesionar vt to injure.
letal a lethal.
letargo m lethargy.
letra f letter; (escritura) (handwriting); (de canción) lyrics pl; **l. de imprenta** block capitals; **l. mayúscula** capital letter; **l. minúscula** small letter; **l. (de cambio)** bill of exchange; (carrera) **letras** arts.
letrero m (aviso) notice; (cartel) poster.
levadura f yeast; **l. en polvo** baking powder.
levantamiento m lifting; (insurrección) uprising; **l. de pesos** weightlifting.
levantar 1 vt to lift; (mano, voz) to raise; (edificio) to erect; (ánimos) to raise. 2 vr **levantarse** to get up; (ponerse de pie) to stand up.
levante m (el) **L.** Levante, the regions of Valencia and Murcia.
leve a (ligero) light; (de poca importancia) slight.
levemente adv slightly.
ley f law; **aprobar una l.** to pass a bill; **oro de l.** pure gold; **plata de l.** sterling silver.
leyenda f (relato) legend; (bajo ilustración) caption.
liar 1 vt (envolver) to wrap up; (cigarrillo) to roll; (enredar) to muddle up; (confundir) to confuse. 2 **liarse** vr (embarullarse) to get muddled up.
liberal a liberal; (generoso) generous; (carácter) open-minded; **profesión l.** profession. 2 mf liberal.
liberar vt (país) to liberate; (prisionero) to release.
libertad f freedom; **(en) l. bajo palabra/fianza** (on) parole/bail; **(en) l. condicional** (on) parole.
libio,-a a & mf Libyan.
libra f pound; **l. esterlina** pound sterling.
librar 1 vt to free; (preso) to release. 2 **librarse** vr to escape; **librarse de algn** to get rid of sb.
libre a free; (sin restricción) open to

the public; **entrada l.** admission free; **l. de impuestos** tax-free.

librería f (tienda) bookstore; (estante) bookcase.

libreta f notebook.

libro m book; **l. de texto** textbook.

licencia f (permiso) permission; (documentos) licence; Am driver's license.

licenciado,-a mf graduate; Am lawyer; **l. en Ciencias** Bachelor of Science.

licenciatura f (título) (bachelor's) degree (course); (carrera) degree (course).

licor m liquor.

licuadora f liquidizer.

líder mf leader.

lidia f bullfighting.

lidiar vt to fight.

liebre f hare.

liga f league.

ligar [7] 1 vt to join. 2 vi fam **l. con una chica** to flirt with a girl.

ligereza f lightness; (frivolidad) flippancy; (acto) indiscretion; (rapidez) speed.

ligeramente adv (levemente) lightly; (un poco) slightly.

ligero,-a 1 a (peso) light; (veloz) quick; (leve) slight; **l. de ropa** lightly clad; **brisa/comida ligera** light breeze/meal. 2 adv **ligero** (rápido) fast.

liguero m garter belt.

lija f sandpaper; **papel de l.** sandpaper.

lima f (herramienta) file; **l. de uñas** nailfile.

limar vt to file.

limitar 1 vt to restrict. 2 vi **l. con** to border on.

límite m limit; (de país) border; **fecha l.** deadline; **velocidad l.** maximum speed.

limón m lemon.

limonada f lemon squash.

limonero m lemon tree.

limpiaparabrisas m inv windshield wiper.

limpiar vt to clean; (con un trapo) to wipe; (zapatos) to polish.

limpieza f (calidad) cleanliness; (acción) cleaning.

limpio,-a 1 a (aseado) clean; (neto) net; **juego l.** fair play. 2 adv **limpio** fairly; **jugar l.** to play fair.

lindar vi **l. con** to border on.

lindo,-a 1 a (bonito) pretty; **de lo l.** a great deal. 2 adv Am (bien) nicely.

línea f line; **l. aérea** airline; **en líneas generales** roughly speaking; **guardar la l.** to watch one's figure.

lino m (fibra) linen.

linterna f torch.

lío m (paquete) bundle; (embrollo) mess; **hacerse un l.** to get mixed up; **meterse en líos** to get into trouble.

liquidación f (saldo) clearance sale; (de deuda) settling.

liquidar 1 vt (deuda, cuenta) to settle; (mercancías) to sell off. 2 vr **liquidarse a algn** (matar) to bump sb off.

líquido,-a 1 a liquid; (cantidad) net. 2 m liquid.

lirio m iris.

lisiado,-a 1 a crippled. 2 mf cripple.

liso,-a a (superficie) smooth; (pelo, falda) straight; (tela) self-colored; Am (desvergonzado) rude.

lista f (relación) list; (franja) stripe; **l. de espera** waiting list; (en avión) standby; **pasar l.** to call the register; **de/a listas** striped.

listín m **l. telefónico** telephone directory.

listo,-a **ser l.** to be clever; **estar l.** to be ready.

litera f (cama) bunk bed; (en tren) couchette.

literatura f literature.

litigio m lawsuit.

litoral 1 m coast. 2 a coastal.

litro m litre.

llaga f (sore); (herida) wound.

llama f flame; **en llamas** in flames.

llamada f call; **l. interurbana** long-distance call.

llamar 1 vt to call; **l. (por teléfono)**

to call; **l. la atención** to attract attention. **2** vi (a la puerta) to knock. **3 llamarse** vr to be called; **¿cómo te llamas?** what's your name?

llano,-a 1 a (superficie) flat. **2** m plain.

llanta f (de rueda) wheel rim; Am tire.

llanto m crying.

llanura f plain.

llave f key; (interruptor) switch; (herramienta) spanner; **cerrar con l.** to lock; (de coche) **l. de contacto** ignition key; **l. inglesa** adjustable spanner; **l. de paso** stopcock.

llavero m key ring.

llegada f arrival; (meta) finish.

llegar [7] vi to arrive; **l. a Madrid** to arrive in Madrid; **¿llegas al techo?** can you reach the ceiling?; **l. a** + infinitivo to go so far as to; **l. a ser** to become.

llenar 1 vt to fill; (satisfacer) to satisfy. **2** vi (comida) to be filling. **3 llenarse** vr to fill (up).

lleno,-a a full (up).

llevar 1 vt to take; (hacia el oyente) to bring; (transportar) to carry; (prenda) to wear; (negocio) to be in charge of; **llevo dos años aquí** I've been here for two years; **esto lleva mucho tiempo** this takes a long time. **2** v aux **l.** + gerundio to have been + present participle; **llevo dos años estudiando español** I've been studying Spanish for two years. ■ **l.** + participio pasado = to have + past participle; **llevaba escritas seis cartas** I had written six letters. **3 llevarse** vr to take away; (premio) to win; (estar de moda) to be fashionable; **llevarse bien con algn** to get along well with sb.

llorar vi to cry.

llover [4] v impers to rain.

llovizna f drizzle.

lluvia f rain.

lluvioso,-a a rainy.

lo¹ art def neutro the; **lo mismo** the same thing; **lo mío** mine; **lo tuyo** yours.

lo² pron pers m & neutro (cosa) it; **debes hacerlo** you must do it; (no se traduce) **no se lo dije** I didn't tell her; **lo que . . .** what . . .; **lo cual . . .** which . . .; **lo de . . .** the business of . . .; **cuéntame lo del juicio** tell me about the trial.

lobo m wolf; **como boca de l.** pitch-dark.

local 1 a local. **2** m (recinto) premises pl.

localidad f (pueblo) locality; (asiento) seat.

localizar [4] vt (encontrar) to find; (fuego, dolor) to localize.

loción f lotion.

loco,-a 1 a mad; **a lo l.** crazily; **l. por** crazy about; **volverse l.** to go mad. **2** mf madman; madwoman.

locomotora f locomotive.

locura f madness.

locutor,-a mf presenter.

locutorio m telephone booth.

lodo m mud.

lógico,-a a logical; **era l. que ocurriera** it was bound to happen.

lograr vt to get, obtain; (premio) to win; (meta) to achieve; **l. hacer algo** to manage to do something.

lombriz f earthworm.

lomo m back; (para filete) loin.

lona f canvas.

loncha f slice.

lonchería f Am snack bar.

longaniza f spicy (pork) sausage.

longitud f length; **dos metros de l.** two meters long; **salto de l.** long jump.

lonja f market.

loquería f Am mental hospital.

lord m (pl **lores**) lord.

loro m parrot.

los¹ art def mpl the. **2** pron **l. que** (personas) those who; (cosas) the ones (that); **toma l. que quieras** take whichever ones you want. **esos son l. míos/tuyos** these are mine/yours.

los² pron pers mpl them; **¿l. has visto?** have you seen them?

losa f slab.

lote m set; (de productos) lot.

lotería f lottery; **tocarle la l. a algn** to win a prize in the lottery.

loza f (material) earthenware; (vajilla) crockery.

lubricante m lubricant.

lucir **1** vi (brillar) to shine. **2** vt (ropas) to sport. **3** **lucirse** vr (hacer buen papel) to do very well; (pavonearse) to show off.

lucha f fight; (deporte) wrestling; **l. libre** free-style o all-in wrestling.

luchar vi to fight; (como deporte) to wrestle.

luego **1** adv (después) then, next; (más tarde) later (on); **¡hasta l.!** so long!; Am **l. de** after; **desde l.** of course. **2** conj therefore.

lugar m place; **en primer l.** in the first place; **en l. de** instead of; **sin l. a dudas** without a doubt; **tener l.** to take place; **dar l. a** to give rise to.

lujo m luxury.

lujuria f lust.

lumbre f fire.

luminoso,-a a luminous; fig bright.

luna f moon; (espejo) mirror; fig **estar en la l.** to have one's head in the clouds; **l. llena** full moon; **l. de miel** honeymoon.

lunar m (en la ropa) dot; (en la piel) mole.

lunes m inv Monday.

lupa f magnifying glass.

lustre m shine.

luto m mourning.

luz f light; **apagar la l.** to put out the light; **dar a l.** (parir) to give birth to; **luces de cruce** dipped headlights; **luces de posición** sidelights; **luces largas** headlights pl; **traje de luces** bullfighter's costume.

luzco indic pres de **lucir.**

M

macana f Am (palo) club; (trasto) rubbish.

macanear vt Am to make up.

macarrones mpl macaroni sing.

macedonia f fruit salad.

maceta f flowerpot.

machacar [1] vt to crush.

machista a & m male chauvinist.

macho **1** a male; fam (viril) manly. **2** m male; fam (hombre viril) macho.

machote m Am rough draft.

macizo,-a **1** a solid. **2** m massif.

macuto m haversack.

madeja f hank.

madera f wood; (de construcción) lumber; **de m.** wooden.

madrastra f stepmother.

madre **1** f mother; **m. de familia** housewife; **m. política** mother-in-law; **m. soltera** unmarried mother. **2** interj **¡m. mía!** good heavens!

madrina f (de bautizo) godmother; (de boda) ≈ bridesmaid.

madrugada f small hours pl; **de m.** in the small hours; **las tres de la m.** three o'clock in the morning.

madrugador,-a **1** a early rising. **2** mf early riser.

madrugar [7] vi to get up early.

madurar vi (persona) to mature; (fruta) to ripen.

maduro,-a a mature; (fruta) ripe; **de edad madura** middle-aged.

maestro,-a **1** mf teacher; (especialista) master; (músico) maestro. **2** a **obra maestra** masterpiece.

magdalena f bun.

magia f magic; **por arte de m.** as if by magic.

magnetofón, magnetófono m tape recorder.

magnífico,-a a magnificent.

mago,-a mf wizard; **los (tres) Reyes Magos** the Three Wise Men, the Three Kings.

magullar **1** vt to bruise. **2** **magullarse** vr to get bruised.

mahonesa f mayonnaise.

maíz m corn.

majestad f majesty.

majo,-a a (bonito) pretty, nice; fam (simpático) nice.

mal **1** m evil; (daño) harm; (enfermedad) illness. **2** a bad; **un m.**

año a bad year; *ver* **malo,-a. 3** *adv* badly; **menos m. que** . . . it's a good job (that) . . .; **no está (nada) m.** it is not bad (at all); **te oigo/veo (muy) m.** I can hardly hear/see you.

malabarista *mf* juggler.

malcriado,-a 1 *a* ill-mannered. **2** *mf* ill-mannered person.

maldad *f* badness; (*acción perversa*) evil thing.

maldecir *vti* to curse.

maldición 1 *f* curse. **2** *interj* damnation!

maldito,-a *a fam* (*molesto*) damned; **¡maldita sea!** damn it!

maleducado,-a 1 *a* bad-mannered. **2** *mf* bad-mannered person.

malentendido *m* misunderstanding.

malestar *m* (*molestia*) discomfort; (*inquietud*) uneasiness.

maleta *f* suitcase; **hacer la m.** to pack one's case.

maletero *m* (*de coche*) trunk.

maletín *m* briefcase.

maleza *f* (*arbustos*) undergrowth; (*malas hierbas*) weeds *pl.*

malgastar *vt* to waste.

malhablado,-a 1 *a* foul-mouthed. **2** *mf* foul-mouthed person.

malhechor,-a *mf* wrongdoer.

malhumor *m* bad mood; **de m.** in a bad mood.

malicia *f* (*mala intención*) malice; (*astucia*) cunning; (*maldad*) badness.

malintencionado,-a 1 *a* ill-intentioned. **2** *mf* ill-intentioned person.

malla *f;* (*red*) mesh; *Am* (*bañador*) swimsuit; (*mallas*) leotard *pl.*

malo,-a *a* bad; (*persona*) (*malvado*) wicked; (*travieso*) naughty; (*enfermo*) ill; (*cosa*) bad; (*perjudicial*) harmful; **por las malas** by force; **lo m. es que** . . . the problem is that . . .

malpensado,-a 1 *a* nastyminded. **2** *mf* nasty-minded person.

malta *f* malt.

maltratado,-a *a* battered.

maltratar *vt* to ill-treat.

mama *f* (*de mujer*) breast; (*de animal*) teat; (*mamá*) mum.

mamá *f fam* mum, mummy.

mamadera *f Am* feeding bottle.

mamar *vt* to suck.

mamífero,-a *mf* mammal.

mampara *f* screen.

manada *f* (*de vacas, elefantes*) herd; (*de ovejas*) flock; (*de lobos, perros*) pack; (*de leones*) pride.

manantial *m* spring.

mancha *f* stain.

manchar 1 *vt* to stain. **2 mancharse** *vr* to get dirty.

manco,-a 1 *a* (*de un brazo*) one-armed; (*de una mano*) one-handed. **2** *mf* (*de un brazo*) one-armed person; (*de una mano*) one-handed person.

mancornas *fpl Am* cufflinks.

mandado *m* (*recado*) errand; **hacer un m.** to run an errand.

mandar *vt* (*ordenar*) to order; (*dirigir*) to be in charge of; (*ejército*) to command; (*enviar*) to send; **m. (a) por** to send for; **m. algo por correo** to send sth by post.

mandarina *f* mandarin.

mandíbula *f* jaw.

mando *m* (*autoridad*) command; (*control*) controls *pl;* **cuadro** *o* **tablero de mandos** dashboard; **m. a distancia** remote control.

manecilla *f* (*de reloj*) hand.

manejar 1 *vt* (*máquina, situación*) to handle; (*dirigir*) to manage; *Am* (*coche*) to drive. **2 manejarse** *vr* to manage.

manera *f* way, manner; **de cualquier m.** (*mal*) carelessly; (*en cualquier caso*) in any case; **de esta m.** in this way; **de ninguna m.** certainly not; **de todas maneras** anyway; **de m. que** so; **de tal m. que** in such a way that; **maneras** manners; **con buenas maneras** politely.

manga *f* sleeve; (*de riego*) hose; (*vuelta*) leg; (*en tenis*) set; **de m.**

corta/larga short-/long-sleeved; **sin mangas** sleeveless; *fig* **sacarse algo de la m.** to pull sth out of one's hat.

mango *m* handle.

manguera *f* hose.

maní *m* (*pl* **manises**) *Am* peanut.

maniático,-a **1** *a* fussy. **2** *mf* fusspot.

manicomio *m* mental hospital.

manifestación *f* demonstration; (*expresión*) expression.

manifestar [1] **1** *vt* (*declarar*) to state; (*mostrar*) to show. **2 manifestarse** *vr* (*por la calle*) to demonstrate.

manilla *f* (*de reloj*) hand; *Am* (*palanca*) lever.

manillar *m* handlebar.

maniobra *f* maneuver.

manipular *vt* to manipulate; (*máquina*) to handle.

maniquí *m* dummy.

manivela *f* crank.

manjar *m* delicacy, dish.

mano *f* hand; **a m.** (*sin máquina*) by hand; (*asequible*) at hand; **escrito a m.** hand-written; **hecho a m.** hand-made; **estrechar la m. a algn** to shake hands with sb; **de segunda m.** second-hand; **¡manos a la obra!** hands on the wheel!; **equipaje de m.** hand luggage; **a m. derecha/izquierda** on the right/left(-hand side); **m. de pintura** coat of paint; **m. de obra** labor (force).

manojo *m* bunch.

manopla *f* mitten.

manso,-a *a* (*animal*) tame.

manta *f* blanket.

manteca *f* fat; **m. de cacao/cacahuete** cocoa/peanut butter.

mantecado *m* shortcake.

mantel *m* tablecloth.

mantener **1** *vt* (*conservar*) to keep; (*entrevista, reunión*) to have; (*familia*) to support; (*sostener*) to hold up; **m. la línea** to keep in trim. **2 mantenerse** *vr* (*sostenerse*) to stand; (*sustentarse*) to live (**de** on);

mantenerse firme (*perseverar*) to hold one's ground.

mantenimiento *m* (*de máquina*) maintenance; (*alimento*) sustenance.

mantequilla *f* butter.

manto *m* cloak.

mantón *m* shawl.

mantuve *pt indef de* **mantener.**

manual **1** *a* manual; **trabajos manuales** handicrafts. **2** *m* (*libro*) manual.

manufactura *f* manufacture.

manzana *f* apple; (*de edificios*) block.

manzanilla *f* (*infusión*) camomile tea; (*vino*) manzanilla.

maña *f* (*astucia*) cunning; (*habilidad*) skill.

mañana **1** *f* (*parte de día*) morning; **de m.** early in the morning; **por la m.** in the morning. **2** *m* el m. tomorrow. **3** *adv* tomorrow; **¡hasta m.!** see you tomorrow! **m. por la m.** tomorrow morning; **pasado m.** the day after tomorrow.

mañoso,-a *a* skillful.

mapa *m* map.

maquillaje *m* make-up.

maquillar **1** *vt* to make up. **2 maquillarse** *vr* (*ponerse maquillaje*) to put one's make-up on; (*usar maquillaje*) to wear make-up.

máquina *f* machine; **escrito a m.** typewritten; **hecho a m.** machine-made; **m. de afeitar (eléctrica)** (electric) shaver; **m. de coser** sewing machine; **m. de escribir** typewriter; **m. fotográfica** o **de fotos** camera.

maquinaria *f* machinery; (*mecanismo*) mechanism.

maquinilla *f* **m. de afeitar** safety razor.

mar *m* & *f* sea; **en alta m.** on the high seas; *fam* **está la m. de guapa** she's looking really beautiful; **llover a mares** to rain cats and dogs.

maratón *mf* marathon.

maravilla *f* marvel; **de m.** wonder-

fully; **¡qué m. de película!** what a
wonderful film!

marca f mark; (de producto) brand;
(récord) record; **m. registrada** registered trademark.

marcar [1] vt to mark; (número) to
dial; (indicar) to indicate; (gol,
puntos) to score; (cabello) to set.

marcha f march; (de coche) gear;
hacer algo sobre la m. to do sth as
one goes along; **estar en m.** (vehículo) to be in motion; (máquina) to
be working; **poner en m.** to start;
m. atrás reverse (gear).

marchar 1 vi (ir) to walk; (aparato)
to be on; **m. bien** (negocio) to be going well. 2 **marcharse** vr to leave,
go away.

marco m (de cuadro etc) frame;
(moneda) mark.

marea f tide; **m. alta/baja** high/low
tide; **m. negra** oil slick.

marear 1 vt to make sick; (en el
mar) to make seasick; (en un
avión) to make airsick; (en un
coche) to make carsick; (aturdir) to
make dizzy; fam (fastidiar) to
annoy. 2 **marearse** vr to get sick/
seasick/airsick/carsick; (quedar
aturdido) to get dizzy.

marejada f swell.

mareo m (náusea) sickness; (en el
mar) seasickness; (en un avión)
airsickness; (en un coche) carsickness; (aturdimiento) dizziness.

marfil m ivory.

margarina f margarine.

margarita f daisy.

margen m edge; (de folio) margin;
fig **mantenerse al m.** not to get involved.

marginado,-a 1 a excluded. 2 mf
dropout.

marginar vt (a una persona) to exclude.

marido m husband.

mariguana, marihuana, marijuana f marijuana.

marinero,-a m sailor.

marioneta f marionette.

mariposa f butterfly.

mariquita f ladybird.

marisco m shellfish; **mariscos**
seafood.

marítimo,-a a maritime; **paseo
m.** promenade.

mármol m marble.

marqués m marquis.

marrano,-a 1 a (sucio) filthy. 2 mf
(animal) pig; (persona) fam slob.

marrón a & m brown.

marroquí a & mf Moroccan.

Marte m Mars.

martes m inv Tuesday.

martillo m hammer.

mártir mf martyr.

marzo m March.

más 1 adv more; **m. gente de la que
esperas** more people than you're
expecting; **m. de** more than, over;
cada día o **vez m.** more and more;
es m. what's more, furthermore; **lo
m. posible** as much as possible; **m.
bien** rather; **m. o menos** more or
less; **m. aún** even more; **¿qué m.
da?** what's the difference? ▪ (comparativo) **es m. alta/inteligente
que yo** she's taller/more intelligent than me. ▪ (superlativo) **el m.
bonito/caro** the prettiest/most expensive. ▪ (exclamación) **¡qué casa
m. bonita!** what a lovely house!;
¡está m. guapa! she looks so beautiful!. ▪ (después de pron interr e indef) else; **¿algo m.?** anything else?;
no, nada m. no, nothing else;
quién m.? who else?; **nadie/alguien m.** nobody/somebody else. ▪
por m. + (a /adv +) **que** + subjuntivo however (much); **por m. fuerte
que sea** however strong he may
be. 2 m inv **los/las m.** most people.
3 prep (en sumas) plus.

masa f mass; (de cosas) bulk; (de
pan etc) dough; **medios de comunicación de masas** mass media.

masaje m massage; **dar masaje(s)
(a)** to massage.

mascar [1] vti to chew.

máscara f mask; **m. de gas** gas
mask.

mascarilla f mask; **m. de oxígeno** oxygen mask; (*cosmética*) face pack.

masculino,-a a male; (*para hombre*) men's; (*género*) masculine.

máster m master's degree.

masticar [1] vt to chew.

mástil m mast.

mastín m mastiff.

mata f (*matorral*) shrub.

matador m matador, bullfighter.

matar vt to kill.

mate[1] a (*sin brillo*) matt.

mate[2] m mate; **jaque m.** checkmate.

matemática f, **matemáticas** fpl mathematics sing.

materia f matter; (*tema*) question; (*asignatura*) subject; **m. prima** raw material; **índice de materias** table of contents.

material 1 a material. **2** m material; **m. escolar/de construcción** teaching/building materials; **m. de oficina** office equipment.

materialmente adv physically.

maternal a maternal.

materno,-a a maternal; **abuelo m.** maternal grandfather; **lengua materna** mother tongue.

matiz m (*de color*) shade.

matorral m thicket.

matrero,-a mf Am (*bandolero*) bandit.

matrícula f registration; (*de coche*) (*número*) registration number; (*placa*) license plate.

matrimonio m marriage; (*pareja casada*) married couple; **m. civil/ religioso** civil/church wedding; **contraer m.** to marry; **cama de m.** double bed.

matriz f matrix, (*útero*) womb.

matrona f (*comadrona*) midwife.

maullar vi to mew.

maxilar 1 a maxillary. **2** jaw.

máximo,-a 1 a maximum. **2** m maximum; **al m.** to the utmost; **como m.** (*como mucho*) at the most; (*lo más tarde*) at the latest.

mayo m May.

mayonesa f mayonnaise.

mayor a (*comparativo*) (*tamaño*) bigger (**que** than); (*edad*) older, elder; (*superlativo*) (*tamaño*) biggest; (*edad*) oldest, eldest; (*adulto*) grown-up; (*maduro*) mature; (*principal*) major; **la m. parte** the majority; **la m. parte de las veces** most often; **ser m. de edad** to be of age; **al por m.** wholesale.

mayoría f majority; **la m. de los niños** most children; **m. de edad** majority.

mayúscula f capital letter.

mazapán m marzipan.

me pron pers (*objeto directo*) me; **no me mires** don't look at me. ▪ (*objeto indirecto*) me, to me, for me; **¿me das un caramelo?** will you give me a sweet?; **me lo dio** he gave it to me. ▪ (*pron reflexivo*) myself; **me he cortado** I've cut myself; **me voy/muero** (*no se traduce*) I'm off/dying.

mecánico,-a 1 a mechanical. **2** mf mechanic.

mecanismo m mechanism.

mecanografía f typing.

mecanógrafo,-a mf typist.

mecedora f rocking chair.

mecer [2] **1** vt to rock. **2 mecerse** vr to rock.

mecha f (*de vela*) wick; (*de pelo*) streak.

mechero,-a m (cigarette) lighter.

mechón m (*de pelo*) lock; (*de lana*) tuft.

medalla f medal.

media f stocking; Am (*calcetín*) sock; (*promedio*) average; **a medias** (*incompleto*) unfinished; (*entre dos*) half and half.

mediano,-a a (*tamaño*) medium-sized.

medianoche f midnight.

mediante prep by means of.

medicación f medication.

medicamento m medicine.

medicina f medicine; **estudiante de m.** medical student.

médico,-a 1 *mf* doctor; **m. de cabecera** family doctor. **2** *a* medical.
medida *f* measure; (*dimensión*) measurement; (*ropa*) made-to-measure; **a m. que avanzaba** as he advanced; **adoptar** o **tomar medidas** to take steps.
medieval *a* medieval.
medio,-a 1 *a* half; (*intermedio*) middle; (*normal*) average; **una hora y media** an hour and a half; **a media mañana/tarde** in the middle of the morning/afternoon; **clase media** middle class; **salario m.** average wage. **2** *adv* half; **está m. muerta** she is half dead. **3** *m* (*mitad*) half; (*centro*) middle; **en m. (de)** (*en el centro*) in the middle (of); (*entre dos*) in between; **medios de transporte** means of transport; **por m. de** by means of; **medios de comunicación** (mass) media; **m. ambiente** environment.
medioambiental *a* environmental.
mediocre *a* mediocre.
mediodía *m* (*hora exacta*) midday; (*período aproximado*) early afternoon; (*sur*) south.
medir [6] **1** *vt* to measure. **2** *vi* to measure; **mide 2 metros** he is 2 meters tall; **mide dos metros de alto/ancho/largo** it is two meters high/wide/long.
médula *f* marrow; **m. ósea** bone marrow.
megafonía *f* public-address system.
mejicano,-a *a* & *mf* Mexican.
mejilla *f* cheek.
mejillón *m* mussel.
mejor 1 *a* (*comparativo*) better (**que** than); (*superlativo*) best; **tu m. amiga** your best friend; **lo m.** the best thing. **2** *adv* (*comparativo*) better (**que** than); (*superlativo*) best; **cada vez m.** better and better; **m. dicho** or rather; **es el que m. canta** he is the one who sings the best; **a lo m.** (*quizás*) perhaps; (*ojalá*) hopefully.

mejora *f* improvement.
mejorar 1 *vti* to improve. **2 mejorarse** *vr* to get better; **¡que te mejores!** get well soon!
melancolía *f* melancholy.
melancólico,-a *a* melancholic.
melena *f* (head of) hair; (*de león*) mane.
mellizo,-a *a* & *mf* twin.
melocotón *m* peach.
melodía *f* tune.
melón *m* melon.
membrana *f* membrane.
membrillo *m* quince.
memoria *f* memory; (*informe*) report; **memorias** (*biografía*) memoirs; **aprender/saber algo de m.** to learn/know sth by heart.
mencionar *vt* to mention.
mendigo,-a *mf* beggar.
mendrugo *m* crust (of stale bread).
menear 1 *vt* to shake; (*cola*) to wag. **2 menearse** *vr* to shake.
menestra *f* vegetable stew.
menguar *vti* to diminish.
meñique *a* & *m* (**dedo**) **m.** little finger.
menor 1 *a* (*comparativo*) (*de tamaño*) smaller (**que** than); (*de edad*) younger (**que** than); (*superlativo*) (*de tamaño*) smallest; (*de intensidad*) least, slightest; (*de edad*) youngest; **ser m. de edad** to be a minor, to be under age; **al por m.** retail. **2** *mf* minor.
menos 1 *a* (*comparativo*) (*con singular*) less; (*con plural*) fewer; **m. dinero/leche/tiempo que** less money/milk/time than; **m. libros que** fewer books than; **tiene m. años de lo que parece** he's younger than he looks; (*superlativo*) **fui el que perdí m. dinero** I lost the least money. **2** *adv* **m. de** (*con singular*) less than; (*con plural*) fewer than, less than. ▪ (*superlativo*) (*con singular*) least; **el m. inteligente de la clase** the least intelligent boy in the class. ▪ (*con plural*) the fewest; **ayer fue**

cuando vinieron m. personas yesterday was when the fewest people came. ▪ (*locuciones*) **a m. que** + *subjuntivo* unless; **al** *o* **por lo m.** at least; **echar a algn de m.** to miss sb; **¡m. mal!** just as well! **ni mucho m.** far from it. **3** *prep* except; (*en restas*) minus.

menosprecio *m* contempt.

mensaje *m* message.

mensajero,-a *mf* messenger.

mensual *a* monthly.

menta *f* mint; (*licor*) crème de menthe.

mental *a* mental.

mente *f* mind.

mentir [5] *vi* to lie.

mentira *f* lie.

mentón *m* chin.

menú *m* menu.

menudo,-a **1** *a* minute; **¡m. lío/susto!** what a mess/fright! **2** *adv* **a m.** often.

mercado *m* market; **M. Común** Common Market.

mercadotecnia *f* marketing.

mercancías *fpl* goods.

mercantil *a* commercial.

merecer *vt* **1** to deserve; (*uso impers*) **no merece la pena hacerlo** it's not worth while doing it. **2 merecerse** *vr* to deserve.

merendar [1] **1** *vt* to have for tea. **2** *vi* to have tea.

merendero *m* (*en el campo*) picnic spot.

merezco *indic pres de* **merecer.**

meridional *a* southern.

merienda *f* afternoon snack.

mérito *m* merit.

merluza *f* hake.

mermelada *f* jam; (*de agrios*) marmalade; **m. de fresa** strawberry jam; **m. de naranja** orange marmalade.

mes *m* month; **el m. pasado/que viene** last/next month.

mesa *f* table; (*de despacho etc*) desk; **poner/recoger la m.** to set/clear the table.

meseta *f* plateau.

mesilla *f* **m. de noche** bedside table.

mesón *m* old-style tavern.

meta *f* (*objetivo, portería*) goal; (*de carrera*) finishing line.

metal *m* metal.

metálico,-a *a* metallic. **2** *m* **pagar en m.** to pay (in) cash.

meteorológico,-a *a* meteorological; **parte m.** weather report.

meter **1** *vt* (*poner*) to put (**en**, in); (*comprometer*) to involve (**en** in). **2 meterse** *vr* (*entrar*) to go/come in; (*entrometerse*) to meddle; (*estar*) **¿dónde te habías metido?** where have you been (all this time)?; **meterse con algn** (*en broma*) to get at sb.

método *m* method.

métrico,-a *a* metric; **sistema m.** metric system.

metro *m* meter; (*tren*) subway.

mexicano,-a *a* & *mf* Mexican.

mezcla *f* (*producto*) mixture; (*acción*) mixing.

mezclar **1** *vt* to mix; (*involucrar*) to involve. **2 mezclarse** *vr* (*cosas*) to get mixed up; (*gente*) to mingle.

mezquino,-a *a* (*tacaño*) mean; (*escaso*) miserable.

mezquita *f* mosque.

mi *a* my; **mis cosas/libros** my things/books.

mí *pron pers* me; **a mí me dio tres** he gave me three; **compra otro para mí** buy one for me too; **por mí mismo** by myself.

mía *a* & *pron pos f ver* **mío.**

microbús *m* minibus.

micrófono *m* microphone.

microonda *f* **un (horno) microondas** a microwave (oven).

microprocesador *m* microprocessor.

microscopio *m* microscope.

miedo *m* (*pavor*) fear; (*temor*) apprehension; **una película de m.** a horror film; **tener m. de algo/algn** to be afraid of sth/sb.

miedoso,-a *a* fearful.

miel *f* honey.

miembro *m* (*socio*) member; (*de cuerpo*) limb.

mientras 1 *conj* while; (*cuanto*) **m. más/menos . . .** the more/less . . . **2** *adv* **m. (tanto)** meanwhile, in the meantime.

miércoles *m inv* Wednesday; **M. de Ceniza** Ash Wednesday.

miga *f* (*de pan etc*) crumb.

mil *a & m* thousand; **m. pesetas** a o one thousand pesetas.

milagro *m* miracle.

milésimo,-a *a & mf* thousandth.

mili *f* military service; **hacer la m.** to do one's military service.

milímetro *m* millimeter.

militar 1 *a* military. **2** *mf* soldier.

milla *f* mile.

millar *m* thousand.

millón *m* million.

millonario,-a *a & mf* millionaire.

mimar *vt* to spoil.

mimbre *m* wicker.

mina *f* mine; (*de lápiz*) lead.

mineral 1 *a* mineral. **2** *m* ore.

minero,-a 1 *m* miner. **2** *a* mining.

miniatura *f* miniature.

minifalda *f* miniskirt.

mínimo,-a 1 *a* (*muy pequeño*) minute; (*en matemáticas*) minimum. **2** *m* minimum; **como m.** at least.

ministerio *m* department.

ministro,-a *mf* minister; **primer m.** Prime Minister.

minoría *f* minority; **m. de edad** minority.

minúsculo,-a *a* minute; **letra minúscula** small letter.

minusválido,-a 1 *a* disabled. **2** *mf* disabled person.

minuto *m* minute.

mío,-a 1 *a pos* of mine; **un amigo m.** a friend of mine; **no es asunto m.** it is none of my business. **2** *pron pos* mine.

miope *mf* short-sighted person.

mirada *f* look; **lanzar** *o* **echar una m. a** to glance at.

mirar 1 *vt* to look at; (*observar*) to watch; (*cuidar*) **mira que no le pase nada** see that nothing happens to him. **2** *vi* **la casa mira al norte** the house faces north.

mirlo *m* blackbird.

misa *f* mass.

miserable *a* (*mezquino*) (*persona*) despicable; (*sueldo etc*) miserable; (*pobre*) wretched.

miseria *f* (*pobreza extrema*) extreme poverty; (*insignificancia*) pittance; (*tacañería*) meanness.

misión *f* mission.

mismo,-a 1 *a* same; (*uso enfático*) **yo m.** I myself; **por eso m.** that is why; **por uno** *o* **sí m.** by oneself; **aquí m.** right here. **2** *pron* same; **es el m. de ayer** it's the same one as yesterday; **lo m.** the same (thing); **dar** *o* **ser lo m.** to make no difference. **3** *adv* **así m.** likewise.

misterio *m* mystery.

mitad *f* half; (*centro*) middle; **a m. de camino** half-way there; **a m. de precio** half price; **en la m. del primer acto** half-way through the first act.

mitote *m Am* uproar.

mixto *a* mixed.

mobiliario *m* furniture.

moca *m* mocha.

mochila *f* rucksack.

moco *m* snot; **sonarse los mocos** to blow one's nose.

mocoso,-a *mf fam* brat.

moda *f* fashion; **a la m., de m.** in fashion; **pasado de m.** old-fashioned.

modales *mpl* manners.

modelo 1 *a inv & m* model. **2** *mf* (fashion) model; **desfile de modelos** fashion show.

módem *m* modem.

moderado,-a *a* moderate.

modernizar [4] *vt*, **modernizarse** *vr* to modernize.

moderno,-a *a* modern.

modesto,-a *a* modest.

modificar [1] *vt* to modify.

modisto,-a *mf* fashion designer.

modo *m* (*manera*) way, manner;

mofarse vr to laugh (**de** at).

moflete m chubby cheek.

mohoso,-a a moldy; (oxidado) rusty.

mojar 1 vt to wet; (humedecer) to dampen. **2 mojarse** vr to get wet.

molde m mold.

moldeador m (del pelo) wave.

mole f mass.

moler [4] vt to grind.

molestar 1 vt (incomodar) to disturb; (causar malestar) to hurt; **¿le molestaría esperar fuera?** would you mind waiting outside? **2 molestarse** vr (tomarse la molestia) to bother; (ofenderse) to take offense.

molestia f bother; (dolor) slight pain.

molesto,-a a (irritante) annoying; **estar m. con algn** (enfadado) to be annoyed with sb.

molino m mill; **m. de viento** windmill.

momentáneo,-a a momentary.

momento m (instante) moment; (periodo) time; **al m.** at once; **de m.** for the time being; **en cualquier m.** at any time.

monasterio m monastery.

mondar 1 vt to peel. **2 mondarse** vr fam **m. (de risa)** to laugh one's head off.

moneda f (pieza) coin; (dinero) currency; **m. suelta** small change.

monedero m purse.

monetario,-a a monetary.

monigote m (persona) wimp; (dibujo) rough sketch (of a person).

monitor,-a mf monitor; (profesor) instructor.

monja f nun.

monje m monk.

mono,-a 1 m monkey; (prenda) (de trabajo) overalls pl; (de vestir) catsuit. **2** a fam (bonito) pretty.

monopolio m monopoly.

monótono,-a a monotonous.

monstruo m monster; (genio) genius.

montaje m (instalación) fitting; (ensamblaje) assembling.

montaña f mountain; **m. rusa** big dipper.

montañismo m mountaineering.

montañoso,-a a mountainous.

montar 1 vi (en bici, a caballo) to ride; (en coche, tren) to travel; (subirse) to get in. **2** vt (colocar) to put on; (máquina etc) to assemble; (negocio) to set up. **3 montarse** vr (subirse) to get on; (en coche) to get in.

monte m (montaña) mountain; (con nombre propio) mount.

montón m heap; **un m. de** a load of.

montura f (cabalgadura) mount; (de gafas) frame.

monumento m monument.

moño m bun.

moqueta f fitted carpet.

mora f (zarzamora) blackberry.

morado,-a a & m purple.

moral 1 a moral. **2** f (ética) morals pl; (ánimo) morale.

morboso,-a a (malsano) morbid.

morcilla f black pudding.

mordaz a biting.

morder [4] vt to bite.

mordida f Am (soborno) bribe.

mordisco m bite.

moreno,-a 1 a (pelo) dark-haired; (piel) dark-skinned; (bronceado) tanned; **ponerse m.** to get a suntan; **pan/azúcar m.** brown bread/ sugar. **2** mf (persona) (de pelo) dark-haired person; (mujer) brunette; (de piel) dark-skinned person.

morgue f Am morgue.

morir [7] **1** vi to die; **m. de frío/ hambre/cáncer** to die of cold/hunger/cancer. **2 morirse** vr to die; **morirse de hambre** to starve to death; fig to be starving; **morirse de aburrimiento** to be bored to death; **morirse de risa** to die laughing.

moro,-a a & mf Moor; fam (musulmán) Muslim; (árabe) Arab.

morocho,-a a Am (moreno) swarthy.

morro m (hocico) snout.

mortadela f mortadella.

mortal a mortal; (mortífero) fatal; **un accidente m.** a fatal accident.

mosca f fly; fam **estar m.** (suspicaz) to be suspicious; fam **por si las moscas** just in case.

moscardón m blowfly.

mosquito m mosquito.

mostaza f mustard.

mostrador m (de tienda) counter; (de bar) bar.

mostrar 1 vt to show. 2 **mostrarse** vr to be; **se mostró muy comprensiva** she was very understanding.

mota f speck.

mote[1] m (apodo) nickname.

mote[2] m Am boiled salted corn.

motín m (amotinamiento) mutiny; (disturbio) riot.

motivo m (causa) reason; **motivos** grounds; **con m. de** on the occasion of; **sin m.** for no reason at all.

moto f motorbike.

motocicleta f motorbike.

motociclista mf motorcyclist.

motor,-a a (grande) engine; (pequeño) motor; **m. de reacción** jet engine.

motora f motorboat.

motorista mf motorcyclist.

mover [4] 1 vt to move; (hacer funcionar) to drive. 2 **moverse** vr to move.

movimiento m movement; (en física) motion; (actividad) activity; **(poner algo) en m.** (to set sth) in motion.

moza f young girl.

mozo m boy; (de estación) porter; (de hotel) bellboy.

mucamo,-a mf Am servant.

muchacha f girl.

muchacho m boy.

muchedumbre f crowd.

mucho,-a 1 a sing lots of; (en frases negativas e interrogativas)

much; **hay m. tonto suelto** there are lots of idiots around; **no tengo m. dinero** I don't have much money; **¿bebes m. café?** do you drink a lot of coffee?; **m. tiempo** a long time; **tengo m. sueño/mucha sed** I am very sleepy/thirsty. ■ **muchos,-as** lots of; (en frases negativas e interrogativas) many; **no hay muchas chicas** there aren't many girls; **¿tienes muchos amigos?** do you have many friends?; **tiene muchos años** he is very old. 2 pron lots; **¿cuánta leche queda? — mucha** how much milk is there left?—a lot; **muchos,-as** lots; **¿cuántos libros tienes? — muchos** how many books have you got?— lots; **muchos creemos que . . .** many of us believe that . . . 3 adv a lot; **lo siento m.** I'm very sorry; **como m.** at the most; **con m.** by far; **m. antes/después** long before/ after; **¡ni m. menos!** no way!; **por m. (que)** + subj however much; **hace m. que no viene por aquí** he has not been to see us for a long time.

mudanza f move; **estar de m.** to be moving; **camión de m.** removal van.

mudar 1 vt (ropa) to change; (plumas, pelo) to molt; (de piel) to shed. 2 **mudarse** vr **mudarse de casa/ropa** to move house/to change one's clothes.

mudo,-a 1 a (que no habla) dumb. 2 mf mute.

mueble m piece of furniture; **muebles** furniture sing; **con/sin muebles** furnished/unfurnished.

muela f molar; **dolor de muelas** toothache; **m. del juicio** wisdom tooth.

muelle[1] m spring.

muelle[2] m (en puerto) dock.

muerte f death; **dar m. a algn** to kill sb; **odiar a algn a m.** to loathe sb; **un susto de m.** the fright of one's life.

muerto,-a 1 a dead; **m. de hambre**

starving; **m. de frío** frozen to death; **m. de miedo** scared stiff; **m. de risa** laughing one's head off; **(en) punto m.** (in) neutral. **2** *mf* (*difunto*) dead person; **hacerse el m.** to pretend to be dead.

muestra *f* (*espécimen*) sample; (*modelo a copiar*) model; (*prueba, señal*) sign; **dar muestras de** to show signs of; **m. de cariño/respeto** token of affection/respect.

mugido *m* (*de vaca*) moo; (*de toro*) bellow.

mugre *f* filth.

mujer *f* woman; (*esposa*) wife; **m. de la limpieza** cleaning lady; **m. de su casa** houseproud woman.

muleta *f* (*prótesis*) crutch; (*de torero*) muleta.

mulo,-a *mf* mule.

multa *f* fine; (*de tráfico*) ticket.

multicopista *f* duplicator.

multinacional *a* & *f* multinational.

múltiple *a* multiple.

multiplicación *f* multiplication.

multiplicar [1] **1** *vti* to multiply (**por** by). **2 multiplicarse** *vr* to multiply.

multitud *f* (*de personas*) crowd; (*de cosas*) multitude.

mundial 1 *a* worldwide; **campeón m.** world champion; **de fama m.** world-famous. **2** *m* world championship.

mundialmente *adv* **m. famoso** world-famous.

mundo *m* world; **todo el m.** everyone.

muñeca *f* wrist; (*juguete, muchacha*) doll.

muñeco *m* (*juguete*) (little) boy doll; **m. de trapo** rag doll; **m. de nieve** snowman.

munición *f* ammunition.

municipal *a* municipal; (*policía*) local.

municipio *m* municipality; (*ayuntamiento*) town council.

murciélago *m* bat.

murmullo *m* murmur.

murmurar *vi* (*criticar*) to gossip; (*susurrar*) to whisper; (*producir murmullo*) to murmur.

muro *m* wall.

músculo *m* muscle.

museo *m* museum.

musgo *m* moss.

música *f* music; **m. clásica** classical music.

musical *a* musical.

músico,-a *mf* musician.

muslo *m* thigh.

musulmán,-ana *a* & *mf* Muslim.

mutilado,-a *mf* disabled person.

mutuo,-a *a* mutual.

muy *adv* very; **m. bueno/malo** very good/bad; **¡m. bien!** very good!; **M. señor mío** Dear Sir; **m. de mañana/noche** very early/late.

N

nabo *m* turnip.

nácar *m* mother-of-pearl.

nacer *vi* to be born; (*pelo*) to begin to grow; (*río*) to rise; **nací en Montoro** I was born in Montoro.

nacimiento *m* birth; (*de río*) source; (*belén*) Nativity scene; **lugar de n.** place of birth.

nación *f* nation; **las Naciones Unidas** the United Nations.

nacional 1 *a* national; (*producto, mercado, vuelo*) domestic. **2** *mf* national.

nacionalidad *f* nationality.

nada 1 *pron* nothing; (*con verbo*) not . . . anything, nothing; **no sé n.** I don't know anything; **yo no digo n.** I'm saying nothing, I'm not saying anything; **más que n.** more than anything; **sin decir n.** without saying anything; **casi n.** hardly anything; **gracias — de n.** thanks —don't mention it; **para n.** not at all; **como si n.** just like that; **n. de eso** nothing of the kind; **n. de n.** nothing at all; **n. más verla** as soon as he saw her. **2** *adv* not at all; **no me gusta n.** I don't like it at all.

nadar *vi* to swim; **n. a braza** to do the breaststroke.

nadie *pron* no one, nobody; (*con verbo*) not . . . anyone, anybody; **no conozco a n.** I don't know anyone *o* anybody; **más que n.** more than anyone; **sin decírselo a n.** without telling anyone; **casi n.** hardly anyone.

nafta *f Am* (*gasolina*) gasoline.

nailon *m* nylon; **medias de n.** nylons.

naipe *m* playing card.

nalga *f* buttock.

nana *f* lullaby.

naranja 1 *f* orange. **2** *a & m* (*color*) orange.

naranjada *f* orangeade.

naranjo *m* orange tree.

narcotráfico *m* drug trafficking.

nariz *f* nose; **narices** nose *sing; fam* **meter las narices en algo** to poke one's nose into sth.

nata *f* cream; (*de leche hervida*) skin; **n. batida/montada** whipped cream.

natación *f* swimming.

natillas *fpl* custard *sing*.

natural 1 *a* natural; (*fruta, flor*) fresh; (*bebida*) at room temperature; **de tamaño n.** life-size. **2** *mf* native.

naturaleza *f* nature; **en plena n.** in unspoilt countryside.

naturalidad *f* (*sencillez*) naturalness; (*espontaneidad*) ease; **con n.** straightforwardly.

naturalizar [4] **1** *vt* to naturalize. **2 naturalizarse** *vr* to become naturalized.

naturalmente *adv* naturally; **¡n.!** of course!

naturismo *m* naturism.

naufragar [7] *vi* (*barco*) to be wrecked.

naufragio *m* shipwreck.

náusea *f* nausea; **me da n.** it makes me sick; **sentir náuseas** to feel sick.

navaja *f* (*cuchillo*) penknife; **n. de afeitar** razor.

nave *f* ship; (*de iglesia*) nave; **n. (espacial)** spaceship; **n. industrial** plant.

navegar [7] *vi* to sail.

Navidad(es) *f(pl)* Christmas; **árbol de Navidad** Christmas tree; **Feliz Navidad/Felices Navidades** Merry Christmas.

navideño,-a *a* Christmas.

navío *m* ship.

neblina *f* mist.

necesario,-a *a* necessary; **es n. hacerlo** it has to be done; **es n. que vayas** you must go; **no es n. que vayas** it's not necessary for you to go; **si fuera n.** if need be.

neceser *m* make-up bag.

necesidad *f* need; **por n.** of necessity; **tener n. de** to need.

necesitar *vt* to need.

necio,-a 1 *a* silly. **2** *mf* fool.

nectarina *f* nectarine.

neerlandés,-esa 1 *a* Dutch. **2** *mf* (*hombre*) Dutchman; (*mujer*) Dutchwoman; **los neerlandeses** the Dutch. **3** *m* (*idioma*) Dutch.

nefasto,-a *a* (*perjudicial*) harmful; (*funesto*) ill-fated.

negación *f* negation; (*negativa*) denial; (*gramatical*) negative.

negar [1] **1** *vt* to deny; (*rechazar*) to refuse; **negó haberlo robado** he denied stealing it; **le negaron la beca** they refused him the grant. **2 negarse** *vr* to refuse (**a** to).

negativo,-a *a & m* negative.

negligencia *f* negligence.

negociación *f* negotiation.

negociar 1 *vt* to negotiate. **2** *vi* (*comerciar*) to do business.

negocio *m* business; (*transacción*) deal; (*asunto*) affair; **hombre de negocios** businessman; **mujer de negocios** businesswoman.

negro,-a 1 *a* black; **verlo todo n.** to be very pessimistic. **2** *mf* (*hombre*) black; (*mujer*) black (woman); *fam* **trabajar como un n.** to work like a dog. **3** *m* (*color*) black.

nene,-a *mf* (*niño*) baby boy; (*niña*) baby girl.

neocelandés,-esa 1 *a* New Zealand. **2** *mf* New Zealander.

neoyorkino,-a 1 *a* New York. **2** *mf* New Yorker.

neozelandés,-esa *a* & *mf* = **neocelandés,-esa.**

nervio *m* nerve; (*de la carne*) sinew; **nervios** nerves; **ataque de n.** a fit of hysterics; **ser un manojo de n.** to be a bundle of nerves.

nervioso,-a *a* nervous; **poner n. a algn** to get on sb's nerves.

neto,-a *a* (*peso, cantidad*) net.

neumático,-a 1 *a* pneumatic. **2** *m* tire; **n. de recambio** spare tire.

neumonía *f* pneumonia.

neurótico,-a *a* & *mf* neurotic.

neutral *a* neutral.

neutro,-a *a* (*imparcial*) neutral; (*género*) neuter.

nevada *f* snowfall.

nevar [1] *v impers* to snow.

nevera *f* (*frigorífico*) fridge; (*portátil*) cool box.

ni *conj* no . . . ni, ni . . . ni neither . . . nor, not . . . or; **ni se te ocurra** don't even think about it

nicaragüense, nicaragüeño,-a *a* & *mf* Nicaraguan.

nido *m* nest.

niebla *f* fog; **hay mucha n.** it is very foggy.

nieto,-a *mf* (*niño*) grandson; (*niña*) granddaughter; **mis nietos** my grandchildren.

nieve *f* snow.

nigeriano,-a *a* & *mf* Nigerian.

ningún *a* (*delante de m sing*) ver **ninguno,-a.**

ninguno,-a 1 *a* (*con verbo*) not . . . any; **en ninguna parte** nowhere; **de ningún modo** no way. **2** *pron* (*persona*) nobody, no one; **n. de los dos** neither of the two; **n. de ellos** none of them; (*cosa*) not . . . any of them; (*enfático*) none of them; **no me gusta** I don't like any of them; **no vi n.** I saw none of them.

niña *f* girl; (*pupila*) pupil.

niñera *f* nanny.

niño,-a *mf* child; (*bebé*) baby; (*mu-*chacho) (small) boy; (*muchacha*) (little) girl; **de n.** as a child; **niños** children.

nitrógeno *m* nitrogen.

nivel *m* (*altura*) level; (*categoría*) standard; **a n. del mar** at sea level; **n. de vida** standard of living.

nº *abr de* **número** number, n.

no *adv* not; (*como respuesta*) no; **no vi a nadie** I did not see anyone, I didn't see anyone; **aún no** not yet; **ya no** no longer; **¿por qué no?** why not?; **no fumar/aparcar** no smoking/parking; **no sea que** + *subjuntivo* in case; **es rubia, ¿no?** she's blonde, isn't she?; **llegaron anoche, ¿no?** they arrived yesterday, didn't they?

noble 1 *a* noble. **2** *mf* (*hombre*) nobleman; (*mujer*) noblewoman; **los nobles** the nobility *sing*.

noche *f* evening; (*después de las diez*) night; **de n., por la n.** at night; **esta n.** tonight; **mañana por la n.** tomorrow night/evening; **buenas noches** (*saludo*) good evening; (*despedida*) good night.

nochebuena *f* Christmas Eve.

nochevieja *f* New Year's Eve.

nocturno,-a *a* night; **clases nocturnas** evening classes.

nombrar *vt* to name.

nombre *m* name; (*sustantivo*) noun; **n. de pila** Christian name; **n. y apellidos** full name; **n. propio** proper noun.

nordeste *a* & *m* northeast.

nórdico,-a 1 *a* (*del norte*) northern; (*escandinavo*) Nordic. **2** *m* Nordic person.

noreste *a* & *m* northeast.

norma *f* norm.

normal *a* normal; **lo n.** the usual.

normalizar [4] **1** *vt* to normalize. **2 normalizarse** *vr* to return to normal.

noroeste *a* & *m* northwest.

norte *m* north; **al n. de** to the north of.

norteafricano,-a *a* & *mf* North African.

norteamericano,-a *a & mf* (North) American.

noruego,-a 1 *a* Norwegian. **2** *mf* Norwegian. **3** *m* (*idioma*) Norwegian.

nos *pron pers* us; (*con verbo reflexivo*) ourselves; (*con verbo recíproco*) each other; **n. hemos divertido mucho** we enjoyed ourselves a lot; **n. queremos mucho** we love each other very much.

nosotros,-as *pron pers* (*sujeto*) we; (*complemento*) us; **con n.** with us.

nostalgia *f* nostalgia; (*morriña*) homesickness.

nota *f* note; (*de examen*) mark, grade; **sacar buenas notas** to get good grades.

notable 1 *a* (*apreciable*) noticeable; (*digno de notar*) outstanding. **2** *m* (*nota*) very good.

notar 1 *vt* (*percibir*) to notice. **2 notarse** *vr* (*percibirse*) to show; **no se nota** it doesn't show.

notario,-a *mf* notary (public).

noticia *f* news *sing;* **una n.** a piece of news; **una buena n.** (some) good news.

notificar [1] *vt* to notify.

novato,-a 1 *a* (*persona*) inexperienced. **2** *mf* (*principiante*) novice.

novecientos,-as *a inv & mf inv* nine hundred.

novedad *f* (*cosa nueva*) novelty; (*cambio*) change; (*cualidad*) newness.

novela *f* novel; (*corta*) story.

noveno,-a *a & m* ninth; **novena parte** ninth.

noventa *a & m inv* ninety.

novia *f* (*amiga*) girlfriend; (*prometida*) fiancée; (*en boda*) bride.

noviembre *m* November.

novillada *f* bullfight with young bulls.

novillo,-a *mf* (*toro*) young bull; (*vaca*) young cow; **hacer novillos** to play hooky.

novio *m* (*amigo*) boyfriend; (*prometido*) fiancé; (*en boda*) bride-groom; **los novios** the bride and groom.

nube *f* cloud.

nublarse *vr* to cloud over.

nuca *f* back of the neck.

nuclear *a* nuclear; **central n.** nuclear power station.

núcleo *m* nucleus; (*parte central*) core.

nudillo *m* knuckle.

nudista *a & mf* nudist.

nudo *m* knot; **hacer un n.** to tie a knot.

nuera *f* daughter-in-law.

nuestro,-a 1 *a pos* our; **un amigo n.** a friend of ours. **2** *pron pos* ours; **este libro es n.** this book is ours.

nuevamente *adv* again.

nueve *a & m inv* nine.

nuevo,-a *a* new.

nuez *f* walnut; **n. (de Adán)** Adam's apple.

numérico,-a *a* digital.

número *m* number; (*de zapatos*) size; **n. de matrícula** license number.

numeroso,-a *a* numerous.

nunca *adv* never; (*enfático*) not . . . ever; **no he estado n. en España** I've never been to Spain; **yo no haría n. eso** I wouldn't ever do that; **casi n.** hardly ever; **más que n.** more than ever; **n. jamás** never ever; (*futuro*) never again.

nutrición *f* nutrition.

nutritivo,-a *a* nutritious; **valor n.** nutritional value.

ñame *m Am* yarn.

ñapa *f Am* bonus.

ñato,-a *a Am* snub-nosed.

ñoño,-a 1 *a* (*soso*) dull. **2** *mf* dullard.

O

o *conj* or; **o . . . o** either . . . or; **o sea** in other words.

oasis *m inv* oasis.

obedecer *vt* to obey.

obediente *a* obedient.

obeso,-a *a* obese.

obispo *m* bishop.

objetivo,-a 1 *m* (*fin, meta*) objective; (*de cámara*) lens. **2** *a* objective.

objeto *m* object; (*fin*) purpose; **con o. de . . .** in order to . . .

obligación *f* (*deber*) obligation; **por o.** out of a sense of duty.

obligar [7] *vt* to force.

obligatorio,-a *a* obligatory.

obra *f* (*trabajo*) work; **o. maestra** masterpiece; (*acto*) deed; (*construcción*) building site; **'carretera en o.'** 'roadworks'.

obrar *vi* (*proceder*) to act; **o. bien/mal** to do the right/wrong thing.

obrero,-a 1 *mf* worker. **2** *a* working; **clase obrera** working class.

obsceno,-a *a* obscene.

obsequio *m* gift.

observador,-a 1 *mf* observer. **2** *a* observant.

observar *vt* (*mirar*) to watch; (*notar*) to notice; (*cumplir*) to observe.

obsesión *f* obsession.

obstáculo *m* obstacle.

obstante (no) 1 *adv* nevertheless. **2** *prep* notwithstanding.

obstinado,-a *a* obstinate.

obstinarse *vr* to persist (**en** in).

obstruir 1 *vt* (*salida, paso*) to block. **2 obstruirse** *vr* to get blocked up.

obtener *vt* (*alcanzar*) to obtain, get.

obvio,-a *a* obvious.

oca *f* goose.

ocasión *f* (*momento*) occasion; (*oportunidad*) opportunity; (*saldo*) bargain; **en cierta o.** once; **aprovechar la o.** to make the most of an opportunity.

ocasional *a* (*eventual*) occasional; **de forma o.** occasionally.

ocasionar *vt* to cause.

occidental *a* western.

occidente *m* West.

océano *m* ocean.

ochenta *a & m inv* eighty.

ocho *a & m inv* eight.

ochocientos,-as *a & m inv* eight hundred.

ocio *m* leisure.

octavo,-a *a & mf* eighth.

octubre *m* October.

oculista *mf* ophthalmologist.

ocultar 1 *vt* to conceal; **o. algo a algn** to hide sth from sb. **2 ocultarse** *vr* to hide.

ocupación *f* (*tarea*) occupation.

ocupado,-a *a* (*persona*) busy; (*asiento*) taken; (*aseos, teléfono*) engaged; (*puesto de trabajo*) filled.

ocupante *mf* occupant; (*ilegal*) squatter.

ocupar 1 *vt* to occupy; (*espacio, tiempo*) to take up; (*cargo*) to hold. **2 ocuparse** *vr* **ocuparse de** (*cuidar*) to look after; (*encargarse*) to see to.

ocurrencia *f* (*agudeza*) witty remark; (*idea*) idea.

ocurrente *a* witty.

ocurrir 1 *v impers* to happen; **¿qué te ocurre?** what's the matter with you? **2 ocurrirse** *vr* **no se me ocurre nada** I can't think of anything.

odiar *vt* to hate.

odio *m* hatred.

odontólogo,-a *mf* dental surgeon.

oeste *a & m* west.

ofender 1 *vt* to offend. **2 ofenderse** *vr* to take offense (**con, por** at).

ofensa *f* offense.

oferta *f* offer; (*presupuesto*) bid.

oficial,-a 1 *a* official. **2** *m* (*rango*) officer; (*obrero*) skilled worker.

oficialismo *m Am* (*gobierno*) government.

oficina *f* office; **o. de turismo** tourist office; **o. de correos** post office.

oficinista *mf* office worker.

oficio *m* (*ocupación*) occupation; (*profesión*) trade.

ofrecer 1 *vt* to offer; (*aspecto*) to present. **2 ofrecerse** *vr* (*prestarse*) to offer; (*situación*) to present itself.

ofrezco *indic pres de* **ofrecer.**

oftalmólogo,-a *mf* ophthalmologist.

oído *m* (*sentido*) hearing; (*órgano*) ear.

oír *vt* to hear; ¡**oye!** hey!; ¡**oiga!** excuse me!

ojal *m* buttonhole.

ojalá 1 *interj* let's hope so! **2** *conj* + *subjuntivo* ¡**o. sea cierto!** I hope it is true!

ojeada *f* **echar una o.** to have a quick look (**a** at).

ojeras *fpl* bags under the eyes.

ojo 1 *m* eye; (*de cerradura*) keyhole; **calcular a o.** to guess. **2** *interj* careful!

ojota *f Am* sandal.

ola *f* wave.

oleaje *m* swell.

oleoducto *m* pipeline.

oler [4] **1** *vt* to smell. **2** *vi* (*exhalar*) to smell; **o. a** to smell of; **o. bien/mal** to smell good/bad.

olfato *m* sense of smell.

olimpiada *f* Olympic Games *pl*; **las olimpiadas** the Olympic Games.

olímpico,-a *a* Olympic.

oliva *f* olive; **aceite de o.** olive oil.

olivo *m* olive (tree).

olmo *m* elm.

olor *m* smell.

olvidar 1 *vt* to forget; (*dejar*) to leave. **2 olvidarse** *vr* **olvidarse de algo** to forget sth.

olla *f* saucepan; **o. exprés** *o* **a presión** pressure cooker.

ombligo *m* navel.

omisión *f* omission.

omitir *vt* to omit.

omnipotente *a* almighty.

omóplato, omoplato *m* shoulder blade.

once *inv a & m* eleven.

onda *f* wave; (*en el agua*) ripple; **o. larga/media/corta** long/medium/short wave.

ondulado,-a *a* (*pelo*) wavy; (*paisaje*) rolling.

ONU *f abr de* **Organización de las Naciones Unidas** United Nations (Organization), UN(O).

opaco,-a *a* opaque.

opcional *a* optional.

ópera *f* opera.

operación *f* operation; (*financiera*) transaction.

operador,-a *mf* operator; (*de la cámara*) (*hombre*) cameraman; (*mujer*) camerawoman.

operar 1 *vt* to operate (**a** on). **2 operarse** *vr* to have an operation (**de** for); (*producirse*) to take place.

opinar *vi* (*pensar*) to think; (*declarar*) to give one's opinion.

opinión *f* opinion; **cambiar de o.** to change one's mind.

oponer (*pp* **opuesto**) **1** *vt* (*resistencia*) to offer. **2 oponerse** *vr* (*estar en contra*) to be against.

oporto *m* (*vino*) port.

oportunidad *f* opportunity.

oportuno,-a *a* timely; (*conveniente*) appropriate.

oposición *f* opposition; (*examen*) competitive examination.

opresión *f* oppression.

oprimir *vt* (*pulsar*) to press; (*subyugar*) to oppress.

optativo,-a *a* optional.

óptica *f* (*tienda*) optician's (shop).

óptico,-a 1 *a* optical. **2** *mf* optician.

optimista 1 *a* optimistic. **2** *mf* optimist.

óptimo,-a *a* excellent; (*condiciones*) optimum.

opuesto,-a *a* (*contrario*) contrary; (*de enfrente*) opposite; **en direcciones opuestas** in opposite directions.

opuse *pt indef de* **oponer.**

oración *f* (*plegaria*) prayer.

oral *a* oral; **por vía o.** to be taken orally.

orar *vi* to pray.

orden 1 *m* order; **o. público** law and order; **por o. alfabético** in alphabetical order; **del o. de** in the order of. **2** *f* order; (*judicial*) warrant; ¡**a la o.!** sir!

ordenado,-a *a* tidy.

ordenador,-a *m* computer; **o. de sobremesa** desktop (computer); **o. doméstico** home computer.

ordenanza 1 *m* (*empleado*) office boy. **2** *f* regulations *pl*.

ordenar *vt* (*organizar*) to put in order; (*habitación*) to tidy up; (*mandar*) to order.

ordeñar *vt* to milk.

ordinario,-a *a* (*corriente*) ordinary; (*grosero*) common.

orégano *m* oregano.

oreja *f* ear.

orejero,-a *a* (*soplón*) grass.

orfanato, orfelinato *m* orphanage.

orgánico,-a *a* organic.

organismo *m* organism; (*institución*) body.

organización *f* organization.

organizar [4] **1** *vt* to organize. **2 organizarse** *vr* (*armarse*) to happen.

órgano *m* organ.

orgullo *m* (*propia estima*) pride; (*arrogancia*) arrogance.

orgulloso,-a *a* estar o. (*satisfecho*) to be proud; ser o. (*arrogante*) to be arrogant.

orientación *f* (*dirección*) orientation; (*guía*) guidance.

oriental 1 *a* eastern. **2** *mf* Oriental.

orientar 1 *vt* (*indicar camino*) to give directions to; **una casa orientada al sur** a house facing south. **2 orientarse** *vr* (*encontrar el camino*) to get one's bearings.

oriente *m* East; **el Extremo** *o* **Lejano/Medio/Próximo O.** the Far/Middle/Near East.

orificio *m* hole; (*del cuerpo*) orifice.

origen *m* origin; **dar o. a** to give rise to.

original *a & mf* original.

orilla *f* (*borde*) edge; (*del río*) bank; (*del mar*) shore.

orinal *m* chamberpot; *fam* potty.

orinar 1 *vi* to urinate. **2 orinarse** *vr* to wet oneself.

oro *m* gold; **de o.** golden; **o. de ley** fine gold.

orquesta *f* orchestra; (*de verbena*) dance band.

ortiga *f* (stinging) nettle.

ortodoxo,-a *a & mf* orthodox.

ortografía, *f* spelling.

ortográfico,-a *a* spelling.

ortopédico,-a *a* orthopedic.

oruga *f* caterpillar.

orzuelo *m* sty(e).

os *pron pers* (*complemento directo*) you; (*complemento indirecto*) (to) you; (*con verbo reflexivo*) yourselves; (*con verbo recíproco*) each other; **os veo mañana** I'll see you tomorrow; **os daré el dinero** I'll give you the money; **os escribiré** I'll write to you.

osadía *f* (*audacia*) daring; (*desvergüenza*) impudence.

oscilar *vi* (*variar*) to fluctuate.

oscuras (a) *adv* in the dark.

oscurecer 1 *vi impers* to get dark. **2** *vt* (*ensombrecer*) to darken. **3 oscurecerse** *vr* (*nublarse*) to become cloudy.

oscuridad *f* darkness; *fig* obscurity.

oscuro,-a *a* dark; (*origen, idea*) obscure; (*nublado*) overcast.

oscuro,-a *a* = obscuro,-a.

osito *m* **o.** (**de peluche**) teddy bear.

oso *m* bear; **o. polar** polar bear.

ostentación *f* ostentation.

osteópata *mf* osteopath.

ostra *f* oyster; **aburrirse como una o.** to be bored stiff.

OTAN *f abr de* **Organización del Tratado del Atlántico Norte** North Atlantic Treaty Organization, NATO.

otoño *m* autumn, fall.

otorgar [7] *vt* (*premio*) to award (**a** to).

otorrinolaringólogo,-a *mf* ear, nose and throat specialist.

otro,-a 1 *a indef* **otro/otra . . .** another . . .; **otros/otras . . .** other . . .; **el otro/la otra . . .** the other . . .; **otra cosa** something else; **otra vez** again. **2** *pron indef* another (one); **otros/otras** others; **el otro/la otra** the other (one); **los otros/las otras** the others.

oval, ovalado,-a a oval.
oveja f sheep; (hembra) ewe; **la o. negra** the black sheep.
overol m Am overalls pl.
ovillo m ball (of wool).
OVNI m abr de **objeto volador no identificado** UFO.
oxidar 1 vt (metales) to rust. **2 oxidarse** vr (metales) to rust.
oxígeno m oxygen.
oye indic pres & imperativo de **oír.**
ozono m ozone; **capa** f **de o.** ozone layer.

P

pabellón m (en feria) stand; (bloque) wing; **p. de deportes** sports center.
paciencia f patience.
pacificar [1] vt to pacify.
pacotilla f **de p.** second-rate.
pactar vt to agree.
padecer vti to suffer; **padece del corazón** he suffers from heart trouble.
padrastro m stepfather; (pellejo) hangnail.
padre m father; **padres** parents.
padrenuestro m Lord's Prayer.
padrino m (de bautizo) godfather; (de boda) best man; **padrinos** godparents.
padrón m census.
paella f paella (rice dish made with vegetables, meat and/or seafood).
pág abr de **página** page, p.
paga f (salario) wage; **p. extra** bonus.
pagar [7] vti to pay; (recompensar) to repay; **p. en metálico** o **al contado** to pay cash.
página f page.
pago m payment; **p. adelantado** o **anticipado** advance payment.
paila f Am (frying) pan.
país m country; **P. Vasco** Basque Country; **P. Valenciano** Valencia.
paisaje m landscape.
paja f straw.

pajarita f bow tie; (de papel) paper bird.
pájaro m bird; **p. carpintero** woodpecker.
pakistaní a & mf Pakistani.
pala f shovel; (de jardinero) spade; (de ping-pong, frontón) bat; (de remo) blade.
palabra f word; **dirigir la p. a algn** to address sb; **juego de palabras** pun; **p. de honor** word of honor.
palabrota f swearword.
palacio m (grande) palace; (más pequeño) mansion.
paladar m palate.
paladear vt to savor.
palanca f lever; (manecilla) handle; **p. de cambio** gearshift.
palco m box.
palestino,-a a & mf Palestinian.
paleta f (espátula) slice; (de pintor) palette; (de albañil) trowel; (de ping-pong) bat.
paletilla f shoulder blade.
paleto,-a 1 a boorish. **2** mf country bumpkin.
paliar vt to alleviate.
palidecer vi (persona) to turn pale.
palidez f paleness.
pálido,-a a pale.
palillero m toothpick case.
palillo m (mondadientes) toothpick; **palillos chinos** chopsticks; (de tambor) drumstick.
paliza f beating; **darle a algn una p.** to give sb a thrashing.
palma f palm; (árbol) palm tree; **hacer palmas** to applaud.
palmada f slap.
palmera f palm tree.
palmo m **p. a p.** inch by inch.
palo m stick; (vara) rod; (de escoba) broomstick; (golpe) blow; (madera) wood; (de portería) woodwork; (de golf) club.
paloma f pigeon; (como símbolo) dove.
palomar m pigeon house.
palomitas (de maíz) fpl popcorn sing.

palpar vt to feel.

palpitar vi to palpitate.

palurdo,-a a boorish.

pamela f broad-brimmed hat.

pampa f pampa, pampas pl.

pan m bread; **p. de molde** loaf of sliced bread; **p. integral** whole-wheat bread; **p. rallado** bread-crumbs pl.

pana f corduroy.

panadería f bakery.

panameño,-a a & mf Panamanian.

pancarta f placard; (en manifestación) banner.

panda[1] m panda.

panda[2] f (de amigos) gang.

pandilla f gang.

panfleto m pamphlet.

pánico m panic; **sembrar el p.** to cause panic.

panorama m panorama.

pantaletas fpl Am panties.

pantalones mpl trousers pl; **p. vaqueros** jeans pl.

pantalla f (monitor) screen; (de lámpara) shade.

pantano m (natural) marsh; (artificial) reservoir.

pantera f panther.

pantorrilla f calf.

pantufla f slipper.

panty m (pair of) tights pl.

panza f fam belly.

pañal m diaper.

paño m cloth.

pañuelo m handkerchief; (pañoleta) shawl.

papa[1] f (patata) potato.

Papa m **el P.** the Pope.

papá m fam dad, daddy.

papada f double chin.

papagayo m parrot.

papel m paper; (hoja) piece of paper; (rol) role; **papeles** (documentos) identification papers; **p. higiénico** toilet paper; **p. de aluminio** aluminum foil; **p. pintado** wallpaper.

papelera f (en despacho) wastepaper basket; (en calle) trash can.

papelería f (tienda) stationer's.

papeleta f (de rifa) ticket; (de votación) ballot.

paperas fpl mumps sing.

papilla f mush; (de niños) baby food.

paquete m packet; (postal) parcel.

paquistaní a & mf Pakistani.

par 1 a (número) even. 2 m (pareja) pair; (dos) couple; **a la p.** (a la vez) at the same time; **de p. en p.** wide open.

para prep for; (finalidad) to, in order to; (tiempo) by; (a punto de) **está p. salir** it's about to leave; **p. terminar antes** (in order) to finish earlier; **p. entonces** by then; **¿p. qué?** what for?; **ir p. viejo** to be getting old; **no es p. tanto** it's not as bad as all that; **p. mí** in my opinion.

parabólico,-a a **antena parabólica** satellite dish.

parabrisas m inv windshield.

paracaidista mf parachutist; (soldado) paratrooper.

parachoques m inv bumper, fender.

parada f stop; **p. de autobús** bus stop; **p. de taxis** taxi rank.

paradero m (lugar) whereabouts pl; (apeadero) stop.

parado,-a 1 a stopped; (quieto) still; (fábrica) at a standstill; (desempleado) unemployed; Am (de pie) standing; fig **salir bien/mal p.** to come off well/badly. 2 mf unemployed person.

parador m roadside inn; **p. nacional** o **de turismo** luxury hotel.

paraguas m inv umbrella.

paraíso m paradise.

paralelo,-a a & m parallel.

paralítico,-a a & mf paralytic.

paralizar [1] vt to stop; (circulación) to stop. 2 **paralizarse** vr to come to a standstill.

parapeto m parapet; (de defensa) barricade.

parar 1 vt to stop; (balón) to save.

2 vi to stop; (alojarse) to stay; **sin p.** nonstop; **fue a p. a la cárcel** he ended up in jail. **3 pararse** vi to stop; Am (ponerse en pie) to stand up.

pararrayos m inv lightning rod.

parásito,-a a & m parasite.

parcela f plot.

parche m patch; (emplasto) plaster.

parchís m ≈ ludo.

parcial a (partidario) biased; (no completo) partial; **a tiempo p.** part-time.

parcialmente adv partly.

pardo,-a a (marrón) brown; (gris) dark grey.

parecer 1 vi to seem; **parece que no arranca** it looks as if it won't start; **como te parezca** whatever you like; **¿te parece?** is that okay with you?; **¿qué te parece?** what do you think of it? **2 parecerse** vr to be alike; **parecerse a** to look like.

parecido,-a a similar; **bien p.** good-looking. **2** m resemblance.

pared f wall.

pareja f pair; (hombre y mujer) couple; (de baile, juego) partner; **por parejas** in pairs; **hacen buena p.** they make a nice couple.

parentesco m relationship.

paréntesis m inv bracket; **entre p.** in brackets.

parezco indic pres de **parecer.**

pariente mf relative, relation.

parir 1 vt to give birth to. **2** vi to give birth.

parlamento m parliament.

paro m (huelga) strike; (desempleo) unemployment; **estar en p.** to be unemployed; **cobrar el p.** to be on the dole.

parpadear vi (ojos) to blink; (luz) to flicker.

párpado m eyelid.

parque m park; (de niños) playpen; **p. de atracciones** amusement park; **p. zoológico** zoo; **p. nacional/natural** national park/nature reserve.

parquear vti Am to park.

parquímetro m parking meter.

parra f grapevine.

párrafo m paragraph.

parrilla f grill; **pescado a la p.** grilled fish.

párroco m parish priest.

parroquia f parish; (iglesia) parish church.

parte 1 f (sección) part; (en una repartición) share; (lugar) place; (en juicio) party; **en** o **por todas partes** everywhere; **por mi p.** as far as I am concerned; **de p. de . . .** on behalf of . . . ; **¿de p. de quién?** who's calling?; **en gran p.** to a large extent; **en p.** partly; **la mayor p.** the majority; **por otra p.** on the other hand. **2** m (informe) report.

participación f participation; (acción) share; (notificación) notification.

participar 1 vi to take part, participate (**en** in). **2** vt (notificar) to notify.

participio m participle.

particular 1 a (concreto) particular; (privado) private; (raro) peculiar. **2** mf (individuo) private individual.

partida f (salida) departure; (remesa) batch; (juego) game; (certificado) certificate; **p. de nacimiento** birth certificate.

partidario,-a a **ser/no ser p. de algo** to be for/against sth. **2** mf supporter.

partido,-a m party; (de fútbol) match, game; **sacar p. de** to profit from.

partir 1 vt to break; (dividir) to split; (cortar) to cut. **2** vi (marcharse) to leave; **a p. de** from. **3 partirse** vr to split (up); **partirse de risa** to split one's sides laughing.

partitura f score.

parto m labor; childbirth.

pasa f raisin.

pasadizo m corridor.

pasado,-a 1 a (último) last; (anticuado) old-fashioned; (alimento) bad; (*cocido*) cooked; **p. (de moda)** out of date; **p. mañana** the day after tomorrow. **2** *m* past.

pasaje *m* passage; (*calle*) alley; (*pasajeros*) passengers *pl*; (*billete*) ticket.

pasajero,-a 1 *a* passing. **2** *mf* passenger.

pasamanos *m inv* (*barra*) handrail; (*de escalera*) banister.

pasaporte *m* passport.

pasar 1 *vt* to pass; (*página*) to turn; (*trasladar*) to move; (*tiempo*) to spend, pass; (*padecer*) to suffer; (*cruzar*) to cross; (*límite*) to go beyond; **p. hambre** to go hungry. **2** *vi* to pass; (*entrar*) to come in; **p. a** (*continuar*) to go on to; **p. de largo** to go by (without stopping). **3** *v impers* (*suceder*) to happen; **¿qué pasa aquí?** what's going on here?; **¿qué te pasa?** what's the matter?; **pase lo que pase** come what may. **4 pasarse** *vr* (*comida*) to go off; (*excederse*) to go too far; **se me pasó la ocasión** I missed my chance; **se le pasó llamarme** he forgot to phone me; **pasarse el día haciendo algo** to spend the day doing sth; **pasárselo bien/mal** to have a good/bad time.

pasatiempo *m* pastime, hobby.

pascua *f* Easter; **pascuas** (*Navidad*) Christmas *sing*; **¡Felices Pascuas!** Merry Christmas!

pasear 1 *vi* to go for a walk. **2** *vt* (*perro*) to walk. **3 pasearse** *vr* to go for a walk.

paseo *m* walk; (*en bicicleta, caballo*) ride; (*en coche*) drive; (*avenida*) avenue; **dar un p.** to go for a walk/ride/drive.

pasillo *m* corridor.

pasión *f* passion.

pasivo,-a *a* passive; (*inactivo*) inactive.

paso *m* step; (*modo de andar*) gait; (*ruido al andar*) footstep; (*camino*) way; (*acción*) passage; (*de montaña*) mountain pass; **abrirse p.** to force one's way through; **'ceda el**

p.' 'give way'; **'prohibido el p.'** 'no entry'; **p. de peatones** pedestrian crossing, crosswalk; **el p. del tiempo** the passage of time; **estar de p.** to be just passing through.

pasta *f* paste; (*italiana*) pasta; (*galleta*) biscuit; *fam* (*dinero*) dough; **p. de dientes** *o* **dentífrica** toothpaste.

pastel *m* cake; (*de carne, fruta*) pie.

pastelería *f* pastry shop, bakery.

pastilla *f* tablet; (*de jabón*) bar; **pastillas para la tos** cough drops.

pastor,-a 1 *mf* shepherd; (*mujer*) shepherdess; **p. alemán** Alsatian. **2** *m* (*sacerdote*) pastor.

pata *f* leg; **patas arriba** upside down; **mala p.** bad luck; **meter la p.** to put one's foot in it.

patada *f* kick; (*en el suelo*) stamp.

patalear *vi* to stamp one's feet (with rage).

patán *m* bumpkin.

patata *f* potato; **patatas fritas** French fries; (*de bolsa*) potato chips.

paté *m* pâté.

patentar *vt* to patent.

paternal *a* paternal.

paterno,-a *a* paternal.

patilla *f* (*de gafas*) leg; **patillas** (*pelo*) sideburns.

patín *m* skate; (*hidropedal*) pedal boat; **p. de ruedas/de hielo** roller/ice skate.

patinaje *m* skating; **p. artístico** figure skating; **p. sobre hielo/ruedas** ice-/roller-skating.

patinar *vi* to skate; (*sobre ruedas*) to roller-skate; (*sobre hielo*) to ice-skate; (*deslizarse*) to slide; *resbalar*) to slip; (*vehículo*) to skid.

patinete *m* scooter.

patio *m* (*de una casa*) patio; (*de recreo*) playground; **p. de butacas** stalls.

pato *m* duck.

patria *f* homeland.

patrimonio *m* (*bienes*) wealth; (*heredado*) inheritance.

patriotismo *m* patriotism.
patrocinar *vt* to sponsor.
patrón,-ona 1 *mf* (*jefe*) boss; (*de pensión*) (*hombre*) landlord; (*mujer*) landlady. 2 *m* pattern.
patronal 1 *a* employers'. 2 *f* employers' organization.
patronato, patronazgo *m* (*institución benéfica*) foundation; (*protección*) patronage.
patrono,-a *mf* boss; (*empresario*) employer.
patrulla *f* patrol.
paulatino,-a *a* gradual.
pausa *f* pause; (*musical*) rest.
pavimento *m* (*de calle*) paving.
pavo *m* turkey.
pavor *m* terror.
payaso *m* clown.
payo,-a *mf* non-Gipsy.
paz *f* peace; (*sosiego*) peacefulness; **¡déjame en p.!** leave me alone!
peaje *f* toll; **autopista de p.** turnpike.
peatón *m* pedestrian.
peca *f* freckle.
pecado *m* sin.
pecera *f* fishtank.
pecho *m* chest; (*de mujer, animal*) breast; **dar el p. (a un bebé)** to breast-feed (a baby).
pechuga *f* (*de ave*) breast.
pectoral *a* chest.
peculiar *a* (*raro*) peculiar; (*característico*) characteristic.
pedagógico,-a *a* pedagogical.
pedal *m* pedal.
pedante 1 *a* pedantic. 2 *mf* pedant.
pedazo *m* piece, bit; **hacer pedazos** to smash to pieces; (*papel, tela*) to tear to pieces.
pediatra *mf* pediatrician.
pedido *m* (*remesa*) order.
pedir [6] *vt* to ask (for); (*en bar etc*) to order; (*mendigar*) to beg; **p. algo a algn** to ask sb for sth; **p. prestado** to borrow; **p. cuentas** to ask for an explanation.
pedrada *f* (*golpe*) blow from a stone; (*lanzamiento*) throw of a stone.

pega *f fam* (*objeción*) objection; **de p.** (*falso*) sham.
pegajoso,-a *a* (*pegadizo*) sticky.
pegamento *m* glue.
pegar [7] 1 *vt* (*adherir*) to stick; (*con pegamento*) to glue; (*golpear*) to hit; *fam* **no pegó ojo** he didn't sleep a wink; **p. un grito** to shout; **p. un salto** to jump. 2 *vi* (*adherirse*) to stick; (*armonizar*) to match; (*sol*) to beat down. 3 **pegarse** *vr* (*adherirse*) to stick; (*pelearse*) to fight; (*comida*) to get burnt; (*arrimarse*) to get close; **pegarse un tiro** to shoot oneself; **se me ha pegado el sol** I've got a touch of the sun.
pegatina *f* sticker.
peinado,-a *m* hairstyle, *fam* hairdo.
peinar 1 *vt* (*pelo*) to comb. 2 **peinarse** *vr* to comb one's hair.
peine *m* comb.
pelado,-a *a* (*fruta, patata*) peeled; (*cabeza*) shorn.
pelar 1 *vt* (*cortar el pelo a*) to cut the hair of; (*fruta, patata*) to peel. 2 **pelarse** *vr* (*cortarse el pelo*) to get one's hair cut.
peldaño *m* step; (*de escalera de mano*) rung.
pelea *f* fight; (*riña*) row.
pelear 1 *vi* to fight; (*reñir*) to quarrel. 2 **pelearse** *vr* to fight; (*reñir*) to quarrel; (*enemistarse*) to fall out.
peletería *f* (*tienda*) fur shop.
película *f* film, movie; (*fotográfica*) film; **p. de miedo** *o* **terror** horror film; **p. del Oeste** Western.
peligro *m* danger; (*riesgo*) risk; **correr (el) p. de . . .** to run the risk of . . . ; **poner en p.** to endanger.
peligroso,-a *a* dangerous.
pelirrojo,-a 1 *a* red-haired; (*anaranjado*) ginger-haired. 2 *mf* redhead.
pellejo *m* (*piel*) skin; **jugarse el p.** to risk one's neck.
pellizco *m* pinch.
pelma *mf*, **pelmazo,-a** *mf* (*persona*) bore.
pelo *m* hair; (*de animal*) coat; **cor-**

tarse el p. (*uno mismo*) to cut one's hair; (*en la peluquería*) to have one's hair cut; **tomar el p. a algn** to pull sb's leg; **por los pelos** by the skin of one's teeth.

pelota *f* ball; **hacer la p. a algn** to suck up to sb.

pelotón *m* squad.

pelotudo,-a *a Am* slack.

peluca *f* wig.

peluche *m* **osito de p.** teddy bear.

peludo,-a *a* hairy.

peluquería *f* hairdresser's (shop).

pena *f* (*tristeza*) sorrow; **¡qué p.!** what a pity!; **no merece** *o* **vale la p. (ir)** it's not worthwhile (going); **a duras penas** with great difficulty; **p. de muerte** *o* **capital** death penalty.

penalti *m* (*pl* **penaltis**) penalty.

pendejo *m Am* jerk.

pendiente 1 *a* (*por resolver*) pending; (*colgante*) hanging (**de** from); **asignatura p.** (*en colegio*) subject not yet passed; **estar p. de** (*esperar*) to be waiting for; (*vigilar*) to be on the lookout for. **2** *m* (*joya*) earring. **3** *f* slope.

penetrante *a* penetrating; (*frío, voz, mirada*) piercing.

penetrar 1 *vt* to penetrate. **2** *vi* (*entrar*) to enter (**en** -).

penicilina *f* penicillin.

península *f* peninsula.

penique *m* penny, *pl* pence.

penitenciario,-a *a* prison.

pensamiento *m* thought; (*flor*) pansy.

pensar [1] **1** *vi* to think (**en** of, about; **sobre** about, over); **sin p.** (*con precipitación*) without thinking; (*involuntariamente*) involuntarily. **2** *vt* (*considerar*) to think about; (*proponerse*) to intend; (*concebir*) to make; *fam* **¡ni pensarlo!** not on your life!

pensativo,-a *a* thoughtful.

pensión *f* (*residencia*) boarding house; (*hotel*) guesthouse; (*paga*) allowance; **media p.** half board; **p. completa** full board.

pensionista *mf* pensioner.

penúltimo,-a *a* & *mf* penultimate.

penumbra *f* half-light.

peña *f* rock; (*de amigos*) club.

peñón *m* rock; **el P. de Gibraltar** the Rock of Gibraltar.

peón *m* unskilled laborer; (*en ajedrez*) pawn.

peor *a* & *adv* (*comparativo*) worse; (*superlativo*) worst; **en el p. de los casos** if the worst comes to the worst.

pepinillo *m* gherkin.

pepino *m* cucumber.

pequeño,-a 1 *a* small, little; (*bajo*) short. **2** *mf* child; **de p.** as a child.

pera *f* pear.

peral *m* pear tree.

percance *m* mishap.

percha *f* (*colgador*) (coat) hanger.

perchero *m* clothes rack.

percibir *vt* (*notar*) to perceive; (*cobrar*) to receive.

percusión *f* percussion.

perder [3] **1** *vt* to lose; (*tren, autobús, oportunidad*) to miss; (*tiempo*) to waste. **2** *vi* to lose; **echar (algo) a p.** to spoil (sth); **echarse a p.** to be spoiled; **salir perdiendo** to come off worst. **3 perderse** *vr* (*extraviarse*) (*persona*) to get lost; **se me ha perdido la llave** I've lost my key.

pérdida *f* loss; (*de tiempo, esfuerzos*) waste.

perdiz *f* partridge.

perdón *m* pardon; **¡p.!** sorry!; **pedir p.** to apologize

perdonar *vt* to forgive; (*eximir*) to pardon; **¡perdone!** sorry!; **perdonarle la vida a algn** to spare sb's life.

perecedero,-a *a* perishable; **artículos perecederos** perishables.

perecer *vi* to perish.

perejil *m* parsley.

perenne *a* perennial.

perezoso,-a *a* (*vago*) lazy.

perfección *f* perfection; **a la p.** to perfection.

perfeccionar vt to perfect; (mejorar) to improve.
perfeccionista a & mf perfectionist.
perfectamente adv perfectly; **¡p.!** (de acuerdo) agreed!, all right!
perfecto,-a a perfect.
perfil m profile; (contorno) outline; **de p.** in profile.
perforar vt to perforate.
perfume 1 vti to perfume. **2 perfumarse** vr to put on perfume.
perfume m perfume.
pericia f expertise.
periferia f periphery; (alrededores) outskirts pl.
periférico m peripheral.
periódico,-a 1 m newspaper. **2** a periodic.
periodista mf journalist.
periodo, período m period.
periquito m budgerigar, fam budgie.
perjudicar [1] vt to harm; (intereses) to prejudice.
perjudicial a harmful.
perjuicio m damage.
perla f pearl.
permanecer vi to remain, stay.
permanente 1 a permanent. **2** f (de pelo) perm; **hacerse la p.** to have one's hair permed.
permiso m (autorización) permission; (licencia) license; **p. de conducir** driver's license.
permitir 1 vt to permit, allow. **2 permitirse** vr (costearse) to afford; **'no se permite fumar'** 'no smoking'.
pero conj but.
perpendicular a & f perpendicular.
perpetuo,-a a perpetual; **cadena perpetua** life imprisonment.
perplejo,-a a perplexed.
perra f bitch.
perrera f kennel; (para muchos perros) kennels pl.
perro m dog; **vida de perros** dog's life; **p. caliente** hot dog.
persecución f pursuit; (represión) persecution.

perseguir [6] vt to pursue; (seguir) to run after; (reprimir) to persecute.
perseverar vi to persevere; (durar) to last.
persiana f blinds pl.
persistente a persistent.
persistir vi to persist.
persona f person; fam **p. mayor** grown-up.
personaje m character; (celebridad) celebrity.
personal 1 a personal. **2** m (plantilla) personnel.
personalidad f personality.
perspectiva f perspective; (futuro) prospect.
perspicaz a perspicacious.
persuadir vt to persuade.
persuasión f persuasion.
pertenecer vi to belong (a to).
pertinaz a persistent; (obstinado) obstinate.
perturbación f disturbance.
peruano,-a a & mf Peruvian.
perverso,-a a perverse.
pervertir [5] vt to pervert.
pesa f weight; **levantamiento m de pesas** weightlifting.
pesadez f heaviness; (de estómago) fullness; (fastidio) drag.
pesadilla f nightmare.
pesado,-a a heavy; (aburrido) tedious.
pésame m **dar el p.** to offer one's condolences.
pesar 1 vt to weigh; (entristecer) to grieve. **2** vi to weigh; (ser pesado) to be heavy. **3** m (pena) sorrow; (arrepentimiento) regret; **a p. de** in spite of.
pesca f fishing.
pescadería f fish shop.
pescadilla f young hake.
pescado m fish.
pescador,-a 1 a fishing. **2** mf (hombre) fisherman; (mujer) fisherwoman.
pescar [1] vti to fish.
pescuezo m fam neck.
peseta f peseta.
pesimismo m pessimism.

pesimista 1 *a* pessimistic. **2** *mf* pessimist.

pésimo,-a *a* awful.

peso *m* weight; **p. bruto/neto** gross/net weight; **de p.** (*razón*) convincing.

pestaña *f* eyelash.

peste *f* (*hedor*) stench; (*epidemia*) plague.

pesticida *m* pesticide.

pestillo *m* bolt.

petaca *f* (*para cigarrillos*) cigarette case; (*para bebidas*) flask; *Am* (*maleta*) suitcase.

pétalo *m* petal.

petardo *m* firecracker.

petición *f* request.

petróleo *m* oil.

petrolero *m* oil tanker.

pez *m* fish.

pezón *m* nipple.

pezuña *f* hoof.

piadoso,-a *a* (*devoto*) pious; (*compasivo*) compassionate; **mentira piadosa** white lie.

pianista *mf* pianist.

piano *m* piano.

pibe,-a *mf Am* (*niño*) kid.

picadero *m* riding school.

picado,-a 1 *a* (*carne*) ground; (*fruta*) bad; (*diente*) decayed; (*mar*) choppy. **2** *m* **caer en p.** to plummet.

picador *m* picador.

picadora *f* mincer.

picadura *f* (*de insecto, serpiente*) bite; (*de avispa, abeja*) sting; (*en fruta*) spot.

picante *a* hot; (*chiste etc*) risqué.

picaporte *m* (*aldaba*) door knocker; (*pomo*) door handle.

picar [1] **1** *vt* (*insecto, serpiente*) to bite; (*avispas, abejas*) to sting; (*comer*) (*aves*) to peck (at); (*persona*) to pick at; (*anzuelo*) to bite; (*perforar*) to prick; (*carne*) to mince. **2** *vi* (*escocer*) to itch; (*herida*) to smart; (*el sol*) to burn; (*estar picante*) to be hot; (*pez*) to bite; *fig* (*dejarse engañar*) to swallow it. **3 picarse** *vr* (*fruta*) to spot;

(*dientes*) to decay; (*enfadarse*) to get cross.

pícaro,-a 1 *a* (*travieso*) mischievous; (*astuto*) crafty. **2** *mf* rogue.

pico *m* (*de ave*) beak, bill; (*punta*) corner; (*de montaña*) peak; (*herramienta*) pick; **cincuenta y p.** fifty odd; **las dos y p.** a little after two.

picor *m* tingling.

pie *m* foot; (*de instrumento*) stand; (*de copa*) stem; (*de una ilustración*) caption; **a p.** on foot; **de p.** standing up; **de pies a cabeza** from head to foot; **en p.** standing; **hacer p.** to touch the bottom; **perder p.** to get out of one's depth; **al p. de la letra** to the letter.

piedad *f* piety; (*compasión*) pity.

piedra *f* stone; (*de mechero*) flint.

piel *f* skin; (*de patata*) peel; (*cuero*) leather; (*con pelo*) fur; **p. de gallina** goose pimples *pl*.

pienso *m* fodder.

pierna *f* leg.

pieza *f* piece, part; (*habitación*) room; (*teatral*) play; **p. de recambio** spare part.

pijama *m* pajamas *pl*.

pila *f* battery; (*montón*) pile; (*de la cocina*) sink; **nombre de p.** Christian name.

píldora *f* pill.

pileta *f* (*pila*) sink; *Am* (*piscina*) swimming pool.

pillar 1 *vt* (*coger*) to catch; (*alcanzar*) to catch up with; **lo pilló un coche** he was run over by a car. **2 pillarse** *vr* to catch; **pillarse un dedo/una mano** to catch one's finger/hand.

pillo,-a 1 *a* (*travieso*) naughty; (*astuto*) cunning. **2** *mf* rogue.

piloto *m* (*de avión, barco*) pilot; (*de coche*) driver; (*de moto*) rider; (*luz*) pilot lamp; **piso p.** show apartment.

pimentón *m* red pepper.

pimienta *f* pepper.

pimiento *m* (*fruto*) pepper; (*planta*) pimiento.

pinar *m* pine wood.

pincel *m* paintbrush.

pinchadiscos *mf inv* disc jockey, DJ.

pinchar 1 *vt* (*punzar*) to jag; (*balón, globo*) to burst; (*rueda*) to puncture. **2** *vi* (*coche*) to get a puncture.

pinchazo *m* (*punzadura*) prick; (*de rueda*) puncture; (*de dolor*) sharp pain.

pincho *m* (*púa*) barb; **p. moruno** shish kebab.

ping-pong *m* table tennis.

pingüino *m* penguin.

pino *m* pine; *fig* **hacer el p.** to do a handstand.

pinole *m Am* corn drink.

pinta *f* (*medida*) pint; *fam* (*aspecto*) look.

pintada *f* graffiti.

pintar 1 *vt* (*dar color*) to paint; (*dibujar*) to draw. **2 pintarse** *vr* (*maquillarse*) to put make-up on.

pintor,-a *mf* painter.

pintoresco,-a *a* (*lugar*) picturesque; (*persona*) eccentric.

pintura *f* painting; (*materia*) paint.

pinza *f* (*para depilar*) tweezers *pl*; (*para tender*) clothes pin; (*de animal*) pincer.

piña *f* (*de pino*) pine cone; (*ananás*) pineapple.

piñón *m* pine seed.

piojo *m* louse.

pipa *f* (*de fumar*) pipe; (*de fruta*) seed; (*de girasol*) sunflower seed.

piragua *f* canoe.

piragüismo *m* canoeing.

pirámide *f* pyramid.

piraña *f* piranha.

pirata *a & mf* pirate.

piropo *m* **echar un p.** to pay a compliment.

pisada *f* footstep; (*huella*) footprint.

pisapapeles *m inv* paperweight.

pisar *vt* to step on.

piscifactoría *f* fish farm.

piscina *f* swimming pool.

piso *m* apartment; (*planta*) floor; (*de carretera*) surface.

pisotear *vt* (*aplastar*) to stamp on; (*pisar*) to trample on.

pisotón *m* **me dio un p.** he stood on my foot.

pista *f* track; (*rastro*) trail; (*indicio*) clue; **p. de baile** dance floor; **p. de esquí** ski slope; **p. de patinaje** ice rink; **p. de tenis** tennis court; **p. de aterrizaje** landing strip; **p. de despegue** runway.

pistacho *m* pistachio (nut).

pistola *f* pistol.

pitar 1 *vt* (*silbato*) to blow. **2** *vi* to whistle; (*coche*) to toot one's horn.

pitillo *m* cigarette.

pito *m* whistle; (*de vehículo*) horn.

pizarra *f* (*encerado*) blackboard; (*piedra*) slate.

pizca *f* little bit; **ni p.** not a bit.

placa *f* plate; (*conmemorativa*) plaque.

placer *m* pleasure; **tengo el p. de . . .** it gives me great pleasure to . . .

plaga *f* plague.

plagiario,-a *mf Am* (*secuestrador*) kidnapper.

plagio *m* plagiarism.

plan *m* (*proyecto*) plan; (*programa*) program; **p. de estudios** syllabus; **estar a p.** to be on a diet.

plana *f* page; **primera p.** front page.

plancha *f* iron; (*de metal*) plate; (*de cocina*) hotplate; **sardinas a la p.** grilled sardines.

planchar *vt* to iron.

planeta *m* planet.

planificación *f* planning.

planilla *f Am* application form.

plano,-a 1 *m* (*de ciudad*) map; (*proyecto*) plan. **2** *a* flat.

planta *f* plant; (*del pie*) sole; (*piso*) floor, story; **p. baja** first floor.

plantar 1 *vt* (*árboles, campo*) to plant; (*poner*) to put, place; **2 plantarse** *vr* to stand; (*llegar*) to arrive.

plantear 1 *vt* (*problema*) to raise; (*proponer*) to put forward; (*exponer*) to present. **2 plantearse** *vr* (*considerar*) to consider; (*problema*) to arise.

plantilla f (personal) staff; (de zapato) insole.

plantón m fam **dar un p. a algn** to stand sb up.

plástico,-a a & m plastic.

plastilina® f Plasticine®.

plata f silver; (objetos de plata) silverware; Am money; **p. de ley** sterling silver.

plataforma f platform.

plátano m (fruta) banana; (árbol) plane tree.

platillo m saucer; **p. volante** flying saucer.

platina f (de tocadiscos) deck.

plato m plate, dish; (parte de una comida) course; (guiso) dish; (de balanza) tray; (de tocadiscos) turntable; **de primer p.** for starters; **p. combinado** one-course meal.

playa f beach; (costa) seaside; Am **p. de estacionamiento** parking lot.

playera f sneaker; Am (camiseta) teeshirt.

plaza f square; (mercado) marketplace; (de vehículo) seat; (laboral) post; **p. de toros** bullring.

plazo m (periodo) period; (término) deadline; **a corto/largo p.** in the short term/in the long run; **comprar a plazos** buy on an installment plan.

plegable a folding.

plegar vt to fold.

pleito m lawsuit; **poner un p. (a algn)** to sue (sb).

pleno,-a 1 a full. **2** m plenary meeting.

pliego m sheet of paper.

pliegue m fold; (de vestido) pleat.

plomero,-a m Am plumber.

plomo m (metal) lead; (fusible) fuse.

pluma f feather; (de escribir) fountain pen.

plumero m feather duster.

plumier m pencil box.

plural a & m plural.

pluriempleo m moonlighting.

población f (ciudad) town; (pueblo) village; (habitantes) population.

poblado,-a 1 a populated. **2** m village.

pobre 1 a poor; **¡p.!** poor thing! **2** mf poor person; **los pobres** the poor.

pobreza f (indigencia) poverty; (escasez) scarcity.

pocillo m Am cup.

poco,-a 1 m **un p.** a little; **un p. de azúcar** a little sugar. **2** a not much, little; **p. sitio/tiempo** not much space/time, little space/time; **pocos,-as** not many, few; **pocas personas** not many people, few people; **unos,-as pocos,-as** a few. **3** pron not much; **pocos,-as** few, not many; **queda p.** there isn't much left. **4** adv (con verbo) not (very) much, little; (con a) not very; **p. generoso** not very generous; **un p. tarde/frío** a little late/ cold; **dentro de p.** soon; **p. a p.** little by little; **p. antes/después** shortly before/afterwards; **por p.** almost.

pocho,-a a (fruta) overripe.

poder¹ m power.

poder² vt to be able to; **no puede hablar** she can't speak; **no podré llamar** I won't be able to phone. ▪ (permiso) may, can; **¿se puede (entrar)?** may o can I (come in)?; **aquí no se puede fumar** you can't smoke here. ▪ (posibilidad) may, might; **puede que no lo sepan** they may o might not know; **no puede ser** that's impossible; **puede (ser) (que sí)** maybe, perhaps. ▪ (deber) **podrías haberme advertido** you might have warned me. **2** vi to cope (**con** with).

poderoso,-a a powerful.

podré indic fut de **poder**.

podrido,-a a rotten.

podrir vt defectivo de **pudrir**.

poesía f (género) poetry; (poema) poem.

poeta mf poet.

póker m poker.

polaco,-a 1 *a* Polish. **2** *mf* Pole. **3** *m* (*idioma*) Polish.
polea *f* pulley.
polémica *f* controversy.
polémico,-a *a* controversial.
polen *m* pollen.
policía 1 *f* police (force). **2** *mf* (*hombre*) policeman; (*mujer*) policewoman.
polideportivo *m* sports center.
poliéster *m* polyester.
polietileno *m* polyethene.
polígono *m* polygon; **p. industrial** industrial estate.
polilla *f* moth.
politécnico,-a *a* & *m* polytechnic.
política *f* politics *sing*; (*estrategia*) policy.
político,-a 1 *a* political; (*pariente*) in-law; **su familia política** her in-laws. **2** *mf* politician.
póliza *f* (*sello*) stamp; **p. de seguros** insurance policy.
polo *m* pole; (*helado*) Popsicle®; (*deporte*) polo; **P. Norte/Sur** North/South Pole.
polución *f* pollution.
polvera *f* powder compact.
polvo *m* dust; **limpiar** *o* **quitar el p.** to dust; **en p.** powdered; **polvo(s) de talco** talcum powder; *fam* **estar hecho p.** (*deprimido*) to be depressed.
pólvora *f* gunpowder.
polvoriento,-a *a* dusty.
polvorón *m* sweet pastry.
pollo *m* chicken.
pomada *f* ointment.
pomelo *m* (*fruto*) grapefruit; (*árbol*) grapefruit tree.
pómez *a inv* **piedra p.** pumice (stone).
pomo *m* (*de puerta*) knob.
pómulo *m* cheekbone.
ponche *m* punch.
poncho *m* poncho.
pondré *indic fut de* poner.
poner (*pp* **puesto**) **1** *vt* to put; (*mesa, huevo*) to lay; (*gesto*) to make; (*multa*) to impose; (*telegrama*) to send; (*negocio*) to set up;

(*encender*) to switch on; (*película*) to put on; (+ *adjetivo*) to make; **p. triste a algn** to make sb sad; **¿qué llevaba puesto?** what was he wearing?; (*decir*) **¿qué pone aquí?** what does it say here? **2 ponerse** *vr* to put oneself; (*vestirse*) to put on; (+ *adjetivo*) to become; (*sol*) to set; **p. al teléfono** to answer the phone; **p. a** to start to; **p. a trabajar** to start down to work.
poney *m* pony.
pongo *indic pres de* poner.
poniente *m* (*occidente*) West.
popa *f* stern.
popular *a* (*música, costumbre*) folk; (*famoso*) popular.
póquer *m* poker.
por *prep* (*agente*) by; **pintado p. Picasso** painted by Picasso; **p. qué** why ▪ (*causa*) because of; **p. necesidad/amor** out of need/love. ▪ (*tiempo*) **p. la mañana/noche** in the morning/at night; **p. ahora** for the time being. ▪ (*en favor de*) for; **lo hago p. mi hermano** I'm doing it for my brother('s sake). ▪ (*lugar*) **pasamos p. Córdoba** we went through Cordoba; **p. ahí** over there; **¿p. dónde vamos?** which way are we taking?; **mirar p. la ventana** to look out of the window; **entrar p. la ventana** to get in through the window. ▪ (*medio*) by; **p. avión/correo** by plane/post. ▪ (*a cambio de*) for; **cambiar algo p. algo** to exchange sth for sth. ▪ (*distributivo*) **p. cabeza** per person; **p. hora/mes** per hour/month. ▪ (*multiplicación*) **dos p. tres, seis** two times three is six; **un diez p. ciento** ten percent. ▪ (*con infinitivo*) in order to. ▪ **p. más/muy . . . que sea** no matter how . . . he/she is; **p. mí** as far as I'm concerned.
porcelana *f* porcelain.
porcentaje *m* percentage.
porción *f* portion.
porche *m* porch.
pormenor *m* detail; **venta al p.** retail.

porno *a inv* porn.

pornográfico,-a *a* pornographic.

poro *m* pore.

porque *conj* because; **¡p. no!** just because!

porqué *m* reason.

porquería *f* (*suciedad*) dirt; (*birria*) garbage.

porra *f* (*de policía*) nightstick; *fam* **¡vete a la p.!** get lost!

porrazo *m* thump.

porrón *m* glass bottle with a spout coming out of its base, used for drinking wine.

portada *f* (*de libro etc*) cover; (*de periódico*) front page; (*de disco*) sleeve; (*fachada*) facade.

portaequipajes *m inv* (*maletero*) trunk; (*baca*) roof rack.

portal *m* entrance hall; (*porche*) porch; (*puerta de la calle*) main door.

portarse *vr* to behave.

portátil *a* portable.

portazo *m* slam of a door; **dar un p.** to slam the door.

portento *m* (*cosa*) marvel; (*persona*) genius.

portería *f* porter's lodge; (*de fútbol etc*) goal.

portero,-a *mf* (*de vivienda*) caretaker; (*de edificio público*) doorman; (*guardameta*) goalkeeper; **p. automático** entryphone.

portorriqueño,-a *a & mf* Puerto Rican.

portugués,-a *a & mf* Portuguese.

porvenir *m* future.

posada *f* inn.

posar 1 *vi* (*para retrato etc*) to pose. **2** *vt* to put down. **3 posarse** *vr* to settle.

posdata *f* postscript.

poseer *vt* to possess.

posibilidad *f* possibility; (*oportunidad*) chance.

posible *a* possible; **de ser p.** if possible; **lo antes p.** as soon as possible; **es p. que venga** he might come.

posición *f* position.

positivo,-a *a* positive.

posponer *vt* (*aplazar*) to postpone; (*relegar*) to relegate.

postal 1 *a* postal. **2** *f* postcard.

poste *m* pole; (*de portería*) post.

póster *m* poster.

posterior *a* (*lugar*) rear; (*tiempo*) subsequent (**a** to).

posteriormente *adv* subsequently.

postgraduado,-a *a & mf* postgraduate.

postigo *m* (*de puerta*) wicket; (*de ventana*) shutter.

postizo,-a *a* false; **dentadura postiza** dentures *pl*.

postre *m* dessert.

póstumo,-a *a* posthumous.

postura *f* position.

potable *a* drinkable; **agua p./no p.** drinking water/not drinking water.

potaje *m* hotpot.

potencia *f* power; **en p.** potential.

potencial *a & m* potential.

potente *a* powerful.

potro *m* colt; (*de gimnasia*) horse.

pozo *m* well; (*minero*) shaft.

PP *m abr de* **Partido Popular.**

práctica *f* practice; **en la p.** in practice.

practicar [1] *vti* to practice; (*operación*) to carry out.

práctico,-a *a* practical; (*útil*) handy.

pradera *f*, **prado** *m* meadow.

pragmático,-a 1 *a* pragmatic. **2** *mf* pragmatist.

preámbulo *m* (*introducción*) preamble; (*rodeo*) circumlocution.

precario,-a *a* precarious.

precaución *f* (*cautela*) caution; (*medida*) precaution; **con p.** cautiously.

precavido,-a *a* cautious.

precedente 1 *a* preceding. **2** *m* precedent; **sin p.** unprecedented.

precepto *m* precept.

precintar *vt* to seal off.

precinto *m* seal.

precio *m* price.

preciosidad *f* (*cosa*) lovely thing; (*persona*) darling.

precioso,-a *a* (*hermoso*) lovely, beautiful; (*valioso*) precious.

precipicio *m* precipice.

precipitación *f* (*prisa*) haste; (*lluvia*) rainfall.

precipitado,-a *a* (*apresurado*) hurried; (*irreflexivo*) rash.

precipitar 1 *vt* (*acelerar*) to hurry; (*arrojar*) to hurl down. 2 **precipitarse** *vr* (*persona*) to hurl oneself; (*acontecimientos*) to gather speed; (*actuar irreflexivamente*) to rush.

precisamente *adv* (*con precisión*) precisely; (*exactamente*) exactly.

precisar *vt* (*especificar*) to specify; (*necesitar*) to require.

precisión *f* (*exactitud*) precision; (*aclaración*) clarification; **con p.** precisely.

preciso,-a *a* (*necesario*) necessary; (*exacto*) accurate; (*claro*) clear.

precoz *a* (*persona*) precocious.

predecesor,-a *mf* predecessor.

predecir (*pp* **predicho**) *vt* to predict.

predicado *m* predicate.

predicción *f* prediction.

predigo *indic pres de* **predecir**.

predije *pt indef de* **predecir**.

predilecto,-a *a* favorite.

predisponer (*pp* **predispuesto**) *vt* to predispose.

predominar *vi* to predominate.

preescolar *a* preschool.

preferencia *f* preference.

preferible *a* preferable; **es p. que no vengas** you'd better not come.

preferido,-a *mf* favorite.

preferir [5] *vt* to prefer.

prefijo *m* (*telefónico*) area code; (*gramatical*) prefix.

pregunta *f* question; **hacer una p.** to ask a question.

preguntar 1 *vti* to ask; **p. algo a algn** to ask sb sth; **p. por algn** to ask about sb. 2 **preguntarse** *vr* to wonder.

prehistórico,-a *a* prehistoric.

prejuicio *m* prejudice.

preliminar *a & m* preliminary.

prematuro,-a *a* premature.

premeditado,-a *a* premeditated.

premiar *vt* to award a prize (**a** to); (*recompensar*) to reward.

premio *m* prize; (*recompensa*) reward.

prenatal *a* prenatal.

prenda *f* garment.

prender 1 *vt* (*sujetar*) to fasten; (*con alfileres*) to pin; **p. fuego a** to set fire to. 2 *vi* (*fuego*) to catch; (*madera*) to catch fire. 3 **prenderse** *vr* to catch fire.

prensa *f* press.

prensar *vt* to press.

preñado,-a *a* pregnant.

preocupación *f* worry.

preocupar 1 *vt* to worry. 2 **preocuparse** *vr* to worry (**por** about); **no te preocupes** don't worry.

preparación *f* preparation; (*formación*) training.

preparar 1 *vt* to prepare. 2 **prepararse** *vr* to get ready.

preparativo *m* preparation.

preposición *f* preposition.

presa *f* prey; (*embalse*) dam; *fig* **ser p. de** to be a victim of.

presagiar *vt* to predict.

presagio *m* (*señal*) omen; (*premonición*) premonition.

prescindir *vi* **p. de** to do without.

presencia *f* presence; **p. de ánimo** presence of mind.

presenciar *vt* to witness.

presentación *f* presentation; (*de personas*) introduction.

presentador,-a *mf* presenter.

presentar 1 *vt* to present; (*una persona a otra*) to introduce. 2 **presentarse** *vr* (*comparecer*) to present oneself; (*inesperadamente*) to turn up; (*ocasión, oportunidad*) to arise; (*candidato*) to stand; (*darse a conocer*) to introduce oneself (**a** to).

presente 1 *a* present; **tener p.** (*tener en cuenta*) to bear in mind. 2 *m* present.

presentimiento *m* premonition.

preservar *vt* to preserve (**de** from; **contra** against).

preservativo *m* condom.

presidente,-a *mf* president; (*de una reunión*) chairperson.

presidiario,-a *mf* prisoner.

presidio *m* prison.

presidir *vt* to head; (*reunión*) to chair.

presión *f* pressure; **a** *o* **bajo p.** under pressure.

presionar *vt* to press; *fig* to pressurize.

preso,-a 1 *a* imprisoned. 2 *mf* prisoner.

préstamo *m* loan.

prestar 1 *vt* to lend; (*atención*) to pay; (*ayuda*) to give; (*servicio*) to do. 2 **prestarse** *vr* (*ofrecerse*) to offer oneself (**a** to).

prestidigitador,-a *mf* conjuror.

prestigio *m* prestige.

presumido,-a 1 *a* conceited. 2 *mf* vain person.

presumir 1 *vt* (*suponer*) to presume. 2 *vi* (*ser vanidoso*) to show off.

presuntuoso,-a *a* (*vanidoso*) conceited; (*pretencioso*) pretentious.

presupuesto,-a *m* budget; (*cálculo*) estimate.

pretender *vt* (*intentar*) to try; (*aspirar a*) to try for; (*cortejar*) to court.

pretendiente,-a *mf* (*al trono*) pretender; (*amante*) suitor.

pretérito *m* preterite.

pretexto *m* pretext.

prevenir *vt* (*precaver*) to prevent; (*evitar*) to avoid; (*advertir*) to warn.

prever (*pp* **previsto**) *vt* to forecast.

previo,-a *a* prior; **sin p. aviso** without notice.

previsible *a* predictable.

previsto,-a *a* forecast.

primario,-a *a* primary.

primavera *f* spring.

primer *a* (*delante de m*) first.

primera *f* (*en tren*) first class; (*marcha*) first (gear).

primero,-a 1 *a* first; **de primera necesidad** basic. 2 *mf* first; **a primero(s) de mes** at the beginning of the month. 3 *adv* first.

primitivo,-a *a* primitive; (*tosco*) rough.

primo,-a 1 *mf* cousin; **p. hermano** first cousin. 2 *a* **materia prima** raw material.

primogénito,-a *a & mf* first-born.

primoroso,-a *a* exquisite.

princesa *f* princess.

principal *a* main, principal; **puerta p.** front door.

príncipe *m* prince.

principiante 1 *a* novice. 2 *mf* beginner.

principio *m* beginning, start; (*fundamento*) principle; **a principio(s) de** at the beginning of; **al p., en un p.** at first; **en p.** in principle; **principios** basics.

pringar [7] 1 *vt* (*ensuciar*) to make greasy. 2 **pringarse** *vr* (*ensuciarse*) to get greasy.

pringoso,-a *a* (*grasiento*) greasy.

prisa *f* hurry; **date p.** hurry up; **tener p.** to be in a hurry; **de** *o* **a p.** in a hurry.

prisión *f* prison.

prisionero,-a *mf* prisoner.

prismáticos *mpl* binoculars.

privado,-a *a* private.

privar 1 *vt* (*despojar*) to deprive (**de** of). 2 **privarse** *vr* (*abstenerse*) to go without.

privilegio *m* privilege.

pro 1 *m* advantage; **los pros y los contras** the pros and cons. 2 *prep* in favor of.

proa *f* prow.

probable *a* probable, likely; **es p. que llueva** it'll probably rain.

probador *m* fitting room.

probar [2] 1 *vt* to try; (*comprobar*) to check; (*demostrar*) to prove. 2 *vi* to try. 3 **probarse** *vr* (*ropa*) to try on.

probeta f test tube.
problema m problem.
proceder 1 vi (actuar) to act; (ser oportuno) to be advisable; **p. de** (provenir) to come from; **p. a** (continuar) to go on to. **2** m (comportamiento) behavior.
procedimiento m (método) procedure.
procesador m processor; **p. de textos** word processor.
procesar vt to prosecute; (información) to process.
procesión f procession.
proceso m process; (juicios) trial; **p. de datos** data processing.
proclamar vt to proclaim.
procurar vt (intentar) to attempt; (proporcionar) to manage) to get; **procura que no te vean** make sure they don't see you.
prodigioso,-a a (sobrenatural) prodigious; (maravilloso) wonderful.
producción f (acción) production; (producto) product; **p. en cadena/ serie** assembly-line/mass production.
producir 1 vt to produce; (fruto, cosecha, rendir) to yield; (originar) to bring about. **2 producirse** vr to take place.
productivo,-a a productive; (beneficioso) profitable.
producto m product; (producción) produce.
productor,-a 1 a producing. **2** mf producer.
profesión f profession.
profesional a & mf professional.
profesor,-a mf teacher; (de universidad) lecturer.
profesorado m (grupo de profesores) staff.
profetizar [4] vt to prophesy.
prófugo,-a a & mf fugitive.
profundidad f depth; **un metro de p.** one meter deep.
profundo,-a a deep; (idea, sentimiento) profound.
progenitor,-a mf **progenitores** (padres) parents.

programa m program; (informático) program; (de estudios) syllabus.
programación f programming.
programar vt program; (para ordenador) to program.
progresar vi to make progress.
progresivamente adv progressively.
progresivo,-a a progressive.
progreso m progress.
prohibido,-a a forbidden; 'prohibida la entrada' 'no admittance'; **p. aparcar/fumar** no parking/ smoking.
prohibir vt to forbid.
prójimo,-a mf one's fellow man.
proliferar vi to proliferate.
prólogo m prologue.
prolongar [7] **1** vt (alargar) to extend. **2 prolongarse** vr (continuar) to carry on.
promedio m average.
promesa f promise.
prometer 1 vt to promise. **2** vi to be promising. **3 prometerse** vr to get engaged.
prometido,-a 1 a promised. **2** mf (hombre) fiancé; (mujer) fiancée.
promocionar vt to promote.
pronombre m pronoun.
pronosticar [1] vt to forecast.
pronóstico m (del tiempo) forecast; (médico) prognosis.
pronto,-a 1 a quick, prompt. **2** adv (deprisa) quickly; (temprano) early; **de p.** suddenly; **por de** o **lo p.** (para empezar) to start with; **¡hasta p.!** see you soon!
pronunciación f pronunciation.
pronunciar vt to pronounce; (discurso) to deliver.
propaganda f (política) propaganda; (comercial) advertising.
propagar [7] **1** vt to spread. **2 propagarse** vr to spread.
propiamente adv **p. dicho** strictly speaking.
propiedad f (posesión) ownership; (cosa poseída) property; **con p.** properly.
propietario,-a mf owner.

propina f tip.
propio,-a a (de uno) own; (correcto) suitable; (característico) typical; (mismo)(hombre) himself; (mujer) herself; (animal, cosa) itself; **el p. autor** the author himself; **propios,-as** themselves.
proponer (pp **propuesto**) **1** vt to propose. **2 proponerse** vr to intend.
proporción f proportion; **proporciones** (tamaño) size sing.
proporcional a proportional.
proporcionar vt (dar) to give; (suministrar) to supply.
proposición f (propuesta) proposal.
propósito m (intención) intention; **a p.** (por cierto) by the way; (adrede) on purpose.
propuesta f suggestion.
propuse pt indef de **proponer.**
prórroga f (prolongación) extension; (en partido) overtime; (aplazamiento) postponement.
prosa f prose.
proseguir [6] vti to carry on.
prospecto m leaflet.
prosperar vi (negocio, país) to prosper; (propuesta) to be accepted.
próspero,-a a prosperous.
prostitución f prostitution.
prostituta f prostitute.
protagonista mf main character.
protección f protection; **p. de escritura** write protection.
protector,-a 1 a protective. **2** mf protector.
proteger [5] vt to protect.
protesta f protest.
protestante a & mf Protestant.
protestar vi to protest; (quejarse) to complain.
protocolo m protocol.
protuberante a bulging.
provecho m benefit; **¡buen p.!** enjoy your meal!; **sacar p. de algo** to benefit from sth.
proveedor,-a mf supplier.
proveer (pp **provisto**) vt to supply.
provenir vi **p. de** to come from.

proverbio m proverb.
provincia f province.
provisional a provisional.
provisto,-a a **p. de** equipped with.
provocación f provocation.
provocador,-a 1 mf instigator. **2** a provocative.
provocar [1] vt (causar) to cause; (instigar) to provoke; Am **si no le provoca** if he doesn't feel like it.
provocativo,-a a provocative.
próximamente adv soon.
proximidad f closeness; **en las proximidades de** in the vicinity of.
próximo,-a a (cercano) near, close; (siguiente) next.
proyección f projection; (de película) showing.
proyectar vt (luz) to project; (planear) to plan; (película) to show.
proyectil m projectile.
proyecto m project.
proyector m projector.
prudencia f prudence; (moderación) care.
prudente a prudent; (conductor) careful.
prueba f (argumento) proof; (examen etc) test; **a p. de agua/balas** waterproof/bullet-proof.
psicoanálisis m inv psychoanalysis.
psicología f psychology.
psicológico,-a a psychological.
psicólogo,-a mf psychologist.
psicópata mf psychopath.
psiquiatra mf psychiatrist.
psiquiátrico,-a 1 a psychiatric. **2** m mental hospital.
psíquico,-a a psychic.
PSOE m abr de **Partido Socialista Obrero Español** Socialist Workers' Party of Spain.
pta(s). abr de **peseta(s)** peseta(s).
pts abr de **pesetas.**
púa f (de planta) thorn; (de animal) spine; (de peine) tooth.
pub m (pl pubs, pubes) pub.
publicación f publication.
publicar [1] vt to publish; (divulgar) to publicize.

publicidad *f* advertising; (*conocimiento público*) publicity.

público,-a 1 *a* public. **2** *m* public; (*de teatro*) audience; (*de estadio*) spectators *pl*.

puchero *m* (*olla*) cooking pot; (*cocido*) stew; **hacer pucheros** to pout.

pucho *m Am* dog-end.

pude *pt indef de* **poder.**

pudor *m* modesty.

pudrir *vt defectivo,* **pudrirse** *vr* to rot.

pueblo *m* village; (small) town; (*gente*) people.

puente *m* bridge; **p. aéreo** (*civil*) air shuttle service.

puerco,-a 1 *a* filthy. **2** *m* pig; *f* sow.

puericultura *f* pediatrics *sing.*

pueril *a* childish.

puerro *m* leek.

puerta *f* door; (*verja*) gate.

puerto *m* (*de mar, ordenador*) port; (*de montaña*) (mountain) pass; (*de deportivo*) marina.

puertorriqueño,-a *a & mf* Puerto Rican.

pues *conj* (*puesto que*) as, since; (*por lo tanto*) therefore; (*entonces*) so; (*para reforzar*) **¡p. claro que sí!** but of course!; **p. como iba diciendo** well, as I was saying; **¡p. no!** certainly not!

puestero,-a *mf Am* stallholder.

puesto,-a 1 *conj* **p. que** since, as. **2** *m* (*lugar*) place; (*empleo*) post; (*tienda*) stall; **p. de trabajo** job. **3** *a* (*colocado*) put; **llevar p.** (*ropa*) to have on, to wear.

pugna *f* fight.

pulcro,-a (extremely) neat.

pulga *f* flea.

pulgada *f* inch.

pulgar *m* thumb.

pulir *vt* (*metal, madera*) to polish.

pulmón *m* lung.

pulpería *f Am* store.

pulpo *m* octopus.

pulsación *f* pulsation; (*en mecanografía*) keystroke.

pulsar *vt* (*timbre, botón*) to press; (*tecla*) to hit.

pulsera *f* (*aro*) bracelet; **reloj de p.** wristwatch.

pulso *m* pulse; (*mano firme*) steady hand; **echarse un p.** to arm-wrestle.

puma *m* puma.

puna *f Am* high moor; (*mal*) mountain sickness.

punta *f* (*extremo*) tip; (*extremo afilado*) point; (*de cabello*) end; **sacar p. a un lápiz** to sharpen a pencil; **tecnología p.** state-of-the-art technology; **hora p.** rush hour.

puntapié *m* kick.

puntería *f* aim; **tener buena/mala p.** to be a good/bad shot.

puntiagudo,-a *a* sharp.

puntilla *f* (*encaje*) lace; **dar la p.** to finish (the bull) off; **de puntillas** on tiptoe.

punto *m* point; (*marca*) dot; (*lugar*) point; (*de costura, sutura*) stitch; **a p.** ready; **a p. de** on the point of; **hasta cierto p.** to a certain extent; **p. muerto** neutral; **p. de vista** point of view; **p. y seguido** period; **p. y coma** semicolon; **dos puntos** colon; **p. y aparte** full stop, new paragraph; **las ocho en p.** eight o'clock sharp; **hacer p.** to knit.

puntuación *f* (*ortográfica*) punctuation; (*deportiva*) score; (*nota*) mark.

puntual 1 *a* punctual. **2** *adv* punctually.

puntualidad *f* punctuality.

puñado *m* handful.

puñal *m* dagger.

puñalada *f* stab.

puñetazo *m* punch.

puño *m* fist; (*de camisa etc*) cuff; (*de herramienta*) handle.

pupa *f* (*herida*) sore.

pupila *f* pupil.

pupitre *m* desk.

puré *m* purée; **p. de patata** mashed potatoes.

pureza *f* purity.

purificar [1] *vt* to purify.

puritano,-a *a* puritanical. **2** *m* puritan.

puro,-a 1 *a* (*sin mezclas*) pure; (*mero*) sheer; **aire p.** fresh air; **la pura verdad** the plain truth. **2** *m* (*cigarro*) cigar.

púrpura *a inv* purple.

puse *pt indef de* **poner.**

puzzle *m* jigsaw puzzle.

P.V.P. *m abr de* **precio de venta al público** recommended retail price.

Pza., Plza. *abr de* **plaza** square, Sq.

Q

que¹ *pron rel* (*sujeto, persona*) who, that; (*cosa*) that, which. ▪ (*complemento, persona*) *no se traduce o* that; (*cosa*) *no se traduce o* that, which; **la chica q. conocí** the girl (that) I met; **el coche q. compré** the car (that *o* which) I bought. ▪ **lo q.** what. ▪ (*con infinitivo*) **hay mucho q. hacer** there's a lot to do.

que² *conj se traduce o* that; **dijo que llamaría** he said (that) he would call. ▪ (*consecutivo*) *no se traduce o* that; **habla tan bajo q. no se le oye** he speaks so quietly (that) he can't be heard. ▪ (*en comparativas*) than; **mejor q. tú** better than you ▪ (*causal*) because; **date prisa q. no tenemos mucho tiempo** hurry up, because we haven't got much time. ▪ (*enfático*) **¡q. no!** no! ▪ (*deseo, mandato*) (+ *subjuntivo*) **¡q. te diviertas!** enjoy yourself! ▪ (*final*) so that; **ven q. te dé un beso** come and let me give you a kiss. ▪ (*disyuntivo*) whether; **me da igual q. suba o no** I couldn't care whether he comes up or not. ▪ (*locuciones*) **q. yo sepa** as far as I know; **yo q. tú** if I were you.

qué 1 *pron interr* what; **¡q. quieres?** what do you want? ▪ (*exclamativo*) (+ *a*) how; (+ *n*) what a; **¡q. bonito!** how pretty!; **¡q. lástima!** what a pity! **2** *a interr* which; **¡q. libro quieres?** which book do you want?

quebrada *f Am* stream.

quebrar [1] **1** *vt* (*romper*) to break. **2** *vi* (*empresa*) to go bankrupt. **3 quebrarse** *vr* to break.

quedar 1 *vi* (*restar*) to be left; (*con amigo*) to arrange to meet; (*acordar*) to agree (**en** to); (*estar situado*) to be; **quedan dos** there are two left; **quedaría muy bien allí** it would look very nice there; **q. en ridículo** to make a fool of oneself; **q. bien/mal** to make a good/bad impression. **2 quedarse** *vr* (*permanecer*) to stay; **quedarse sin dinero/pan** to run out of money/bread; **quedarse con hambre** to be still hungry; **quedarse (con)** (*retener*) to keep; **quédese (con) el cambio** keep the change.

quehacer *m* chore.

queja *f* complaint; (*de dolor*) groan.

quejarse *vr* to complain (**de** about).

quemadura *f* burn.

quemar 1 *vt* to burn. **2** *vi* to be burning hot. **3 quemarse** *vr fig* to burn oneself out.

quemazón *f* smarting.

quepo *indic pres de* **caber.**

querella *f* lawsuit.

querer 1 *vt* to want; (*amar*) to love; **sin q.** without meaning to; **¡por lo que más quieras!** for heaven's sake!; **¡quiere pasarme el pan?** would you pass me the bread?; **q. decir** to mean; **no quiso darme permiso** he refused me permission. **2 quererse** *vr* to love each other.

querido,-a *a* dear.

querré *indic fut de* **querer.**

queso *m* cheese.

quicio *m* (*de puerta*) doorpost; **sacar de q. (a algn)** to infuriate (sb).

quien *pron rel* **el hombre con q. vino** the man she came with, (*formal*) the man with whom she came. ▪ (*indefinido*) **q. quiera venir . . .** whoever wants to come . . .; **hay q. dice lo contrario** there are some people who say the opposite.

quién *pron interr* who; **¡q. es?** who

is it?; **¿para q. es?** who is it for?; **¿de q. es esa bici?** whose bike is that?

quienquiera *pron indef* (*pl* **quienesquiera**) whoever.

quieto,-a *a* still; **¡estáte q.!** keep still!

quilo *m* = **kilo.**

químico,-a 1 *a* chemical *mf* chemist.

quince *a & m inv* fifteen.

quiniela *f* sports lottery *pl.*

quinientos,-as *a & mf inv* five hundred.

quinqué *m* oil lamp.

quintal *m* (*medida*) 46 kg; **q. métrico** = 100 kg.

quinto,-a *a & mf* fifth.

quiosco *m* kiosk; **q. de periódicos** newspaper stand.

quirófano *m* operating room.

quirúrgico,-a *a* surgical.

quise *indic fut de* **querer.**

quitaesmalte(s) *m inv* nail varnish remover.

quitamanchas *m inv* stain remover.

quitanieves *m* (**máquina**) **q.** snowplow.

quitar 1 *vt* to remove, take away; (*ropa*) to take off; (*dolor*) to relieve; (*sed*) to quench; (*hambre*) to take away; (*robar*) to steal; (*tiempo*) to take up; (*asiento*) to take; (*cantidad*) to take away. **2** *vi* **¡quita!** get out of the way! **3 quitarse** *vr* (*apartarse*) to move away; (*mancha*) to come out; (*dolor*) to go away; (*ropa, gafas*) to take off; **quitarse de fumar** to give up smoking; **quitarse a algn de encima** to get rid of sb.

quizá(s) *adv* perhaps, maybe.

R

rábano *m* radish.

rabia *f* (*ira*) rage; (*enfermedad*) rabies *sing;* **¡qué r.!** how annoying!; **me da r.** it makes me mad.

rabiar *vi* (*enfadarse*) to rage; **hacer r. a algn** to make sb see red.

rabioso,-a *a* rabid; (*enfadado*) furious.

rabo *m* tail; (*de fruta etc*) stalk.

racha *f* (*de viento*) gust; (*período*) spell.

racial *a* racial.

racimo *m* bunch.

ración *f* portion.

racionar *vt* to ration.

racismo *m* racism.

racista *a & mf* racist.

radar *m* (*pl* **radares**) radar.

radiación *f* radiation.

radiactividad *f* radioactivity.

radiactivo,-a *a* radioactive.

radiador *m* radiator.

radiante *a* radiant (**de** with).

radical *a* radical.

radio 1 *f* radio. **2** *m* radius; (*de rueda*) spoke.

radioactividad *f* radioactivity.

radiocasete *m* (*pl* **radiocasetes**) radio cassette.

radiografía *f* (*imagen*) X-ray.

ráfaga *f* (*de viento*) gust; (*de disparos*) burst.

raído,-a *a* (*gastado*) worn.

raíz *f* (*pl* **raíces**) root; **r. cuadrada** square root; **a r. de** as a result of.

raja *f* (*corte*) cut; (*hendidura*) crack.

rajar 1 *vt* (*tela*) to tear; (*hender*) to crack. **2 rajarse** *vr* (*tela*) to tear; (*partirse*) to crack; *fam* (*echarse atrás*) to back out; *Am* (*acobardarse*) to chicken out.

rallado,-a *a* **queso r.** grated cheese; **pan r.** breadcrumbs *pl.*

rallador *m* grater.

rallar *vt* to grate.

ralo,-a *a* thin.

rama *f* branch.

ramillete *m* (*de flores*) posy.

ramo *m* (*de flores*) bunch; (*sector*) branch.

rampa *f* ramp.

rana *f* frog.

rancho *m* (*granja*) ranch.

rancio,-a *a* (*comida*) stale.

rango *m* rank; (*jerarquía elevada*) high social standing.

ranura *f* slot; **r. de expansión** expansion slot.

rapar vt to crop.
rapaz 1 a predatory; **ave r.** bird of prey. **2** mf youngster; (muchacho) lad; (muchacha) lass.
rape m (pez) angler fish; **cortado al r.** close-cropped.
rapidez f speed.
rápido,-a 1 a quick, fast. **2** adv quickly. **3** m fast train.
raptar vt to kidnap.
rapto m (secuestro) kidnapping.
raqueta f (de tenis) racket; (de ping-pong) paddle.
raquítico,-a a (delgado) emaciated; fam (escaso) meager.
raro,-a a rare; (extraño) strange.
rascacielos m inv skyscraper.
rascar [1] vt (con las uñas) to scratch.
rasgar [7] vt to tear.
rasgo m feature.
rasguño m scratch.
raso,-a 1 a (llano) flat; (cielo) clear. **2** m satin.
raspa f (de pescado) bone.
raspar 1 vt (limar) to scrape (off). **2** vi (ropa etc) to chafe.
rastrear vt (zona) to comb.
rastrillo m rake; (mercadillo) flea market.
rastro m trace; (en el suelo) trail.
rasurar vt, **rasurarse** vr to shave.
rata f rat.
ratero,-a mf pickpocket.
ratificar [1] vt to ratify.
rato m (momento) while; **a ratos** at times; **al poco r.** shortly after; **pasar un buen/mal r.** to have a good/ bad time; **ratos libres** free time sing.
ratón m (también de ordenador) mouse.
raya f (línea) line; (del pantalón) crease; (del pelo) part; **camisa a rayas** striped shirt.
rayar vt to scratch.
rayo m ray; (relámpago) (flash of) lightning.
raza f (humana) race; (de animal) breed.
razón f reason; (justicia) justice; (proporción) rate; **uso de r.** power

of reasoning; **dar la r. a algn** to say that sb is right; **tener r.** to be right.
razonable a reasonable.
razonar 1 vt (argumentar) to reason out. **2** vi (discurrir) to reason.
reacción f reaction; **avión de r.** jet (plane).
reaccionar vi to react.
reactor m reactor; (avión) jet (plane).
reajuste m readjustment.
real[1] a (efectivo, verdadero) real.
real[2] a (regio) royal.
realidad f reality; **en r.** in fact.
realismo m realism.
realizador,-a mf producer.
realizar [4] **1** vt (hacer) to carry out; (ambición) to achieve; **2 realizarse** vr (persona) to fulfill oneself; (sueño) to come true.
realmente adv really.
realzar [4] vt (recalcar) to highlight; (belleza, importancia) to heighten.
reanimar vt, **reanimarse** vr to revive.
reanudar 1 vt to renew. **2 reanudarse** vr to resume.
rebaja f (descuento) reduction; **rebajas** sales.
rebajar 1 vt (precio) to cut; (tanto por ciento) to take off. **2 rebajarse** vr (humillarse) to humble oneself.
rebanada f slice.
rebaño m herd; (de ovejas) flock.
rebasar vt (exceder) to exceed.
rebeca f cardigan.
rebelarse vr to rebel.
rebelde 1 mf rebel. **2** a rebellious.
rebelión f rebellion.
rebobinar vt to rewind.
rebosar vi to overflow.
rebotar vi (pelota) to bounce; (bala) to ricochet.
rebuznar vi to bray.
recado m (mandado) errand; (mensaje) message; **dejar un r.** to leave a message.
recalcar [1] vt fig to stress.
recalentar [1] vt (comida) to reheat.
recambio m (repuesto) spare

(part); (*de pluma etc*) refill; **rueda de r.** spare wheel.

recapacitar *vt* to think over.

recargado,-a *a* (*estilo*) overelaborate.

recargar [7] *vt* (*batería*) to recharge; (*adornar mucho*) to overelaborate.

recatado,-a *a* (*prudente*) cautious; (*modesto*) modest.

recaudador,-a *mf* tax collector.

recaudar *vt* to collect.

recelar *vt* **r. de** to distrust.

receloso,-a *a* suspicious.

recepción *f* reception.

recepcionista *mf* receptionist.

receptor,-a 1 *mf* (*persona*) recipient. **2** *m* (*aparato*) receiver.

receta *f* recipe; **r. (médica)** prescription.

recetar *vt* to prescribe.

rechazar [4] *vt* to reject.

rechinar *vi* (*metal*) to squeak; (*dientes*) to chatter.

rechoncho,-a *a* chubby.

recibidor *m* entrance hall.

recibimiento *m* reception.

recibir 1 *vt* to receive; (*acoger*) to welcome. **2 recibirse** *vr Am* **recibirse de** to qualify as.

recibo *m* (*factura*) bill; (*resguardo*) receipt.

reciclar *vt* to recycle.

recién *adv* recently; **r. casados** newlyweds; **r. nacido** newborn baby.

reciente *a* recent.

recientemente *adv* recently.

recinto *m* (*cercado*) enclosure; **r. comercial** shopping precinct.

recio,-a *a* (*robusto*) sturdy; (*grueso*) thick; (*voz*) loud.

recipiente *m* container.

recíproco,-a *a* reciprocal.

recitar *vt* to recite.

reclamación *f* (*demanda*) claim; (*queja*) complaint.

reclamar 1 *vt* to claim. **2** *vi* to protest (**contra** against).

reclinar 1 *vt* to lean (**sobre** on). **2 reclinarse** *vr* to lean back.

recluir *vt* to shut away.

recluso,-a *mf* inmate.

recobrar 1 *vt* to recover; (*conocimiento*) to regain; **r. el aliento** to get one's breath back. **2 recobrarse** *vr* to recover.

recodo *m* bend.

recoger [5] **1** *vt* to pick up; (*datos etc*) to collect; (*ordenar, limpiar*) to clean; (*cosecha*) to gather. **2 recogerse** *vr* (*pelo*) to lift up.

recogida *f* collection; (*cosecha*) harvest.

recomendación *f* recommendation; (*para persona*) reference.

recomendar [1] *vt* to recommend.

recompensa *f* reward.

reconciliar 1 *vt* to reconcile. **2 reconciliarse** *vr* to be reconciled.

reconfortante *a* comforting.

reconocer *vt* to recognize; (*admitir*) to admit; (*paciente*) to examine.

reconocimiento *m* recognition; (*médico*) examination.

reconstituyente *m* tonic.

reconstruir *vt* to reconstruct.

recopilación *f* compilation.

recopilar *vt* to compile.

récord *m* record.

recordar [2] *vti* to remember; **r. algo a algn** to remind sb of sth.

recorrer *vt* (*distancia*) to travel; (*país*) to tour; (*ciudad*) to walk round.

recorrido *m* (*trayecto*) journey; (*itinerario*) route.

recortar *vt* to cut out.

recorte *m* cutting; (*de pelo*) trim.

recostar [2] **1** *vt* to lean. **2 recostarse** *vr* (*tumbarse*) to lie down.

recreo *m* recreation; (*en colegio*) break, playtime.

recriminar *vt* to recriminate; (*reprochar*) to reproach.

recrudecer *vt*, **recrudecerse** *vr* to worsen.

recta *f* (*de carretera*) straight stretch.

rectangular *a* rectangular.

rectángulo *m* rectangle.

rectificar [1] *vt* to rectify; (*corregir*) to remedy.
recto,-a 1 *a* (*derecho*) straight; (*ángulo*) right. 2 *adv* straight (on).
rector,-a *mf* rector.
recuerdo *m* (*memoria*) memory; (*regalo etc*) souvenir; **recuerdos** regards.
recuperación *f* recovery.
recuperar 1 *vt* (*salud*) to recover; (*conocimiento*) to regain; (*tiempo, clases*) to make up. 2 **recuperarse** *vr* to recover.
recurrir *vi* (*sentencia*) to appeal; **r. a** (*a algn*) to turn to; (*a algo*) to resort to.
recurso *m* resource; (*de sentencia*) appeal.
red *f* net; (*sistema*) network; **r. local** local area network, LAN.
redacción *f* (*escrito*) composition; (*acción*) writing.
redactar *vt* to draft.
redactor,-a *mf* editor.
redondel *m* (*círculo*) ring.
redondo,-a *a* round; (*rotundo*) categorical.
reducción *f* reduction.
reducir 1 *vt* (*disminuir*) to reduce. 2 **reducirse** *vr* (*disminuirse*) to diminish; (*limitarse*) to confine oneself (**a** to).
reembolso *m* reimbursement; **contra r.** cash on delivery.
reemplazar [4] *vt* to replace (**con** with).
ref. *abr de* **referencia** reference, ref.
refaccionar *vt Am* to repair.
refectorio *m* refectory.
referencia *f* reference.
referéndum *m* (*pl* **referéndums**) referendum.
referente **r. a** concerning, regarding.
referir [5] 1 *vt* to tell. 2 **referirse** *vr* (*aludir*) to refer (**a** to).
refilón de r. (*de pasada*) briefly.
refinería *f* refinery.
reflector *m* spotlight.

reflejar 1 *vt* to reflect. 2 **reflejarse** *vr* to be reflected (**en** in).
reflejo,-a 1 *m* (*imagen*) reflection; (*destello*) gleam; **reflejos** (*en el cabello*) highlights. 2 *a* (*movimiento*) reflex.
reflexión *f* reflection.
reflexionar *vi* to think (**sobre** about).
reflexivo,-a *a* (*persona*) thoughtful; (*verbo etc*) reflexive.
reforma *f* reform; (*reparación*) repair.
reformar *vt* to reform; (*edificio*) to renovate.
reformatorio *m* reform school.
reforzar [2] *vt* to strengthen.
refrán *m* saying.
refrescante *a* refreshing.
refrescar [1] 1 *vt* to refresh. 2 *vi* (*bebida*) to be refreshing. 3 **refrescarse** *vr* to cool down.
refresco *m* soft drink.
refrigeración *f* refrigeration; (*aire acondicionado*) air conditioning.
refrigerado,-a *a* (*local*) air-conditioned.
refuerzo *m* strengthening.
refugiarse *vr* to take refuge.
refugio *m* refuge.
refunfuñar *vi* to grumble.
regadera *f* watering can.
regalar *vt* (*dar*) to give (as a present).
regaliz *m* licorice.
regalo *m* present.
regañadientes a r. reluctantly.
regañar 1 *vt* to tell off. 2 *vi* to nag.
regar [1] *vt* to water.
regata *f* regatta.
regatear *vi* to haggle; (*en fútbol*) to dribble.
regazo *m* lap.
regeneración *f* regeneration.
régimen *m* (*pl* **regímenes**) regime; (*dieta*) diet; **estar a r.** to be on a diet.
regio,-a *a* (*real*) regal; *Am* (*magnífico*) majestic.

región f region.

regional a regional.

registrado,-a a **marca registrada** registered trademark.

registrar 1 vt (examinar) to inspect; (cachear) to frisk; (inscribir) to register. **2 registrarse** vr (detectarse) to be recorded; (inscribirse) to register.

registro m inspection; (inscripción) registration.

regla f (norma) rule; (instrumento) ruler; (periodo) period; **por r. general** as a (general) rule.

reglamentario,-a a statutory.

reglamento m regulations pl.

regocijar vt to delight.

regocijo m (placer) delight; (alborozo) rejoicing.

regresar vi to return.

regreso m return.

regular 1 vt to regulate; (ajustar) to adjust. **2** a regular; (mediano) so-so; **vuelo r.** scheduled flight. **3** adv so-so.

regularidad f regularity; **con r.** regularly.

regularizar [4] vt to regularize.

rehabilitar vt to rehabilitate; (edificio) to convert.

rehacer (pp **rehecho**) **1** vt to redo. **2 rehacerse** vr (recuperarse) to recover.

rehén m hostage.

rehogar [7] vt to brown.

rehuir vt to shun.

rehusar vt to refuse.

reina f queen.

reinar vi to reign.

reincidir vi to relapse (**en** into).

reincorporarse vr **r. al trabajo** to return to work.

reino m kingdom; **el R. Unido** the United Kingdom.

reír [6] vi, **reírse** vr to laugh (**de** at).

reiterar vt to reiterate.

reivindicación f demand.

reivindicar [1] vt to demand.

reja f (de ventana) grating.

rejilla f grill; (de horno) gridiron; (para equipaje) luggage rack.

rejoneador,-a mf bullfighter on horseback.

relación f relationship; (conexión) connection; **relaciones públicas** public relations.

relacionado,-a a related (**con** to).

relacionar 1 vt to relate (**con** to). **2 relacionarse** vr to be related; (alternar) to get acquainted.

relajación f relaxation.

relajar vt, **relajarse** vr to relax.

relamerse vr to lick one's lips.

relámpago m flash of lightning.

relatar vt to tell, relate.

relativo,-a a relative (**a** to).

relato m story.

relax m relaxation.

relegar [7] vt to relegate.

relevante a important.

relevar vt (sustituir) to take over from.

relevo m relief; (en carrera) relay.

religión f religion.

relinchar vi to neigh.

rellano m landing.

rellenar vt (impreso etc) to fill in; (llenar) to pack (**de** with).

relleno,-a 1 m (de aves) stuffing; (de pasteles) filling. **2** a stuffed.

reloj m clock; (de pulsera) watch.

relojería f (tienda) watchmaker's.

relucir vi to shine.

reluzco indic pres de **relucir**.

remache m rivet.

remangarse vr (mangas, pantalones) to roll up.

remar vi to row.

rematar vt to finish off.

remate m (final) finish; (en fútbol) shot at goal; **para r.** to crown it all; **de r.** utter.

remediar vt to remedy; (enmendar) to repair; **no pude remediarlo** I couldn't help it.

remedio m (cura) remedy; (solución) solution; **¡qué r.!** what else can I do!; **no hay más r.** there's no choice; **sin r.** without fail.

remendar [1] vt (ropa) to patch.

remesa f (de mercancías) consignment.

remiendo *m* (*arreglo*) mend; (*parche*) patch.

remilgado,-a *a* (*melindroso*) fussy.

remite *m* (*en carta*) sender's name and address.

remitente *mf* sender.

remitir 1 *vt* (*enviar*) to send. **2** *vi* (*fiebre, temporal*) to subside.

remo *m* oar.

remodelación *f* (*modificación*) reshaping; (*reorganización*) reorganization.

remojar *vt* to soak (**en** in).

remojón *m* fam **darse un r.** to go for a dip.

remolacha *f* red beet.

remolcador *m* tug.

remolcar [1] *vt* to tow.

remolino *m* (*de agua*) whirlpool; (*de aire*) whirlwind.

remolque *m* (*acción*) towing; (*vehículo*) trailer.

remordimiento *m* remorse.

remoto,-a *a* remote.

remover [4] *vt* (*tierra*) to turn over; (*líquido*) to shake up; (*comida etc*) to stir.

remuneración *f* remuneration.

remunerar *vt* to remunerate.

renacuajo *m* tadpole; fam (*niño pequeño*) shrimp.

rencor *m* resentment; **guardar r. a algn** to have a grudge against sb.

rencoroso,-a *a* resentful.

rendido,-a *a* (*muy cansado*) exhausted.

rendija *f* crack.

rendimiento *m* (*de máquina, motor*) performance.

rendir [6] **1** *vt* (*fruto, beneficios*) to yield; (*cansar*) to exhaust. **2** *vi* (*dar beneficios*) to pay. **3 rendirse** *vr* to surrender.

RENFE *abr de* **Red Nacional de Ferrocarriles Españoles** Spanish railroad network.

renglón *m* line.

reno *m* reindeer.

renombre *m* renown.

renovación *f* (*de contrato, pasaporte*) renewal.

renovar [2] *vt* to renew; (*edificio*) to renovate.

renta *f* (*ingresos*) income; (*beneficio*) interest; (*alquiler*) rent.

rentable *a* profitable.

renunciar *vi* (*dimitir*) to resign; (*no aceptar*) to decline; **r. a** to give up.

reñido,-a *a* (*disputado*) hard-fought.

reñir [6] **1** *vt* (*regañar*) to tell off. **2** *vi* (*discutir*) to argue; (*pelear*) to fight.

reo *mf* (*acusado*) accused; (*culpable*) culprit.

reojo mirar algo de r. to look at sth out of the corner of one's eye.

reparar 1 *vt* to repair. **2** *vi* **r. en** (*darse cuenta de*) to notice.

reparo *m* **no tener reparos en** not to hesitate to; **me da r.** I am embarrassed.

repartidor,-a *mf* distributor.

repartir *vt* (*dividir*) to share out; (*regalo, premio*) to give out; (*correo*) to deliver.

reparto *m* distribution; (*distribución*) handing out; (*de mercancías*) delivery; (*de actores*) cast.

repasar *vt* to revise.

repecho *m* short steep slope.

repeler *vt* (*repugnar*) to disgust.

repente de r. suddenly.

repentino,-a *a* sudden.

repercutir 1 *vt* (*subida de precio*) to pass on. **2** *vi* **r. en** to affect.

repertorio *m* repertoire.

repetición *f* repetition.

repetir [6] **1** *vt* to repeat; (*plato*) to have a second helping of. **2** *vi* (*en colegio*) to repeat a year. **3 repetirse** *vr* (*hecho*) to recur.

repicar [1] *vti* (*campanas*) to ring.

repisa *f* shelf.

replegarse [1] *vr* to fall back.

repleto,-a *a* full (up); **r. de** packed with.

réplica *f* answer; (*copia*) replica.

replicar [1] **1** *vt* (*objetar*) to argue. **2** *vi* to reply.

repollo *m* cabbage.

reponer 1 *vt* to replace. **2 reponerse** *vr* **reponerse de** to recover from.

reportaje *m* report; (*noticias*) news item.

reportero,-a *mf* reporter.

reposar *vti* to rest (**en** on).

reposo *m* rest.

repostar *vti* (*gasolina*) to fill up.

repostería *f* confectionery.

reprender *vt* to reprimand.

represalias *fpl* reprisals.

representante *mf* representative.

representar *vt* to represent; (*significar*) to mean; (*obra*) to perform.

represión *f* repression.

reprimenda *f* reprimand.

reprimir *vt* to repress.

reprochar *vt* **r. algo a algn** to reproach sb for sth.

reproducción *f* reproduction.

reproducir *vt*, **reproducirse** *vr* to reproduce.

reptil *m* reptile.

república *f* republic.

repuesto *m* (*recambio*) spare (part); **rueda de r.** spare wheel.

repugnante *a* disgusting.

repugnar *vt* to disgust.

repulsivo,-a *a* repulsive.

repuse *pt indef de* **reponer.**

reputación *f* reputation.

requesón *m* cottage cheese.

requisar *vt* to requisition.

requisito *m* requirement.

res *f* animal.

resaca *f* hangover.

resaltar *vi* (*sobresalir*) to project; *fig* to stand out.

resbaladizo,-a *a* slippery.

resbalar *vi*, **resbalarse** *vr* to slip.

resbalón *m* slip.

rescatar *vt* (*liberar*) to rescue.

rescate *m* rescue; (*dinero pagado*) ransom.

rescindir *vt* (*contrato*) to cancel.

rescoldo *m* embers *pl*.

reseco,-a *a* parched.

resentimiento *m* resentment.

reserva *f* (*de entradas etc*) booking; (*provisión*) reserve.

reservado,-a *a* reserved.

reservar *vt* (*billetes etc*) to reserve, book; (*guardar*) to keep.

resfriado,-a 1 *m* (*catarro*) cold; **coger un r.** to catch (a) cold. **2** *a* **estar r.** to have a cold.

resfriarse *vr* to catch (a) cold.

resguardo *m* (*recibo*) receipt.

residencia *f* residence; **r. de ancianos** old people's home.

residir *vi* to reside (**en** in).

resignarse *vr* to resign oneself (**a** to).

resina *f* resin.

resistencia *f* resistance; (*aguante*) endurance; (*de bombilla etc*) element.

resistir 1 *vi* to resist; (*soportar*) to hold (out). **2** *vt* (*situación, persona*) to put up with; (*tentación*) to resist. **3 resistirse** *vr* to resist; (*oponerse*) to offer resistance; (*negarse*) to refuse.

resolver [4] (*pp* **resuelto**) **1** *vt* (*solucionar*) to solve; (*asunto*) to settle. **2 resolverse** *vr* (*solucionarse*) to be solved.

resonar [6] *vi* to resound; (*tener eco*) to echo.

resoplar *vi* (*respirar*) to breathe heavily; (*de cansancio*) to puff and pant.

resorte *m* (*muelle*) spring; (*medio*) means.

respaldo *m* (*de silla etc*) back.

respecto *m* **al r., a este r.** in this respect; **con r. a, r. a** with regard to.

respetable *a* respectable.

respetar *vt* to respect.

respeto *m* respect.

respetuoso,-a *a* respectful.

respingo *m* start.

respiración *f* (*acción*) breathing; (*aliento*) breath.

respirar *vti* to breathe.

resplandecer *vi* to shine.

resplandor *m* (*brillo*) brightness;

(muy intenso) brilliance; *(de fuego)* blaze.

responder 1 *vt* to answer. **2** *vi (a una carta)* to reply; *(reaccionar)* to respond; *(corresponder)* to answer; *(protestar)* to answer back.

responsabilidad *f* responsibility.

responsabilizar [4] **1** *vt* to make responsible **(de** for); *(culpar)* hold responsible **(de** for). **2 responsabilizarse** *vr* to claim responsibility **(de** for).

responsable 1 *a* responsible. **2** *mf* **el/la r.** *(de robo etc)* the perpetrator.

respuesta *f* answer, reply; *(reacción)* response.

resquicio *m* chink.

resta *f* subtraction.

restablecer 1 *vt* to re-establish; *(el orden)* to restore. **2 restablecerse** *vr* (mejorarse) to recover.

restante *a* remaining.

restar *vt* to subtract.

restaurante *m* restaurant.

restaurar *vt* to restore.

resto *m* rest; *(en resta)* remainder; **restos** remains; *(de comida)* leftovers.

restregar [1] *vt* to scrub.

restricción *f* restriction.

restringir [6] *vt* to restrict.

resucitar *vti* to revive.

resuello *m* gasp.

resultado *m* result; *(consecuencia)* outcome.

resultar *vi (ser)* to turn out; **me resultó fácil** it turned out to be easy for me.

resumen *m* summary; **en r.** in short.

resumir *vt* to sum up.

retaguardia *f* rearguard.

retahíla *f* series *sing.*

retal *m (pedazo)* scrap.

retar *vt* to challenge.

retazo *m (pedazo)* scrap.

retención *f* retention; **r. de tráfico** (traffic) hold-up.

retener *vt (conservar)* to retain; *(detener)* to detain.

retirada *f* withdrawal.

retirar 1 *vt (apartar, alejar)* to take away; *(dinero)* to withdraw. **2 retirarse** *vr (apartarse)* to withdraw; *(irse, jubilarse)* to retire.

retiro *m (lugar tranquilo)* retreat.

reto *m* challenge.

retoque *m* final touch.

retorcer [4] *vt (cuerda, hilo)* to twist; *(ropa)* to wring (out). **2 retorcerse** *vr* to become twisted.

retorno *m* return.

retortijón *m (dolor)* stomach cramp.

retraído,-a *a* reserved.

retransmisión *f* broadcast.

retrasado,-a 1 *a (tren etc)* late; *(reloj)* slow; **estar r.** *(en el colegio)* to be behind. **2** *mf* **r. (mental)** mentally retarded person.

retrasar 1 *vt (retardar)* to slow down; *(atrasar)* to postpone; *(reloj)* to put back. **2 retrasarse** *vr* to be delayed; *(reloj)* to be slow.

retraso *m (demora)* delay; **con r.** late; **una hora de r.** an hour behind schedule.

retrato *m (pintura)* portrait; *(fotografía)* photograph.

retrete *m* toilet.

retribución *f (pago)* pay; *(recompensa)* reward.

retroceder *vi* to back away.

retroceso *m (movimiento)* backward movement.

retrospectivo,-a *a & f* retrospective.

retrovisor *m* rear-view mirror.

retumbar *vi (resonar)* to resound; *(tronar)* to thunder.

retuve *pt indef de* **retener.**

reúma, reumatismo *m* rheumatism.

reunión *f* meeting.

reunir 1 *vt* to gather together; *(dinero)* to raise; *(cualidades)* to possess; *(requisitos)* to fulfill. **2 reunirse** *vr* to meet.

revelar *vt* to reveal; *(película)* to develop.

reventar 154

reventar [1] *vti*, **reventarse** *vr* to burst.

reventón *m* (*de neumático*) blow-out.

reverencia *f* (*de hombre*) bow; (*de mujer*) curtsy.

reversible *a* reversible.

reverso *m* back.

revés *m* (*reverso*) reverse; (*contrariedad*) setback; **al o del r.** (*al contrario*) the other way round; (*la parte interior en el exterior*) inside out; (*boca abajo*) upside down; (*la parte de detrás delante*) back to front.

revisar *vt* to check; (*coche*) to service.

revisión *f* checking; (*de coche*) service; **r. médica** checkup.

revisor,-a *mf* corrector, inspector.

revista *f* magazine.

revivir *vti* to revive.

revolcarse [2] *vr* to roll about.

revoltijo, revoltillo *m* jumble.

revoltoso,-a *a* (*travieso*) mischievous.

revolución *f* revolution.

revolver [4] (*pp* **revuelto**) **1** *vt* (*desordenar*) to mess up; **me revuelve el estómago** it turns my stomach. **2 revolverse** *vr* (*agitarse*) to roll; (*el mar*) to become rough.

revólver *m* (*pl* **revólveres**) revolver.

revuelo *m* (*agitación*) stir.

revuelto,-a *a* (*desordenado*) in a mess; (*tiempo*) unsettled; (*mar*) rough; (*huevos*) scrambled.

rey *m* king; (**el día de**) **Reyes** Epiphany, January 6.

rezagarse *vr* to fall behind.

rezar [4] **1** *vi* (*orar*) to pray. **2** *vt* (*oración*) to say.

rezumar *vt* to ooze.

ría *f* estuary.

riada *f* flood.

ribera *f* (*de río*) bank; (*zona*) riverside.

rico,-a **1** *a* **ser r.** to be rich; **estar r.** (*delicioso*) to be delicious. **2** *mf* rich person; **los ricos** the rich.

ridiculizar [4] *vt* to ridicule.

ridículo,-a **1** *a* ridiculous. **2** *m* ridicule; **hacer el r., quedar en r.** to make a fool of o.eself; **poner en r.** to make a fool of sb.

riego *m* irrigation.

rienda *f* rein.

riesgo *m* risk; **correr el r. de** to run the risk of.

rifa *f* raffle.

rifle *m* rifle.

rigidez *f* rigidity; (*severidad*) inflexibility.

rigor *m* rigor; (*severidad*) severity.

rigurosamente *adv* rigorously; (*meticulosamente*) meticulously; (*severamente*) severely.

riguroso,-a *a* rigorous; (*severo*) severe.

rimar *vti* to rhyme (**con** with).

rímel *m* mascara.

rincón *m* corner.

rinoceronte *m* rhinoceros.

riña *f* (*pelea*) fight; (*discusión*) row.

riñón *m* kidney.

río *m* river; **r. abajo** downstream; **r. arriba** upstream.

riqueza *f* wealth.

risa *f* laugh; (*carcajadas*) laughter; **me da r.** it makes me laugh; **morirse o mondarse de r.** to die laughing.

risueño,-a *a* (*sonriente*) smiling.

ritmo *m* rhythm; (*paso*) rate.

rival *a & mf* rival.

rivalizar [4] *vi* to rival (**en** in).

rizado,-a *a* (*pelo*) curly; (*mar*) choppy.

rizar [4] *vt*, **rizarse** *vr* (*pelo*) to curl.

rizo *m* (*de pelo*) curl.

robar *vt* (*objeto*) to steal; (*banco, persona*) to rob; (*casa*) to burgle.

roble *m* oak (tree).

robo *m* robbery, theft; (*en casa*) burglary; **r. a mano armada** armed robbery.

robot *m* (*pl* **robots**) robot; **r. de cocina** food processor.

robusto,-a *a* robust.

roca *f* rock.

roce *m* (*fricción*) friction; (*en la piel*) chafing; (*contacto ligero*) brush.

rociar vt to sprinkle.
rocío m dew.
rocoso,-a a rocky.
rodaja f slice.
rodaje m shooting.
rodar [2] **1** vt (película etc) to shoot. **2** vi to roll.
rodear 1 vt to surround. **2 rodearse** vr to surround oneself (**de** with).
rodeo m (desvío) detour; (al hablar) evasiveness; rodeo; **no andarse con rodeos** to get straight to the point.
rodilla f knee; **de rodillas** kneeling; **hincarse** o **ponerse de rodillas** to kneel down.
roer vt (hueso) to gnaw; (galleta) to nibble at.
rogar [2] vt (pedir) to ask; (implorar) to beg; **hacerse de r.** to play hard to get.
rojo,-a a red; **estar en números rojos** to be in the red. **2** m (color) red.
rollizo,-a a chubby.
rollo m roll; fam (pesadez) drag.
romance m (aventura amorosa) romance.
romántico,-a a & mf romantic.
rombo m diamond; (en geometría) rhombus.
rompecabezas m inv (juego) (jigsaw) puzzle.
romper (pp roto) **1** vt to break; (papel, tela) to tear; (vajilla, cristal) to smash; (pantalones) to split; (relaciones) to break off. **2** vi to break; **r. a llorar** to burst out crying. **3 romperse** vr to break; (papel, tela) to tear; **romperse la cabeza** to rack one's brains.
ron m rum.
roncar [1] vi to snore.
roncha f (en la piel) swelling.
ronco,-a a hoarse; **quedarse r.** to lose one's voice.
ronda f round; (patrulla) patrol; (carretera) ring road; (paseo) avenue.
rondar vti (merodear) to prowl around; (estar cerca de) to be about.
ronquido m snore.

ronronear vi to purr.
roñoso,-a a (mugriento) filthy; (tacaño) mean.
ropa f clothes pl, clothing; **r. interior** underwear.
ropero m (armario) **r.** wardrobe, closet.
rosa 1 a inv (color) pink; **novela r.** romantic novel. **2** f (flor) rose. **3** m (color) pink.
rosado,-a 1 a (color) pink; (vino) rosé. **2** m (vino) rosé.
rosal m rosebush.
rosbif m roast beef.
rosco m (pastel) ring-shaped pastry.
rosquilla f ring-shaped pastry; **venderse como rosquillas** to sell like hot cakes.
rostro m (cara) face; fam **tener mucho r.** to have a lot of nerve.
roto,-a 1 a broken; (papel) torn; (gastado) worn out; (ropa) in tatters. **2** m (agujero) hole.
rótula f kneecap.
rotulador m felt-tip pen.
rótulo m (letrero) sign; (titular) heading.
rotundo,-a a categorical; **éxito r.** resounding success.
rotura f (ruptura) breaking; (de hueso) fracture.
rozadura f scratch.
rozar [4] **1** vt to brush against. **2** vi to rub. **3 rozarse** vr to brush (**con** against).
Rte. abr de **remite, remitente** sender.
rubí m (pl **rubíes**) ruby.
rubio,-a 1 a (pelo, persona) blond; **tabaco r.** Virginia tobacco. **2** m blond; f blonde.
ruborizarse [4] vr to blush.
rudimentario,-a a rudimentary.
rudo,-a a rough.
rueda f wheel; **r. de recambio** spare wheel; **r. de prensa** press conference.
ruedo m bullring.
ruego m request.
rugido m (de animal) roar.
rugir [6] vi to roar.

ruido *m* noise; (*sonido*) sound;
  hacer r. to make a noise.
ruidoso,-a *a* noisy.
ruin *a* (*vil*) vile; (*tacaño*) mean.
ruina *f* ruin.
ruiseñor *m* nightingale.
ruleta *f* roulette.
rulo *m* (*para el pelo*) roller.
rumba *f* rumba.
rumbo *m* direction; (**con**) **r. a**
  bound for.
rumor *m* rumor; (*murmullo*)
  murmur.
rumorearse *v impers* to be ru-
  mored.
ruptura *f* breaking; (*de relaciones*)
  breaking-off.
rural *a* rural.
ruso,-a *a* a & *mf* Russian.
rústico,-a *a* rustic.
ruta *f* route.
rutina *f* routine.

S

S.A. *abr de* **Sociedad Anónima** ≈
  PLC, ≈ Ltd, ≈ Inc.
sábado *m* Saturday.
sábana *f* sheet; *fam* **se me pegaron
  las sábanas** I overslept.
sabañón *m* chilblain.
saber¹ *m* knowledge.
saber² [1] *vt* to know; (*tener habilidad*) to be able to; (*enterarse*) to
  learn; **que yo sepa** as far as I
  know; **vete tú a s.** goodness knows;
  a s. namely; **¿sabes cocinar?** can
  you cook? 2 *vi* (*tener sabor*) to taste
  (**a** of); (*soler*) to be accustomed to;
  sabe a fresa it tastes of straw-
  berries.
sabiduría *f* wisdom.
sabio,-a 1 *a* (*prudente*) wise. 2 *mf*
  scholar.
sable *m* sabre.
sabor *m* (*gusto*) flavor; **con s. a limón** lemon-flavored.
saborear *vt* (*degustar*) to taste.
sabotaje *m* sabotage.

sabré *indic fut de* **saber.**
sabroso,-a *a* tasty; (*delicioso*) delicious.
sacacorchos *m inv* corkscrew.
sacapuntas *m inv* pencil sharpener.
sacar [1] *vt* to take out; (*con más
  fuerza*) to pull out; (*obtener*) to get;
  (*conclusiones*) to draw; (*entrada*)
  to buy; (*libro, disco*) to bring out;
  (*fotografía*) to take; **s. la lengua** to
  stick one's tongue out; **s. provecho
  de algo** to benefit from sth.
sacarina *f* saccharin.
sacerdote *m* priest.
saciar *vt* (*sed*) to quench; (*deseos,
  hambre*) to satisfy.
saco *m* sack; (*jersey*) pullover; **s.
  de dormir** sleeping bag.
sacrificar [1] **1** *vt* to sacrifice.
  2 sacrificarse *vr* to make sacri-
  fices.
sacrificio *m* sacrifice.
sacudida *f* shake; (*espasmo*) jolt;
  (*de terremoto*) tremor.
sacudir *vt* (*agitar*) to shake; (*alfombra, sábana*) to shake out;
  (*arena, polvo*) to shake off; (*golpear*) to beat.
sádico,-a 1 *a* sadistic. **2** *mf* sadist.
saeta *f* (*dardo*) dart.
safari *m* (*cacería*) safari; (*parque*)
  safari park.
sagaz *a* (*listo*) clever; (*astuto*)
  shrewd.
sagrado,-a *a* sacred.
sal¹ *f* salt; **s. de mesa** table salt; **s.
  gorda** cooking salt.
sal² *imperativo de* **salir.**
sala *f* room; (*en un hospital*) ward;
  s. de estar living room; **s. de
  espera** waiting room; **s. de exposi-
  ciones** exhibition hall; **s. de fiestas** nightclub.
salado,-a *a* (*con sal*) salted; (*con
  exceso de sal*) salty; (*infortunado*)
  unlucky; **agua salada** salt water.
salario *m* salary.
salchicha *f* sausage.
salchichón *m* (*salami-type*) sausage.

saldar vt (cuenta) to settle; (deuda) to pay off.

saldo m (de cuenta) balance; **saldos** sales.

saldré indic fut de **salir.**

salero m (recipiente) saltcellar.

salgo indic pres de **salir.**

salida f (partida) departure; (puerta etc) exit, way out; (de carrera) start; (de un astro) rising; (perspectiva) opening; (en ordenador) output; **callejón sin s.** dead end; **s. de emergencia** emergency exit; **te vi a la s. del cine** I saw you leaving the cinema; **s. del sol** sunrise.

salir 1 vi (de un sitio, tren etc) to leave; (venir de dentro, revista, disco) to come out; (novios) to go out; (aparecer) to appear; (ley) to come in; (trabajo, vacante) to come up; (resultar) to turn out (to be); (problema) to work out; **salió de la habitación** she left the room; **¿cómo te salió el examen?** how did your exam go?; **s. ganando** to come out on top; **s. barato/caro** to work out cheap/expensive; **esta cuenta no me sale** I can't work this calculation out. 2 **salirse** vr (líquido, gas) to leak (out); **salirse de lo normal** to be out of the ordinary; **salirse con la suya** to get one's own way.

saliva f saliva.

salmón 1 m (pescado) salmon. 2 a inv (color) salmon pink.

salmonete m (pescado) red mullet.

salobre a (agua) brackish; (gusto) salty.

salón m (en una casa) lounge; **s. de actos** assembly hall; **s. de belleza** beauty salon; **s. del automóvil** motor show.

salpicar [1] vt (rociar) to splash; **me salpicó el abrigo de barro** he splashed mud on my coat.

salsa f sauce; (de carne) gravy.

saltamontes m inv grasshopper.

saltar 1 vt (obstáculo, valla) to jump (over). 2 vi to jump; (romperse) to break; (plomos) to blow; (desprenderse) to come off; **s. a la vista** to be obvious; **s. saltarse** vr (omitir) to skip; (no hacer caso) to ignore; **saltarse el semáforo** to run the lights; **se me saltaron las lágrimas** tears came to my eyes.

salto m (acción) jump, leap; **a saltos** in leaps and bounds; **dar un s.** to jump, leap; **de un s.** in a flash; **s. de altura** high jump; **s. de longitud** long jump; **s. mortal** somersault.

salud f health; **beber a la s. de algn** to drink to sb's health; **¡s.!** cheers!

saludable a (sano) healthy.

saludar vt (decir hola a) to say hello to; **saluda de mi parte a** give my regards to; **le saluda atentamente** (en una carta) yours faithfully.

saludo m greeting; **un s. de** best wishes from.

salvado m bran.

salvaguardar vt to safeguard (de from).

salvaje a (planta, animal) wild; (pueblo, tribu) savage.

salvam(i)ento m rescue.

salvar 1 vt to save (de from); (obstáculo) to clear; (dificultad) to overcome. 2 **salvarse** vr (sobrevivir) to survive; (escaparse) to escape (de from); **¡sálvese quien pueda!** every man for himself!

salvavidas m inv life preserver.

salvo,-a 1 a safe; **a s.** safe. 2 adv (exceptuando) except (for). 3 conj **s. que** unless.

san a saint; ver **santo,-a.**

sanar 1 vt (curar) to heal. 2 vi (persona) to recover; (herida) to heal.

sanción f sanction.

sancionar vt (castigar) to penalize.

sandalia f sandal.

sándalo m sandalwood.

sandía f watermelon.

sandwich m sandwich.

sangrar vi to bleed.

sangre f blood; **donar s.** to give blood; **a s. fría** in cold blood.

sangría f (bebida) sangria.

sangriento,-a a (cruel) cruel.

sanguíneo,-a a blood; **grupo s.** blood group.

sano,-a a healthy; **s. y salvo** safe and sound.

santiguarse vr to cross oneself.

santo,-a 1 a holy. **2** mf saint; (día onomástico) saint's day; **se me fue el s. al cielo** I completely forgot; **¿a s. de qué?** why on earth?

santuario m shrine.

sapo m toad.

saque m (en tenis) service; (en fútbol) **s. inicial** kick-off; **s. de esquina** corner kick.

saquear vt (casas y tiendas) to loot.

sarampión m measles.

sarcástico,-a a sarcastic.

sardina f sardine.

sargento m sergeant.

sarpullido m rash.

sarro m (en los dientes) tartar; (en la lengua) fur.

sartén f frying pan, skillet.

sastre m tailor.

satélite m satellite; **televisión vía s.** satellite television.

satén m satin.

sátira f satire.

satisfacción f satisfaction.

satisfacer (pp **satisfecho**) vt to satisfy; (deuda) to pay.

satisfecho,-a a satisfied; **me doy por s.** that's good enough for me.

sauce m willow; **s. llorón** weeping willow.

sauna f sauna.

saxofón m saxophone.

sazonar vt to season.

se[1] pron (reflexivo) (a él mismo) himself; (a ella misma) herself; (animal) itself; (a usted mismo) yourself; (a ellos / ellas mismos / mismas) themselves; (a ustedes mismos) yourselves; **se afeitó** he shaved; **se compró un nuevo coche** he bought himself a new

car. ▪ (recíproco) one another, each other. ▪ (voz pasiva) **el vino se guarda en cubas** wine is kept in casks. ▪ (impersonal) **nunca se sabe** you never know; **se habla inglés** English spoken; **se dice que . . .** it is said that . . .

se[2] pron pers (a él) (to o for) him; (a ella) (to o for) her; (a usted o ustedes) (to o for) you; (a ellos) (to o for) them; **se lo diré en cuanto les vea** I'll tell them as soon as I see them; **¿se lo explico?** shall I explain it to him/her etc?

sé[1] indic pres de **saber.**

sé[2] imperativo de **ser.**

sea subj pres de **ser.**

secador m dryer; **s. de pelo** hairdryer.

secadora f tumble dryer.

secar [1] **1** vt to dry. **2 secarse** vr to dry; (marchitarse) to dry up; **secarse las manos** to dry one's hands.

sección f section.

seco,-a a dry; (tono) curt; (golpe, ruido) sharp; **frutos secos** dried fruit; **limpieza en s.** dry-cleaning; **frenar en s.** to pull up sharply.

secretaría f (oficina) secretary's office.

secretario,-a mf secretary.

secreto,-a 1 a secret; **en s.** in secret. **2** m secret.

secta f sect.

sector m sector; (zona) area.

secuencia f sequence.

secuestrar vt (persona) to kidnap; (avión) to hijack.

secuestro m (de persona) kidnapping; (de avión) hijacking.

secundario,-a a secondary.

sed f thirst; **tener s.** to be thirsty.

seda f silk.

sedal m fishing line.

sedante a & m sedative.

sede f headquarters; (de gobierno) seat.

sedentario,-a a sedentary.

sedimento m sediment.

sedoso,-a a silky.

seducir vt to seduce.

seductor,-a 1 a seductive. **2** mf seducer.

segar [1] vt to cut.

seglar 1 a secular. **2** mf lay person; m layman; f laywoman.

segmento m segment.

seguida en s. immediately, straight away.

seguido adv straight; **todo s.** straight ahead.

seguir [6] **1** vt to follow; (camino) to continue. **2** vi to follow; **siguió hablando** he went on o kept on speaking; **sigo resfriado** I've still got the cold.

según 1 prep according to; (en función de) depending on; (tal como) just as; **estaba s. lo dejé** it was just as I had left it. **2** conj (a medida que) as; **s. iba leyendo . . .** as I read . . . **3** adv ¿**vendrás? - s.** are you coming?—it depends.

segundo,-a¹ a second.

segundo² m (tiempo) second.

seguramente adv (probablemente) most probably; (seguro) surely.

seguridad f security; (física) safety; (confianza) confidence; (certeza) sureness; **s. en carretera** road safety; **s. en sí mismo** self-confidence; **con toda s.** most probably; **tener la s. de que . . .** to be certain that . . .; **S. Social** ≈ Social Security.

seguro,-a 1 a (cierto) sure; (libre de peligro) safe; (protegido) secure; (fiable) reliable; (firme) steady; **estoy s. de que . . .** I am sure that . . .; **está segura de ella misma** she has self-confidence. **2** m (de accidentes etc) insurance; (dispositivo) safety device; **s. de vida** life insurance. **3** adv definitely.

seis a & m inv six.

seiscientos,-as a & mf inv six hundred.

seleccionar vt to select.

selecto,-a a select.

self-service m self-service restaurant.

selva f jungle.

sello m (de correos) stamp; (para documentos) seal.

semáforo m traffic lights pl.

semana f week; **S. Santa** Holy Week.

semanal a & m weekly.

semanario m weekly magazine.

sembrar vt to sow; **s. el pánico** to spread panic.

semejante 1 a (parecido) similar. **2** m (prójimo) fellow being.

semestre m semester.

semifinal f semifinal.

semilla f seed.

seminario m (en colegio) seminar; (para sacerdotes) seminary.

sémola f semolina.

sencillo,-a a (fácil) simple; (natural) unaffected; (billete) single; (sin adornos) plain.

senda f, **sendero** m path.

seno m (pecho) breast; (interior) heart.

sensación f sensation; **tengo la s. de que . . .** I have a feeling that . . .; **causar s.** to cause a sensation.

sensacional a sensational.

sensato,-a a sensible.

sensible a sensitive; (perceptible) perceptible.

sensiblemente adv noticeably.

sensualidad f sensuality.

sentar [1] **1** vt to sit; (establecer) to establish. **2** vi (color, ropa) to suit; **el pelo corto te sienta mal** short hair doesn't suit you; **s. bien/mal a** (comida) to agree/disagree with; **la sopa te sentará bien** the soup will do you good. **3 sentarse** vr to sit (down).

sentencia f (condena) sentence.

sentido m sense; (significado) meaning; (dirección) direction; (conciencia) consciousness; **s. común** common sense; **no tiene s.** it doesn't make sense; (de) **s. único** one-way; **perder el s.** to faint.

sentimental 1 *a* sentimental; **vida s.** love life. **2** *mf* sentimental person.

sentimiento *m* feeling; (*pesar*) sorrow.

sentir [5] **1** *vt* to feel; (*lamentar*) to regret; **lo siento (mucho)** I'm (very) sorry; **siento molestarle** I'm sorry to bother you. **2 sentirse** *vr* to feel; **me siento mal** I feel ill.

seña *f* mark; (*gesto, indicio*) sign; **hacer señas a algn** to signal to sb; **señas** (*dirección*) address.

señal *f* sign; (*marca*) mark; (*vestigio*) trace; **s. de llamada** dial tone; **s. de tráfico** road sign.

señalar *vt* (*indicar*) to indicate; (*identificar, comunicar*) to point out; **s. con el dedo** to point at.

señor *m* (*hombre*) man; (*caballero*) gentleman; (*con apellido*) Mr; (*tratamiento de respeto*) sir; **el Sr. Gutiérrez** Mr Gutiérrez.

señora *f* (*mujer*) woman; (*trato formal*) lady; (*con apellido*) Mrs; (*tratamiento de respeto*) madam; (*esposa*) wife; **¡señoras y señores!** ladies and gentlemen!; **la Sra. Salinas** Mrs Salinas.

señorita *f* (*joven*) young woman; (*trato formal*) young lady; (*tratamiento de respeto*) Miss; **la S. Padilla** Miss Padilla.

sepa *subj pres de* **saber.**

separación *f* separation; (*espacio*) space.

separar 1 *vt* to separate; (*desunir*) to detach; (*dividir*) to divide; (*apartar*) to move away. **2 separarse** *vr* to separate; (*apartarse*) to move away (**de** from).

septentrional *a* northern.

septiembre *m* September.

séptimo,-a *a & mf* seventh.

sepultura *f* grave.

sequía *f* drought.

séquito *m* entourage.

ser[1] *m* being; **s. humano** human being; **s. vivo** living being.

ser[2] *vi* to be; **ser músico** to be a mu-

sician; **s. de** (*procedencia*) to be from; (+ *material*) to be made of; (+ *poseedor*) to belong to; **el perro es de Miguel** the dog belongs to Miguel; **hoy es dos de noviembre** today is the second of November; **son las cinco de la tarde** it's five o'clock; **¿cuántos estaremos en la fiesta?** how many of us will there be at the party?; **¿cuánto es?** how much is it?; **el estreno será mañana** tomorrow is the opening night; **es que . . .** it's just that . . .; **como sea** anyhow; **lo que sea** whatever; **o sea** that is (to say); **por si fuera poco** to top it all; **sea como sea** be that as it may; **a no s. que** unless; **de no s. por . . .** had it not been for . . . ▪ (*auxiliar en pasiva*) to be; **fue asesinado** he was murdered.

sereno,-a *a* calm.

serial *m* serial.

serie *f* series *sing*; **fabricación en s.** mass production.

seriedad *f* (*severidad*) seriousness; (*gravedad*) gravity; **falta de s.** irresponsibility.

serio,-a *a* serious; **en s.** seriously.

sermón *m* sermon.

serpiente *f* snake; **s. de cascabel** rattlesnake; **s. pitón** python.

serrín *m* sawdust.

serrucho *m* handsaw.

servicial *a* helpful.

servicio *m* service; (*retrete*) rest room; **s. a domicilio** delivery service; **s. militar** military service.

servidor,-a 1 *m* server. **2** *mf* (*criado*) servant.

servilleta *f* napkin.

servir [6] **1** *vt* to serve. **2** *vi* to serve; (*valer*) to be suitable; **ya no sirve** it's no use; **¿para qué sirve esto?** what is this (used) for?; **s. de** to serve as. **3 servirse** *vr* (*comida etc*) to help oneself.

sesenta *a & m inv* sixty.

sesión *f* (*reunión*) session; (*pase*) showing.

seso *m* brain.

seta *f* (*comestible*) mushroom; **s. venenosa** toadstool.

setecientos,-as *a* & *mf inv* seven hundred.

setenta *a* & *m inv* seventy.

setiembre *m* = **septiembre.**

seto *m* hedge.

seudónimo *m* pseudonym; (*de escritor*) pen name.

severidad *f* severity; (*rigurosidad*) strictness.

sexo *m* sex; (*órgano*) genitals *pl.*

sexto,-a *a* & *mf* sixth.

sexual *a* sexual; **vida s.** sex life.

si *conj* if; **como si** as if; **si no** if not; **me preguntó si me gustaba** he asked me if o whether I liked it.

sí[1] *pron pers* (*sing*) (*él*) himself; (*ella*) herself; (*cosa*) itself; (*pl*) themselves; (*uno mismo*) oneself; **por sí mismo** by himself.

sí[2] *adv* yes; **porque sí** just because; **¡que sí!** yes, I tell you!; **un día sí y otro no** every other day; (*uso enfático*) **sí que me gusta** of course I like it; **¡eso sí que no!** certainly not!

sico- = **psico-.**

sida *m* AIDS.

siderúrgico,-a *a* iron and steel.

sidra *f* cider.

siempre 1 *adv* always; **como s.** as usual; **a la hora de s.** at the usual time; **para s.** forever. 2 *conj* **s. que** (*cada vez que*) whenever; (*a condición de que*) provided, as long as; **s. y cuando** provided, as long as.

sien *f* temple.

sierra *f* saw; (*montañosa*) mountain range.

siesta *f* siesta; **dormir la s.** to have a siesta.

siete *a* & *m inv* seven.

sigilo *m* secrecy.

sigilosamente *adv* (*secretamente*) secretly.

sigiloso,-a *a* secretive.

sigla *f* acronym.

siglo *m* century.

significado *m* meaning.

significar [1] *vt* to mean.

significativo,-a *a* significant; (*expresivo*) meaningful.

signo *m* sign; **s. de interrogación** question mark.

sigo *indic pres de* **seguir.**

siguiente *a* following, next; **al día s.** the following day.

sílaba *f* syllable.

silbar *vi* to whistle.

silbato *m* whistle.

silbido *m* whistle.

silencio *m* silence.

silencioso,-a *a* (*persona*) quiet; (*motor etc*) silent.

silicona *f* silicone.

silla *f* chair; (*de montura*) saddle; **s. de ruedas** wheelchair.

sillín *m* saddle.

sillón *m* armchair.

silueta *f* silhouette; (*de cuerpo*) figure.

silvestre *a* wild.

símbolo *m* symbol.

simétrico,-a *a* symmetrical.

simiente *f* seed.

similar *a* similar.

similitud *f* similarity.

simio *m* monkey.

simpatía *f* (*de persona, lugar*) charm; **tenerle s. a algn** to like sb.

simpático,-a *a* nice.

simpatizar [4] *vi* to sympathize (**con** with); (*llevarse bien*) to hit it off (**con** with), to get along well (**con** with).

simple 1 *a* simple; (*mero*) mere. 2 *m* (*persona*) simpleton.

simulacro *m* sham.

simular *vt* to simulate.

simultáneo,-a *a* simultaneous.

sin *prep* without; **cerveza s.** alcohol-free beer; **s. más ni más** without further ado.

sinagoga *f* synagogue.

sinceridad *f* sincerity.

sincero,-a *a* sincere.

sincronizar [4] *vt* to synchronize.

sindicato *m* labor union.

sinfonía *f* symphony.

singular 1 *a* singular; (*excepcio-*

nal) exceptional; (*raro*) odd. **2** *m*
(*número*) singular; **en s.** in the singular.

siniestro,-a *a* sinister. **2** *m* disaster.

sino *conj* but; **nadie s. él** no one but him; **no quiero s. que me oigan** I only want them to listen (to me).

sinónimo,-a 1 *a* synonymous. **2** *m* synonym.

sintético,-a *a* synthetic.

sintetizar [4] *vt* to synthesize.

síntoma *m* symptom.

sintonía *f* (*de programa*) tuning.

sintonizador *m* (*de radio*) tuning knob.

sintonizar [4] *vt* (*radio*) to tune in.

sinvergüenza 1 *a* (*desvergonzado*) shameless; (*descarado*) rude. **2** *mf* (*desvergonzado*) rogue; (*caradura*) cheeky devil.

siquiera *adv* (*por lo menos*) at least; **ni s.** not even.

sirena *f* mermaid; (*señal acústica*) siren.

sirviente,-a *mf* servant.

sistema *m* system; **por s.** as a rule; **s. nervioso** nervous system; **s. operativo** operating system.

sitio *m* (*lugar*) place; (*espacio*) room; **en cualquier s.** anywhere; **hacer s.** to make room.

situación *f* situation; (*ubicación*) location.

situar 1 *vt* to locate. **2 situarse** *vr* to be situated.

slogan *m* slogan.

smoking *m* tuxedo.

s/n. *abr de* **sin número.**

snob *a* & *mf* = **esnob.**

sobaco *m* armpit.

soberanía *f* sovereignty.

soberano,-a *a* & *mf* sovereign.

soberbio,-a *a* proud; (*magnífico*) splendid.

sobornar *vt* to bribe.

sobra *f* **de s.** (*no necesario*) superfluous; **tener de s.** to have plenty; **saber algo de s.** to know sth only too well; **sobras** (*restos*) leftovers.

sobrante 1 *a* remaining. **2** *m* surplus.

sobrar *vi* to be more than enough; (*quedar*) to be left over; **sobran tres sillas** there are three chairs too many; **ha sobrado carne** there's still some meat left (over).

sobrasada *f* sausage spread.

sobre[1] *m* (*para carta*) envelope; (*de sopa etc*) packet.

sobre[2] *prep* (*encima*) on, on top of; (*por encima*) over, above; (*acerca de*) about, on; (*aproximadamente*) about; **s. todo** above all.

sobrecogedor,-a *a* awesome.

sobredosis *f inv* overdose.

sobreentenderse *vr* **se sobreentiende** that goes without saying.

sobrehumano,-a *a* superhuman.

sobrenatural *a* supernatural.

sobrepasar 1 *vt* to exceed. **2 sobrepasarse** *vr* to go too far.

sobreponerse *vr* (*superar*) to overcome; (*animarse*) to pull oneself together.

sobresaliente 1 *m* (*nota*) A. **2** *a* (*que destaca*) excellent.

sobresalir *vi* to protrude; *fig* (*destacar*) to stand out.

sobresalto *m* (*movimiento*) start; (*susto*) fright.

sobrevenir *vi* to happen unexpectedly.

sobreviviente 1 *a* surviving. **2** *mf* survivor.

sobrevivir *vi* to survive.

sobrevolar [2] *vt* to fly over.

sobrina *f* niece.

sobrino *m* nephew.

sobrio,-a *a* sober.

socarrón,-ona *a* (*sarcástico*) sarcastic.

socavón *m* (*bache*) pothole.

sociable *a* sociable.

social *a* social.

socialista *a* & *mf* socialist.

sociedad *f* society; (*empresa*) company.

socio,-a *mf* (*miembro*) member; (*de empresa*) partner; **hacerse s. de un club** to join a club.

sociológico,-a *a* sociological.
socorrer *vt* to assist.
socorrista *mf* lifeguard.
socorro *m* assistance; **¡s.!** help!;
puesto de s. first-aid post.
soda *f* (*bebida*) soda water.
soez *a* vulgar.
sofá *m* (*pl* **sofás**) sofa; **s. cama** sofa
bed.
sofisticado,-a *a* sophisticated.
sofocado,-a *a* suffocated. **estar s.**
to be out of breath; (*preocupado*)
to be upset.
sofocante *a* stifling.
sofocar [1] **1** *vt* (*ahogar*) to suffocate; (*incendio*) to extinguish.
2 sofocarse *vr* (*ahogarse*) to suffocate; (*irritarse*) to get upset.
soga *f* rope.
soja *f* soybean.
sol *m* sun; (*luz*) sunlight; (*luz y calor*) sunshine; **hace s.** it's sunny;
tomar el s. to sunbathe; **al o bajo el
s.** in the sun.
solamente *adv* only; **no s.** not
only; **s. que . . .** except that . . .
solapa *f* (*de chaqueta*) lapel; (*de sobre, bolsillo, libro*) flap.
solar[1] *a* solar; **luz s.** sunlight.
solar[2] *m* (*terreno*) plot; (*en obras*)
building site.
soldado *m* soldier.
soldar [2] *vt* (*cable*) to solder;
(*chapa*) to weld.
soleado,-a *a* sunny.
soledad *f* (*estado*) solitude; (*sentimiento*) loneliness.
solemne *a* (*majestuoso*) solemn.
soler [4] *vi* defectivo to be in the
habit of; **solemos ir en coche** we
usually go by car; **solía pasear por
aquí** he used to walk round here.
solicitar *vt* (*información etc*) to request; (*trabajo*) to apply for.
solicitud *f* (*petición*) request; (*de
trabajo*) application.
solidaridad *f* solidarity.
sólido,-a *a* solid.
solitario,-a *a* (*que está solo*) solitary; (*que se siente solo*) lonely.
sollozar [4] *vi* to sob.

sollozo *m* sob.
solo,-a **1** *a* only; (*solitario*) lonely;
una sola vez only once; **se en-
ciende s.** it switches itself on automatically; **a solas** alone, by oneself. **2** *m* (*musical*) solo.
sólo *adv* only; **tan s.** only; **no s. . . .
sino (también)** not only . . . but
(also); **con s., (tan) s. con** just by.
solomillo *m* sirloin.
soltar [2] **1** *vt* (*desasir*) to let go of;
(*prisionero*) to release; (*humo,
olor*) to give off; (*carcajada*) to let
out; **¡suéltame!** let me go! **2 soltarse** *vr* (*desatarse*) to come loose;
(*perro etc*) to get loose; (*desprenderse*) to come off.
soltero,-a 1 *a* single. **2** *m* (*hombre*)
bachelor. **3** *f* (*mujer*) single woman.
solterón,-ona 1 *m* (*hombre*) old
bachelor. **2** *f* (*mujer*) old maid.
soluble *a* soluble; **café s.** instant
coffee.
solución *f* solution.
solucionar *vt* to solve; (*arreglar*)
to settle.
sombra *f* shade; (*silueta proyec-
tada*) shadow; **s. de ojos** eyeshadow.
sombrero *m* (*prenda*) hat; **s. de
copa** top hat; **s. hongo** derby hat.
sombrilla *f* sunshade.
sombrío,-a *a* (*oscuro*) dark; (*tenebroso*) gloomy.
someter 1 *vt* to subject; (*rebeldes*)
to put down; **s. a prueba** to put to
the test. **2 someterse** *vr* (*subordi-
narse*) to submit; (*rendirse*) to surrender; **someterse a un tratamiento** to undergo treatment.
somnífero *m* sleeping pill.
somnoliento,-a *a* sleepy.
sonar [2] **1** *vi* to sound; (*timbre, teléfono*) to ring; **suena bien** it
sounds good; **tu nombre/cara me
suena** your name/face rings a bell.
2 sonarse *vr* **sonarse (la nariz)** to
blow one's nose.
sondeo *m* (*encuesta*) poll.
sonido *m* sound.

sonoro,-a a (resonante) resounding; **banda sonora** soundtrack.

sonreír [6] vi, **sonreírse** vr to smile; **me sonrió** he smiled at me.

sonrisa f smile.

sonrojarse vr to blush.

soñar [2] vti to dream; **s. con** to dream of o about.

soñoliento,-a a sleepy.

sopa f soup.

sopera f soup tureen.

soplar 1 vi (viento) to blow. **2** vt (polvo etc) to blow away; (para enfriar) to blow on; (para apagar) to blow out; (para inflar) to blow up.

soplo m (acción) puff; (de viento) gust.

soplón,-ona mf fam (niño) telltale; (delator) informer.

soportar vt (sostener) to support; (tolerar) to endure; (aguantar) to put up with.

soporte m support.

sorber vt (beber) to sip; (absorber) to soak up.

sorbete m sorbet.

sorbo m sip; (trago) gulp.

sórdido,-a a sordid.

sordo,-a 1 a (persona) deaf; (ruido, dolor) dull. **2** mf deaf person.

sordomudo,-a 1 a deaf and dumb. **2** mf deaf and dumb person.

sorprender vt to surprise; (coger desprevenido) to take by surprise.

sorpresa f surprise; **coger por s.** to take by surprise.

sorpresivo,-a a Am unexpected.

sortear vt to draw lots for; (rifar) to raffle (off).

sorteo m draw; (rifa) raffle.

sortija f ring.

sosegar [1] **1** vt to calm. **2** **sosegarse** vr to calm down.

soso,-a a lacking in salt; (persona) dull.

sospechar 1 vi (desconfiar) to suspect; **s. de algn** to suspect sb. **2** vt (pensar) to suspect.

sospechoso,-a 1 a suspicious. **2** mf suspect.

sostén m (apoyo) support; (prenda) bra, brassiere.

sostener 1 vt to hold; (sustentar) to hold up; **s. que ...** to maintain that ... **2 sostenerse** vr (mantenerse) to support oneself; (permanecer) to remain.

sostuve pt indef de **sostener.**

sota f (de baraja) jack.

sotana f cassock.

sótano m basement.

soviético,-a a & mf Soviet; **la Unión Soviética** the Soviet Union.

soy indic pres de **ser.**

spray m (pl sprays) spray.

Sr. abr de **Señor** Mister, Mr.

Sra. abr de **Señora** Mrs.

Srta. abr de **Señorita** Miss.

standard a & m standard.

su a pos (de él) his; (de ella) her; (de usted, ustedes) your; (de animales o cosas) its; (impersonal) one's; (de ellos) their.

suave a smooth; (luz, voz etc) soft; (templado) mild.

suavizante m (para el pelo) (hair) conditioner; (para la ropa) fabric softener.

suavizar [4] **1** vt to smooth (out). **2 suavizarse** vr (temperatura) to get milder.

subalterno,-a a & mf subordinate.

subasta f auction.

subcampeón,-ona mf runner-up.

subconsciente a & m subconscious.

subdesarrollado,-a a underdeveloped.

subdirector,-a mf assistant director.

súbdito,-a mf subject.

subestimar vt to underestimate.

subir 1 vt to go up; (llevar arriba) to take up, bring up; (precio, salario, voz) to raise; (volumen) to turn up. **2** vi (ir arriba) to go/come up; (al autobús, barco etc) to get on; (aumentar) to go up; **s. a** (un coche) to get into. **3 subirse** vr to climb up;

(*al autobús, avión, tren, bici*) to get on; (*cremallera*) to do up; (*mangas*) to roll up; **subirse a** (*un coche*) to get into.

súbitamente *adv* suddenly.

súbito,-a *a* sudden.

sublevarse *vr* to rebel.

sublime *a* sublime.

submarinismo *m* skin-diving.

submarino,-a **1** *a* underwater. **2** *m* submarine.

subnormal **1** *a* mentally handicapped. **2** *mf* mentally handicapped person.

subordinado,-a *a & mf* subordinate.

subrayar *vt* to underline; *fig* (*recalcar*) to stress.

subscripción *f* subscription.

subsecretario,-a *mf* undersecretary.

subsidiario,-a *a* subsidiary.

subsidio *m* allowance; **s. de desempleo** unemployment benefit.

subsistencia *f* subsistence.

subterráneo,-a *a* underground.

suburbio *m* (*barrio pobre*) slum; (*barrio periférico*) suburb.

subvención *f* subsidy.

suceder **1** *vi* (*ocurrir*) (*uso impers*) to happen; **¿qué sucede?** what's going on?; **s. a** (*seguir*) to follow. **2 sucederse** *vr* to follow one another.

sucesión *f* (*serie*) succession.

sucesivamente *adv* **y así s.** and so on.

sucesivo,-a *a* (*siguiente*) following; **en lo s.** from now on.

suceso *m* (*acontecimiento*) event; (*incidente*) incident.

sucesor,-a *mf* successor.

suciedad *f* dirt; (*calidad*) dirtiness.

sucio,-a *a* dirty.

suculento,-a *a* succulent.

sucumbir *vi* to succumb.

sucursal *f* (*de banco etc*) branch.

sudadera *f* sweatshirt.

sudafricano,-a *a & mf* South African.

sudamericano,-a *a & mf* South American.

sudar *vti* to sweat.

sudeste *a & m* southeast.

sudoeste *a & m* southwest.

sudor *m* sweat.

sueco,-a **1** *a* Swedish. **2** *mf* (*persona*) Swede. **3** *m* (*idioma*) Swedish.

suegra *f* mother-in-law.

suegro *m* father-in-law; **mis suegros** my in-laws.

suela *f* sole.

sueldo *m* wages *pl*.

suelo *m* (*superficie*) ground; (*de interior*) floor.

suelto,-a **1** *a* loose; (*en libertad*) free; (*huido*) at large; (*desatado*) undone; **dinero s.** loose change. **2** *m* (*dinero*) (loose) change.

sueño *m* sleepiness; (*cosa soñada*) dream; **tener s.** to be sleepy.

suerte *f* (*fortuna*) luck; **por s.** fortunately; **tener s.** to be lucky; **¡que tengas s.!** good luck!

suéter *m* sweater.

suficiente **1** *a* (*bastante*) sufficient, enough. **2** *m* (*nota*) pass.

suficientemente *adv* sufficiently; **no es lo s. rico como para ...** he isn't rich enough to ...

sufragio *m* (*voto*) vote.

sufrimiento *m* suffering.

sufrir **1** *vi* to suffer. **2** *vt* (*accidente*) to have; (*dificultades, cambios*) to experience; (*aguantar*) to put up with.

sugerencia *f* suggestion.

sugerir [5] *vt* to suggest.

sugestión *f* suggestion.

suicida **1** *mf* (*persona*) suicide. **2** *a* suicidal.

suicidarse *vr* to commit suicide.

suicidio *m* suicide.

suizo,-a **1** *a* Swiss. **2** *mf* (*persona*) Swiss. **3** *m* (*pastel*) eclair.

sujetador *m* (*prenda*) bra, brassiere.

sujetar **1** *vt* (*agarrar*) to hold; (*fijar*) to hold down; (*someter*) to restrain. **2 sujetarse** *vr* (*agarrarse*) to hold on.

sujeto,-a 1 *m* subject; (*individuo*) fellow. **2** *a* (*atado*) secure.

suma *f* (*cantidad*) sum; (*cálculo*) addition.

sumar *vt* (*cantidades*) to add (up).

sumergir [6] **1** *vt* to submerge; (*hundir*) to sink. **2 sumergirse** *vr* to submerge; (*hundirse*) to sink.

sumidero *m* drain.

suministrar *vt* to supply; **s. algo a algn** to supply sb with sth.

suministro *m* supply.

sumiso,-a *a* submissive.

supe *pt indef de* **saber.**

súper *m* (*gasolina*) premium; *fam* (*supermercado*) supermarket.

superar *vt* (*obstáculo etc*) to overcome; (*prueba*) to pass; (*aventajar*) to surpass.

superdotado,-a 1 *a* exceptionally gifted. **2** *mf* genius.

superficial *a* superficial.

superficie *f* surface; (*área*) area.

superfluo,-a *a* superfluous.

superior 1 *a* (*posición*) top, upper; (*cantidad*) greater (**a** than); (*calidad*) superior; (*estudios*) higher. **2** *m* (*jefe*) superior.

supermercado *m* supermarket.

supersónico,-a *a* supersonic.

supersticioso,-a *a* superstitious.

supervisar *vt* to supervise.

supervivencia *f* survival.

súpito,-a *a Am* sudden.

suplantar *vt* to supplant.

suplementario,-a *a* supplementary.

suplemento *m* supplement.

suplicar [1] *vt* to beg.

suplicio *m* (*tortura*) torture; (*tormento*) torment.

suplir *vt* (*reemplazar*) to replace; (*compensar*) to make up for.

suponer (*pp* **supuesto**) *vt* to suppose; (*significar*) to mean; (*implicar*) to entail; **supongo que sí** I suppose so.

supositorio *m* suppository.

supremo,-a *a* supreme.

suprimir *vt* (*ley*) to abolish; (*restricción*) to lift; (*palabra*) to delete.

supuesto,-a *a* (*asumido*) supposed; (*presunto*) alleged; **¡por s.!** of course!; **dar algo por s.** to take sth for granted.

supuse *pt indef de* **suponer.**

sur *a & m* south.

suramericano,-a *a & mf* South American.

surco *m* (*en tierra*) furrow; (*en disco*) groove.

sureste *a & m* southeast.

surf(ing) *m* surfing.

surgir [6] *vi* (*problema, dificultad*) to crop up; (*aparecer*) to arise.

suroeste *a & m* southwest.

surtido,-a 1 *a* (*variado*) assorted. **2** *m* selection.

surtidor *m* spout; **s. de gasolina** gas pump.

susceptible *a* susceptible; (*quisquilloso*) touchy; **s. de** (*capaz*) capable of.

suscitar *vt* (*provocar*) to cause; (*rebelión*) to stir up; (*interés etc*) to arouse.

suscribirse *vr* to subscribe (**a** to).

suscripción *f* subscription.

suspender 1 *vt* (*reunión*) to adjourn; (*examen*) to fail; (*colgar*) to hang; **me han suspendido** I've failed (the exam). **2** *vi* (*en colegio*) **he suspendido** I've failed.

suspense *m* suspense; **novela/película de s.** thriller.

suspensión *f* (*levantamiento*) hanging (up); (*de coche*) suspension.

suspenso *m* (*nota*) fail.

suspicaz *a* suspicious; (*desconfiado*) distrustful.

suspirar *vi* to sigh.

suspiro *m* sigh.

sustancia *f* substance.

sustantivo,-a *m* noun.

sustento *m* (*alimento*) sustenance.

sustituir *vt* to substitute.

sustituto,-a *mf* substitute.

susto *m* fright; **llevarse** *o* **darse un s.** to be frightened.

sustraer *vt* to subtract; (*robar*) to steal.

susurrar *vi* to whisper.

sutil *a* (*diferencia, pregunta*) subtle; (*aroma*) delicate.

suyo,-a *a & pron pos* (*de él*) his; (*de ella*) hers; (*de animal o cosa*) its; (*de usted, ustedes*) yours; (*de ellos, ellas*) theirs.

T

tabaco *m* tobacco; (*cigarrillos*) cigarettes *pl*; **t. rubio** Virginia tobacco.

taberna *f* bar.

tabique *m* (*pared*) partition (wall).

tabla *f* board; (*de vestido*) pleat; (*de sumar etc*) table; **t. de surf** surfboard; **t. de windsurf** sailboard.

tablero *m* (*tablón*) panel; (*en juegos*) board; **t. de mandos** (*de coche*) dash(board).

tableta *f* (*de chocolate*) bar.

tablón *m* plank; (*en construcción*) beam; **t. de anuncios** notice bulletin board.

taburete *m* stool.

tacaño,-a 1 *a* mean. **2** *mf* miser.

tachar *vt* to cross out.

tacho *m Am* bucket.

taco *m* (*tarugo*) plug; (*de jamón, queso*) cube; (*palabrota*) swearword.

tacón *m* heel; **zapatos de t.** high-heeled shoes.

táctica *f* tactics *pl*.

táctico,-a *a* tactical.

tacto *m* (*sentido*) touch; (*delicadeza*) tact.

tajada *f* slice.

tal 1 *a* (*semejante*) such; (*más sustantivo singular contable*) such a; (*indeterminado*) such and such; **en tales condiciones** in such conditions; **nunca dije t. cosa** I never said such a thing; **t. vez** perhaps, maybe; **como si t. cosa** as if nothing had happened. **2** *adv* **t. (y) como** just as; **¿qué t.?** how are things?; **¿qué t. ese vino?** how do you find this wine? **3** *conj as* **con t. (de) que** + *subjuntivo* so long as, provided. **4** *pron* (*cosa*) something; (*persona*) someone, somebody.

taladro *m* (*herramienta*) drill.

talante *m* (*carácter*) disposition; **de mal t.** unwillingly.

talar *vt* (*árboles*) to fell.

talco *m* talc; **polvos de t.** talcum powder.

talega *f* sack.

talento *m* talent.

Talgo *m* fast passenger train.

talla *f* (*de prenda*) size; (*estatura*) height.

tallar *vt* (*madera, piedra*) to carve; (*piedras preciosas*) to cut; (*metales*) to engrave.

tallarines *mpl* noodles, tagliatelle *sing*.

talle *m* (*cintura*) waist.

taller *m* (*obrador*) workshop; **t. de reparaciones** (*garaje*) garage.

tallo *m* stem.

talón *m* heel; (*cheque*) check.

talonario *m* (*de cheques*) check book.

tamaño *m* size; **de gran t.** large; **del t. de** as big as.

tambalearse *vr* (*persona*) to stagger; (*mesa*) to wobble.

también *adv* too, also; **yo t.** me too.

tambor *m* drum.

tampoco *adv* (*en afirmativas*) nor, neither; (*en negativas*) not . . . either; **no lo sé, — yo t.** I don't know, neither *o* nor do I.

tampón *m* tampon.

tan *adv* so; **¡es t. listo!** he's so clever; **¡qué gente t. agradable!** such nice people; **¡qué vestido t. bonito!** such a beautiful dress. ■ (*consecutivo*) so . . . (that); **iba t. deprisa que no lo ví** he was going so fast that I couldn't see him. ■ (*comparativo*) **t. . . . como** as . . .

as; **t. alto como tú** as tall as you (are). ▪ **t. sólo** only.

tango *m* tango.

tanque *m* tank.

tanto,-a 1 *m* (*punto*) point; **un t. para cada uno** so much for each; **t. por ciento** percentage; **estar al t.** (*informado*) to be informed; (*pendiente*) to be on the lookout. 2 *a* (+ *sing*) so much; (+ *pl*) so many; **t. dinero** so much money; **¡ha pasado t. tiempo!** it's been so long!; **tantas manzanas** so many apples; **cincuenta y tantas personas** fifty odd people; **t. . . . como** as much . . . as; **tantos,-as . . . como** as many . . . as. 3 *pron* (+ *sing*) so much; (+ *pl*) so many; **otro t.** the same again; **no es** *o* **hay para t.** it's not that bad; **otros tantos** as many again; **uno de tantos** run-of-the-mill. 4 *adv* (*cantidad*) so much; (*tiempo*) so long; (*frecuencia*) so often; **t. mejor/peor** so much the better/worse; **t. . . . como** both . . . and; **t. tú como yo** both you and I; **por lo t.** therefore.

tapa *f* (*cubierta*) lid; (*de libro*) cover; (*aperitivo*) appetizer.

tapadera *f* cover.

tapar 1 *vt* to cover; (*botella etc*) to put the lid on; (*con ropas o mantas*) to wrap up; (*ocultar*) to hide; (*vista*) to block. 2 **taparse** *vr* (*cubrirse*) to cover oneself; (*abrigarse*) to wrap up.

tapete *m* (*table*) cover.

tapia *f* wall; (*cerca*) garden wall.

tapizar [4] *vt* to upholster.

tapón *m* (*de lavabo etc*) plug; (*de botella*) cap; (*de tráfico*) traffic jam.

taponar 1 *vt* (*tubería, hueco*) to plug; (*poner el tapón a*) to put the plug in. 2 **taponarse** *vr* **se me han taponado los oídos** my ears are blocked up.

taquigrafía *f* shorthand.

taquilla *f* ticket office; (*de cine, teatro*) box-office.

tararear *vt* to hum.

tardar 1 *vt* **tardé dos horas en venir** it took me two hours to get here. 2 *vi* (*demorar*) to take long; **no tardes** don't be long; **a más t.** at the latest. 3 **tardarse** *vr* **¿cuánto se tarda en llegar?** how long does it take to get there?

tarde 1 *f* (*hasta las cinco*) afternoon; (*después de las cinco*) evening. 2 *adv* late; **(más) t. o (más) temprano** sooner or later.

tarea *f* task; **tareas** (*de ama de casa*) housework *sing*; (*de estudiante*) homework *sing*.

tarifa *f* (*precio*) rate; (*en transportes*) fare; (*lista de precios*) price list.

tarjeta *f* card; **t. postal** postcard; **t. de crédito** credit card.

tarro *m* (*vasija*) jar; *Am* (*lata*) tin.

tarta *f* (*tart*) (*pastel*) cake.

tartamudear *vi* to stutter, stammer.

tartamudo,-a 1 *a* stuttering, stammering. 2 *mf* stutterer, stammerer.

tartera *f* lunch box.

tasa *f* (*precio*) fee; (*impuesto*) tax; (*índice*) rate; **tasas académicas** course fees; **t. de natalidad/mortalidad** birth/death rate.

tasar *vt* (*valorar*) to value; (*poner precio*) to fix the price of.

tasca *f* bar.

tatarabuelo,-a *mf* (*hombre*) great-great-grandfather; (*mujer*) great-great-grandmother; **tatarabuelos** great-great-grandparents.

tataranieto,-a *mf* (*hombre*) great-great-grandson; (*mujer*) great-great-granddaughter; **tataranietos** great-great-grandchildren.

tatuaje *m* tattoo.

taurino,-a *a* bullfighting.

taxi *m* taxi.

taxista *mf* taxi driver.

taza *f* cup; **una t. de café** (*recipiente*) a coffee cup; (*contenido*) a cup of coffee.

tazón *m* bowl.

te *pron pers* 1 (*complemento di-*

recto) you; (*complemento indirecto*) (to o for) you; (*reflexivo*) yourself; **no quiero verte** I don't want to see you; **te compraré uno** I'll buy you one; **te lo dije** I told you so; **lávate** wash yourself; **no te vayas** don't go.

té m (pl **tés**) tea.

teatro m theatre; **obra de t.** play.

tebeo m children's comic.

techo m (de habitación) ceiling; (*tejado*) roof.

tecla f key.

teclado m keyboard; **t. numérico** numeric keypad.

técnica f (*tecnología*) technology; (*método*) technique; (*habilidad*) skill.

técnico,-a 1 a technical. **2** mf technician.

tecnología f technology.

tedio m tedium.

teja f tile.

tejado m roof.

tejanos mpl jeans.

tejer vt (en el telar) to weave; (*hacer punto*) to knit.

tejido m fabric.

tela f cloth; **t. de araña** cobweb; **t. metálica** gauze.

telaraña f spider's web.

telecabina f cable car.

telediario m television news bulletin.

telefax m fax.

teleférico m cable car.

telefilm(e) m TV film.

telefonear vti to telephone, phone.

teléfono m telephone, phone; **t. portátil** portable telephone; **t. móvil** car phone; **le llamó por t.** she phoned you; **al t.** on the phone.

telegrama m telegram.

telenovela f television serial.

teleobjetivo m telephoto lens.

telescopio m telescope.

telesilla m chair lift.

telespectador,-a mf TV viewer.

telesquí m ski lift.

televidente mf TV viewer.

televisión f television; **ver la t.** to watch television.

televisivo,-a a television.

televisor m television set.

télex m inv telex.

telón m curtain.

tema m subject.

temblar [1] vi (de frío) to shiver; (*de miedo*) to tremble (**de** with); (*voz, pulso*) to shake.

temblor m tremor; **t. de tierra** earth tremor.

temer 1 vt to fear. **2** vi to be afraid. **3 temerse** vr to fear; **¡me lo temía!** I was afraid this would happen!

temerario,-a a reckless.

temor m fear; (*recelo*) worry.

témpano m ice block.

temperamento m temperament.

temperatura f temperature.

tempestad f storm.

templado,-a a (agua) lukewarm; (*clima*) mild.

templo m temple.

temporada f season; (*período*) period; **t. alta** high season; **t. baja** low season.

temporal 1 a temporary. **2** m storm.

temprano,-a a & adv early.

tenaz a tenacious.

tenaza f, **tenazas** fpl (*herramienta*) pliers.

tendencia f tendency.

tender [3] **1** vt (extender) to spread out; (*para secar*) to hang out; (*trampa*) to set; (*mano*) to hold out; (*tumbar*) to lay. **2** vi **a** to tend to. **3 tenderse** vr to stretch out.

tendero,-a mf shopkeeper.

tendón m tendon.

tenebroso,-a a (sombrío) dark; (*siniestro*) sinister.

tenedor m fork.

tener 1 vt to have, have got; **va a t. un niño** she's going to have a baby. ▪ (*sostener*) to hold; **tenme el bolso un momento** hold my bag a minute. ▪ **t. calor/frío** to be hot/cold; **t.**

cariño a algn to be fond of sb; **t. miedo** to be frightened. ■ *(edad)* to be; **tiene dieciocho (años)** he's eighteen (years old). ■ *(medida)* **la casa tiene cien metros cuadrados** the house is 100 square meters. ■ *(contener)* to hold. ■ *(mantener)* to keep; **me tuvo despierto toda la noche** he kept me up all night. ■ *(considerar)* to consider; **ten por seguro que lloverá** you can be sure it'll rain. ■ **t. que** to have (got) to; **tengo que . . .** I have to . . ., I must . . . **2 tenerse** *vr* **tenerse en pie** to stand (up).

tenga *subj pres de* **tener.**

tengo *indic pres de* **tener.**

teniente *m* lieutenant.

tenis *m* tennis.

tenor *m* tenor.

tensión *f* tension; *(eléctrica)* voltage; **t. arterial** blood pressure.

tenso,-a *a (cuerda, cable)* taut; *(persona, relaciones)* tense.

tentación *f* temptation.

tentar [1] *vt (incitar)* to tempt; *(atraer)* to attract.

tentativa *f* attempt.

tentempié *m (pl* **tentempiés)** *(comida)* snack; *(juguete)* tumbler.

tenue *a (luz, sonido)* faint.

teñir [6] **1** *vt (pelo etc)* to dye. **2 teñirse** *vr* **teñirse el pelo** to dye one's hair.

teoría *f* theory; **en t.** theoretically.

terapia *f* therapy.

tercer *a* third; **el t. mundo** the third world.

tercero,-a *a & mf* third.

tercio *m (one)* third; *(de cerveza)* medium-size bottle of beer.

terciopelo *m* velvet.

terco,-a *a* stubborn.

tergiversar *vt* to distort; *(declaraciones)* to twist.

terminal 1 *a* terminal. **2** *f* terminal; *(de autobús)* terminal. **3** *m (de ordenador)* terminal.

terminar 1 *vt* to finish. **2** *vi (acabarse)* to finish; *(ir a parar)* to end up **(en** in); **terminó por comprarlo**

he ended up buying it. **3 terminarse** *vr* to finish; *(vino etc)* to run out.

término *m (final)* end; *(palabra)* term; **en términos generales** generally speaking; **por t. medio** on average.

termo *m* thermos (flask).

termómetro *m* thermometer.

termostato *m* thermostat.

ternera *f* calf; *(carne)* veal.

ternura *f* tenderness.

terraplén *m* embankment.

terremoto *m* earthquake.

terreno *m (tierra)* land; *(campo)* field; *(deportivo)* ground; *(ámbito)* field.

terrestre *a (de la tierra)* terrestrial; *(transporte, ruta)* by land.

terrible *a* terrible.

territorio *m* territory.

terrón *m (de azúcar)* lump.

terror *m* terror; **película de t.** horror film.

terrorismo *m* terrorism.

terrorista *a & mf* terrorist.

terso,-a *a (liso)* smooth.

tertulia *f* get-together.

tesis *f inv* thesis; *(opinión)* point of view.

tesoro *m* treasure.

test *m* test.

testamento *m* will; **hacer t.** to make one's will.

testarudo,-a *a* obstinate.

testificar [1] *vi* to testify.

testigo *mf* witness.

testimonio *m* testimony; *(prueba)* evidence.

tétano *m* tetanus.

tetera *f* teapot.

tetina *f* (rubber) teat.

texto *m* text; **libro de t.** textbook.

tez *f* complexion.

ti *pron pers* you; **es para ti** it's for you; **piensas demasiado en ti mismo** you think too much about yourself.

tía *f* aunt; *fam (mujer)* woman.

tibio,-a *a* tepid.

tiburón *m* shark.

tic *m* (*pl* **tiques**) twitch; **t. nervioso** nervous twitch.

tiempo *m* time; (*meteorológico*) weather; (*de partido*) half; (*verbal*) tense; **a t.** in time; **a su (debido) t.** in due course; **al mismo t.** at the same time; **al poco t.** soon afterwards; **con t.** in advance; **¿cuánto t.?** how long?; **¿cuánto t. hace?** how long ago?; **estar a t. de** to still have time to; **¿nos da t. de llegar?** have we got (enough) time to get there?; **t. libre** free time; **¿qué t. hace?** what's the weather like?; **hace buen/mal t.** the weather is good/bad.

tienda *f* store; **ir de tiendas** to go shopping; **t. (de campaña)** tent.

tienta *a tientas* by touch; **andar a tientas** to feel one's way; **buscar (algo) a tientas** to grope (for sth).

tierno,-a *a* tender; (*reciente*) fresh.

tierra *f* land; (*planeta*) earth; (*suelo*) ground; **tocar t.** to land.

tieso,-a *a* (*rígido*) stiff; (*erguido*) upright.

tiesto *m* flowerpot.

tifus *m inv* typhus (fever).

tigre *m* tiger; *Am* jaguar.

tijeras *fpl* pair of scissors, scissors *pl.*

tila *f* lime tea.

timar *vt* to swindle.

timbre *m* (*de puerta*) bell; (*sonido*) timbre.

timidez *f* shyness.

tímido,-a *a* shy.

timo *m* swindle.

timón *m* (*de barco, avión*) rudder; (*de coche*) steering wheel.

tímpano *m* eardrum.

tinieblas *fpl* darkness.

tino *m* (*puntería*) **tener buen t.** to be a good shot.

tinta *f* ink; **t. china** Indian ink.

tinte *m* dye.

tintero *m* inkwell.

tintinear *vi* (*vidrio*) to clink; (*campana*) to tinkle.

tinto 1 *a* (*vino*) red. **2** *m* (*vino*) red wine.

tintorería *f* dry-cleaner's.

tío,-a *m* uncle; *fam* guy; **mis tíos** (*tío y tía*) my uncle and aunt.

tiovivo *m* merry-go-round.

típico,-a *a* typical; (*baile, traje*) traditional.

tipo *m* (*clase*) type, kind; *fam* (*persona*) guy; (*figura*) (*de hombre*) build; (*de mujer*) figure; **jugarse el t.** to risk one's neck; **t. bancario** o **de descuento** bank rate; **t. de cambio/interés** exchange/interest rate.

tira *f* strip.

tirabuzón *m* ringlet.

tirachinas *m inv* slingshot.

tirada *f* printrun.

tiranía *f* tyranny.

tirante 1 (*cable etc*) taut. **2** *m* (*de vestido etc*) strap; **tirantes** suspenders.

tirar 1 *vt* (*echar*) to throw, fling; (*dejar caer*) to drop; (*desechar*) to throw away; (*derribar*) to knock down. **2** *vi* **t. de** (*cuerda, puerta*) to pull; (*disparar*) to shoot; **ir tirando** to get by; **tira a la izquierda** turn left. **3** *tirarse vr* (*lanzarse*) to throw oneself; (*tumbarse*) to lie down; **tirarse de cabeza al agua** to dive into the water.

tirita® *f* Band-Aid®.

tiritar *vi* to shiver.

tiro *m* (*lanzamiento*) throw; (*disparo, ruido*) shot; (*de chimenea*) draft; **t. al blanco** target shooting; **t. al plato** clay pigeon shooting.

tirón *m* pull; (*del bolso*) snatch; *fam* **de un t.** in one go.

titubear *vi* (*dudar*) to hesitate.

titular¹ 1 *mf* (*persona*) holder. **2** *m* (*de periódico*) headline.

titular² 1 *vt* (*poner título*) to call. **2** *titularse vr* (*película etc*) to be called.

título *m* title; (*diploma*) diploma; (*titular*) headline.

tiza *f* chalk.

tiznar *vt* to blacken (with soot).

toalla *f* towel.

toallero *m* towel rail.

tobillo m ankle.

tobogán m slide; (en piscina) chute.

tocadiscos m inv record player.

tocador m (mueble) dressing table; (habitación) dressing room.

tocar [1] **1** vt to touch; (instrumento, canción) to play; (timbre, campana) to ring; (bocina) to blow; (tema, asunto) to touch on. **2** vi (entrar en contacto) to touch; ¿a quién le toca? (en juegos) whose turn is it?; **me tocó el gordo** (en rifa) I won the jackpot. **3 tocarse** vr (una cosa con otra) to touch each other.

tocino m lard; **t. de cielo** sweet made with egg yolk.

tocólogo,-a m obstetrician.

todavía adv (aún) still; (en negativas) yet; (para reforzar) even, still; **t. la quiere** he still loves her; **t. no** not yet; **t. más/menos** even more/less.

todo,-a 1 a all; (cada) every; **t. el mundo** everybody; **t. el día** all day, the whole day; **t. ciudadano de más de dieciocho años** every citizen over eighteen years of age; **todos,-as** all; **t. los niños** all the children; **t. los martes** every Tuesday. **2** pron all, everything; **t. aquél** o **el que quiera** anybody who wants (to); **todos,-as** all of them; **hablé con todos** I spoke to everybody; **todos aprobamos** we all passed; **ante t.** first of all; **del t.** completely; **después de t.** after all; **eso es t.** that's all; **hay de t.** there are all sorts; **lo sé t.** I know all about it; **lo contrario** quite the opposite; **t. lo más** at the most. **3** adv completely; **t. sucio** all dirty.

toldo m (cubierta) awning; (en la playa) sunshade; Am (cabaña) tent.

tolerar vt to tolerate.

toma f (acción) taking; **t. de corriente** socket.

tomar 1 vt to take; (comer, beber) to have; **toma** here (you are); **t. el sol** to sunbathe; **t. en serio/broma** to take seriously/as a joke. **2 tomarse** vr (comer) to eat; (beber) to drink; **no te lo tomes así** don't take it like that.

tomate m tomato; **salsa de t.** (de lata) tomato sauce; (de botella) ketchup.

tómbola f tombola.

tomo m volume.

tonel m cask.

tonelada f ton; **t. métrica** tonne.

tónico,-a 1 m tonic. **2** f (bebida) tonic (water); **tónica general** overall trend.

tono m tone; **un t. alto/bajo** a high/low pitch.

tontería f silliness; (dicho, hecho) silly thing; (insignificancia) trifle.

tonto,-a 1 a silly. **2** mf fool.

topacio m topaz.

toparse vr **t. con** to bump into; (dificultades) to run up against.

tope m (límite) limit; **estar hasta los topes** to be full up; **fecha t.** deadline.

tópico m cliché.

topo m (animal) mole; (espía) spy, inside informer.

topónimo m place name.

torbellino m (de viento) whirlwind.

torcer [4] **1** vt (tobillo) to sprain; (esquina) to turn; (inclinar) to slant. **2** vi to turn. **3 torcerse** vr (doblarse) to twist; (tobillo, mano) to sprain; (desviarse) to go off to the side.

torear vi to fight.

torero,-a mf bullfighter.

tormenta f storm.

tormento m (tortura) torture; (padecimiento) torment.

tornillo m screw.

torno m (de alfarero) wheel; **en t. a** around.

toro m bull; ¿te gustan los toros? do you like bullfighting?

torpe a (sin habilidad) clumsy; (tonto) thick; (movimiento) slow.

torre f tower; (en ajedrez) rook.

torrente *m* torrent.

tórrido,-a *a* torrid.

torso *m* torso.

torta *f* (*pastel*) cake; (*golpe*) slap.

tortazo *m* (*bofetada*) slap.

tortícolis *f inv* crick in the neck.

tortilla *f* omelet; *Am* tortilla; **t. francesa/española** (plain)/potato omelette.

tortuga *f* turtle.

tortura *f* torture.

tos *f* cough; **t. ferina** whooping cough.

tosco,-a *a* (*basto*) rough; (*persona*) uncouth.

toser *vi* to cough.

tostada *f* **una t.** some toast, a slice of toast.

tostador *m* toaster.

tostar [2] *vt* (*pan*) to toast; (*café*) to roast.

total **1** *a* total. **2** *m* (*todo*) whole; (*cantidad*) total; **en t.** in all. **3** *adv* anyway; (*para resumir*) in short.

totalidad *f* whole; **la t. de** all of; **en su t.** as a whole.

tóxico,-a *a* toxic. **2** *m* poison.

toxicómano,-a **1** *a* addicted to drugs. **2** *mf* drug addict.

tozudo,-a *a* stubborn.

traba *f* (*obstáculo*) hindrance.

trabajador,-a **1** *mf* worker. **2** *a* hard-working.

trabajar **1** *vi* to work; **t. de camarera** to work as a waitress. **2** *vt* to work (on).

trabajo *m* work; (*esfuerzo*) effort; **un t.** a job; **t. eventual** casual labor; **trabajos manuales** arts and crafts.

trabalenguas *m inv* tongue twister.

trabar **1** *vt* (*conversación, amistad*) to start. **2** **trabarse** *vr* **se le trabó la lengua** he got tongue-tied.

tractor *m* tractor.

tradición *f* tradition.

tradicional *a* traditional.

traducción *f* translation.

traducir *vt* to translate (**a** into). **2** **traducirse** *vr* to result (**en** in).

traductor,-a *mf* translator.

traer **1** *vt* to bring; (*llevar consigo*) to carry; (*problemas*) to cause; (*noticia*) to feature; **trae** give it to me. **2** **traerse** *vr* (*llevar consigo*) to bring along.

traficante *mf* (*de drogas etc*) trafficker.

tráfico *m* traffic; **t. de drogas** drug traffic.

tragaperras *f inv* (**máquina**) **t.** slot machine.

tragar [7] *vt*, **tragarse** *vr* to swallow.

tragedia *f* tragedy.

trágico,-a *a* tragic.

trago *m* (*bebida*) swig; **de un t.** in one go; **pasar un mal t.** to have a bad time.

traición *f* betrayal.

traicionar *vt* to betray.

traidor,-a **1** *a* treacherous. **2** *mf* traitor.

traigo *indic pres de* **traer**.

traje[1] *m* (*de hombre*) suit; (*de mujer*) dress; **t. de baño** swimsuit; **t. de chaqueta** two-piece suit; **t. de novia** wedding dress.

traje[2] *pt indef de* **traer**.

trama *f* plot.

tramar *vt* to plot.

trámite *m* (*paso*) step; (*formalidad*) formality.

tramo *m* (*de carretera*) stretch; (*de escalera*) flight.

trampa *f* (*de caza*) trap; (*engaño*) fiddle; **hacer trampa(s)** to cheat.

trampilla *f* trap door.

trampolín *m* springboard.

tramposo,-a **1** *a* deceitful. **2** *mf* cheat.

tranquilizante *m* tranquillizer.

tranquilizar [4] **1** *vt* to calm down; **lo dijo para tranquilizarme** he said it to reassure me. **2** **tranquilizarse** *vr* (*calmarse*) to calm down.

tranquilo,-a *a* (*persona, lugar*) calm; (*agua*) still; (*conciencia*) clear.

transatlántico,-a **1** *m* (ocean) liner. **2** *a* transatlantic.

transbordador *m* (car) ferry; **t. espacial** space shuttle.

transbordo m (de trenes) **hacer t.** to change.

transcurrir vi (tiempo) to pass, go by; (acontecer) to take place.

transcurso m **en el t. de** in the course of.

transeúnte mf (peatón) passer-by.

transferencia f transference; (de dinero) transfer; **t. bancaria** bank transfer.

transformación f transformation.

transformador m transformer.

transformar 1 vt to transform. **2 transformarse** vr to turn (en into).

transfusión f transfusion.

transición f transition.

transistor m transistor.

transitado,-a a (carretera) busy.

transitivo,-a a transitive.

tránsito m (tráfico) traffic; (movimiento) passage; **pasajeros en t.** passengers in transit.

transitorio,-a a transitory.

transmisión f transmission; (emisión) broadcast.

transmisor m transmitter.

transmitir vt to pass on; (emitir) to transmit.

transparentarse vr to be transparent; **se le transparentaban las bragas** you could see her panties.

transparente a transparent.

transpiración f perspiration.

transplante m transplant.

transportar vt to transport; (pasajeros) to carry; (mercancías) to ship.

transporte m transport.

transversal a cross.

tranvía m streetcar.

trapo m (viejo, roto) rag; (bayeta) cloth; **t. de cocina** dishcloth; **t. del polvo** duster.

tráquea f trachea.

tras prep (después de) after; (detrás) behind.

trascendencia f (importancia) significance.

trascendental, trascendente a significant.

trasero,-a 1 a back, rear; **en la parte trasera** at the back. **2** m fam bottom.

trasladar 1 vt (cosa) to move; (trabajador) to transfer. **2 trasladarse** vr to move.

traslado m (de casa) move; (de personal) transfer.

trasnochar vi to stay up (very) late.

traspié m (pl **traspiés**) stumble; **dar un t.** to trip.

trastero m (cuarto) **t.** junk room.

trastienda f back room.

trasto m thing; (cosa inservible) piece of junk.

trastornar 1 vt (planes) to disrupt; fig (persona) to unhinge. **2 trastornarse** vr (enloquecer) to go mad.

trastorno m (molestia) trouble; **t. mental** mental disorder.

tratado m (pacto) treaty; (estudio) treatise.

tratamiento m treatment; (de textos etc) processing.

tratar 1 vt to treat; (asunto) to discuss; (manejar) to handle; (textos etc) to process; **me trata de 'tú'** he calls me 'tu'. **2** vi **t. de** (intentar) to try to; **t. de** o **sobre** o **acerca de** to be about. **3 tratarse** vr (relacionarse) to be on speaking terms; **se trata de** (es cuestión de) it's a question of; (es) it is.

trato m (contacto) contact; (acuerdo) agreement; (comercial) deal; **malos tratos** ill-treatment; **¡t. hecho!** it's a deal!

traumático,-a a traumatic.

través 1 prep **a t. de** (superficie) across, over; (agujero etc) through; (por medio de) through; **a t. del periódico** through the newspaper. **2** adv **de t.** (transversalmente) crosswise; (de lado) sideways.

travesía f (viaje) crossing.

travestí, travesti mf transvestite.

travesura f mischief.

travieso,-a a mischievous.

trayecto m (distancia) distance; (recorrido) route; (viaje) journey.

trazar [4] *vt* (*línea*) to draw; (*plano*) to design.

trébol *m* trefoil; (*en naipes*) club.

trece *a & m inv* thirteen.

trecho *m* (*distancia*) distance; (*tramo*) stretch.

tregua *f* truce.

treinta *a & m inv* thirty.

tremendo,-a *a* (*terrible*) terrible; (*muy grande*) enormous; (*excelente*) tremendous.

tren *m* train.

trenca *f* (*prenda*) duffle coat.

trenza *f* (*de pelo*) braid.

trepar *vti* to climb.

tres *a & m inv* three; **t. en raya** tick-tack-toe.

trescientos,-as *a & mf* three hundred.

tresillo *m* three-piece suite.

treta *f* ruse.

triángulo *m* triangle.

tribu *f* tribe.

tribuna *f* (*plataforma*) dais; (*en estadio*) stand.

tribunal *m* court; (*de examen*) board of examiners; **T. Supremo** Supreme Court.

tributo *m* tribute; (*finanzas*) tax.

triciclo *m* tricycle.

trienio *m* three-year period.

trigésimo,-a *a & mf* thirtieth; **t. primero** thirty-first.

trigo *m* wheat.

trimestral *a* quarterly.

trimestre *m* quarter; (*escolar*) term.

trinchar *vt* (*carne*) to carve.

trinchera *f* trench.

trineo *m* sledge; (*grande*) sleigh.

tripa *f* (*intestino*) gut; *fam* tummy; **dolor de t.** stomachache.

triple *a & m* triple.

trípode *m* tripod.

tripulación *f* crew.

tripulante *mf* crew member.

tripular *vt* to man.

triquiñuela *f* dodge.

triste *a* (*infeliz*) sad; (*sombrío*) gloomy.

tristeza *f* sadness.

triturar *vt* to grind (up).

triunfador,-a 1 *a* winning. **2** *mf* winner.

triunfar *vi* to triumph.

triunfo *m* (*victoria*) triumph; (*deportiva*) win; (*éxito*) success.

trivial *a* trivial.

triza *f* **hacer trizas** to tear to shreds.

trocear *vt* to cut up (into pieces).

trofeo *m* trophy.

tromba *f* **t. de agua** violent downpour.

trombón *m* trombone.

trompa *f* (*instrumento*) horn; (*de elefante*) trunk; *fam* **estar t.** to be sloshed.

trompeta *f* trumpet.

tronchar 1 *vt* (*rama, tronco*) to cut down. **2 troncharse** *vr* **troncharse de risa** to split one's sides laughing.

tronco *m* (*torso, de árbol*) trunk; (*leño*) log.

trono *m* throne.

tropa *f* troops *pl*.

tropel *m* **en t.** in a mad rush.

tropezar [1] *vi* (*trompicar*) to stumble (**con** on); **t. con algn/dificultades** to run into sb/difficulties.

tropezón *m* (*traspié*) stumble; **dar un t.** to trip.

tropical *a* tropical.

trópico *m* tropics *pl*.

tropiezo[1] *m* (*obstáculo*) trip.

tropiezo[2] *indic pres de* **tropezar**.

trotar *vi* to trot.

trote *m* trot; **al t.** at a trot.

trozo *m* piece.

truco *m* (*ardid*) trick; (*manera de hacer algo*) knack; **coger el t. (a algo)** to get the knack *o* hang (of sth).

trucha *f* trout.

trueno *m* thunder; **un t.** a thunderclap.

trufa *f* truffle.

tu *a pos* your; **tu libro** your book; **tus libros** your books.

tú *pron* you.

tubería *f* (*de agua*) pipes *pl*; (*de gas, petróleo*) pipeline.

tubo *m* tube; (*tubería*) pipe; **t. de ensayo** test tube; **t. de escape** exhaust (pipe).

tuerca *f* nut.

tuerto,-a 1 *a* blind in one eye. **2** *mf* person who is blind in one eye.

tuerzo *indic pres de* **torcer.**

tulipán *m* tulip.

tullido,-a *a* crippled.

tumba *f* grave.

tumbar 1 *vt* to knock down. **2 tumbarse** *vr* (*acostarse*) to lie down.

tumbona *f* easy chair; (*de lona*) deckchair.

tumor *m* tumor.

tumulto *m* commotion.

túnel *m* tunnel; **el t. del Canal de la Mancha** the Channel Tunnel.

túnica *f* tunic.

tupé *m* (*pl* **tupés**) (*flequillo*) fringe.

tupido,-a *a* thick.

turba *f* (*combustible*) peat.

turbado,-a *a* (*alterado*) disturbed; (*desconcertado*) confused.

turbar 1 *vt* (*alterar*) to unsettle; (*desconcertar*) to baffle. **2 turbarse** *vr* (*preocuparse*) to become upset; (*desconcertarse*) to become confused.

turbio,-a *a* (*agua*) cloudy; (*negocio etc*) dubious.

turbulencia *f* turbulence.

turco,-a 1 *a* Turkish. **2** *mf* (*persona*) Turk; *fig* **cabeza de t.** scapegoat. **3** *m* (*idioma*) Turkish.

turismo *m* tourism; (*coche*) car; **ir de t.** to go touring.

turista *mf* tourist.

turístico,-a *a* tourist; **de interés t.** of interest to tourists.

turnarse *vr* to take turns.

turno *m* (*en juegos etc*) turn; (*de trabajo*) shift; **t. de día/noche** day/night shift.

turquesa *a & f* turquoise.

turrón *m* nougat.

tutear 1 *vt* to address as 'tú'. **2 tutearse** *vr* to call (each other) 'tú'.

tutela *f* guidance.

tutor, -a *mf* (*de huérfano*) guardian; (*de estudiante*) tutor.

tuve *pt indef de* **tener.**

tuyo,-a 1 *a pos* (*con personas*) of yours; (*con objetos*) one of your; **¿es amigo t.?** is he a friend of yours?; **un libro t.** one of your books. **2** *pron pos* yours.

U

u *conj* (*before words beginning with* o *or* ho) or.

ubicación *f* location.

ubicar [1] **1** *vt* (*situar*) to locate. **2 ubicarse** *vr* (*en un lugar*) to be located.

Ud. *abr de* **usted** you.

Uds. *abr de* **ustedes** you.

úlcera *f* ulcer.

últimamente *adv* recently.

ultimar *vt* (*terminar*) to finalize; (*matar*) to finish off.

ultimátum *m* (*pl* **ultimátums**) ultimatum.

último,-a *a* last; (*más reciente*) latest; (*más alto*) top; (*más bajo*) lowest; (*definitivo*) final; (*más lejano*) back; **por ú.** finally; **a últimos de mes** at the end of the month; **últimas noticias** latest news; **el u. piso** the top apartment; **el u. de la lista** the lowest on the list; **la última fila** the back row.

ultraderecha *f* extreme right.

ultramarinos *m* groceries; **tienda de u.** greengrocer.

ultrasónico,-a *a* ultrasonic.

ultravioleta *a inv* ultraviolet.

ulular *vi* (*viento*) to howl; (*búho*) to hoot.

umbral *m* threshold.

un,-a 1 *art indet* a, (*antes de vocal*) an; **unos,-as** some. **2** *a* (*delante de m sing*) one; **un chico y dos chicas** one boy and two girls.

unánime *a* unanimous.

unanimidad *f* unanimity; **por u.** unanimously.

undécimo,-a a eleventh.

únicamente adv only.

único,-a a (solo) only; (extraordinario) unique; **hijo ú.** only child; **lo ú. que quiero** the only thing I want.

unidad f unit; (cohesión) unity; **u. de disquete** disk drive.

unido,-a a united; **están muy unidos** they are very attached to one another; **una familia muy unida** a very close family.

unificación f unification.

uniforme 1 m (prenda) uniform. **2** a uniform; (superficie) even.

unilateral a unilateral.

unión f union.

UE Unión Europea.

unir vt, **unirse** vr to unite.

unísono m **al u.** in unison.

universal a universal.

universidad f university.

universitario,-a 1 a university. **2** mf university student.

universo m universe.

uno,-a 1 m inv one; **el u. de mayo** the first of May. **2** f (hora) **es la una** it's one o'clock. **3** a **unos,-as** some; **unas cajas** some boxes; **debe haber unos/unas veinte** there must be around twenty. **4** pron one; (persona) someone, somebody; (impers) you, one; **u. (de ellos), una (de ellas)** one of them; **unos cuantos** a few; **se miraron el u. al otro** they looked at each other; **de u. en u.** one by one; **u. tras otro** one after the other; **vive con u.** she's living with some man; **u. tiene que . . .** you have to . . .

untar vt to smear; (mantequilla) to spread.

uña f nail; **morderse o comerse las uñas** to bite one's nails.

uperizado,-a a **leche uperizada** UHT milk.

urbanismo m town planning.

urbanización f (barrio) housing estate; (proceso) urbanization.

urbano,-a a urban.

urbe f large city.

urgencia f urgency; (emergencia) emergency.

urgente a urgent; **correo u.** express mail.

urgir [6] vi to be urgent.

urna f (para votos) ballot box.

urraca f magpie.

uruguayo,-a a & mf Uruguayan.

usado,-a a (ropa) second-hand.

usar 1 vt to use; (prenda) to wear. **2 usarse** vr to be used.

usina f Am (central eléctrica) power station.

uso m use; **u. externo** for external use only; **u. tópico** local application; **haga u. del casco** wear a helmet.

usted (pl **ustedes**) pron pers you; **¿quién es u.?, ¿quiénes son ustedes?** who are you?

usual a usual.

usuario,-a mf user.

utensilio m utensil; (herramienta) tool.

útil a useful; (día) working.

utilidad f utility; **tener u.** to be useful.

utilitario,-a 1 m (coche) utility vehicle. **2** a utilitarian.

utilización f use.

utilizar [4] vt to use.

utópico,-a a & mf utopian.

uva f grape; **u. blanca** green grape.

UVI f abr de **unidad de vigilancia intensiva** intensive care unit.

V

vaca f cow; (carne) beef.

vacaciones fpl vacation; (viaje) holiday; **estar/irse de v.** to be/go on holiday.

vacante 1 a vacant. **2** f vacancy.

vaciar vt, **vaciarse** vr to empty.

vacilar vi (dudar) to hesitate; (voz) to falter; **sin v.** without hesitation.

vacío,-a 1 a empty; (hueco) hollow; (sin ocupar) vacant. **2** m void; (hueco) gap; (espacio) (empty) space.

vacuna f vaccine.

vado m (de un río) ford; **'v. permanente'** 'keep clear'.

vagabundo,-a 1 a (errante) wandering. **2** mf wanderer; (sin casa) hobo.

vagar [7] vi to wander about.

vago,-a 1 a (perezoso) lazy; (indefinido) vague. **2** mf (holgazán) layabout.

vagón m (para pasajeros) car; (para mercancías) freight car.

vaho m (de aliento) breath; (vapor) vapor.

vaina f (de guisante etc) pod; Am (molestia) nuisance.

vainilla f vanilla.

vajilla f dishes pl.

valdré indic fut de **valer**.

vale¹ interj all right, OK.

vale² m (comprobante) voucher; (pagaré) IOU (I owe you).

valer 1 vt to be worth; (costar) to cost; **no vale nada** it is worthless; **no vale la pena (ir)** it's not worthwhile (going); **¿cuánto vale?** how much is it? **2** vi (servir) to be useful; (ser válido) to count; **más vale** it is better; **más vale que te vayas ya** you had better leave now. **3 valerse** vr **valerse por sí mismo** to be able to manage on one's own.

valgo indic pres de **valer**.

válido,-a a valid.

valiente a (valeroso) brave.

valioso,-a a valuable.

valor m value; (precio) price; (valentía) courage; **objetos de v.** valuables; **sin v.** worthless.

valoración f appraisal.

valorar vt to value.

vals m waltz.

válvula f valve; **v. de seguridad** safety valve.

valla f (cerca) fence; (muro) wall; **v. publicitaria** billboard.

valle m valley.

vampiro m vampire.

vandalismo m vandalism.

vanguardia f vanguard; (artística) avant-garde.

vanidad f vanity.

vanidoso,-a a conceited.

vano,-a a (vanidoso) vain; (esfuerzo, esperanza) futile; **en v.** in vain.

vapor m (de agua hirviendo) steam; (gas) vapor; **al v.** steamed; **v. de agua** water vapor.

vaporizador m vaporizer.

vaquero,-a 1 m cowboy. **2** a pantalón **v.** jeans pl. **3** mpl **vaqueros** (prenda) jeans.

vara f rod.

variable a & f variable.

variado,-a a varied.

variante f (carretera) detour.

variar vti to vary; (con ironía) **para v.** just for a change.

varicela f chickenpox.

variedad f variety; (espectáculo) **variedades** variety show.

varilla f (vara) rod; (de abanico, paraguas) rib.

varios,-as a several.

variz f varicose vein.

varón m (hombre) man; (chico) boy.

vas indic pres de **ir**.

vascuence m (idioma) Basque.

vaselina f Vaseline®.

vasija f pot.

vaso m (para beber) glass.

vaticinar vt to predict.

vatio m watt.

vaya¹ interj **¡v. lío!** what a mess!

vaya² subj pres de **ir**.

Vd., Vds. abr de **usted, ustedes** you.

ve 1 imperativo de **ir**. **2** indic pres de **ver**.

vecindad f, **vecindario** m (área) neighborhood; (vecinos) residents pl.

vecino,-a 1 mf (persona) neighbor; (residente) resident. **2** a neighboring.

vega f fertile plain.

vegetación f vegetation; (en nariz) **vegetaciones** adenoids.

vegetal a & m vegetable.

vegetariano,-a a & mf vegetarian.

zócalo m (de pared) baseboard.
zodiaco, zodíaco m zodiac; **signo del z.** sign of the zodiac.
zona f zone.
zoo m zoo.
zoológico,-a 1 a zoological; **parque z.** zoo. **2** m zoo.
zopilote m Am buzzard.
zoquete mf fam blockhead.
zorra f vixen.
zorro m fox.
zueco m clog.
zumbar vi to buzz; **me zumban los oídos** my ears are buzzing.
zumbido m buzzing.
zumo m juice.
zurcir [3] vt to darn.
zurdo,-a 1 mf (persona) left-handed person. **2** a left-handed.

...oe shop.
... mf (vendedor) shoe ...r; (fabricante) shoe-...arador) cobbler.
...slipper; **zapatillas de de-**...iners.
...n shoe.
...ear vt to shake.
...o m (pendiente) earring.
...f claw.
...ar vi to set sail.
...a f bramble.
...zamora f (zarza) blackberry ...ush; (fruto) blackberry.
...arzuela f Spanish operetta; **la Z.** ...royal residence in Madrid.
...igzag m (pl **zigzags** o **zigzagues**) zigzag.

---

vehemente a vehement.
vehículo m vehicle.
veinte a & m inv twenty.
vejez f old age.
vejiga f bladder.
vela[1] f candle; **pasar la noche en v.** to have a sleepless night.
vela[2] f (de barco) sail.
velador m Am (mesilla de noche) bedside table.
velar 1 vt (difrento) to hold a wake; (enfermo) to watch over. **2** vi (no dormir) to stay awake. **3 velarse** vr to blur.
velatorio m vigil.
velero m sailing boat.
veleta f weather vane.
velo m veil.
velocidad f (rapidez) speed; (marcha) gear; **v. máxima** speed limit.
velocímetro m speedometer.
veloz a rapid.
vello m hair.
vena f vein.
venado m deer; (carne) venison.
vencedor,-a 1 mf winner. **2** a winning.
vencer [2] **1** vt to defeat; (dificultad) to overcome. **2** vi (pago, deuda) to be payable; (plazo) to expire.
vencido,-a a (derrotado) defeated; (equipo etc) beaten; **darse por v.** to give up.
venda f bandage.
vendaje m dressing.
vendar vt to bandage; **v. los ojos a algn** to blindfold sb.
vendaval m gale.
vendedor,-a mf seller; (hombre) salesman; (mujer) saleswoman.
vender vt, **venderse** vr to sell; '**se vende**' for sale.
vendimia f grape harvest.
vendré indic fut de venir.
veneno m poison; (de serpiente) venom.
venenoso,-a a poisonous.
venéreo,-a a venereal.
venezolano,-a a & mf Venezuelan.

venga subj pres de venir.
venganza f vengeance, revenge.
vengo indic pres de venir.
venir 1 vi to come; **el año que viene** next year; fam **¡venga ya!** (expresa incredulidad) come off it!; (vamos) come on!; **v. grande/pequeño** (ropa) to be too big/small; **v. mal/bien** to be inconvenient/convenient. ▪ (en pasivas) **esto vino provocado por . . .** this was brought about by . . . ▪ **esto viene ocurriendo desde hace mucho tiempo** this has been going on for a long time now. **2 venirse** vr **venirse abajo** to collapse.
venta f sale; (posada) country inn; **en v.** for sale; **a la v.** on sale; **v. a plazos/al contado** credit/cash sale; **v. al por mayor/al por menor** wholesale/retail.
ventaja f advantage; **llevar v. a** to have the advantage over.
ventana f window; (de la nariz) nostril.
ventanilla f window; (de la nariz) nostril.
ventilador m ventilator; (de coche) fan.
ventilar vt to ventilate.
ventisca f blizzard; (de nieve) snowstorm.
ver 1 vt to see; (televisión) to watch; **a v.** let's see; **a v. si escribes** I hope you'll write; **(ya) veremos** we'll see; **no tener nada que v. con** to have nothing to do with. **2 verse** vr (imagen etc) to be seen; (encontrarse con algn) to see each other; **¡nos vemos!** see you later!; Am **te ves divina** you look divine.
veraneante mf vacationist, tourist.
veranear vi to spend one's summer vacation.
veraniego,-a a summer.
verano m summer.
veras de v. really.
verbena f street o night party.
verbo m verb.
verdad f truth; **es v.** it is true; **¡de v!** really!, truly!; **un amigo de v.** a

real friend; (*en frase afirmativa*) **está muy bien, ¿(no es) v.?** it is very good, isn't it?; (*en frase negativa*) **no te gusta, ¿v.?** you don't like it, do you?

verdaderamente *adv* truly.

verdadero,-a *a* true.

verde 1 *a* green; (*fruta*) unripe; (*chiste, película*) blue. **2** (*color*) green.

verdoso,-a *a* greenish.

verdura *f* vegetables *pl.*

vereda *f* path; *Am* (*acera*) sidewalk.

veredicto *m* verdict.

vergonzoso,-a *a* (*penoso*) disgraceful; (*tímido*) shy.

vergüenza *f* shame; (*timidez*) shyness; **¿no te da v.?** aren't you ashamed?; **es una v.** it's a disgrace; **me da v.** I'm too embarrassed.

verificar [1] *vt* to check.

verja *f* (*reja*) grating; (*cerca*) railing; (*puerta*) iron gate.

vermut, vermú *m* (*pl* **vermús**) vermouth.

verosímil *a* probable, likely; (*creíble*) credible.

verruga *f* wart.

versión *f* version.

verso *m* (*poesía*) verse.

vertebrado,-a *a* & *m* vertebrate.

vertedero *m* (*de basura*) tip.

verter [3] *vt* to pour (out); (*basura*) to dump.

vertical *a* vertical.

vertiente *f* (*de montaña, tejado*) slope; *Am* (*manantial*) spring.

vertiginoso,-a *a* (*velocidad*) breakneck.

vértigo *m* vertigo; **me da v.** it makes me dizzy.

vespa® *f* (motor) scooter.

vespino® *m* moped.

vestíbulo *m* (*de casa*) hall; (*de edificio público*) foyer.

vestido,-a 1 *m* (*de mujer*) dress. **2** *a* dressed.

vestigio *m* trace.

vestir [6] **1** *vt* (*a alguien*) to dress; (*llevar puesto*) to wear. **2** *vi* to

dress; **ropa de (mucho) v.** formal dress. **3** **vestirse** *vr* to get dressed, dress; **vestirse de** to wear; (*disfrazarse*) to dress up as.

vestuario *m* (*conjunto de vestidos*) wardrobe; (*para teatro*) costumes *pl;* (*camerino*) dressing room; (*en estadio*) changing room.

veterano,-a *a* & *mf* veteran.

veterinario,-a 1 *mf* vet, veterinarian. **2** *f* veterinary medicine.

veto *m* veto.

vez *f* time; (*turno*) turn; **una v.** once; **dos veces** twice; **cinco veces** five times; **a** *o* **algunas veces** sometimes; **cada v.** each *o* every time; **cada v. más** more and more; **de v. en cuando** now and again; **¿le has visto alguna v.?** have you ever seen him?; **otra v.** again; **a la v.** at the same time; **tal v.** perhaps, maybe; **de una v.** in one go; **en v. de** instead of.

vía 1 *f* (*del tren*) track; (*camino*) road; **(por) v. oral** to be taken orally; **por v. aérea/marítima** by air/sea. **2** *prep* (*a través de*) via.

viajar *vi* to travel.

viaje *m* journey, trip; (*largo, en barco*) voyage; **¡buen v.!** have a good trip!; **estar de v.** to be away (on a trip); **v. de negocios** business trip; **v. de novios** honeymoon.

viajero,-a *mf* traveler; (*en transporte público*) passenger.

víbora *f* viper.

vibración *f* vibration.

vibrar *vti* to vibrate.

vicepresidente,-a *mf* vice president; (*de compañía, comité*) vicechairman, vice president.

viceversa *adv* vice versa.

vicio *m* vice; (*mala costumbre*) bad habit.

vicioso,-a 1 *a* (*persona*) depraved; **círculo v.** vicious circle. **2** *mf* depraved person.

víctima *f* victim.

victoria *f* victory.

vid *f* vine.

vida *f* life; **en mi v.** never in my life;

ganarse la v. to earn one's living; **¿qué es de tu v.?** how's life?

vídeo *m* video; **grabar en ·** video.

videocámara *f* video camera.

videoclub *m* video club.

videojuego *m* video game.

vidriera *f* stained-glass window; *Am* (*escaparate*) shop window.

vidrio *m* glass.

viejo,-a 1 *a* old; **hacerse v.** to grow old; **un v. amigo** an old friend. **2** *mf* (*hombre*) old man; (*mujer*) old woman; **los viejos** old people.

viento *m* wind; **hace** *o* **sopla mucho v.** it is very windy.

vientre *m* belly.

viernes *m inv* Friday; **V. Santo** Good Friday.

vietnamita *a* & *mf* Vietnamese.

viga *f* (*de madera*) beam; (*de hierro*) girder.

vigencia *f* validity; **entrar en v.** to come into force.

vigésimo,-a *a* & *mf* twentieth.

vigilante *m* guard; (*nocturno*) night watchman.

vigilar 1 *vt* to watch; (*lugar*) to guard. **2** *vi* to keep watch.

vigor *m* vigor; (*fuerza*) strength; **en v.** in force.

vil *a* vile.

villa *f* (*población*) town; (*casa*) villa.

villancico *m* (Christmas) carol.

vinagre *m* vinegar.

vinagreras *fpl* oil and vinegar cruets.

vinagreta *f* vinaigrette.

vincha *f* *Am* headband.

vínculo *m* link.

vine *pt indef de* **venir.**

vino *m* wine; **v. blanco/tinto** white/red wine; **v. rosado** rosé.

viña *f* vineyard.

viñedo *m* vineyard.

viñeta *f* illustration.

violación *f* (*de persona*) rape; (*de ley, derecho*) violation.

violar *vt* (*persona*) to rape; (*ley, derecho*) to violate.

v.

virg
(*acei*

viril *a* v.

virtud *f* v.

virtuoso,-a
virtuoso.

viruela *f* small

virus *m inv* virus.

visa *f Am visa.*

visado *m* visa.

visera *f* (*de gorra*) peak, visor.

visibilidad *f* visibility.

visible *adj* visible.

visillo *m* small net curtain.

visión *f* vision; (*vista*) sight.

visita *f* visit; (*invitado*) visitor; **hacer una v.** to pay a visit; **estar de v.** to be visiting.

visitante 1 *mf* visitor. **2** *a* (*equipo*) away.

visitar *vt* to visit.

vislumbrar *vt* to glimpse.

visón *m* mink.

víspera *f* (*día anterior*) day before; (*de festivo*) eve.

vista *f* sight; (*panorama*) view; **a la v.** visible; **a primera** *o* **simple v.** on the face of it; **en v. de** in view of, considering; **corto de v.** short-sighted; **conocer a algn de v.** to know sb by sight; **perder de v. a** to lose sight of; **¡hasta la v.!** see you!; **con vista(s) al mar** overlooking the sea.

vistazo *m* glance; **echar un v. a algo** (*ojear*) to have a (quick) look at sth.

visto,-a 1 *a* **está v. que . . .** it is obvious that . . .; **por lo v.** apparently; **estar bien v.** to be well looked upon; **estar mal v.** to be

vehemente *a* vehement.
vehículo *m* vehicle.
veinte *a & m inv* twenty.
vejez *f* old age.
vejiga *f* bladder.
vela[1] *f* candle; **pasar la noche en v.** to have a sleepless night.
vela[2] *f* (*de barco*) sail.
velador *m Am* (*mesilla de noche*) bedside table.
velar 1 *vt* (*difrento*) to hold a wake; (*enfermo*) to watch over. **2** *vi* (*no dormir*) to stay awake. **3 velarse** *vr* to blur.
velatorio *m* vigil.
velero *m* sailing boat.
veleta *f* weather vane.
velo *m* veil.
velocidad *f* (*rapidez*) speed; (*marcha*) gear; **v. máxima** speed limit.
velocímetro *m* speedometer.
veloz *a* rapid.
vello *m* hair.
vena *f* vein.
venado *m* deer; (*carne*) venison.
vencedor,-a 1 *mf* winner. **2** *a* winning.
vencer [2] **1** *vt* to defeat; (*dificultad*) to overcome. **2** *vi* (*pago, deuda*) to be payable; (*plazo*) to expire.
vencido,-a *a* (*derrotado*) defeated; (*equipo etc*) beaten; **darse por v.** to give up.
venda *f* bandage.
vendaje *m* dressing.
vendar *vt* to bandage; **v. los ojos a algn** to blindfold sb.
vendaval *m* gale.
vendedor,-a *mf* seller; (*hombre*) salesman; (*mujer*) saleswoman.
vender *vt*, **venderse** *vr* to sell; 'se vende' for sale.
vendimia *f* grape harvest.
vendré *indic fut de* venir.
veneno *m* poison; (*de serpiente*) venom.
venenoso,-a *a* poisonous.
venéreo,-a *a* venereal.
venezolano,-a *a & mf* Venezuelan.

venga *subj pres de* venir.
venganza *f* vengeance, revenge.
vengo *indic pres de* venir.
venir 1 *vi* to come; **el año que viene** next year; *fam* **¡venga ya!** (*expresa incredulidad*) come off it!; (*vamos*) come on!; **v. grande/pequeño** (*ropa*) to be too big/small; **v. mal/bien** to be inconvenient/convenient. ■ (*en pasivas*) **esto vino provocado por . . .** this was brought about by . . . ■ **esto viene ocurriendo desde hace mucho tiempo** this has been going on for a long time now. **2 venirse** *vr* **venirse abajo** to collapse.
venta *f* sale; (*posada*) country inn; **en v.** for sale; **a la v.** on sale; **v. a plazos/al contado** credit/cash sale; **v. al por mayor/al por menor** wholesale/retail.
ventaja *f* advantage; **llevar v. a** to have the advantage over.
ventana *f* window; (*de la nariz*) nostril.
ventanilla *f* window; (*de la nariz*) nostril.
ventilador *m* ventilator; (*de coche*) fan.
ventilar *vt* to ventilate.
ventisca *f* blizzard; (*de nieve*) snowstorm.
ver 1 *vt* to see; (*televisión*) to watch; **a v.** let's see; **a v. si escribes** I hope you'll write; **(ya) veremos** we'll see; **no tener nada que v. con** to have nothing to do with. **2 verse** *vr* (*imagen etc*) to be seen; (*encontrarse con algn*) to see each other; **¡nos vemos!** see you later!; *Am* **te ves divina** you look divine.
veraneante *mf* vacationist, tourist.
veranear *vi* to spend one's summer vacation.
veraniego,-a *a* summer.
verano *m* summer.
veras de v. really.
verbena *f* street o night party.
verbo *m* verb.
verdad *f* truth; **es v.** it is true; **¡de v!** really!, truly!; **un amigo de v.** a

real friend; (en frase afirmativa) **está muy bien, ¿(no es) v.?** it is very good, isn't it?; (en frase negativa) **no te gusta, ¿v.?** you don't like it, do you?

verdaderamente adv truly.

verdadero,-a a true.

verde 1 a green; (fruta) unripe; (chiste, película) blue. **2** m (color) green.

verdoso,-a a greenish.

verdura f vegetables pl.

vereda f path; Am (acera) sidewalk.

veredicto m verdict.

vergonzoso,-a a (penoso) disgraceful; (tímido) shy.

vergüenza f shame; (timidez) shyness; **¡no te da v.?** aren't you ashamed?; **es una v.** it's a disgrace; **me da v.** I'm too embarrassed.

verificar [1] vt to check.

verja f (reja) grating; (cerca) railing; (puerta) iron gate.

vermut, vermú m (pl **vermús**) vermouth.

verosímil a probable, likely; (creíble) credible.

verruga f wart.

versión f version.

verso m (poesía) verse.

vertebrado,-a a & m vertebrate.

vertedero m (de basura) tip.

verter [3] vt to pour (out); (basura) to dump.

vertical a vertical.

vertiente f (de montaña, tejado) slope; Am (manantial) spring.

vertiginoso,-a a (velocidad) breakneck.

vértigo m vertigo; **me da v.** it makes me dizzy.

vespa® f (motor) scooter.

vespino® m moped.

vestíbulo m (de casa) hall; (de edificio público) foyer.

vestido,-a 1 m (de mujer) dress. **2** a dressed.

vestigio m trace.

vestir [6] **1** vt (a alguien) to dress; (llevar puesto) to wear. **2** vi to

dress; **ropa de (mucho) v.** formal dress. **3** vestirse vr to get dressed, dress; **vestirse de** to wear; (disfrazarse) to dress up as.

vestuario m (conjunto de vestidos) wardrobe; (para teatro) costumes pl; (camerino) dressing room; (en estadio) changing room.

veterano,-a a & mf veteran.

veterinario,-a 1 mf vet, veterinarian. **2** f veterinary medicine.

veto m veto.

vez f time; (turno) turn; **una v.** once; **dos veces** twice; **cinco veces** five times; **a o algunas veces** sometimes; **cada v.** each o every time; **cada v. más** more and more; **de v. en cuando** now and again; **¿le has visto alguna v.?** have you ever seen him?; **otra v.** again; **a la v.** at the same time; **tal v.** perhaps, maybe; **de una v.** in one go; **en v. de** instead of.

vía 1 f (del tren) track; (camino) road; **(por) v. oral** to be taken orally; **por v. aérea/marítima** by air/sea. **2** prep (a través de) via.

viajar vi to travel.

viaje m journey, trip; (largo, en barco) voyage; **¡buen v.!** have a good trip!; **estar de v.** to be away (on a trip); **v. de negocios** business trip; **v. de novios** honeymoon.

viajero,-a mf traveler; (en transporte público) passenger.

víbora f viper.

vibración f vibration.

vibrar vti to vibrate.

vicepresidente,-a mf vice president; (de compañía, comité) vice-chairman, vice president.

viceversa adv vice versa.

vicio m vice; (mala costumbre) bad habit.

vicioso,-a 1 a (persona) depraved; **círculo v.** vicious circle. **2** mf depraved person.

víctima f victim.

victoria f victory.

vid f vine.

vida f life; **en mi v.** never in my life;

ganarse la v. to earn one's living; **¿qué es de tu v.?** how's life?

vídeo m video; **grabar en v.** to video.

videocámara f video camera.

videoclub m video club.

videojuego m video game.

vidriera f stained-glass window; Am (escaparate) shop window.

vidrio m glass.

viejo,-a 1 a old; **hacerse v.** to grow old; **un v. amigo** an old friend. **2** mf (hombre) old man; (mujer) old woman; **los viejos** old people.

viento m wind; **hace** o **sopla mucho v.** it is very windy.

vientre m belly.

viernes m inv Friday; **V. Santo** Good Friday.

vietnamita a & mf Vietnamese.

viga f (de madera) beam; (de hierro) girder.

vigencia f validity; **entrar en v.** to come into force.

vigésimo,-a a & mf twentieth.

vigilante m guard; (nocturno) night watchman.

vigilar 1 vt to watch; (lugar) to guard. **2** vi to keep watch.

vigor m vigor; (fuerza) strength; **en v.** in force.

vil a vile.

villa f (población) town; (casa) villa.

villancico m (Christmas) carol.

vinagre m vinegar.

vinagreras fpl oil and vinegar cruets.

vinagreta f vinaigrette.

vincha f Am headband.

vínculo m link.

vine pt indef de **venir.**

vino m wine; **v. blanco/tinto** white/red wine; **v. rosado** rosé.

viña f vineyard.

viñedo m vineyard.

viñeta f illustration.

violación f (de persona) rape; (de ley, derecho) violation.

violar vt (persona) to rape; (ley, derecho) to violate.

violencia f violence.

violento,-a a violent; (situación) embarrassing; **sentirse v.** to feel awkward.

violeta 1 a violet. **2** m (color) violet. **3** f (flor) violet.

violín m violin.

violonc(h)elo m cello.

virar vi to turn round.

virgen a (persona, selva) virgin; (aceite, lana) pure; (cinta) blank.

viril a virile.

virtud f virtue; (propiedad) ability.

virtuoso,-a a virtuous; (músico) virtuoso.

viruela f smallpox.

virus m inv virus.

visa f Am visa.

visado m visa.

visera f (de gorra) peak; (de casco) visor.

visibilidad f visibility.

visible adj visible.

visillo m small net curtain.

visión f vision; (vista) sight.

visita f visit; (invitado) visitor; **hacer una v.** to pay a visit; **estar de v.** to be visiting.

visitante 1 mf visitor. **2** a (equipo) away.

visitar vt to visit.

vislumbrar vt to glimpse.

visón m mink.

víspera f (día anterior) day before; (de festivo) eve.

vista f sight; (panorama) view; **a la v.** in sight; **a primera** o **simple v.** on the face of it; **en v. de** in view of, considering; **corto de v.** short-sighted; **conocer a algn de v.** to know sb by sight; **perder de v. a** to lose sight of; **¡hasta la v.!** see you!; **con vista(s) al mar** overlooking the sea.

vistazo m glance; **echar un v. a algo** (ojear) to have a (quick) look at sth.

visto,-a 1 a **está v. que . . .** it is obvious that . . .; **por lo v.** apparently; **estar bien v.** to be well looked upon; **estar mal v.** to be frowned upon. **2** *m* **v. bueno** approval.

vitalicio,-a *a* lifelong.

vitalidad *f* vitality.

vitamina *f* vitamin.

viticultor,-a *mf* wine grower.

vitorear *vt* to cheer.

vitrina *f* (*aparador*) display cabinet; (*de exposición*) showcase; *Am* (*escaparate*) shop window.

viudo,-a *mf* (*hombre*) widower; (*mujer*) widow.

viva *interj* hurrah!

vivaracho,-a *a* lively.

vivaz *a* vivacious; (*perspicaz*) quick-witted.

víveres *mpl* provisions.

vivero *m* (*de plantas*) nursery.

vivienda *f* housing; (*casa*) house; (*piso*) apartment.

vivir 1 *vi* to live. **2** *vt* (*guerra etc*) to live through.

vivo,-a *a* alive; (*vivaz*) lively; (*listo*) clever; (*color*) vivid; **en v.** (*programa*) live; **al rojo v.** red-hot.

vocabulario *m* vocabulary.

vocación *f* vocation.

vocal 1 *f* vowel. **2** *m* member. **3** *a* vocal.

voceador,-a *mf Am* vendor.

vocero,-a *mf Am* spokesperson; (*hombre*) spokesman; (*mujer*) spokeswoman.

vociferar *vi* to shout.

vodka *m* vodka.

volandas en v. flying through the air.

volante 1 *m* steering wheel; (*de vestido*) frill; **ir al v.** to be at the wheel. **2** *a* flying; **platillo v.** flying saucer.

volantín *m Am* (*cometa*) small kite.

volar [2] **1** *vi* to fly; *fam* **lo hizo volando** he did it in a flash. **2** *vt* (*explotar*) to blow up; (*caja fuerte*) to blow open; (*terreno*) to blast. **3 volarse** *vr* (*papel etc*) to be blown away.

volcán *m* volcano.

volcar [2] **1** *vt* (*cubo etc*) to knock

over; (*barco, bote*) to capsize; (*vaciar*) to empty out. **2** *vi* (*coche*) to turn over; (*barca*) to capsize. **3 volcarse** *vr* (*vaso, jarra*) to fall over; (*coche*) to turn over; (*barca*) to capsize.

voleibol *m* volleyball.

voltaje *m* voltage.

voltereta *f* somersault.

voltio *m* volt.

volumen *m* volume.

voluminoso,-a *a* voluminous; (*enorme*) massive.

voluntad *f* will; **fuerza de v.** willpower; **tiene mucha v.** he is very strong-willed.

voluntario,-a 1 *a* voluntary; **ofrecerse v.** to volunteer. **2** *mf* volunteer.

volver [4] (*pp* **vuelto**) **1** *vi* to return; (*venir de vuelta*) to come back; (*ir de vuelta*) to go back; **v. en sí** to come round; **v. a hacer algo** to do sth again. **2** *vt* (*convertir*) to make; (*dar vuelta a*) to turn; (*boca abajo*) to turn upside down; (*de fuera adentro*) to turn inside out; (*de atrás adelante*) to turn back to front; (*cinta, disco*) to turn over; **volverle la espalda a algn** to turn one's back on sb; **al v. la esquina** on turning the corner. **3 volverse** *vr* to turn; (*venir de vuelta*) to come back; (*ir de vuelta*) to go back; (*convertirse*) to become; **volverse loco** to go mad.

vomitar 1 *vi* to vomit; **tengo ganas de v.** I feel sick. **2** *vt* to bring up.

voraz *a* voracious.

vosotros,-as *pron pers pl* you.

votación *f* (*voto*) vote; (*acción*) voting.

votante *mf* voter.

votar *vi* to vote; **v. a algn** to vote for sb.

voto *m* vote.

voy *indic pres de* **ir.**

voz *f* voice; (*grito*) shout; **en v. alta** aloud; **en v. baja** in a low voice; **a media v.** in a low voice; **a voces** shouting; **dar voces** to shout; **no**

tener ni v. ni voto to have no say in the matter.
vuelo *m* flight; **v. chárter/regular** charter/scheduled flight; **una falda de v.** a full skirt.
vuelta *f(regreso)* return; *(viaje)* return journey; *(giro)* turn; *(en carreras)* lap; *(ciclista)* tour; *(dinero)* change; **a v. de correo** by return post; **estar de v.** to be back; **dar media v.** to turn round; **la cabeza me da vueltas** my head is spinning; **no le des más vueltas** stop worrying about it; **dar una v.** *(a pie)* to go for a walk; *(en coche)* to go for a drive.
vuestro,-a 1 *a pos (antes del sustantivo)* your; *(después del sustantivo)* of yours. **2** *pron pos* yours; **lo v.** what is yours.
vulgar *a* vulgar.
vulnerable *a* vulnerable.

W

walkman® *m* Walkman®.
wáter *m* *(pl wáteres)* toilet.
whisky *m* whisky; *(irlandés, US)* whiskey.
windsurf(ing) *m* windsurfing.

X

xenofobia *f* xenophobia.

Y

y *conj* and; **son las tres y cuarto** it's a quarter past three; **¿y qué?** so what?; **¿y tú?** what about you?; **¿y eso?** how come?; *ver* **e.**
ya 1 *adv* already; *(ahora mismo)* now; **ya lo sabía** I already knew; **¡hazlo ya!** do it at once!; **ya mismo** right away; **ya hablaremos luego** we'll talk about it later; **ya verás** you'll see; **ya no** no longer; **ya no viene por aquí** he doesn't come round here any more; **ya era hora** about time too; **ya lo creo** I should

think so; **¡ya voy!** coming!; **¡ya está!** that's it! **2** *conj* **ya que** since.
yacaré *m Am* alligator.
yacer *vi* to lie.
yacimiento *m* deposit.
yanqui 1 *a* Yankee. **2** *mf* Yank.
yarda *f* yard.
yate *m* yacht.
yedra *f* ivy.
yegua *f* mare.
yema *f(de huevo)* yolk; *(de planta)* bud; *(pastel)* sweet made from sugar and egg yolk; **y. del dedo** fingertip.
yendo *gerundio de* **ir.**
yerba *f* = **hierba.**
yerbatero,-a *mf Am (curandero)* witch doctor who uses herbs.
yerno *m* son-in-law.
yerro *indic pres de* **errar.**
yeso *m* plaster.
yo *pron pers* I; **entre tú y yo** between you and me; **¿quién es?— soy yo** who is it?—it's me; **yo no** not me; **yo que tú** if I were you; **yo mismo** I myself.
yoga *m* yoga.
yogur *m* yogurt.
yuca *f* yucca.
yudo *m* judo.
yugo *m* yoke.
yugo(e)slavo,-a *a & mf* Yugoslav, Yugoslavian.

Z

zafarse *vr* to get away (**de** from).
zafiro *m* sapphire.
zalamero,-a 1 *mf* crawler. **2** *a* crawling.
zamarra *f* *(prenda)* sheepskin jacket.
zambo,-a *a* knock-kneed; *Am* half Indian and half Negro.
zambullirse *vr* to jump.
zanahoria *f* carrot.
zancada *f* stride.
zancadilla *f* **ponerle la z. a algn** to trip sb up.
zanco *m* stilt.
zancudo *m Am* mosquito.

zanja *f* ditch.

zapatería *f* shoe shop.

zapatero,-a *mf* (*vendedor*) shoe shop owner; (*fabricante*) shoemaker; (*reparador*) cobbler.

zapatilla *f* slipper; **zapatillas de deporte** trainers.

zapato *m* shoe.

zarandear *vt* to shake.

zarcillo *m* (*pendiente*) earring.

zarpa *f* claw.

zarpar *vi* to set sail.

zarza *f* bramble.

zarzamora *f* (*zarza*) blackberry bush; (*fruto*) blackberry.

zarzuela *f* Spanish operetta; **la Z.** royal residence in Madrid.

zigzag *m* (*pl* **zigzags** *o* **zigzagues**) zigzag.

zócalo *m* (*de pared*) baseboard.

zodiaco, zodíaco *m* zodiac; **signo del z.** sign of the zodiac.

zona *f* zone.

zoo *m* zoo.

zoológico,-a **1** *a* zoological; **parque z.** zoo. **2** *m* zoo.

zopilote *m Am* buzzard.

zoquete *mf fam* blockhead.

zorra *f* vixen.

zorro *m* fox.

zueco *m* clog.

zumbar *vi* to buzz; **me zumban los oídos** my ears are buzzing.

zumbido *m* buzzing.

zumo *m* juice.

zurcir [3] *vt* to darn.

zurdo,-a **1** *mf* (*persona*) left-handed person. **2** *a* left-handed.

SPANISH VERBS

Models for regular conjugation

TOMAR to take

INDICATIVE

PRESENT	FUTURE	CONDITIONAL
1. tomo	tomare	tomaría
2. tomas	tomarás	tomarías
3. toma	tomara	tomaría
1. tomamos	tomaremos	tomaríamos
2. tomáis	tomaréis	tomaríais
3. toman	tomarán	tomarían

IMPERFECT	PRETERITE	PERFECT
1. tomaba	tome	he tomado
2. tomabas	tomaste	has tomado
3. tomaba	tomo	ha tomado
1. tomábamos	tomamos	hemos tomado
2. tomabais	tomasteis	habéis tomado
3. tomaban	tomaron	han tomado

	CONDITIONAL	
FUTURE PERFECT	PERFECT	PLUPERFECT
1. habré tomado	habría tomado	había tomado
2. habrás tomado	habrías tomado	habías tomado
3. habrá tomado	habría tomado	había tomado
1. habremos tomado	habríamos tomado	habíamos tomado
2. habréis tomado	habríais tomado	habíais tomado
3. habrán tomado	habrían tomado	habían tomado

SUBJUNCTIVE

PRESENT	IMPERFECT	PERFECT/PLUPERFECT
1. tome	tom-ara/ase	haya/hubiera* tomado
2. tomes	tom-aras/ases	hayas/hubieras tomado
3. tome	tom-ara/ase	haya/hubiera tomado

*the alternative form 'hubiese' etc is also possible

1. tomemos	tom-áramos/ásemos	hayamos/hubiéramos tomado
2. toméis	tom-arais/aseis	hayáis/hubierais tomado
3. tomen	tom-aran/asen	hayan/hubieran tomado

IMPERATIVE	INFINITIVE	PARTICIPLE
(tú) toma	PRESENT	PRESENT
(Vd) tome	tomar	tomando
(nosotros) tomemos		
(vosotros) tomad	PERFECT	PAST
(Vds) tomen	haber tomado	tomado

COMER to eat

INDICATIVE

PRESENT	FUTURE	CONDITIONAL
1. como	comere	comería
2. comes	comerás	comerías
3. come	comera	comería
1. comemos	comeremos	comeríamos
2. coméis	comeréis	comeríais
3. comen	comerán	comerían

IMPERFECT	PRETERITE	PERFECT
1. comía	comí	he comido
2. comías	comiste	has comido
3. comía	comio	ha comido
1. comíamos	comimos	hemos comido
2. comíais	comisteis	habéis comido
3. comían	comieron	han comido

	CONDITIONAL	
FUTURE PERFECT	**PERFECT**	**PLUPERFECT**
1. habré comido	habría comido	había comido
2. habrás comido	habrías comido	habías comido
3. habrá comido	habría comido	había comido
1. habremos comido	habríamos comido	habíamos comido
2. habréis comido	habríais comido	habíais comido
3. habrán comido	habrían comido	habían comido

SUBJUNCTIVE

PRESENT	**IMPERFECT**	**PERFECT/PLUPERFECT**
1. coma	com-iera/iese	haya/hubiera* comido
2. comas	com-ieras/ieses	hayas/hubieras comido
3. coma	com-iera/iese	haya/hubiera comido
1. comamos	com-iéramos/ iésemos	hayamos/hubiéramos comido
2. comáis	com-ierais/ieseis	hayáis/hubierais comido
3. coman	com-ieran/iesen	hayan/hubieran comido

*the alternative form 'hubiese' etc is also possible.

IMPERATIVE	*INFINITIVE*	*PARTICIPLE*
(tú) come	**PRESENT**	**PRESENT**
(Vd) coma	comer	comiendo
(nosotros) comamos		
(vosotros) comed	**PERFECT**	**PAST**
(Vds) coman	haber comido	comido

PARTIR to leave

INDICATIVE

PRESENT	**FUTURE**	**CONDITIONAL**
1. parto	partiré	partiría
2. partes	partirás	partirías
3. parte	partirá	partiría

1. partimos	partiremos	partiríamos
2. partís	partiréis	partiríais
3. parten	partirán	partirían

IMPERFECT	**PRETERITE**	**PERFECT**
1. partía	partí	he partido
2. partías	partiste	has partido
3. partía	partió	ha partido
1. partíamos	partimos	hemos partido
2. partíais	partisteis	habéis partido
3. partían	partieron	han partido

CONDITIONAL

FUTURE PERFECT	**PERFECT**	**PLUPERFECT**
1. habré partido	habría partido	había partido
2. habrás partido	habrías partido	habías partido
3. habrá partido	habría partido	había partido
1. habremos partido	habríamos partido	habíamos partido
2. habréis partido	habríais partido	habíais partido
3. habrán partido	habrían partido	habían partido

SUBJUNCTIVE

PRESENT	**IMPERFECT**	**PERFECT/PLUPERFECT**
parta	parti-era/ese	haya/hubiera* partido
partas	parti-eras/eses	hayas/hubieras partido
parta	parti-era/ese	haya/hubiera partido
partamos	parti-éramos/ésemos	hayamos/hubiéramos partido
partáis	parti-erais/eseis	hayáis/hubierais partido
partan	parti-eran/esen	hayan/hubieran partido

*the alternative form 'hubiese' etc is also possible

IMPERATIVE	INFINITIVE	PARTICIPLE
(tú) parte	**PRESENT**	**PRESENT**
(Vd) parta	partir	partiendo
(nosotros)		
partamos	**PERFECT**	**PAST**
(vosotros) partid	haber partido	partido
(Vds) partan		

ESTAR to be

INDICATIVE

PRESENT	FUTURE	CONDITIONAL
1. estoy	estaré	estaría
2. estás	estarás	estarías
3. está	estará	estaría
1. estamos	estaremos	estaríamos
2. estáis	estaréis	estaríais
3. están	estarán	estarían

IMPERFECT	PRETERITE	PERFECT
1. estaba	estuve	he estado
2. estabas	estuviste	has estado
3. estaba	estuvo	ha estado
1. estábamos	estuvimos	hemos estado
2. estabais	estuvisteis	habéis estado
3. estaban	estuvieron	han estado

	CONDITIONAL	
FUTURE PERFECT	PERFECT	PLUPERFECT
1. habré estado	habría estado	había estado
2. habrás estado	habrías estado	habías estado
3. habrá estado	habría estado	había estado
1. habremos estado	habríamos estado	habíamos estado
2. habréis estado	habríais estado	habíais estado
3. habrán estado	habrían estado	habian estado

SUBJUNCTIVE

PRESENT	IMPERFECT	PERFECT/PLUPERFECT
1. este	estuv-iera/iese	haya/hubiera* estado
2. estés	estuv-ieras/ieses	hayas/hubieras estado
3. este	estuv-iera/iese	haya/hubiera estado
1. estemos	estuv-iéramos/iésemos	hayamos/hubiéramos estado
2. estéis	estuv-ierais/ieseis	hayáis/hubierais estado
3. estén	estuv-ieran/iesen	hayan/hubieran estado

*the alternative form 'hubiese' etc is also possible

IMPERATIVE	INFINITIVE	PARTICIPLE
(tú) esta	**PRESENT**	**PRESENT**
(Vd) esté	estar	estando
(nosotros) estemos		
(vosotros) estad	**PERFECT**	**PAST**
(vds) esten	haber estado	estado

HABER to have (auxiliary)
INDICATIVE

PRESENT	FUTURE	CONDITIONAL
1. he	habré	habría
2. has	habrás	habrías
3. ha/hay*	habrá	habría
1. hemos	habremos	habríamos
2. habéis	habréis	habríais
3. han	habrán	habrían

IMPERFECT	PRETERITE	PERFECT
1. había	hube	
2. habías	hubiste	

3. había	hubo	ha habido*
1. habíamos	hubimos	
2. habíais	hubisteis	
3. habían	hubieron	

FUTURE PERFECT	CONDITIONAL PERFECT	PLUPERFECT
1.		
2.		
3. habrá habido*	habría habido*	había habido*
1.		
2.		
3.		

SUBJUNCTIVE

PRESENT	IMPERFECT	PERFECT/PLUPERFECT
1. haya	hub-iera/iese	
2. hayas	hub-ieras/ieses	
3. haya	hub-iera/iese	haya/hubiera** habido*
1. hayamos	hub-iéramos/iésemos	
2. hayáis	hub-ierais/ieseis	
3. hayan	hub-ieran/iesen	

INFINITIVE PARTICIPLE

PRESENT	PRESENT
haber	habiendo
PERFECT	**PAST**
haber habido*	habido

* 'haber' is an auxiliary verb used with the participle of another verb to form compound tenses (eg he bebido—I have drunk). 'hay' means ' there is/are' and all third person singular forms in their respective tenses have this meaning. The forms highlighted with an asterisk are used only for this latter construction.

**the alternative form 'hubiese' is also possible

Models for irregular conjugation

[1] **pensar** *PRES* pienso, piensas, piensa, pensamos, pensáis, piensan; *PRES SUBJ* piense, pienses, piense, pensemos, penséis, piensen; *IMPERAT* piensa, piense, pensemos, pensad, piensen

[2] **contar** *PRES* cuento, cuentas, cuenta, contamos, contáis, cuentan; *PRES SUBJ* cuente, cuentes, cuente, contemos, contéis, cuenten; *IMPERAT* cuenta, cuente, contemos, contad, cuenten

[3] **perder** *PRES* pierdo, pierdes, pierde, perdemos, perdéis, pierden; *PRES SUBJ* pierda, pierdas, pierda, perdamos, perdáis, pierdan; *IMPERAT* pierde, pierda, perdamos, perded, pierdan

[4] **morder** *PRES* muerdo, muerdes, muerde, mordemos, mordéis, muerden; *PRES SUBJ* muerda, muerdas, muerda, mordamos, mordáis, muerdan; *IMPERAT* muerde, muerda, mordamos, morded, muerdan

[5] **sentir** *PRES* siento, sientes, siente, sentimos, sentís, sienten; *PRES SUBJ* sienta, sientas, sienta, sintamos, sintáis, sientan; *PRES P* sintiendo; *IMPERAT* siente, sienta, sintamos, sentid, sientan

[6] **vestir** *PRES* visto, vistes, viste, vestimos, vestís, visten; *PRES SUBJ* vista, vistas, vista, vistamos, vistáis, vistan; *PRES P* vistiendo; *IMPERAT* viste, vista, vistamos, vestid, vistan

[7] **dormir** *PRES* duermo, duermes, duerme, dormimos, dormís, duermen; *PRES SUBJ* duerma, duermas, duerma, durmamos, durmáis, duerman; *PRES P* durmiendo; *IMPERAT* duerme, duerma, durmamos, dormid, duerman

caer *PRES* caigo, caes, cae, caemos, caéis, caen; *PRES SUBJ* caiga, caigas, caiga, caigamos, caigáis, caigan; *PRES P* cayendo; *PP* caído; *IMPERAT* cae, caiga, caigamos, caed, caigan

conocer *PRES* conozco, conoces, conoce, conocemos, conocéis, conocen; *PRES SUBJ* conozca, conozcas, conozca, conozcamos, conozcáis, conozcan; *IMPERAT* conoce, conozca, conozcamos, conoced, conozcan

dar *PRES* doy, das, da, damos, dais, dan; *PRES SUBJ* dé, des, dé, demos, deis, den; *PRET* di, diste, dio, dimos, disteis, dieron; *IMPERF SUBJ* diera/diese; *IMPERAT* da, dé, demos, dad, den

decir *PRES* digo, dices, dice, decimos, decís, dicen; *PRES SUBJ* diga, digas, diga, digamos, digáis, digan; *FUT* diré; *COND* diría; *PRET* dije, dijiste, dijo, dijimos, dijisteis, dijeron; *IMPERF SUBJ* dijera/dijese; *PRES P* diciendo; *PP* dicho; *IMPERAT* di, diga, digamos, decid, digan

hacer *PRES* hago, haces, hace, hacemos, hacéis, hacen; *PRES SUBJ* haga, hagas, haga, hagamos, hagáis, hagan; *FUT* haré; *COND* haría; *PRET* hice, hiciste, hizo, hicimos, hicisteis, hicieron; *IMPERF SUBJ* hiciera/hiciese; *PP* hecho; *IMPERAT* haz, haga, hagamos, haced, hagan

ir *PRES* voy, vas, va, vamos, vais, van; *PRES SUBJ* vaya, vayas, vaya, vayamos, vayáis, vayan; *IMPERF* iba, ibas, iba, íbamos, ibais, iban; *PRET* fui, fuiste, fue, fuimos, fuisteis, fueron; *IMPERF SUBJ* fuera/fuese; *PRES P* yendo; *IMPERAT* ve, vaya, vamos, id, vayan

leer *PRET* leí, leíste, leyó, leímos, leísteis, leyeron; *IMPERF SUBJ* leyera/leyese; *PRES P* leyendo; *PP* leído; *IMPERAT* lee, lea, leamos, leed, lean

poder *PRES* puedo, puedes, puede, podemos, podéis, pueden; *PRES SUBJ* pueda, puedas, pueda, podamos, podáis, puedan; *FUT* podré; *COND* podría; *PRET* pude, pudiste, pudo, pudimos, pudisteis, pudieron; *IMPERF SUBJ* pudiera/pudiese; *PRES P* pudiendo; *IMPERAT* puede, pueda, podamos, poded, puedan

poner *PRES* pongo, pones, pone, ponemos, ponéis, ponen; *PRES SUBJ* ponga, pongas, ponga, pongamos, pongáis, pongan; *FUT* pondré; *COND* pondría; *PRET* puse, pusiste, puso, pusimos, pusisteis, pusieron; *IMPERF SUBJ* pusiera/pusiese; *PP* puesto; *IMPERAT* pon, ponga, pngamos, poned, pongan

querer *PRES* quiero, quieres, quiere, queremos, queréis, quieren; *PRES SUBJ* quiera, quieras, quiera, queramos, queráis, quieran; *FUT* querré; *COND* querría; *PRET* quise, quisiste, quiso, quisimos, quisisteis, quisieron; *IMPERF SUBJ* quisiera/quisiese; *IMPERAT* quiere, quiera, queramos, quered, quieran

saber *PRES* sé, sabes, sabe, sabemos, sabéis, saben; *PRES SUBJ* sepa, sepas, sepa, sepamos, sepáis, sepan; *FUT* sabré; *COND* sabría; *PRET* supe, supiste, supo, supimos, supisteis, supieron; *IMPERF SUBJ* supiera/supiese; *IMPERAT* sabe, sepa, sepamos, sabed, sepan

ser *PRES* soy, eres, es, somos, sois, son; *PRES SUBJ* sea, seas, sea, seamos, seáis, sean; *IMPERF* era, eras, era, éramos, erais, eran; *PRET* fui, fuiste, fue, fuimos, fuisteis, fueron; *IMPERF SUBJ* fuera/fuese; *IMPERAT* sé, sea, seamos, sed, sean

tener *PRES* tengo, tienes, tiene, tenemos, tenéis, tienen; *PRES SUBJ* tenga, tengas, tenga, tengamos, tengáis, tengan; *FUT* tendré; *COND* tendría; *PRET* tuve, tuviste, tuvo, tuvimos, tuvisteis, tuvieron; *IMPERF SUBJ* tuviera/tuviese; *IMPERAT* ten, tenga, tengamos, tened, tengan

venir *PRES* vengo, vienes, viene, venimos, venís, vienen; *PRES SUBJ* venga, vengas, venga, vengamos, vengáis, vengan; *FUT* vendré; *COND* vendría; *PRET* vine, viniste, vino, vinimos, vinisteis, vinieron; *IMPERF SUBJ* viniera/viniese; *PRES P* viniendo; *IMPERAT* ven, venga, vengamos, venid, vengan

VERBOS IRREGULARES INGLESES

infinitive	*past simple*	*past participle*
arise	arose	arisen
awake	awoke	awoken
be	was, were	been
bear	bore	borne
beat	beat	beaten
become	became	become
begin	began	begun
bend	bent	bent
bet	bet, betted	bet, betted
bid (*offer*)	bid	bid
bind	bound	bound
bite	bit	bitten
bleed	bled	bled
blow	blew	blown
break	broke	broken
breed	bred	bred
bring	brought	brought
broadcast	broadcast	broadcast
build	built	built
burn	burnt, burned	burnt, burned
burst	burst	burst
buy	bought	bought
cast	cast	cast
catch	caught	caught
choose	chose	chosen
cling	clung	clung
come	came	come
cost	cost	cost
creep	crept	crept
cut	cut	cut
deal	dealt	dealt

infinitive	*past simple*	*past participle*
dig	dug	dug
dive	dove	dived
do	did	done
draw	drew	drawn
dream	dreamt, dreamed	dreamt, dreamed
drink	drank	drunk
drive	drove	driven
eat	ate	eaten
fall	fell	fallen
feed	fed	fed
feel	felt	felt
fight	fought	fought
find	found	found
flee	fled	fled
fling	flung	flung
fly	flew	flown
forbid	forbad(e)	forbidden
forecast	forecast	forecast
foresee	foresaw	foreseen
forget	forgot	forgotten
forgive	forgave	forgiven
freeze	froze	frozen
get	got	gotten
give	gave	given
go	went	gone
grind	ground	ground
grow	grew	grown
hang	hung, hanged	hung, hanged
have	had	had
hear	heard	heard
hide	hid	hidden
hit	hit	hit
hold	held	held
hurt	hurt	hurt

infinitive	*past simple*	*past participle*
keep	kept	kept
kneel	knelt, kneeled	knelt, kneeled
know	knew	known
lay	laid	laid
lead	led	led
lean	leant, leaned	leant, leaned
leap	leapt, leaped	leapt, leaped
learn	learnt, learned	learnt, learned
leave	left	left
lend	lent	lent
let	let	let
lie	lay	lain
light	lit, lighted	lit, lighted
lose	lost	lost
make	made	made
mean	meant	meant
meet	met	met
mislay	mislaid	mislaid
mislead	misled	misled
mistake	mistook	mistaken
misunderstand	misunderstood	misunderstood
mow	mowed	mown, mowed
outdo	outdid	outdone
overcome	overcame	overcome
overdo	overdid	overdone
overtake	overtook	overtaken
pay	paid	paid
put	put	put
quit	quit	quit
read	read	read
redo	redid	redone
rend	rent	rent
rewind	rewound	rewound
ride	rode	ridden

infinitive	past simple	past participle
ring	rang	rung
rise	rose	risen
run	ran	run
saw	sawed	sawn, sawed
say	said	said
see	saw	seen
seek	sought	sought
sell	sold	sold
send	sent	sent
set	set	set
sew	sewed	sewn, sewed
shake	shook	shaken
shear	sheared	shorn, sheared
shed	shed	shed
shine	shone	shone
shoot	shot	shot
show	showed	shown, showed
shrink	shrank, shrunk	shrunk
shut	shut	shut
sing	sang	sung
sink	sank	sunk
sit	sat	sat
sleep	slept	slept
slide	slid	slid
sling	slung	slung
slink	slunk	slunk
slit	slit	slit
smell	smelt, smelled	smelt, smelled
sneak	snuck	snuck
sow	sowed	sown, sowed
speak	spoke	spoken
speed	sped, speeded	sped, speeded
spell	spelt, spelled	spelt, spelled
spend	spent	spent

infinitive	past simple	past participle
spill	spilt, spilled	spilt, spilled
spin	spun	spun
spit	spat	spat
split	split	split
spoil	spoilt, spoiled	spoilt, spoiled
spread	spread	spread
spring	sprang	sprung
stand	stood	stood
steal	stole	stolen
stick	stuck	stuck
sting	stung	stung
stink	stank	stunk
stride	strode	stridden
strike	struck	struck, stricken
string	strung	strung
strive	strove	striven
swear	swore	sworn
sweep	swept	swept
swell	swelled	swollen, swelled
swim	swam	swum
swing	swung	swung
take	took	taken
teach	taught	taught
tear	tore	torn
tell	told	told
think	thought	thought
throw	threw	thrown
thrust	thrust	thrust
tread	trod	trodden
undergo	underwent	undergone
understand	understood	understood
undertake	undertook	undertaken
undo	undid	undone
upset	upset	upset

infinitive	past simple	past participle
wake	woke	woken
wear	wore	worn
weave	wove	woven
weep	wept	wept
wet	wet, wetted	wet, wetted
win	won	won
wind	wound	wound
withdraw	withdrew	withdrawn
wring	wrung	wrung
write	wrote	written

COUNTRIES and REGIONS	PAISES Y REGIONES
Africa (*African*)	Africa *f* (*africano,-a*)
Albania (*Albanian*)	Albania *f* (*albanés,-esa*)
Algeria (*Algerian*)	Argelia *f* (*argelino,-a*)
America (*American*)	América *f* (*americano,-a*)
Central/North/South America (*Central/North/South American*)	A. Central/del Norte/del Sur *f*
Antarctica, the Antarctic (*Antarctic*)	Antártida, *f* el Antártico *m* (*antártico,-a*)
Arabia (*Arab, Arabic*)	Arabia *f* (*árabe*)
the Arctic (*Arctic*)	el Artico *m* (*ártic,-a*)
Argentina (*Argentinian, Argentine*)	Argentina *f* (*argentino,-a*)
Asia (*Asian*)	Asia *f* (*asiático,-a*)
Australia (*Australian*)	Australia *f* (*australiano, -a*)
Austria (*Austrian*)	Austria *f* (*austríaco,-a*)
the Balearic Islands (*Balearic*)	Baleares *fpl* (*balear*)
Belgium (*Belgian*)	Bélgica *f* (*belga*)
Bolivia (*Bolivian*)	Bolivia *f* (*boliviano,-a*)
Brazil (*Brazilian*)	Brasil *m* (*brasileño,-a, brasilero,-a*)
Bulgaria (*Bulgarian*)	Bulgaria *f* (*búlgaro,-a*)
Burma (*Burmese*)	Birmania *f* (*birmano,-a*)
Canada (*Canadian*)	Canadá *m* (*canadiense*)
Canaries	Canarias *fpl* (*canario,-a*)
Central America (*Central American*)	Centroamérica *f* (*centroamericano,-a*)
Chile (*Chilean*)	Chile *m* (*chileno,-a*)
China (*Chinese*)	China *f* (*chino,-a*)

Colombia (*Colombian*)	Colombia *f* (*colombiano, -a*)
Corsica (*Corsican*)	Córcega *f* (*corso, -a*)
Costa Rica (*Costa Rican*)	Costa Rica *f* (*costarricense, costarriqueño, -a*)
Crete (*Cretan*)	Creta *f* (*cretense*)
Cuba (*Cuban*)	Cuba *f* (*cubano, -a*)
Cyprus (*Cypriot*)	Chipre *m* (*chipriota*)
Czech Republic (*Czech*)	República Checa *f* (*checo, -a*)
Denmark (*Danish*)	Dinamarca *f* (*danés, -esa*)
Dominican Republic (*Dominican*)	República Dominicana *f* (*dominicano, -a*)
Ecuador (*Ecuadorian*)	Ecuador *m* (*ecuatoriano, -a*)
Egypt (*Egyptian*)	Egipto *m* (*egipcio, -a*)
Eire, Republic of Ireland (*Irish*)	Eire *m* (*irlandés, -esa*)
El Salvador (*Salvadoran, Salvadorian*)	El Salvador *m* (*salvadoreño, -a*)
England (*English*)	Inglaterra *f* (*inglés, -esa*)
Ethiopia (*Ethiopian*)	Etiopía *f* (*etiope, etíope*)
Europe (*European*)	Europa *f* (*europeo, -a*)
Finland (*Finnish*)	Finlandia *f* (*finlandés, -a*)
France (*French*)	Francia *f* (*francés, -a*)
Germany (*German*)	Alemania *f* (*alemán, -ana*)
Gibraltar (*Gibraltarian*)	Gibraltar *m* (*gibraltaneño, -a*)
Great Britain (*British*)	Gran Bretaña *f* (*británico, -a*)
Greece (*Greek*)	Grecia *f* (*griego, -a*)
Holland (*Dutch*)	Holanda *f* (*holandés, -esa*)
Honduras (*Honduran*)	Honduras *f* (*hondureño, -a*)

Hungary (*Hungarian*)	Hungría f (*húngaro,-a*)
Iceland (*Icelandic*)	Islandia f (*islandés,-esa*)
India (*Indian*)	India f (*indio,-a*)
Indonesia (*Indonesian*)	Indonesia f (*indonesio,-a*)
Iran (*Iranian*)	Irán m (*iraní*)
Iraq (*Iraqi*)	Irak, Iraq m (*iraquí*)
Ireland (*Irish*)	Irlanda f (*irlandés,-esa*)
Israel (*Israeli*)	Israel m (*israelí*)
Italy (*Italian*)	Italia f (*italiano,-a*)
Jamaica (*Jamaican*)	Jamaica f (*jamaicano,-a*)
Japan (*Japanese*)	Japón m (*japonés,-esa*)
Kenya (*Kenyan*)	Kenia f (*keniano,-a*)
Korea (*Korean*)	Corea f (*coreano,-a*)
Latin America (*Latin American*)	Latinoamérica f (*latinoaméricano,-a*); Hispanoamérica f (*hispanoamericano,-a*); Iberoamérica f (*iberoamericano,-a*)
Latvia (*Latvian*)	Letonia f (*letón,-ona*)
the Lebanon (*Lebanese*)	Líbano m (*libanés,-esa*)
Libya (*Libyan*)	Libia f (*libio,-a*)
Lithuania (*Lithuanian*)	Lituania f (*lituano,-a*)
Luxembourg	Luxemburgo m (*luxemburgués,-a*)
Majorca (*Majorcan*)	Mallorca f (*mallorquín,-ina*)
Malaysia (*Malay*)	Malasia f (*malayo,-a*)
Mexico (*Mexican*)	Méjico, México m (*mejicano,-a, mexicano,-a*)
Mongolia (*Mongolian*)	Mongolia f (*mongol*)
Morocco (*Moroccan*)	Marruecos m (*marroquí*)
the Netherlands, the Low Countries (*Dutch*)	Países Bajos mpl (*neerlandés,-esa*)

Nicaragua (*Nicaraguan*)	Nicaragua *f* (*nicaragüense, nicaragüeño,-a*)
North Africa (*North African*)	Norteáfrica *f* (*norteafricano,-a*)
North America ((*North*) *American*)	Norteamérica *f* (*norteamericano,-a*)
Northern Ireland (*Northern Irish*)	Irlanda del Norte *f*
Norway (*Norwegian*)	Noruega *f* (*noruego,-a*)
Pakistan (*Pakistani*)	Pakistán, Paquistán *m* (*pakistani, paquistani*)
Palestine (*Palestinian*)	Palestina *f* (*palestino,-a*)
Panama (*Panamanian*)	Panamá *m* (*panameño,-a*)
Paraguay (*Paraguayan*)	Paraguay *m* (*paraguayo, -a*)
Peru (*Peruvian*)	Perú (el) *m* (*peruano,-a*)
(the) Philippines (*Philippine, Filipino*)	Filipinas *fpl* (*filipino,-a*)
Poland (*Polish*)	Polonia *f* (*polaco,-a*)
Portugal (*Portuguese*)	Portugal *m* (*portugués,-a*)
Puerto Rico (*Puerto Rican*)	Puerto Rico *m* (*portorriqueño,-a, puertorriqueño,-a*)
Rumania, Roumania (*R(o)umanian*)	Rumanía *f* (*rumano,-a*)
Russia (*Russian*)	Rusia *f* (*ruso,-a*)
Saudi Arabia (*Saudi Arabian, Saudi*)	Arabia Saudita *f* (*saudita, saudi*)
Scandinavia (*Scandinavian*)	Escandinavia *f* (*escandinavo,-a*)
Scotland (*Scottish, Scots*)	Escocia *f* (*escocés,-a*)
Sicily (*Sicilian*)	Sicilia *f* (*siciliano,-a*)
Slovakia (*Slovak*)	Eslovaquia *f* (*eslovaco,-a*)
South Africa (*South African*)	Sudáfrica *f* (*sudafricano, -a*)

South America (*South American*)	Sudamérica *f* (*sudamericano,-a*); Suramérica *suramericano,-a*)
Spain (*Spanish*)	España *f* (*español,-a*)
Sweden (*Swedish*)	Suecia *f* (*sueco,-a*)
Switzerland (*Swiss*)	Suiza *f* (*suizo,-a*)
Syria (*Syrian*)	Siria *f* (*sirio,-a*)
Thailand (*Thai*)	Tailandia *f* (*tailandés, -esa*)
Tunisia (*Tunisian*)	Túnez *m* (*tunecino,-a*)
Turkey (*Turkish*)	Turquía *f* (*turco,-a*)
Ukraine (*Ukrainian*)	Ucrania *f* (*ucraniano,-a*)
the United States (*United States, American*)	Estados Unidos *mpl* (*estadounidense*)
Uruguay (*Uruguayan*)	Uruguay *m* (*uruguayo,-a*)
Venezuela (*Venezuelan*)	Venezuela *f* (*venezolano, -a*)
Vietnam (*Vietnamese*)	Vietnam *m* (*vietnamita*)
Wales (*Welsh*)	Gales *f* (el país de *m*) (*galés,-esa*)
the West Indies (*West Indian*)	Antillas *f* (*antillano,-a*)

NUMBERS

LOS NÚMEROS

zero	0	cero
one	1	uno, una
two	2	dos
three	3	tres
four	4	cuatro
five	5	cinco
six	6	seis
seven	7	siete
eight	8	ocho
nine	9	nueve
ten	10	diez
eleven	11	once
twelve	12	doce
thirteen	13	trece
fourteen	14	catorce
fifteen	15	quince
sixteen	16	dieciséis
seventeen	17	diecisiete
eighteen	18	dieciocho
nineteen	19	diecinueve
twenty	20	viente
twenty-one	21	veintiuno
twenty-two	22	veintidós
thirty	30	treinta
thirty-one	31	treinta y uno
thirty-two	32	treinta y dos
forty	40	cuarenta
fifty	50	cincuenta
sixty	60	sesenta
seventy	70	setenta
eighty	80	ochenta
ninety	90	noventa

a *or* one hundred	100	cien
a *or* one hundred and one	101	ciento uno
a *or* one hundred and ten	110	ciento diez
two hundred	200	doscientos, doscientas
five hundred	500	quinientos, quinientas
seven hundred	700	setecientos, setecientas
a *or* one thousand	1,000	mil
two hundred thousand	200,000	doscientos mil
one million	1,000,000	un millón

A

a *indef art (before vowel or silent h* **an)** un, una; **he has a big nose** tiene la nariz grande; **half a liter/ an hour** medio litro/media hora; **he's a teacher** es profesor; **60 cents a kilo** 60 centavos el kilo; **three times a week** tres veces a la semana.

abandon *vt* abandonar.

abbey abadía *f.*

abbreviation abreviatura *f.*

ability capacidad *f.*

able *a (capable)* capaz; **to be a. to do sth** poder hacer algo.

abnormal *a* anormal.

abnormally *adv* anormalmente.

aboard 1 *adv* a bordo; **to go a.** *(ship)* embarcarse; *(train)* subir. **2** *prep* a bordo de.

abolish *vt* abolir.

abortion aborto *m;* **to have an a.** abortar.

about 1 *adv (approximately)* más o menos; **he's a. 40** tendrá unos 40 años; **it's a. time you got up** ya es hora de que te levantes. **2** *prep (concerning)* acerca de; **a program a. New York** un programa sobre Nueva York; **to speak a. sth** hablar de algo; **what's it all a.?** ¿de qué se trata? **how a. a game of tennis?** ¿qué te parece un partido de tenis? ▪ **it's a. to start** está a punto de empezar.

above 1 *adv* arriba; **the apartment a.** el piso de arriba; **a policy imposed from a.** una política impuesta desde arriba. **2** *prep (higher than)* encima de; *(greater than)* superior a; **100 meters a. sea level** 100 metros sobre el nivel del mar; **it's a. the door** está encima de la puerta; **a. all** sobre todo; **he's not a. stealing** es capaz incluso de robar.

above-mentioned *a* susodicho,-a.

abreast *adv* **to keep a. of things** mantenerse al día.

abroad *adv* en el extranjero; **to go a.** irse al extranjero.

abrupt *a (manner)* brusco,-a; *(change)* súbito,-a.

abruptly *adv (act)* bruscamente; *(speak)* con aspereza.

abscess absceso *m.*

absence *(of person)* ausencia *f;* *(of thing)* falta *f.*

absent *a* ausente.

absent-minded *a* distraído,-a.

absolute *a* absoluto,-a; *(failure)* total; *(truth)* puro,-a.

absolutely *adv* completamente; **a. not** en absoluto; **you're a. right** tienes toda la razón; **a.!** ¡desde luego!

absorb *vt (liquid)* absorber; **to be absorbed in sth** estar absorto, -a en algo.

absurd *a* absurdo,-a.

abuse 1 *n (ill-treatment)* malos tratos *mpl;* *(misuse)* abuso *m;* *(insults)* injurias *fpl.* **2** *vt (ill-treat)* maltratar; *(misuse)* abusar de; *(insult)* injuriar.

abusive *a (insulting)* grosero,-a.

academic 1 *a* académico,-a; *(career)* universitario,-a; **a. year** año *m* escolar. **2** *n* académico,-a *mf.*

accelerate *vi* acelerar.

accelerator acelerador *m.*

accent acento *m.*

accept *vt* aceptar; *(theory)* admitir.

acceptable *a* admisible.

access acceso *m.*

accessible *a* accesible; *(person)* asequible.

accessory *(to crime)* cómplice *mf;* **accessories** accesorios *mpl;* *(for outfit)* complementos *mpl.*

access time tiempo *m* de acceso.

accident accidente *m;* **by a.** por casualidad.

accidental *a* fortuito,-a; *(unintended)* imprevisto,-a.

accidentally *adv (by chance)* por casualidad.

accommodation(s) alojamiento *m.*

accompany *vt* acompañar.

accomplish vt (aim) conseguir; (task, mission) llevar a cabo.

accord of his own a. espontáneamente.

accordance in a. with de acuerdo con.

according to prep según.

accordion acordeón m.

account (report) informe m; (at bank, in business) cuenta f; **on a. of** a causa de; **to take a. of, to take into a.** tener en cuenta; **accounts department** servicio m de contabilidad; **current a.** cuenta f corriente.

• **account for** vt (explain) explicar.

accountant contable mf.

accumulate 1 vt acumular. **2** vi acumularse.

accurate a (number) exacto,-a; (answer) correcto,-a; (observation) acertado,-a; (translation) fiel.

accurately adv con precisión.

accusation acusación f.

accuse vt acusar.

accustomed a **to be a. to sth** estar acostumbrado a algo; **to get a. to sth** acostumbrarse a algo.

ace (card & fig) as m; (in tennis) ace m.

ache 1 n dolor m. **2** vi doler; **my back aches** me duele la espalda.

achieve vt (attain) conseguir; (accomplish) llevar a cabo.

achievement (attainment) logro m; (feat) hazaña f.

acid 1 a ácido,-a. **2** n ácido m.

acid rain lluvia f ácida.

acknowledge vt (recognize) reconocer; (letter) acusar recibo de; (greet) saludar.

acne acné m.

acorn bellota f.

acoustics npl acústica f sing.

acquaint vt **to be acquainted with sb** conocer a algn; **to be acquainted with sth** estar al corriente de algo.

acquaintance conocimiento m; (person) conocido,-a mf; **to make sb's a.** conocer a algn.

acquire vt adquirir.

acre acre m (approx 40,47 áreas).

acrobatic a acrobático,-a.

across 1 adv a través; **to go a.** atravesar; **to run a.** atravesar corriendo. **2** prep a través de; (at the other side of) al otro lado de; **they live a. the road** viven enfrente; **to go a. the street** cruzar la calle.

acrylic a acrílico,-a.

act 1 n (action) acto m; (parliamentary) ley f; (of play) acto m; **a. of God** caso m de fuerza mayor. **2** vt (part) interpretar; (character) representar; **to a. like a fool** hacer el tonto. **3** vi (pretend) fingir; (behave) comportarse; (take action) actuar; (work) funcionar.

• **act for** vt obrar en nombre de.

• **act out** vt exteriorizar.

• **act up** vi fam (machine) funcionar mal; (child) dar guerra.

action (deed) acción f; (in war) acción f de combate; **to be out of a.** (person) estar fuera de servicio; (machine) estar estropeado,-a; **to take a.** tomar medidas.

active a activo,-a; (energetic) vigoroso,-a; (interest) vivo,-a.

activity actividad f; (on street etc) bullicio m.

actor actor m.

actress actriz f.

actual a verdadero,-a.

actually adv (really) en efecto; (even) incluso.

acute a agudo,-a; (pain) intenso, -a; (hearing) muy fino,-a.

ad fam anuncio m.

AD abbr of **Anno Domini** después de Cristo, d.C.

adapt 1 vt adaptar (**to** a). **2** vi adaptarse.

adaptable a **he's very a.** se amolda fácilmente a las circunstancias.

adapter, adaptor (plug) ladrón m.

add 1 vt (numbers) sumar; (one thing to another) añadir. **2** vi (count) sumar.

• **add in** vt (include) incluir.

• **add to** vt aumentar.

- **add together** vt (numbers) sumar.
- **add up 1** vt (numbers) sumar. **2** vi **it doesn't a. up** no tiene sentido.

addict adicto,-a mf; **drug a.** drogadicto,-a mf; **television a.** teleadicto,-a mf.

addicted a adicto,-a.

addiction (to gambling etc) vicio m; (to drugs) adicción f.

addition adición f; **in a. to** además de.

additional a adicional.

additive aditivo m.

address 1 n (on letter) dirección f; (speech) discurso m. **2** vt (letter) dirigir; (speak to) dirigirse (**to** a).

adenoids npl vegetaciones fpl (adenoideas).

adequate a (enough) suficiente; (satisfactory) adecuado,-a.

adequately adv suficientemente.

adhesive 1 a adhesivo,-a. **2** n adhesivo m.

adjective adjetivo m.

adjust 1 vt (machine etc) ajustar; (methods) variar. **2** vi (person) adaptarse (**to** a).

adjustable a ajustable.

adjustment (by person) adaptación f; (change) modificación f.

administer vt (country) gobernar; (justice) administrar.

administration (of country) gobierno m; (of justice) administración f.

administrative a administrativo,-a.

admiral almirante m.

admiration admiración f.

admire vt admirar.

admission (to school etc) ingreso m; (price) entrada f; (of fact) reconocimiento m.

admit vt (person) dejar entrar; (crime, guilt) confesar.

admittance (entry) entrada f.

adolescent adolescente mf.

adopt vt adoptar.

adopted a **a. child** hijo,-a mf adoptivo,-a.

adoption adopción f.

adorable a adorable.

adore vt adorar.

adult 1 n (person) adulto,-a mf. **2** a (film, education) para adultos.

advance 1 n (movement) avance m; (progress) progreso m; **in a. de** antemano. **2** a (before time) adelantado,-a; **a. payment** pago m por adelantado. **3** vt (troops) avanzar; (time, date) adelantar; (idea) proponer; (loan) prestar. **4** vi (move forward, make progress) avanzar.

advanced a (developed) avanzado,-a; (student) adelantado,-a; (course) superior.

advantage ventaja f; **to take a. of sb** abusar de algn; **to take a. of sth** aprovechar algo.

adventure aventura f.

adventurous a (character) aventurero,-a; (bold) atrevido, -a.

adverb adverbio m.

advertise 1 vt anunciar. **2** vi hacer publicidad; (in newspaper) poner un anuncio; **to a. for sth/sb** buscar algo/a algn mediante un anuncio.

advertisement anuncio m; **advertisements** publicidad f sing.

advice consejos mpl; **a piece of a.** un consejo.

advisable a aconsejable.

advise vt aconsejar; (on business etc) asesorar.

- **advise against** vt desaconsejar.

adviser consejero,-a mf; (in business etc) asesor,-a mf.

aerial antena f.

aerobics aerobic m.

aeroplane avión m.

aerosol aerosol m.

affair (matter) asunto m; **business affairs** negocios mpl; **love a.** aventura f amorosa.

affect vt (person, health) afectar; (prices, future) influir en.

affection afecto m.

affectionate a cariñoso,-a.

affluent a (society) opulento,-a; (person) rico,-a.

afford vt (be able to buy) permitirse el lujo de.

affordable a (price etc) asequible.

afloat *adv* **to keep a.** mantenerse a flote.

afraid *a* **to be a.** tener miedo (**of sb** a algn; **of sth** de algo); **I'm a. of it** me da miedo; **I'm a. not/so** me temo que no/sí.

African *a* & *n* africano,-a (*mf*).

after 1 *adv* después; **the day a.** el día siguiente. **2** *prep* (*later*) después de; (*behind*) detrás de; **the day a. tomorrow** pasado mañana; **a. you!** ¡pase usted!; **they asked a. you** preguntaron por ti; **what's he a.?** ¿qué pretende?; **he takes a. his uncle** se parece a su tío. **3** *conj* después (de) que; **a. it happened** después de que ocurrió.

after-effects *npl* consecuencias *fpl*; (*of drug*) efectos *mpl* secundarios.

afternoon tarde *f*; **good a.!** ¡buenas tardes!; **in the a.** por la tarde.

after-sales service servicio *m* posventa.

aftershave (lotion) loción *f* para después del afeitado.

afterwards *adv* después.

again *adv* otra vez; **a. and a.** repetidas veces; **to do sth a.** volver a hacer algo; **never a.!** ¡nunca más!; **now and a.** de vez en cuando.

against *prep* contra; **a. the law** ilegal.

age 1 *n* edad *f*; *fam* (*long time*) eternidad *f*; **underage** menor de edad; **old a.** vejez *f*; **the Iron A.** la Edad del Hierro. **2** *vti* envejecer.

aged[1] *a* de *or* a la edad de; (*old*) viejo,-a; anciano,-a.

aged[2] *npl* **the a.** los ancianos.

agency agencia *f*.

agenda orden *m* del día.

agent agente *m*; (*representative*) representante *mf*.

aggravate *vt* (*worsen*) agravar; (*annoy*) molestar.

aggression agresión *f*.

aggressive *a* agresivo,-a.

agile *a* ágil.

agitated *a* inquieto.

ago *adv* **a week a.** hace una semana; **how long a.?** ¿hace cuánto tiempo?

agony dolor *m* muy fuerte; (*mental*) angustia *f*.

agree *vi* (*be in agreement*) estar de acuerdo; (*reach agreement*) ponerse de acuerdo; **to a. to do sth** consentir en hacer algo; **onions don't a. with me** la cebolla no me sienta bien.

• **agree (up)on** *vt* (*decide*) ponerse de acuerdo en.

agreeable *a* (*pleasant*) agradable; (*person*) simpático,-a; (*in agreement*) de acuerdo.

agreed *a* (*time, place*) acordado.

agreement (*arrangement*) acuerdo *m*; (*contract etc*) contrato *m*.

agricultural *a* agrícola.

agriculture agricultura *f*.

ahead *adv* delante; (*early*) antes; **go a.!** ¡adelante!; **to be a.** (*in race etc*) llevar la ventaja; **to look a.** pensar en el futuro.

aid 1 *n* ayuda *f*; (*rescue*) auxilio *m*; **in a. of** a beneficio de. **2** *vt* ayudar.

AIDS SIDA *m*.

aim 1 *n* (*with weapon*) puntería *f*; (*objective*) propósito *m*. **2** *vti* (*gun*) apuntar (**at** a, hacia).

• **aim at** *vt* (*target*) apuntar a.

• **aim to** *vt* **a. to do sth** tener la intención de hacer algo.

air 1 *n* aire *m*; **to travel by a.** viajar en avión; **to be on the a.** (*program*) estar emitiendo. **2** *vt* (*bed, clothes*) airear; (*room*) ventilar.

air-conditioned *a* climatizado,-a.

air conditioning aire *m* acondicionado.

aircraft *inv* avión *m*.

aircraft carrier portaaviones *m inv*.

airfare precio *m* del billete de avión.

air force fuerzas *fpl* aéreas.

air freshener ambientador *m*.

airline línea *f* aérea.

airline ticket billete *m* de avión.

air mail correo *m* aéreo; **by a.** por avión.

airplane avión *m*.

airport aeropuerto *m*.

air raid ataque *m* aéreo.

airsickness mareos *mpl* (del avión).

airtight *a* hermético,-a.

air traffic control control *m* de tráfico aéreo.

air traffic controller controlador *m* aéreo.

aisle (*in church*) nave *f*; (*in theater*) pasillo *m*.

ajar *a & adv* entreabierto,-a.

alarm 1 *n* alarma *f*; (*fear*) inquietud *f*. **2** *vt* alarmar.

alarm clock despertador *m*.

album álbum *m*.

alcohol alcohol *m*.

alcoholic *a & n* alcohólico,-a (*mf*).

alert 1 *a* alerta; (*lively*) despabilado,-a. **2** *n* alerta *m*.

algebra álgebra *f*.

Algerian *a & n* argelino,-a (*mf*).

alibi coartada *f*.

alien *a & n* extranjero,-a (*mf*); (*from space*) extraterrestre *mf*.

alight *a* (*on fire*) ardiendo,-a.

alike 1 *a* (*similar*) parecidos,-as; (*the same*) iguales. **2** *adv* (*in the same way*) de la misma manera, igualmente.

alive *a* vivo,-a; *fig* (*teeming*) lleno, -a (**with** de).

all 1 *a* todo,-a, todos,-as; **a. year** (*durante*) todo el año; **a. kinds of things** todo tipo de cosas; **at a. times** siempre; **a. six of us were there** los seis estábamos allí. **2** *pron* todo,-a, todos,-as; **after a.** al fin y al cabo; **a. who saw it** todos los que lo vieron; **it's a. you can do** es lo único que puedes hacer; **I don't like it at a.** no me gusta en absoluto; **most of a., above a.** sobre todo; **once and for a.** de una vez para siempre; **thanks — not at a.** gracias—de nada; **a. in a.** en conjunto; **that's a.** ya está; **the score was one a.** empataron a uno; **it's still 3 a.** siguen empatados a tres. **3** *adv* **a. by myself** completamente solo,-a; **a. at once** (*suddenly*) de repente; (*altogether*) de una vez; **a.**

the better tanto mejor; **a. the same** de todos modos; **if it's a. the same to you** si no te importa. **4** *n* **to give one's a.** darse por completo.

all-around *a* (*athlete etc*) completo,-a.

allergic *a* alérgico,-a (**to** a).

alley callejón *m*.

alleyway callejón *m*.

alliance alianza *f*.

alligator caimán *m*.

allocate *vt* destinar (**to** para).

allotment (*land*) parcela *f*.

allow *vt* (*permit*) permitir; (*a request*) acceder a; (*allot*) (*time*) dejar; (*money*) destinar; **you're not allowed to do that** no puedes hacer eso; **I wasn't allowed to go** no me dejaron ir.

• **allow for** *vt* tener en cuenta.

allowance (*payment*) subsidio *m*; (*discount*) descuento *m*; **to make allowances for sb** disculpar a algn; **travel a.** dietas *fpl* de viaje.

all-purpose *a* (*tool*) multiuso, de uso universal.

all right 1 *a* (*okay*) bien; **thank you very much — that's a.** muchas gracias—de nada. **2** *adv* (*well*) bien; (*definitely*) sin duda; (*okay*) de acuerdo.

ally aliado,-a *mf*.

almond almendra *f*.

almost *adv* casi.

alone 1 *a* solo,-a; **let a.** ni mucho menos; **leave it a.!** ¡no lo toques!; **leave me a.** déjame en paz. **2** *adv* solamente.

along 1 *adv* **come a.!** ¡anda, ven!; **a. with** junto con. **2** *prep* (*the length of*) a lo largo de; **to walk a. the street** andar por la calle.

alongside 1 *adv* de costado. **2** *prep* al lado de.

aloud *adv* en voz alta.

alphabet alfabeto *m*.

alphabetical *a* alfabético,-a.

alphabetically *adv* por orden alfabético.

Alps *npl* **the A.** los Alpes.

already *adv* ya.

alright *a* & *adv* = **all right.**

Alsatian pastor *m* alemán.

also *adv* también.

altar altar *m*.

alter 1 *vt* (*plan*) cambiar; (*law, draft etc*) modificar. 2 *vi* cambiar(se).

alteration (*to plan*) cambio *m*; (*to law etc*) modificación *f*; (*to timetable*) revisión *f*.

alternate 1 *a* alterno,-a; **on a. days** cada dos días. 2 *vt* alternar; **a alternates with b** a alterna con b.

alternately *adv* **a. hot and cold** ahora caliente, ahora frío.

alternative 1 *a* alternativo,-a. 2 *n* alternativa *f*; **I have no a.** no tengo más remedio.

alternatively *adv* o bien.

although *conj* aunque.

altogether *adv* (*in total*) en total; (*completely*) completamente.

aluminum aluminio *m*.

always *adv* siempre.

am *1st person sing pres of* **be.**

a.m. *abbr of* **ante meridiem** de la mañana; **2 a. m.** las dos de la mañana.

amateur 1 *n* aficionado,-a *mf*. 2 *a* aficionado,-a; (*pejorative*) chapucero,-a.

amaze *vt* asombrar; **to be amazed at sth** quedar pasmado,-a de algo.

amazing *a* asombroso,-a.

ambassador embajador,-a *mf*.

amber 1 *a* (*traffic light*) amarillo, -a, ámbar. 2 *n* ámbar.

ambition ambición *f*.

ambitious *a* ambicioso,-a.

ambulance ambulancia *f*; **a. man** ambulanciero *m*.

American *a* & *n* americano,-a (*mf*); (*of USA*) norteamericano,-a (*mf*), estadounidense (*mf*).

ammunition municiones *fpl*.

among(st) *prep* entre.

amorous *a* (*person*) ligón,-ona; (*feelings, relationship*) amoroso.

amount cantidad *f*; (*of money*) suma *f*; (*of bill*) importe *m*.

• **amount to** *vt* ascender a; (*be equivalent to*) equivaler a.

ample *a* (*enough*) bastante; (*more than enough*) abundante; (*large*) amplio,-a.

amplifier amplificador *m*.

amputate *vt* amputar.

amuse *vt* divertir.

amusement diversión *f*.

amusement park parque *m* de atracciones.

amusing *a* divertido,-a.

an *indef art see* **a.**

analysis (*pl* analyses) análisis *m inv*.

analyze *vt* analizar.

anarchy anarquía *f*.

anatomy anatomía *f*.

ancestor antepasado *m*.

anchor 1 *n* ancla *f*. 2 *vt* anclar; *fig* (*fix securely*) sujetar.

anchovy anchoa *f*.

ancient *a* antiguo,-a.

and *conj* y; (*before stressed i-, hi-*) e; **a hundred a.** one ciento uno; **a. so on** etcétera; **come a. see us** ven a vernos; **she cried a. cried** no paró de llorar; **try a. help me** trata de ayudarme; **wait a. see** espera a ver; **worse a. worse** cada vez peor.

anesthetic anestesia *f*.

angel ángel *m*.

anger cólera *f*.

angle ángulo *m*; (*point of view*) punto *m* de vista.

angler pescador,-a *mf* de caña.

angling pesca *f* con caña.

angrily *adv* furiosamente.

angry *a* enfadado,-a; **to get a.** enfadarse.

animal *a* & *n* animal (*m*).

ankle tobillo *m*; **a. socks** calcetines *mpl* cortos.

annex (*building*) (edificio *m*) anexo *m*.

anniversary aniversario *m*.

announce *vt* anunciar; (*news*) comunicar.

announcement anuncio *m*; (*news*) comunicación *f*; (*statement*) declaración *f*.

announcer (*on TV*) locutor,-a *mf*.

annoy *vt* molestar; **to get annoyed** molestarse.

annoying *a* molesto,-a.

annual 1 *a* anual. **2** *n* (*book*) anuario *m*.

annually *adv* anualmente.

anonymous *a* anónimo,-a.

anorak anorak *m*.

another 1 *a* otro,a; **a. one** otro,a; **a. 15** otros quince. **2** *pron* otro,-a; **to love one a.** quererse el uno al otro.

answer 1 *n* (*to letter etc*) contestación *f*; (*to question*) respuesta *f*; (*to problem*) solución *f*; **there's no a.** (*on telephone*) no contestan; (*at door*) no abren. **2** *vt* contestar a; (*problem*) resolver; (*door*) abrir; (*phone*) contestar. **3** *vi* contestar.

• **answer back** *vi* replicar; **don't a. back!** ¡no repliques!

• **answer for** *vt* responder de; **he's got a lot to a. for** es responsable de muchas cosas.

• **answer to** *vt* (*name*) responder a; (*description*) corresponder a.

answering machine contestador *m* automático.

ant hormiga *f*.

Antarctic 1 *a* antártico,-a; **A. Ocean** océano *m* Antártico. **2** *n* **the A.** La Antártida.

antelope antílope *m*.

antenna (*pl* **antennae**) antena *f*.

anthem national a. himno *m* nacional.

anthology antología *f*.

antibiotic *a* & *n* antibiótico,-a (*m*).

antibody anticuerpo *m*.

anticipate *vt* (*expect*) esperar; (*problems*) anticipar.

anticipation (*excitement*) ilusión *f*.

antics *npl* payasadas *fpl*; (*naughtiness*) travesuras *fpl*.

antifreeze anticongelante *m*.

antihistamine *n* antihistamínico *m*.

antique 1 *a* antiguo,-a. **2** *n* antigüedad *f*.

antique dealer anticuario,-a *mf*.

antique shop tienda *f* de antigüedades.

antiseptic *a* & *n* antiséptico,-a (*m*).

anxiety (*concern*) inquietud *f*; (*worry*) preocupación *f*; (*eagerness*) ansia *f*.

anxious *a* (*concerned*) inquieto,-a; (*worried*) preocupado,-a; (*fearful*) angustiado,-a; (*eager*) ansioso,-a.

anxiously *adv* (*to wait*) con impaciencia.

any 1 *a* (*in questions, conditionals*) algún,-una; **are there a. seats left?** ¿quedan plazas?; **is there a. water left?** ¿queda agua?; **if you see a. blouses you like** si ves algunas blusas que te gusten. ▪ (*in negative clauses*) ningún,-una; **there aren't a. others** no hay otros. ▪ (*no matter which*) cualquier,-a; (*every*) todo, -a; **a. doctor will say the same** cualquier médico te dirá lo mismo; **at a. moment** en cualquier momento; **in a. case** de todas formas. **2** *pron* (*in questions, conditionals*) alguno,-a; **do they have a.?** ¿tienen alguno?; **I need some paper, do you have a.?** necesito papel, ¿tienes?; **if you see a., let me know** si ves alguno,-a, dímelo. ▪ (*in negative clauses*) ninguno,-a; **I don't want a.** no quiero ninguno,-a. ▪ (*no matter which*) cualquiera; **a. of them will do** cualquiera vale. **3** *adv* **is there a. more?** ¿hay más?; **not a. more/longer** ya no; **is that a. better?** ¿está mejor así?

anybody *pron* (*in questions, conditionals*) alguien; (*in negative clauses*) nadie; (*no matter who*) cualquiera; **bring a. you like** trae a quien quieras.

anyhow *adv* (*in spite of that*) de todas formas; (*changing the subject*) bueno; (*carelessly*) de cualquier forma.

anyone *pron* = **anybody**.

anyplace *adv* = **anywhere**.

anything *pron* (*in questions, conditionals*) algo, alguna cosa; (*in* *negative clauses*) nada; (*no matter what*) cualquier cosa; **a. but that** cualquier cosa menos eso; **a. else?** ¿algo más?; **hardly a.** casi nada; **to run/work like a.** correr/trabajar a más no poder.

anyway *adv* = **anyhow.**

anywhere *adv* (*in questions, conditionals*) (*position*) en alguna parte; (*movement*) a alguna parte; **could it be a. else?** ¿podría estar en otro sitio? ▪ (*in negative clauses*) (*position*) en ninguna parte; (*movement*) a ninguna parte. ▪ (*no matter where*) en cualquier parte; **go a. you like** a donde quieras.

apart *adv* **you should keep them a.** debes mantenerlos aparte; **to fall a.** deshacerse; **to take sth a.** desmontar algo; **with his feet a.** con los pies separados; **a. from** aparte de.

apartment piso *m*; **a. complex** bloque *m* de pisos.

apartment house casa *f* de pisos.

ape mono *m*.

aperitif aperitivo *m*.

apologetic *a* **he was very a.** pidió mil perdones.

apologize *vi* disculparse (**for** por).

apology disculpa *f*.

apostrophe apóstrofo *m*.

appall *vt* horrorizar.

appalling *a* (*horrifying*) horroroso,-a; (*very bad*) fatal.

apparatus aparato *m*; (*equipment*) equipo *m*.

apparent *a* (*obvious*) evidente; (*seeming*) aparente; **to become a.** ponerse de manifiesto.

apparently *adv* (*seemingly*) por lo visto.

appeal **1** *n* (*request*) solicitud *f*; (*plea*) súplica *f*; (*interest*) interés *m*; (*in law*) apelación *f*. **2** *vi* (*plead*) rogar (**to** a); **to a. for help** solicitar ayuda; **it doesn't a. to me** no me dice nada.

appear *vi* (*become visible*) aparecer; (*publicly*) presentarse; (*seem*) parecer; **so it appears** según parece.

appearance (*becoming visible*) aparición *f*; (*publicly*) presentación *f*; (*of book etc*) publicación *f*; (*look*) aspecto *m*; **to all appearances** al parecer.

appendicitis apendicitis *f*.

appendix (*pl* **appendices**) apéndice *m*.

appetite apetito *m*; (*sexual*) deseo *m*; **he's lost his a. for this sort of job** se le han quitado las ganas de un trabajo de este tipo.

appetizing *a* apetitoso.

applaud *vti* aplaudir.

applause aplausos *mpl*, aplauso *m*.

apple manzana *f*; **a. pie** tarta *f* de manzana; **a. tree** manzano *m*.

appliance dispositivo *m*.

applicant (*for post*) candidato,-a *mf*.

application (*of cream*) aplicación *f*; (*for post etc*) solicitud *f*; **a. form** solicitud *f*.

apply **1** *vt* aplicar; (*brake*) echar; (*law*) recurrir a; (*force*) usar; **to a. oneself to sth** dedicarse a algo. **2** *vi* (*for job*) presentar una solicitud.

• **apply for** *vt* (*post, information*) solicitar.

appoint *vt* (*person*) nombrar.

appointment (*to post*) nombramiento *m*; (*meeting*) cita *f*.

appreciate **1** *vt* (*be thankful for*) agradecer; (*understand*) entender; (*value*) apreciar. **2** *vi* (*increase in value*) apreciarse.

appreciation (*of help, advice*) agradecimiento *m*; (*of difficulty*) comprensión *f*; (*increase in value*) apreciación *f*.

apprentice aprendiz,-a *mf*.

apprenticeship aprendizaje *m*.

approach **1** *n* (*coming near*) acercamiento *m*; (*to town*) acceso *m*; (*to problem*) enfoque *m*. **2** *vt* (*come near to*) acercarse a; (*problem*) abordar. **3** *vi* acercarse.

appropriate *a* (*suitable*) apropiado,-a; (*convenient*) oportuno,-a.

appropriately *adv* adecuadamente.

approval aprobación f; **on a.** sin compromiso de compra.

approve vt aprobar.

• **approve of** vt aprobar.

approximate a aproximado,-a.

approximately adv aproximadamente.

apricot albaricoque m.

April abril m; **A. Fools' Day** día m uno de abril, ≈ día de los Inocentes (28 de diciembre).

apron delantal m.

apt a (suitable) apropiado,-a; (description) exacto,-a; **to be a. to do sth** (liable) tener tendencia a hacer algo.

aptitude capacidad f.

aquarium acuario m.

Arab a & n árabe (mf).

Arabian a árabe.

Arabic 1 a árabe; **A. numerals** numeración arábiga. **2** n (language) árabe m.

arc arco m.

arcade arcada f; **shopping a.** galerías fpl (comerciales); **amusement a** salón m de juegos.

arch 1 n (of bridge etc) arco m; (roof) bóveda f. **2** vt (back) arquear.

archer arquero,-a mf.

archery tiro m con arco.

architect arquitecto,-a mf.

architecture arquitectura f.

arctic the **A.** el Ártico.

are 2nd person sing pres, 1st, 2nd, 3rd person pl pres of **be**.

area zona f; (of surface) superficie f.

area code prefijo m local.

Argentinian a & n argentino,-a (mf).

argue 1 vi (quarrel) discutir; (reason) argumentar. **2** vt discutir; (point of view) mantener; **to a. that . . .** sostenar que . . .

argument (quarrel) discusión f, disputa f; (reason) argumento m (**for** a favor de; **against** en contra de).

arise* vi (get up) levantarse; (problem, need) surgir.

arithmetic aritmética f.

arm 1 n brazo m; (of garment) manga f; **arms** (weapons) armas fpl. **2** vt armar.

armband brazalete m; (for swimming) manguito m.

armchair sillón m.

armor (of tank etc) blindaje m; **(suit of) a.** armadura f.

armored car coche m blindado.

armpit axila f.

army ejército m.

around 1 adv alrededor; **all a.** por todos lados. **2** prep alrededor de; (approximately) aproximadamente; **a. the corner** a la vuelta de la esquina; **a. here** por aquí; **there's nobody a.** no hay nadie; **to rush a.** correr de un lado para otro.

arrange 1 vt (order) ordenar; (hair, flowers) arreglar; (music) adaptar; (plan) organizar; (agree on) quedar en; **to a. a time** fijar una hora. **2** vi **I shall a. for him to be there** lo arreglaré para que pueda asistir.

arrangement (display) colocación f; (of music) adaptación f; (agreement) acuerdo m; **arrangements** (plans) planes mpl.

arrears npl atrasos mpl; **to be paid in a.** cobrar con retraso; **salaries are paid monthly in a.** los salarios se pagan mensualmente con un mes de retraso.

arrest 1 n detención f; **to be under a.** estar detenido,-a. **2** vt (criminal) detener.

arrival llegada f.

arrive vi llegar (**at, in** a).

arrow flecha f.

art arte m; (drawing) dibujo m; **arts** (branch of knowledge) letras fpl.

artery arteria f.

arthritis artritis f.

article artículo m.

articulate vti articular; (words) pronunciar.

artificial a artificial.

artist artista mf; (painter) pintor, -a mf.

artistic a artístico,-a.

as adv & conj (comparison) **as . . . as . . .** tan . . . como . . .; **as far as** hasta; **as far as I'm concerned** por lo que a mí respecta; **as many as** tantos,-as como; **as much as** tanto,-a como; **as opposed to** a diferencia de; **as little as $5** tan sólo cinco dólares; **as soon as they arrive** en cuanto lleguen; **I'll stay as long as I can** me quedaré todo el tiempo que pueda; **just as big** igual de grande; **three times as fast** tres veces más rápido; **the same as** igual que. ■ (manner) como; **as you like** como quieras; **leave it as it is** déjalo tal como está; **do as I say** haz lo que yo te digo; **it serves as a table** sirve de mesa; **she was dressed as a gypsy** iba vestida de gitana; **to act as if** actuar como si (+ subjunctive). ■ (time) mientras; **as a child** de niño,-a; **as I was eating** mientras comía; **as we were leaving we saw Pat** al salir vimos a Pat; **as from, as of** a partir de. ■ (because) como, ya que; **as it is getting late** ya que se está haciendo tarde. ■ (and so) igual que; **as well** también. ■ (concerning) **as for my brother** en cuanto a mi hermano.

ASAP abbr (as soon as possible) lo antes posible.

ash[1] (tree) fresno m.

ash[2] ceniza f.

ashamed a avergonzado,-a; **you ought to be a. of yourself!** ¿no te da vergüenza?

ashore adv en tierra; **to go a.** desembarcar.

ashtray cenicero m.

Ash Wednesday miércoles m inv de ceniza.

Asian a & n asiático,-a (mf).

aside 1 adv aparte; **to stand a.** apartarse. 2 prep **a. from** (apart from) aparte de; (as well as) además de. 3 n aparte m.

ask 1 vt preguntar; (request) pedir; (invite) invitar; **to a. sb a question**
preguntar algo a algn; **to a. sb how to do sth** preguntar a algn cómo se hace algo. 2 vi (inquire) preguntar; (request) pedir.

• **ask after** vt preguntar por.

• **ask for** vt (help) pedir; (person) preguntar por; **to a. sb for sth** pedir algo a algn.

asleep a dormido,-a; **to fall a.** quedarse dormido,-a.

asparagus n inv espárrago m.

aspect aspecto m.

aspirin aspirina f.

assault 1 n ataque m (**on** a); (crime) agresión f. 2 vt atacar; (sexually) violar.

assemble 1 vt (people) reunir; (furniture) montar. 2 vi (people) reunirse.

assembly asamblea f; (of machinery etc) montaje m; **morning a.** servicio m matinal.

assess vt (estimate value) valorar; (damages, price) calcular; (effect) evaluar.

asset ventaja f; **to be an a.** (person) ser de gran valor; **assets** activo m.

assign vt asignar.

assignment (task) tarea f.

assist vti ayudar.

assistance ayuda f.

assistant ayudante mf; **a. manager** subdirector,-a mf; **shop a.** dependiente,-a mf.

associate[1] 1 vt (ideas) relacionar. 2 vi **to a. with** tratar con.

associate[2] (colleague) colega mf; (partner) socio,-a mf; (accomplice) cómplice mf.

association asociación f; (company) sociedad f.

assorted a surtido,-a.

assortment surtido m.

assume vt (suppose) suponer; (power) asumir; (attitude, name) adoptar.

assurance (guarantee) garantía f; (confidence) confianza f; (insurance) seguro m.

assure vt asegurar.

asterisk asterisco m.

asthma asma f.

asthmatic a & n asmático,-a (mf).

astonish vt asombrar.

astonishing a asombroso,-a.

astray adv **to go a.** extraviarse; fig equivocarse.

astrology astrología f.

astronaut astronauta mf.

astronomy astronomía f.

at prep (position) en, a; **at school/work** en el colegio/trabajo; **at the window** a la ventana; **at the top** en lo alto. ▪ (direction) a; **to look at sth/sb** mirar algo/a algn; **to shout at sb** gritarle a algn. ▪ (time) a; **at Easter/Christmas** en Semana Santa/Navidad; **at six o'clock** a las seis. ▪ **at best/worst** en el mejor/peor de los casos; **not at all** en absoluto; (don't mention it) de nada. ▪ (rate) a; **at 100 pesetas each** a 100 pesetas la unidad; **two at a time** de dos en dos.

athlete atleta mf.

athletic a atlético,-a; (sporty) deportista.

athletics npl atletismo m sing.

Atlantic the A. (Ocean) el (océano) Atlántico.

atlas atlas m.

atmosphere (air) atmósfera f; (ambience) ambiente m.

atom átomo m; **a. bomb** bomba f atómica.

atomic a atómico,-a.

attach vt (stick) pegar; (document) adjuntar; **to be attached to** (be fond of) tener cariño a.

attaché agregado,-a mf; **a. case** maletín m.

attack 1 n ataque m. **2** vt (assault) atacar; (problem) abordar.

attacker agresor,-a mf.

attempt 1 n intento m; **at the second a.** a la segunda. **2** vt intentar.

attend 1 vt (school) frecuentar; (meeting) asistir a. **2** vi (at meeting) asistir.

• **attend to** vt (business) ocuparse de; (in shop) atender a.

attendance asistencia f.

attendant (in museum) guía mf; (in parking lot) vigilante,-a mf.

attention atención f; **for the a. of** a la atención de.

attentive a (listener) atento,-a; (helpful) solícito,-a.

attic ático m.

attitude actitud f; (position of body) postura f.

attorney abogado,-a mf; **A. General** ≈ Ministro,-a mf de Justicia; **district a.** fiscal mf.

attract vt atraer; **to a. attention** llamar la atención.

attraction (attractive thing) atractivo m; (charm) encanto m.

attractive a (person) guapo,-a; (idea, proposition) atrayente.

auction 1 n subasta f. **2** vt subastar.

auctioneer subastador,-a mf.

audible a audible.

audience (spectators) público m; (at concert, conference) auditorio m; (television) telespectadores mpl; (meeting) audiencia f.

audio a de sonido.

audio-visual a audiovisual.

August agosto m.

aunt (also fam **auntie, aunty**) tía f.

au pair a. (girl) au pair f.

Australian a & n australiano,-a (mf).

Austrian a & n austríaco,-a (mf).

author autor,-a mf.

authority autoridad f; **local a.** ayuntamiento m.

authorize vt autorizar; (payment etc) aprobar.

autobiography autobiografía f.

autograph 1 n autógrafo m. **2** vt (book, photo) dedicar.

automatic 1 a automático,-a. **2** n (car) coche m automático.

automatically adv automáticamente.

automobile automóvil m, Am carro m.

autumn otoño m.

auxiliary a auxiliar.

available a (thing) disponible; (person) libre.

avalanche avalancha f.

avenue avenida f; fig vía f.

average 1 n promedio m; **on a.** por término medio. **2** a medio,-a; (middle) regular.

aviation aviación f.

avocado (also **avocado pear**) aguacate m.

avoid vt evitar; **to a. doing sth** evitar hacer algo.

awake 1 a despierto,-a. **2** vi* despertarse.

award 1 n (prize) premio m; (medal) condecoración f; (grant) beca f. **2** vt (prize) otorgar; (medal) dar; (damages) adjudicar.

aware a (informed) enterado,-a; **not that I'm a. of** que yo sepa no; **to become a. of sth** darse cuenta de algo.

away adv **far a.** lejos; **go a.!** ¡lárgate!; **it's 3 miles a.** está a 3 millas (de distancia); **keep a. from the fire!** ¡no te acerques al fuego!; **right a.** en seguida; **to be a.** (absent) estar ausente; **to go a.** irse; **to play a.** (in sport) jugar fuera; **to turn a.** volver la cara; **to chatter/work a.** hablar/trabajar sin parar.

awful a espantoso,-a; fam **an a. lot of work** muchísimo trabajo.

awfully adv fam terriblemente.

awkward a (clumsy) torpe; (difficult) pesado,-a; (moment) inoportuno,-a.

awning (on shop) marquesina f.

ax 1 n hacha f. **2** vt (jobs) suprimir; (cut back) reducir; (plan) cancelar.

axle eje m.

B

BA abbr of **Bachelor of Arts.**

baby bebé m; (young child) niño, -a mf.

baby carriage cochecito m de niño.

babysit vi hacer de canguro.

babysitter canguro mf.

bachelor soltero m; **B. of Arts/ Science** licenciado,-a mf en Filosofía y Letras/Ciencias.

back 1 n (of person) espalda f; (of chair) respaldo m; (of hand) dorso m; (of house, car) parte f de atrás; (of stage, cupboard) fondo m; **b. to front** al revés. **2** a trasero,-a; **b. door** puerta f de atrás; **b. seat** asiento m de detrás; **b. wheel** rueda f trasera; **b. number** número m atrasado. **3** adv (at the rear) atrás; (towards the rear) hacia atrás. **4** vt (support) apoyar; (financially) financiar; (bet on) apostar por.

• **back out** vi (withdraw) volverse atrás.

• **back up** vt (support) apoyar a.

backache dolor m de espalda.

backfire vi (car) petardear.

background fondo m; (origin) origen m; (past) pasado m; (education) formación f; (circumstances) antecedentes mpl; **b. music** hilo m musical.

backing (support) apoyo m; (financial) respaldo m financiero.

backlog **to have a b. of work** tener un montón de trabajo atrasado.

backside fam trasero m.

backstage adv entre bastidores.

back-up (of disk) copia f de seguridad.

backward 1 a (movement) hacia atrás; (child, country) retrasado, -a. **2** adv (hacia) atrás.

backwards adv hacia atrás; **to walk b.** andar de espaldas.

backyard jardín m trasero.

bacon tocino m, beicon m.

bad a malo,-a; (decayed) podrido, -a; (accident) grave; (headache) fuerte; (ill) enfermo,-a.

badge insignia f; (metal disc) chapa f.

badger tejón m.

badly adv mal; (seriously) gravemente; (*very much*) mucho; **we need it b.** nos hace mucha falta; **to be b. off** (*financially*) andar mal de dinero.

bad-mannered *a* maleducado.

badminton bádminton *m*.

bad-tempered *a* **to be b.** (*temperament*) tener mal genio; (*temporarily*) estar de mal humor.

baffle *vt* desconcertar.

bag (*plastic, paper, shopping*) bolsa *f*; (*handbag*) bolso *m*; *fam* **bags of** montones de; **bags** (*under eyes*) ojeras *fpl*.

baggage equipaje *m*.

baggy *a* holgado,-a; **b. trousers** pantalones *mpl* anchos.

bagpipes *npl* gaita *f sing*.

bail fianza *f*; **on b.** bajo fianza.

bait cebo *m*.

bake *vt* cocer al horno.

baked *a* al horno; **b. potato** patata *f* asada.

baked beans alubias *fpl* cocidas en salsa de tomate.

baker panadero,-a *mf*.

bakery panadería *f*.

balance 1 *n* (*equilibrium*) equilibrio *m*; (*financial*) saldo *m*; (*remainder*) resto *m*. **2** *vt* poner en equilibrio; (*budget*) equilibrar. **3** *vi* guardar el equilibrio.

balance sheet balance *m*.

balcony balcón *m*.

bald *a* calvo,-a.

baldness calvicie *f*.

Balkans *npl* **the Balkans** los Balcanes.

ball¹ (*in baseball, tennis etc*) pelota *f*; (*football*) balón *m*; (*in billiards, golf etc*) bola *f*; (*of wool*) ovillo *m*; **to be on the b.** *fam* ser un espabilado.

ball² (*dance*) baile *m*.

ballerina bailarina *f*.

ballet ballet *m*.

balloon globo *m*.

ballot votación *f*.

ballpoint (pen) bolígrafo *m*.

ballroom salón *m* de baile.

ban 1 *n* prohibición *f*. **2** *vt* (*prohibit*) prohibir; (*exclude*) excluir.

banana plátano *m*, *Am* banana *f*.

band (*strip*) tira *f*; (*group*) grupo *m*; (*of musicians*) banda *f*.

bandage 1 *n* venda *f*. **2** *vt* vendar.

Band-Aid® tirita® *f*.

bang *n* (*blow*) golpe *m*; (*noise*) ruido *m*; (*explosion*) estallido *m*; (*of gun*) estampido *m*.

• **bang into** *vt* golpearse contra.

banger *fam* (*firework*) petardo *m*; **old b.** (*car*) coche *m* destartalado.

bangle brazalete *m*.

banister(s) pasamanos *m inv*.

bank¹ (*for money*) banco *m*.

bank² (*of river*) ribera *f*, orilla *f*.

• **bank on** *vt* contar con.

bank account cuenta *f* bancaria.

bank card tarjeta *f* bancaria.

banker banquero,-a *mf*.

banking banca *f*.

bankrupt *a* en quiebra; **to go b.** quebrar.

bankruptcy bancarrota *f*.

banner (*in demonstration*) pancarta *f*.

bar 1 *n* (*of gold*) barra *f*; (*of chocolate*) tableta *f*; (*of cage*) barrote *m*; (*pub*) bar *m*; (*counter*) barra *f*; (*of soap*) pastilla *f*. **2** *vt* (*door*) atrancar; (*road*) cortar; (*exclude*) excluir (**from** de); (*prohibit*) prohibir.

barbecue barbacoa *f*.

barbed *a* **b. wire** alambre *m* de espino.

barber barbero,-a *mf*; **b.'s (shop)** barbería *f*.

bare *a* desnudo,-a; (*head*) descubierto,-a; (*foot*) descalzo,-a; (*room*) sin muebles; **with his b. hands** sólo con las manos.

barefoot *a & adv* descalzo,-a.

barely *adv* apenas.

bargain 1 *n* (*deal*) negocio *m*; (*cheap purchase*) ganga *f*; **b. price** precio *m* de oferta. **2** *vi* negociar.

- **bargain for** vt esperar; **I hadn't bargained for this** no contaba con esto.
barge n gabarra f.
- **barge in** vi (go in) entrar sin permiso.
- **barge into** vt (room) irrumpir en; (person) tropezar con.
bark¹ vi (dog) ladrar.
bark² (of tree) corteza f.
barking ladridos mpl.
barley cebada f.
barn granero m.
barometer barómetro m.
barracks npl cuartel m sing.
barrage (dam) presa f.
barrel (of wine) tonel m; (of beer, oil) barril m; (of firearm) cañón m.
barren a estéril; (land) yermo,-a.
barrette pasador m (del pelo).
barricade 1 n barricada f. 2 vt cerrar con barricadas.
barrier barrera f.
bartender camarero m.
base 1 n base f; (foot) pie m; (of column) basa f. 2 vt basar (**on** en).
baseball béisbol m.
basement sótano m.
bash 1 n (heavy blow) golpetazo m; (dent) bollo m. 2 vt golpear.
- **bash up** vt **to b. sb up** darle a algn una paliza.
basic 1 a básico,-a; **b. pay** sueldo m base. 2 npl **basics** lo fundamental.
basically adv fundamentalmente.
basin (washbowl) palangana f; (for washing up) barreño m; (in bathroom) lavabo m.
basis (pl **bases**) base f; **on the b. of** en base a.
bask vi (in sunlight) tostarse.
basket (big) cesta f; (small) cesto m.
bat¹ (in baseball) bate m.
bat² (animal) murciélago m.
bat³ vt **without batting an eyelid** sin pestañear.
batch (of bread) hornada f; (of goods) lote m.
bath 1 n baño m; (tub) bañera f; **to have a b.** bañarse. 2 vt bañar.

bathe vi bañarse.
bathing baño m.
bathing suit traje m de baño.
bathing trunks npl bañador m.
bathrobe albornoz m.
bathroom cuarto m de baño.
bathtub bañera f.
batter 1 n pasta para rebozar. 2 vt (baby) maltratar.
- **batter down** vt (door) derribar.
- **battered** a (car) desvencijado, -a.
battery (for radio) pila f; (for car) batería f.
battle 1 n batalla f; fig lucha f. 2 vi luchar.
battleship acorazado m.
baud baudio m.
bawl vi gritar.
bay bahía f; (large) golfo m.
BC abbr of **before Christ** a.C.
be* 1 vi (permanent state) ser; **he is very tall** es muy alto; **Washington is the capital** Washington es la capital; **sugar is sweet** el azúcar es dulce. ▪ (temporary state, location) estar; **how are you?** ¿cómo estás?; **this soup is cold** esta sopa está fría. ▪ (cost) **a return ticket is $24** un billete de ida y vuelta cuesta 24 dólares; **how much is it?** ¿cuánto es? ▪ (weather) **it's foggy** hay niebla; **it's cold/hot** hace frío/calor. ▪ (time, date) **it's one o'clock** es la una; **it's four o'clock** son las cuatro; **it's the 11th/Tuesday today** hoy es 11/martes. ▪ **to be cold/afraid/hungry** tener frío/miedo/hambre; **she is thirty (years old)** tiene treinta años. 2 v aux estar; **he is writing a letter** está escribiendo una carta; **she was singing** cantaba; **they are leaving next week** se van la semana que viene; **we have been waiting for a long time** hace mucho que estamos esperando. ▪ (passive) ser; **he was murdered** fue asesinado. ▪ (obligation) **I am to see him this afternoon** debo verle esta tarde. ▪ **there is, there are** hay; **there was, there were** había; **there**

will be habrá; **there would be** habría; **there have been a lot of complaints** ha habido muchas quejas; **there were ten of us** éramos diez. ■ *(in tag questions)* ¿verdad?, ¿no?; **it's lovely, isn't it?** es bonito, ¿no?; **you're happy, aren't you?** estás contento, ¿verdad?

beach playa *f*.

beacon baliza *f*; *(lighthouse)* faro *m*.

bead *(of necklace etc)* cuenta *f*; *(of liquid)* gota *f*.

beak *(of bird)* pico *m*.

beam *(in building)* viga *f*; *(of light)* rayo *m*.

beaming *a (smiling)* radiante.

bean alubia *f*, judía *f*; *Am* frijol *m*; **broad b.** haba *f*; **coffee b.** grano *m* de café; **green** *or* **runner b.** judía *f* verde.

bear* *1 vt (carry)* llevar; *(endure)* soportar; **to b. in mind** tener presente. *2 vi* **to b. left** girar a la izquierda.
• **bear out** *vt* confirmar.

bear² *(animal)* oso *m*.

bearable *a* soportable.

beard barba *f*.

bearded *a* barbudo,-a.

bearing *(relevance)* relación *f*; **to have a b. on** estar relacionado,-a con; **to get one's bearings** orientarse.

beast bestia *f*.

beastly *a fam* asqueroso,-a.

beat* *1 vt (hit)* pegar; *(drum)* tocar; *(in cooking)* batir; *(defeat)* vencer. *2 vi (heart)* latir. *3 n (of heart)* latido *m*; *(of policeman)* ronda *f*.
• **beat down** *vi (sun)* caer a plomo.
• **beat off** *vt* rechazar.
• **beat up** *vt* dar una paliza a.

beating *(thrashing)* paliza *f*; *(defeat)* derrota *f*.

beautiful *a* hermoso,-a, bello,-a; *(place)* lugar *m* pintoresco.

beauty belleza *f*, hermosura *f*.

beauty spot *(on face)* lunar *m*.

beaver castor *m*.

because 1 *conj* porque. **2** *prep* **b. of** a causa de.

become* *vi (doctor, priest)* hacerse; *(mayor, officer)* llegar a ser; *(angry, sad)* ponerse; **what has b. of him?** ¿qué ha sido de él?

bed cama *f*; **to get out of b.** levantarse de la cama; **to go to b.** acostarse; **b. and breakfast** *(service)* cama *f* y desayuno *m*; *(sign)* 'pensión'.

bedding ropa *f* de cama.

bedroom dormitorio *m*.

bedside b. table mesilla *f* de noche.

bedtime hora *f* de acostarse.

bee abeja *f*.

beech haya *f*.

beef carne *f* de vaca, *Am* carne *f* de res.

been *pp* of **be**.

beep 1 *n* pitido *m*. **2** *vi* pitar.

beeper *(busca)*personas *m inv*.

beer cerveza *f*; **a glass of b.** una caña.

beet red b. remolacha *f*.

beetle escarabajo *m*.

before 1 *conj (earlier than)* antes de que (+ *subjunctive*), antes de (+ *infinitive*); **b. she goes** antes de que se vaya; **b. leaving** antes de salir. **2** *prep (place)* delante de; *(in the presence of)* ante; *(order, time)* antes de. **3** *adv (time)* antes; *(place)* (por) delante; **I have met him b.** ya le conozco; **the night b.** la noche anterior.

beg 1 *vt (money etc)* pedir; *(beseech)* rogar. **2** *vi (solicit)* mendigar; **to b. for money** pedir limosna.

beggar mendigo,-a *mf*.

begin* *vti* empezar, comenzar; **to b. doing** *or* **to do sth** empezar a hacer algo; **to b. with . . .** para empezar . . .

beginner principiante *mf*.

beginning principio *m*, comienzo *m*; **at the b. of May** a principios de mayo.

begrudge *vt* dar de mala gana;

(*envy*) envidiar; **to b. sb sth** envidiarle algo a algn.

behalf nombre *m*; **on b. of, in b. of** de parte de.

behave *vi* (*person*) (com)portarse; **b. yourself!** ¡pórtate bien!

behavior comportamiento *m*.

behind 1 *prep* detrás de. **2** *adv* (*in the rear*) detrás, atrás; **I've left my umbrella b.** se me ha olvidado el paraguas; **to be b. with one's payments** estar atrasado,-a en los pagos. **3** *n fam* trasero *m*.

beige *a & n* beige (*m*).

belch 1 *vi* eructar. **2** *n* eructo *m*.

Belgian *a & n* belga (*mf*).

belief creencia *f*; (*opinion*) opinión *f*; (*faith*) fe *f*; (*confidence*) confianza *f* (**in** en).

believable *a* creíble.

believe *vti* creer; **I b. so** creo que sí; **to b.in sb/sth** creer en algn/algo.

believer (*religious*) creyente *mf*.

belittle *vt* (*person*) restar importancia a.

bell (*of church*) campana *f*; (*small*) campanilla *f*; (*of school, door, bicycle etc*) timbre *m*; (*on animal*) cencerro *m*.

bellboy botones *m inv*.

belly (*of person*) barriga *f*, tripa *f*.

bellyache *fam* dolor *m* de barriga.

belong *vi* pertenecer (**to** a); (*be a member*) ser socio,-a (**to** de).

belongings *npl* efectos *mpl* personales.

below 1 *prep* debajo de. **2** *adv* abajo.

belt cinturón *m*; (*in machine*) correa *f*; (*area*) zona *f*.

• **belt along** *vi fam* ir a todo gas.

bench (*seat*) banco *m*.

bend 1 *vt** doblar; (*back*) encorvar; (*head*) inclinar. **2** *vi** doblarse; (*road*) torcerse; **to b. (over)** inclinarse. **3** *n* (*in river, road*) curva *f*; (*in pipe*) recodo *m*.

• **bend down** *vi* inclinarse.

beneath 1 *prep* (*below*) bajo, debajo de. **2** *adv* debajo.

beneficial *a* (*doing good*) bené-

fico,-a; (*advantageous*) beneficioso,-a.

benefit 1 *vt* beneficiar. **2** *vi* sacar provecho (**from** *or* **by** de). **3** *n* (*advantage*) beneficio *m*; (*allowance*) subsidio *m*; **I did it for your b.** lo hice por tu bien.

bent *a* (*curved*) curvado,-a; **to be b. on doing sth** (*determined*) estar empeñado,-a en hacer algo.

bereavement duelo *m*.

berry baya *f*.

berserk *a* **to go b.** volverse loco,-a.

berth (*bed*) litera *f*.

beside *prep* (*next to*) al lado de, junto a; (*compared with*) comparado con; **that's b. the point** eso no viene al caso.

besides 1 *prep* (*in addition to*) además de; (*except*) excepto. **2** *adv* además.

best 1 *a* mejor; **the b. thing would be to phone them** lo mejor sería llamarles; **the b. part of a year** casi un año. **2** *adv* mejor; **as b. I can** lo mejor que pueda. **3** *n* lo mejor; **to do one's b.** hacer todo lo posible; **to make the b. of sth** sacar el mejor partido de algo.

best man ≈ padrino *m* de boda.

best-seller *n* best-seller *m*.

bet 1 *n* apuesta *f*. **2** *vti** apostar (**on** a).

betray *vt* traicionar.

betrayal traición *f*.

better 1 *a* mejor; **that's b.!** ¡eso es!; **to get b.** mejorar; (*healthier*) mejor; **b. off** (*richer*) más rico,-a; **the b. part of the day** la mayor parte del día. **2** *adv* mejor; **we had b. leave** más vale que nos vayamos. **3** *vt* (*improve*) mejorar; (*surpass*) superar.

betting apuestas *fpl*.

between 1 *prep* entre; **b. you and me** entre nosotros; **closed b. 1 and 3** cerrado de 1 a 3. **2** *adv* en, medio; **in b.** (*position*) en medio; (*time*) mientras (tanto).

beware *vi* tener cuidado (**of** con); **b.!** ¡cuidado!

bewilder *vt* desconcertar.

beyond 1 *prep* más allá de; **it is b. me why . . .** no comprendo por qué . . . ; **this task is b. me** no puedo con esta tarea. **2** *adv* más allá.

bias (*tendency*) tendencia *f* (**towards** hacia); (*prejudice*) prejuicio *m*.

bias(s)ed *a* parcial; **to be b. against sth/sb** tener prejuicio en contra de algo/algn.

bib (*for baby*) babero *m*.

Bible Biblia *f*.

bicycle bicicleta *f*.

bid 1 *vti** (*at auction*) pujar (**for** por). **2** *n* (*offer*) oferta *f*; (*at auction*) puja *f*.

big *a* grande (**gran** *before sing noun*); **a b. clock** un reloj grande; **a b. surprise** una gran sorpresa; **my b. brother** mi hermano mayor; *fam* **b. deal!** ¿y qué?

bighead *fam* engreído,-a *mf*.

bike (*bicycle*) bici *f*; (*motorcycle*) moto *f*.

bike path/track carril *m* de bicicletas.

bikini bikini *m*.

bile bilis *f*.

bilingual *a* bilingüe.

bill *n* (*for gas etc*) factura *f*; (*in restaurant*) cuenta *f*; (*in Congress*) proyecto *m* de ley; (*currency*) billete *m* (de banco).

billboard cartelera *f*.

billfold billetero *m*.

billiards billar *m*.

billion (*thousand million*) mil millones *mpl*.

bin (*for storage*) cajón *m*; (**garbage**) **b.** cubo *m* de la basura.

bind* *vt* (*tie up*) atar; (*book*) encuadernar.

binder (*file*) carpeta *f*.

bingo bingo *m*.

binoculars *npl* prismáticos *mpl*.

biological *a* biológico,-a.

biology biología *f*.

birch (*tree*) abedul *m*.

bird (*small*) pájaro *m*; (*large*) ave *f*.

bird's-eye view vista *f* de pájaro.

birth nacimiento *m*; **to give b. to a child** dar a luz a un niño.

birth certificate partida *f* de nacimiento.

birthday cumpleaños *m inv*.

biscuit bizcocho *m*.

bishop obispo *m*; (*chess*) alfil *m*.

bit (*small piece*) trozo *m*; (*small quantity*) poco *m*; **a b. of sugar** un poco de azúcar; **b. by b.** poco a poco; **a b.** (*slightly*) un poco.

bite 1 *n* (*act*) mordisco *m*; (*wound*) mordedura *f*; (*mouthful, snack*) bocado *m*; (**insect**) **b.** picadura *f*. **2** *vti** morder; (*insect*) picar; **to b. one's nails** morderse las uñas.

bitter *a* amargo,-a; (*weather*) glacial; (*wind*) cortante; (*person*) amargado,-a; (*struggle*) enconado,-a; (*hatred*) implacable.

bitterness amargura *f*; (*of weather*) crudeza *f*; (*of person*) rencor *m*.

bizarre *a* (*odd*) extraño,-a; (*eccentric*) estrafalario,-a.

black 1 *a* (*color*) negro,-a; *fig* **b. and blue** amoratado,-a. **2** *n* (*color*) negro *m*; (*person*) negro, -a *mf*.

• **black out** *vi* (*faint*) desmayarse.

blackberry zarzamora *f*.

blackbird mirlo *m*.

blackboard pizarra *f*, encerado *m*.

blackcurrant grosella *f* negra.

black eye ojo *m* amoratado.

blacklist lista *f* negra.

blackmail 1 *n* chantaje *m*. **2** *vt* chantajear.

blackmailer chantajista *mf*.

blackout (*of lights*) apagón *m*; (*fainting*) pérdida *f* de conocimiento.

bladder vejiga *f*.

blade (*of grass*) brizna *f*; (*of knife etc*) hoja *f*.

blame 1 *n* culpa *f*. **2** *vt* echar la culpa a; **he is to b.** él tiene la culpa.

blameless *a* (*person*) inocente; (*conduct*) intachable.

bland *a* (*food*) soso,-a.

blank 1 a (*without writing*) en blanco; **b. check** cheque m en blanco. **2** n (*space*) espacio m en blanco.

blanket manta f.

blare vi resonar.

• **blare out** vt pregonar.

blast 1 n (*of wind*) ráfaga f; (*of horn etc*) toque m; (*explosion*) explosión f; (*shock wave*) onda f de choque. **2** vt fam **(it)!** ¡maldito sea!

blasted a maldito,-a.

blast-off n despegue m.

blaze 1 n (*burst of flame*) llamarada f; (*fierce fire*) incendio m; (*of sun*) resplandor m. **2** vi (*fire*) arder; (*sun etc*) brillar.

blazer chaqueta f sport.

bleach (*household*) lejía f.

bleak a (*countryside*) desolado,-a.

bleed* vti sangrar.

blemish (*flaw*) defecto m; (*on fruit*) maca f; *fig* **without b.** sin tacha.

blend 1 n mezcla f. **2** vt (*mix*) mezclar; (*match*) armonizar. **3** vi (*mix*) mezclarse.

blender (*for food*) licuadora f.

bless vt bendecir; **b. you!** (*after sneeze*) ¡Jesús!

blessing bendición f; (*advantage*) ventaja f.

blew pt of **blow**.

blind 1 a (*without sight*) ciego,-a; **a b. man** un ciego; **a b. woman** una ciega. **2** n (*on window*) persiana f; pl **the b.** los ciegos.

blindfold 1 n venda f. **2** vt vendar los ojos a.

blindly adv a ciegas; (*love*) ciegamente.

blindness ceguera f.

blink vi (*eyes*) pestañear; (*lights*) parpadear.

bliss felicidad f.

blister (*on skin*) ampolla f.

blizzard ventisca f.

blob (*drop*) gota f; (*spot*) mancha f.

block 1 n bloque m; (*of wood*) taco m; (*group of buildings*) manzana

f; **a b. of apartments** un bloque de pisos. **2** vt (*obstruct*) obstruir.

• **block up** vt bloquear; **to get blocked up** (*pipe*) obstruirse.

blockage bloqueo m.

bloke fam tío m, tipo m.

blond a & n rubio (m).

blonde a & n rubia (f).

blood sangre f; **b. donor** donante mf de sangre; **b. group** grupo m sanguíneo; **b. pressure** tensión f arterial; **high/low b. pressure** hipertensión f/hipotensión f.

bloodshed derramamiento m de sangre.

bloodshot a inyectado,-a de sangre.

bloody a (*battle*) sangriento, -a; (*bloodstained*) manchado,-a de sangre.

bloom 1 n (*flower*) flor f; **in full b.** en flor. **2** vi (*blossom*) florecer.

blossom 1 n (*flower*) flor f. **2** vi florecer.

blot (*of ink*) borrón m.

blotchy a (*skin*) enrojecido,-a; (*paint*) cubierto,-a de manchas.

blouse blusa f.

blow¹ golpe m.

blow² * **1** vi (*wind*) soplar. **2** (*trumpet etc*) tocar; (*smoke*) echar; (*of wind*) llevarse; **to b. one's nose** sonarse la nariz.

• **blow away** vt **the wind blew it away** el viento se lo llevó.

• **blow down** vt derribar.

• **blow off 1** vt (*remove*) quitar. **2** vi (*hat*) salir volando.

• **blow out 1** vt apagar. **2** vi apagarse.

• **blow up 1** vt (*building*) volar; (*inflate*) inflar. **2** vi (*explode*) explotar.

blow dry 1 vt secar con secador, marcar. **2** n marcado m.

blowtorch soplete m.

blue 1 a azul; (*sad*) triste. **b. jeans** vaqueros mpl, tejanos mpl. **2** n azul m.

blueberry arándano m.

bluff 1 n (*deception*) farol m. **2** vi tirarse un farol.

blunder 1 n metedura f de pata, *fam* patinazo m. **2** vi meter la pata.

blunt a (*knife*) embotado,-a; (*pencil*) despuntado,-a; (*frank*) directo,-a; (*statement*) tajante.

blur 1 n **he was just a b.** apenas se le veía. **2** vt (*shape*) desdibujar; (*memory*) enturbiar.

blurred a borroso,-a.

blush vi ruborizarse.

blustery a borrascoso,-a.

board 1 n (*plank*) tabla f; (*meals*) pensión f; **full b.** pensión completa; **room and b.** casa f y comida; **b. of directors** consejo m de administración; **on b.** a bordo. **2** vt (*ship, plane etc*) embarcarse en.

boarder (*in boarding house*) huésped mf; (*at school*) interno,-a mf.

boarding (*embarkation*) embarque m.

boarding pass tarjeta f de embarque.

boarding house pensión f.

boarding school internado m.

boast vi jactarse (**about** de).

boat barco m; (*small*) barca f; (*large*) buque m.

bodily a físico,-a.

body cuerpo m; (*corpse*) cadáver m; (*organization*) organismo m.

bodyguard guardaespaldas mf inv.

bodywork carrocería f.

bogus a falso,-a.

boil¹ 1 n **to come to a b.** empezar a hervir. **2** vt (*water, egg*) hervir; (*food*) cocer. **3** vi hervir.

• **boil over** vi (*milk*) salirse.

boil² (*on skin*) furúnculo m.

boiled a **b. egg** huevo m pasado por agua.

boiler caldera f.

boiling a (*water*) hirviente; **it's b. hot** (*food*) quema; (*weather*) hace un calor agobiante.

bold a (*courageous*) valiente; (*dress, proposition etc*) audaz, atrevido.

boldness audacia f, descaro m, osadía f.

Bolivian a & n boliviano,-a (mf).

bolt 1 n (*on door*) cerrojo m; (*small*) pestillo m; (*with nut*) tornillo m. **2** vt (*lock*) cerrar con cerrojo; (*food*) engullir. **3** vi (*person*) largarse; (*horse*) desbocarse.

bomb 1 n bomba f. **2** vt (*city etc*) bombardear; (*by terrorists*) volar.

bomber bombardero m.

bombing bombardeo m.

bond (*link*) vínculo m; (*financial*) bono m.

bone hueso m; (*in fish*) espina f.

bonfire hoguera f.

bonnet (*child's*) gorro f.

bonus plus m; (*on wages*) prima f; (*on shares*) dividendo m extraordinario.

bony a (*person*) huesudo,-a; (*fish*) lleno,-a de espinas.

boo 1 interj ¡bu! **2** vt abuchear.

booby trap trampa f; (*bomb etc*) trampa f explosiva.

book 1 n libro m; (*of stamps*) carpeta f; (*in commerce*) **books** cuentas fpl. **2** vt (*reserve*) reservar.

bookcase estantería f.

booked up a completo.

booking (*reservation*) reserva f.

booking office taquilla f.

bookkeeper contable mf.

bookkeeping contabilidad f.

booklet (*pamphlet*) folleto m.

bookmaker corredor,-a mf de apuestas.

bookseller librero,-a mf.

bookshelf estantería f.

bookstore librería f.

boom (*noise*) estampido m; (*sudden prosperity*) auge m.

boost 1 n estímulo m. **2** vt (*increase*) aumentar; (*tourism, exports*) fomentar; **to b. sb's confidence** subirle la moral a algn.

boot n bota f; (*short*) botín m; *fam* **she got the b.** la echaron (del trabajo).

• **boot out** vt *fam* echar a patadas.

booth (*in language lab etc*) cabina

f; **telephone b.** cabina *f* telefónica.

booze *fam* **1** *n* priva *f.* **2** *vi* privar.

border *n* borde *m;* (*frontier*) frontera *f.*

• **border on** *vi* (*country*) lindar con.

borderline 1 *a* (*case etc*) dudoso, -a. **2** *n* línea *f* divisoria, frontera *f.*

bore 1 *vt* aburrir. **2** *n* (*person*) pesado,-a *mf;* (*thing*) lata *f;* **what a b.!** ¡qué rollo!

boredom aburrimiento *m.*

boring *a* aburrido,-a, pesado,-a.

born to be b. nacer; **I was b. in 1969** nací en 1969.

borrow *vt* pedir prestado; **can I b. your pen?** ¿me dejas tu bolígrafo?

boss *n* (*head*) jefe,-a *mf;* (*factory owner etc*) patrón,-ona *mf.*

• **boss around** *vt* ser mandón, -ona a.

bossy *a* mandón,-ona.

botch *vt* chapucear; **a botched job** una chapuza.

both 1 *a* ambos,-as, los/las dos; **b. men are teachers** ambos son profesores; **hold it with b. hands** sujétalo con las dos manos. **2** *pron* **b. (of them)** ambos,-as, los/las dos; **b. of you** vosotros dos. **3** *adv* a la vez; **b. New York and Ohio are in the U.S.** tanto Nueva York como Ohio están en los Estados Unidos.

bother 1 *vt* (*disturb*) molestar; (*be a nuisance to*) dar la lata a; (*worry*) preocupar; **I can't be bothered** no tengo ganas; **he didn't b. shaving** no se molestó en afeitarse. **2** *vi* **. don't b.** no te molestes **3** *n* (*disturbance*) molestia *f;* (*nuisance*) lata *f;* (*trouble*) problemas *mpl.* **4** *interj* ¡maldito sea!

bottle botella *f;* (*of perfume, ink*) frasco *m;* **baby's b.** biberón *m.*

bottle opener abrebotellas *m inv.*

bottom 1 *a* (*lowest*) más bajo,-a. **2** *n* parte *f* inferior; (*of sea, garden, street, box, bottle*) fondo *m;* (*of page, hill*) pie *m;* (*buttocks*) tra-

sero *m;* **to be at the b. of the class** ser el último/la última de la clase.

boulder canto *m* rodado.

bounce 1 *vi* (*ball*) rebotar; (*check*) ser rechazado (por el banco). **2** *vt* (*ball*) botar.

bound¹ *a* **he's b. to know it** seguro que lo sabe; **it's b. to happen** sucederá con toda seguridad; **it was b. to fail** estaba destinado al fracaso.

bound² *a* **to be b. for** dirigirse a.

boundary límite *m.*

bounds *npl* **the river is out of b.** está prohibido bajar al río.

bouquet (*of flowers*) ramillete *m.*

boutique boutique *f.*

bow¹ *a* **1** *vi* hacer una reverencia. **2** *n* (*with head, body*) reverencia *f.*

bow² (*for violin, arrows*) arco *m;* (*knot*) lazo *m.*

bowels *npl* entrañas *fpl.*

bowl¹ (*dish*) cuenco *m;* (*for soup*) tazón *m;* (*for washing clothes, dishes*) barreño *m.*

bowl² *vi* (*in cricket*) lanzar la pelota.

bowler (*hat*) bombín *m.*

bowling (*game*) bolos *mpl.*

bowling alley bolera *f.*

bowling pin bolo *m.*

bowls *npl* bolos *mpl.*

bow tie pajarita *f.*

box¹ caja *f;* (*large*) cajón *m.*

box² **1** *vi* boxear. **2** *vt* (*hit*) pegar.

• **box in** *vt* (*enclose*) aprisionar.

boxer boxeador *m;* (*dog*) bóxer *m.*

boxing boxeo *m;* **b. ring** cuadrilátero *m.*

box office taquilla *f.*

boy (*child*) chico *m;* (*youth*) joven *m.*

boycott 1 *n* boicot *m.* **2** *vt* boicotear.

boyfriend novio *m;* (*live-in*) compañero *m.*

bra sostén *m.*

bracelet pulsera *f.*

bracket (*round*) paréntesis *m;* (*square*) corchete *m.*

brag *vi* jactarse (**about** de).

bragging fanfarronería *f.*

braid 1 vt trenzar. **2** n trenza f.

brain cerebro m; **brains** inteligencia f; **to have brains** ser inteligente.

brainwash vt lavar el cerebro a.

brainy a fam inteligente.

brake 1 n freno m. **2** vi frenar.

brake light luz f de freno.

branch 1 n (of tree) rama f; (of road) bifurcación f; **b. (office)** sucursal f. **2** vi (road) bifurcarse.

• **branch off** vi desviarse.

• **branch out** vi diversificarse.

brand marca f; **b. name** marca f de fábrica.

brand-new a flamante.

brandy brandy m.

brass latón m.

brave a valiente.

bravery valentía f.

brawl reyerta f.

brawny a fornido,-a.

Brazilian a & n brasileño,-a (mf).

bread pan m; **b. and butter** pan con mantequilla.

breadbox panera f.

breadcrumb miga f de pan; **breadcrumbs** pan m sing rallado.

breadth (width) anchura f; (extent) amplitud f.

breadwinner cabeza mf de familia.

break 1 vt* romper; (fail to keep) faltar a; (destroy) destrozar; (financially) arruinar; (journey) interrumpir; (record) batir; **to b. a leg** romperse la pierna; **to b. the law** violar la ley; **she broke the news to him** le comunicó la noticia. **2** vi* romperse; (storm) estallar; (story) divulgarse. **3** n (fracture) rotura f; (crack) grieta f; (opening) abertura f; (in a relationship) ruptura f; (pause) pausa f; (at school) recreo m; fam (chance) oportunidad f; **to take a b.** descansar un rato; (holiday) tomar unos días libres; **a lucky b.** un golpe de suerte.

• **break away** vi (become separate) desprenderse (from de).

• **break down 1** vt (door) derribar; (resistance) acabar con. **2** vi (in car) tener una avería; (weep) ponerse a llorar.

• **break in** vi (burglar) entrar a la fuerza.

• **break into** vt (house) allanar; (safe) forzar.

• **break loose** vi escaparse.

• **break off 1** vt (relations) romper. **2** vi (become detached) desprenderse; (talks) interrumpirse; (stop) pararse.

• **break out** vi (prisoners) escaparse; (war etc) estallar.

• **break up 1** vt (object) romper; (car) desguazar; (crowd) disolver. **2** vi romperse; (crowd) disolverse; (meeting) levantarse; (relationship) fracasar; (couple) separarse; (at end of term) terminar.

breakdown avería f; (in communications) ruptura f; **(nervous) b.** crisis f nerviosa.

breakfast desayuno m; **to have b.** desayunar.

break-in robo m (con allanamiento de morada).

breakthrough avance m.

breakup (in marriage) separación f.

breast (chest) pecho m; (of chicken etc) pechuga f.

breast-feed vt dar el pecho a.

breaststroke braza f.

breath aliento m; **out of b.** sin aliento.

Breathalyzer® alcoholímetro m.

breathe vti respirar.

• **breathe in** vi aspirar.

• **breathe out** vi espirar.

breathing respiración f; **b. space** respiro m.

breathtaking a impresionante.

breed 1 n (of animal) raza f. **2** vt* (animals) criar. **3** vi* (animals) reproducirse.

breeder (person) criador,-a mf.

breeze brisa f.

breezy a (weather) ventoso,-a.

brew 1 vt (beer) elaborar; (hot drink) preparar. **2** vi (tea) reposar; **a storm is brewing** se prepara una tormenta; **something's brewing** algo se está cociendo.

brewery cervecería f.

bribe 1 vt sobornar. **2** n soborno m.

brick ladrillo m.

bricklayer albañil m.

bride novia f; **the b. and groom** los novios.

bridegroom novio m.

bridesmaid dama f de honor.

bridge puente m.

brief 1 a (short) breve; (concise) conciso,-a. **2** n **briefs** (for men) calzoncillos mpl; (for women) bragas fpl. **3** vt (inform) informar; (instruct) dar instrucciones a.

briefcase cartera f.

briefing (meeting) reunión f informativa.

briefly adv brevemente.

bright a (light, sun, eyes) brillante; (color) vivo,-a; (day) claro,-a; (cheerful) alegre; (clever) listo,-a.

brighten vi (prospects) mejorar; (face) iluminarse.

• **brighten up 1** vt (room etc) hacer más alegre. **2** vi (weather) despejarse; (person) animarse.

brightly adv brillantemente.

brightness (of sun) resplandor m; (of color) viveza f.

brilliance (of light) brillo m; (of color) viveza f; (of person) brillantez f.

brilliant a brillante; (idea) genial; (very good) estupendo,-a.

bring* vt traer; (take to a different position) llevar; (cause) provocar; **could you b. that book?** ¿podrías traerme el libro?

• **bring about** vt provocar.

• **bring along** vt traer.

• **bring around** vt (revive) hacer volver en sí; (persuade) convencer.

• **bring back** vt (return) devolver; (reintroduce) volver a introducir; (make one remember) traer a la memoria.

• **bring down** vt (from upstairs) bajar (algo); (government) derribar; (reduce) rebajar.

• **bring forward** vt (meeting etc) adelantar.

• **bring in** vt (yield) dar; (show in) hacer entrar; (law etc) introducir.

• **bring out** vt (publish) publicar; (emphasize) recalcar.

• **bring to** vt reanimar.

• **bring together** vt (reconcile) reconciliar.

• **bring up** vt (educate) educar; (subject) plantear; (vomit up) vomitar.

brink (edge) borde m.

brisk a enérgico,-a; (pace) rápido, -a; (trade) activo,-a.

briskly adv (to walk) rápidamente.

bristle cerda f.

British 1 a británico,-a; **the B. Isles** las Islas Británicas. **2** npl **the B.** los británicos.

Briton británico,-a mf.

brittle a quebradizo,-a.

broad a (road, river) ancho,-a; (not detailed) general; **in b. daylight** a plena luz del día.

broadcast 1 n emisión f. **2** vt* emitir.

broccoli brécol m.

brochure folleto m.

broke a **to be (flat) b.** estar sin blanca.

broken a roto,-a; (machinery) averiado,-a; (leg) fracturado,-a; **a b. home** una familia deshecha.

broken-down a (machine) averiado,-a.

bronchitis bronquitis f.

bronze bronce m.

brooch broche m.

brood 1 n (of birds) cría f. **2** vi (ponder) rumiar; **to b. over a problem** darle vueltas a un problema.

broody a (pensive) pensativo,-a; (moody) melancólico,-a; fam (woman) con ganas de tener hijos.

brook arroyo m.

broom escoba f; (plant) retama f.

broomstick palo m de escoba.

brother hermano m; **brothers and sisters** hermanos.

brother-in-law cuñado m.

brought pt & pp of **bring.**
brown 1 a marrón; (hair) castaño, -a; (tanned) moreno,-a. **2** n marrón m.
browse vi (person in shop) mirar; (through book) hojear.
bruise 1 n morado m, cardenal m. **2** vt contusionar.
bruised a amoratado,-a.
brunch combinación f de desayuno y almuerzo.
brunette a & n morena (f).
brush 1 n (for hair, teeth) cepillo m; (artist's) pincel m; (for house-painting) brocha f. **2** vt cepillar; **to b. one's hair/teeth** cepillarse el pelo/los dientes.
• **brush aside** vt dejar de lado.
• **brush off** vt ignorar.
• **brush up (on)** vt repasar.
brutal a brutal, cruel.
brutality brutalidad f.
brute (animal) bruto m; (person) bestia f.
BS abbr of **Bachelor of Science.**
bubble burbuja f.
• **bubble over** vi rebosar.
buck fam dólar m.
bucket cubo m.
buckle 1 n hebilla f. **2** vt abrochar (con hebilla). **3** vi (wall, metal) combarse.
buck up 1 vt **b. your ideas up!** ¡espabílate! **2** vi (cheer up) animarse.
bud 1 n (shoot) brote m; (flower) capullo m. **2** vi brotar.
Buddhist a & n budista (mf).
budge vi (move) moverse.
budgerigar periquito m.
budget 1 n presupuesto m; **the B.** (of the state) los presupuestos del Estado. **2** vi hacer un presupuesto (**for** para).
buffalo (pl **buffaloes**) búfalo m.
buffet (snack bar) bar m; (self-service meal) bufet m libre.
bug 1 n (insect) bicho m; (microbe) microbio m; **I've got a b.** tengo alguna infección; (hidden microphone) micrófono m oculto; (in computer program) error m. **2** vt fam (annoy) fastidiar.
buggy (baby's stroller) cochecito m de niño.
bugle bugle m.
build 1 vt* construir. **2** n (physique) físico m.
builder constructor,-a mf; (contractor) contratista mf.
building edificio m.
built-in a (cupboard) empotrado,-a; (incorporated) incorporado,-a.
built-up a urbanizado,-a.
bulb (of plant) bulbo m; (lightbulb) bombilla f.
Bulgarian a & n búlgaro,-a (mf).
bulge 1 n protuberancia f; (in pocket) bulto m. **2** vi (swell) hincharse; (be full) estar repleto,-a.
bulging a abultado,-a; (eye) saltón.
bulk (mass) masa f, volumen m; (greater part) mayor parte f.
bulky a voluminoso,-a.
bull toro m.
bulldog buldog m.
bulldozer bulldozer m.
bullet bala f.
bulletin boletín m.
bulletin board tablón m de anuncios.
bullet-proof a a prueba de balas; **b. vest** chaleco m antibalas.
bullfight corrida f de toros.
bullfighter torero,-a mf.
bullfighting los toros mpl; (art) tauromaquia f.
bullring plaza f de toros.
bully 1 n matón m. **2** vt intimidar.
bum fam (tramp) vagabundo m; (idler) holgazán,-ana mf.
• **bum around** vi fam vaguear.
bumblebee abejorro m.
bump 1 n (swelling) chichón m; (on road) bache m; (blow) golpe m; (jolt) sacudida f. **2** vt golpear; **to b. one's head** darse un golpe en la cabeza.
• **bump into** vt (meet) tropezar con.

bumper (*on vehicle*) parachoques *m inv.*

bumpy *a* (*road*) con muchos baches.

bun (*bread*) panecillo *m*; (*sweet*) magdalena *f.*

bunch (*of keys*) manojo *m*; (*of flowers*) ramo *m*; (*of grapes*) racimo *m*; (*of people*) grupo *m.*

bundle 1 *n* (*of clothes*) bulto *m*; (*of papers*) fajo *m.* **2** *vt* (*make bundle of*) liar; (*push*) empujar.

bungalow bungalow *m.*

bunk (*bed*) litera *f.*

bunny *fam* **b. (rabbit)** conejito *m.*

buoy boya *f.*

burden 1 *n* carga *f.* **2** *vt* cargar (**with** con).

bureaucracy burocracia *f.*

burger *fam* hamburguesa *f.*

burglar ladrón,-ona *mf.*

burglar alarm alarma *f* antirrobo.

burglarize *vt* robar.

burglary robo *m* en una casa.

burgle *vt* robar.

burial entierro *m.*

burn 1 *n* quemadura *f.* **2** *vt** quemar. **3** *vi** (*fire*) arder; (*building, food*) quemarse; (*ointment etc*) escocer.

• **burn down 1** *vt* incendiar. **2** *vi* incendiarse.

burner (*on stove*) quemador *m.*

burning *a* (*on fire*) ardiendo,-a en llamas.

burp 1 *n* eructo *m.* **2** *vi* eructar.

burst 1 *n* (*explosion*) estallido *m*; (*of tire*) reventón *m*; **b. of laughter** carcajada *f.* **2** *vt** (*balloon*) reventar. **3** *vi** reventarse; (*shell*) estallar.

• **burst into** *vi* to **b. into laughter/ tears** echarse a reír/llorar; **to b. into a room** irrumpir en una habitación.

• **burst out** *vi* to **b. out laughing** echarse a reír.

bursting *a* **the bar was b. with people** el bar estaba atestado de gente.

bury *vt* enterrar; (*hide*) ocultar; **to be buried in thought** estar absorto en pensamientos.

bus (*pl* **buses** or **busses**) autobús *m.*

bus shelter marquesina *f* (de autobús).

bus station estación *f* de autobuses.

bush (*shrub*) arbusto *m.*

bushy *a* espeso,-a.

business (*commerce*) negocios *mpl*; (*firm*) empresa *f*; (*matter*) asunto *m*; **on b.** de negocios; **b. hours** horas *fpl* de oficina; **b. trip** viaje *m* de negocios; **it's no b. of mine** no es asunto mío; **mind your own b.** no te metas en donde no te llaman.

businessman hombre *m* de negocios.

businesswoman mujer *f* de negocios.

bus stop parada *f* de autobús.

bust[1] (*of woman*) pecho *m*; (*sculpture*) busto *m.*

bust[2] *fam* **to go b.** quebrar.

bustle (*activity, noise*) bullicio *m.*

• **bustle about** *vi* ir y venir.

bustling *a* bullicioso,-a.

busy *a* ocupado,-a; (*life*) ajetreado,-a; (*street*) concurrido,-a; (*telephone*) ocupado,-a; **b. signal** señal *f* de comunicado.

busybody entrometido,-a *mf*, cotilla *mf.*

but 1 *conj* pero; (*after negative*) sino; **not two b. three** no dos sino tres. **2** *prep* menos; **everyone b. her** todos menos ella.

butcher carnicero,-a *mf*; **b.'s (shop)** carnicería *f.*

butler mayordomo *m.*

butt (*of cigarette*) colilla *f*; *fam* (*bottom*) culo *m.*

butter 1 *n* mantequilla *f.* **2** *vt* untar con mantequilla.

buttercup botón *m* de oro.

butterfly mariposa *f.*

buttock nalga *f*; **buttocks** nalgas *fpl.*

button 1 *n* botón *m.* **2** *vt* **to b. (up) one's jacket** abotonarse la chaqueta.

buttonhole ojal *m.*

buy 1 *n* **a good b.** una ganga. **2** *vt** comprar; **she bought that car from a neighbor** compró ese coche a un vecino.

buyer comprador,-a *mf.*

buzz 1 *n* (*of bee*) zumbido *m;* (*of conversation*) rumor *m.* **2** *vi* zumbar.

• **buzz off** *vi fam* largarse.

by 1 *prep* (*indicating agent*) por; **composed by Bach** compuesto,-a por Bach; **a film by Almodóvar** una película de Almodóvar. ▪ (*via*) por; **he left by the back door** salió por la puerta trasera. ▪ (*manner*) en, con, por; **by car/train** en coche/tren; **by credit card** con tarjeta de crédito; **by chance** por casualidad; **by oneself** solo,-a; **you can obtain a ticket by filling in the coupon** puede conseguir una entrada rellenando el cupón. ▪ (*amount*) por; **little by little** poco a poco; **they are sold by the dozen** se venden por docenas; **to be paid by the hour** cobrar por horas; **he won by a foot** ganó por un pie. ▪ (*beside*) al lado de, junto a; **side by side** juntos. ▪ (*past*) **to walk by a building** pasar por delante de un edificio. ▪ (*time*) para; **by now** ya; **by then** para entonces; **we have to be there by nine** tenemos que estar allí para las nueve; **by the time we arrive** (para) cuando lleguemos. ▪ (*during*) de; **by day/night** de día/noche. ▪ (*according to*) según; **is that O.K by you?** ¿te viene bien? **2** *adv* **to go by** (*past*) pasar; **she just walked by** pasó de largo; **by and by** con el tiempo; **by and large** en conjunto.

bye(-bye) ¡adiós!, ¡hasta luego!

by-election elección *f* parcial.

bypass 1 *n* (*road*) carretera *f* de circunvalación. **2** *vt* evitar.

bystander mirón,-ona *mf.*

C

cab taxi *m.*

cabbage col *f.*

cabin (*hut*) choza *f;* (*on ship*) camarote *m.*

cabinet (*furniture*) armario *m;* (*glass-fronted*) vitrina *f;* (*in government*) gabinete *m.*

cabinet meeting consejo *m* de ministros.

cable cable *m.*

cable car teleférico *m.*

cable TV televisión *f* por cable.

cactus (*pl* **cacti**) cactus *m.*

café, cafetería cafetería *f,* bar *m.*

caffeine cafeína *f.*

cage jaula *f.*

cake pastel *m.*

calculate *vt* calcular.

calculation cálculo *m.*

calculator calculadora *f.*

calendar calendario *m.*

calf (*pl* **calves**) (*of cattle*) becerro,-a *mf,* ternero,-a *mf;* (*part of leg*) pantorrilla *f.*

call 1 *vt* llamar; (*meeting etc*) convocar; **what's he called?** ¿cómo se llama? **2** *vi* llamar; **to c. at sb's (house)** pasar por casa de algn. **3** *n* llamada *f;* (*visit*) visita *f;* (**phone**) **c.** llamada *f.*

• **call back** *vti* (*phone again*) llamar otra vez.

• **call in 1** *vt* (*doctor*) llamar; (*visit*) ir a ver. **2** *vi* entrar.

• **call on** *vt* visitar; **to c. on sb for support** recurrir a algn en busca de apoyo.

• **call out 1** *vt* (*shout*) gritar; (*doctor*) hacer venir. **2** *vi* gritar.

• **call (up)** *vt* llamar (por teléfono).

call box cabina *f* telefónica.

calm 1 *a* (*weather, sea*) en calma; (*relaxed*) tranquilo,-a; **keep c.!** ¡tranquilo,-a! **2** *n* (*of weather, sea*) calma *f.* **3** *vt* calmar.

• **calm down** *vi* calmarse.

calmly *adv* con calma, tranquilamente.

calorie caloría f.
camcorder videocámara f.
came pt of **come**.
camel camello,-a mf.
camera cámara f.
camp 1 n campamento m. **2** vi **to go camping** ir de camping.
campaign campaña f.
camp bed cama f plegable.
camper (person) campista mf; (vehicle) caravana f.
campfire fogata f.
camp(ing) site camping m.
can¹ v aux (pt **could**) poder; (know how to) saber; **I'll phone you as soon as I c.** te llamaré en cuanto pueda; **she can't do it** no puede hacerlo; **I cannot understand why** no entiendo por qué; **he could have come** podría haber venido; **c. you ski?** ¿sabes esquiar?; **she could have forgotten** puede (ser) que lo haya olvidado; **they can't be very poor** no deben ser muy pobres; **what c. it be?** ¿qué será?
can² (tin) lata f.
Canadian a & n canadiense (mf).
canal canal m.
canary canario m.
cancel vt (train, booking) cancelar; (contract) anular; (permission) retirar.
cancellation cancelación f; (of contract) anulación f.
cancer cáncer m.
candid a franco,-a.
candidate candidato,-a mf; (in state exam) opositor,-a mf.
candle vela f; (in church) cirio m.
candlestick palmatoria f; (in church) cirial m.
candy caramelo m.
cane 1 n (walking stick) bastón m; (for punishment) palmeta f. **2** vt castigar con la palmeta.
cannabis canabis m.
canned a enlatado,-a; **c. foods** conservas fpl.
cannibal a & n caníbal (mf).
canoe canoa f; (for sport) piragua f.

canoeing piragüismo m.
can opener abrelatas m.
canopy (awning) toldo m.
canteen (restaurant) comedor m, cantina f.
canvas lona f; (painting) lienzo m.
canyon cañón m.
cap gorro m; (soldier's) gorra f; (of pen) capuchón m; (of bottle) chapa f.
capability habilidad f.
capable a (skillful) hábil; (able) capaz (**of** de).
capacity capacidad f; (position) puesto m; **in her c. as manageress** en calidad de gerente.
cape (garment) capa f.
capital (town) capital f; (money) capital m; (letter) mayúscula f.
capsize 1 vt hacer zozobrar. **2** vi zozobrar.
capsule cápsula f.
captain capitán m.
capture vt capturar; (of troops) (town) tomar.
car coche m, Am carro m; **by c.** en coche.
caramel azúcar m quemado; (sweet) caramelo m.
caravan (vehicle) caravana f.
carbon carbono m; **c. copy** copia f al papel carbón.
carburetor carburador m.
card tarjeta f; (of cardboard) cartulina f; (in file) ficha f.
cardboard cartón m.
cardigan rebeca f.
cardinal 1 n cardenal m. **2** a **c. numbers** números mpl cardinales.
care 1 vi (be concerned) preocuparse (**about** por); **I don't c.** no me importa; **who cares?** ¿qué más da? **2** n (attention, protection) cuidado m; (worry) preocupación f; **to take c. of** cuidar; (business) ocuparse de; **take c.** (be careful) ten cuidado; (as farewell) ¡cuídate!; **to take c. not to do sth** guardarse de hacer algo.
• **care about** vt (something) preocuparse de; (somebody) tener cariño a.

- **care for** vt (look after) cuidar; **I don't c. for that sort of thing** no me hace gracia una cosa así; **would you c. for a coffee?** ¿te apetece un café?

career carrera f.

carefree a despreocupado,-a.

careful a cuidadoso,-a; (cautious) prudente; **to be c.** tener cuidado; **be c.!** ¡ojo!

carefully adv (painstakingly) cuidadosamente; (cautiously) con cuidado.

careless a descuidado,-a; (about clothes) desaliñado,-a; (driving) negligente.

car ferry transbordador m para coches.

cargo (pl **cargoes** or **cargos**) carga f.

caring a humanitario,-a, afectuoso,-a.

carnation clavel m.

carnival carnaval m.

carol villancico m.

carp (fish) carpa f.

carpenter carpintero,-a mf.

carpentry carpintería f.

carpet alfombra f; (fitted) moqueta f.

carpeting (wall to wall) c. moqueta f.

carpet sweeper barredora f para alfombras.

carriage (horse-drawn) carruaje m; (on train) vagón m, coche m.

carrier bag bolsa f de plástico.

carrot zanahoria f.

carry 1 vt llevar; (goods) transportar; (stock) tener; (responsibility, penalty) conllevar; (disease) ser portador,-a de. **2** vi (sound) oírse.

- **carry away** vt llevarse; **to get carried away** entusiasmarse.
- **carry off** vt (prize) llevarse; **to c. it off** salir airoso,-a.
- **carry on** vt continuar; (conversation) mantener. **2** vi continuar; **c. on!** ¡adelante! **3** n (baggage) bolsa f de viaje.

- **carry out** vt (plan) llevar a cabo; (order) cumplir; (repairs) hacer.
- **carry through** vt (plan) completar.

cart 1 n (horse-drawn) carro m; (handcart) carretilla f. **2** vt acarrear.

- **cart around** vt fam llevar y traer.

carton (of cream etc) paquete m.

cartoon (strip) tira f cómica; (animated) dibujos mpl animados.

cartridge cartucho m; (for pen) recambio m.

carve vt (wood) tallar; (stone, metal) esculpir; (meat) trinchar.

car wash túnel m or tren m de lavado.

case[1] (instance, medical) caso m; (legal) causa f; **in any c.** en cualquier caso; **just in c.** por si acaso.

case[2] (suitcase) maleta f; (small) estuche m; (soft) funda f.

cash 1 n dinero m efectivo; **to pay c.** pagar al contado or en efectivo. **2** vt (check) cobrar.

cash box caja f.

cashier cajero,-a mf.

cash price precio m al contado.

cash register caja f registradora.

casino casino m.

casserole (container) cacerola f; (food) guisado m.

cassette casete f.

cassette player cassette m.

cassette recorder casete m.

cast 1 vt* (net, fishing line) echar; (light) proyectar; (glance) lanzar; (vote) emitir; **to c. suspicion on sb** levantar sospechas sobre algn; (play, film) hacer el reparto de. **2** n (plaster) c. escayola f; (of play) reparto m.

castle castillo m; (in chess) torre f.

castor ruedecilla f.

casual a informal; (worker) eventual; (clothes) (de) sport; (unimportant) casual.

casualty (injured) herido,-a mf; **casualties** víctimas fpl.

cat gato,-a *mf*.

catalog catálogo *m*.

catapult tirachinas *m inv*.

catastrophe catástrofe *f*.

catch 1 *vt* (thief, bus etc)* coger, *Am* agarrar; *(fish)* pescar; *(mouse etc)* atrapar; *(surprise)* sorprender; *(hear)* entender; **to c. fire** *(log)* prenderse; *(building)* incendiarse; **to c. one's breath** *(recover)* recuperar el aliento. **2** *vi* (sleeve etc)* engancharse **(on** en**)**; *(fire)* encenderse. **3** *n (of ball)* parada *f*; *(of fish)* presa *f*; *(on door)* pestillo *m*; *(drawback)* pega *f*.

• **catch on** *vi (become popular)* ganar popularidad; *(understand)* caer en la cuenta.

• **catch up** *vi* **to c. up (with) sb** *(reach)* alcanzar a algn; *(with news)* ponerse al corriente **(on** de**)**; **to c. up with work** ponerse al día con el trabajo.

catching *a (disease)* contagioso,-a.

category categoría *f*.

cater for *vt (wedding etc)* proveer comida para; *(taste)* atender a.

caterpillar oruga *f*.

cathedral catedral *f*.

Catholic *a & n* católico,-a *(mf)*.

cauliflower coliflor *f*.

cause 1 *n (of event etc)* causa *f*; *(reason)* motivo *m*. **2** *vt* provocar; **to c. sb to do sth** hacer que algn haga algo.

caution *n (care)* cautela *f*; *(warning)* aviso *m*.

cautious *a* cauteloso,-a.

cautiously *adv* con precaución.

cave cueva *f*.

• **cave in** *vi (roof etc)* derrumbarse.

cavity *(hole)* cavidad *f*.

CD *abbr of* **compact disc** CD *m*.

cease 1 *vt* **to c. doing** *or* **to do sth** dejar de hacer algo. **2** *vi* cesar.

cease-fire alto *m* el fuego.

ceiling techo *m*.

celebrate 1 *vt* celebrar. **2** *vi* divertirse.

celebration celebración *f*.

celebrity celebridad *f*.

celery apio *m*.

cell *(in prison)* celda *f*; *(in organism)* célula *f*.

cellar sótano *m*; *(for wine)* bodega *f*.

cellophane celofán *m*.

cement 1 *n* cemento *m*. **2** *vt (fix with cement)* unir con cemento.

cement mixer hormigonera *f*.

cemetery cementerio *m*.

cent centavo *m*, céntimo *m*.

center centro *m*.

centigrade *a* centígrado,-a.

centimeter centímetro *m*.

centipede ciempiés *m inv*.

central *a* central.

Central American *a & n* centroamericano,-a *(mf)*.

century siglo *m*.

ceramic *a* de cerámica.

cereal cereal *m*.

ceremony ceremonia *f*.

certain 1 *a (sure)* seguro,-a; *(true)* cierto,-a; **to make c. of sth** asegurarse de algo; **to a c. extent** hasta cierto punto. **2** *adv* **for c.** a ciencia cierta.

certainly *adv* desde luego; **c. not** de ninguna manera.

certainty certeza *f*; *(assurance)* seguridad *f*.

certificate certificado *m*; *(from college)* diploma *m*.

certify *vt* certificar.

chain 1 *n* cadena *f*; *(of events)* serie *f*; *(of mountains)* cordillera *f*. **2** *vt* **to c. (up)** encadenar.

chair *n* silla *f*; *(with arms)* sillón *m*; *(of meeting)* presidente *mf*.

chair lift telesilla *m*.

chairman presidente *m*.

chalet chalet *m*, chalé *m*.

chalk *(for writing)* tiza *f*.

challenge 1 *vt* desafiar; *(authority etc)* poner a prueba; *(statement)* poner en duda; **to c. sb to do sth** retar a algn a que haga algo. **2** *n* desafío *m*.

challenging *a (idea)* desafiante; *(task)* que presenta un desafío.

chamber **C. of Commerce** Cámara *f* de Comercio.

champagne (*French*) champán *m*; (*from Catalonia*) cava *m*.
champion campeón,-ona *mf*.
championship campeonato *m*.
chance 1 *n* (*fortune*) azar *m*; (*opportunity*) oportunidad *f*; **by c.** por casualidad; **to take a c.** arriesgarse; **(the) chances are that . . .** lo más probable es que . . . 2 *vt* arriesgar.
chandelier araña *f* (de luces).
change 1 *vt* cambiar; **to c. gear** cambiar de marcha; **to c. one's mind/the subject** cambiar de opinión/de tema; **to c. trains** hacer trasbordo; **to get changed** cambiarse de ropa. 2 *vi* cambiar(se); **I think he's changed** le veo cambiado. 3 *n* cambio *m*; (*money after purchase*) vuelta *f*; **for a c.** para variar; **c. of scene** cambio de aires; **small c.** suelto *m*.
• **change over** *vi* **to c. over to sth** cambiar a algo, adoptar algo.
changeable *a* (*weather*) variable; (*person*) inconstante.
changeover conversión *f*.
changing room vestuario *m*.
channel canal *m*; (*administrative*) vía *f*; **the English C.** el Canal de la Mancha.
chant 1 *n* (*of demonstrators*) eslogan *m*. 2 *vti* (*demonstrators*) corear.
chaos caos *m*.
chaotic *a* caótico,-a.
chapel capilla *f*.
chapped *a* agrietado,-a.
chapter capítulo *m*.
char *vt* carbonizar.
character carácter *m*; (*in play*) personaje *m*; (*person*) tipo *m*.
characteristic 1 *n* característica *f*. 2 *a* característico,-a.

charge 1 *vt* cobrar; (*the enemy*) cargar contra; (*battery*) cargar; **to c. sb with a crime** acusar a algn de un crimen. 2 *vi* (*battery, troops*) cargar; **to c. about** andar a lo loco. 3 *n* (*cost*) precio *m*; (*in court*) acusación *f*; **bank charges** comisión *f*; **free of c.** gratis; **service c.** servicio

m; **to be in c. of** estar a cargo de; **to take c. of** hacerse cargo de.
charity (*organization*) institución *f* benéfica.
charm 1 *n* (*quality*) encanto *m*; **lucky c.** amuleto *m*. 2 *vt* encantar.
charming *a* encantador,-a.
chart (*giving information*) tabla *f*; (*graph*) gráfico *m*; (*map*) carta *f* de navegación; (*of hit records*) **the charts** la lista de éxitos.
charter flight vuelo *m* chárter.
chase *vt* perseguir; (*hunt*) cazar.
• **chase after** *vt* (*someone*) correr detrás de; (*something*) andar tras.
• **chase away** *or* **off** *vt* ahuyentar.
chasm sima *f*; *fig* abismo *m*.
chassis chasis *m inv*.
chat 1 *n* charla *f*. 2 *vi* charlar.
chatter 1 *vi* (*person*) parlotear; (*teeth*) castañetear. 2 *n* (*of person*) parloteo *m*; (*of teeth*) castañeteo *m*.
chatterbox parlanchín,-ina *mf*.
chatty *a* hablador,-a.
chauffeur chófer *m*.
cheap 1 *a* barato,-a; (*fare*) económico,-a; (*contemptible*) bajo,-a. 2 *adv* barato.
cheaply *adv* en plan económico.
cheat 1 *vt* engañar; **to c. sb out of sth** estafar algo a algn. 2 *vi* (*at games*) hacer trampa; (*on an exam etc*) copiar(se). 3 *n* (*trickster*) tramposo,-a.
check 1 *vt* verificar; (*facts*) comprobar; (*tickets*) controlar; (*tires, oil*) revisar; (*stop*) detener; (*in chess*) dar jaque a. 2 *vi* comprobar. 3 *n* (*of documents etc*) revisión *f*; (*of facts*) comprobación *f*; (*in chess*) jaque *m*; (*in restaurant etc*) cuenta *f*.
• **check in** *vi* (*at airport*) facturar; (*at hotel*) registrarse (**at** en).
• **check off** *vt* (*names on list etc*) tachar.
• **check on** *vt* verificar.
• **check out** *vi* (*of hotel*) dejar el hotel. 2 *vt* (*facts*) verificar.
• **check up** *vi* **to c. up on sth** comprobar algo.

checkbook talonario *m* de cheques.

checkers (*game*) damas *fpl*.

check in **c. desk** (*at airport*) mostrador *m* de facturación.

checkmate jaque mate *m*.

checkout (*counter*) caja *f*.

checkroom guardarropa *f*; (*for luggage*) consigna *f*.

checkup (*medical*) chequeo *m*.

cheddar queso *m* cheddar.

cheek mejilla *f*; (*nerve*) cara *f*; **what c.!** ¡vaya jeta!

cheeky *a* fresco,-a.

cheer 1 *vi* aclamar. **2** *vt* (*applaud*) aclamar. **3** *n* viva *m*; **cheers** aplausos *mpl*; **cheers!** (*before drinking*) ¡salud!

• **cheer up 1** *vi* animarse. **2** *vt* **to c. sb up** animar a algn.

cheerful *a* alegre.

cheering ovación *f*.

cheese queso *m*.

cheeseburger hamburguesa *f* de queso.

cheesecake tarta *f* de queso.

chef chef *m*.

chemical 1 *n* sustancia *f* química. **2** *a* químico,-a.

chemist farmacéutico. -a *mf*; (*scientist*) químico,-a *mf*.

chemistry química *f*.

cherry cereza *f*.

cherry brandy licor *m* de cerezas.

chess ajedrez *m*.

chessboard tablero *m* de ajedrez.

chest pecho *m*; (*for linen*) arca *f*; (*for valuables*) cofre *m*; **c. of drawers** cómoda *f*.

chestnut (*nut*) castaña *f*.

chew *vt* masticar.

chewing gum chicle *m*.

chick pollito *m*.

chicken *n* pollo *m*; *fam* (*coward*) gallina *m*.

• **chicken out** *vi* rajarse (por miedo).

chickenpox varicela *f*.

chickpea garbanzo *m*.

chicory achicoria *f*.

chief 1 *n* jefe *m*. **2** *a* principal.

chiefly *adv* (*above all*) sobre todo; (*mainly*) principalmente.

chilblain sabañón *m*.

child (*pl* **children**) niño,-a *mf*; (*son*) hijo *m*; (*daughter*) hija *f*.

child care (*for working parents*) servicio *m* de guardería.

childhood infancia *f*, niñez *f*.

childish *a* pueril.

Chilean *adj* & *n* chileno,-a (*mf*).

chill 1 *n* (*illness*) resfriado *m*; (*coldness*) fresco *m*. **2** *vt* (*meat*) refrigerar; (*wine*) enfriar.

chilled *a* (*wine*) frío,-a.

chil(l)i chile *m*.

chilly *a* frío,-a.

chime *vi* repicar, sonar.

chimney chimenea *f*.

chimney flue cañón *m*.

chimpanzee chimpancé *m*.

chin barbilla *f*.

china loza *f*; **bone c.** porcelana *f*.

Chinese 1 *a* chino,-a. **2** *n* (*person*) chino,-a *mf*; (*language*) chino *m*.

chip 1 *n* (*in cup*) mella *f*; (*microchip*) chip *m*; (*in gambling*) ficha *f*; **chips** patatas *fpl* fritas. **2** *vt* (*china, glass*) mellar.

chiropodist pedicuro,-a *mf*.

chisel cincel *m*.

chives *npl* cebollino *m sing*.

choc-ice (*ice cream*) helado *m* cubierto de chocolate.

chock-a-block, **chock-full** *a* hasta los topes.

chocolate 1 *n* chocolate *m*; **chocolates** bombones *mpl*. **2** *a* de chocolate.

choice elección *f*; **a wide c.** un gran surtido; **there's no c.** no hay más remedio.

choir coro *m*.

choke 1 *vt* (*person*) ahogar; (*obstruct*) obstruir. **2** *vi* ahogarse.

cholesterol colesterol *m*.

choose* **1** *vt* elegir; (*decide on*) optar por. **2** *vi* elegir.

choos(e)y *a* exigente.

chop 1 *vt* (*wood*) cortar; (*tree*) talar; (*food*) cortar a pedacitos. **2** *n* (*of lamb, pork etc*) chuleta *f*.

- **chop down** *vt* (*tree*) talar.
- **chop off** *vt* (*branch, finger etc*) cortar.
- **chop up** *vt* cortar en pedazos.
chopper *fam* (*helicopter*) helicóptero *m*.
chopsticks *npl* palillos *mpl*.
chord (*musical*) acorde *m*.
chore tarea *f*.
chorus coro *m*; (*in a song*) estribillo *m*.
christen *vt* bautizar.
christening bautizo *m*.
Christian *n* & *a* cristiano,-a (*mf*).
Christian name nombre *m* de pila.
Christmas Navidad *f*; **Merry C.** feliz Navidad; **C. Day** (día *m* de) Navidad *f*; **C. Eve** Nochebuena *f*.
chrome cromo *m*.
chrysanthemum crisantemo *m*.
chubby *a* rellenito,-a.
chuck *vt fam* tirar.
chum compañero,-a *mf*.
chunk pedazo *m*.
church iglesia *f*.
chute (*for refuse*) conducto *m*; (*slide*) tobogán *m*.
cider sidra *f*.
cigar puro *m*.
cigarette cigarrillo *m*.
cigarette butt colilla *f*.
cigarette lighter mechero *m*.
cinema cine *m*.
cinnamon canela *f*.
circle 1 *n* círculo *m*; (*of people*) corro *m*; **in business circles** en el mundo de los negocios. **2** *vt* (*move round*) dar la vuelta a. **3** *vi* dar vueltas.
circuit circuito *m*.
circular *a* & *n* circular (*f*).
circulate 1 *vt* (*news*) hacer circular. **2** *vi* circular.
circulation (*of blood*) circulación *f*; (*of newspaper*) tirada *f*.
circumference circunferencia *f*.
circumstance circunstancia *f*; **under no circumstances** en ningún caso.
circus circo *m*.
citizen ciudadano,-a *mf*.

city ciudad *f*.
city center centro *m* urbano.
city hall ayuntamiento *m*.
civil *a* civil; (*polite*) educado,-a; **c. rights** derechos *mpl* civiles.
civilian *a* & *n* civil (*mf*).
civilization civilización *f*.
civil servant funcionario,-a *mf*.
civil service administración *f* pública.
claim 1 *vt* (*benefits, rights*) reclamar; (*assert*) afirmar. **2** *n* (*demand*) reclamación *f*; (*right*) derecho *m*; (*assertion*) pretensión *f*; **to put in a c.** pedir una indemnización.
clam almeja *f*.
clamp wheel c. cepo *m*.
clap *vi* aplaudir.
clapping aplauso(s) *m*(*pl*).
clarinet clarinete *m*.
clash 1 *vi* (*disagree*) estar en desacuerdo; (*colors*) desentonar; (*dates*) coincidir. **2** *n* (*sound*) sonido *m*; (*fight*) choque *m*; (*conflict*) conflicto *m*.
clasp 1 *n* (*on belt*) cierre *m*; (*on necklace*) broche *m*. **2** *vt* (*object*) agarrar.
class 1 *n* clase *f*; **second c. ticket** billete *m* de segunda (clase). **2** *vt* clasificar.
classic 1 *a* clásico,-a. **2** *n* (*author*) autor *m* clásico; (*work*) obra *f* clásica.
classical *a* clásico,-a.
classmate compañero,-a *mf* de clase.
classroom aula *f*.
clause oración *f*.
claw (*of bird, lion*) garra *f*; (*of cat*) uña *f*; (*of crab*) pinza *f*.
clay arcilla *f*.
clean 1 *a* limpio,-a; (*unmarked, pure*) sin defecto. **2** *adv* por completo; **it went c. through the middle** pasó justo por el medio. **3** *vt* (*room*) limpiar; **to c. one's teeth** lavarse los dientes.
cleaner limpiador,-a *mf*.
cleaning limpieza *f*.

cleaning woman señora *f* de la limpieza.

cleanly *adv* (*to break, cut*) limpiamente.

cleansing c. lotion leche *f* limpiadora.

clear 1 *a* claro,-a; (*road, day*) despejado,-a; (*obvious*) claro,-a; (*majority*) absoluto; (*profit*) neto; **to make sth c.** aclarar algo. **2** *adv* **stand c.!** ¡apártese!; **to stay c. of** evitar. **3** *vt* (*room*) vaciar; (*authorize*) autorizar; (*hurdle*) salvar; **to c. one's throat** aclararse la garganta; **to c. the table** quitar la mesa; **to c. sb of a charge** exculpar a algn de un delito. **4** *vi* (*sky*) despejarse.

• **clear away** *vt* quitar.

• **clear off** *vi fam* largarse.

• **clear out** *vt* (*room*) limpiar a fondo; (*cupboard*) vaciar.

• **clear up 1** *vt* (*tidy*) recoger; (*arrange*) ordenar; (*mystery*) resolver. **2** *vi* (*weather*) despejarse.

clearance (*of area*) despeje *m*.

clearance sale liquidación *f* (de existencias).

clear-cut *a* claro,-a.

clearly *adv* claramente; (*at start of sentence*) evidentemente.

clearway carretera *f* donde está prohibido parar.

clementine clementina *f*.

clench *vt* (*teeth, fist*) apretar.

clerical *a* (*of an office*) de oficina.

clerk (*office worker*) oficinista *mf*; (*civil servant*) funcionario,-a *mf*; (*in shop*) dependiente,-a *mf*.

clever *a* (*person*) inteligente; (*argument*) ingenioso,-a; **to be c. at sth** tener aptitud para algo.

click (*sound*) clic *m*.

client cliente *mf*.

cliff acantilado *m*.

climate clima *m*.

climax (*peak*) punto *m* culminante.

climb 1 *vt* (*ladder*) subir por; (*mountain*) escalar; (*tree*) trepar a. **2** *vi* (*plants*) trepar.

• **climb down** *vi* bajar.

climber alpinista *mf*, *Am* andinista *mf*.

cling* *vi* (*hang on*) agarrarse (**to** a); (*clothes*) ajustarse; **to c. together** unirse.

clinic (*in state hospital*) ambulatorio *m*; (*specialized*) clínica *f*.

clip¹ *vt* (*cut*) cortar; (*ticket*) picar.

clip² *n* (*for hair*) pasador *m*; (*for paper*) sujetapapeles *m inv*; (*brooch*) clip *m*.

• **clip on** *vt* (*brooch*) prender (**to** a); (*documents*) sujetar (**to** a).

clippers *npl* (*for hair*) maquinilla *f* para rapar; (*for nails*) cortaúñas *m inv*; (*for hedge*) tijeras *fpl* de podar.

clipping (*newspaper*) recorte *m*.

cloak (*garment*) capa *f*.

cloakroom guardarropa *m*; (*toilets*) servicios *mpl*.

clock reloj *m*; **to be open round the c.** estar abierto las 24 horas (del día).

clockwise *a & adv* en el sentido de las agujas del reloj.

close¹ 1 *a* (*in space, time*) cercano, -a; (*contact*) directo,-a; **c. to** cerca de; (*relationship*) estrecho,-a; (*friend*) íntimo; (*weather*) bochornoso,-a; **c. together** juntos. **2** *adv* cerca; **they live c. by** *or* **c. at hand** viven cerca.

close² 1 *vt* cerrar; (*bring to a close*) concluir; (*meeting*) levantar. **2** *vi* (*shut*) cerrar(se). **3** *n* fin *m*, final *m*.

• **close down** *vti* (*business*) cerrar para siempre.

• **close in** *vi* **to c. in on sb** rodear a algn.

• **close up 1** *vt* cerrar del todo. **2** *vi* cerrarse; (*ranks*) apretarse.

closely *adv* (*listen*) con atención; **c. contested/connected** muy reñido -a/relacionado,-a; **to follow (events) c.** seguir de cerca (los acontecimientos).

closet armario *m*.

closing time hora *f* de cierre.

clot 1 *n* (*of blood*) coágulo *m*. **2** *vi* coagularse.

cloth paño *m*; (*rag*) trapo *m*; (*tablecloth*) mantel *m*.

clothes *npl* ropa *f sing*.

clothes hanger percha *f*.

clothes line tendedero *m*.

clothes peg pinza *f*.

clothes shop tienda *f* de ropa.

clothing ropa *f*.

cloud *n* nube *f*.

• **cloud over** *vi* nublarse.

cloudy *a* (*sky*) nublado,-a.

clove (*of garlic*) diente *f*.

clown payaso *m*.

club (*society*) club *m*; (*for golf*) palo *m*; (*in cards*) trébol *m*.

clue (*sign*) indicio *m*; (*to mystery*) pista *f*; (*in crossword*) clave *f*; *fam* **I haven't a c.** no tengo (ni) idea.

clumsy *a* torpe; (*awkward*) tosco, -a.

clutch 1 *vt* agarrar. **2** *n* (*in vehicle*) embrague *m*.

clutter *vt* **to c. (up)** llenar de cosas.

Co *Com abbr of* **Company** C., Cª.
Cía.

coach 1 *n* autocar *m*; (*carriage*) carruaje *m*; (*of train*) coche *m*, vagón *m*. **2** *vt* (*student*) dar clases particulares a; (*team*) entrenar.

coal carbón *m*.

coal mine mina *f* de carbón.

coarse *a* (*material*) basto,-a; (*language*) grosero,-a.

coast costa *f*.

coat 1 *n* (*overcoat*) abrigo *m*; (*short*) chaquetón *m*; (*of animal*) pelo *m*; (*of paint*) capa *f*. **2** *vt* cubrir (**with** de); (*with liquid*) bañar (**with** en).

coat hanger percha *f*.

coating capa *f*.

cob mazorca *f*.

cobbled *a* adoquinado,-a.

cobweb telaraña *f*.

cocaine cocaína *f*.

cock (*bird*) gallo *m*.

cockle berberecho *m*.

cockpit cabina *f* del piloto.

cockroach cucaracha *f*.

cocktail cóctel *m*.

cocoa cacao *m*.

coconut coco *m*.

cod bacalao *m*.

code código *m*; (*symbol*) clave *f*; (*for telephone*) prefijo *m*.

cod-liver oil aceite *m* de hígado de bacalao.

co-ed 1 *a* mixto,-a. **2** *n* colegio *m* mixto.

coffee café *m*.

coffee bar cafetería *f*.

coffee break pausa *f* para el café.

coffeepot cafetera *f*.

coffee table mesita *f* de café.

coffin ataúd *m*.

cognac coñac *m*.

coil 1 *vt* **to c. (up)** enrollar. **2** *n* (*loop*) vuelta *f*; (*of rope*) rollo *m*.

coin moneda *f*.

coincide *vi* coincidir (**with** con).

coincidence coincidencia *f*.

Coke® (*abbr of* **Coca-Cola®**) coca-cola *f*.

cold 1 *a* frío,-a; **I'm c.** tengo frío; **it's c.** (*weather*) hace frío. **2** *n* frío *m*; (*illness*) resfriado *m*; **to catch a c.** resfriarse, acatarrarse; **to have a c.** estar resfriado,-a.

coldness frialdad *f*.

coleslaw ensalada *f* de col.

collaborate *vi* colaborar (**with** con).

collaboration colaboración *f*.

collapse 1 *vi* (*fall down*) derrumbarse; (*cave in*) hundirse. **2** *n* (*falling down*) derrumbamiento *m*; (*caving in*) hundimiento *m*.

collar *n* (*of garment*) cuello *m*; (*for dog*) collar *m*.

collarbone clavícula *f*.

colleague colega *mf*.

collect 1 *vt* (*gather*) recoger; (*stamps etc*) coleccionar; (*taxes*) recaudar. **2** *vi* (*for charity*) hacer una colecta (**for** para). **3** *adv* **to call c.** llamar a cobro revertido.

collection (*of mail*) recogida *f*; (*of*

money) colecta *f*; *(of stamps)* colección *f*; *(of taxes)* recaudación *f*.

collector *(of stamps)* coleccionista *mf*.

college ≈ centro *m* de enseñanza superior, ≈ politécnico *m*; **to go to c.** seguir estudios superiores.

collide *vi* chocar.

collision choque *m*.

colloquial *a* coloquial.

cologne (agua *f* de) colonia *f*.

Colombian *a* & *n* colombiano,-a *(mf)*.

colon *(punctuation)* dos puntos *mpl*.

colonel coronel *m*.

colony colonia *f*.

color 1 *n* color *m*; **c. film/television** película *f*/televisión *f* en color. 2 *vt* colorear.

colored *a* *(pencil)* de color; *(photograph)* en color.

colorful *a* *(with color)* lleno,-a de color; *(person)* pintoresco,-a.

column columna *f*.

coma coma *m*; **to go into a c.** entrar en coma.

comb 1 *n* peine *m*. 2 *vt* **to c. one's hair** peinarse.

combination combinación *f*.

combine 1 *vt* combinar. 2 *vi* combinarse; *(companies)* asociarse.

come* *vi* venir; *(arrive)* llegar; *(happen)* suceder; **to c. apart/undone** desatarse/ soltarse; **that's what comes of being too impatient** es lo que pasa por ser demasiado impaciente.

• **come about** *vi* ocurrir, suceder.

• **come across** *vt* *(thing)* encontrar por casualidad; **to c. across sb** tropezar con algn.

• **come along** *vi* *(arrive)* venir; *(make progress)* progresar; **c. along!** ¡venga!

• **come around** 1 *vt* *(corner)* dar la vuelta a. 2 *vi* *(visit)* venir; *(regain consciousness)* volver en sí.

• **come away** *vi* *(leave)* salir; *(part)* desprenderse **(from** de).

• **come back** *vi* *(return)* volver.

• **come by** 1 *vt* *(acquire)* adquirir. 2 *vi* *(visit)* **why don't you c. by?** ¿por qué no te pasas por casa?

• **come down** *vi* bajar; *(rain)* caer.

• **come forward** *vi* *(advance)* avanzar; *(volunteer)* ofrecerse.

• **come in** *vi* *(enter)* entrar; *(arrive)* *(train)* llegar; *(tide)* subir.

• **come into** *vt* *(enter)* entrar en; *(inherit)* heredar.

• **come off** 1 *vt* *(fall from)* caerse de. 2 *vi* *(button)* caerse; *(succeed)* salir bien.

• **come on** *vi* *(make progress)* progresar; **c. on!** *(hurry)* ¡venga!

• **come out** *vi* salir **(of** de); *(book)* aparecer; *(stain)* quitarse; **to c. out (on strike)** declararse en huelga.

• **come over** 1 *vi* venir. 2 *vt* **what's c. over you?** ¿qué te pasa?

• **come through** *vt* *(cross)* cruzar; *(illness)* recuperarse de; *(accident)* sobrevivir a.

• **come to** 1 *vi* *(regain consciousness)* volver en sí. 2 *vt* *(amount to)* ascender a; *(arrive at)* llegar a.

• **come up** *vi* *(rise)* subir; *(sun)* salir; *(approach)* acercarse **(to** a); *(difficulty, question)* surgir.

• **come up against** *vt* *(problems etc)* encontrarse con.

• **come upon** *vt see* **come across.**

• **come up to** *vt* *(equal)* igualar.

• **come up with** *vt* *(solution etc)* encontrar.

comedian cómico *m*.

comedy comedia *f*.

comfort 1 *n* comodidad *f*; *(consolation)* consuelo *m*. 2 *vt* consolar.

comfortable *a* cómodo,-a; *(temperature)* agradable.

comforter edredón *m*.

comic 1 *a* cómico,-a. 2 *n* tebeo *m*, comic *m*.

comic strip tira *f* cómica.

coming comings and goings idas y venidas *fpl*.

comma coma *f*.

command 1 *vt* mandar. **2** *n* (*order*) orden *f*; (*authority*) mando *m*; (*of language*) dominio *m*.

commemorate *vt* conmemorar.

commence *vti* comenzar.

comment *n* comentario *m*.

• **comment on** *vt* (*event etc*) comentar.

commentary comentario *m*.

commentator comentarista *mf*.

commerce comercio *m*.

commercial *a* comercial.

commission comisión *f*.

commit *vt* (*crime*) cometer; **to c. suicide** suicidarse.

commitment compromiso *m*.

committee comisión *f*, comité *m*.

commodity artículo *m*.

common *a* común; (*ordinary*) corriente.

commonly *adv* (*generally*) en general.

commonplace *a* corriente.

common sense sentido *m* común.

commotion alboroto *m*.

communal *a* (*bathroom etc*) comunitario,-a.

communicate 1 *vi* comunicarse (**with** con). **2** *vt* comunicar.

communication comunicación *f*.

communion comunión *f*.

community comunidad *f*; (*people*) colectividad *f*.

community center centro *m* social.

commute *vi* viajar diariamente al lugar de trabajo.

commuter persona *f* que viaja diariamente al lugar de trabajo.

commuting desplazarse diariamente al lugar de trabajo.

compact 1 *a* compacto,-a; (*style*) conciso,-a. **2** *n* (*for powder*) polvera *f*.

compact disc disco *m* compacto.

companion compañero,-a.

company compañía *f*; (*business*) empresa *f*; **to keep sb c.** hacer compañía algn.

comparative 1 *a* comparativo,-a;

(*relative*) relativo,-a. **2** *n* (*in grammar*) comparativo *m*.

comparatively *adv* relativamente.

compare 1 *vt* comparar (**to, with** con); (**as) compared with** en comparación con. **2** *vi* compararse.

comparison comparación *f*.

compartment (*on train*) departamento *m*.

compass brújula *f*; (**pair of) compasses** compás *m*.

compatible *a* compatible.

compel *vt* (*oblige*) obligar; **to c. sb to do sth** obligar a algn a hacer algo.

compensate *vti* compensar; **to c. sb for sth** indemnizar a algn de algo.

compensation (*for loss*) indemnización *f*.

compete *vi* competir.

competent *a* competente.

competition competencia *f*; (*contest*) concurso *m*.

competitive *a* competitivo,-a.

competitor competidor,-a *mf*.

compile *vt* compilar.

complain *vi* quejarse (**of, about** de).

complaint queja *f*; (*formal*) reclamación *f*; (*illness*) enfermedad *f*.

complete 1 *a* (*entire*) completo,-a; (*absolute*) total. **2** *vt* completar; (*form*) rellenar.

completely *adv* completamente, por completo.

complex 1 *a* complejo,-a. **2** *n* complejo *m*.

complexion tez *f*; *fig* aspecto *m*.

complicate *vt* complicar.

complicated *a* complicado,-a.

complication complicación *f*.

compliment cumplido *m*.

comply *vi* obedecer; **to c. with** (*order*) cumplir con.

compose *vti* componer; **to be composed of** componerse de; **to c. oneself** calmarse.

composed *a* (*calm*) sereno,-a.

composer compositor,-a *mf.*

composition (*essay*) redacción *f.*

compound compuesto *m.*

comprehensive *a* completo,-a; (*insurance*) a todo riesgo; **c. school** escuela *f* secundaria.

comprise *vt* (*include*) comprender; (*consist of*) constar de; (*constitute*) constituir.

compromise acuerdo *m.*

compulsive *a* compulsivo,-a.

compulsory *a* obligatorio,-a.

computer ordenador *m.*

computerized *a* informatizado,-a.

computer programmer programador,-a *mf* de ordenadores.

computer science informática *f.*

con *vt fam* estafar.

conceal *vt* ocultar; (*emotions*) disimular.

conceited *a* presuntuoso,-a.

conceivable *a* concebible.

concentrate 1 *vt* concentrar. **2** *vi* **to c. on sth** concentrarse en algo.

concentration concentración *f.*

concern 1 *vt* concernir; (*worry*) preocupar. **2** *n* (*worry*) preocupación *f*; (*business*) negocio *m.*

concerned *a* (*worried*) preocupado,-a (**about** por).

concerning *prep* con respecto a.

concert concierto *m.*

concise *a* conciso,-a.

conclude *vti* concluir.

conclusion conclusión *f.*

concrete 1 *n* hormigón *m.* **2** *a* (*made of concrete*) de hormigón; (*definite*) concreto,-a.

condemn *vt* condenar.

condensation condensación *f.*

condition condición *f*; **on c. that . . .** a condición de que . . .

conditioner acondicionador *m.*

condominium condominio *m.*

condom preservativo *m.*

conduct 1 *n* (*behavior*) conducta *f.* **2** *vt* (*lead*) guiar; (*business, orchestra*) dirigir.

conducted tour visita *f* acompañada.

conductor (*on bus*) cobrador *m*; (*on train*) revisor,-a *mf*; (*of orchestra*) director,-a *mf.*

cone cono *m*; **ice-cream c.** cucurucho *m.*

conference congreso *m.*

confess *vti* confesar; (*to priest*) confesarse.

confession confesión *f.*

confetti confeti *m.*

confidence confianza *f*; **in c.** en confianza.

confident *a* seguro,-a.

confidential *a* (*secret*) confidencial; (*entrusted*) de confianza.

confidently *adv* con seguridad.

confine *vt* limitar.

confirm *vt* confirmar.

confirmation confirmación *f.*

confirmed *a* empedernido,-a.

confiscate *vt* confiscar.

conflict 1 *n* conflicto *m.* **2** *vi* chocar (**with** con).

conflicting *a* contradictorio,-a.

conform *vi* conformarse; **to c. to** or **with** (*customs*) amoldarse a; (*rules*) someterse a.

confront *vt* hacer frente a.

confuse *vt* (*person*) despistar; (*thing*) confundir (**with** con); **to get confused** confundirse.

confused *a* (*person*) confundido,-a; (*mind, ideas*) confuso,-a.

confusing *a* confuso,-a.

confusion confusión *f.*

congested *a* (*street*) repleto,-a de gente.

congestion congestión *f.*

congratulate *vt* felicitar.

congratulations *npl* felicitaciones *fpl*; **c.!** ¡enhorabuena!

congregate *vi* congregarse.

congress congreso *m.*

congressman diputado *m*, miembro *m* del Congreso.

congresswoman diputada *f*, miembro *f* del Congreso.

conjugate *vt* conjugar.

conjugation conjugación *f.*

conjunction conjunción *f.*

conjurer prestidigitador,-a *mf.*

conjuring trick juego *m* de manos.

con man estafador *m*.

connect 1 *vt* unir; (*wires*) empalmar; (*install*) instalar; (*electricity*) conectar; (*on phone*) poner. **2** *vi* (*train, flight*) enlazar (**with** con).

connected *a* unido,-a; (*events*) relacionado,-a.

connection conexión *f*; (*installation*) instalación *f*; (*rail, flight*) enlace *m*; (*of ideas*) relación *f*; (*person*) contacto *m*; **in c. with** (*regarding*) con respecto a.

conquer *vt* (*enemy, bad habit*) vencer; (*country*) conquistar.

conscience conciencia *f*.

conscientious *a* concienzudo,-a.

conscious *a* (*aware*) consciente; (*choice etc*) deliberado,-a.

consent 1 *n* consentimiento *m*. **2** *vi* consentir (**to** en).

consequence consecuencia *f*.

consequently *adv* por consiguiente.

conservation conservación *f*.

conservative *a & n* conservador, -a (*mf*).

conservatory (*greenhouse*) invernadero *m*.

conserve 1 *vt* conservar. **2** *n* conserva *f*.

consider *vt* (*ponder on, regard*) considerar; (*keep in mind*) tener en cuenta; **to c. doing sth** pensar hacer algo.

considerable *a* considerable.

considerate *a* considerado,-a.

consideration consideración *f*.

considering *prep* teniendo en cuenta.

consignment envío *m*.

consist *vi* **to c. of** consistir en.

consistent *a* consecuente; **c. with** de acuerdo con.

consolation consuelo *m*; **c. prize** premio *m* de consolación.

console¹ *vt* consolar.

console² consola *f*.

consonant consonante *f*.

conspicuous *a* (*striking*) llamativo,-a; (*easily seen*) visible.

constable policía *m*.

constant *a* constante; (*continuous*) incesante; (*loyal*) fiel.

constantly *adv* constantemente.

constipated *a* estreñido,-a.

constitution constitución *f*.

construct *vt* construir.

construction construcción *f*.

consul cónsul *mf*.

consulate consulado *m*.

consult *vti* consultar (**about** sobre).

consultancy (**firm**) asesoría *f*, consulting *m*.

consultant (*doctor*) especialista *mf*; (*in business*) asesor,-a *mf*.

consultation consulta *f*.

consume *vt* consumir.

consumer consumidor,-a *mf*.

consumption consumo *m*.

contact 1 *n* contacto *m*. **2** *vt* ponerse en contacto con.

contact lenses lentes *fpl* de contacto.

contagious *a* contagioso,-a.

contain *vt* contener.

container (*box, package*) recipiente *m*; (*for shipping*) contenedor *m*.

contemporary *a & n* contemporáneo,-a (*mf*).

contempt desprecio *m*.

contend *vi* competir; **there are many problems to c. with** se han planteado muchos problemas.

content¹ contenido *m*; **table of contents** índice *m* de materias.

content² *a* contento,-a.

contented *a* satisfecho,-a.

contest prueba *f*.

contestant concursante *mf*.

context contexto *m*.

continent continente *m*; **(on) the C.** (en) Europa.

continental *a* continental; (*European*) **C.** europeo,-a.

continual *a* continuo,-a, constante.

continually *adv* continuamente.

continuously *adv* continuamente.

continue *vti* continuar, seguir; **to c. to do sth** seguir *or* continuar haciendo algo.

continuous *a* continuo,-a.

contraceptive *a & n* anticonceptivo (*mf*).

contract contrato *m*.

contradict *vt* contradecir.

contradiction contradicción *f*.

contrary **1** *n* **on the c.** todo lo contrario. **2** *adv* **c.** **to** en contra de.

contrast contraste *m*.

contrasting *a* opuesto,-a.

contribute **1** *vt* (*money*) contribuir; (*ideas, information*) aportar. **2** *vi* contribuir; (*in discussion*) participar; (*to publication*) colaborar (**to** en).

contribution (*of money*) contribución *f*; (*to publication*) colaboración *f*.

contrive *vi* **to c. to do sth** buscar la forma de hacer algo.

contrived *a* artificial.

control **1** *vt* controlar; (*person, animal*) dominar; (*vehicle*) manejar; **to c. one's temper** controlarse. **2** *n* (*power*) control *m*; (*authority*) autoridad *f*; (*in car, plane*) (*device*) mando *m*; (*on TV*) botón *m* de control; **out of c.** fuera de control; **to be in c.** estar al mando; **to be under c.** (*situation*) estar bajo control; **to go out of c.** descontrolarse; **to lose c.** perder los estribos.

control tower torre *f* de control.

convalesce *vi* convalecer.

convalescence convalecencia *f*.

convalescent home clínica *f* de reposo.

convenience comodidad *f*.

convenience food comida *f* precocinada.

convenient *a* (*arrangement*) conveniente; (*time*) oportuno,-a; (*place*) bien situado,-a.

convent convento *m*.

conversation conversación *f*.

converse *vi* conversar.

convert *vt* convertir (**into** en).

convertible **1** *a* convertible. **2** *n* (*car*) descapotable *m*.

convey *vt* (*carry*) transportar; (*sound*) transmitir; (*idea*) comunicar.

conveyor belt cinta *f* transportadora.

convict *vt* declarar culpable a.

conviction (*belief*) creencia *f*, convicción *f*; (*for crime*) condena *f*.

convince *vt* convencer.

convincing *a* convincente.

convoy convoy *m*.

cook **1** *vt* cocinar, guisar; (*dinner*) preparar. **2** *vi* (*person*) cocinar, guisar; (*food*) cocerse. **3** *n* cocinero,-a *mf*.

cookbook libro *m* de cocina.

cooker cocina *f*.

cookery cocina *f*.

cookie galleta *f*.

cooking cocina *f*.

cooking apple manzana *f* ácida para cocinar.

cool **1** *a* fresco,-a; (*calm*) tranquilo,-a; (*reserved*) frío,-a; **it's c.** (*weather*) hace fresquito. **2** *n* (*coolness*) fresco *m*; **to lose one's c.** perder la calma. **3** *vt* (*air*) refrescar; (*drink*) enfriar.

• **cool down** *or* **off** *vi* (*something hot*) enfriarse; *fig* calmarse; (*feelings*) enfriarse.

cooler (*for food*) nevera *f* portátil.

coolness (*calmness*) calma *f*; (*composure*) aplomo *m*.

cooperate *vi* cooperar.

cooperation cooperación *f*.

coop up *vt* encerrar.

cop *fam* (*policeman*) poli *m*.

cope *vi* arreglárselas; **to c. with** (*person, work*) poder con; (*problem*) hacer frente a.

copper (*metal*) cobre *m*.

copy **1** *n* copia *f*; (*of book*) ejemplar *m*. **2** *vti* copiar.

• **copy down** *vt* (*letter etc*) pasar a limpio.

cord (*string*) cuerda *f*; (*electrical*) cordón *m*.

cordial (*drink*) licor *m*.

cordon off *vt* acordonar.

corduroy pana *f*.

core (*of fruit*) corazón *m*; *fig* centro *m*.

cork corcho *m*.

corkscrew sacacorchos *m inv*.

corn[1] (*maize*) maíz *m*; (*grain*) granos *mpl*; (*seed*) cereal *m*.

corn[2] (*on foot*) callo *m*.

corned beef carne *f* acecinada.

corner 1 *n* (*of street*) esquina *f*; (*bend in road*) curva *f*; (*of room*) rincón *m*; (*in soccer*) **c. (kick)** córner *m*. **2** *vt* (*enemy*) arrinconar; (*market*) acaparar.

cornet (*for ice cream*) cucurucho *m*.

cornflakes *npl* copos *mpl* de maíz, cornflakes *mpl*.

corny *a* gastado,-a.

corporal cabo *m*.

corpse cadáver *m*.

correct 1 *vt* (*mistake*) corregir; (*child*) reprender. **2** *a* correcto, -a; (*behavior*) formal.

correction corrección *f*.

correctly *adv* correctamente.

correspond *vi* corresponder; (*by letter*) escribirse; **to c. to** equivaler a.

correspondence correspondencia *f*; **c. course** curso *m* por correspondencia.

corresponding *a* (*matching*) correspondiente.

corridor pasillo *m*.

corrugated *a* **c. iron** hierro *m* ondulado.

corrupt *a* (*person*) corrupto,-a; (*actions*) deshonesto,-a.

cosmetic cosmético *m*.

cosmonaut cosmonauta *mf*.

cost 1 *n* (*price*) precio *m*; coste *m*; **at all costs** a toda costa. **2** *vti** costar, valer; **how much does it c.?** ¿cuánto cuesta?

Costa Rican *a & n* costarricense (*mf*).

costly *a* costoso,-a.

costume traje *m*; **c. jewelery** bisutería *f*.

cot cuna *f*.

cottage casa *f* de campo.

cottage cheese requesón *m*.

cotton algodón *m*; (*thread*) hilo *m*.

cotton wool algodón *m* hidrófilo.

couch sofá *m*.

couchette litera *f*.

cough 1 *vi* toser. **2** *n* tos *f*.

• **cough up** *vt fam* **to c. up the money** soltar la pasta.

cough syrup jarabe *m* para la tos.

could *v aux of* **can**[1].

council (*body*) consejo *m*; **town c.** consejo *m* municipal.

council house ≈ vivienda *f* de protección oficial.

councilor concejal *mf*.

count[1] **1** *vt* contar. **2** *vi* contar; **that doesn't c.** eso no vale.

• **count in** *vt* incluir a, contar con.

• **count on** *vt* contar con.

• **count out** *vt* (*banknotes*) contar uno por uno.

count[2] (*nobleman*) conde *m*.

countdown cuenta *f* atrás.

counter (*in shop*) mostrador *m*; (*in bank*) ventanilla *f*; (*in board games*) ficha *f*.

counter- *prefix* contra-.

counterattack contraataque *m*.

counter clockwise *a & adv* en sentido inverso a las agujas del reloj.

counterfoil (*of check*) matriz *f*.

country (*state*) país *m*; (*rural area*) campo *m*; **native c.** patria *f*.

countryside (*area*) campo *m*; (*scenery*) paisaje *m*.

county condado *m*.

couple (*of people*) pareja *f*; (*of things*) par *m*; **a married c.** un matrimonio; **a c. of times** un par de veces.

coupon cupón *m*.

courage valor *m*.

courageous *a* valiente.

courier (*messenger*) mensajero,-a *mf*; (*guide*) guía *mf* turístico,-a.

course (*of river*) curso *m*; (*of ship, plane*) rumbo *m*; (*series*) ciclo *m*; (*for golf*) campo *m*; (*of meal*) plato *m*; (*degree*) carrera *f*; (*in single subject*) curso *m*; (*short course*) cursillo *m*; **in the c. of construction** en vías de construcción; **a c. of treatment** un tratamiento; **of c.** claro, por supuesto; **of c. not!** ¡claro que no!

court (*of law*) tribunal *m*; (*royal*) corte *f*; (*for sport*) pista *f*, cancha *f*.

courteous *a* cortés.

courtroom sala *f* de justicia.

courtyard patio *m*.

cousin primo,-a *mf*.

cover 1 *vt* cubrir (**with** de); (*with lid*) tapar; (*hide*) disimular; (*protect*) abrigar; (*include*) abarcar. **2** *n* cubierta *f*; (*lid, of book*) tapa *f*; (*on bed*) manta *f*; (*of chair etc*) funda *f*; (*of magazine*) portada *f*; (*in restaurant*) cubierto *m*; (*in insurance*) cobertura *f* completa; **to take c.** refugiarse.

• **cover over** *vt* (*floor etc*) recubrir.

• **cover up 1** *vt* cubrir; (*crime*) encubrir. **2** *vi* (*person*) abrigarse; **to c. up for sb** encubrir a algn.

coveralls *npl* mono *m* sing.

cover charge (*in restaurant*) precio *m* del cubierto.

covering 1 *n* cubierta *f*. **2** *a* (*letter*) explicatorio,-a.

cow vaca *f*.

coward cobarde *mf*.

cowardice cobardía *f*.

cowardly *a* cobarde.

cowboy vaquero *m*.

cozy *a* (*atmosphere*) acogedor,-a; (*bed*) calentito,-a.

crab cangrejo *m*.

crack 1 *vt* (*cup*) partir; (*nut*) cascar; (*whip*) hacer restallar; (*joke*) contar. **2** *vi* (*glass*) partirse; (*wall*) agrietarse; *fam* **to get cracking on sth** ponerse a hacer algo. **3** *n* (*in cup*) raja *f*; (*in wall, ground*) grieta *f*; (*of whip*) restallido *m*;

(*of gun*) detonación *f*; *fam* (*drug*) crack *m*.

• **crack up** *vi* (*go insane*) desquiciarse; (*with laughter*) partirse de risa.

cracker galleta *f* seca; (*firework*) petardo *m*.

crackpot *fam* chiflado,-a.

cradle (*baby's*) cuna *f*.

craft (*occupation*) oficio *m*; (*art*) arte *m*; (*skill*) destreza *f*.

craftsman artesano *m*.

crafty *a* astuto,-a.

cram 1 *vt* atiborrar; **crammed with** atestado,-a de. **2** *vi* (*for exam*) empollar.

cramp (*in leg etc*) calambre *m*.

cramped *a* apretado,-a.

crane (*device*) grúa *f*.

crash 1 *vt* **to c. one's car** tener un accidente con el coche. **2** *vi* (*car, plane*) estrellarse; (*collide*) chocar; **to c. into** estrellarse contra. **3** *n* (*noise*) estrépito *m*; (*collision*) choque *m*; (*of market*) quiebra *f*; **car/plane c.** accidente *m* de coche/avión.

crash course curso *m* intensivo.

crash helmet casco *m* protector.

crash-land *vi* hacer un aterrizaje forzoso.

crash landing aterrizaje *m* forzoso.

crate caja *f* (para embalaje).

craving ansia *f*.

crawl 1 *vi* (*baby*) gatear; (*vehicle*) avanzar lentamente. **2** *n* (*swimming*) crol *m*.

crayon cera *f*.

craze manía *f*; (*fashion*) moda *f*.

crazy *a* loco,-a.

creak *vi* (*hinge*) chirriar.

cream (*of milk*) nata *f*; **c. colored** color crema.

cream cheese queso *m* crema.

creamy *a* cremoso,-a.

crease 1 *n* (*wrinkle*) arruga *f*; (*on trousers*) raya *f*. **2** *vt* (*clothes*) arrugar. **3** *vi* arrugarse.

create *vt* crear.

creation creación *f*.

creative a (person) creativo,-a.
creature (animal) criatura f.
crèche guardería f.
credible a creíble.
credit 1 n (financial) crédito m;
(merit) honor m; **on c.** a crédito; **to
be a c. to** hacer honor a. **2** vt hacer
honor a. **2** vt abonar en cuenta a
algn.
credit card tarjeta f de crédito.
credit facilities facilidades fpl de
pago.
creditworthy a solvente.
creek cala f; riachuelo m.
creep* vi (insect) arrastrarse; (cat)
deslizarse; (person) arrastrarse.
creepy a fam espeluznante.
cremate vt incinerar.
crematorium crematorio m.
crepe paper papel m crespón.
cress berro m.
crest (of cock, wave) cresta f; (of
hill) cima f.
crew (of plane, yacht) tripulación f.
crib 1 n (for baby) cuna f. **2** vt
(copy) copiar.
cricket¹ (insect) grillo m.
cricket² (game) cricket m.
crime delincuencia f; (offence) delito m.
criminal a & n criminal (mf).
cripple lisiado,-a mf.
crisis (pl **crises**) crisis f inv.
crisp a crujiente; (lettuce) fresco, -a.
critic crítico,-a mf.
critical a crítico,-a.
critically adv **c. ill** gravemente
enfermo,-a.
criticism crítica f.
criticize vt criticar.
crochet ganchillo m.
crockery loza f.
crocodile cocodrilo m.
crocus crocus m.
crook fam caco m.
crooked a (stick, picture) torcido,
-a; (path) tortuoso,-a.
crop cultivo m; (harvest) cosecha f.
• **crop up** vi surgir.
croquet croquet m.
cross 1 n cruz f; (of breeds) cruce m;

c. section sección f transversal.
2 vt cruzar. **3** vi cruzar; (roads)
cruzarse. **4** a (angry) enfadado,-a.
• **cross off** or **out** vt tachar.
• **cross over** vi cruzar.
cross-country race cros m.
cross-eyed a bizco,-a.
crossing pedestrian c. paso m de
peatones; **sea c.** travesía f.
cross-reference referencia f cru-
zada.
crossroads cruce m; fig encrucijada f.
crosswalk paso m de peatones.
crossword (puzzle) crucigrama
m.
crouch vi **to c. (down)** agacharse.
crow cuervo m.
crowbar palanca f.
crowd 1 n muchedumbre f; (gang)
pandilla f; **the c.** el vulgo; **there
was such a c. there** había tantí-
sima gente allí. **2** vi **to c. in/out** en-
trar/salir en tropel.
• **crowd round** vt apiñarse alrededor de.
crowded a lleno,-a, atestado,-a.
crown corona f.
crucial a decisivo,-a.
crude a (manners, style) grosero,
-a.
cruel a cruel (**to** con).
cruelty crueldad f (**to** hacia).
cruet set vinagreras fpl.
cruise 1 vi (ship) hacer un crucero;
(car) viajar a velocidad constante;
(plane) viajar a velocidad de crucero. **2** n (on ship) crucero m.
crumb miga f.
crumble 1 vt desmigar. **2** vi (wall)
desmoronarse; (bread) desmiga-
jarse.
crumbly a que se desmigaja.
crummy a fam chungo,-a.
crumple vt (clothes) arrugar.
crunch 1 vt (food) mascar. **2** n cru-
jido m.
crunchy a crujiente.
crush 1 vt aplastar; (wrinkle) arrugar; (grind) moler. **2** n (of people)
gentío m.

crust corteza *f.*
crutch (*for walking*) muleta *f.*
cry 1 *vi* gritar; (*weep*) llorar. **2** *n* grito *m*; (*weep*) llanto *m.*
• **cry off** *vi* rajarse.
• **cry out** *vi* gritar; **to c. out for sth** pedir algo a gritos.
• **cry over** *vt* llorar por.
crystal cristal *m.*
cub (*young animal*) cachorro,-a *mf*; (*junior scout*) niño *m* explorador.
Cuban *a & n* cubano,-a (*mf*).
cube cubo *m*; (*of sugar*) terrón *m.*
cubic *a* cúbico,-a.
cubicle cubículo *m.*
cuckoo cuco *m.*
cucumber pepino *m.*
cuddle 1 *vt* abrazar. **2** *vi* abrazarse.
• **cuddle up to** *vt* acurrucarse contra.
cuddly toy muñeco *m* de peluche.
cue (*in play*) pie *m*; indicación *f.*
cuff (*of sleeve*) puño *m*; (*of trousers*) dobladillo *m.*
cufflinks *npl* gemelos *mpl.*
cul-de-sac callejón *m* sin salida.
culprit culpable *mf.*
cultivate *vt* cultivar.
cultivated *a* (*person*) culto,-a.
cultural *a* cultural.
culture cultura *f.*
cultured *a* (*person*) culto,-a.
cumbersome *a* (*bulky*) voluminoso,-a.
cunning 1 *a* astuto,-a. **2** *n* astucia *f.*
cup taza *f*; (*trophy*) copa *f.*
cupboard armario *m*; (*on wall*) alacena *f.*
curable *a* curable.
curb bordillo *m.*
cure 1 *vt* curar. **2** *n* (*remedy*) cura *f*, remedio *m.*
curiosity curiosidad *f.*
curious *a* (*inquisitive*) curioso,-a; (*odd*) extraño,-a.
curl 1 *vt* (*hair*) rizar. **2** *vi* rizarse. **3** *n* (*of hair*) rizo *m.*

• **curl up** *vi* (*cat etc*) enroscarse; (*person*) hacerse un ovillo.
curly *a* rizado,-a.
currant pasa *f* (de Corinto).
currency moneda *f*; **foreign c.** divisas *fpl.*
current *a* actual; (*opinion*) general; (*year*) en curso.
current account cuenta *f* corriente.
current affairs actualidad *f sing* (política).
currently *adv* actualmente.
curriculum (*pl* curricula) plan *m* de estudios; **c. vitae** (*resume*) currículum *m* (vitae).
curry curry *m.*
curse *vi* blasfemar.
cursor cursor *m.*
curtain cortina *f.*
curts(e)y 1 *n* reverencia *f.* **2** *vi* hacer una reverencia (**to** a).
curve 1 *n* curva *f.* **2** *vi* (*road, river*) describir una curva.
cushion cojín *m*; (*large*) almohadón *m.*
custard natillas *fpl.*
custom (*habit*) costumbre *f.*
customer cliente *mf.*
customs *n sing or pl* aduana *f.*
customs duty derechos *mpl* de aduana.
customs officer agente *mf* de aduana.
cut 1 *vt** cortar; (*stone*) tallar; (*reduce*) reducir; (*divide up*) dividir (**into** en). **2** *vi** cortar. **3** *n* corte *m*; (*in skin*) cortadura *f*; (*wound*) herida *f*; (*with knife*) cuchillada *f*; (*of meat*) clase *f* de carne; (*reduction*) reducción *f.*
• **cut away** (*remove*) cortar.
• **cut back** *vt* (*expenses*) reducir; (*production*) disminuir.
• **cut down** *vt* (*tree*) talar.
• **cut down on** *vt* reducir.
• **cut off** *vt* (*water etc*) cortar; (*place*) aislar; (*heir*) excluir.
• **cut out 1** *vt* (*from newspaper*) recortar; (*delete*) suprimir; (*person*)

to be c. out for sth estar hecho,-a
para algo; *fam* c. it out! ¡basta ya!
2 *vi* (engine) calarse.
• **cut up** *vt* cortar en pedazos.
cutback reducción *f* (in de).
cute *a* mono,-a, lindo,-a.
cutlery cubiertos *mpl.*
cutlet chuleta *f.*
cutting (from newspaper) recorte
m.
CV, cv *abbr of* **curriculum vitae.**
cycle 1 *n* ciclo *m*; (bicycle) bicicleta
f; (motorcycle) moto *f*. 2 *vi* ir en bicicleta.
cycling ciclismo *m.*
cyclist ciclista *mf.*
cylinder cilindro *m*; (for gas) bombona *f.*
cymbal platillo *m.*
Czech 1 *a* checo,-a. 2 *n* (person)
checo,-a (mf); (language) checo *m.*

D

dab *vt* (apply) aplicar; (touch
lightly) tocar ligeramente.
dad, daddy *fam* papá *m*, papi *m.*
daffodil narciso *m.*
daft *a* (idea) tonto,-a.
daily 1 *a* diario,-a. 2 *adv* diariamente. 3 *n* (newspaper) diario *m.*
dairy lechería *f*; **d. farming** industria *f* lechera; **d. produce** productos *mpl* lácteos.
daisy margarita *f.*
dam (barrier) dique *m*; (lake)
presa *f.*
damage 1 *n* daño *m*; (to health,
reputation) perjuicio *m*. 2 *vt*
(harm) dañar; (spoil) estropear.
damn *fam* 1 *interj* d. (it)! ¡maldito,
-a sea! 2 *n* I don't give a d. me importa un bledo. 3 *a* maldito,-a.
4 *adv* (very) muy, sumamente.
damp 1 *a* húmedo,-a; (wet) mojado,-a. 2 *n* humedad *f.*
dampen *vt* humedecer.
dampness humedad *f.*
dance 1 *n* baile *m*; (classical, tri-
bal) danza *f*. 2 *vti* bailar.

dance hall salón *m* de baile.
dancer (by profession) bailarín,
-ina *mf*; **she's a good d.** baila muy
bien.
dandelion diente *m* de león.
dandruff caspa *f.*
Dane danés,-esa *mf.*
danger (peril) peligro *m*; (risk)
riesgo *m*; (of war etc) amenaza *f*;
out of d. fuera de peligro.
dangerous *a* peligroso,-a; (risky)
arriesgado,-a; (harmful) nocivo,
-a; (illness) grave.
dangerously *adv* peligrosamente.
Danish 1 *a* danés,-esa. 2 *n* (language) danés *m.*
dare 1 *vi* atreverse, osar. 2 *vt* (challenge) desafiar; **to d. to do sth** atreverse a hacer algo.
daring *a* osado,-a.
dark 1 *a* (unlit, color) oscuro,-a;
(hair, complexion) moreno,-a;
(eyes, future) negro,-a. 2 *n* (darkness) oscuridad *f.*
dark-haired *a* moreno,-a.
darkness oscuridad *f.*
dark-skinned *a* de piel oscura.
darling *a & n* querido,-a (mf).
dart (missile) dardo *m*; **darts** *sing*
(game) dardos *mpl.*
dartboard diana *f.*
dash 1 *n* (hyphen) guión *m*. 2 *vi*
(rush) correr.
• **dash off** *vi* salir corriendo.
dashboard salpicadero *m.*
data *npl* datos *mpl.*
database base *m* de datos.
data processing (act) proceso *m*
de datos; (science) informática *f.*
date¹ *n* fecha *f*; (social event) compromiso *m*; (with girl, boy) cita *f*;
(person dated) ligue *m*; **what's the
d. today?** ¿qué día es hoy?; **out
of d.** (ideas) anticuado,-a; (expression) desusado,-a; (invalid)
caducado,-a; **to be up to d.** estar
al día.
• **date back to, date from** *vt* datar de; (origins etc) remontarse a.
date² (fruit) dátil *m.*
daughter hija *f.*

daughter-in-law nuera *f.*

dawdle *vi* (*walking*) andar despacio; (*waste time*) perder el tiempo.

dawn amanecer *m.*

day día *m;* **(on) the next** or **following d.** el or al día siguiente; **the d. after tomorrow** pasado mañana; **the d. before yesterday** anteayer.

daylight luz *f* del día.

day return (*ticket*) billete *m* de ida y vuelta para el mismo día.

daytime día *m.*

dead 1 *a* muerto,-a; **he was shot d.** le mataron a tiros. **2** *adv fam* (*tired, easy*) muy.

dead end (*street*) callejón *m* sin salida.

deadline (*date*) fecha *f* tope; (*time*) hora *f* tope.

deaf 1 *a* sordo,-a; **d. mute** sordomudo,-a *mf.* **2** *npl* **the d.** los sordos.

deafness sordera *f.*

deal (*in business, politics*) trato *m;* (*amount*) cantidad *f;* (*at cards*) reparto *m;* **business d.** contrato *m;* **to do a d. with sb** (*transaction*) cerrar un trato con algn; (*agreement*) pactar algo con algn; **it's a d.!** ¡trato hecho!; **a good d. (of sth)** una gran parte (de algo); **a good d. slower** mucho más despacio.

• **deal* in** *vt* (*goods*) comerciar en; (*drugs*) traficar con.

• **deal* out** *vt* repartir.

• **deal* with** *vt* (*firm, person*) tratar con; (*subject, problem*) abordar; (*in book etc*) tratar de.

dealer (*in goods*) comerciante *mf;* (*in drugs*) traficante *mf.*

dealings *npl* (*relations*) trato *m sing;* (*in business*) negocios *mpl.*

dear 1 *a* (*loved*) querido,-a; (*expensive*) caro,-a; (*in letter*) **D. Andrew** Querido Andrew; **D. Madam** Estimada señora; **D. Sir(s)** Muy señor(es) mío(s). **2** *n* querido,-a *mf;* **my d.** mi vida. **3** *interj* **oh d.!, d. me!** (*surprise*) ¡vaya por Dios!; (*disappointment*) ¡qué pena!

death muerte *f.*

death certificate certificado *m* de defunción.

debate 1 *n* debate *m.* **2** *vti* discutir.

debit 1 *n* débito *m.* **2** *vt* **to d. sb's account** cargar una suma en la cuenta de algn.

debt deuda *f.*

decade década *f,* decenio *m.*

decaffeinated *a* descafeinado,-a.

decay 1 (*of food, body*) descomposición *f;* (*of teeth*) caries *f inv;* (*of buildings*) desmoronamiento *m.*

deceive *vt* (*mislead*) engañar; (*lie to*) mentir.

December diciembre *m.*

decent *a* decente; (*person*) honrado,-a; (*kind*) simpático,-a.

decide 1 *vt* decidir; **to d. to do sth** decidir hacer algo. **2** *vi* (*reach decision*) decidirse.

• **decide on** *vt* (*choose*) optar por.

decimal 1 *a* decimal; **d. point** coma *f* (de fracción decimal). **2** *n* decimal *m.*

decision decisión *f.*

decisive *a* (*resolute*) decidido,-a; (*conclusive*) decisivo,-a.

deck (*of ship*) cubierta *f.*

deckchair tumbona *f.*

declare *vt* declarar; (*winner, innocence*) proclamar.

decline *vi* (*decrease*) disminuir; (*amount*) bajar; (*business*) decaer; (*deteriorate*) deteriorarse; (*health*) empeorar.

decorate *vt* (*adorn*) decorar (**with** con); (*paint*) pintar; (*wallpaper*) empapelar.

decoration (*decor*) decoración *f.*

decorative *a* decorativo,-a.

decorator decorador,-a *mf;* (*painter*) pintor,-a *mf;* (*paper-hanger*) empapelador,-a *mf.*

decrease 1 *n* disminución *f;* (*in speed, size, price*) reducción *f.* **2** *vi* disminuir; (*price, temperature*) bajar; (*speed, size*) reducirse. **3** *vt* disminuir; (*price, temperature*) bajar.

dedicated *a* dedicado,-a, entregado,-a.

deduct vt descontar (**from** de).

deduction (conclusion) conclusión f; (subtraction) descuento m.

deed (act) acto m; (legal document) escritura f.

deep a profundo,-a; (breath, sigh) hondo,-a; (voice) bajo,-a; **it's ten meters d.** tiene diez metros de profundidad.

deep-freeze 1 n congelador m. **2** vt congelar.

deer n inv ciervo m.

defeat 1 vt derrotar. **2** n (of army, team) derrota f.

defect n defecto m.

defective a (faulty) defectuoso,-a.

defend vt defender.

defendant n acusado,-a mf.

defense n defensa f.

defiant a (behavior) desafiante; (person) insolente.

defense n defensa f.

deficiency n falta f, carencia f.

deficient a deficiente; **to be d. in sth** carecer de algo.

deficit n déficit m.

define vt definir; (duties, powers) delimitar.

definite a (clear) claro,-a; (progress) notable; (date, place) determinado,-a.

definitely adv sin duda.

definition n definición f.

deformed a deforme.

defrost vt (freezer, food) descongelar.

defy vt desafiar; (law, order) contravenir.

degenerate vi degenerar (**into** en).

degree n grado m; (qualification) título m; **to some d.** hasta cierto punto; **to have a d. in science** ser licenciado en ciencias.

de-icer n anticongelante m.

dejected a deprimido,-a.

delay 1 vt (flight, train) retrasar; (person) entretener; (postpone) aplazar. **2** n retraso m.

delegate 1 n delegado,-a mf. **2** vt

delegar (**to** en); **to d. sb to do sth** encargar a algn que haga algo.

delegation n delegación f.

delete vt suprimir; (cross out) tachar.

deliberate a (intentional) deliberado,-a.

deliberately adv (intentionally) a propósito; (unhurriedly) pausadamente.

delicacy (food) manjar m (exquisito).

delicate a delicado,-a; (handwork) fino,-a; (instrument) sensible; (flavor) fino,-a.

delicatessen n delicatessen m.

delicious a delicioso,-a.

delight 1 n (pleasure) placer m; (source of pleasure) encanto m; **he took d. in it** le encantó. **2** vt encantar.

delighted a encantado,-a.

delightful a (person) encantador, -a; (view) muy agradable; (meal, weather) delicioso,-a.

delinquent a & n delincuente (mf).

deliver vt (goods, letters) repartir; (parcel, manuscript etc) entregar; (speech, verdict) pronunciar; (baby) dar a luz.

delivery (of goods) reparto m; (of package, manuscript etc) entrega f; (of baby) parto m.

delude vt engañar; **don't d. yourself** no te hagas ilusiones.

deluxe a de lujo inv.

demand 1 n (request) petición f; (for pay rise, rights) reclamación f; (need) necesidad f; (claim) exigencia f; (economic) demanda f; **to be in d.** ser solicitado,-a. **2** vt exigir; (rights) reclamar; **to d. that . . .** insistir en que . . . (+ subjunctive).

demanding a (hard to please) exigente; (job) agotador,-a.

demerara (sugar) azúcar m moreno.

democracy n democracia f.

democratic a democrático,-a.

demolish vt (building) derribar.

demolition demolición f.
demonstrate 1 vt demostrar. **2** vi (politically) manifestarse.
demonstration (proof) demostración f.; (explanation) explicación f.; (political) manifestación f.
demonstrative a franco,-a.
demonstrator manifestante mf.
demoralize vt desmoralizar.
den (of animal) guarida f.; (study) estudio m.
denial (of charge) desmentido m.; (of rights) denegación f.
denim dril m.; **denims** tejanos mpl, vaqueros mpl.
denounce vt denunciar.
dent 1 n abolladura f. **2** vt abollar.
dental a dental.
dentist dentista mf.
dentures npl dentadura f postiza.
deny vt (refuse) negar; (rumor, report) desmentir; (charge) rechazar; **to d. sb sth** negarle algo a algn.
deodorant desodorante m.
depart vi marcharse, irse; (from subject) desviarse (**from** de).
department sección f.; (in university) departamento m.; (in government) ministerio m.
department store grandes almacenes mpl.
departure partida f.; (of plane, train) salida f.
depend 1 vi (rely) fiarse (**on, upon** de). **2** v impers (be determined by) depender (**on** de); **it depends on the weather** según el tiempo que haga; **that depends** según.
dependable a (person) fiable.
dependent dependiente mf.
depict vt (in painting) representar; (describe) describir.
deplorable a lamentable.
deplore vt deplorar.
deposit 1 n (in bank, on rented car) depósito m.; (in river, test tube) sedimento m.; (in wine) poso m.; (on purchase) señal f.; (on house) entrada f. **2** vt depositar; (into account) ingresar.

depot almacén m.; (bus garage) cochera f (de autobuses).
depress vt (discourage) deprimir.
depressed a (person) deprimido, -a; **to get d.** deprimirse.
depression depresión f.
deprive vt privar (**of** de).
deprived a necesitado,-a.
depth profundidad f.; (of emotion) intensidad f.
deputy (substitute) suplente mf.; **d. head** subdirector,-a mf.
derailment descarrilamiento m.
derelict a abandonado,-a.
derive vt sacar, obtener.
descend 1 vi descender; **to d. from** (be related to) descender de. **2** vt (stairs) bajar.
• **descend upon** vt (area) invadir.
descendant descendiente mf.
descent descenso m.
describe vt describir.
description descripción f.; (type) clase f.
desert¹ desierto m.
desert² vt (place, family) abandonar.
deserve vt (rest, punishment) merecer; (prize, praise) ser digno,-a de.
design 1 n diseño m.; (of building etc) plano m.; (of room) disposición f.; (pattern) dibujo m. **2** vt diseñar.
designer diseñador,-a mf.; **d. jeans** vaqueros mpl de marca.
designer clothes ropa f de marca.
desirable a deseable; (asset, offer) atractivo,-a.
desire 1 n deseo m.; **I haven't the slightest d. to go** no me apetece nada ir. **2** vt desear.
desk (in school) pupitre m.; (in office) escritorio m.; (reception) **d.** recepción f.
desk clerk recepcionista mf.
desktop computer ordenador m de sobremesa.
despair 1 n desesperación f. **2** vi desesperar(se) (**of** de).

despatch n & vt see **dispatch**.

desperate a (person, situation, action) desesperado,-a; (need) apremiante; **to be d. for sth** necesitar algo con urgencia.

desperately adv (need) urgentemente; (bad, busy) terriblemente.

despicable a despreciable; (behavior) indigno,-a.

despise vt despreciar.

despite prep a pesar de.

dessert postre m.

dessert spoon cuchara f de postre.

destination destino m.

destitute a indigente.

destroy vt destruir; (vehicle, old furniture) destrozar.

destruction destrucción f.

destructive a (gale etc) destructor,-a.

detach vt (remove) separar.

detachable a separable (**from** de).

detached a (separated) separado,-a.

detached house casa f independiente.

detail detalle m, pormenor m.

detailed a detallado,-a.

detain vt (police etc) detener; (delay) retener.

detect vt (error, movement) advertir; (difference) notar; (smell, sound) percibir; (discover) descubrir.

detective detective mf; **d. story** novela f policíaca.

detector aparato m detector.

detention (of suspect etc) detención f.

deter vt (dissuade) disuadir (**from** de); **to d. sb from doing sth** impedir a algn hacer algo.

detergent detergente m.

deteriorate vi deteriorarse.

deterioration empeoramiento m; (of substance, friendship) deterioro m.

determination (resolution) resolución f.

determine vt determinar.

determined a (person) decidido, -a; (effort) enérgico,-a.

deterrent fuerza f disuasoria.

detour desvío m.

develop 1 vt desarrollar; (trade) fomentar; (plan) elaborar; (illness, habit) contraer; (interest) mostrar; (natural resources) aprovechar; (build on) (site) urbanizar. 2 vi (body, industry) desarrollarse; (system) perfeccionarse; (interest) crecer.

• **develop into** vt transformarse en.

development desarrollo m; (of trade) fomento m; (of skill) perfección f; (of character) formación f; (advance) avance m; (exploitation) explotación f; (of land, site) urbanización f; **there are no new developments** no hay ninguna novedad.

deviate vi desviarse (**from** de).

device aparato m; (mechanism) mecanismo m.

devil diablo m, demonio m; fam **where the d. did you put it?** ¿dónde demonios lo pusiste?

devise vt idear.

devote vt dedicar.

devoted a dedicado,-a (**to** a).

devotion devoción f; (to cause) dedicación f.

dew rocío m.

diabetes diabetes f.

diabetic a & n diabético,-a (mf).

diagnosis (pl **diagnoses**) diagnóstico m.

diagonal a & n diagonal (f).

diagonally adv en diagonal, diagonalmente.

diagram diagrama m; (of process, system) esquema m; (of workings) gráfico m.

dial 1 n (of clock) esfera f; (on machine) botón m selector; (on radio) dial m. 2 vti marcar.

dial tone señal f de marcar.

dialect dialecto m.

dialog diálogo m.

diameter diámetro m.

diamond diamante m; (shape) rombo m.

diaper pañal m.

diarrhea diarrea f.

diary diario m; (for appointments) agenda f.

dice 1 n dado m. **2** vt (food) cortar en cuadritos.

dictate 1 vt (letter, order) dictar. **2** vi (order about) dar órdenes.

dictation dictado m.

dictionary diccionario m.

did pt of **do.**

die vi morir(se); **to be dying for sth/to do sth** morirse por algo/de ganas de hacer algo.

• **die down** vi (wind) amainar; (noise, excitement) disminuir.

• **die out** vi extinguirse.

diesel (oil) gasoil m; **d. engine** motor m diesel.

diet 1 n (normal food) dieta f; (selected food) régimen m. **2** vi estar a régimen.

differ vi (be unlike) ser distinto,-a; (disagree) discrepar.

difference diferencia f; (disagreement) desacuerdo m; **it makes no d. (to me)** (me) da igual; **what d. does it make?** ¿qué más da?

different a distinto,-a.

differently adv de otra manera.

difficult a difícil.

difficulty dificultad f; (problem) problema m.

dig* 1 vt (earth) cavar; (tunnel) excavar; (hole) hacer. **2** vi cavar.

• **dig out** vt fig (find) sacar; (information) descubrir.

• **dig up** vt (weeds) arrancar; (buried object) desenterrar.

digest vt (food) digerir; (facts) asimilar.

digestion digestión f.

digger excavadora f.

digit (number) dígito m.

digital a digital.

dilapidated a en mal estado.

dilute vt diluir; (wine, milk) aguar.

dim 1 a (light) tenue; (room) os-

curo,-a; (outline) borroso,-a; (memory) vago,-a; fam (stupid) torpe. **2** vt (light) bajar.

dime moneda f de diez centavos.

dimension dimensión f.

din estrépito m.

dine vi (formal use) cenar.

diner (person) comensal mf; (restaurant) restaurante m barato.

dinghy bote m; **(rubber) d.** bote m neumático.

dingy a (street, house) oscuro,-a; (dirty) sucio,-a; (colour) desteñido,-a.

dining car vagón m restaurante.

dining room comedor m.

dinner (at midday) comida f; (in evening) cena f.

dinner jacket smoking m.

dinner party cena f.

dinner service vajilla f.

dinosaur dinosaurio m.

dip 1 n (bathe) chapuzón m; (of road) pendiente f. **2** vi (road) bajar.

• **dip into** vt (savings) echar mano de.

diphthong diptongo m.

diploma diploma m.

direct 1 a directo,-a. **2** adv directamente. **3** vt dirigir; **can you d. me to a bank?** ¿me puede indicar dónde hay un banco?

direction dirección f; **directions** (to place) señas fpl; **directions for use** modo m de empleo.

directly 1 adv (above etc) justo; (speak) directamente; (at once) en seguida. **2** conj en cuanto.

director director,-a mf.

directory (for telephone) guía f telefónica.

directory assistance (servicio m de) información f.

dirt suciedad f.

dirt-cheap adv & a fam tirado, -a.

dirty 1 a sucio,-a; (joke) verde; (mind) pervertido,-a; **d. word** palabrota f; **to get sth d.** ensuciar algo. **2** vt ensuciar.

disability discapacidad f.
disabled 1 a minusválido,-a. **2** npl **the d.** los minusválidos mpl.
disadvantage desventaja f; (obstacle) inconveniente m.
disagree vi (differ) no estar de acuerdo (**with** con); (quarrel) reñir (**about** por); **garlic disagrees with me** el ajo no me sienta bien.
disagreeable a desagradable.
disagreement desacuerdo m; (argument) riña f.
disappear vi desaparecer.
disappearance desaparición f.
disappoint vt decepcionar.
disappointing a decepcionante.
disappointment decepción f.
disapproval desaprobación f.
disapprove vi **to d. of** desaprobar.
disarm 1 vt desarmar. **2** vi desarmarse.
disaster desastre m.
disastrous a desastroso,-a.
disc disco m.
discard vt (old things) deshacerse de; (plan) descartar.
discharge vt (prisoner) soltar; (patient) dar de alta; (soldier) licenciar; (dismiss) despedir.
discontinued a (article) que no se fabrica más.
discipline 1 n disciplina f. **2** vt (child) castigar; (worker) sancionar.
disc jockey disc-jockey mf, pinchadiscos mf inv.
disclose vt revelar.
disco discoteca f.
discomfort (pain) malestar m.
disconnect vt desconectar (**from** de); (gas, electricity) cortar.
discontented a descontento,-a.
discotheque discoteca f.
discount descuento m.
discourage vt (dishearten) desanimar; (advances) rechazar.
discover vt descubrir; (missing person, object) encontrar.
discovery descubrimiento m.
discreet a discreto,-a.
discriminate vi distinguir (between entre); **to d. against sth/sb** discriminar algo/a algn.
discrimination (bias) discriminación f.
discuss vt discutir; (in writing) tratar de.
discussion discusión f.
disease enfermedad f.
disembark vti desembarcar.
disfigured a desfigurado,-a.
disgrace 1 n desgracia f. **2** vt deshonrar.
disgraceful a vergonzoso,-a.
disguise 1 n disfraz m; **in d.** disfrazado,-a. **2** vt (person) disfrazar (**as** de).
disgust 1 n repugnancia f, asco m. **2** vt (revolt) dar asco a.
disgusted a disgustado,-a, indignado,-a.
disgusting a repugnante; (behavior, state of affairs) intolerable.
dish (for serving) fuente f; (course) plato m; **to wash** or **do the dishes** fregar los platos.
• **dish up** vt (meal) servir.
dishcloth trapo m de fregar.
disheveled a (hair) despeinado, -a; (appearance) desaliñado,-a.
dishonest a (person) poco honrado,-a; (means) fraudulento,-a.
dishwasher lavaplatos m inv.
disillusioned a desilusionado,-a.
disincentive freno m.
disinfect vt desinfectar.
disinfectant desinfectante m.
disk disco m; (for computer) disquete m.
disk drive unidad f de disquete, disquetera f.
dislike 1 n antipatía f (**for, of** a, hacia). **2** vt tener antipatía hacia.
dislocate vt (joint) dislocar.
dismal a (prospect) sombrío,-a; (place, weather) deprimente; (person) triste.
dismantle vt desmontar.
dismay 1 n consternación f. **2** vt consternar.
dismiss vt (employee) despedir.
dismissal (of employee) despido m.

disobedience desobediencia f.
disobedient a desobediente.
disobey vt desobedecer; (law) violar.
disorder (untidiness) desorden m; (riot) disturbio m; (illness) trastorno m.
disorganized a desorganizado,-a.
dispatch vt (mail) enviar; (goods) expedir.
dispel vt disipar.
dispenser (device) máquina f expendedora; **cash d.** cajero m automático.
disperse 1 vt dispersar. 2 vi dispersarse.
display 1 n (exhibition) exposición f; (on computer screen) visualización f. 2 vt mostrar; (goods) exponer; (on computer screen) visualizar; (feelings) manifestar.
displeased a contrariado,-a.
disposable a desechable.
disposal **at my d.** a mi disposición.
dispose vi **to d. of** (trash) tirar; (unwanted object) deshacerse de.
dispute 1 n (disagreement) discusión f; (quarrel) disputa f; **industrial d.** conflicto m laboral. 2 vt refutar.
disqualify vt (team) descalificar; (make ineligible) incapacitar.
disregard vt (ignore) ignorar.
disrupt vt (meeting, traffic) interrumpir; (order) trastornar; (schedule etc) desbaratar.
disruption (of meeting, traffic) interrupción f; (of schedule etc) desbaratamiento m.
dissatisfaction descontento m.
dissatisfied a descontento,-a.
dissolve 1 vt disolver. 2 vi disolverse.
dissuade vt disuadir (**from** de).
distance distancia f; **in the d.** a lo lejos.
distant a (place, time) lejano,-a; (look) distraído,-a; (aloof) distante.
distaste aversión f.
distasteful a desagradable.

distinct a (different) diferente; (smell, change) marcado,-a; (idea, intention) claro,-a; **as d. from** a diferencia de.
distinction (difference) diferencia f; (excellence) distinción f; (in exam) sobresaliente m.
distinctive a distintivo,-a.
distinctly adv (clearly) claramente; (definitely) sensiblemente.
distinguish vt distinguir.
distinguished a distinguido,-a.
distort vt (misrepresent) deformar.
distract vt distraer.
distraction (interruption) distracción f; **to drive sb to d.** volver loco a algn.
distress (mental) angustia f; (physical) dolor m.
distressing a penoso,-a.
distribute vt distribuir.
distribution distribución f.
distributor distribuidor,-a mf; (in car engine) delco m.
district (of country) región f; (of town) barrio m; **d. attorney** fiscal mf.
distrust vt desconfiar de.
disturb vt (inconvenience) molestar; (silence) romper; (sleep) interrumpir; (worry) perturbar; (papers) desordenar.
disturbance (commotion) disturbio m.
disturbing a inquietante.
ditch zanja f; (at roadside) cuneta f; (for irrigation) acequia f.
ditto ídem.
divan diván m.
dive 1 n (into water) zambullida f; (of diver) buceo m; (of plane) picado m; (in sport) salto m. 2 vi* zambullirse; (diver) bucear; (plane) bajar en picado; (in sport) saltar; **he dived for the phone** se precipitó hacia el teléfono.
diver (person) buceador,-a mf; (professional) buzo m; (from diving board) saltador,-a mf.
diversion (distraction) distracción f.

divert vt desviar.

divide 1 vt dividir. **2** vi (road, stream) bifurcarse.
• **divide off** vt separar.
• **divide up** vt (share out) repartir.

diving submarinismo m; (sport) salto m de trampolín.

diving board trampolín m.

division división f; (sharing) reparto m; (of organization) sección f.

divorce 1 n divorcio m. **2** vt **she divorced him** se divorció de él.

divorced divorciado,-a; **to get d.** divorciarse.

dizziness vértigo m.

dizzy a (person) (unwell) mareado,-a.

DJ abbr of **disc jockey**.

do* **1** v aux (in negatives and questions) (not translated in Spanish) **do you drive?** ¿tienes carnet de conducir?; **don't you want to come?** ¿no quieres venir?; **he doesn't smoke** no fuma. ■ (emphatic) (not translated in Spanish) **do come with us!** ¡ánimo, vente con nosotros!; **I do like your bag** me encanta tu bolso. ■ (substituting main verb) (not translated in Spanish) **I don't believe him — neither do I** no le creo—yo tampoco; **I'll go if you do** si vas tú, voy yo; **I think it's dear, but he doesn't** a mí me parece caro pero a él no; **who went? — I did** ¿quién asistió?—yo. ■ (in question tags) **he refused, didn't he?** dijo que no, ¿verdad?; **I don't like it, do you?** a mí no me gusta, ¿y a ti? **2** vt hacer; (task) realizar; (duty) cumplir con; (distance) recorrer; **what can I do for you?** ¿en qué puedo servirle?; **what do you do (for a living)?** ¿a qué te dedicas?; **he's done it!** ¡lo ha conseguido!; **we were doing eighty** íbamos a ochenta. **3** vi (act) hacer; **do as I tell you** haz lo que te digo; **how are you doing?** ¿qué tal?; **to do well** (person) tener éxito; (business) ir bien; **five pounds will do**

con cinco libras será suficiente; **that will do!** ¡basta ya!; **this cushion will do as a pillow** este cojín servirá de almohada.
• **do away with** vt (abolish) abolir; (discard) deshacerse de.
• **do for** vt (destroy, ruin) arruinar; **I'm done for if I don't finish this** estoy perdido,-a si no acabo esto.
• **do in** vt **I'm done in** (exhausted) estoy hecho,-a polvo.
• **do out** vt (clean) limpiar a fondo.
• **do over** vt (repeat) repetir.
• **do up** vt (wrap) envolver; (belt etc) abrochar; (laces) atar; (dress up) arreglar; (redecorate) renovar.
• **do with** vt **I could do with a rest** (need) un descanso no me vendría nada mal; **to have** or **be to do with** (concern) tener que ver con.
• **do without** vt pasar sin, prescindir de.

dock 1 n **the docks** el muelle. **2** vi (ship) atracar.

docker estibador m.

dockyard astillero m.

doctor médico,-a mf; (academic) doctor,-a mf.

doctorate doctorado m.

document documento m.

documentary a & n documental (m).

dodge vt (blow) esquivar; (pursuer) despistar; (tax) evadir.

dodgem coche m de choque.

does 3rd person sing pres of **do**.

dog perro,-a mf.

doggy bag (in restaurant) bolsita f para llevarse los restos de la comida.

doghouse perrera f; fam **to be in the d.** estar en desgracia.

doing it was none of my d. yo no tuve nada que ver.

do-it-yourself bricolaje m.

doll (toy) muñeca f.

dollar dólar m.

dollhouse casa f de muñecas.

dolphin delfín m.

dome cúpula f.

domestic a (appliance, pet) doméstico,-a; (*flight, news*) nacional; (*trade, policy*) interior.

dominant *a* dominante.

dominate *vti* dominar.

Dominican *a & n* dominicano,-a (*mf*).

domino (*pl* dominoes) (*piece*) ficha *f* de dominó; **dominoes** (*game*) dominó *m sing*.

donate *vt* donar.

donation donativo *m*.

done 1 *pp* of **do. 2** *a* (*finished*) terminado,-a; (*meat*) hecho,-a; (*vegetables*) cocido,-a.

donkey burro,-a *mf*.

door puerta *f*.

doorbell timbre *m* (de la puerta).

doorknob pomo *m*.

door knocker picaporte *m*.

doorman portero *m*.

doormat felpudo *m*.

doorstep peldaño *m*.

doorway entrada *f*.

dope 1 *n fam* (*drug*) chocolate *m*. **2** *a* tonto,-a.

dormitory (*in school*) dormitorio *m*; (*in university*) colegio *m* mayor.

dosage (*amount*) dosis *f inv*.

dose dosis *f inv*.

dot punto *m*.

dotted line línea *f* de puntos.

double 1 *a* doble. **2** *adv* doble; **folded d.** doblado,-a por la mitad; **it's d. the price** cuesta dos veces más. **3** *n* **to earn d.** ganar el doble.

• **double back** *vi* **to d. back on one's tracks** volver sobre sus pasos.

• **double up** *vi* (*bend*) doblarse.

double bed cama *f* de matrimonio.

double-breasted *a* cruzado,-a.

double glazing doble acristalamiento *m*.

doubt 1 *n* duda *f*; **no d.** sin duda; **to be in d. about sth** dudar algo. **2** *vt* dudar.

doubtful *a* **I'm a bit d. about it** no me convence del todo; **it's d. whether . . .** no se sabe seguro si . . .

dough (*for bread*) masa *f*; (*for*

pastries) pasta *f*; *fam* (*money*) pasta *f*.

doughnut rosquilla *f*, dónut® *m*.

dove paloma *f*.

down 1 *adv* (*to or at lower level*) abajo; (*to floor*) al suelo; (*to ground*) a tierra; **to go d.** (*price, person*) bajar; **d. there** allí abajo; **to be d. with a cold** estar resfriado,-a; **to feel d.** estar deprimido,-a. **2** *prep* (*along*) por; **to go d. the road** bajar la calle.

down-and-out vagabundo,-a *mf*.

downhill *adv* **to go d.** ir cuesta abajo.

down payment entrada *f*, fianza *f*.

downpour chaparrón *m*.

downright 1 *a* (*liar, rogue*) declarado,-a; (*lie*) manifesto,-a. **2** *adv* (*totally*) completamente.

downstairs 1 *adv* abajo; (*to first floor*) a la planta baja; **to go d.** bajar la escalera. **2** *a* (*on first floor*) de la planta baja.

downtown *adv* en el centro (de la ciudad).

downward(s) *adv* hacia abajo.

doze 1 *vi* dormitar. **2** *n* cabezada *f*; **to have a d.** echar una cabezada.

• **doze off** *vi* quedarse dormido,-a.

dozen docena *f*; **half a d./a d. eggs** media docena/una docena de huevos.

Dr *abbr of* **Doctor** Doctor,-a *mf*, Dr., Dra.

drab *a* (*dreary*) gris; (*color*) pardo, -a.

draft (*of cold air*) corriente *f* (de aire); **d.** (*beer*) cerveza *f* de barril.

drafty *a* **this room is very d.** en esta habitación hay mucha corriente.

drag 1 *vt* (*pull*) arrastrar. **2** *vi* (*trail*) arrastrarse; (*person*) rezagarse.

• **drag on** *vi* (*war, strike*) hacerse interminable.

• **drag out** *vt* (*speech etc*) alargar.

• **drag along** *vt* arrastrar.

dragon dragón *m*.

drain 1 *n* (*for water*) desagüe *m*;

(*grating*) sumidero *m*. **2** *vt* (*marsh etc*) avenar; (*reservoir*) desecar. **3** *vi* **to d. (away)** (*liquid*) irse.

draining board escurridero *m*.

drainpipe tubo *m* de desagüe.

drama (*play*) obra *f* de teatro; (*subject*) teatro *m*; (*tense situation*) drama *m*.

dramatic *a* (*change*) impresionante; (*moment*) emocionante; (*of the theater*) dramático,-a.

dramatically *adv* (*to change*) de forma espectacular.

drapes *npl* cortinas *fpl*.

drastic *a* (*severe*) drástico,-a; (*change*) radical.

drastically *adv* radicalmente.

draw 1 *vt** (*picture*) dibujar; (*line*) trazar; (*curtains*) (*open*) descorrer; (*close*) correr; (*attract*) atraer; (*attention*) llamar. **2** *vi** (*sketch*) dibujar; **they drew two all** empataron a dos. **3** *n* (*score*) empate *m*.

• **draw in** *vi* (*days*) acortarse.

• **draw near (to)** *vt* acercarse (a).

• **draw on** *vt* (*savings*) recurrir a; (*experience*) aprovecharse de.

• **draw out** *vt* (*withdraw*) sacar.

• **draw up** *vt* (*contract*) preparar; (*plan*) esbozar.

drawback inconveniente *m*.

drawer cajón *m*.

drawing dibujo *m*.

drawing pin chincheta *f*.

drawing room sala *f* de estar.

dread 1 *vt* temer. **2** *n* temor *m*.

dreadful *a* (*shocking*) espantoso, -a; (*awful*) fatal.

dreadfully *adv* (*horribly*) terriblemente; (*very*) muy.

dream 1 *n* sueño *m*; (*marvel*) maravilla *f*. **2** *vti** soñar (**of, about** con).

• **dream up** *vt* (*excuse*) inventarse; (*plan*) idear.

dreary *a* (*gloomy*) triste; (*boring*) aburrido,-a.

drench *vt* empapar.

dress 1 *n* vestido *m*; (*clothing*) ropa *f*. **2** *vt* (*person*) vestir; (*wound*) vendar; (*salad*) aliñar; **he was dressed in a gray suit** llevaba (puesto) un traje gris. **3** *vi* vestirse.

• **dress up** *vi* (*in disguise*) disfrazarse (**as** de); (*in best clothes*) vestirse elegante.

dresser (*in bedroom*) tocador *m*.

dressing (*bandage*) vendaje *m*; (**salad**) **d.** aliño *m*.

dressing table tocador *m*.

dressmaker modista *mf*.

drew *pt* of **draw**.

dribble 1 *vi* (*baby*) babear; (*liquid*) gotear. **2** *vt* (*ball*) regatear.

dried *a* (*fruit*) seco,-a; (*milk*) en polvo.

drier *see* **dryer**.

drift *vi* (*boat*) ir a la deriva; (*person*) ir sin rumbo, vagar; **they drifted away** se marcharon poco a poco.

drill 1 *n* (*handtool*) taladro *m*; **dentist's d.** fresa *f*; **pneumatic d.** martillo *m* neumático. **2** *vt* (*wood etc*) taladrar.

drink 1 *vti** beber; **to have sth to d.** tomarse algo; **to d. to sth/sb** brindar por algo/algn. **2** *n* bebida *f*; (*alcoholic*) copa *f*.

• **drink up 1** *vt* beberse todo. **2** *vi* **d. up!** ¡bébelo todo!

drinkable *a* potable; (*not unpleasant*) agradable.

drinking water agua *f* potable.

drip 1 *n* goteo *m*; *fam* (*person*) necio,-a *mf*. **2** *vi* gotear; **he was dripping with sweat** el sudor le caía a gotas.

drip-dry *a* que no necesita planchado.

drive 1 *vt* (*vehicle*) conducir, *Am* manejar; (*person*) llevar; (*stake*) hincar; (*nail*) clavar; (*compel*) forzar; **to d. sb mad** volver loco,-a a algn. **2** *vi** (*in car*) conducir, *Am* manejar. **3** *n* camino *m* de entrada; (*energy*) energía *f*; **to go for a d.** dar una vuelta en coche; **left-hand d.** conducción *f* por la izquierda.

• **drive along** *vti* (*in car*) conducir.

• **drive back 1** *vt* (*enemy*) recha-

zar; (*passenger*) llevar de vuelta a.
2 *vi* volver en coche.
• **drive in** *vt* (*nail*) clavar.
• **drive off** *vi* salir (en coche).
• **drive on** *vi* (*after stopping*) continuar.
• **drive out** *vt* expulsar.
• **drive up** *vi* llegar en coche.
driveway *n* camino *m* de entrada.
drivel tonterías *mpl*.
driver (*of car, bus*) conductor,-a *mf*; (*of train*) maquinista *mf*; (*of lorry*) camionero,-a *mf*.
driver's license carnet *m* de conducir.
driving lesson clase *f* de conducir.
driving school autoescuela *f*.
driving test examen *m* de conducir.
drizzle 1 *n* llovizna *f*. **2** *vi* lloviznar.
droop *vi* (*flower*) marchitarse.
drop 1 *n* (*liquid*) gota *f*; (*descent*) desnivel *m*; (*in price*) bajada *f*; (*in temperature*) descenso *m*. **2** *vt* (*let fall*) dejar caer; (*lower*) bajar; (*reduce*) disminuir; (*abandon*) (*subject, charge etc*) abandonar. **3** *vi* (*object*) caerse; (*voice, price, temperature*) bajar; (*speed*) disminuir.
• **drop behind** *vi* quedarse atrás.
• **drop in** or **round** *vi* (*visit*) pasarse (**at** por).
• **drop off 1** *vi* (*fall asleep*) quedarse dormido,-a. **2** *vt* (*deliver*) dejar en casa (de algn).
• **drop out** *vi* (*of college*) dejar los estudios; (*of society*) marginarse; (*of competition*) retirarse.
drought sequía *f*.
drown 1 *vt* ahogar; (*place*) inundar. **2** *vi* ahogarse; **he drowned** murió ahogado.
drowsy *a* soñoliento,-a; **to feel d.** tener sueño.
drug 1 *n* (*medicine*) medicamento *m*; (*narcotic*) droga *f*; **to be on drugs** drogarse. **2** *vt* (*person*) drogar; (*food, drink*) adulterar con drogas.
drug addict drogadicto,-a *mf*.
drugstore establecimiento *m*

donde se compran medicamentos, periódicos etc.
drum tambor *m*; (*container*) bidón *m*; **to play the drums** tocar la batería.
drummer (*in band*) tambor *mf*; (*in pop group*) batería *mf*.
drunk 1 *a* borracho,-a; **to get d.** emborracharse. **2** *n* borracho,-a *mf*.
drunkard borracho,-a *mf*.
drunken *a* (*driver*) borracho,-a; **d. driving** conducir en estado de embriaguez.
dry 1 *a* seco,-a. **2** *vt* secar. **3** *vi* **to d. (off)** secarse.
• **dry up 1** *vt* secar. **2** *vi* secarse.
dry-clean *vt* lavar en seco.
dry-cleaner (*shop*) tintorería *f*.
dryer secadora *f*.
dual *a* doble, dual.
dub *vt* (*subtitle*) doblar (**into** a).
dubious *a* (*morals etc*) dudoso,-a; (*doubting*) indeciso,-a.
duchess duquesa *f*.
duck¹ pato,-a *mf*; (*as food*) pato *m*.
duck² *vi* (*bow down*) agacharse. **2** *vt* (*evade*) esquivar.
due *a* (*expected*) esperado,-a; (*money*) pagadero,-a; **the train is d. (to arrive) at ten** el tren debe llegar a las diez; **in d. course** a su debido tiempo; **to be d. to** deberse a. **2** *adv* (*north etc*) derecho hacia.
duel duelo *m*.
duffel coat trenca *f*.
duke duque *m*.
dull *a* (*boring*) pesado,-a; (*place*) sin interés; (*light*) apagado,-a; (*weather*) gris; (*sound, ache*) sordo,-a.
dumb *a* mudo,-a; (*stupid*) tonto,-a.
dump 1 *n* (*tip*) vertedero *m*; *fam* (*place*) lugar *m* de mala muerte; (*town*) poblacho *m*; (*dwelling*) tugurio *m*. **2** *vt* (*garbage*) verter.
dump truck volquete *m*.
dungarees *npl* mono *m sing*.
duplex casa *f* adosada; **d. apartment** dúplex *m inv*.
duplicate duplicado *m*; **in d.** por duplicado.

durable a duradero,-a.

duration duración f.

during prep durante.

dusk crepúsculo m; **at d.** al anochecer.

dust 1 n polvo m. **2** vt (furniture) quitar el polvo a.

duster (for housework) trapo m (del polvo).

dusty a polvoriento,-a.

Dutch 1 a holandés,-esa. **2** n (language) holandés m; **the D.** los holandeses mpl.

Dutchman holandés m.

Dutchwoman holandesa f.

duty deber m; (task) función f; (tax) impuesto m; **to be on d.** estar de servicio; (doctor, soldier) estar de guardia; **d. chemist** farmacia f de guardia; **customs d.** derechos mpl de aduana.

duty-free a libre de impuestos.

duvet edredón m.

dwarf (pl **dwarves**) enano,-a mf.

dye 1 n tinte m. **2** vt teñir; **to d. one's hair black** teñirse el pelo de negro.

dynamic a dinámico,-a.

dynamite dinamita f.

dynamo dínamo f.

dyslexic a disléxico,-a.

E

each 1 a cada; **e. day/month** todos los días/meses. **2** pron cada uno,-a; **we bought one e.** nos compramos uno cada uno,-a; **e. other** el uno al otro; **they hate e. other** se odian.

eager a (anxious) impaciente (**to** por); (keen) deseoso,-a.

eagerly adv (anxiously) con impaciencia; (keenly) con ilusión.

eagerness impaciencia f (**to do** por hacer); (keenness) afán m.

eagle águila f.

ear oreja f; (inner ear) oído m; (of corn) espiga f.

earache dolor m de oídos.

early 1 a (before usual time) temprano,-a; **to have an e. night** acostarse pronto; **you're e.!** ¡qué pronto has venido! ▪ (at first stage, period) in her e. forties a los cuarenta y pocos; **in e. July** a principios de julio. ▪ (in the near future) **an e. reply** una respuesta pronta. **2** adv (before the expected time) temprano; **to leave e.** irse pronto; **e. on** al principio; **earlier on** antes; **five minutes e.** con cinco minutos de adelanto; **as e. as possible** tan pronto como sea posible; **to book e.** reservar con tiempo; **at the earliest** cuanto antes.

earn vt ganarse; (money) ganar; **to e. one's living** ganarse la vida.

earnings npl ingresos mpl.

earphones npl auriculares mpl, cascos mpl.

earplug tapón m para los oídos.

earring pendiente m.

earth n tierra f; (electric) toma f de tierra; **to be down to e.** ser práctico; fam **where/why on e. . . . ?** ¿pero dónde/por qué demonios . . . ?

earthquake terremoto m.

ease 1 n (lack of difficulty) facilidad f; (affluence) comodidad f; (freedom from discomfort) tranquilidad f; **at e.** relajado,-a. **2** vt (pain) aliviar; (move gently) deslizar con cuidado.

• **ease off** or **up** vi (decrease) disminuir; (slow down) ir más despacio.

easel caballete m.

easily adv fácilmente; **e. the best** con mucho el mejor.

east 1 n este m. **2** a del este, oriental. **3** adv al este.

eastbound a (con) dirección este.

Easter Semana Santa f; **E. Sunday** Domingo m de Resurrección.

eastern a oriental, del este.

eastward(s) adv hacia el este.

easy 1 a fácil; (comfortable) cómodo,-a; **take I'm e.!** me da lo mismo; **e. chair** butacón m. **2** adv **go e. on the wine** no te pases con el vino; **to take things e.** tomarse las cosas con calma; **take it e.!** ¡tranquilo!

easy-going a (*calm*) tranquilo, -a; (*lax*) despreocupado,-a; (*undemanding*) poco exigente.

eat* vt comer.

• **eat away** vt desgastar; (*metal*) corroer.

• **eat out** vi comer fuera.

• **eat up** vt (*meal*) terminar; (*petrol*) consumir; (*miles*) tragar.

eau de Cologne colonia f.

eccentric a & n excéntrico,-a (*mf*).

echo 1 n (*pl* echoes) eco m. 2 vt (*repeat*) repetir. 3 vi resonar.

economic a económico,-a; (*profitable*) rentable.

economical a económico,-a.

economize vi economizar (**on** en).

economy (*national*) economía f; (*saving*) ahorro m; **e. class** (clase f) turista f.

edge 1 n borde m; (*of knife*) filo m; (*of water*) orilla f; **on the e. of town** en las afueras de la ciudad; **to have the e. on sb** llevar ventaja a algn; **to be on e.** tener los nervios de punta. 2 vi **to e. closer** acercarse lentamente; **to e. forward** avanzar poco a poco.

edible a comestible.

edit vt editar; (*proofs*) corregir; (*newspaper*) ser redactor,-a de; (*film, TV program*) montar; (*cut*) cortar.

• **edit out** vt suprimir.

edition edición f.

editor (*of book*) editor,-a mf; (*of newspaper*) redactor,-a mf; (*of film, TV program*) montador,-a mf.

editorial 1 a **e. staff** redacción f. 2 n editorial m.

educate vt educar.

educated a culto,-a.

education (*schooling*) enseñanza f; (*training*) formación f; (*studies*) estudios mpl; (*culture*) cultura f.

educational a educativo,-a.

eel anguila f.

effect efecto m; (*impression*) impresión f; **in e.** efectivamente; **to come into e.** entrar en vigor; **to have an e. on** afectar a; **to no e.** sin resultado alguno; **effects** (*possessions*) efectos mpl.

effective a (*successful*) eficaz; (*impressive*) impresionante.

effectively adv (*successfully*) eficazmente; (*in fact*) en efecto.

efficiency (*of person*) eficacia f; (*of machine*) rendimiento m.

efficient a eficaz; (*person*) eficiente; (*machine*) de buen rendimiento.

efficiently adv eficazmente; **to work e.** tener buen rendimiento.

effort esfuerzo m; (*attempt*) intento m; **to make an e.** hacer un esfuerzo.

eg abbr p. ej.

egg 1 n huevo m. 2 vt **to e. sb on (to do sth)** empujar a algn (a hacer algo).

egg cup huevera f.

eggplant berenjena f.

egg timer reloj m de arena.

egg white clara f de huevo.

Egyptian a & n egipcio,-a (*mf*).

eiderdown edredón m.

eight a & n ocho (m) inv.

eighteen a & n dieciocho (m) inv.

eighth a & n octavo,-a (*mf*).

eighty a & n ochenta (m) inv.

either 1 pron (*affirmative*) cualquiera; (*negative*) ninguno, ninguna, ni el uno ni el otro, ni la una ni la otra; **e. of them** cualquiera de los dos; **I don't want e. of them** no quiero ninguno de los dos. 2 a (*both*) cada, los dos, las dos; **on e. side** en ambos lados. 3 conj o; **e. . . . or . . . o . . . o . . .** ; **e. Friday or Saturday** o (bien) el viernes o el sábado. 4 adv (*after negative*) tampoco; **I don't want to do it e.** yo tampoco quiero hacerlo.

elastic 1 a elástico,-a; fig flexible; **e. band** goma elástica. 2 n elástico m.

elbow 1 n codo m. 2 vt **to e. sb** dar un codazo a algn.

elder a mayor.

elderly 1 a anciano,-a. **2** npl **the e.** los ancianos.

eldest 1 a mayor. **2** n el/la mayor.

elect vt elegir.

election 1 n elección f; **general e.** elecciones fpl generales. **2** a electoral.

electric a eléctrico,-a; fig electrizante.

electrical a eléctrico,-a.

electric blanket manta f eléctrica.

electric chair silla f eléctrica.

electrician electricista mf.

electricity electricidad f; **e. bill** recibo m de la luz.

electric shock electrochoque m.

electrocute vt electrocutar.

electronic a electrónico,-a.

electronics electrónica f.

elegance elegancia f.

elegant a elegante.

elegantly adv con elegancia.

element elemento m; (electrical) resistencia f.

elementary a (not developed) rudimentario,-a; (easy) fácil; **e. school** escuela f primaria.

elephant elefante m.

elevator ascensor m.

eleven a & n once (m) inv.

eleventh a & n undécimo,-a (mf).

eligible a apto,-a; **he isn't e. to vote** no tiene derecho al voto.

eliminate vt eliminar.

else adv **anything e.?** ¿algo más?; **everything e.** todo lo demás; **no-one e.** nadie más; **someone e.** otro,-a; **something e.** otra cosa; **somewhere e.** en otra parte; **what e.?** ¿qué mas?; **where e.?** ¿en qué otro sitio?; **or e.** si no.

elsewhere adv en otra parte.

elude vt (avoid) esquivar; **his name eludes me** no consigo acordarme de su nombre.

embark vi embarcar(se); **to e. upon sth** emprender algo.

embarrass vt avergonzar.

embarrassing a embarazoso,-a; (situation) violento,-a.

embarrassment vergüenza f.

embassy embajada f.

emblem emblema m.

embrace 1 vt abrazar; (include) abarcar. **2** vi abrazarse. **3** n abrazo m.

embroider vt bordar; (story, truth) adornar.

embroidery bordado m.

emerald esmeralda f.

emerge vi salir; (problem) surgir; **it emerged that . . .** resultó que . . .

emergency emergencia f; (medical) urgencia f; **in an e.** en caso de emergencia; **e. exit** salida f de emergencia; **e. landing** aterrizaje m forzoso; **state of e.** estado m de excepción.

emigrate vi emigrar.

emotion emoción f.

emotional a emocional; (moving) conmovedor,-a.

emperor emperador m.

emphasis énfasis m; **to place e. on sth** hacer hincapié en algo.

emphasize vt subrayar.

empire imperio m.

employ vt emplear; (time) ocupar.

employee empleado,-a mf.

employer empresario,-a mf.

employment empleo m.

employment agency agencia f de colocaciones.

empty 1 a vacío,-a; **e. promises** promesas fpl vanas. **2** vt vaciar. **3** vi vaciarse. **4** npl **empties** envases mpl.

empty-handed adv con las manos vacías.

emulsion **e. (paint)** pintura f mate.

enable vt **to e. sb to do sth** permitir a algn hacer algo.

enamel esmalte m.

enchanting a encantador,-a.

enclose vt (surround) rodear; (fence in) cercar; (in envelope) adjuntar; **please find enclosed** le enviamos adjunto.

enclosure (fenced area) cercado m; (in envelope) documento m adjunto.

encounter 1 n encuentro m. **2** vt

encontrarse con; (*problems*) tropezar con.

encourage *vt* (*urge*) animar; (*help to develop*) fomentar.

encouragement estímulo *m*.

encyclopedia enciclopedia *f*.

end 1 *n* (*of stick*) punta *f*; (*of street*) final *m*; (*conclusion*) fin *m*, final *m*; (*aim*) objetivo *m*; **in the e.** al final; **for hours on e.** hora tras hora; **to put an e. to** acabar con; **it makes my hair stand on e.** me pone el pelo de punta. 2 *vt* acabar, terminar. 3 *vi* acabarse, terminarse.

• **end up** *vi* terminar; **to e. up doing sth** terminar por hacer algo.

endanger *vt* poner en peligro.

ending final *m*.

endive escarola *f*.

endless *a* interminable.

endorse *vt* (*check etc*) endosar; (*approve*) aprobar; (*support*) apoyar.

endorsement (*on check etc*) endoso *m*; (*approval*) aprobación *f*.

endurance resistencia *f*.

endure 1 *vt* (*bear*) aguantar. 2 *vi* perdurar.

enemy *a & n* enemigo,-a (*mf*).

energetic *a* enérgico,-a.

energy 1 *n* energía *f*. 2 *a* energético,-a.

enforce *vt* (*law*) hacer cumplir.

engaged *a* prometido,-a; (*busy*) ocupado,-a; **to get e.** prometerse; **it's e.** (*phone*) está comunicando.

engagement (*to marry*) noviazgo *m*; (*appointment*) cita *f*.

engagement ring anillo *m* de compromiso.

engine motor *m*; (*of train*) locomotora *f*.

engine driver maquinista *mf*.

engineer ingeniero,-a *mf*; (*on train*) maquinista *mf*.

engineering ingeniería *f*.

English 1 *a* inglés,-esa. 2 *n* (*language*) inglés *m*; **the E.** los ingleses *mpl*.

Englishman inglés *m*.

English-speaking *a* de habla inglesa.

Englishwoman inglesa *f*.

engrave *vt* grabar.

engraving grabado *m*.

enjoy *vt* disfrutar; **to e. oneself** pasarlo bien; **he enjoys swimming** le gusta nadar.

enjoyable *a* agradable.

enjoyment disfrute *m*.

enlarge *vt* ampliar.

enlighten *vt* iluminar.

enormous *a* enorme.

enormously *adv* enormemente; **I enjoyed myself e.** lo pasé genial.

enough 1 *a* bastante, suficiente; **e. books** bastantes libros; **have we got e. gas?** ¿tenemos suficiente gasolina? 2 *adv* bastante; **sure e.** en efecto. 3 *n* lo suficiente; **e. to live on** lo suficiente para vivir; **it isn't e.** no basta; **I've had e.!** ¡estoy harto!

enquire = **inquire.**

enquiry = **inquiry.**

enroll 1 *vt* matricular. 2 *vi* matricularse.

enrollment matrícula *f*.

ensure *vt* asegurar.

entail *vt* suponer.

enter 1 *vt* (*go into*) entrar en; (*data into computer*) introducir; (*join*) ingresar en; **to e. one's name for a course** matricularse en un curso. 2 *vi* entrar.

• **enter into** *vt* (*agreement*) firmar; (*negotiations*) iniciar.

enterprise empresa *f*; **free e.** libre empresa.

enterprising *a* emprendedor,-a.

entertain 1 *vt* (*amuse*) divertir; (*consider*) considerar. 2 *vi* (*have guests*) tener invitados.

entertainer artista *mf*.

entertaining *a* divertido,-a.

entertainment diversión *f*; (*show*) espectáculo *m*.

enthusiasm entusiasmo *m*.

enthusiast entusiasta *mf*.

enthusiastic *a* entusiasta; (*praise*) caluroso,-a; **to be e. about sth** entusiasmarse por algo.

enthusiastically *adv* con entusiasmo.

entire a todo,-a; **the e. family** toda la familia.

entirely adv (completely) totalmente; (solely) exclusivamente.

entitle vt (permit) dar derecho a; **to be entitled to** tener derecho a.

entrance entrada f; (admission) ingreso m; **e. examination** examen m de ingreso.

entrant (in competition) participante mf.

entry (entrance) entrada f; **no e.** dirección prohibida.

entry form hoja f de inscripción.

envelope sobre m.

envious a envidioso,-a; **to feel e.** tener envidia.

environment entorno m; (natural) medio ambiente m.

environmental a medio ambiental.

envy 1 n envidia f. **2** vt **to e. sb sth** envidiar algo a algn.

epidemic 1 n epidemia f. **2** a epidémico,-a.

episode episodio m.

equal 1 a igual; **to be e. to the occasion** estar a la altura de las circunstancias. **2** n igual mf; **to treat sb as an e.** tratar a algn de igual a igual. **3** vt equivaler a.

equality igualdad f.

equalize vi (in sport) empatar.

equally adv igualmente; **e. pretty** igual de bonito; **to share sth e.** dividir algo en partes iguales.

equation ecuación f.

equator ecuador m.

equip vt (supply) equipar; (person) proveer.

equipment (materials) equipo m.

equivalent a & n equivalente (m).

erase vt borrar.

eraser goma f de borrar.

erect 1 a (upright) erguido,-a. **2** vt (monument) erigir.

errand recado m.

erratic a (performance, behavior) irregular; (weather) muy variable; (person) caprichoso,-a.

error error m.

escalator escalera f mecánica.

escape 1 n fuga f; (of gas) escape m. **2** vi escaparse. **3** vt (avoid) evitar; **the name escapes me** se me escapa el nombre.

escort 1 n (bodyguard etc) escolta f. **2** vt (protect) escoltar.

Eskimo a & n esquimal (mf).

especially adv especialmente.

espresso café m exprés.

essay (at school) redacción f.

essential a esencial.

essentially adv esencialmente.

establish vt (found) establecer; (business) montar; **to e. the truth** demostrar la verdad.

establishment establecimiento m; **the E.** el sistema.

estate (land) finca f; (property) bienes mpl; (inheritance) herencia f; (housing) **e.** urbanización f.

estimate 1 n (calculation) cálculo m; (likely cost of work) presupuesto m. **2** vt calcular.

etiquette etiqueta f.

EU abbr **European Union** UE.

Euro- prefix Euro-.

European a & n europeo,-a (mf).

evacuate vt evacuar.

evade vt evadir.

evaluate vt evaluar.

evaporate 1 vi evaporarse. **2** vt evaporar.

eve víspera f; **on the e. of** en vísperas de.

even 1 a (smooth) liso,-a; (regular) uniforme; (equally balanced) igual; (number) par; (in football game etc) **to be e.** ir empatados, -as; **to get e. with sb** desquitarse con algn. **2** adv aun; **e. now** incluso ahora; **e. the children knew** hasta los niños lo sabían; **e. as** mientras; **e. if** incluso si; **e. though** aunque. ▪ (with negative) ni siquiera; **she can't e. write her name** ni siquiera sabe escribir su nombre. ▪ (before comparative) aun, todavía; **e. worse** aun peor.

evening (early) tarde f; (late) noche f; **in the e.** por la tarde/noche; **tomorrow e.** mañana por la tarde/noche.

evening class clase *f* nocturna.

evenly *adv* (*uniformly*) de modo uniforme; (*fairly*) equitativamente.

event (*happening*) suceso *m*; (*in sport*) prueba *f*; **at all events** en todo caso; **in the e. of fire** en caso de incendio.

eventual *a* (*ultimate*) final; (*resulting*) consiguiente.

eventually *adv* finalmente.

ever *adv* (*always*) siempre; **for e.** para siempre; **stronger than e.** más fuerte que nunca; **have you e. been there?** ¿has estado allí alguna vez?; **how e. did you manage it?** ¿cómo diablos lo conseguiste?; *fam* **e. so . . .** muy . . . ; **thank you e. so much** muchísimas gracias.

every *a* (*each*) cada; (*all*) todos,-as; **e. now and then or e. now and again** de vez en cuando; **e. day** todos los días; **e. other day** cada dos días; **e. one of you** todos, -as vosotros,-as; **e. citizen** todo ciudadano.

everybody *pron* todo el mundo, todos,-as; **e. who . . .** todos los que . . .

everyday *a* de todos los días; **an e. occurrence** un suceso cotidiano.

everyone *pron* = **everybody.**

everyplace *adv* en todos sitios.

everything *pron* todo; **he eats e.** come de todo; **e. I have** todo lo que tengo.

everywhere *adv* por *or* en todas partes; **e. I go** por todas partes adonde voy.

evidence *n* (*proof*) evidencia *f*; (*in court case*) testimonio *m*; (*sign*) indicio *m*; **to give e.** prestar declaración.

evident *a* evidente.

evidently *adv* evidentemente.

evil 1 *a* (*wicked*) malvado,-a; (*harmful*) nocivo,-a. 2 *n* mal *m*.

ewe oveja *f*.

ex *her* **e.** su ex marido; **his e.** su ex mujer.

ex- *prefix* ex-; **ex-minister** ex ministro *m*.

exact *a* exacto,-a; **this e. spot** ese mismo lugar.

exactly *adv* exactamente; **e.!** ¡exacto!

exaggerate *vti* exagerar.

exaggeration exageración *f*.

exam examen *m*.

examination examen *m*; (*medical*) reconocimiento *m*; **to sit an e.** hacer un examen.

examine *vt* examinar; (*customs*) registrar; (*medically*) reconocer a.

examiner examinador,-a *mf*.

example ejemplo *m*; **for e.** por ejemplo.

exceed *vt* exceder.

exceedingly *adv* extremadamente.

excel *vi* sobresalir.

excellent *a* excelente.

except *prep* excepto; **e. for the little ones** excepto los pequeños; **e. that . . .** salvo que . . .

exception excepción *f*; **with the e. of** a excepción de; **to take e. to sth** ofenderse por algo.

exceptional *a* excepcional.

exceptionally *adv* excepcionalmente.

excerpt extracto *m*.

excess 1 *n* exceso *m*. 2 *a* excedente; **e. baggage** exceso *m* de equipaje; **e. fare** suplemento *m*.

excessive *a* excesivo,-a.

excessively *adv* excesivamente, en exceso.

exchange 1 *n* cambio *m*; (*telephone*) **e.** central *f* telefónica; **in e. for** a cambio de. 2 *vt* intercambiar; **to e. blows** golpearse.

exchange rate tipo *m* de cambio.

excite *vt* (*enthuse*) entusiasmar; (*arouse*) provocar; **to get excited** entusiasmarse.

excited *a* ilusionado,-a; emocionado,-a.

excitement (*emotion*) emoción *f*.

exciting *a* emocionante.

exclaim *vi* exclamar.

exclamation exclamación *f*.

exclamation point signo *m* de admiración.

exclude vt excluir; (*from club*) no admitir.

exclusive 1 a exclusivo,-a; (*select*) selecto,-a. **2** n (*in newspaper*) exclusiva f.

exclusively adv exclusivamente.

excursion excursión f.

excuse 1 vt disculpar; (*exempt*) dispensar; (*justify*) justificar; **e. me!** con permiso. **2** n excusa f; **to make excuses** dar excusas.

execute vt (*order*) cumplir; (*task*) realizar; (*person*) ejecutar.

execution (*of order*) cumplimiento m; (*of task*) realización f; (*of person*) ejecución f.

executive a & n ejecutivo,-a (*mf*).

exempt 1 vt eximir (**from** de). **2** a exento,-a; **e. from tax** libre de impuesto.

exemption exención f.

exercise 1 n ejercicio m. **2** vt (*rights, duties*) ejercer. **3** vi hacer ejercicio.

exercise book cuaderno m.

exert vt (*influence*) ejercer; **to e. oneself** esforzarse.

exertion esfuerzo m.

exhaust 1 vt agotar. **2** n (*gas*) gases mpl de combustión; **e. pipe** tubo m de escape.

exhausting a agotador,-a.

exhibit 1 n objeto m expuesto. **2** vt exponer; (*manifest*) mostrar.

exhibition exposición f.

exhibitor expositor,-a mf.

exist vi existir; (*stay alive*) subsistir.

existence existencia f.

existing a actual.

exit salida f.

exorbitant a exorbitante.

expand 1 vt ampliar. **2** vi (*grow*) ampliarse; (*metal*) dilatarse.

• **expand on** vt ampliar.

expanse extensión f.

expansion (*in size*) expansión f; (*of gas, metal*) dilatación f.

expansion slot ranura f de expansión.

expect 1 vt (*anticipate*) esperar; (*suppose*) suponer; **to e. sth from sb/sth** esperar algo de algn/algo; **to e. to do sth** contar con hacer algo; **she's expecting a baby** está esperando un niño. **2** vi **to be expecting** estar embarazada.

expectation esperanza f; **contrary to e.** contrariamente a lo que se esperaba.

expedition expedición f.

expel vt expulsar.

expenditure desembolso m.

expense gasto m; **to spare no e.** no escatimar gastos; *fig* **at the e. of** a costa de.

expensive a caro,-a.

experience 1 n experiencia f. **2** vt (*sensation*) experimentar; (*difficulty, loss*) sufrir.

experienced a experimentado,-a.

experiment 1 n experimento m. **2** vi experimentar (**on, with** con).

expert a & n experto,-a (*mf*).

expertise pericia f.

expiration vencimiento m.

expiration date fecha f de caducidad.

expire vi (*come to an end*) terminar; (*policy, contract*) vencer; (*ticket*) caducar.

expired (*ticket*) caducado,-a.

explain vt explicar; (*clarify*) aclarar; **to e. oneself** justificarse.

• **explain away** vt justificar.

explanation explicación f; (*clarification*) aclaración f.

explode 1 vt hacer explotar. **2** vi (*bomb*) explotar; **to e. with anger** montar en cólera.

exploit 1 n hazaña f. **2** vt explotar.

exploration exploración f.

explore vt explorar.

explorer explorador,-a mf.

explosion explosión f.

explosive 1 a explosivo,-a. **2** n explosivo m.

export 1 vt exportar. **2** n exportación f.

expose vt (*uncover*) exponer; (*secret*) revelar; (*plot*) descubrir.

express 1 a (*explicit*) expreso,-a;

(*letter*) urgente. **2** *n* (*train*) expreso *m*. **3** *vt* expresar.

expression expresión *f*.

expressway autopista *f*.

extend **1** *vt* (*enlarge*) ampliar; (*lengthen*) alargar; (*prolong*) prolongar; (*increase*) aumentar. **2** *vi* (*stretch*) extenderse; (*last*) prolongarse.

extension extensión *f*; (*of time*) prórroga *f*; (*of building*) anexo *m*.

extensive *a* extenso,-a.

extensively *adv* extensamente; (*frequently*) con frecuencia.

extent (*area*) extensión *f*; to some **e.** hasta cierto punto; **to a large e.** en gran parte; **to such an e.** hasta tal punto.

exterior *a* & *n* exterior (*m*).

external *a* externo,-a.

extinguisher extintor *m*.

extra **1** *a* extra; (*spare*) de sobra. **2** *adv* extra; **e. fine** extra fino. **3** *n* (*additional charge*) suplemento *m*; (*in film*) extra *mf*.

extract **1** *n* extracto *m*. **2** *vt* (*tooth, information*) extraer.

extracurricular *a* extracurricular.

extraordinary *a* extraordinario, -a; (*strange*) raro,-a.

extravagant *a* (*wasteful*) derrochador,-a; (*excessive*) exagerado, -a.

extreme **1** *a* extremo,-a; **an e. case** un caso excepcional. **2** *n* extremo *m*; **in the e.** en sumo grado.

extremely *adv* extremadamente; **I'm e. sorry** lo siento de veras.

eye *n* ojo *m*; **I couldn't believe my eyes** no podía creerlo; **not to take one's eyes off sb/sth** no quitar la vista de encima a algn/algo; **to catch sb's e.** llamar la atención de algn; **to turn a blind e.** hacer la vista gorda (**to** a); **with an e. to** con miras a; **to keep an e. on sb/sth** vigilar a algn/algo.

eyebrow ceja *f*.

eyeglasses *npl* gafas *fpl*.

eyelash pestaña *f*.

eyelid párpado *m*.

eyeliner lápiz *m* de ojos.

eyeshadow sombra *f* de ojos.

eyesight vista *f*.

F

fabulous *a* fabuloso,-a.

face **1** *n* cara *f*; (*surface*) superficie *f*; **f. to f.** cara a cara; **she slammed the door in my f.** me dio con la puerta en las narices; **in the f. of danger** ante el peligro; **to pull faces** hacer muecas; **f. down/up** boca abajo/arriba; **to save f.** salvar las apariencias. **2** *vt* (*look onto*) dar a; (*be opposite*) estar enfrente de; (*problem*) hacer frente a; **to f. up to** hacer cara a; (*tolerate*) aguantar. **3** *vi* **to f. on to** dar a; **to f. towards** mirar hacia.

facility (*ease*) facilidad *f*; **facilities** (*means*) facilidades *fpl*; (*rooms, equipment*) instalaciones *fpl*.

fact hecho *m*; (*reality*) realidad *f*; **as a matter of f.** de hecho; **in f.** en realidad.

factor factor *m*.

factory fábrica *f*.

fade *vi* (*colour*) desteñirse; (*flower*) marchitarse; (*light*) apagarse.

• **fade away/out** *vi* desvanecerse.

• **fade in** *vt* hacer aparecer gradualmente.

fail **1** *n* (*at school*) suspenso *m*; **without f.** sin falta. **2** *vt* (*exam*) suspender; **to f. to do sth** (*be unable*) no poder hacer algo; (*neglect*) dejar de hacer algo. **3** *vi* (*show, film*) fracasar; (*brakes*) fallar; (*at school*) suspender; (*health*) deteriorarse.

failed *a* (*attempt, poet*) fracasado, -a.

failing **1** *n* (*shortcoming*) defecto *m*; (*weakness*) punto *m* débil. **2** *prep* a falta de.

failure fracaso *m*; (*at school*) suspenso *m*; (*person*) fracasado, -a *mf*; (*breakdown*) avería *f*; **power f.** apagón *m*; **heart f.** paro *m* cardíaco; **her f. to answer** el hecho de que no contestara.

faint 1 a (sound) débil; (color) pálido,-a; (outline) borroso,-a; (recollection) vago,-a; (giddy) mareado,-a; **I haven't the faintest idea** no tengo la más mínima idea. **2** n desmayo m. **3** vi desmayarse.

faintly adv (with little strength) débilmente; (unclear) vagamente.

fair¹ 1 a (impartial) imparcial; (just) justo,-a; (hair) rubio,-a; (weather) bueno,-a; **it's not f.** no hay derecho; **f. enough!** ¡vale!; **a f. number** un buen número. **2** adv **to play f.** jugar limpio.

fair² feria f; **trade f.** feria f de muestras.

fair-haired a rubio,-a.

fairly adv (justly) justamente; (moderately) bastante.

fair play juego m limpio.

fair-sized a bastante grande.

fairy hada f; **f. tale** cuento m de hadas.

faith fe f; (trust) confianza f.

faithful a fiel.

faithfully adv **yours f.** (in letter) le saluda atentamente.

fake 1 a falso,-a. **2** n (object) falsificación f; (person) impostor,-a mf. **3** vt (forge) falsificar; (feign) fingir.

fall 1 n caída f; (decrease) baja f; otoño m; **falls** (waterfall) cascada f; **Niagara Falls** las cataratas del Niágara. **2** vi* caer, caerse; (temperature, prices) bajar; **night was falling** anochecía; **to f. asleep** dormirse; **to f. ill** caer enfermo,-a; **to f. in love** enamorarse.

• **fall apart** vi (of machine) deshacerse.

• **fall back on** vt (as last resort) recurrir a.

• **fall behind** vi (in race) quedarse atrás; **to f. behind with one's work** retrasarse en el trabajo.

• **fall down** vi (picture etc) caerse; (building) derrumbarse.

• **fall for** vt (person) enamorarse de; (trick) dejarse engañar por.

• **fall in** vi (roof) desplomarse.

• **fall off** vi (drop off) caer; (part) desprenderse; (diminish) disminuir.

• **fall out** vi (hair) caerse; (quarrel) pelearse.

• **fall over** vi caerse.

• **fall through** vi (plan) fracasar.

false a falso,-a; **f. teeth** dentadura f postiza; **f. alarm** falsa alarma f.

fame fama f.

familiar a (common) conocido,-a; **his face is f.** su cara me suena; **to be on f. terms with sb** (know well) tener confianza con algn.

familiarity familiaridad f (with con); (intimacy) confianza f.

familiarize vt (make acquainted) familiarizar (with con); **to become familiarized with sth** familiarizarse con algo.

family familia f; **f. doctor** médico m de cabecera; **f. planning** planificación f familiar; **f. tree** árbol m genealógico.

famous a famoso,-a (for por).

fan (held in hand) abanico m; (electric) ventilador m; (person) aficionado,-a mf; (of pop star etc) fan mf; **football f.** hincha mf.

fancy 1 a de fantasía; **f. goods** artículos mpl de fantasía. **2** n (whim) capricho m; **to take a f. to sth** encapricharse con algo; **what takes your f.?** ¿qué se le antoja? **3** vt (imagine) imaginarse; (like, want) apetecer; **fam f. that!** ¡fíjate!; **do you f. a drink?** ¿te apetece una copa?

fan heater estufa f de aire.

fantastic a fantástico,-a.

far 1 a (distant) lejano,-a; **at the f. end** en el otro extremo. **2** adv (distant) lejos; **f. off** a lo lejos; **farther back** más atrás; **how f. is it to Chicago?** ¿cuánto hay de aquí a Chicago; **as f. as I can** en lo que puedo; **as f. as I know** que yo sepa; **as f. as possible** en lo posible; **f. from complaining, he seemed pleased** lejos de quejarse, parecía contento; **in so f. as . . .** en la medida en que

. . . ; **to go too f.** pasarse de la raya;
f. into the night hasta muy entrada la noche; **so f.** (*in time*) hasta
ahora; **by f.** con mucho; **f. cleverer**
mucho más listo,-a; **f. too much**
demasiado.

faraway *a* lejano,-a.

farce farsa *f*.

fare (*ticket price*) tarifa *f*, precio *m*
del billete; (*for boat*) pasaje *m*;
(*passenger*) pasajero,-a *mf*.

farewell 1 *interj* (*old use*) ¡adiós!
2 *n* despedida *f*.

far-fetched *a* rebuscado,-a.

farm 1 *n* granja *f*, Am hacienda *f*. **2**
vt cultivar.

• **farm out** *vt* encargar fuera.

farmer granjero,-a *mf*, Am hacen-
dado,-a *mf*.

farmhouse granja *f*, Am hacienda *f*.

farming 1 *n* (*agriculture*) agricultura *f*; (*of land*) cultivo *m*. **2** *a*
agrícola.

farmyard corral *m*.

far-off *a* lejano,-a.

farther *adv* más lejos.

farthest 1 *a* más lejano,-a. **2** *adv*
más lejos.

fascinate *vt* fascinar.

fascination fascinación *f*.

fashion (*manner*) manera *f*; (*latest
style*) moda *f*; **to go/be out of f.** pa-
sar/no estar de moda; **f. parade**
desfile *m* de modelos.

fashion show pase *m* de modelos.

fast 1 *a* (*quick*) rápido,-a; (*clock*)
adelantado,-a. **2** *adv* rápidamente,
deprisa; **how f.?** ¿a qué velocidad?;
f. asleep profundamente dormido,-a.

fasten *vt* (*attach*) sujetar; (*fix*) fijar; (*belt*) abrochar; (*bag*) asegurar; (*shoelaces*) atar.

fastener cierre *m*.

fat 1 *a* gordo,-a; (*thick*) grueso,
-a; (*meat*) poco magra. **2** *n* grasa *f*;
cooking f. manteca *f* de cerdo.

fatal *a* (*accident, illness*) mortal;
(*ill-fated*) funesto,-a.

fatally *adv* **f. wounded** mortal-
mente herido,-a.

fate destino *m*.

father padre *m*; **my f. and mother**
mis padres.

Father Christmas Papá *m* Noel.

father-in-law suegro *m*.

fatigue fatiga *f*.

fattening *a* que engorda.

fatty 1 *a* (*food*) graso,-a. **2** *n* fam
(*person*) gordinflón,-ona *mf*.

faucet grifo *m*.

fault (*defect*) defecto *m*; (*in mer-
chandise*) desperfecto *m*; (*blame*)
culpa *f*; **to find f. with** poner reparos a; **to be at f.** tener la culpa.

faulty *a* defectuoso,-a.

favor 1 *n* favor *m*; **in f. of** a favor de;
to ask sb a f. pedirle un favor a
algn. **2** *vt* (*treat favorably*) favorecer; (*approve*) estar a favor de.

favorable *a* favorable.

favorite *a & n* favorito,-a (*mf*).

fax 1 *n* fax *m*. **2** *vt* (*document*) mandar por fax; **to f. sb** mandar un fax
a algn.

fear 1 *n* miedo *m*; **for f. of** por temor
a. **2** *vt* temer; **I f. it's too late** me
temo que ya es tarde.

fearless *a* intrépido,-a.

feast banquete *m*.

feat hazaña *f*.

feather pluma *f*; **f. duster** plumero
m.

feature 1 *n* (*of face*) facción *f*; (*characteristic*) característica *f*; **f. film**
largometraje *m*. **2** *vi* figurar.

February febrero *m*.

fed up *a* fam harto,-a (**with** de).

fee (*of lawyer, doctor*) honorarios
mpl.

feeble *a* débil.

feed [1] *vt* (*give food to*) dar de comer a; **to f. a baby** (*breast-feed*)
amamantar a un bebé; (*with bottle*) dar el biberón a un bebé. **2** *vi*
comer; (*cows, sheep*) pacer.

feedback feedback *m*; fig reacción *f*.

feel 1 *vi** (*have emotion, sensation*)
sentirse; (*have opinion*) opinar;
how do you f.? ¿qué tal te encuen-
tras?; **I f. bad about it** me da pena;
to f. happy sentirse feliz; **to f. cold/**

sleepy tener frío/sueño; **to f. up to sth** sentirse con ánimos para hacer algo; **I feel that . . .** me parece que . . . ; **it feels like summer** parece verano; **I f. sure that . . .** estoy seguro,-a de que . . . ; **I f. like an ice cream** me apetece un helado; **to f. like doing sth** tener ganas de hacer algo. **2** *vt** (*touch*) tocar; (*sense*) sentir; (*the cold*) notar; **she feels like a failure** se siente inútil. **3** *n* (*touch, sensation*) tacto *m*.

• **feel for** *vt* (*have sympathy for*) compadecer.

• **feel up to** *vt* tener ánimos para.

feeling (*emotion*) sentimiento *m*; (*physical*) sensación *f*; (*opinion*) opinión *f*; **I had the f. that . . .** (*impression*) tuve la impresión de que . . . ; **to express one's feelings** expresar sus opiniones.

feet *npl see* **foot.**

fell *pt of* **fall.**

fellow 1 *n* tipo *m*, tío *m*. **2 f. citizen** conciudadano,-a *mf*; **f. countryman/countrywoman** compatriota *mf*.

felt¹ *pt & pp of* **feel.**

felt² fieltro *m*.

felt-tip(ped) pen rotulador *m*.

female 1 *a* femenino,-a; (*animal*) hembra. **2** *n* (*animal*) hembra *f*; (*woman*) mujer *f*; (*girl*) chica *f*.

feminine *a* femenino,-a.

fence 1 *n* cerca *f*. **2** *vi* (*in sport*) practicar la esgrima.

• **fence in** *vt* meter en un cercado.

fencing (*sport*) esgrima *f*.

fend *vi* **to f. for oneself** valerse por sí mismo.

• **fend off** *vt* (*blow*) parar; (*attack*) rechazar.

fender (*on car*) parachoques *m inv.*

fern helecho *m*.

ferocious *a* feroz.

ferry 1 *n* (*small*) barca *f* de pasaje; (*large, for cars*) ferry *m*. **2** *vt* transportar.

fertile *a* fértil.

fertilizer abono *m*.

festival festival *m*.

festive *a* festivo,-a; **the f. season** las fiestas de Navidad.

festivity the festivities las fiestas.

fetch *vt* (*go for*) ir a buscar; (*bring*) traer.

fete fiesta *f*.

fever fiebre *f*.

feverish *a* febril.

few *a* (*not many*) pocos,-as; **as f. as** solamente; **a f.** unos,-as, algunos, -as; **in the next f. days** dentro de unos días; **she has fewer books than I thought** tiene menos libros de lo que pensaba; **quite a f.** un buen número. **2** *pron* (*not many*) pocos,-as; **there are too f.** no hay suficientes; **a f.** (*some*) algunos,-as; **who has the fewest?** ¿quién tiene menos?

fiancé prometido *m*.

fiancée prometida *f*.

fiber fibra *f*.

fiction ficción *f*.

fiddle *fam n* (*musical instrument*) violín *m*.

• **fiddle about** *vi* juguetear (**with** con).

fidget *vi* moverse; **stop fidgeting!** ¡estate quieto!; **to f. with sth** jugar con algo.

field 1 *n* campo *m*; (*oil field, coal field etc*) yacimiento *m*. **2** *vt* (*in sport*) (*ball*) parar y devolver; (*team*) presentar.

field trip viaje *m* de estudios.

field work trabajo *m* de campo.

fierce *a* (*animal*) feroz; (*argument*) acalorado,-a; (*heat, competition*) intenso,-a.

fifteen *a & n* quince *m inv.*

fifteenth *a & n* decimoquinto,-a (*mf*).

fifth *a & n* quinto,-a (*mf*).

fiftieth *adj & n* quincuagésimo,-a (*mf*).

fifty 1 *a* cincuenta *inv; a* **f.-f. chance** una probabilidad del cincuenta por ciento; **to go f.-f.** ir a medias. **2** *n* cincuenta *m inv.*

fig (*fruit*) higo *m*.

fight 1 *vt** combatir; (*bull*) lidiar. **2** *vi** pelear(se); (*quarrel*) reñir; *fig* (*struggle*) luchar (**for/against** por/contra). **3** *n* pelea *f*; (*boxing*) combate *m*; (*quarrel*) riña *f*; *fig* (*struggle*) lucha *f*.
• **fight back 1** *vt* (*tears*) contener. **2** *vi* (*recover ground*) resistir.
• **fight off** *vt* (*attack*) rechazar.
• **fight out** *vt* arreglar discutiendo o peleando.
fighter (*person*) combatiente *mf*; (*boxing*) púgil *m*; *fig* luchador,-a *mf*; **f. (plane)** (avión *m* de) caza *m*.
figure¹ 1 *n* (*numeral*) cifra *f*; (*form, outline*) forma *f*; (*shape, statue, character*) figura *f*; **she has a good f.** tiene buen tipo; **f. of speech** figura retórica. **2** *vt fam* imaginarse. **3** *vi* (*appear*) figurar; *fam* **that figures** eso tiene sentido.
figure² *vt* (*guess*) imaginar.
• **figure on** *vt* **to f. on doing sth** esperar hacer algo.
• **figure out** *vt* comprender; **I can't f. it out** no me lo explico.
file 1 *n* (*tool*) lima *f*; (*folder*) carpeta *f*; (*archive*) archivo *m*; (*of computer*) fichero *m*; (*line*) fila *m*; **on f.** archivado,-a; **in single f.** en fila india. **2** *vt* (*smooth*) limar; (*put away*) archivar. **3** *vi* **to f. past** desfilar.
• **file away** *vt* (*put away*) archivar; (*in card catalog*) clasificar.
• **file down** *vt* limar.
• **file in/out** *vi* entrar/salir en fila.
filing clasificación *f*.
filing cabinet archivador *m*; (*for cards*) fichero *m*.
fill 1 *vt* (*space, time*) llenar (**with** de); (*post, requirements*) cubrir. **2** *vi* llenarse (**with** de).
• **fill in 1** *vt* (*space, form*) rellenar; (*time*) pasar; (*inform*) *fam* poner al corriente (**on** de). **2** *vi* **to f. in for sb** sustituir a algn.
• **fill out** *vt* (*form*) rellenar.
• **fill up 1** *vt* llenar hasta arriba; **f. her up!** ¡llénelo! **2** *vi* llenarse.
fillet filete *m*; **f. steak** filete *m*.
filling 1 *a* que llena mucho. **2** *n*

(*stuffing*) relleno *m*; (*in tooth*) empaste *m*.
filling station gasolinera *f*.
film 1 *n* película *f*. **2** *vt* filmar. **3** *vi* rodar.
film star estrella *f* de cine.
filter 1 *n* filtro *m*; **f. lane** carril *m* de acceso. **2** *vt* filtrar. **3** *vi* (*traffic*) **to f. to the right** girar a la derecha.
filth (*dirt*) porquería *f*; *fig* porquerías *fpl*.
filthy *a* (*dirty*) asqueroso,-a; (*obscene*) obsceno,-a.
fin (*of fish*) aleta *f*.
final 1 *a* último,-a; (*definitive*) definitivo,-a. **2** *n* (*sport*) final *f*.
finalize *vt* ultimar; (*date*) fijar.
finally *adv* finalmente.
finance 1 *n* finanzas *fpl*; **finances** fondos *mpl*. **2** *vt* financiar.
financial *a* financiero,-a.
find 1 *vt** (*locate, think*) encontrar; (*discover*) descubrir; **it has been found that . . .** se ha comprobado que . . . ; **I found it impossible to get away** me resultó imposible irme. **2** *n* hallazgo *m*.
• **find out 1** *vt* (*inquire*) averiguar; (*discover*) descubrir. **2** *vi* **to f. out about sth** informarse sobre algo; (*discover*) enterarse de algo.
fine¹ 1 *n* (*sum of money*) multa *f*. **2** *vt* multar.
fine² 1 *a* (*delicate etc*) fino,-a; (*excellent*) excelente; (*weather*) bueno; **it was f.** hacía buen tiempo. **2** *adv* muy bien. **3** *interj* ¡vale!
finger dedo *m* (de la mano); **to keep one's fingers crossed** esperar que todo salga bien.
fingernail uña *f*.
fingerprint huella *f* dactilar.
fingertip punta *f* or yema *f* del dedo.
finish 1 *n* fin *m*; (*of race*) llegada *f*. **2** *vt* (*complete*) acabar, terminar; (*use up*) agotar; **to f. doing sth** terminar de hacer algo. **3** *vi* acabar, terminar.
• **finish off** *vt* (*complete*) terminar completamente; (*kill*) rematar.
• **finish up 1** *vt* acabar; **to f. up**

doing sth acabar haciendo algo. **2** *vi* **to f. up in jail** ir a parar a la cárcel.

Finn finlandés,-esa *mf*.

Finnish 1 *a* finlandés,-esa. **2** *n* (*language*) finlandés *m*.

fir abeto *m*.

fire 1 *n* fuego *m*; (*accident etc*) incendio *m*; (*heater*) estufa *f*; (*gunfire*) fuego *m*; **to open f.** abrir fuego. **2** *vt* (*gun*) disparar (**at** a); (*dismiss*) despedir. **3** *vi* (*shoot*) disparar (**at** sobre).

fire alarm alarma *f* de incendios.

fire brigade (cuerpo *m* de) bomberos *mpl*.

firecracker petardo *m*.

fire exit salida *f* de emergencia.

fire extinguisher extintor *m*

fireman bombero *m*.

fireplace chimenea *f*; (*hearth*) hogar *m*.

firewood leña *f*.

fireworks *npl* fuegos *mpl* artificiales.

firm 1 *a* firme. **2** *n* empresa *f*.

first 1 *a* primero,-a; (*before masculine singular noun*) primer; **for the f. time** por primera vez; **in the f. place** en primer lugar. **2** *adv* (*before anything else*) primero; **f. and foremost** ante todo; **at f.** al principio. **3** *n* **the f.** el primero, la primera; **the f. of April** el uno *or* el primero de abril; **from the (very) f.** desde el principio.

firstly *adv* en primer lugar.

first aid primeros auxilios.

first-class 1 *a* de primera clase. **2** *adv* **to travel f.** viajar en primera.

fish 1 *n* (*pl* **fish**) pez *m*; (*as food*) pescado *m*. **2** *vi* pescar.

fisherman pescador *m*.

fishing pesca *f*; **to go f.** ir de pesca.

fishing rod caña *f* de pescar.

fish shop pescadería *f*.

fish stick palito *m* de pescado.

fist puño *m*.

fit¹ *vt* (*clothes*) ir bien a; (*slot*) encajar; (*install*) colocar; **that suit doesn't f. you** ese traje no te queda bien; **a car fitted with a radio** un co-

che provisto de radio; **she doesn't f. the description** no responde a la descripción. **2** *vi* (*be of right size*) caber; (*be suitable*) (*facts etc*) cuadrar. **3** *a* (*suitable*) apto,-a (**for** para); (*healthy*) en (plena) forma; **are you f. to drive?** ¿estás en condiciones de conducir?; **to keep f.** mantenerse en forma. **4** *n* **to be a good f.** encajar bien.

fit² (*attack*) ataque *m*; *fig* arrebato *m*; **by fits and starts** a trompicones.

• **fit in 1** *vi* (*tally*) cuadrar (**with** con); **he didn't f. in with his colleagues** no encajó con sus compañeros de trabajo. **2** *vt* (*find time for*) encontrar un hueco para.

• **fit on** *vt* **to f. sth onto sth** colocar *o* encajar algo en algo.

• **fit out** *vt* equipar.

fitness (*health*) (buen) estado *m* físico.

fitted *a* empotrado,-a; **f. carpet** moqueta *f*.

fitting room probador *m*.

fittings *npl* accesorios *mpl*; **light f.** apliques *mpl* eléctricos.

five *a* & *n* cinco (*m*) *inv*; **f. hundred** quinientos,-as.

fix 1 *n* **to be in a f.** estar en un apuro. **2** *vt* (*fasten*) fijar; (*date, price*) fijar; (*repair*) arreglar; (*food, drink*) preparar; **he'll f. it with the boss** (*arrange*) se las arreglará con el jefe.

• **fix on** *vt* (*lid etc*) encajar.

• **fix up** *vt* (*arrange*) arreglar; **to f. sb up with sth** proveer a algn de algo.

fizzy *a* (*water*) con gas.

flag 1 *n* bandera *f*; (*on ship*) pabellón *m*. **2** *vi* (*interest*) decaer; (*conversation*) languidecer.

flake 1 *n* (*of snow*) copo *m*; (*of skin, soap*) escama *f*. **2** *vi* (*paint*) desconcharse.

flame llama *f*; **to go up in flames** incendiarse.

flammable *a* inflamable.

flan tarta *f* rellena; **fruit f.** tarta *f* de fruta.

flannel (*material*) franela *f*.

flap 1 vt (wings, arms) batir. **2** vi (wings) aletear; (flag) ondear. **3** n (of envelope, pocket) solapa f; **to get into a f.** ponerse nervioso,-a.

flare 1 n (distress signal) bengala f. **2** vi (fire) llamear; (trouble) estallar.

flash 1 n (of light) destello m; (of lightning) relámpago m; (for camera) flash m. **2** vt (torch) dirigir; **he flashed his card** enseñó rápidamente su carnet. **3** vi (sudden light) destellar; (shine) brillar; **a car flashed past** un coche pasó como un rayo.

flashlight linterna f.

flask frasco m; **(thermos) f.** termo m.

flat 1 a (surface) llano,-a; (beer) sin gas; (battery) descargado,-a; (tire) desinflado,-a; (dull) soso,-a; (in music) **B f.** si m bemol. **2** adv **to fall f. on one's face** caerse de bruces; **to go f. out** ir a todo gas. **3** n (flat tire) pinchazo m.

flatly adv rotundamente.

flatten vt (make level) allanar; (crush) aplastar.

flatter vt halagar; (clothes, portrait) favorecer.

flavor 1 n sabor m. **2** vt (food) sazonar (with con).

flavoring condimento m; **artificial f.** aroma m artificial.

flaw (failing) defecto m; (fault) desperfecto m.

flea pulga f.

flea market rastro m.

flee* 1 vt huir. **2** vi huir (from de).

fleet flota f.

Flemish 1 a flamenco,-a. **2** n (language) flamenco m.

flesh carne f; (of fruit) pulpa f; **in the f.** en persona.

flex vt (muscles) flexionar.

flexible a flexible.

flick 1 n (of finger) capirotazo m. **2** vt (finger) dar un capirotazo a.

• **flick off** vt (piece of fluff) quitar con un dedo.

• **flick through** vt hojear.

flies npl (on trousers) bragueta f.

flight vuelo m; (escape) huida f; (of stairs) tramo m; **to take f.** darse a la fuga.

flight attendant azafata f.

flimsy a (cloth) ligero,-a; (structure) poco sólido,-a; (excuse) poco convincente.

fling* vt arrojar.

flint (in lighter) piedra f de mechero.

flip-flop (footwear) chancleta f.

flip through vt (book) hojear.

float 1 n flotador m; (in procession) carroza f. **2** vi flotar.

flock 1 n rebaño m; (of birds) bandada f. **2** vi acudir en masa.

flood 1 n inundación f; (of river) riada f. **2** vt inundar. **3** vi (river) desbordarse.

floodlight foco m.

floor (of room) suelo m; (storey) piso m; **first f.** planta f baja.

floorboard tabla f (del suelo).

flop 1 n (failure) fracaso m. **2** vi fracasar.

floppy a flojo,-a.

floppy disk disquete m, disco m flexible.

florist florista mf; **f.'s** floristería f.

flounder inv (fish) platija f.

flour harina f.

flow 1 n flujo m; (of traffic) circulación f; (of people, goods) movimiento m. **2** vi (blood, river) fluir; (traffic) circular.

flow chart organigrama m.

flower 1 n flor f. **2** vi florecer.

flower bed arriate m.

flower shop floristería f.

flu gripe f.

fluent a (eloquent) fluido,-a; **he speaks f. German** habla el alemán con soltura.

fluently adv (to speak) con soltura.

fluff (down) pelusa f.

fluid líquido m.

flunk vt fam catear.

fluorescent a fluorescente.

flush 1 a **f. with** (level) a ras de. **2** n

(blush) rubor m. **3** vt **to f. the lavatory** tirar de la cadena. **4** vi (blush) ruborizarse.

flute flauta f.

flutter vi (leaves, birds) revolotear; (flag) ondear.

fly¹* **1** vt (plane) pilotar. **2** vi (bird, plane) volar; (go by plane) ir en avión; (flag) ondear.

• **fly over** vt (country etc) sobrevolar.

fly² (insect) mosca f; **f. spray** spray m matamoscas.

fly³ (on trousers) bragueta f.

flying **1** a (soaring) volante; (rapid) rápido,-a. **2** n (action) vuelo m; (aviation) aviación f.

flying saucer platillo m volante.

flyover paso m elevado.

foam espuma f; **f. rubber** goma f espuma.

focus **1** vt centrar (**on** en). **2** vi **to f. on sth** enfocar algo; fig centrarse en algo. **3** n foco m.

fog niebla f; (at sea) bruma f.

foggy a **it is f.** hay niebla.

foil **1** n **aluminum f.** papel m de aluminio. **2** vt (plot) frustrar.

fold **1** n (crease) pliegue m. **2** vt doblar; **to f. one's arms** cruzar los brazos. **3** vi **to f. (up)** (chair etc) plegarse.

• **fold away** vt plegar.

folder carpeta f.

folding a (chair etc) plegable.

folk npl (people) gente f.

folk music música f folk.

follow **1** vt seguir; (understand) comprender. **2** vi (come after) seguir; (result) resultar; (understand) entender; **that doesn't f.** eso no es lógico.

• **follow around** vt **to f. sb around** seguir a algn por todas partes.

• **follow on** vi (come after) venir detrás.

• **follow up** vt (idea) llevar a cabo; (clue) investigar.

follower seguidor,-a mf.

following **1** a siguiente. **2** n seguidores mpl.

fond a **to be f. of sb** tenerle mucho cariño a algn; **to be f. of doing sth** ser aficionado,-a a hacer algo.

font (of characters) fuente f.

food comida f.

food poisoning intoxicación f alimenticia.

fool **1** n tonto,-a mf; **to play the f.** hacer el tonto. **2** vt (deceive) engañar. **3** vi (joke) bromear.

• **fool around** vi hacer el tonto.

foolish a (silly) tonto,-a; (unwise) estúpido,-a.

foolishly adv estúpidamente.

foot **1** n (pl **feet**) pie m; (of animal) pata f; **on f.** a pie; **to put one's f. in it** meter la pata. **2** vt **to f. the bill** (pay) pagar la cuenta.

football fútbol americano m; (ball) balón m.

footbridge puente m para peatones.

footpath sendero m.

footprint pisada f.

footstep paso m.

for prep (purpose) para; **what's this f.?** ¿para qué sirve esto?; **f. sale** en venta. ▪ (because of, on behalf of) por; **famous f. its cuisine** famoso,-a por su cocina; **will you do it f. me?** ¿lo harás por mí? ▪ (instead of) por; **can you go f. me?** puede ir por mí? ▪ (during) por, durante; **I was ill f. a month** estuve enfermo,-a durante un mes; **I've been here f. three months** hace tres meses que estoy aquí. ▪ (distance) por; **I walked f. ten kilometers** caminé diez kilómetros. ▪ (at a point in time) por; **I can do it f. next Monday** puedo hacerlo para el lunes que viene; **f. the last time** por última vez. ▪ (in exchange for) por; **I got the car f. five hundred dollars** conseguí el coche por quinientos dólares. ▪ (in favor of) a favor de; **are you f. or against?** ¿estás a favor o en contra? ▪ (towards) hacia, por; **affection f. sb** cariño hacia algn. ▪ **it's time f. you to go** es hora de que os marchéis.

forbid* vt prohibir; **to f. sb to do sth** prohibirle a algn hacer algo.

force 1 n fuerza f; **to come into f.** entrar en vigor; **the (armed) forces** las fuerzas armadas. **2** vt forzar; **to f. sb to do sth** forzar a algn a hacer algo.

forecast 1 n pronóstico m, previsión f. **2** vt* pronosticar.

forehead frente f.

foreign a extranjero,-a; (trade, policy) exterior.

foreigner extranjero,-a mf.

foreman capataz m.

foremost a principal; **first and f.** ante todo.

forerunner precursor,-a mf.

foresee* vt prever.

forest bosque m.

forever adv (constantly) siempre; (for good) para siempre.

forge vt (counterfeit) falsificar; (metal) forjar.

• **forge ahead** vi hacer grandes progresos.

forgery falsificación f.

forget* 1 vt olvidar; **I forgot to close the window** se me olvidó cerrar la ventana. **2** vi olvidarse.

• **forget about** vt olvidar.

forgetful a olvidadizo,-a.

forgive* vt perdonar; **to f. sb for sth** perdonarle algo a algn.

fork 1 n (cutlery) tenedor m; (farming) horca f; (in road) bifurcación f. **2** vi (roads) bifurcarse.

• **fork out** vt fam (money) soltar.

form 1 n forma f; (type) clase f; (document) formulario m; (at school) clase f; **on/on top/off f.** en/en plena/en baja forma. **2** vt formar. **3** vi formarse.

formal a (official) oficial; (party, dress) de etiqueta; (person) formalista.

formality formalidad f.

formally adv oficialmente.

format formato m.

formation formación f.

former a (time) anterior; (one-

time) antiguo,-a; (first) aquél, aquélla; **the f. champion** el ex-campeón.

formerly adv antes, antiguamente.

formula fórmula f.

fort fortaleza f.

fortieth adj & n cuadragésimo,-a (mf).

fortnight quincena f.

fortress fortaleza f.

fortunate a afortunado,-a; **it was f. that he came** fue una suerte que viniera.

fortunately adv afortunadamente.

fortune (luck, fate) suerte f; (money) fortuna f.

forty a & n cuarenta (m) inv.

forward 1 adv (also **forwards**) (direction and movement) hacia adelante; **from this day f.** de ahora en adelante. **2** a (person) fresco,-a. **3** n (in sport) delantero,-a mf. **4** vt (send on) remitir; (goods) expedir.

foul 1 a (smell) fétido,-a; (taste) asqueroso,-a; (language) grosero, -a. **2** n (in football etc) falta f.

found[1] pt & pp of **find.**

found[2] vt (establish) fundar.

fountain fuente f.

fountain pen pluma estilográfica f.

four a & n cuatro (m) inv; **on all fours** a gatas.

fourteen a & n catorce (m) inv.

fourth a & n cuarto,-a (mf).

fowl aves fpl de corral.

fox zorro,-a mf.

foyer vestíbulo m.

fraction fracción f.

fracture 1 n fractura f. **2** vt fracturar.

fragile a frágil.

fragment fragmento m.

fragrance fragancia f.

frail a frágil.

frame 1 n (of window, door, picture) marco m; (of machine) armazón m; **f. of mind** estado m de ánimo.

2 vt (picture) enmarcar; (question) formular; (innocent person) incriminar.

framework within the f. of . . . dentro del marco de . . .

franc franco m.

frank a franco,-a.

frankly adv francamente.

frankness franqueza f.

frantic a (anxious) desesperado,-a; (hectic) frenético,-a.

frantically adv desesperadamente.

fraud fraude m; (person) impostor,-a mf.

fray vi (cloth) deshilacharse.

freckle peca f.

freckled a pecoso,-a.

free **1** a libre; **f. (of charge)** gratuito,-a; (generous) generoso,-a. **2** adv **(for) f.** gratis. **3** vt (liberate) poner en libertad.

freedom libertad f.

freeway autopista f.

freeze* **1** vt congelar. **2** vi (liquid) helarse; (food) congelarse.

• **freeze up** or **over** vi helarse, (windshield) cubrirse de hielo.

freezer congelador m.

freezing a glacial; **above/below f. point** sobre/bajo cero.

French **1** a francés,-esa. **2** n (language) francés m; pl the **F.** los franceses.

French fries npl patatas fpl fritas.

Frenchman francés m.

Frenchwoman francesa f.

frequent a frecuente.

frequently adv frecuentemente.

fresh a fresco,-a; (new) nuevo,-a; **in the f. air** al aire libre.

freshen up vi asearse.

fret vi preocuparse (**about** por).

Friday viernes m.

fridge nevera f, frigorífico m.

fried a frito,-a.

friend amigo,-a mf; **a f. of mine** un,-a amigo,-a mío,-a.

friendly a (person) simpático,-a; (atmosphere) acogedor,-a.

friendship amistad f.

fright (fear) miedo m; (shock) susto m; **to get a f.** pegarse un susto.

frighten vt asustar.

• **frighten away** or **off** vt ahuyentar.

frightened a asustado,-a; **to be f. of sb** tenerle miedo a algn.

frightening a espantoso,-a.

frill (dress) volante m.

fringe (of hair) flequillo m.

frog rana f.

from prep (time) desde, a partir de; **f. the eighth to the seventeenth** desde el ocho hasta el diecisiete; **f. time to time** de vez en cuando. ▪ (price, number) desde, de; **dresses f. ten dollars** vestidos desde díez dólares. ▪ (origin) de; **he's f. Malaga** es de Málaga; **the train f. Bilbao** el tren procedente de Bilbao ▪ (distance) de; **the town is four miles f. the coast** el pueblo está a cuatro millas de la costa. ▪ (remove, subtract) a; **he took the book f. the child** le quitó el libro al niño. ▪ (according to) según, por; **f. what the author said** según lo que dijo el autor. ▪ (position) desde, de; **f. here** desde aquí.

front **1** n parte f delantera; (of building) fachada f; (military, political, of weather) frente m; **in f. (of)** delante (de). **2** a delantero,-a.

front door puerta f principal.

frost n (covering) escarcha f; (freezing) helada f.

frostbite congelación f.

frosty a fig glacial; **it will be a f. night tonight** esta noche habrá helada.

froth espuma f.

frown vi fruncir el ceño.

• **frown upon** vt desaprobar.

frozen a (liquid, feet, etc) helado,-a; (food) congelado,-a.

fruit fruta f; **fruits** (rewards) frutos mpl.

fruit salad macedonia f de frutas

frustrated a frustrado,-a.

frustrating *a* frustrante.

fry *vt* freír.

frying pan sartén *f*.

fuel combustible *m*; (*for engines*) carburante *m*.

fugitive fugitivo,-a *mf*.

fulfill *vt* (*task, ambition*) realizar; (*promise*) cumplir; (*wishes*) satisfacer.

fulfilling *a* que llena.

full 1 *a* lleno,-a (**of** de); (*complete*) completo,-a; **I'm f. (up)** no puedo más. **2** *n* **in f.** en su totalidad.

full board pensión *f* completa.

full-scale *a* (*model*) de tamaño natural.

full stop punto *m*.

full-time 1 *a* de jornada completa. **2** *adv* **to work f.** trabajar aa jornada completa.

fully *adv* completamente.

fumes *npl* humo *m*.

fun (*amusement*) diversión *f*; **in** or **for f.** en broma; **to have f.** pasarlo bien; **to make f. of sb** reírse de algn.

function 1 *n* función *f*; (*ceremony*) acto *m*; (*party*) recepción *f*. **2** *vi* funcionar.

fund 1 *n* fondo *m*; **funds** fondos *mpl*. **2** *vt* (*finance*) financiar.

funeral funeral *m*.

funnel (*for liquids*) embudo *m*; (*of ship*) chimenea *f*.

funny *a* (*peculiar*) raro,-a; (*amusing*) divertido,-a; (*ill*) mal; **I found it very f.** me hizo mucha gracia.

fur (*of living animal*) pelo *m*; (*of dead animal*) piel *f*.

furious *a* (*angry*) furioso,-a.

furnish *vt* (*house*) amueblar.

furniture muebles *mpl*; **a piece of f.** un mueble.

further 1 *a* (*new*) nuevo,-a; (*additional*) otro,-a. **2** *adv* más lejos; (*more*) más; **f. back** más atrás.

further education estudios *mpl* superiores.

furthermore *adv* además.

furthest *a* más lejano,-a.

fury furia *f*.

fuse 1 *n* fusible *m*; (*of bomb*) mecha *f*. **2** *vi* **the lights fused** se fundieron los plomos.

fuss 1 *n* (*commotion*) jaleo *m*; **to kick up a f.** armar un escándalo; **to make a f. of** (*pay attention to*) mimar a. **2** *vi* preocuparse (**about** por).

• **fuss over** *vt* consentir a.

fussy *a* (*nitpicking*) quisquilloso,-a; (*thorough*) exigente.

future 1 *n* futuro *m*; **in the near f.** en un futuro próximo. **2** *a* futuro, -a.

fuzzy *a* (*hair*) muy rizado,-a; (*blurred*) borroso,-a.

G

gadget aparato *m*.

Gaelic 1 *a* gaélico,-a. **2** *n* (*language*) gaélico *m*.

gag 1 *n* mordaza *f*; (*joke*) chiste *m*. **2** *vt* amordazar.

gaiety regocijo *m*.

gaily *adv* alegremente.

gain 1 *n* ganancia *f*; (*increase*) aumento *m*. **2** *vt* (*obtain*) ganar; (*increase*) aumentar; **to g. weight** aumentar de peso.

• **gain on** *vt* ganar terreno a.

gala gala *f*.

galaxy galaxia *f*.

gale vendaval *m*.

gallant *a* (*chivalrous*) galante.

gallery galería *f*.

gallivant *vi fam* callejear.

gallon galón *m*.

gallop 1 *n* galope *m*. **2** *vi* galopar.

gamble 1 *n* (*risk*) riesgo *m*; (*bet*) apuesta *f*. **2** *vi* (*bet*) jugar; (*take a risk*) arriesgarse.

• **gamble away** *vt* (*lose*) perder en el juego.

gambler jugador,-a *mf*.

gambling juego *m*.

game juego *m*; (*match*) partido *m*; (*of bridge*) partida *f*.

gang (*of criminals*) banda *f*; (*of youths*) pandilla *f*.

- **gang up** *vi* confabularse (**on** contra).

gangster gángster *m*.

gangway pasarela *f*.

gap hueco *m*; (*blank space*) blanco *m*; (*in time*) intervalo *m*; (*gulf*) diferencia *f*; (*deficiency*) laguna *f*.

gape *vi* (*person*) mirar boquiabierto,-a.

garage garaje *m*; (*for repairs*) taller *m* mecánico; (*gas station*) gasolinera *f*.

garbage basura *f*; **g. can** cubo *m* de la basura.

garden jardín *m*.

gardener jardinero,-a *mf*.

gardening jardinería *f*.

gargle *vi* hacer gárgaras.

garland guirnalda *f*.

garlic ajo *m*.

garment prenda *f*.

gas *n* gas *m*; gasolina *f*; **g. cooker** cocina *f* de gas; **g. fire** estufa *f* de gas. **2** *vt* (*asphyxiate*) asfixiar con gas.

gash 1 *n* herida *f* profunda. **2** *vt* **he gashed his forehead** se hizo una herida en la frente.

gasoline gasolina *f*.

gasp 1 *n* (*cry*) grito *m* sordo; (*breath*) bocanada *f*. **2** *vi* (*in surprise*) quedar boquiabierto,-a; (*breathe*) jadear.

gas station gasolinera *f*.

gassy *a* gaseoso,-a.

gas tank depósito *m* de gasolina.

gasworks fábrica *f* de gas.

gate puerta *f*; (*at stadium*) entrada *f*.

gatecrash *vti* colarse.

gather 1 *vt* (*collect*) juntar; (*pick up*) recoger; (*bring together*) reunir; (*understand*) suponer; **to g. speed** ir ganando velocidad; **I g. that . . .** tengo entendido que . . . **2** *vi* (*come together*) reunirse.

- **gather around** *vi* agruparse.

gathering reunión *f*.

gaudy *a* chillón,-ona.

gauge 1 *n* (*of railway*) ancho *m* de vía; (*calibrator*) indicador *m*. **2** *vt* (*judge*) juzgar.

gaunt *a* (*lean*) demacrado,-a; (*desolate*) lúgubre.

gauze gasa *f*.

gave *pt* of **give**.

gay *a* (*homosexual*) gay; (*happy*) alegre.

gaze 1 *n* mirada *f* fija. **2** *vi* mirar fijamente.

- **gaze at** *vt* mirar fijamente.

GB *abbr of* **Great Britain**.

gear 1 *n* (*equipment*) equipo *m*; (*belongings*) bártulos *mpl*; (*clothing*) ropa *f*; (*in car etc*) marcha *f*. **2** *vt* adaptar (**to** a).

gearbox caja *f* de cambios.

geese *npl* see **goose**.

gel gel *m*; (*for hair*) gomina *f*.

gem piedra *f* preciosa.

gender género *m*.

general 1 *a* general; **in g.** en general; **the g. public** el público. **2** *n* (*in army*) general *m*.

generally *adv* generalmente.

generation generación *f*.

generation gap abismo *m* or conflicto *m* generacional.

generator generador *m*.

generosity generosidad *f*.

generous *a* generoso,-a; (*plentiful*) copioso,-a.

generously *adv* generosamente.

genius (*person*) genio *m*; (*gift*) don *m*.

gentle *a* dulce; (*breeze*) suave.

gentleman caballero *m*.

gentleness (*mildness*) ternura *f*; (*kindness*) amabilidad *f*.

gently con cuidado.

gents *npl* servicio *m* de caballeros.

genuine *a* auténtico,-a; (*sincere*) sincero,-a.

genuinely *adv* auténticamente.

geographic(al) *a* geográfico,-a.

geography geografía *f*.

geometric(al) *a* geométrico,-a.

geometry geometría *f*.

germ microbio *m*.

German 1 *a* alemán, -ana; **G. measles** rubeola *f*. **2** *n* alemán, -ana *mf*; (*language*) alemán *m*.

German shepherd (*dog*) pastor *m* alemán.

gesture gesto m.

get* 1 vt (obtain) obtener, conseguir; (earn) ganar; (fetch) (something) traer; (somebody) ir a por; (receive) recibir; (bus, train, thief etc) coger, Am agarrar; (understand) entender; (on phone) **g. me Mr Brown** póngame con el Sr. Brown; **can I g. you something to eat?** ¿te traigo algo de comer?; **g. him to call me** dile que me llame; **to g. one's hair cut** cortarse el pelo; **to g. sb to do sth** (ask) persuadir a algn de que haga algo. **2** vi (become) ponerse; **to g. late** hacerse tarde; **to g. dressed** vestirse; **to g. married** casarse; **to g. to** (come to) llegar a; **to g. to know sb** llegar a conocer a algn.

• **get across** vt (idea etc) hacer comprender.

• **get along** vi (manage) arreglárselas; (two people) llevarse bien.

• **get around 1** vi (person) salir; (news) difundirse. **2** vt (problem) salvar; (difficulty) vencer.

• **get around to** vi **if I g. around to it** si tengo tiempo; **I'll g. around to it later** encontraré tiempo para hacerlo más tarde.

• **get at** vt (reach) alcanzar; (criticize) criticar.

• **get away** vi escaparse.

• **get back 1** vi (return) volver; **g. back!** (move backwards) ¡atrás! **2** vt (recover) recuperar.

• **get by** vi (manage) arreglárselas; **she can g. by in French** sabe defenderse en francés.

• **get down 1** vt (depress) deprimir. **2** vi (descend) bajar.

• **get in 1** vi (arrive) llegar; (politician) ser elegido,-a. **2** vt (buy) comprar; (collect) recoger.

• **get off 1** vt (bus etc) bajarse de; (remove) quitarse. **2** vi (escape) escaparse; **to g. off lightly** salir bien librado,-a.

• **get on 1** vt (board) subir a. **2** vi (board) subirse; (make progress) hacer progresos; **how are you get-**

ting on? ¿cómo te van las cosas?; **to g. on (well with sb)** llevarse bien (con algn); (continue) **to g. on with sth** seguir con algo.

• **get on to** vt (find) (person) localizar; (find out) descubrir; (continue) pasar a.

• **get out 1** vt (object) sacar. **2** vi (of room etc) salir (**of** de); (of train) bajar (**of** de); (news) difundirse; (secret) hacerse público.

• **get over** vt (illness) recuperarse de; (difficulty) vencer; (convey) hacer comprender.

• **get through 1** vi (message) llegar; (on phone) **to g. through to sb** conseguir comunicar con algn. **2** vt (consume) consumir; **to g. through a lot of work** trabajar mucho.

• **get together** vi (people) reunirse.

• **get up 1** vi (rise) levantarse. **2** vt (wake up) despertar.

• **get up to** vi hacer; **to g. up to mischief** hacer de las suyas.

get-together reunión f.

ghastly a espantoso,-a.

gherkin pepinillo m.

ghetto gueto m.

ghost fantasma m.

giant a & n gigante (m).

giddy a mareado,-a; **it makes me g.** me da vértigo; **to feel g.** sentirse mareado,-a.

gift regalo m; (talent) don m.

gifted a dotado,-a.

gigantic a gigantesco,-a.

giggle vi reírse tontamente.

gimmick truco m; (in advertising) reclamo m.

gin ginebra f; **g. and tonic** gin tonic m.

ginger 1 a (hair) pelirrojo,-a. **2** n jengibre m.

giraffe jirafa f.

girl chica f; (child) niña f; (daughter) hija f.

girlfriend novia f; (female friend) amiga f.

give* vt dar; **to g. sb sth as a present** regalar algo a algn.

- **give away** *vt* (*present*) regalar; (*disclose*) revelar.
- **give back** *vt* devolver.
- **give in** *vi* (*admit defeat*) darse por vencido,-a; (*surrender*) rendirse. **2** *vt* (*hand in*) entregar.
- **give off** *vt* (*smell etc*) despedir.
- **give out** *vt* repartir.
- **give up** *vt* (*idea*) abandonar; **to g. up smoking** dejar de fumar; **to g. oneself up** entregarse.

glad *a* contento,-a; **to be g.** alegrarse.

gladly *adv* con mucho gusto.

glamorous *a* atractivo,-a.

glamour atractivo *m*; (*charm*) encanto *m*.

glance 1 *n* vistazo *m*. **2** *vi* echar un vistazo (**at** a).

gland glándula *f*.

glaring *a* (*light*) deslumbrante; (*obvious*) evidente.

glass (*material*) vidrio *m*; (*drinking vessel*) vaso *m*; **pane of g.** cristal *m*; **wine g.** copa *f* (para vino); **glasses** (*spectacles*) gafas *fpl*.

glee gozo *m*.

glide *vi* (*plane*) planear.

gliding vuelo *m* sin motor.

glimmer *fig* (*trace*) destello *m*.

glimpse 1 *n* atisbo *m*. **2** *vt* atisbar.

glittering *a* reluciente.

globe globo *m*.

gloom (*obscurity*) penumbra *f*; (*melancholy*) melancolía *f*.

gloomy *a* (*dismal*) deprimente; (*despondent*) pesimista; (*sad*) triste.

glorified *a fam* con pretensiones; **a g. boarding house** una pensión con pretensiones.

glorious *a* (*momentous*) glorioso, -a; (*splendid*) espléndido,-a.

glory gloria *f*; (*splendor*) esplendor *m*.

gloss (*sheen*) brillo *m*; **g. (paint)** esmalte *m*.

glossy *a* lustroso,-a; **g. magazine** revista *f* de lujo.

glove guante *m*; **g. compartment** guantera *f*.

glow 1 *n* brillo *m*. **2** *vi* brillar.

glue 1 *n* pegamento *m*. **2** *vt* pegar (**to** a).

glum *a* alicaído,-a.

glutton glotón,-ona *mf*.

gnat mosquito *m*.

gnaw *vti* (*chew*) roer.

go* 1 *vi* ir; (*depart*) irse, marcharse; (*bus*) salir; (*disappear*) desaparecer; (*function*) funcionar; (*become*) quedarse, volverse; (*fit*) caber; (*time*) pasar; **how's it going?** qué tal (te van las cosas)?; **to get** *or* **be going** marcharse; **to be going to** (*in the future*) ir a; (*on the point of*) estar a punto de; **there are only two weeks to go** sólo quedan dos semanas; **to let sth go** soltar algo. **2** *n* (*try*) intento *m*; (*turn*) turno *m*; **to have a go at sth** probar suerte con algo; **it's your go** te toca a ti; **to have a go at sb** criticar a algn.

- **go about 1** *vt* (*task*) emprender; **how do you go about it?** ¿cómo hay que hacerlo? **2** *vi* (*rumor*) correr.
- **go after** *vt* (*pursue*) andar tras.
- **go against** *vt* (*oppose*) ir en contra de.
- **go ahead** *vi* (*proceed*) proceder; **we'll go on ahead** iremos adelante.
- **go along** *vt* (*street*) ir por.
- **go along with** *vt* (*agree*) estar de acuerdo con; (*accompany*) acompañar.
- **go around** *vi* (*revolve*) dar vueltas; **to go around to sb's house** pasar por casa de algn.
- **go away** *vi* marcharse.
- **go back** *vi* (*return*) volver.
- **go back on** *vt* **to go back on one's word** faltar a su palabra.
- **go back to** *vt* volver a; (*date from*) datar de.
- **go by** *vi* pasar.
- **go down** *vi* (*descend*) bajar; (*sun*) ponerse; (*ship*) hundirse; (*diminish*) disminuir; (*temperature*) bajar.
- **go down with** *vt* (*disease*) coger.

• **go for** vt (fetch) ir por; (attack) atacar.

• **go in** vi entrar.

• **go in for** vt (exam) presentarse a.

• **go into** vt (enter) entrar en; (matter) investigar.

• **go off** vi (leave) irse, marcharse; (bomb) explotar; (gun) dispararse; (alarm) sonar; (food) pasarse.

• **go on** vi (continue) seguir, continuar; (happen) pasar; (light) encenderse; **to go on talking** seguir hablando.

• **go out** vi (leave) salir; (fire, light) apagarse.

• **go over** vt (cross) atravesar; (revise) repasar.

• **go over to** vt (switch to) pasar a; **to go over to the enemy** pasarse al enemigo.

• **go through** vt (endure) sufrir; (examine) examinar; (search) registrar; (spend) gastar.

• **go under** vi (ship) hundirse; (business) fracasar.

• **go up** vi subir.

• **go without** vt pasarse sin.

go-ahead **to give sb the g.** dar luz verde a algn.

goal gol m; (aim, objective) meta f.

goalkeeper portero,-a mf.

goat (male) macho cabrío m; (female) cabra f.

god dios m.

goddaughter ahijada f.

godfather padrino m.

godmother madrina f.

godsend **to be a g.** venir como agua de mayo.

godson ahijado m.

goggles npl (for diving) gafas fpl de bucear; (protective) gafas fpl protectoras.

going a (price) corriente.

goings-on npl tejemanejes mpl.

gold 1 n oro m. 2 a de oro; (color) dorado,-a.

golden a de oro; (color) dorado, -a.

goldfish pez m de colores.

gold-plated a chapado,-a en oro.

golf golf m.

golfer golfista mf.

gone pp of **go**.

good 1 a (before noun) buen, -a; (after noun) bueno,-a; (kind) amable; (generous) generoso,-a; (morally correct) correcto,-a; **g. afternoon, g. evening** buenas tardes; **g. morning** buenos días; **g. night** buenas noches; **to have a g. time** pasarlo bien; **be g.!** ¡pórtate bien!; **he's g. at languages** tiene facilidad para los idiomas; **he's in a g. mood** está de buen humor. 2 n bien m; **for your own g.** por tu propio bien; **it's no g. waiting** no sirve de nada esperar. 3 adv **she's gone for g.** se ha ido para siempre. 4 interj **g.!** ¡muy bien!

goodbye interj ¡adiós!

good-looking a guapo,-a.

goods npl (possessions) bienes mpl; (commercial) mercancías fpl.

good will buena voluntad f.

goose (pl **geese**) ganso m, oca f.

gooseberry grosella f espinosa.

gooseflesh, goosepimples npl carne f de gallina.

gorge desfiladero m.

gorgeous a magnífico,-a; (person) atractivo,-a.

gorilla gorila m.

gospel **the G.** el Evangelio.

gossip (rumor) cotilleo m; (person) chismoso,-a mf.

got pt & pp of **get**.

gotten pp **get**.

gourmet gourmet mf.

govern vt gobernar; (determine) determinar.

government gobierno m.

governor (ruler) gobernador,-a mf; (of school) administrador,-a mf.

gown (dress) vestido m largo; (of lawyer, professor) toga f.

GP abbr of **general practitioner** médico m de cabecera.

grab vt agarrar; **to g. hold of sb** agarrarse a algn.

grace gracia f; (elegance) elegancia f.

graceful *a* elegante; *(movement)* garboso,-a.

grade 1 *n* *(rank)* categoría *f*; *(in army)* rango *m*; *(mark)* nota *f*; *(class)* clase *f*. **2** *vt* clasificar.

gradual *a* gradual.

gradually *adv* poco a poco.

graduate 1 *n* licenciado,-a *mf*. **2** *vi* *(from university)* licenciarse **(in** en).

graduation ceremony ceremonia *f* de entrega de los títulos.

graffiti *npl* grafiti *mpl*.

graft 1 *n* injerto *m*. **2** *vt* injertar **(on to** en).

grain *(cereals)* cereales *mpl*; *(particle)* grano *m*.

gram gramo *m*.

grammar gramática *f*.

grammar school ≈ instituto *m* de Bachillerato.

grammatical *a* gramatical.

grand *a* *(splendid)* grandioso,-a; *(impressive)* impresionante.

grandchild nieto,-a *mf*.

granddad *fam* abuelo *m*.

granddaughter nieta *f*.

grandfather abuelo *m*.

grandma *fam* abuelita *f*.

grandmother abuela *f*.

grandparents *npl* abuelos *mpl*.

grandson nieto *m*.

granny *fam* abuelita *f*.

grant 1 *vt* *(give)* conceder; *(accept)* admitir; **to take for granted** dar por sentado. **2** *n* *(for study)* beca *f*; *(subsidy)* subvención *f*.

grape uva *f*; **g. juice** mosto *m*.

grapefruit pomelo *m*.

graph gráfica *f*.

graphics *npl* gráficos *mpl*.

grasp 1 *vt* agarrar; *(understand)* comprender. **2** *n* *(grip)* agarrón *m*; *(understanding)* comprensión *f*.

grass hierba *f*; *(lawn)* césped *m*.

grasshopper saltamontes *m inv*.

grate 1 *vt* *(food)* rallar. **2** *vi* chirriar. **3** *n* *(in fireplace)* rejilla *f*.

grateful *a* agradecido,-a; **to be g. for** agradecer.

grater rallador *m*.

gratifying *a* grato,-a.

gratitude agradecimiento *m*.

grave¹ tumba *f*.

grave² *a* *(situation)* grave.

gravel gravilla *f*.

graveyard cementerio *m*.

gravity gravedad *f*.

gravy salsa *f*.

gray *a* *(color)* gris; *(hair)* cano,-a; *(sky)* nublado,-a.

graze 1 *vt* *(scratch)* rasguñar; *(brush against)* rozar. **2** *vi* *(cattle)* pacer. **3** *n* rasguño *m*.

grease 1 *n* grasa *f*. **2** *vt* engrasar.

greaseproof paper papel *m* apergaminado.

greasy *a* *(hair, food)* graso,-a.

great *a* grande; *(before sing noun)* gran; *fam (excellent)* estupendo,-a; **a g. many** muchos,-as; **to have a g. time** pasarlo en grande.

great-grandfather bisabuelo *m*.

great-grandmother bisabuela *f*.

greatly *adv* *(with adjective)* muy; *(with verb)* mucho.

greed, greediness *(for food)* gula *f*; *(for money)* codicia *f*.

greedy *a* *(for food)* glotón,-ona; *(for money)* codicioso,-a **(for** de).

Greek 1 *a* griego,-a. **2** *n* *(person)* griego,-a *mf*; *(language)* griego *m*.

green 1 *(color)* verde *m*; *(for golf)* campo *m*; **greens** verduras *fpl*. **2** *a* verde.

greenhouse invernadero *m*; **g. effect** efecto *m* invernadero.

greet *vt* saludar.

greeting saludo *m*.

grenade granada *f*.

grey *a* & *n* see **gray**.

greyhound galgo *m*.

grief pena *f*, dolor *m*.

grieve *vi* **to g. for sb** llorar la muerte de algn.

grill 1 *vt* *(food)* asar a la parrilla. **2** *n* parrilla *f*; *(dish)* parrillada *f*.

grim *a* *(landscape)* lúgubre; *(manner)* severo,-a; *(unpleasant)* desagradable.

grime mugre *f*.

grimy *a* mugriento,-a.

grin 1 vi sonreír abiertamente. **2** n sonrisa abierta.

grind* vt moler; **to g. one's teeth** hacer rechinar los dientes.

grip 1 n (hold) agarrón m; (handle) asidero m. **2** vt agarrar; **to be gripped by fear** ser presa del miedo.

gripping a (film, story) apasionante.

groan 1 n gemido m. **2** vi gemir.

grocer tendero,-a mf.

grocery (shop) tienda f de ultramarinos; **g. store** supermercado m.

groin ingle f.

groom (bridegroom) novio m.

groove (furrow etc) ranura f; (of record) surco m.

grope vi **to g. for sth** buscar algo a tientas.

• **grope about** vi andar a tientas; (looking for sth) buscar a tientas.

gross a grosero,-a; (not net) bruto, -a.

grossly adv enormemente.

gross national product producto m nacional bruto.

ground¹ suelo m; (terrain) terreno m; **grounds** (gardens) jardines mpl; (reason) motivo m sing.

ground² a (coffee) molido,-a; (meat) picado,-a.

groundwork trabajo m preparatorio.

group grupo m.

grow* **1** vt (cultivate) cultivar; **to g. a beard** dejarse (crecer) la barba. **2** vi crecer; (increase) aumentar; (become) volverse.

• **grow into** vi convertirse en.

• **grow out of** vt (phase etc) superar; **he's grown out of his shirt** se le ha quedado pequeña la camisa.

• **grow up** vi crecer.

growl 1 vi gruñir. **2** n gruñido m.

grown a crecido,-a.

grown-up a & n adulto,-a (mf); **the grown-ups** los mayores.

growth crecimiento m; (increase) aumento m; (development) desarrollo m; (diseased part) bulto m.

grub fam (food) comida f.

grubby a sucio,-a.

grudge 1 n rencor m; **to bear sb a g.** guardar rencor a algn. **2** vt **he grudges me my success** me envidia el éxito.

grueling a penoso,-a.

gruesome a espantoso,-a.

grumble vi refunfuñar.

grumpy a gruñón,-ona.

grunt 1 vi gruñir. **2** n gruñido m.

guarantee 1 n garantía f. **2** vt garantizar; (assure) asegurar.

guard 1 vt (protect) proteger; (keep watch over) vigilar; (control) guardar. **2** n (sentry) guardia mf; (on train) jefe m de tren; **to be on one's g.** estar en guardia; **to stand g.** montar la guardia.

Guatemalan adj & n guatemalteco,-a (mf).

guess 1 vti adivinar; fam suponer. **2** n conjetura f; (estimate) cálculo m; **to have** or **make a g.** intentar adivinar.

guesswork conjetura f.

guest invitado,-a mf; (in hotel) cliente,-a mf, huésped,-a mf.

guesthouse casa f de huéspedes.

guidance orientación f.

guide 1 vt guiar. **2** n (person) guía mf; (guidebook) guía f.

guideline pauta f.

guilt culpabilidad f.

guilty a culpable (**of** de).

guinea pig conejillo m de Indias.

guitar guitarra f.

guitarist guitarrista mf.

gulf golfo m; fig abismo m.

gull gaviota f.

gulp trago m.

gum¹ 1 n goma f. **2** vt pegar con goma.

gum² (around teeth) encía f.

gun (handgun) pistola f; (rifle) fusil m; (cannon) cañón m.

• **gun down** vt matar a tiros.

gunfire tiros mpl.

gunman pistolero m.

gunpoint **at g.** a punta de pistola.

gunpowder pólvora f.

gunshot tiro m.

gush *vi* brotar.

gust (*of wind*) ráfaga *f*.

guts *npl* (*entrails*) tripas *fpl*.

gutter (*in street*) cuneta *f*; (*on roof*) canalón *m*.

guy *fam* tipo *m*, tío *m*.

gym (*gymnasium*) gimnasio *m*; (*gymnastics*) gimnasia *f*.

gynecologist ginecólogo,-a *mf*.

H

habit costumbre *f*; **to be in the h. of doing sth** soler hacer algo; **to get into the h. of doing sth** acostumbrarse a hacer algo.

hack 1 *n* (*cut*) corte *m*; (*with an ax*) hachazo *m*. **2** *vt* (*with knife, ax*) cortar.

had *pt & pp of* **have.**

haddock abadejo *m*.

hag bruja *f*.

haggle *vi* regatear.

hail 1 *n* granizo *m*; **a h. of bullets** una lluvia de balas. **2** *vi* granizar.

hailstone granizo *m*.

hair pelo *m*; (*on arm, leg*) vello *m*; **to have long h.** tener el pelo largo.

hairbrush cepillo *m* (para el pelo).

haircut corte *m* de pelo; **to have a h.** cortarse el pelo.

hairdo *fam* peinado *m*.

hairdresser peluquero,-a *mf*; **h.'s (shop)** peluquería *f*.

hairdryer, hairdrier secador *m* (de pelo).

hairgrip horquilla *f*.

hairpin bend curva *f* muy cerrada.

hair-raising *a* espeluznante.

hairspray laca *f* (para el pelo).

hairstyle peinado *m*.

hairy *a* (*with hair*) peludo,-a; *fam* (*frightening*) espeluznante.

half 1 *n* (*pl* **halves**) mitad *f*; (*period in match*) tiempo *m*; **he's four and a h.** tiene cuatro años y medio; **to cut in h.** cortar por la mitad. **2** *a* medio,-a; **h. a dozen/an hour** media docena/hora; **h. fare** media tarifa *f*. **3** *adv* a medias; **h. asleep** medio dormido,-a. **h. past one** la una y media.

half board media pensión *f*.

half-hour media hora *f*.

half term (*holiday*) vacación *f* a mitad de trimestre.

half-time descanso *m*.

halfway *adv* a medio camino.

halibut mero *m*.

hall (*lobby*) vestíbulo *m*; (*building*) sala *f*; **h. of residence** colegio *m* mayor.

hallstand percha *f*.

Hallowe(')en víspera *f* de Todos los Santos.

hallway vestíbulo *m*.

halt alto *m*; **to call a h. to sth** poner fin a algo.

halve *vt* reducir a la mitad.

ham jamón *m*.

hamburger hamburguesa *f*.

hammer 1 *n* martillo *m*. **2** *vt* (*nail*) clavar; *fig* **to h. home** insistir sobre. **3** *vi* dar golpes.

hammering *fam* (*defeat*) paliza *f*.

hammock hamaca *f*.

hamper[1] cesta *f*.

hamper[2] *vt* dificultar.

hamster hámster *m*.

hand 1 *n* mano *f*; (*worker*) trabajador,-a *mf*; (*of clock*) aguja *f*; **by h.** a mano; (*close*) **at h.** a mano; **on the one/other h.** por una/otra parte; **to get out of h.** descontrolarse; **to be on h.** estar a mano; **to have a h. in** intervenir en; **to give sb a h.** echarle una mano a algn; **to give sb a big h.** (*applause*) dedicar a algn una gran ovación. **2** *vt* (*give*) dar.

• **hand back** *vt* devolver.

• **hand in** *vt* (*homework*) entregar.

• **hand out** *vt* repartir.

• **hand over** *vt* entregar.

handbag bolso *m*.

handbook manual *m*.

handbrake freno *m* de mano.

handcuff 1 *vt* esposar. **2** *npl* **handcuffs** esposas *fpl*.

handful puñado *m*.

hand grenade granada *f* de mano.

handicap 1 n (*physical*) minusvalía f; (*in sport*) hándicap m. **2** vt impedir.

handicapped a (*physically*) minusválido,-a; (*mentally*) retrasado,-a; fig desfavorecido,-a.

handkerchief pañuelo m.

handle 1 n (*of knife*) mango m; (*of cup*) asa f; (*of door*) pomo m; (*of drawer*) tirador m. **2** vt manejar; (*problem*) encargarse de; (*people*) tratar; '**h. with care**' 'frágil'.

handlebars npl manillar m.

hand luggage equipaje m de mano.

handmade a hecho,-a a mano.

handout (*leaflet*) folleto m; (*charity*) limosna f.

handrail pasamanos m sing inv.

handshake apretón m de manos.

handsome a (*person*) guapo,-a; (*substantial*) considerable.

handwriting letra f.

handy a (*useful*) útil; (*nearby*) a mano; (*dexterous*) diestro,-a.

handyman manitas m inv.

hang* 1 vt colgar; (*head*) bajar. **2** vi colgar (**from** de); (*in air*) flotar; (*criminal*) ser ahorcado,-a; **to h. oneself** ahorcarse.

• **hang around 1** vi fam no hacer nada; (*wait*) esperar. **2** vt (*bar etc*) frecuentar.

• **hang on** vi agarrarse; (*wait*) esperar; **to h. on to sth** (*keep*) guardar.

• **hang out 1** vt (*washing*) tender. **2** vi his tongue was hanging out le colgaba la lengua.

• **hang up** vt (*picture, telephone*) colgar.

hangar hangar m.

hanger percha f.

hang-glider ala f delta.

hangover resaca f.

hang-up fam (*complex*) complejo m.

happen vi suceder, ocurrir; **if you h. to see my friend** si por casualidad ves a mi amigo.

happening acontecimiento m.

happily adv (*with pleasure*) fe-

lizmente; (*fortunately*) afortunadamente.

happiness felicidad f.

happy a feliz; **h. birthday!** ¡feliz cumpleaños!

harass vt acosar.

harbor 1 n puerto m. **2** vt (*criminal*) encubrir; (*doubts*) abrigar.

hard 1 a duro,-a; (*solid*) sólido,-a; (*difficult*) difícil; (*harsh*) severo,-a; (*strict*) estricto,-a; **h. of hearing** duro,-a de oído; **to be h. up** estar sin blanca; **to take a h. line** tomar medidas severas; **h. drugs** droga f dura; **a h. worker** un trabajador concienzudo; **h. luck!** ¡mala suerte!; **h. evidence** pruebas definitivas; **h. currency** divisa f fuerte. **2** adv (*forcibly*) fuerte; (*with application*) mucho.

hard-boiled a duro,-a.

hard-core a irreductible.

hard disk disco m duro.

harden 1 vt endurecer. **2** vi endurecerse.

hardly adv apenas; **h. anyone/ever** casi nadie/nunca; **he had h. begun when . . .** apenas había comenzado cuando . . .

hardness dureza f; (*difficulty*) dificultad f.

hardship privación f.

hardware (*goods*) ferretería f; (*computer equipment*) hardware m; **h. store** ferretería f.

hardwearing a duradero,-a.

hardworking a muy trabajador,-a.

hare liebre f.

harm 1 n daño m. **2** vt hacer daño a.

harmful a perjudicial (**to** para).

harmless a inofensivo,-a.

harmonica armónica f.

harmonious a armonioso,-a.

harmony armonía f.

harness 1 n (*for horse*) arreos mpl. **2** vt (*horse*) enjaezar.

harp arpa f.

• **harp on** vi fam hablar sin parar; **to h. on about sth** hablar sin parar sobre algo.

harsh a severo,-a; (voice) áspero,-a; (sound) discordante.

harshly adv duramente.

harshness dureza f; (discordancy) discordancia f.

harvest 1 n cosecha f; (of grapes) vendimia f. **2** vt cosechar, recoger.

has 3rd person sing pres of **have**.

hassle fam **1** n (nuisance) rollo m; (problem) lío m; (wrangle) bronca f. **2** vt fastidiar.

haste prisa f.

hasten vi apresurarse.

hastily adv (quickly) de prisa.

hasty a apresurado,-a; (rash) precipitado,-a.

hat sombrero m.

hatch[1] escotilla f; **serving h.** ventanilla f.

hatch[2] **1** vt (egg) empollar. **2** vi (bird) salir del huevo.

hatchback coche m de 3/5 puertas.

hate 1 n odio m. **2** vt odiar.

hateful a odioso,-a.

hatred odio m.

haul 1 n (journey) trayecto m. **2** vt tirar; (drag) arrastrar.

haunted a embrujado,-a.

have* 1 vt tener; (party, meeting) hacer; **h. you got a car?** ¿tienes coche?; **to h. a cigarette** fumarse un cigarrillo; **to h. breakfast/lunch/tea/dinner** desayunar/comer/merendar/cenar; **what will you h.?** ¿qué quieres tomar?; **can I h. your pen for a moment?** ¿me dejas tu bolígrafo un momento? ▪ **to h. to** (obligation) tener que, deber; (borrow) ¿me **I h. to go now** tengo que irme ya ▪ (make happen) hacer; **I'll h. someone come around** haré que venga alguien; **2** v aux (compound) haber; **yes I h.!** ¡que sí!; **you haven't seen my book, h. you?** no has visto mi libro, ¿verdad?; **he's been to France, hasn't he?** ha estado en Francia, ¿verdad?

▪ **have on** vt (wear) vestir; fam **to h. sb on** tomarle el pelo a algn.

▪ **have out** vt **to h. it out with sb** ajustar cuentas con algn.

▪ **have over** vt (invite) recibir.

havoc to play h. with hacer estragos en.

hawk halcón m.

hay heno m.

hay fever fiebre f del heno.

haystack almiar m.

hazard peligro m.

haze (mist) neblina f.

hazelnut avellana f.

hazy a nebuloso,-a.

he pers pron él; **he who** el que.

head 1 n cabeza f; (mind) mente f; (of company) director,-a mf; (of coin) cara f; **to be h. over heels in love** estar locamente enamorado, -a; **to keep one's h.** mantener la calma; **to lose one's h.** perder la cabeza; **heads or tails** cara o cruz. **2** a principal; **h. office** sede f. **3** vt (list etc) encabezar.

▪ **head for** vt dirigirse hacia.

headache dolor m de cabeza; fig quebradero m de cabeza.

heading título m; (of letter) membrete m.

headlight faro m.

headline titular m.

headmaster director m.

headmistress directora f.

headphones npl auriculares mpl.

headquarters npl oficina f central; (military) cuartel m general.

head teacher director,-a mf.

head waiter jefe m de comedor.

headway to make h. avanzar.

heal 1 vi cicatrizar. **2** vt curar.

health salud f; fig prosperidad f; **to be in good/bad h.** estar bien/mal de salud; **h. foods** alimentos mpl naturales; **h. service** ≈ Insalud m.

healthy a sano,-a; (good for health) saludable.

heap 1 n montón m. **2** vt amontonar; (praises) colmar de; **to h. praises on sb** colmar a algn de elogios.

hear* vt oír; (listen to) escuchar; (find out) enterarse de; (evidence) oír; **I won't h. of it!** ¡ni hablar!; **to h. from sb** tener noticias de algn.

hearing oído m; (legal) audiencia f.

hearing aid audífono m.

hearse coche m fúnebre.

heart corazón m; **hearts** corazones; **at h.** en el fondo; **to lose h.** desanimarse.

heart attack infarto m (de miocardio).

heartbeat latido m del corazón.

heart-breaking a desgarrador,-a.

heartening a alentador,-a.

hearty a (person) francote; (meal) abundante; **to have a h. appetite** ser de buen comer.

heat 1 n calor m; (in sport) eliminatoria f. **2** vt calentar.
• **heat up** vi (warm up) calentarse.

heater calentador m.

heath (land) brezal m.

heather brezo m.

heating calefacción f.

heatwave ola f de calor.

heave vt (lift) levantar; (haul) tirar; (push) empujar; (throw) arrojar.

heaven cielo m; **for heaven's sake!** ¡por Dios!

heavily adv (rain, meal) mucho; **to sleep h.** dormir profundamente.

heavy 1 a pesado,-a; (rain, meal) fuerte; (traffic) denso,-a; (loss) grande; **is it h.?** ¿pesa mucho?; **a h. drinker/smoker** un,-a bebedor,-a/fumador,-a empedernido,-a.

Hebrew a hebreo,-a mf; (language) hebreo m.

hectic a agitado,-a.

hedge 1 n seto m. **2** vt **to h. one's bets** cubrirse.

hedgehog erizo m.

heel talón m; (of shoe) tacón m.

hefty a (person) fornido,-a; (package) pesado,-a.

height altura f; (of person) estatura f; **what h. are you?** ¿cuánto mides?

heir heredero m.

heiress heredera f.

held pt & pp of **hold**.

helicopter helicóptero m.

hell infierno m; fam **what the h. are you doing?** ¿qué diablos estás haciendo?; fam **go to h.!** ¡vete a hacer puñetas!; fam **a h. of a party** una fiesta estupenda; fam **she's had a h. of a day** ha tenido un día fatal; fam **h.!** ¡demonios!

hello interj ¡hola!; (on phone) ¡diga!; (showing surprise) ¡hala!

helm timón m.

helmet casco m.

help 1 n ayuda f; **h.!** ¡socorro!; (daily) h. asistenta f. **2** vt ayudar; **can I h. you?** (in shop) ¿qué desea?; **h. yourself!** (to food etc) ¡sírvete!; **I couldn't h. laughing** no pude evitar reírme; **I can't h. it** no lo puedo remediar.
• **help out** vt **to h. sb out** echarle una mano a algn.

helper ayudante,-a mf.

helpful a (person) amable; (thing) útil.

helping ración f.

helpless a (defenseless) desamparado,-a; (powerless) impotente.

hem dobladillo m.
■ **hem in** vt cercar, rodear.

hemorrhage hemorragia f.

hen gallina f.

hepatitis hepatitis f.

her 1 poss a (one thing) su; (more than one) sus; (to distinguish male from female) de ella; **are they h. books or his?** ¿los libros son de ella o de él? **2** object pron (direct object) la; **I saw h. recently** la vi hace poco. ■ (indirect object) le; (with other third person pronouns) se; **he gave h. money** le dio dinero; **they handed it to h.** se lo entregaron. ■ (after prep) ella; **for h.** para ella. ■ (emphatic) ella; **look, it's h.!** ¡mira, es ella!

herb hierba f; **herb tea** infusión f.

herd (*of cattle*) manada *f*; (*of goats*) rebaño *m*.

here 1 *adv* aquí; **h.!** ¡presente!; **h. you are!** ¡toma! **2** *interj* **look h., you can't do that!** ¡oiga, no puede hacer eso!

hermit ermitaño,-a *mf*.

hero (*pl* **heroes**) héroe *m*; (*in novel*) protagonista *m*.

heroic *a* heroico,-a.

heroin heroína *f*.

heroine heroína *f*; (*in novel*) protagonista *f*.

herring arenque *m*.

hers *poss pron* (*attribute*) (*one thing*) suyo,-a; (*more than one*) suyos,-as; (*to distinguish male from female*) de ella; **they are h. not his** son de ella, no de él. ▪ (*one thing*) el suyo, la suya; (*more than one*) los suyos, las suyas.

herself *pers pron* (*reflexive*) se; **she dressed h.** se vistió. ▪ (*alone*) ella misma; **she was by h.** estaba sola. ▪ (*emphatic*) **she told me so h.** eso me dijo ella misma.

hesitant *a* vacilante.

hesitate *vi* vacilar.

hesitation indecisión *f*.

het up *a* nervioso,-a.

hey *interj* ¡oye!, ¡oiga!

hi *interj* ¡hola!

hiccup hipo *m*; (*minor problem*) problemilla *m*; **to have hiccups** tener hipo.

hide¹ **1** *vt* (*conceal*) esconder; (*obscure*) ocultar. **2** *vi* esconderse, ocultarse.

hide² (*skin*) piel *f*.

hide-and-seek escondite *m*.

hideous *a* (*horrific*) horroroso,-a; (*extremely ugly*) espantoso,-a.

hideously *adv* horrorosamente.

hide-out escondrijo *m*.

hiding a good h. una buena paliza.

hiding place escondite *m*.

hi-fi hifi *m*.

high 1 *a* alto,-a; (*price*) elevado,-a; (*drugged*) colocado,-a; **how h. is that wall?** ¿qué altura tiene esa pared?; **it's three feet h.** tiene tres pies de alto; **h. wind** viento *m* fuerte; **to have a h. opinion of sb** tener muy buena opinión de algn. **2** *adv* alto; **to fly h.** volar a gran altura.

high-class *a* de alta categoría.

high density *a* de alta densidad.

higher *a* superior; **h. education** enseñanza *f* superior.

highlands *npl* tierras *fpl* altas.

highlight 1 *n* (*in hair*) reflejo *m*; (*of event*) atracción *f* principal. **2** *vt* hacer resaltar; (*with highlighter*) subrayar con marcador.

highlighter marcador *m*.

highly *adv* (*very*) sumamente; **to speak h. of sb** hablar muy bien de algn.

high-pitched *a* estridente.

high-rise *a* **h. building** rascacielos *m inv*.

high school instituto *m* de enseñanza media.

high-speed *a* & *adv* **h. lens** objetivo *m* ultrarrápido; **h. train** tren *m* de alta velocidad.

high street calle *f* mayor.

highway autopista *f*.

hijack 1 *vt* secuestrar. **2** *n* secuestro *m*.

hijacker secuestrador,-a *mf*; (*of planes*) pirata *mf* del aire.

hijacking secuestro *m*.

hike 1 *n* (*walk*) excursión *f*. **2** *vi* ir de excursión.

hiker excursionista *mf*.

hilarious *a* graciosísimo,-a.

hill colina *f*; (*slope*) cuesta *f*.

hillside ladera *f*.

hilly *a* accidentado,-a.

him *object pron* (*direct object*) lo, le; **hit h.!** ¡pégale!; **she loves h.** lo quiere. ▪ (*indirect object*) le; (*with other third person pronouns*) se; **give h. the money** dale el dinero; **give it to h.** dáselo. ▪ (*after prep*) él; **it's not like h. to say that** no es propio de él decir eso. ▪ (*emphatic*) él; **it's h.** es él.

himself *pers pron* (*reflexive*) se; **he hurt h.** se hizo daño. ▪ (*alone*) por sí mismo; **by h. solo.** ▪ (*emphatic*) él mismo. **he told me so h.** me lo dijo él mismo.

hinder *vt* dificultar.

Hindu *a & n* hindú (*mf*).

hinge bisagra *f*.

• **hinge on** *vt* depender de.

hint 1 *n* indirecta *f*; (*clue*) pista *f*; (*advice*) consejo *m*. **2** *vi* lanzar indirectas. **3** *vt* (*imply*) insinuar.

• **hint at** *vt* aludir a.

hip cadera *f*.

hippopotamus hipopótamo *m*.

hire *vt* (*rent*) alquilar; (*employ*) contratar.

his 1 *poss a* (*one thing*) su; (*more than one*) sus; (*to distinguish male from female*) de él; **he washed h. face** se lavó la cara; **is it h. dog or hers?** ¡el perro es de él o de ella? **2** *poss pron* (*attribute*) (*one thing*) suyo,-a; (*more than one*) suyos,-as; (*to distinguish male from female*) de él. ▪ (*one thing*) el suyo, la suya; (*more than one*) los suyos, las suyas.

Hispanic 1 *a* hispánico,-a. **2** *n* hispano,-a *mf*

hiss 1 *n* siseo *m*; (*in theater*) silbido *m*. **2** *vti* silbar.

historic *a* histórico,-a.

historical *a* histórico,-a.

history historia *f*.

hit 1 *n* (*blow*) golpe *m*; (*success*) éxito *m*. **2** *vt** (*strike*) pegar; (*affect*) afectar; **he was h. in the leg** le dieron en la pierna; **the car h. the kerb** el coche chocó contra el bordillo.

• **hit back** *vi* (*reply to criticism*) replicar.

• **hit out** *vi* **to h. out at sb** atacar a algn.

• **hit (up)on** *vt* dar con; **we h. on the idea of . . .** se nos ocurrió la idea de . . .

hit-and-run driver conductor *m* que atropella a algn y no para.

hitch 1 *n* dificultad *f*. **2** *vi* (*hitch-hike*) hacer autostop.

hitchhike *vi* hacer autostop.

hitchhiker autostopista *mf*.

hitchhiking autostop *m*.

hive colmena *f*.

hoard 1 *n* (*provisions*) reservas *fpl*; (*money etc*) tesoro *m*. **2** *vt* (*objects*) acumular; (*money*) atesorar.

hoarding (*billboard*) valla *f* publicitaria.

hoarse *a* ronco,-a; **to be h.** tener la voz ronca.

hoax (*joke*) broma *f* pesada; (*trick*) engaño *m*.

hobby pasatiempo *m*.

hobo vagabundo,-a *mf*.

hockey hockey *m*.

hold* 1 *vt* (*keep in hand*) tener (en la mano); (*grip*) agarrar; (*opinion*) sostener; (*contain*) dar cabida a; (*meeting*) celebrar; (*reserve: ticket*) guardar; (*at police station etc*) detener; (*office*) ocupar; **to h. sb's hand** cogerle la mano a algn; **the jug holds a liter** en la jarra cabe un litro; **to h. one's breath** contener la respiración; **to h. sb hostage** retener a algn como rehén; **to h. the line** no colgar. **2** *vi* (*rope*) aguantar; (*offer*) ser válido,-a. **3** *n* (*in ship*) bodega *f*; (*control*) control *m*; **to get h. of** (*grip*) coger; (*get in touch with*) localizar.

• **hold back** *vt* (*crowd*) contener; (*feelings*) reprimir; (*truth*) ocultar; (*suspect*) retener; (*store*) guardar.

• **hold down** *vt* (*control*) dominar; (*job*) desempeñar.

• **hold on** *vi* (*keep a firm grasp*) agarrarse bien; (*wait*) esperar; **h. on!** (*on phone*) ¡no cuelgue!

• **hold out 1** *vt* (*hand*) tender. **2** *vi* (*last*) (*things*) durar; (*person*) resistir.

• **hold up** *vt* (*support*) apuntalar; (*rob*) (*train*) asaltar; (*bank*) atracar; (*delay*) retrasar; **we were held up for half an hour** sufrimos media hora de retraso.

holder (*receptacle*) recipiente *m*; (*owner*) poseedor,-a *mf*; (*bearer*) portador,-a *mf*; (*of passport*) titular *mf*.

hold-up (*robbery*) atraco *m*; (*delay*) retraso *m*; (*in traffic*) atasco *m*.

hole agujero *m*; (*large, in golf*) hoyo *m*.

holiday (*one day*) día *m* de) fiesta *f*; (*several days*) vacaciones *fpl*.

hollow 1 *a* hueco,-a; (*cheeks, eyes*) hundido,-a. **2** *n* hueco *m*.

holy *a* sagrado,-a; (*blessed*) bendito,-a.

Holy Ghost Espíritu *m* Santo.

home 1 *n* casa *f*, hogar *m*; (*institution*) asilo *m*; (*country*) patria *f*; **at h.** en casa; **make yourself at h.!** ¡estás en tu casa!; **old people's h.** asilo *m* de ancianos; **to play at h.** jugar en casa. **2** *a* (*domestic*) del hogar; (*political*) interior; (*native*) natal; **h. affairs** asuntos *mpl* interiores. **3** *adv* en casa; **to go h.** irse a casa; **to leave h.** irse de casa.

home computer ordenador *m* doméstico.

home help asistenta *f*.

homeless 1 *a* sin hogar. **2** *npl* **the h.** los sin hogar.

home-made *a* casero,-a.

homesick *a* **to be h.** tener morriña.

hometown ciudad *f* natal.

homework deberes *mpl*.

homosexual *a* & *n* homosexual (*mf*).

Honduran *adj* & *n* hondureño,-a (*mf*).

honest *a* honrado,-a; (*sincere*) sincero,-a; (*fair*) justo,-a.

honestly *adv* honradamente; **h.?** ¿de verdad?

honesty honradez *f*.

honey miel *f*; *fam* (*endearment*) cariño *m*.

honeymoon luna *f* de miel.

honk *vi* (*person in car*) tocar la bocina.

honor 1 *n* honor *m*. **2** *vt* (*respect*) honrar; (*obligation*) cumplir.

honorable *a* (*person*) honrado,-a; (*actions*) honroso,-a.

hood (*of garment*) capucha *f*; (*of car*) capota *f*; (*bonnet*) capó *m*.

hoof (*pl* **hoofs** *or* **hooves**) (*of horse*) casco *m*; (*of cow, sheep*) pezuña *f*.

hook gancho *m*; (*for fishing*) anzuelo *m*; **to take the phone off the h.** descolgar el teléfono.

• **hook up** *vti* conectar (**with** con).

hooked *a* (*nose*) aguileño,-a; (*addicted*) enganchado,-a (**on** a); **to get h.** engancharse.

hooky to play h. hacer novillos.

hooligan gamberro,-a *mf*.

hoop aro *m*.

hoot 1 *n* (*owl*) grito *m*; **hoots of laughter** carcajadas *fpl*. **2** *vi* (*owl*) ulular; (*train*) silbar; (*siren*) sonar.

Hoover® **1** *n* aspiradora *f*. **2** *vt* **to h.** pasar la aspiradora a.

hop 1 *vi* saltar; **to h. on one leg** andar a la pata coja. **2** *n* (*small jump*) brinco *m*.

hope 1 *n* esperanza *f*; (*false*) ilusión *f*; **to have little h. of doing sth** tener pocas posibilidades de hacer algo. **2** *vti* esperar; **I h. so/not** espero que sí/no.

• **hope for** *vt* esperar.

hopeful *a* (*confident*) optimista; (*promising*) prometedor,-a.

hopefully *adv* **h. she won't come** esperemos que no venga.

hopeless *a* desesperado,-a; **to be h. at sports** ser negado,-a para los deportes.

hopelessly *adv* desesperadamente; **h. lost** completamente perdido,-a.

hops *npl* lúpulo *m*.

hopscotch to play h. jugar al tejo.

horizon horizonte *m*.

horizontal *a* horizontal.

horn cuerno *m*; (*on car*) bocina *f*.

horrible *a* horrible.

horribly *adv* horriblemente.

horrific *a* horrendo,-a.

horrify *vt* horrorizar.

horror horror *m*; **a little h.** un diablillo.

horror film película *f* de terror.

horse caballo *m*.

horseback on h. a caballo.

horse race carrera *f* de caballos.

horseshoe herradura *f.*
hose (*pipe*) manguera *f.*
hosepipe manguera *f.*
hospitable *a* hospitalario,-a.
hospital hospital *m.*
hospitality hospitalidad *f.*
hospitalize *vt* hospitalizar.
host 1 *n* (*at home*) anfitrión *m*; (*on TV*) presentador *m.* **2** *vt* (*TV show etc*) presentar.
hostage rehén *m*; **to take sb h.** tomar a algn como rehén.
hostel hostal *m.*
hostess (*at home etc*) anfitriona *f*; (*on TV*) presentadora *f.*
hostile *a* hostil.
hostility hostilidad *f.*
hot *a* caliente; (*weather*) caluroso, -a; (*spicy*) picante; (*temper*) fuerte; **it's very h.** hace mucho calor; **to feel h.** tener calor; **it's not so h.** (*not very good*) no es nada del otro mundo.
hot dog perrito *m* caliente.
hotel hotel *m.*
hot-water bottle bolsa *f* de agua caliente.
hound 1 *n* perro *m* de caza. **2** *vt* acosar.
hour hora *f*; **60 miles an h.** 60 millas por hora; **by the h.** por horas.
hourly 1 *a* cada hora. **2** *adv* por horas.
house 1 *n* casa *f*; (*in theater*) sala *f*; **at my h.** en mi casa. **2** *vt* alojar; (*store*) guardar.
household hogar *m*; **h. products** productos *mpl* domésticos.
housekeeping administración *f* doméstica.
house-warming party fiesta *f* que se da al estrenar casa.
housewife ama *f* de casa.
housework trabajo *m* doméstico.
housing vivienda *f.*
housing estate urbanización *f.*
hovel casucha *f.*
hover *vi* (*bird*) cernerse; (*helicopter*) permanecer inmóvil (en el aire).
hovercraft aerodeslizador *m.*

how *adv* ¿cómo?; **h. are you?** ¿cómo estás?; **h. do you do?** mucho gusto; **h. funny!** ¡qué divertido!; **h. about . . . ?** ¿y si . . . ?; **h. about a stroll?** ¿qué te parece un paseo?; **h. old is she?** ¿cuántos años tiene?; **h. tall are you?** ¿cuánto mides?; **h. many?** ¿cuántos,-as?; **h. much?** ¿cuánto, -a?
however *adv* no obstante, sin embargo; **h. difficult it may be** por difícil que sea; **h. much** por mucho que (+ *subjunctive*).
howl 1 *n* aullido *m.* **2** *vi* aullar.
HQ *abbr of* **headquarters.**
hubcap tapacubos *m inv.*
huddle 1 *n* grupo *m.* **2** *vi* **to h. (up** *or* **together)** acurrucarse.
hug 1 *vt* abrazar. **2** *n* abrazo *m.*
huge *a* enorme.
hull casco *m.*
hum 1 *vt* (*tune*) tararear. **2** *vi* (*bees, engine*) zumbar. **3** *n* (*of bees*) zumbido *m.*
human 1 *a* humano,-a; **h. race** raza *f* humana. **2** *n* ser *m* humano.
human being ser *m* humano.
humanity humanidad *f*; **the humanities** las humanidades.
humble *a* humilde.
humid *a* húmedo,-a.
humidity humedad *f.*
humiliate *vt* humillar.
humiliation humillación *f.*
humorous *a* (*person, story*) gracioso,-a; (*writer*) humorístico,-a.
humor humor *m.*
hump (*on back*) joroba *f*; (*small hill*) montículo *m.*
hunch (*idea*) corazonada *f.*
hundred 1 *n* cien *m*, ciento *m*; (*rough number*) centenar *m*; **a h. and twenty-five** ciento veinticinco; **five h.** quinientos. **2** *a* cien; **a h. people** cien personas; **a h. per cent** cien por cien; **two h. chairs** doscientas sillas.
hundredth *a & n* centésimo,-a (*m*).
Hungarian *adj & n* húngaro,-a (*mf*).

hunger hambre *m*; **h. strike** huelga *f* de hambre.
hungry *a* **to be h.** tener hambre.
hunt 1 *vt* cazar. **2** *vi* (*for game*) cazar; (*search*) buscar. **3** *n* caza *f*; (*search*) búsqueda *f*.
• **hunt down** *vt* perseguir.
hunter cazador,-a *mf*.
hunting caza *f*; (*expedition*) cacería *f*.
hurdle (*in sport*) valla *f*; *fig* obstáculo *m*.
hurl *vt* lanzar.
hurrah, hurray *interj* ¡hurra!; **h. for John!** ¡viva John!
hurricane huracán *m*.
hurry 1 *vi* darse prisa. **2** *vt* meter prisa a. **3** *n* **to be in a h.** tener prisa.
• **hurry up** *vi* (*go faster*) darse prisa.
hurt* 1 *vt* hacer daño a; (*wound*) herir; (*mentally*) ofender. **2** *vi* doler; **my arm hurts** me duele el brazo. **3** *a* (*physically*) herido,-a; (*mentally*) dolido,-a.
husband marido *m*, esposo *m*.
hush 1 *n* silencio *m*. **2** *interj* ¡silencio!
hustle 1 *vt* (*jostle*) empujar; (*hurry along*) meter prisa a. **2** *n* **h. and bustle** ajetreo *m*.
hut cabaña *f*; (*shed*) cobertizo *m*.
hygiene higiene *f*.
hygienic *a* higiénico,-a.
hymn himno *m*; **h. book** cantoral *m*.
hypermarket hipermercado *m*.
hyphen guión *m*.
hyphenated *a* (*word*) (escrito,-a) con guión.
hypocrisy hipocresía *f*.
hypocrite hipócrita *mf*.
hysterical *a* histérico,-a.
hysterically *adv* (*to cry*) histéricamente.

I

I *pers pron* yo.
ice hielo *m*.

iceberg iceberg *m*.
ice-cold *a* helado,-a.
ice cream helado *m*.
ice cube cubito *m* de hielo.
ice-skating patinaje *m* sobre hielo.
icicle carámbano *m*.
icing alcorza *f*.
icing sugar azúcar *m* glas.
icon icono *m*.
icy *a* (*road etc*) helado,-a; (*smile*) glacial.
ID ID card documento *m* nacional de identidad, DNI *m*.
idea idea *f*.
ideal *a & n* ideal (*m*).
ideally *adv* (*if possible*) de ser posible.
identical *a* idéntico,-a.
identification identificación *f*; (*papers*) documentación *f*.
identify 1 *vt* identificar. **2** *vi* identificarse (**with** con).
identity identidad *f*.
idiom modismo *m*.
idiot idiota *mf*.
idiotic *a* idiota.
idle *a* holgazán,-ana; (*not working*) (*person*) desempleado,-a.
idol ídolo *m*.
idolize *vt* idolatrar.
i.e. *abbr* a saber.
if *conj* si; **if I were rich** si fuera rico, -a; **if I were you** yo en tu lugar.
igloo iglú *m*.
ignorance ignorancia *f*.
ignorant *a* ignorante (**of** de).
ignore *vt* (*warning, remark*) no hacer caso de; (*behavior, fact*) pasar por alto.
ill 1 *a* enfermo,-a; (*bad*) malo,-a. **2** *n* mal *m*.
illegal *a* ilegal.
illegible *a* ilegible.
illiterate *a* analfabeto,-a.
illness enfermedad *f*.
illusion ilusión *f*.
illustrate *vt* ilustrar.
illustration ilustración *f*.
image imagen *f*.
imaginary *a* imaginario,-a.

imagination imaginación f.
imagine vt imaginarse; (think) suponer.
imbecile fam imbécil mf.
imitate vt imitar.
imitation 1 n imitación f. **2** a de imitación.
immaculate a impecable.
immature a inmaduro,-a.
immediate a inmediato,-a.
immediately 1 adv inmediatamente. **2** conj (as soon as) en cuanto.
immense a inmenso,-a.
immensely adv sumamente.
immigrant a & n inmigrante (mf).
immigration inmigración f.
immortal a inmortal.
immune a inmune.
immunize vt inmunizar (against contra).
impact impacto m; (crash) choque m.
impatience impaciencia f.
impatient a impaciente.
impatiently adv con impaciencia.
imperative (form of verb) imperativo m.
impersonate vt hacerse pasar por; (famous people) imitar.
impersonator (on TV etc) imitador,-a mf.
impertinent a impertinente.
impetus ímpetu m; fig impulso m.
implement 1 n (tool) herramienta f. **2** vt (decision, plan) llevar a cabo.
implication implicación f; (consequence) consecuencia f.
imply vt (hint) dar a entender.
impolite a maleducado,-a.
import 1 n importación f. **2** vt importar.
importance importancia f; **of little i.** de poca importancia.
important a importante; **it's not i.** no importa.
importer importador,-a mf.
impose 1 vt imponer (**on, upon** a). **2** vi **to i. on** or **upon** (take advantage of) abusar de.
imposing a imponente.

imposition would it be an i. if . . . ? ¿le molestaría si . . . ?
impossibility imposibilidad f.
impossible a imposible.
impostor impostor,-a mf.
impractical a poco práctico,-a.
impress vt impresionar.
impression impresión f; **to be under the i. that** . . . tener la impresión de que . . .
impressive a impresionante.
imprison vt encarcelar.
improbable a improbable.
improper a (indecent) indecente.
improve 1 vt mejorar. **2** vi mejorarse.
• **improve on** vt superar.
improvement mejora f.
improvise vti improvisar.
impudent a insolente.
impulse impulso m.
impulsive a irreflexivo,-a.
impulsively adv de forma impulsiva.
impurity impureza f.
in 1 prep (place) en; **in prison** en la cárcel; **in the distance** a lo lejos; **she arrived in New York** llegó a Nueva York. ▪ (time) (during) en, durante; **in May/1945** en mayo/1945; **in spring** en primavera; **in the daytime** durante el día; **in the morning** por la mañana. ▪ (time) (within) dentro de. ▪ (time) (after) al cabo de. ▪ (manner) en, de; **in a loud/quiet voice** en voz alta/baja; **in French** en francés; **dressed in blue** vestido,-a de azul; **in uniform** de uniforme. ▪ (ratio, numbers) de; **one in six** uno de cada seis; **two meters in length** dos metros de largo. ▪ (after superlative) de; **the smallest car in the world** el coche más pequeño del mundo. **2** adv **to be in** (at home) estar (en casa); (in fashion) estar de moda; **the bus is in** el autobús ha llegado.
inability incapacidad f.
inaccessible a inaccesible.
inaccuracy (error) inexactitud f.
inaccurate a incorrecto,-a.

inadequacy (*lack*) insuficiencia *f*; (*inability*) incompetencia *f*.

inadequate *a* (*lacking*) insuficiente; (*unsuitable*) inadecuado,-a.

inappropriate *a* (*behavior*) poco apropiado,-a.

inaugurate *vt* (*building*) inaugurar.

inauguration (*of building*) inauguración *f*.

Inc, inc *abbr of* **Incorporated** ≈ S.A.

incapable *a* incapaz (**of doing sth** de hacer algo).

incense 1 *vt* enfurecer. **2** *n* incienso *m*.

incentive incentivo *m*.

inch pulgada *f* (*approx* 2.54 cm).

incident incidente *m*.

incidentally *adv* por cierto, de paso.

incite *vt* incitar; **to i. sb to do sth** incitar a algn a hacer algo.

incitement incitación *f*.

inclination deseo *m*; **my i. is to stay** yo prefiero quedarme.

incline 1 *vt* **she's inclined to be aggressive** tiende a ser agresiva. **2** *vi* (*slope*) inclinarse.

include *vt* incluir (**in** en); (*in price*) comprender (**in** en).

including *prep* incluso, inclusive.

inclusive *a* inclusivo,-a; **the rent is i. of bills** el alquiler incluye las facturas.

income ingresos *mpl*; (*from investment*) réditos *mpl*.

income tax impuesto *m* sobre la renta.

incompatible *a* incompatible (**with** con).

incompetent *a* incompetente.

incomplete *a* incompleto,-a.

inconceivable *a* inconcebible.

inconsiderate *a* desconsiderado,-a.

inconsistency inconsecuencia *f*.

inconsistent *a* inconsecuente; **your evidence is i. with the facts** su testimonio no concuerda con los hechos.

inconspicuous *a* que pasa desapercibido,-a.

inconvenience 1 *n* molestia *f*; (*disadvantage*) inconvenientes *mpl*; **the i. of living out here** los inconvenientes de vivir aquí. **2** *vt* molestar.

inconvenient *a* molesto,-a; (*time*) inoportuno,-a.

incorporate *vt* (*include*) incluir; (*contain*) contener.

incorrect *a* incorrecto,-a.

increase 1 *n* aumento *m*; (*in number*) incremento; (*in price etc*) subida *f*. **2** *vt* aumentar; (*price etc*) subir. **3** *vi* aumentar.

increasing *a* creciente.

increasingly *adv* cada vez más.

incredible *a* increíble.

incredibly *adv* increíblemente.

incubator incubadora *f*.

incur *vt* (*blame*) incurrir en; (*debt*) contraer; (*loss*) sufrir.

incurable *a* incurable.

indecent *a* indecente.

indecisive *a* indeciso,-a.

indeed *adv* (*in fact*) efectivamente; **it's very hard i.** es verdaderamente difícil; **thank you very much i.** muchísimas gracias.

indefinite *a* indefinido,-a.

indefinitely *adv* indefinidamente.

independence independencia *f*.

independent *a* independiente; **to become i.** independizarse.

independently *adv* independientemente.

index 1 *n* (*in book*) índice *m*; (*in library*) catálogo *m*. **2** *vt* catalogar.

index card ficha *f*.

index finger dedo *m* índice.

index-linked *a* sujeto,-a al aumento de la inflación.

Indian *a* & *n* (*of America*) indio,-a (*mf*); (*of India*) hindú (*mf*).

indicate 1 *vt* indicar. **2** *vi* (*driving*) poner el intermitente.

indication indicio *m*.

indicator indicador *m*; (*on car*) intermitente *m*.

indifference indiferencia *f*.

indifferent a (uninterested) indiferente; (mediocre) regular.

indigestion indigestión f; **to have i.** tener un empacho.

indignant a indignado,-a; **to get i. about sth** indignarse por algo.

indirect a indirecto,-a.

indirectly adv indirectamente.

indiscreet a indiscreto,-a.

indiscriminate a indiscriminado,-a.

indiscriminately adv (at random) indistintamente sin criterio.

indistinguishable a indistinguible.

individual 1 a (separate) individual; (for one) particular; (characteristic) particular. **2** n (person) individuo m.

individually adv individualmente.

indoor a (plant) interior; **i. pool** piscina cubierta.

indoors adv (inside) dentro (de casa).

induce vt (persuade) inducir; (cause) producir.

indulge vt (child) consentir; (person) complacer.

indulgent a indulgente.

industrial a industrial; (accident) laboral; **i. dispute** conflicto m laboral; **i. estate** polígono m industrial.

industry industria f.

inedible a incomible.

ineffective a ineficaz.

inefficiency ineficacia f; (of person) incompetencia f.

inefficient a ineficaz; (person) inepto,-a.

inept a (person) inepto,-a; (remark) estúpido,-a.

inequality desigualdad f.

inevitable a inevitable.

inevitably adv inevitablemente.

inexcusable a inexcusable.

inexpensive a económico,-a.

inexperienced a inexperto,-a.

inexplicable a inexplicable.

infallible a infalible.

infamous a infame.

infancy infancia f.

infant niño,-a mf.

infantry infantería f.

infatuated a encaprichado,-a (with con).

infatuation encaprichamiento m.

infect vt infectar.

infection infección f.

infectious a (disease) infeccioso, -a; fig contagioso,-a.

inferior a inferior (to a).

inferiority inferioridad f.

infest vt infestar (with de).

infinite a infinito,-a.

infinitely adv infinitamente.

infinitive infinitivo m.

infinity infinidad f.

infirm a (ailing) enfermizo,-a; (weak) débil.

inflamed a inflamado,-a; **to become i.** inflamarse.

inflammation inflamación f.

inflate vt inflar.

inflation inflación f.

inflexible a inflexible.

inflict vt (damage) causar (on a); (defeat) infligir (on a).

influence 1 n influencia f; **to be under the i. (of drink)** llevar unas copas de más; (formally) estar en estado de embriaguez. **2** vt influir en.

influential a influyente.

influenza gripe f.

influx afluencia f.

info fam información f.

inform vt informar (**of, about** de, sobre).

informal a (occasion, behavior) informal; (language, treatment) familiar; (unofficial) no oficial.

informally adv (to speak, behave) de manera informal.

information información f; **a piece of i.** un dato.

information technology informática f.

informative a informativo,-a.

infuriate vt poner furioso,-a.

infuriating a exasperante.

ingenious a ingenioso,-a.

ingratitude ingratitud f.
ingredient ingrediente m.
inhabit vt vivir en, ocupar.
inhabitant habitante mf.
inhale vt (gas) inhalar; (air) aspirar.
inherit vt heredar (**from** de).
inheritance herencia f.
inhibit vt (freedom) limitar; (person) cohibir; **to be inhibited** (person) sentirse cohibido,-a.
inhibition cohibición f.
inhospitable a inhospitalario,-a.
inhuman a inhumano,-a.
initial 1 a inicial. **2** n **initials** (of name) iniciales fpl; (of abbreviation) siglas fpl.
initially adv al principio.
inject vt (drug etc) inyectar.
injection inyección f.
injure vt herir; **to i. oneself** hacerse daño.
injured 1 a herido,-a. **2** npl **the i.** los heridos.
injury herida f.
injustice injusticia f.
ink tinta f.
ink-jet printer impresora f de chorro de tinta.
inkling (idea) idea f vaga, indicio m.
inland 1 a (del) interior. **2** adv (travel) tierra adentro.
in-laws npl familia f política.
inmate (of prison) preso,-a mf.
inn (with lodging) posada f.
inner a interior; **i. city** casco m urbano.
innocence inocencia f.
innocent a & n inocente (mf).
inoculate vt inocular.
inoculation inoculación f.
input (of data) input m, entrada f.
inquire 1 vt preguntar. **2** vi preguntar (**about** por); (find out) informarse (**about** de).
• **inquire into** vt investigar.
inquiry pregunta f; (investigation) investigación f; **'inquiries'** 'información'.
inquisitive a curioso,-a; (questioning) preguntón,-ona.

insane a loco,-a.
insanity locura f.
inscription (on stone, coin) inscripción f; (in book, on photo) dedicatoria f.
insect insecto m; **i. bite** picadura f.
insecticide insecticida m.
insecure a inseguro,-a.
insensitive a insensible.
insensitivity insensibilidad f.
insert vt introducir.
inside 1 n interior m; **on the i.** por dentro; **to turn sth i. out** volver algo al revés. **2** a interior; **i. lane** carril m interior. **3** adv (be) dentro, adentro; (run etc) (hacia) adentro. **4** prep (place) dentro de.
insight (quality) perspicacia f.
insignificant a insignificante.
insincere a poco sincero,-a.
insist 1 vi insistir (**on** en). **2** vt **to i. that . . .** insistir en que . . .
insistence insistencia f.
insistent a insistente.
insolence insolencia f.
insolent a insolente.
insomnia insomnio m.
inspect vt inspeccionar.
inspection inspección f.
inspector inspector,-a mf; (on bus, train) revisor,-a mf.
inspiration inspiración f.
inspire vt inspirar; **to i. respect in sb** infundir respeto a algn.
install vt instalar.
installment (of payment) plazo m; (of novel, program) entrega f.
instance caso m; **for i.** por ejemplo.
instant 1 n (moment) instante m. **2** a inmediato,-a; (coffee, meal) instantáneo,-a.
instantly adv inmediatamente.
instant replay repetición f.
instead 1 adv en cambio. **2** prep **i. of** en vez de.
instinct instinto m.
instinctive a instintivo,-a.
instinctively adv instintivamente.
institution institución f.
instruct vt instruir; (order) mandar.

instruction instructions instrucciones *fpl;* '**instructions for use**' 'modo de empleo'.

instructive *a* instructivo,-a.

instructor instructor,-a *mf;* (*of driving*) profesor,-a *mf.*

instrument instrumento *m.*

insufficient *a* insuficiente.

insulate *vt* aislar (**against, from** de).

insulation aislamiento *m.*

insult 1 *n* insulto *m.* **2** *vt* insultar.

insurance seguro *m;* **i. company** compañía *f* de seguros.

insure *vt* asegurar (**against** contra).

intact *a* intacto,-a.

intellect intelecto *m.*

intellectual *a & n* intelectual (*mf*).

intelligence inteligencia *f.*

intelligent *a* inteligente.

intelligible *a* inteligible.

intend *vt* (*mean*) tener la intención de.

intense *a* intenso,-a.

intensely *adv* (*extremely*) sumamente.

intensify *vt* intensificar.

intensity intensidad *f.*

intensive *a* intensivo,-a; **i. care unit** unidad *f* de vigilancia intensiva.

intent *a* **to be i. on doing sth** estar resuelto,-a a hacer algo.

intention intención *f.*

intentional *a* deliberado,-a.

intentionally *adv* a propósito.

intercept *vt* interceptar.

interchange (*on motorway*) cruce *m.*

interchangeable *a* intercambiable.

intercom (*at entrance*) portero automático.

interconnected *a* (*facts etc*) interrelacionado,-a.

interest 1 *n* interés *m;* **i. rate** tipo *m* de interés. **2** *vt* interesar; **to be interested in** interesarse en; **I'm not interested** no me interesa.

interesting *a* interesante.

interfere *vi* (*meddle*) entrometerse (**in** en).

interference (*meddling*) intromisión *f;* (*on radio etc*) interferencia *f.*

interior 1 *a* interior. **2** *n* interior *m.*

intermediary intermediario,-a *mf.*

intermediate *a* intermedio,-a.

intermission (*at cinema, in theater*) intermedio *m;* (*in music*) interludio *m.*

intern (*doctor*) interno,-a *mf.*

internal *a* interior; (*dispute, injury*) interno,-a.

Internal Revenue Service Hacienda *f.*

international *a* internacional.

interpret *vt* interpretar.

interpreter intérprete *mf.*

interrogate *vt* interrogar.

interrogation interrogatorio *m.*

interrupt *vti* interrumpir.

interruption interrupción *f.*

intersect 1 *vt* cruzar. **2** *vi* cruzarse.

intersection (*crossroads*) cruce *m.*

interval (*of time, space*) intervalo *m.*

intervene *vi* (*person*) intervenir (**in** en); (*event*) sobrevenir.

intervention intervención *f.*

interview 1 *n* entrevista *f.* **2** *vt* entrevistar.

interviewer entrevistador,-a *mf.*

intimate *a* íntimo,-a.

intimidate *vt* intimidar.

into *prep* (*motion*) en, a; **to get i. a car** subir a un coche; **to go i. a house** entrar en una casa; **to change dollars i. pesetas** cambiar dólares en *or* por pesetas; **to translate sth i. French** traducir algo al francés; *fam* **to be i. sth** ser aficionado,-a a algo.

intolerable *a* intolerable.

intoxicate *vt* embriagar.

intoxicated *a* borracho,-a.

intransitive *a* intransitivo,-a.

intricate *a* intrincado,-a.

introduce *vt* (*person, program*)

presentar (**to** a); (*bring in*) introducir (**into, to** en).

introduction (*of person, program*) presentación *f*; (*in book, bringing in*) introducción *f*.

intrude *vi* entrometerse (**into, on** en); (*disturb*) molestar.

intruder intruso,-a *mf*.

intrusion intrusión *f*.

intuition intuición *f*.

inundate *vt* inundar (**with** de); **I was inundated with offers** me llovieron las ofertas.

invade *vt* invadir.

invader invasor,-a *mf*.

invalid[1] (*disabled person*) minusválido,-a *mf*; (*sick person*) enfermo,-a *mf*.

invalid[2] *a* nulo,-a.

invaluable *a* inestimable.

invariably *adv* (*always*) invariablemente.

invent *vt* inventar.

invention invento *m*.

inventor inventor,-a *mf*.

inventory inventario *m*.

inverted *a* (**in**) **i. commas** (entre) comillas *fpl*.

invest *vt* invertir (**in** en).

investigate *vt* (*crime, subject*) investigar; (*cause, possibility*) estudiar.

investigation (*of crime*) investigación *f*; (*of cause*) examen *m*.

investigator investigador,-a *mf*.

investor inversor,-a *mf*.

invigorating *a* vigorizante.

invisible *a* invisible.

invitation invitación *f*.

invite *vt* invitar (**to** a); (*comments etc*) solicitar; (*criticism*) provocar.

inviting *a* (*attractive*) atractivo,-a; (*food*) apetitoso,-a.

invoice **1** *n* factura *f*. **2** *vt* facturar.

involve *vt* (*entail*) suponer; (*concern*) implicar (**in** en); **to be involved in an accident** sufrir un accidente.

involved *a* (*complicated*) complicado,-a; (*romantically*) enredado,-a.

involvement (*participation*) participación *f*; (*in crime*) implicación *f*; **emotional i.** relación *f* sentimental.

inwards *adv* hacia dentro.

IQ coeficiente *m* intelectual, CI *m*.

Iranian *a & n* iraní (*mf*).

Iraqi *a & n* iraquí (*mf*).

iris (*of eye*) iris *m inv*; (*plant*) lirio *m*.

Irish **1** *a* irlandés,-esa. **2** *npl* **the I.** los irlandeses.

Irishman irlandés *m*.

Irishwoman irlandesa *f*.

iron **1** *n* hierro *m*; (*for clothes*) plancha *f*; **the i. and steel industry** la industria siderúrgica. **2** *vt* (*clothes*) planchar.

ironic(al) *a* irónico,-a.

ironing **to do the i.** planchar.

ironing board tabla *f* de planchar.

irony ironía *f*.

irrational *a* irracional.

irregular *a* irregular.

irrelevance irrelevancia *f*.

irrelevant *a* no pertinente.

irresistible *a* irresistible.

irrespective *a* **i. of** sin tener en cuenta.

irrigate *vt* regar.

irritable *a* irritable.

irritate *vt* (*annoy*) irritar, fastidiar.

irritating *a* irritante.

irritation (*annoyance*) fastidio *m*; (*bad mood*) mal humor *m*.

is *3rd person sing pres of* **be**.

Islamic *a* islámico,-a.

island isla *f*.

isolate *vt* aislar (**from** de).

isolated *a* aislado,-a.

isolation aislamiento *m*.

issue **1** *n* (*matter*) cuestión *f*; (*of journal etc*) ejemplar *m*. **2** *vt* (*book*) publicar; (*currency etc*) emitir; (*passport*) expedir; (*supplies*) repartir; (*order, instructions*) dar.

it *pers pron* (*subject*) él, ella (*often omitted*); **it's here** está aquí. ▪ (*direct object*) lo, la; **I don't believe it** no me lo creo. ▪ (*indirect object*) le;

give it a kick dale una patada. ■ *(after prep)* él, ella, ello; **we'll talk about it later** ya hablaremos de ello. ■ *(impersonal)* **it's late** es tarde; **it's me** soy yo; **it's raining** está lloviendo; **who is it?** ¿quién es?

Italian 1 *a* italiano,-a. **2** *n (person)* italiano,-a *mf; (language)* italiano *m*.

italic *a* **in italics** en cursiva.

itch 1 *n* picor *m*. **2** *vi (skin)* picar.

itchy *a* que pica.

item *(in list)* artículo *m; (in collection)* pieza *f; (on agenda)* asunto *m*; **i. of clothing** prenda *f* de vestir; **news i.** noticia *f*.

its *poss a (one thing)* su; *(more than one)* sus.

itself *pers pron* ■ *(reflexive)* se; **the cat scratched i.** el gato se rascó. ■ *(emphatic)* él *or* ella mismo,-a.

ivory marfil *m*.

ivy hiedra *f*.

J

jab 1 *n* pinchazo *m; (poke)* golpe *m* seco. **2** *vt* pinchar.

jack *(for car)* gato *m; (cards)* sota *f*.

jacket chaqueta *f; (of suit)* americana *f*; **j. potatoes** patatas *fpl* al horno.

jacuzzi jacuzzi *m*.

jagged *a* dentado,-a.

jail 1 *n* cárcel *f*. **2** *vt* encarcelar.

jam¹ mermelada *f*.

jam² 1 *n (blockage)* atasco *m*. **2** *vt (cram)* meter a la fuerza; *(block)* atascar. **3** *vi (door)* atrancarse; *(brakes)* agarrotarse.

• **jam into** *vt (crowd)* apretarse en; **to j. sth into sth** meter algo a la fuerza en algo.

jam jar pote *m* de mermelada.

jam-packed *a fam (with people)* atestado,-a; *(with things)* atiborrado,-a.

January enero *m*.

Japanese 1 *a* japonés,-esa. **2** *n* *(person)* japonés,-esa *mf; (language)* japonés *m*.

jar *(glass)* tarro *m; (earthenware)* tinaja *f*.

jaundice ictericia *f*.

javelin jabalina *f*.

jaw mandíbula *f*.

jazz jazz *m*.

jealous *a* celoso,-a; *(envious)* envidioso,-a; **to be j. of** tener celos de.

jealousy celos *mpl; (envy)* envidia *f*.

jeans *npl* vaqueros *mpl*, tejanos *mpl*.

jeep jeep *m*.

jeer 1 *n (boo)* abucheo *m*. **2** *vi (boo)* abuchear; *(mock)* burlarse.

jeering *a* burlón,-ona.

jelly gelatina *f*.

jeopardize *vt* poner en peligro; *(agreement etc)* comprometer.

jerk 1 *n (jolt)* sacudida *f; fam (idiot)* imbécil *mf*. **2** *vt (shake)* sacudir.

jersey jersey *m*.

jet reactor *m*; **j. engine** reactor *m*.

jet lag desfase *m* horario.

jet-lagged *a* que sufre los efectos del desfase horario.

Jew judío,-a *m*.

jewel joya *f; (in watch)* rubí *m*.

jeweler joyero,-a *mf*.

jewelry joyas *fpl*.

Jewish *a* judío,-a.

jigsaw *(puzzle)* rompecabezas *m inv*.

jingle *vi* tintinear.

jitters *npl* **to get the j.** ponerse nervioso,-a.

job trabajo *m; (task)* tarea *f; (occupation)* (puesto *m* de) trabajo *m*; **we had a j. to . . .** nos costó (trabajo) . . . ; **it's a good j. that . . .** menos mal que . . .

job center oficina *f* de empleo.

jobless *a* parado,-a.

jockey jinete *m*.

jog 1 *n* trote *m*. **2** *vt* empujar; *(memory)* refrescar. **3** *vi (run)* hacer footing.

john *fam* meódromo *m*.
join 1 *vt* juntar; (*road*) empalmar con; (*river*) desembocar en; (*meet*) reunirse con; (*group*) unirse a; (*institution*) entrar en; (*army*) alistarse a; (*party*) afiliarse a; (*club*) hacerse socio,-a de. **2** *vi* unirse; (*roads*) empalmar; (*rivers*) confluir; (*become a member*) afiliarse; (*club*) hacerse socio,-a. **3** *n* juntura *f*.
• **join in 1** *vi* participar. **2** *vt* participar en.
joint 1 *n* articulación *f*; (*of meat*) corte *m* de carne para asar; (*once roasted*) asado *m*; (*drugs*) porro *m*. **2** *a* colectivo,-a; **j. (bank) account** cuenta *f* conjunta.
joke 1 *n* chiste *m*; (*prank*) broma *f*. **2** *vi* estar de broma.
joker bromista *mf*; (*in cards*) comodín *m*.
jolly *a* alegre.
jolt 1 *n* sacudida *f*. **2** *vi* moverse a sacudidas. **3** *vt* sacudir.
jostle 1 *vt* dar empujones a. **2** *vi* dar empujones.
• **jot down** *vt* apuntar.
journalist periodista *mf*.
journey viaje *m*; (*distance*) trayecto *m*.
joy alegría *f*.
joyful *a* alegre.
joystick palanca *f* de mando; (*of video game*) joystick *m*.
judge 1 *n* juez *mf*, jueza *f*. **2** *vt* juzgar; (*estimate*) considerar; (*assess*) valorar. **3** *vi* juzgar.
judg(e)ment sentencia *f*; (*opinion*) opinión *f*.
judo judo *m*.
jug jarra *f*; **milk j.** jarra de leche.
juggle *vi* hacer juegos malabares (**with** con).
juggler malabarista *mf*.
juice jugo *m*; (*of citrus fruits*) zumo *m*.
juicy *a* jugoso,-a.
July julio *m*.
jumble 1 *n* revoltijo *m*. **2** *vt* revolver.

jumbo *a* gigante.
jumbo jet jumbo *m*.
jump 1 *n* salto *m*; (*sudden increase*) subida repentina *f*. **2** *vi* saltar; (*start*) sobresaltarse; (*increase*) aumentar de golpe. **3** *vt* saltar; **to j. the line** colarse.
• **jump in** or **on 1** *vt* (*train etc*) subirse a. **2** *vi* subir.
jump rope comba *f*.
jumpy *a* fam nervioso,-a.
junction (*of roads*) cruce *m*.
June junio *m*.
jungle jungla *f*.
junior 1 *a* (*lower in rank*) subalterno,-a; (*younger*) menor; **j. team** equipo juvenil. **2** *n* (*of lower rank*) subalterno,-a *mf*; (*younger person*) menor *mf*.
junior high school = instituto *m* de enseñanza secundaria.
junk trastos *mpl*.
junk shop tienda *f* de segunda mano.
jury jurado *m*.
just 1 *a* (*fair*) justo,-a. **2** *adv* (*at this very moment*) ahora mismo, en este momento; (*only*) solamente; (*barely*) por poco; (*exactly*) exactamente; **he had j. arrived** acababa de llegar; **he was j. leaving when Rosa arrived** estaba a punto de salir cuando llegó Rosa; **j. as I came in** justo cuando entré; **I only j. caught the bus** cogí el autobús por los pelos; **j. about** casi; **j. as fast as** tan rápido como.
justice justicia *f*.
justify *vt* justificar.
• **jut out** *vi* sobresalir.

K

kangaroo canguro *m*.
karate kárate *m*.
kebab pincho moruno *m*.
keen *a* (*eager*) entusiasta; (*intense*) profundo,-a; (*mind, senses*) agudo,-a.

keep 1 *n* **to earn one's k.** ganarse el pan. **2** *vt* mantener; (*letters, memories, silence, secret*) guardar; (*retain possession of*) quedarse con; (*hold back*) entretener; (*in prison*) detener; (*promise*) cumplir; (*diary, accounts*) llevar; **to k. sb waiting** hacer esperar a algn; **to k. doing sth** seguir haciendo algo; **she keeps forgetting her keys** siempre se olvida las llaves; **to k. going** seguir adelante. **3** *vi* (*food*) conservarse.
• **keep away 1** *vt* mantener a distancia. **2** *vi* mantenerse a distancia.
• **keep back 1** *vt* (*information*) callar; (*money etc*) retener. **2** *vi* (*crowd*) mantenerse atrás.
• **keep down** *vt* **to k. prices down** mantener los precios bajos.
• **keep off** *vt* **k. off the grass** prohibido pisar la hierba.
• **keep on 1** *vt* (*clothes etc*) no quitarse; (*continue to employ*) mantener a; **it keeps on breaking** siempre se está rompiendo. **2** *vi* **the rain kept on** la lluvia siguió/continuó; **he just kept on** (*talking, complaining*) siguió machacando; **k. straight on** sigue todo derecho.
• **keep out 1** *vt* no dejar pasar. **2** *vi* **k. out!** ¡no entres!
• **keep to** *vt* **to k. to the left** circular por la izquierda.
• **keep up 1** *vt* mantener. **2** *vi* (*in race etc*) no rezagarse.
• **keep up with** *vt* **to k. up with sb** (*in a race*) mantenerse a la altura de algn; **to k. up with the times** estar al día.
kennel caseta *f* para perros.
Kenyan *a & n* keniano,-a (*mf*).
kept *pt & pp of* **keep.**
kerosene queroseno *m.*
ketchup ketchup *m.*
kettle hervidor *m.*
key 1 *n* (*for lock*) llave *f*; (*of piano, typewriter*) tecla *f*. **2** *a* clave.
keyboard teclado *m.*
key ring llavero *m.*

kick 1 *n* (*from person*) puntapié *m.* **2** *vi* (*animal*) cocear; (*person*) dar patadas. **3** *vt* dar un puntapié a.
• **kick down** or **in** *vt* (*door etc*) derribar a patadas.
• **kick out** *vt* echar a patadas.
kick-off saque *m* inicial.
kid[1] *fam* (*child*) niño,-a *mf*; **the kids** los críos.
kid[2] **1** *vt* tomar el pelo a. **2** *vi* tomar el pelo.
kidnap *vt* secuestrar.
kidnapper secuestrador,-a *mf.*
kidney riñón *m.*
kill *vt* matar.
killer asesino,-a *mf.*
kilo kilo *m.*
kilogram kilogramo *m.*
kilometer kilómetro *m.*
kind[1] **1** *n* clase *f*; **what k. of?** ¿qué tipo de? **2** *adv fam* **k. of** en cierta manera.
kind[2] *a* amable.
kindergarten jardín *m* de infancia.
kindness amabilidad *f.*
king rey *m.*
kingdom reino *m.*
kiosk quiosco *m.*
kiss 1 *n* beso *m.* **2** *vt* besar. **3** *vi* besarse.
kit (*gear*) equipo *m*; (*clothing*) ropa *f*; (*toy model*) maqueta *f.*
kitchen cocina *f.*
kite (*toy*) cometa *f.*
kitten gatito,-a *mf.*
knack **to get the k. of doing sth** cogerle el truquillo a algo.
knee rodilla *f.*
kneel* *vi* **to k. (down)** arrodillarse.
knew *pt of* **know.**
knickers *npl* bragas *fpl.*
knife (*pl* **knives**) cuchillo *m.*
knight caballero *m*; (*in chess*) caballo *m.*
knit 1 *vt* tejer; (*join*) juntar. **2** *vi* hacer punto; (*bone*) soldarse.
knitting punto *m.*
knitting needle aguja *f* de hacer punto.

knob (*of stick*) puño *m*; (*of drawer*) tirador *m*; (*button*) botón *m*.

knock 1 *n* golpe *m*; **there was a k. at the door** llamaron a la puerta. **2** *vt* golpear. **3** *vi* chocar (**against**, **into** contra); (*at door*) llamar (**at** a).

• **knock down** *vt* (*demolish*) derribar; (*car*) atropellar.

• **knock off** *vt* tirar.

• **knock out** *vt* (*make unconscious*) dejar sin conocimiento; (*in boxing*) derrotar por K.O.

• **knock over** *vt* volcar; (*car*) atropellar.

knocker (*on door*) aldaba *f*.

knot 1 *n* nudo *m*. **2** *vt* anudar.

know* 1 *vt* saber; (*be acquainted with*) conocer; **she knows how to ski** sabe esquiar; **we got to k. each other at the party** nos conocimos en la fiesta. **2** *vi* saber; **to let sb k.** avisar a algn.

know-how conocimiento *m* práctico.

knowledge conocimiento *m*; (*learning*) conocimientos *mpl*.

known *a* conocido,-a.

knuckle nudillo *m*.

Koran Corán *m*.

Korean *a & n* coreano,-a (*mf*).

L

lab *fam* laboratorio *m*.

label 1 *n* etiqueta *f*. **2** *vt* poner etiqueta a.

laboratory laboratorio *m*.

labor 1 *n* (*work*) trabajo *m*; (*workforce*) mano *f* de obra; **to be in l.** estar de parto. **2** *a* (*market etc*) laboral. **3** *vi* (*work*) trabajar (duro).

laborer peón *m*; **farm l.** peón *m* agrícola.

labor union sindicato *m*.

lace *n* (*fabric*) encaje *m*; **laces** cordones *mpl*; **to do up one's laces** atarse los cordones.

lack 1 *n* falta *f*. **2** *vt* carecer de. **3** *vi* carecer (**in** de).

lad chaval *m*.

ladder escalera *f* (de mano).

ladle cucharón *m*.

lady señora *f*; **'Ladies'** (*restroom*) 'Señoras'.

ladybug mariquita *f*.

lager cerveza *f* (rubia).

lake lago *m*.

lamb cordero *m*; (*meat*) carne *f* de cordero.

lame *a* cojo,-a.

lamp lámpara *f*.

lamp post farola *f*.

lampshade pantalla *f*.

land 1 *n* tierra *f*; (*country*) país *m*; (*property*) tierras *fpl*; **piece of l.** terreno *m*; **by l.** por tierra. **2** *vt* (*plane*) hacer aterrizar. **3** *vi* (*plane*) aterrizar; (*passengers*) desembarcar.

landing (*of staircase*) rellano *m*; (*of plane*) aterrizaje *m*.

landlady (*of apartment*) propietaria *f*, casera *f*; (*of boarding house*) patrona *f*; (*of pub*) dueña *f*.

landlord (*of apartment*) propietario *m*, casero *m*; (*of pub*) dueño *m*.

landscape paisaje *m*.

landslide desprendimiento *m* de tierras.

lane (*in country*) camino *m*; (*in town*) callejón *m*; (*of highway*) carril *m*.

language idioma *m*, lengua *f*.

language laboratory laboratorio *m* de idiomas.

lantern farol *m*.

lap¹ (*knees*) rodillas *fpl*.

lap² (*circuit*) vuelta *f*.

lapel solapa *f*.

larder despensa *f*.

large *a* grande; (*amount*) importante; **by and l.** por lo general.

largely *adv* (*mainly*) en gran parte; (*chiefly*) principalmente.

lark¹ (*bird*) alondra *f*.

laser láser *m*; **l. printer** impresora *f* láser.

last 1 *a* (*final, most recent*) último, -a; (*past*) pasado,-a; (*previous*) anterior; **l. but one** penúltimo,-a; **l. month** el mes pasado; **l. night** anoche. **2** adv (on final occasion) por última vez; (at the end) en último lugar; (in race etc) último; **at (long) l.** por fin. **3** n el último, la última. **4** vi (time) durar; (hold out) aguantar.

lastly adv por último.

latch pestillo m.

late 1 a (not on time) tardío,-a; (hour) avanzado,-a; (far on in time) tarde; **to be five minutes l.** llegar con cinco minutos de retraso; **in the l. afternoon** a última hora de la tarde. **2** adv tarde; **l. at night** a altas horas de la noche.

latecomer rezagado,-a mf.

lately adv últimamente.

Latin 1 a latino,-a; **L. America** América Latina, Latinoamérica f; **L. American** latinoamericano,-a (mf). **2** n latino,-a (mf); (language) latín m.

latter 1 a (last) último,-a; (second of two) segundo,-a. **2** pron éste,-a.

laugh 1 n risa f. **2** vi reír, reírse.
• **laugh about** vt **to l. about sb/sth** reírse de algn/algo.
• **laugh at** vt **to l. at sb/sth** reírse de algn/algo.

laughter risa f.

launch 1 n (vessel) lancha f; (of product) lanzamiento m. **2** vt (rocket, new product) lanzar; (ship) botar; (film, play) estrenar.

Laundromat® lavandería f automática.

laundry (place) lavandería f; (dirty clothes) ropa f sucia; **to do the l.** lavar la ropa.

lavatory retrete m; (room) baño m; **public l.** servicios mpl.

law ley f; (as subject) derecho m.

law court tribunal m de justicia.

lawn césped m.

lawnmower cortacésped m.

lawsuit pleito m.

lawyer abogado,-a mf.

lay* vt (place) poner; (cable, trap) tender; (foundations) echar; (table, eggs) poner; (set down) asentar.

• **lay down** vt (put down) poner.
• **lay off** vt (dismiss) despedir.
• **lay on** vt (provide) proveer de; (food) preparar.
• **lay out** vt (open out) extender; (arrange) disponer; (ideas) exponer; (spend) gastar.

layabout vago,-a mf.

layer capa f.

layout (arrangement) disposición f; (presentation) presentación f.

lazy a vago,-a.

lead¹ (metal) plomo m; (in pencil) mina f.

lead² 1 n (front position) delantera f; (advantage) ventaja f; (leash) correa f; (electric cable) cable m; **to be in the l.** ir en cabeza; **to take the l.** (in race) tomar la delantera; (score) adelantarse. **2** vt* (conduct) conducir; (be the leader of) dirigir; (life) llevar; **to l. sb to think sth** hacer a algn pensar algo. **3** vi* (road) llevar (**to** a); (in race) llevar la delantera.

• **lead away** vt llevar.
• **lead to** vt (result in) dar lugar a

leader jefe,-a mf; (political) líder mf.

leading a (main) principal.

leaf (pl leaves) hoja f.

leaflet folleto m.

leak 1 n (of gas, liquid) escape m; (of information) filtración f. **2** vi (gas, liquid) escaparse. **3** vt (information) filtrar.

lean* 1 vi inclinarse; (thing) estar inclinado; **to l. on/against** apoyarse en/contra. **2** vt apoyar (**on** en).

• **lean forward** vi inclinarse hacia delante.
• **lean over** vi inclinarse.

leap 1 n (jump) salto m. **2** vi* saltar.

leap year año m bisiesto.

learn* 1 vt aprender; (find out about) enterarse de; **to l. (how) to ski** aprender a esquiar. **2** vi aprender; **to l. about or of** (find out) enterarse de.

learner (*beginner*) principiante *mf*.

learning (*knowledge*) conocimientos *mpl*; (*erudition*) saber *m*.

leash correa *f*.

least 1 *a* menor. 2 *adv* menos. 3 *n* lo menos; **at l.** por lo menos.

leather 1 *n* (*fine*) piel *f*; (*heavy*) cuero *m*. 2 *a* de piel.

leave[1]* 1 *vt* dejar; (*go away from*) abandonar; (*go out of*) salir de; **I have two cookies left** me quedan dos galletas. 2 *vi* (*go away*) irse, marcharse; (*go out*) salir; **the train leaves in five minutes** el tren sale dentro de cinco minutos.

• **leave behind** *vt* dejar atrás.

• **leave on** *vt* (*clothes*) dejar puesto,-a; (*lights, radio*) dejar encendido,-a.

• **leave out** *vt* (*omit*) omitir.

leave[2] (*time off*) vacaciones *fpl*.

lecture 1 *n* conferencia *f*; (*at university*) clase *f*; **to give a l.** dar una conferencia (**on** sobre). 2 *vi* (*at university*) dar clases.

lecturer conferenciante *mf*; (*at university*) profesor,-a *mf*.

leek puerro *m*.

left[1] 1 *a* izquierdo,-a. 2 *adv* a la izquierda. 3 *n* izquierda *f*; **on the l.** a mano izquierda.

left[2] *pt* & *pp of* **leave**[1].

left-hand *a* **on the l. side** a mano izquierda.

left-handed *a* zurdo,-a.

leftovers *npl* sobras *fpl*.

leg pierna *f*; (*of animal, table*) pata *f*.

legal *a* legal; (*permitted by law*) lícito,-a; (*relating to the law*) jurídico,-a.

legal holiday fiesta *f* nacional.

legend leyenda *f*.

legible *a* legible.

leisure ocio *m*; (*free time*) tiempo *m* libre; **l. activities** pasatiempos *mpl*.

lemon limón *m*; **l. juice** zumo *m* de limón; **l. tea** té *m* con limón.

lemonade gaseosa *f*.

lend* *vt* prestar.

length largo *m*; (*duration*) duración *f*; (*section of string etc*) trozo *m*.

lengthen 1 *vt* alargar; (*lifetime*) prolongar. 2 *vi* alargarse; (*lifetime*) prolongarse.

lenient *a* indulgente.

lens (*of spectacles*) lente *f*; (*of camera*) objetivo *m*.

lentil lenteja *f*.

leopard leopardo *m*.

leotard mallas *fpl*.

less menos; **l. and l.** cada vez menos; **a year l. two days** un año menos dos días.

lesson clase *f*; (*in book*) lección *f*.

let* 1 *vt* dejar; (*rent out*) alquilar; **to l. sb do sth** dejar a algn hacer algo; **to l. go of sth** soltar algo; **to l. sb know** avisar a algn. 2 *v aux* **l. him wait** que espere; **l.'s go!** ¡vamos!, ¡vámonos!

• **let down** *vt* (*lower*) bajar; (*fail*) defraudar.

• **let in** *vt* (*admit*) dejar entrar.

• **let off** *vt* (*bomb*) hacer explotar; (*fireworks*) hacer estallar; **to l. sb off** (*pardon*) perdonar.

• **let out** *vt* (*release*) soltar; (*news*) divulgar; (*secret*) revelar; (*cry*) soltar.

• **let up** *vi* (*cease*) cesar.

letdown decepción *f*.

letter (*of alphabet*) letra *f*; (*written message*) carta *f*.

letter box buzón *m*.

lettuce lechuga *f*.

level 1 *a* (*flat*) llano,-a; (*even*) nivelado,-a; **to be l. with** estar a nivel de. 2 *n* nivel *m*; **to be on a l. with** estar al mismo nivel que.

level crossing paso *m* a nivel.

lever palanca *f*.

liable *a* **the river is l. to freeze** el río tiene tendencia a helarse.

liar mentiroso,-a *mf*.

liberty libertad *f*; **to be at l. to say sth** ser libre de decir algo.

librarian bibliotecario,-a *mf*.

library biblioteca *f*.

Libyan a & n libio,-a (mf).
lice npl see **louse.**
license (permit) permiso m; **l. number** (of car) matrícula f.
lick vt lamer.
licorice regaliz m.
lid (cover) tapa f; (of eye) párpado m.
lie[1] vi mentir. **2** n mentira f.
lie[2]* vi (act) acostarse; (state) estar acostado,-a.
• **lie around** vi (person) estar tumbado,-a; (things) estar tirado, -a.
• **lie down** vi acostarse.
life (pl **lives**) vida f; **to come to l.** cobrar vida.
life belt cinturón m salvavidas.
lifeboat (on ship) bote m salvavidas; (on shore) lancha f de socorro.
lifeguard socorrista mf.
life insurance seguro m de vida.
life jacket chaleco m salvavidas.
lifetime vida f; **in his l.** durante su vida.
lift 1 vt levantar; (head etc) alzar; (pick up) coger. **2** n **to give sb a l.** llevar a algn en coche.
• **lift out** vt (take out) sacar.
• **lift up** vt levantar.
light[1] **1** n luz f; (lamp) lámpara f; (headlight) faro m; **to set l. to sth** prender fuego a algo; **have you got a l.?** ¿tiene fuego? **2** vt* (illuminate) iluminar; (ignite) encender. **3** a claro,-a; (hair) rubio,-a.
• **light up 1** vt iluminar. **2** vi iluminarse; (light cigarette) encender un cigarrillo.
light[2] **1** a ligero,-a; (rain) fino,-a. **2** adv **to travel l.** ir ligero,-a de equipaje.
light bulb bombilla f.
lighter (cigarette) **l.** mechero m.
lighthouse faro m.
lighting (act) iluminación f.
lightning (flash) relámpago m; (which hits the earth) rayo m.
like[1] **1** prep (similar to) parecido,-a a; (the same as) igual que; **l. that** así; **what's he l.?** ¿cómo es?; **to feel**

l. tener ganas de. **2** a parecido,-a; (equal) igual.
like[2] **1** vt **do you l. chocolate?** ¿te gusta el chocolate?; **he likes dancing** le gusta bailar; **I would l. a coffee** quisiera un café; **would you l. to go now?** ¿quieres que nos vayamos ya? **2** vi querer; **as you l.** como quieras.
likeable a simpático,-a.
likelihood probabilidad f.
likely 1 a probable; **he's l. to cause trouble** es probable que cause problemas. **2** adv probablemente; **not l.!** ¡ni hablar!
likewise adv (also) asimismo.
liking (for thing) afición f; (for person) simpatía f; (for friend) cariño m.
lily lirio m.
limb miembro m.
lime (fruit) lima f; (tree) limero m.
limit 1 n límite m; (maximum) máximo m; (minimum) mínimo m. **2** vt (restrict) limitar (**to** a).
limousine limusina f.
limp 1 vi cojear. **2** n cojera f.
line[1] n línea f; (straight) raya f; (of writing) renglón m; (of poetry) verso m; (row) fila f; (of trees) hilera f; (of people waiting) cola f; (rope) cuerda f; (telephone) línea f; (of railway) vía f.
line[2] vt (clothes) forrar.
• **line up 1** vt (arrange in rows) poner en fila; **he has something lined up for this evening** tiene algo organizado para esta noche. **2** vi (people) ponerse en fila; (in line) hacer cola.
linen (sheets etc) ropa f blanca.
liner transatlántico m.
lining forro m.
link 1 n (of chain) eslabón m; (connection) conexión f. **2** vt unir.
• **link up** vi unirse; (meet) encontrarse.
lino linóleo m.
lint brush cepillo m de la ropa.
lion león m.
lip labio m.

lipstick lápiz m de labios.

liqueur licor m.

liquid a & n líquido,-a (m).

liquor bebidas fpl alcohólicas.

list 1 n lista f; (catalog) catálogo m. **2** vt (make a list of) hacer una lista de; (put on a list) poner en una lista.

listen vi escuchar; (pay attention) prestar atención.

• **listen out** vi estar atento,-a (**for** a).

listener oyente mf.

liter litro m.

literary a literario,-a.

literature literatura f; (documentation) folleto m informativo.

litter (trash) basura f; (papers) papeles mpl; (offspring) camada f.

litter bin papelera f.

little 1 a pequeño,-a; **a l. dog** un perrito; **a l. house** una casita. **2** pron poco m; **save me a l.** guárdame un poco; **a l. cheese** un poco de queso. **3** adv poco; **l. by l.** poco a poco; **as l. as possible** lo menos posible; **l. milk/money** poca leche/poco dinero.

live¹ vti vivir; **to l. an interesting life** llevar una vida interesante.

live² a (TV etc) en directo; (wire) con corriente.

• **live off** or **on** vt vivir de.

• **live through** vt sobrevivir a, vivir.

• **live together** vi vivir juntos.

• **live up to** vt. **l. up to expectations** estar a la altura de lo que se esperaba.

• **live with** vt vivir con.

lively a (person) vivo,-a; (place) animado,-a.

liver hígado m.

living 1 a vivo,-a. **2** n vida f; **to earn** or **make one's l.** ganarse la vida.

living room sala f de estar.

lizard (large) lagarto m; (small) lagartija f.

load 1 n (cargo) carga f; (weight) peso m; fam **loads (of)** montones de; fam **that's a l. of garbage!** ¡no

son más que tonterías! **2** vt cargar.

• **load up** vti cargar.

loaf (pl loaves) pan m.

loan 1 n (to individual) préstamo m; (to company etc) empréstito m; **on l.** prestado,-a. **2** vt prestar.

lobby (hall) vestíbulo m.

lobster langosta f.

local a local; (person) del pueblo.

local area network red f local.

locally adv en or de la localidad.

locate vt (situate) ubicar; (find) localizar.

location ubicación f.

lock¹ 1 n (on door etc) cerradura f; (bolt) cerrojo m; (padlock) candado m; (on canal) esclusa f. **2** vt cerrar con llave or cerrojo or candado.

lock² (of hair) mechón m.

• **lock in** vt (person) encerrar a.

• **lock out** vt (person) cerrar la puerta a.

• **lock up** vt (house) cerrar; (in jail) meter en la cárcel.

locker armario m ropero.

locket medallón m.

lodger huésped,-a mf.

lodging alojamiento m; **l. house** casa f de huéspedes.

loft desván m.

log (wood) tronco m; (for fire) leño m.

logical a lógico,-a.

lollipop chupachup® m.

loneliness soledad f.

lonely a (person) solo,-a; (place) solitario,-a.

long¹ 1 a (size) largo,-a; (time) mucho,-a; **it's three meters l.** tiene tres metros de largo; **it's a l. way** está lejos; **at l. last** por fin; **how l. is the film?** ¿cuánto tiempo dura la película? **2** adv mucho tiempo; **as l. as the exhibition lasts** mientras dure la exposición; **as l. as** or **so l. as you don't mind** con tal de que no te importe; **before l.** dentro de poco; **how l. have you been here?** ¿cuánto tiempo llevas aquí?

long-distance a de larga distancia; **l. call** conferencia interurbana.

long-term *a* a largo plazo.

look 1 *n* (*glance*) mirada *f*; (*appearance*) aspecto *m*; **to take a l. at** echar un vistazo a. **2** *vi* mirar; (*seem*) parecer; **he looks well** tiene buena cara; **she looks like her father** se parece a su padre.

· **look after** *vt* ocuparse de, cuidar de.

· **look around 1** *vi* mirar alrededor; (*turn head*) volver la cabeza. **2** *vt* (*house, shop*) ver.

· **look at** *vt* mirar.

· **look for** *vt* buscar.

· **look forward to** *vt* esperar con ilusión; **I l. forward to hearing from you** (*in letter*) espero noticias suyas.

· **look into** *vt* investigar.

· **look onto** *vt* dar a.

· **look out** *vi* **the bedroom looks out onto the garden** el dormitorio da al jardín; **l. out!** ¡cuidado!, ¡ojo!

· **look over** *vt* (*examine*) revisar; (*place*) inspeccionar.

· **look up 1** *vi* (*glance upwards*) alzar la vista. **2** *vt* (*look for*) buscar.

lookout (*person*) centinela *mf*; (*place*) mirador *m*; **to be on the l. for** estar al acecho de.

loose 1 *a* (*not secure*) flojo,-a; (*papers, hair, clothes*) suelto,-a; (*baggy*) holgado,-a; (*not packaged*) a granel; **to set sb l.** soltar a algn; **l. change** suelto *m*. **2** *n* **to be on the l.** (*prisoner*) andar suelto.

loosen *vt* aflojar; (*belt*) desabrochar.

lord señor *m*.

lose* *vti* perder; **to l. to sb** perder contra algn.

loser perdedor,-a *mf*.

loss pérdida *f*.

lost *a* perdido,-a; **to get l.** perderse; **get l.!** *fam* ¡vete a la porra!

lot **a l. of** (*much*) mucho,-a; (*many*) muchos,-as; **he feels a l. better** se

encuentra mucho mejor; **lots of** montones de; **what a l. of bottles!** ¡qué cantidad de botellas!

lotion loción *f*.

lottery lotería *f*.

loud 1 *a* (*voice*) alto,-a; (*noise*) fuerte; (*protests, party*) ruidoso,-a. **2** *adv* **to read/think out l.** leer/pensar en voz alta.

loudly *adv* (*to speak etc*) en voz alta.

loudspeaker altavoz *m*.

lousy *a fam* fatal; **a l. trick** una cochinada.

love 1 *n* amor *m*; **to be in l. with sb** estar enamorado,-a de algn; **to make l.** hacer el amor. **2** *vt* (*person*) querer; (*sport etc*) ser muy aficionado,-a a; **he loves cooking** le encanta cocinar.

lovely *a* (*charming*) encantador,-a; (*beautiful*) precioso,-a; (*delicious*) riquísimo,-a.

lover (*enthusiast*) aficionado,-a *mf*.

loving *a* cariñoso,-a.

low 1 *a* bajo,-a; (*poor*) pobre; (*reprehensible*) malo,-a; **to feel l.** sentirse deprimido,-a. **2** *adv* bajo.

lower 1 *a* inferior. **2** *vt* bajar; (*reduce*) reducir; (*price*) rebajar.

low-fat *a* (*milk*) desnatado,-a; (*food*) light *inv*.

loyal *a* leal.

lozenge pastilla *f*.

LP LP *m*, elepé *m*.

luck suerte *f*; **bad l.!** ¡mala suerte!; **good l.!** ¡(buena) suerte!

luckily *adv* afortunadamente.

lucky *a* (*person*) afortunado,-a; (*charm*) de la suerte; **that was l.** ha sido una suerte.

ludicrous *a* ridículo,-a.

luggage equipaje *m*.

lukewarm *a* (*water etc*) tibio,-a.

lullaby nana *f*.

luminous *a* luminoso,-a.

lump (*of coal etc*) trozo *m*; (*of sugar, earth*) terrón *m*; (*swelling*) bulto *m*.

lump sum suma *f* global.

lunatic *a & n* loco,-a (*mf*).

lunch comida *f*, almuerzo *m*; **l. hour** hora *f* de comer.
lung pulmón *m*.
luxurious *a* lujoso,-a.
luxury lujo *m*.

M

mac(c)aroni macarrones *mpl*.
machine máquina *f*.
machinery (*machines*) maquinaria *f*; (*workings of machine*) mecanismo *m*.
mackerel *inv* caballa *f*.
mad *a* loco,-a; **to be m. about sth/ sb** estar loco,-a por algo/algn; **to be m. at sb** estar enfadado,-a con algn.
madam señora *f*.
made *pt & pp of* make.
madman loco *m*.
madness locura *f*.
magazine (*periodical*) revista *f*.
maggot gusano *m*.
magic **1** *n* magia *f*. **2** *a* mágico,-a; **m. wand** varita *f* mágica.
magical *a* mágico,-a.
magician (*wizard*) mago,-a *mf*; (*conjuror*) prestigiditador,-a *mf*.
magistrate juez,-a *mf* de paz.
magnet imán *m*.
magnificent *a* magnífico,-a.
magnifying glass lupa *f*.
mahogany caoba *f*.
maid criada *f*.
mail **1** *n* correo *m*; **2** *vt* (*post*) echar (al buzón).
mailbox buzón *m*.
mailman cartero *m*.
main **1** *a* (*problem, door etc*) principal; (*square, mast, sail*) mayor; (*office*) central; **the m. thing is to keep calm** lo esencial es mantener la calma; **m. road** carretera *f* principal. **2** *n* (*pipe, wire*) conducto *m* principal; **the mains** (*water or gas system*) la conducción; (*electrical*) la red (eléctrica).
mainly *adv* principalmente; (*for the most part*) en su mayoría.

maintain *vt* (*road, machine*) conservar en buen estado; **to m. that** sostener que.
maître d' jefe *mf* de sala.
maize maíz *m*.
majesty majestad *f*.
major **1** *a* principal; (*contribution, operation*) importante. **2** *n* (*officer*) comandante *m*.
majorette majorette *f*.
majority mayoría *f*.
make* **1** *vt* hacer; (*manufacture*) fabricar; (*clothes, curtains*) confeccionar; (*meal*) preparar; (*decision*) tomar; (*earn*) ganar; **to be made of** ser de; **to m. sb do sth** obligar a algn a hacer algo; **to m. do with** arreglárselas con algo; **I don't know what to m. of it** no sé qué pensar de eso; **we've made it!** (*succeeded*) ¡lo hemos conseguido! **2** *n* (*brand*) marca *f*.
• **make out** **1** *vt* (*list, receipt*) hacer; (*check*) extender; (*perceive*) distinguir; (*understand*) entender; (*claim*) pretender. **2** *vi* **how did you m. out?** ¿qué tal le fue?
• **make up** *vt* (*list*) hacer; (*assemble*) montar; (*invent*) inventar; (*apply cosmetics to*) maquillar; (*one's face*) maquillarse; (*loss*) compensar; **to m. up (with sb)** hacer las paces (con algn).
• **make up for** *vt* (*loss, damage*) compensar por; (*lost time, mistake*) recuperar.
maker fabricante *mf*.
make-up (*cosmetics*) maquillaje *m*.
malaria malaria *f*.
male **1** *a* (*animal, plant*) macho; (*person*) varón; (*sex*) masculino. **2** *n* (*person*) varón *m*; (*animal, plant*) macho *m*.
malice (*wickedness*) malicia *f*.
malicious *a* (*wicked*) malévolo,-a.
mall (*shopping*) centro *m* comercial.
mammal mamífero *m*.
man (*pl* **men**) hombre *m*; **old m.**

viejo *m*; **young m.** joven *m*; (*humanity*) el hombre; (*human being*) ser *m* humano.
manage 1 *vt* (*company, household*) llevar; (*money, affairs, person*) manejar; (*achieve*) conseguir; **to m. to do sth** lograr hacer algo. **2** *vi* (*cope physically*) poder; (*financially*) arreglárselas.
management dirección *f*.
manager (*of company, bank*) director,-a *mf*; (*of department*) jefe, -a *mf*.
managing director director,-a *mf* gerente.
mandarin (*fruit*) mandarina *f*.
mane (*of horse*) crin *f*; (*of lion*) melena *f*.
maneuver 1 *n* maniobra *f*. **2** *vt* maniobrar; (*person*) manejar. **3** *vi* maniobrar.
maniac maníaco,-a *mf*; *fam* loco, -a *mf*.
man-made *a* (*lake*) artificial; (*fibres, fabric*) sintético,-a.
manner (*way, method*) manera *f*, modo *m*; (*way of behaving*) forma *f* de ser; **(good) manners** buenos modales *mpl*; **bad manners** falta *f* sing de educación.
mantelpiece (*shelf*) repisa *f* de chimenea; (*fireplace*) chimenea *f*.
manual *a & n* manual (*m*).
manufacture 1 *vt* fabricar. **2** *n* fabricación *f*.
manufacturer fabricante *mf*.
manure estiércol *m*.
many 1 *a* muchos,-as; **a great m.** muchísimos,-as; **as m. . . . as . . .** tantos,-as . . . como . . . ; **how m. days?** ¿cuántos días?; **not m. books** pocos libros; **so m. flowers!** ¡cuántas flores!; **too m.** demasiados,-as. **2** *pron* muchos,-as.
map (*of country*) mapa *m*; (*of town, bus*) plano *m*.
marathon maratón *m or f*.
marble (*stone*) mármol *m*; (*glass ball*) canica *f*.
March marzo *m*.

march 1 *n* marcha *f*. **2** *vi* marchar.
mare yegua *f*.
margarine margarina *f*.
margin margen *m*.
mark[1] **1** *n* (*trace*) huella *f*; (*stain*) mancha *f*; (*symbol*) signo *m*; (*sign, token*) señal *f*; (*in exam etc*) nota *f*. **2** *vt* (*make mark on*) marcar; (*stain*) manchar; (*exam*) corregir.
• **mark out** *vt* (*area*) delimitar.
marker (*pen*) rotulador *m*.
market mercado *m*.
marketing marketing *m*.
marmalade mermelada *f* (de cítricos).
marriage (*state*) matrimonio *m*; (*wedding*) boda *f*.
married *a* casado,-a.
marrow (*bone*) *m*. médula *f*; (*vegetable*) calabacín *m*.
marry *vt* casarse con; (*priest*) casar; **to get married** casarse.
marsh pantano *m*; **salt m.** marisma *f*.
Martian *n & a* marciano,-a (*mf*).
marvelous *a* maravilloso,-a.
marzipan mazapán *m*.
mascara rímel *m*.
mascot mascota *f*.
masculine *a* masculino,-a.
mashed potatoes *npl* puré *m* de patatas.
mask máscara *f*.
mass[1] (*in church*) misa *f*; **to say m.** decir misa.
mass[2] **1** *n* masa *f*; (*large quantity*) montón *m*; (*of people*) multitud *f*. **2** *a* masivo,-a.
massacre 1 *n* masacre *f*. **2** *vt* masacrar.
massage 1 *n* masaje *m*. **2** *vt* dar masaje a.
masseur masajista *m*.
masseuse masajista *f*.
massive *a* enorme.
mast mástil *m*; (*radio etc*) torre *f*.
master 1 *n* (*of dog, servant*) amo *m*; (*of household*) señor *m*; (*teacher*) profesor *m*; **m.'s degree** ≈ máster *m*. **2** *vt* (*person, situation*) domi-

nar; (*subject, skill*) llegar a dominar.

masterpiece obra *f* maestra.
mat (*rug*) alfombrilla *f*; (*doormat*) felpudo *m*; (*rush mat*) estera *f*.
match¹ cerilla *f*.
match² **1** *n* (*sport*) partido *m*. **2** *vt* (*be in harmony with*) armonizar con; (*colors, clothes*) hacer juego con; **they are well matched** (*teams*) van iguales; (*couple*) hacen buena pareja. **3** *vi* (*harmonize*) hacer juego.
• **match up to** *vt* estar a la altura de.
matchbox caja *f* de cerillas.
matching *a* a juego.
matchstick cerilla *f*.
material (*substance*) materia *f*; (*cloth*) tejido *m*; **materials** (*ingredients, equipment*) materiales *mpl*.
maternal *a* maternal; (*uncle etc*) materno,-a.
maternity maternidad *f*.
maternity hospital maternidad *f*.
math matemáticas *fpl*.
mathematical *a* matemático,-a.
mathematics matemáticas *fpl*.
matinée (*cinema*) sesión *f* de tarde; (*theater*) función *f* de tarde.
matter 1 *n* (*affair, question*) asunto *m*; (*problem*) problema *m*; (*substance*) materia *f*; **what's the m.?** ¿qué pasa?. **2** *vi* importar; **it doesn't m.** no importa, da igual.
mattress colchón *m*.
mature *a* maduro,-a.
maximum 1 *n* máximo *m*. **2** *a* máximo,-a.
may *v aux* (*pt* **might**) (*possibility, probability*) poder, ser posible; **he m.** *or* **might come** puede que venga; **you m.** *or* **might as well stay** más vale que te quedes. ▪ (*permission*) poder; **m. I?** ¿me permite?; **you m. smoke** pueden fumar. ▪ (*wish*) ojalá (+ *subjunctive*); **m. you always be happy!** ¡ojalá seas siempre feliz!

May mayo *m*.
maybe *adv* quizá(s), tal vez.
mayonnaise mayonesa *f*.
mayor (*man*) alcalde *m*; (*woman*) alcaldesa *f*.
maze laberinto *m*.
me *pron* (*as object*) me; **he gave it to me** me lo dio; **listen to me** escúchame; **she knows me** me conoce. ▪ (*after prep*) mí; **it's for me** es para mí; **with me** conmigo. ▪ (*emphatic*) yo; **it's me** soy yo; **what about me?** y yo, ¿qué?
meadow prado *m*.
meal (*food*) comida *f*.
mean¹* *vt* (*signify*) querer decir; (*intend*) pensar; (*wish*) querer; **what do you m. by that?** ¿qué quieres decir con eso?; **I m. it** (te) lo digo en serio; **she was meant to arrive on the 7th** tenía que *or* debía llegar el día 7; **they m. well** tienen buenas intenciones; **I didn't m. to do it** lo hice sin querer.
mean² *a* (*miserly*) tacaño,-a; (*unkind*) malo,-a; (*bad-tempered*) malhumorado,-a.
meaning sentido *m*.
meaningless *a* sin sentido.
meanness (*miserliness*) tacañería *f*; (*nastiness*) maldad *f*.
means *sing or pl* (*method*) medio *m pl*; (*resources, wealth*) recursos *mpl* (económicos); **by m. of** por medio de, mediante; **by all m.!** ¡por supuesto!; **by no m.** de ninguna manera.
meantime in the m. mientras tanto.
meanwhile *adv* mientras tanto.
measles sarampión *m*.
measure 1 *n* medida *f*; (*ruler*) regla *f*. **2** *vt* (*object, area*) medir.
• **measure up** *vi* to **m. up to sth** estar a la altura de algo.
measurement medida *f*.
meat carne *f*.
mechanic mecánico,-a *mf*.
mechanical *a* mecánico,-a.
mechanism mecanismo *m*.

medal medalla *f.*
medalist medalla *mf;* **to be a gold m.** ser medalla de oro.
media *npl* medios *mpl* de comunicación.
medical *a* (*treatment*) médico,-a; (*book*) de medicina.
medication medicación *f.*
medicine (*science*) medicina *f;* (*drug etc*) medicamento *m.*
medicine cabinet botiquín *m.*
medieval *a* medieval.
Mediterranean 1 *a* mediterráneo,-a. **2** *n* the M. el Mediterráneo.
medium *a* (*average*) mediano,-a.
medium-sized *a* de tamaño mediano.
meet* 1 *vt* (*by chance*) encontrar; (*by arrangement*) reunirse con; (*pass in street etc*) toparse con; (*get to know*) conocer; (*await arrival of*) esperar; (*collect*) ir a buscar; **pleased to m. you!** ¡mucho gusto! **2** *vi* (*by chance*) encontrarse; (*by arrangement*) reunirse; (*formal meeting*) entrevistarse; (*get to know each other*) conocerse.
• **meet with** *vt* (*difficulty*) tropezar con; (*loss*) sufrir; (*success*) tener; (*person*) reunirse con.
meeting (*prearranged*) cita *f;* (*formal*) entrevista *f;* (*of committee etc*) reunión *f;* (*of assembly*) sesión *f.*
melody melodía *f.*
melon melón *m.*
melt 1 *vt* (*metal*) fundir. **2** *vi* (*snow*) derretirse; (*metal*) fundirse.
member miembro *mf;* (*of a society*) socio,-a *mf;* (*of party, union*) afiliado,-a *mf.*
memo (*official*) memorándum *m;* (*personal*) apunte *m.*
memory memoria *f;* (*recollection*) recuerdo *m.*
men *npl see* **man.**
mend *vt* reparar; (*clothes*) remendar; (*socks etc*) zurcir.
mental *a* mental; **m. home, m.**

hospital hospital *m* psiquiátrico; **m. illness** enfermedad *f* mental.
mentally *adv* **to be m. handicapped** ser un,-a disminuido,-a psíquico,-a.
mention 1 *n* mención *f.* **2** *vt* mencionar; **don't m. it!** ¡de nada!
menu (*à la carte*) carta *f;* (*fixed meal*) menú *m;* **today's m.** menú del día; (*computer*) menú *m.*
mercy misericordia *f;* **at the m. of** a la merced de.
mere *a* mero,-a.
merely *adv* simplemente.
merge *vi* unirse; (*roads*) converger; (*companies*) fusionarse.
merger (*of companies*) fusión *f.*
merry *a* alegre; (*tipsy*) achispado, -a; **M. Christmas!** ¡Felices Navidades!
merry-go-round tiovivo *m.*
mesh malla *f.*
mess (*confusion*) confusión *f;* (*disorder*) desorden *m;* (*mix-up*) lío *m;* (*dirt*) suciedad *f.*
• **mess about, mess around 1** *vt* fastidiar. **2** *vi* (*act the fool*) hacer el tonto.
• **mess around with** *vt* (*fiddle with*) manosear.
• **mess up** *vt* (*make untidy*) desordenar; (*dirty*) ensuciar; (*spoil*) estropear.
message recado *m.*
messenger mensajero,-a *mf.*
messy *a* (*untidy*) desordenado,-a; (*dirty*) sucio,-a.
metal 1 *n* metal *m.* **2** *a* metálico,-a.
meter¹ contador *m.*
meter² metro *m.*
method método *m.*
methodical *a* metódico,-a.
metric *a* métrico,-a.
mew maullido *m.*
Mexican *a & n* mejicano,-a (*mf*), mexicano,-a (*mf*).
mice *npl see* **mouse.**
microchip microchip *m.*
microphone micrófono *m.*
microscope microscopio *m.*

microwave (oven) (horno *m*) microondas *m inv*.

mid *a* (in) m. **afternoon** a media tarde; (in) m. **April** a mediados de abril.

midair *a* (collision, explosion) en el aire.

midday mediodía *m*.

middle 1 *a* de en medio; the M. **Ages** la Edad Media. **2** *n* medio *m*; (waist) cintura *f*; in the m. of en medio de; in the m. of winter en pleno invierno.

middle-aged *a* de mediana edad.

middle-class *a* de clase media.

midnight medianoche *f*.

midst in the m. of en medio de.

midwife comadrona *f*.

might *v aux see* **may**.

mild *a* (person, character) apacible; (climate) templado,-a; (punishment) leve; (tobacco, taste) suave.

mile milla *f*; *fam* **miles better** muchísimo mejor.

mileage kilometraje *m*.

military *a* militar.

milk leche *f*.

milk chocolate chocolate *m* con leche.

milkman lechero *m*.

milk shake batido *m*.

mill (grinder) molino *m*; (for coffee) molinillo *m*; (factory) fábrica *f*.

millimeter milímetro *m*.

million millón *m*.

millionaire millonario,-a *mf*.

mime *vt* imitar.

mimic *vt* imitar.

mince(meat) carne *f* picada.

mincer picadora *f* de carne.

mind 1 *n* (intellect) mente *f*; (brain) cabeza *f*; **what kind of car do you have in m.?** ¿en qué clase de coche estás pensando?; **to be in two minds** estar indeciso,-a; **to my m.** a mi parecer. **2** *vt* (child) cuidar; (house) vigilar; (be careful of) tener cuidado con; (object to) tener inconveniente en; **m. the step!** ¡ojo con el escalón!; **I wouldn't m. a cup of coffee** me vendría bien un café; **never m.** no importa. **3** *vi* (object) **do you m. if I open the window?** ¿le importa que abra la ventana?

mine[1] *poss pron* (el) mío, (la) mía, (los) míos, (las) mías; **a friend of m.** un amigo mío; **these gloves are m.** estos guantes son míos; **which is m.?** ¿cuál es el mío?

mine[2] (for coal etc) mina *f*.

miner minero,-a *mf*.

mineral *a* mineral.

mineral water agua *f* mineral.

mini- *prefix* mini-.

miniature 1 *n* miniatura *f*. **2** *a* (en) miniatura.

minimum *a* mínimo,-a.

minister ministro,-a *mf*; (of church) pastor,-a *mf*.

ministry (political) ministerio *m*; (in church) sacerdocio *m*.

minor *a* (lesser) menor; (unimportant) sin importancia.

minority minoría *f*.

mint (herb) menta *f*; (sweet) pastilla *f* de menta.

minus *prep* **5 m. 3** 5 menos 3; **m. 10 degrees** 10 grados bajo cero.

minute[1] minuto *m*; **just a m.** (espera) un momento.

minute[2] *a* (tiny) diminuto,-a.

miracle milagro *m*.

miraculous *a* milagroso,-a.

mirror espejo *m*; **rear-view m.** retrovisor *m*.

misbehave *vi* portarse mal.

miscellaneous *a* variado,-a.

mischief (naughtiness) travesura *f*; (evil) malicia *f*; **to get up to m.** hacer travesuras.

mischievous *a* (naughty) travieso,-a; (playful) juguetón,-ona; (wicked) malicioso,-a.

miser avaro,-a *mf*.

miserable *a* (sad) triste; (wretched) miserable.

miserly *a* tacaño,-a.

misery (sadness) tristeza *f*; (wretchedness) desgracia *f*; (suffer-

ing) sufrimiento *m*; (*poverty*) miseria *f*.

misfortune desgracia *f*.

mishap contratiempo *m*.

mislay* *vt* extraviar.

mislead* *vt* despistar; (*deliberately*) engañar.

misleading *a* (*erroneous*) erróneo,-a; (*deliberately*) engañoso,-a.

miss¹ señorita *f*.

miss² 1 *vt* (*train etc*) perder; (*opportunity*) dejar pasar; (*regret absence of*) echar de menos; **you have missed the point** no has captado la idea. 2 *vi* (*throw etc*) fallar; (*shot*) errar; **is anything missing?** ¿falta algo?

• **miss out** 1 *vt* (*omit*) saltarse; 2 *vi* **don't worry, you're not missing out** no te preocupes, no te pierdes nada.

• **miss out on** *vt* perderse.

missile misil *m*; (*object thrown*) proyectil *m*.

missing *a* (*lost*) perdido,-a; (*disappeared*) desaparecido,-a; (*absent*) ausente; **m. person** desaparecido,-a *mf*; **three cups are m.** faltan tres tazas.

mission misión *f*.

mist (*fog*) niebla *f*; (*thin*) neblina *f*; (*at sea*) bruma *f*.

mistake 1 *n* error *m*; **by m.** por equivocación; (*unintentionally*) sin querer; **to make a m.** cometer un error. 2 *vt** (*meaning*) malentender; **to m. Jack for Bill** confundir a Jack con Bill.

mistaken *a* erróneo,-a; **you are m.** estás equivocado,-a.

mistakenly *adv* por error.

mistreat maltratar.

mistress (*of house*) ama *f*; (*primary school*) maestra *f*; (*secondary school*) profesora *f*; (*lover*) amante *f*.

mistrust 1 *n* recelo *m*. 2 *vt* desconfiar de.

misty *a* (*day*) de niebla; (*window etc*) empañado,-a.

misunderstand* *vti* malentender.

misunderstanding malentendido *m*; (*disagreement*) desavenencia *f*.

mitten manopla *f*.

mix 1 *vt* mezclar. 2 *vi* (*blend*) mezclarse (**with** con).

• **mix up** *vt* (*ingredients*) mezclar bien; (*confuse*) confundir (**with** con); (*papers*) revolver.

mixed *a* (*assorted*) surtido,-a; (*varied*) variado,-a; (*school*) mixto,-a.

mixer (*for food*) batidora *f*.

mixture mezcla *f*.

mix-up confusión *f*.

moan 1 *n* gemido *m*. 2 *vi* (*groan*) gemir; (*complain*) quejarse (**about** de).

mob 1 *n* multitud *f*. 2 *vt* acosar.

mobile *a* móvil.

mobile phone teléfono *m* móvil.

model 1 *n* modelo *mf*; (**scale**) m. maqueta *f*. 2 *a* (*railway*) en miniatura.

modem módem *m*.

moderate *a* moderado,-a; (*reasonable*) razonable; (*average*) regular; (*ability*) mediocre.

moderation moderación *f*.

modern *a* moderno,-a; **m. languages** lenguas *fpl* modernas.

modernize *vt* modernizar.

modest *a* modesto,-a; (*chaste*) púdico,-a; (*price*) módico,-a; (*success*) discreto,-a.

modesty (*humility*) modestia *f*; (*chastity*) pudor *m*.

modification modificación *f*.

modify *vt* modificar.

moist *a* húmedo,-a.

moisture humedad *f*.

mold (*fungus*) moho *m*.

mold² 1 *n* (*shape*) molde *m*. 2 *vt* moldear; (*clay*) modelar.

moldy *a* mohoso,-a; **to go m.** enmohecerse.

mole¹ (*beauty spot*) lunar *m*.

mole² (*animal*) topo *m*.

mom *fam* mamá *f*.

moment momento *m*.
Monday lunes *m*.
money dinero *m*.
money order giro *m* postal.
monitor (*of computer*) monitor *m*.
monk monje *m*.
monkey mono *m*.
monopolize *vt* (*attention etc*) acaparar.
monotonous *a* monótono,-a.
monotony monotonía *f*.
monster monstruo *m*.
month mes *m*.
monthly 1 *a* mensual. **2** *adv* mensualmente.
monument monumento *m*.
moo *vi* mugir.
mood humor *m*; **to be in a good/ bad m.** estar de buen/mal humor; **to be in the m. for (doing) sth** estar de humor para (hacer) algo.
moody *a* (*changeable*) de humor variable; (*bad-tempered*) malhumorado,-a.
moon luna *f*.
moonlight luz *f* de la luna.
moor (*heath*) páramo *m*.
mop (*for floor*) fregona *f*.
• **mop up** *vt* (*liquids*) limpiar.
moped ciclomotor *m*.
moral 1 *a* moral. **2** *n* moraleja *f*; **morals** moral *f sing*, moralidad *f sing*.
morale moral *f*.
more 1 *a* más; **and what is m.** y lo que es más; **is there any m. tea?** ¿queda más té?; **I've no m. money** no me queda más dinero. **2** *pron* más; **how many m.?** ¿cuántos más?; **I need some m.** necesito más; **many/much m.** muchos,-as/ mucho más; **m. than a hundred** más de cien. **3** *adv* más; **I won't do it any m.** no lo volveré a hacer; **m. and m. difficult** cada vez más difícil; **m. or less** más o menos; **she doesn't live here any m.** ya no vive aquí.
moreover *adv* además.
morning mañana *f*; (*before dawn*)

madrugada *f*; **in the m.** por la mañana; **on Monday mornings** los lunes por la mañana; **tomorrow m.** mañana por la mañana.
Moroccan *a & n* marroquí (*mf*).
mortal *a & n* mortal (*mf*).
mortgage hipoteca *f*.
mortgage company sociedad *f* hipotecaria.
Moslem *a & n* musulmán,-ana (*mf*).
mosque mezquita *f*.
mosquito (*pl* **mosquitoes**) mosquito *m*.
moss musgo *m*.
most 1 *a* (*greatest in quantity etc*) más; (*the majority of*) la mayor parte de; **this house suffered (the) m. damage** esta casa fue la más afectada; **who made (the) m. mistakes?** ¿quién cometió más errores?; **m. of the time** la mayor parte del tiempo; **m. people** la mayoría de la gente. **2** *pron* (*greatest part*) la mayor parte; (*greatest number*) lo máximo; (*the majority of people*) la mayoría; **at the (very) m.** como máximo. **3** *adv* más; **the m. intelligent student** el estudiante más inteligente; **what I like m.** lo que más me gusta; **m. of all** sobre todo.
mostly *adv* (*chiefly*) en su mayor parte; (*generally*) generalmente; (*usually*) normalmente.
motel motel *m*.
moth mariposa *f* nocturna; **clothes m.** polilla *f*.
mother madre *f*; **M.'s Day** Día *m* de la Madre.
mother-in-law suegra *f*.
motion 1 *n* (*movement*) movimiento *m*; (*gesture*) ademán *m*. **2** *vi* **to m. (to) sb to do sth** hacer señas a algn para que haga algo.
motivated *a* motivado,-a.
motive (*reason*) motivo *m*.
motor (*engine*) motor *m*.
motorboat (*lancha*) motora *f*.
motorcycle motocicleta *f*.
motorcyclist motociclista *mf*.

motorist automovilista *mf*.
mount 1 *n* (*horse*) montura *f*; (*for photograph*) marco *m*. **2** *vt* (*horse*) subirse *or* montar a; (*photograph*) enmarcar. **3** *vi* (*go up*) subir; (*get on horse, bike*) montar.
• **mount up** *vi* (*increase*) subir; (*accumulate*) acumularse.
mountain montaña *f*; **m. bike** bicicleta *f* de montaña.
mountaineer alpinista *mf*, *Am* andinista *mf*.
mountaineering alpinismo *m*, *Am* andinismo *m*.
mountainous *a* montañoso,-a.
mourn *vti* **to m. (for) sb** llorar la muerte de algn.
mourning luto *m*; **in m.** de luto.
mouse (*pl* **mice**) ratón *m*.
mousse (*dessert*) mousse *f*.
mouth (*pl* **mouths**) boca *f*; (*of river*) desembocadura *f*.
mouthwash enjuague *m* bucal.
move 1 *n* (*movement*) movimiento *m*; (*in game*) jugada *f*; (*turn*) turno *m*; (*course of action*) medida *f*; (*to new home*) mudanza *f*. **2** *vt* mover; (*transfer*) trasladar; (*affect emotionally*) conmover; **to m. house** mudarse (de casa); **to m. job** cambiar de trabajo. **3** *vi* (*change position*) moverse; (*change house*) mudarse (de casa); (*change post*) trasladarse; (*leave*) marcharse; (*in game*) hacer una jugada.
• **move about, move around 1** *vt* cambiar de sitio. **2** *vi* (*be restless*) ir y venir.
• **move along 1** *vt* (*move forward*) hacer avanzar. **2** *vi* (*move forward*) avanzar.
• **move away** *vi* (*move aside*) apartarse; (*change house*) mudarse (de casa).
• **move back 1** *vt* (*to original place*) volver a. **2** *vi* (*withdraw*) retirarse; (*to original place*) volver.
• **move forward** *vti* avanzar.

• **move in** *vi* (*into new home*) instalarse.
• **move on** *vi* (*go forward*) avanzar; (*time*) transcurrir.
• **move out** *vi* (*leave house*) mudarse.
• **move over** *vi* correrse hacia un lado.
• **move up** *vi* (*go up*) subir; (*move along*) correrse hacia un lado, hacer sitio.
movement movimiento *m*; (*gesture*) además *m*; (*trend*) corriente *f*; (*of goods, capital*) circulación *f*.
movie película *f*.
moving *a* (*that moves*) móvil; (*car etc*) en marcha; (*touching*) conmovedor,-a.
mow* *vt* (*lawn*) cortar.
mower cortacésped *m & f*.
Mr *abbr of* **mister** señor *m*, Sr.
Mrs *abbr* señora *f*, Sra.
Ms *abbr* señora *f*, Sra, señorita *f*, Srta.
MS *abbr of* **Master of Science** Licenciado,-a en Ciencias *mf*.
much 1 *a* mucho,-a; **as m. . . . as** tanto,-a . . . como; **how m. chocolate?** ¿cuánto chocolate?; **so m.** tanto,-a. **2** *adv* mucho; **as m. as** tanto como; **as m. as possible** todo lo posible; **how m.?** ¿cuánto?; **how m. is it?** ¿cuánto es?; **m. better** mucho mejor; **m. more** mucho más; **too m.** demasiado. **3** *pron* mucho; **I thought as m.** lo suponía; **m. of the town was destroyed** gran parte de la ciudad quedó destruida.
mud barro *m*.
muddle 1 *n* desorden *m*; (*mix-up*) embrollo *m*; **to get into a m.** hacerse un lío. **2** *vt* **to m. (up)** confundir.
muddy *a* fangoso,-a; (*hands*) cubierto,-a de barro; (*liquid*) turbio,-a.
mug¹ (*large cup*) tazón *m*; (*beer*) jarra *f*.
mug² *vt* (*assault*) asaltar.
mugger asaltante *mf*.

mule mulo,-a *mf*.
multiple 1 *a* múltiple. **2** *n* múltiplo *m*.
multiplication multiplicación *f*.
multiply *vt* multiplicar (**by** por).
mumble 1 *vt* decir entre dientes. **2** *vi* hablar entre dientes.
mummy *fam* mami *f*.
mumps paperas *fpl*.
murder 1 *n* asesinato *m*. **2** *vt* asesinar.
murderer asesino *m*.
murmur *vti* murmurar. **2** *n* murmullo *m*.
muscle músculo *m*.
muscular *a* (*person*) musculoso,-a.
museum museo *m*.
mushroom seta *f*; (*food*) champiñón *m*.
music música *f*.
musical 1 *a* musical; **to be m.** estar dotado,-a para la música. **2** *n* musical *m*.
musician músico,-a *mf*.
Muslim *a* & *n* musulmán,-ana (*mf*).
mussel mejillón *m*.
must *v aux* (*obligation*) deber, tener que; **you m. arrive on time** tienes que *o* debes llegar a la hora. ▪ (*probability*) deber (de); **he m. be ill** debe (de) estar enfermo.
mustache bigote *m*.
mustard mostaza *f*.
musty *a* que huele a cerrado *or* a humedad.
mutter *vti* murmurar.
mutton (carne *f* de) cordero *m*.
mutual *a* mutuo,-a; (*shared*) común.
muzzle (*for animal*) bozal *m*.
my *poss* mi; **I washed my hair** me lavé el pelo; **my cousins** mis primos; **my father** mi padre; **one of my friends** un amigo mío.
myself *pers pron* (*emphatic*) yo mismo,-a; **my husband and m.** mi marido y yo. ▪ (*reflexive*) me; **I hurt m.** me hice daño. ▪ (*after prep*) mí (mismo,-a).

mysterious *a* misterioso,-a.
mystery misterio *m*.

N

nail 1 *n* (*of finger, toe*) uña *f*; (*metal*) clavo *m*. **2** *vt* clavar.
· **nail down** *vt* clavar.
nailfile lima *f* de uñas.
nail polish, nail varnish esmalte *m or* laca *f* de uñas.
naïve *a* ingenuo,-a.
naked *a* desnudo,-a.
name 1 *n* nombre *m*; (*surname*) apellido *m*; (*reputation*) reputación *f*; **what's your n.?** ¿cómo te llamas? **2** *vt* llamar; (*appoint*) nombrar.
nanny niñera *f*.
nap (*sleep*) siesta *f*; **to have a n.** echar la *or* una siesta.
napkin (**table**) **n.** servilleta *f*.
nappy pañal *m*.
narrow 1 *a* (*passage, road etc*) estrecho,-a. **2** *vi* estrecharse.
· **narrow down** *vt* reducir.
narrowly *adv* (*closely*) de cerca; (*by a small margin*) por poco.
nastily *adv* (*to behave*) antipáticamente.
nasty *a* (*unpleasant*) desagradable; (*unfriendly*) antipático,-a; (*malicious*) mal intencionado,-a.
nation nación *f*.
national *a* nacional.
nationality nacionalidad *f*.
native 1 *a* (*place*) natal; **n. language** lengua *f* materna. **2** *n* nativo,-a *mf*.
natural *a* natural; (*normal*) normal; (*born*) nato,-a.
naturally *adv* (*of course*) naturalmente; (*by nature*) por naturaleza; (*in a relaxed manner*) con naturalidad.
nature naturaleza *f*; **n. study** historia *f* natural.
naughty *a* (*child*) travieso,-a.

nauseous *a* **to feel n.** tener ganas de vomitar.

naval *a* naval; **n. officer** oficial *mf* de marina.

navel ombligo *m*.

navigate 1 *vt* (*river*) navegar por; (*ship*) gobernar. 2 *vi* navegar.

navigation navegación *f*.

navy marina *f*; **n. blue** azul *m* marino.

near 1 *a* (*space*) cercano,-a; (*time*) próximo,-a; **in the n. future** en un futuro próximo; **it was a n. thing** poco faltó. 2 *adv* (*space*) cerca; **that's n. enough** ya vale. 3 *prep* cerca de; **n. the end of the film** hacia el final de la película.

nearby 1 *a* cercano,-a. 2 *adv* cerca.

nearly *adv* casi; **very n.** casi, casi; **we haven't n. enough** no alcanza ni con mucho.

neat *a* (*room, habits etc*) ordenado, -a; (*appearance*) pulcro,-a.

neatly *adv* (*carefully*) cuidadosamente; (*cleverly*) hábilmente.

necessarily *adv* necesariamente.

necessary *a* necesario,-a; **to do what is n.** hacer lo que haga falta; **if n.** si es preciso.

necessity necesidad *f*; (*article*) requisito *m* indispensable.

neck cuello *m*; (*of animal*) pescuezo *m*.

necklace collar *m*.

nectarine nectarina *f*.

need 1 *n* necesidad *f*; (*poverty*) indigencia *f*; **if n. be** si fuera necesario; **there's no n. for you to do that** no hace falta que hagas eso. 2 *vt* necesitar; (*require*) requerir; **I n. to see him** tengo que verle. 3 *v aux* tener que, deber; **n. he go?** ¿tiene que ir?; **you needn't wait** no hace falta que esperes.

needle aguja *f*.

needlessly *adv* innecesariamente.

needlework (*sewing*) costura *f*; (*embroidery*) bordado *m*.

negative 1 *a* negativo,-a. 2 *n* (*in grammar*) negación *f*; (*photo*) negativo *m*.

neglect *vt* (*not look after*) descuidar; **to n. to do sth** (*omit to do*) no hacer algo.

neglected *a* (*appearance*) desarreglado,-a; (*garden*) descuidado, -a; **to feel n.** sentirse desatendido,-a.

negligence negligencia *f*.

negligent *a* negligente.

negotiate *vti* negociar.

negotiation negociación *f*.

neigh *vi* relinchar.

neighbor vecino,-a *mf*.

neighborhood (*district*) barrio *m*; (*people*) entorno *m*.

neighboring *a* vecino,-a.

neither 1 *a & pron* ninguno de los dos, ninguna de las dos. 2 *adv & conj* ni; **n. . . . nor** ni . . . ni; **it's n. here nor there** no viene al caso; **she was not there and n. was her sister** ella no estaba, ni su hermana tampoco.

neon neón *m*; **n. light** luz *f* de neón.

nephew sobrino *m*.

nerve nervio *m*; (*courage*) valor *m*; (*cheek*) descaro *m*; **to get on sb's nerves** poner los nervios de punta a algn.

nervous *a* (*apprehensive*) nervioso, -a; (*afraid*) miedoso,-a; (*timid*) tímido,-a; **to be n.** tener miedo.

nest nido *m*.

net¹ red *f*.

net² *a* neto,-a.

netting (*wire*) alambrada *f*.

nettle ortiga *f*.

network red *f*.

neutral 1 *a* neutro,-a. 2 *n* (*gear*) punto *m* muerto.

never *adv* nunca, jamás; **he n. complains** no se queja nunca; **n. again** nunca (ja)más.

never-ending *a* interminable.

nevertheless *adv* sin embargo, no obstante.

new *a* nuevo,-a.

newborn *a* recién nacido,-a.

newcomer recién llegado,-a *mf*; (*to job etc*) nuevo,-a *mf*.

newly *adv* recién.

news noticias *fpl;* **a piece of n.** una noticia.

news bulletin boletín *m* informativo.

newsflash noticia *f* de última hora.

newsletter hoja *f* informativa.

newspaper periódico *m.*

next 1 *a (in position)* de al lado; *(in time)* próximo,-a; *(in order)* siguiente, próximo,-a; **the n. day** el día siguiente; **n. Friday** el viernes que viene. **2** *adv* después; *(next time)* la próxima vez; **what shall we do n.?** ¿qué hacemos ahora? **3** *prep* **n. to** al lado de.

next door *a* & *adv* de al lado; **our n. neighbor** el vecino *or* la vecina de al lado.

nib plumilla *f.*

nibble *vti* mordisquear.

nice *a (person)* simpático,-a; *(thing)* agradable; *(nice-looking)* bonito,-a, *Am* lindo,-a; **n. and cool** fresquito,-a; **to smell/taste n.** oler/saber bien.

nicely *adv* muy bien.

nickel moneda *f* de cinco centavos.

nickname apodo *m.*

niece sobrina *f.*

night noche *f;* **at twelve o'clock at n.** a las doce de la noche; **last n.** anoche; **to have a n. out** salir por la noche.

nightclub sala *f* de fiestas; *(disco)* discoteca *f.*

nightgown camisón *m.*

nightingale ruiseñor *m.*

nightmare pesadilla *f.*

night-time noche *f;* **at n.** por la noche.

night watchman vigilante *m* nocturno.

nil nada *f; (in sport)* cero *m.*

nine *a* & *n* nueve *(m) inv;* **n. hundred** novecientos,-as.

nineteen *a* & *n* diecinueve *(m) inv.*

ninety *a* & *n* noventa *(m) inv.*

ninth *a* & *n* noveno,-a *(mf).*

nip *vt (pinch)* pellizcar; *(bite)* morder.

nipple *(female)* pezón *m; (male)* tetilla *f.*

nitrogen nitrógeno *m.*

no 1 *adv* no; **no longer** ya no; **no less than** no menos de. **2** *a* ninguno,-a; **she has no children** no tiene hijos; **I have no idea** no tengo (ni) idea; **no sensible person** ninguna persona razonable; **'no parking'** 'prohibido aparcar'; **no way!** ¡ni hablar!

noble *a* noble.

nobody *pron* nadie; **there was n. there** no había nadie; **n. else** nadie más.

nod 1 *n (in agreement)* señal *f* de asentimiento. **2** *vi (in agreement)* asentir con la cabeza. **3** *vt* **to n. one's head** inclinar la cabeza.

• **nod off** *vi* dormirse.

noise ruido *m;* **to make a n.** hacer ruido.

noisily *adv* ruidosamente.

noisy *a* ruidoso,-a.

nominate *vt (appoint)* nombrar.

non- *prefix* no.

none *pron* ninguno,-a; **n. at all** nada en absoluto.

nonetheless *adv* no obstante, sin embargo.

non-existent *a* inexistente.

non-fiction literatura *f* no novelesca.

nonsense tonterías *fpl;* **that's n.** eso es absurdo.

nonsmoker no fumador,-a *mf.*

nonstick *a* antiadherente.

nonstop 1 *a* continuo; *(train)* directo,-a. **2** *adv* sin parar.

noodles *npl* fideos *mpl,* tallarines *mpl.*

noon mediodía *m;* **at n.** a mediodía.

nor *conj* ni, ni . . . tampoco; **neither . . . n.** ni . . . ni; **neither you n. I** ni tú ni yo; **neither do I** (ni) yo tampoco.

normal *a* normal.

normally *adv* normalmente.

north 1 *n* norte *m.* **2** *a* hacia el norte. **3** *a* del norte; **n. wind** viento del norte.

northbound *a* (con) dirección norte.

northeast nor(d)este *m.*

northern *a* del norte.

northerner norteño,-a *mf*.
northward *a & adv* hacia el norte.
northwest noroeste *m*.
Norwegian 1 *a* noruego,-a. 2 *n* (*person*) noruego,-a *mf*; (*language*) noruego *m*.
nose nariz *f*; **her n. is bleeding** le está sangrando la nariz.
nosebleed hemorragia *f* nasal.
nostril orificio *m* nasal.
nosy *a* entrometido,-a.
not *adv* no; **he's n. in today** hoy no está; **n. at all** en absoluto; **thank you — n. at all** gracias—no hay de qué; **n. one (of them) said thank you** nadie me dio las gracias.
note 1 *n* (*in music, written*) nota *f*; (*money*) billete *m* (de banco); **to take n. of** (*notice*) prestar atención a; **to take notes** (*at lecture*) tomar apuntes. 2 *vt* (*write down*) anotar; (*notice*) darse cuenta de.
notebook cuaderno *m*.
notepad bloc *m* de notas.
notepaper papel *m* de carta.
nothing 1 *n* nada; **I saw n.** no vi nada; **for n.** (*free*) gratis; **it's n. to do with you** no tiene nada que ver contigo; **n. else** nada más; **n. much** poca cosa. 2 *adv* **she looks n. like her sister** no se parece en nada a su hermana.
notice 1 *n* (*warning*) aviso *m*; (*attention*) atención *f*; (*in newspaper etc*) anuncio *m*; (*sign*) aviso *m*; **he gave a month's n.** presentó la dimisión con un mes de antelación; **at short n.** con poca antelación; **until further n.** hasta nuevo aviso; **to take n. of sth** prestar atención a algo. 2 *vt* darse cuenta de.
noticeable *a* obvio, evidente.
notification aviso *m*.
notify *vt* avisar.
notion idea *f*.
nought cero *m*.
noun sustantivo *m*.
nourishing *a* nutritivo,-a.
novel[1] novela *f*.
novel[2] *a* original.
novelist novelista *mf*.

November noviembre *m*.
now 1 *adv* ahora; (*at present, these days*) actualmente; **just n., right n.** ahora mismo; **from n. on** de ahora en adelante; **n. and then, n. and again** de vez en cuando; **n. (then)** ahora bien; **n., n.!** ¡de eso nada! 2 *conj* **n. (that)** ahora que.
nowadays *adv* hoy (en) día.
nowhere *adv* en ninguna parte; **it's n. near ready** no está preparado, ni mucho menos.
nozzle boquilla *f*.
nuclear *a* nuclear.
nude *a* desnudo,-a; **in the n.** al desnudo.
nudge 1 *vt* dar un codazo a. 2 *n* codazo *m*.
nuisance pesadez *f*; (*person*) pesado,-a *mf*; **what a n.!** ¡qué lata!
numb *a* (*without feeling*) entumecido,-a.
number 1 *n* número *m*; **have you got my (phone) n.?** ¿tienes mi (número de) teléfono?; **a n. of people** varias personas. 2 *vt* (*put a number on*) numerar.
numeral número *m*.
numerous *a* numeroso,-a.
nun monja *f*.
nurse 1 *n* enfermera *f*; (*male*) enfermero *m*. 2 *vt* (*look after*) cuidar.
nursery guardería *f*; (*in house*) cuarto *m* de los niños; (*garden center*) vivero *m*.
nursery rhyme canción *f* infantil.
nursery school jardín *m* de infancia.
nut (*fruit*) fruto *m* seco; (*for bolt*) tuerca *f*.
nutcracker cascanueces *m inv*.
nylon 1 *n* nailon *m*; **nylons** medias *fpl* de nailon. 2 *a* de nailon.

O

oak roble *m*.
oar remo *m*.
oats avena *f*.
obedience obediencia *f*.

obedient *a* obediente.

obey *vt* obedecer; (*law*) cumplir.

object[1] (*thing*) objeto *m*; (*aim, purpose*) objetivo *m*; (*in grammar*) complemento *m*.

object[2] *vi* oponerse (**to** a); **do you o. to my smoking?** ¿le molesta que fume?

objection objeción *f*.

objective objetivo *m*.

obligation obligación *f*.

oblige *vt* (*compel*) obligar; (*do a favor for*) hacer un favor a; **I'm obliged to do it** me veo obligado, -a hacerlo.

obliging *a* solícito, -a.

oblique *a* oblicuo, -a, inclinado, -a.

obscene *a* obsceno, -a.

observant *a* observador, -a.

observation observación *f*; (*surveillance*) vigilancia *f*.

observe *vt* observar; (*on surveillance*) vigilar; (*remark*) advertir.

obstacle obstáculo *m*.

obstinate *a* (*person*) obstinado, -a.

obstruct *vt* obstruir; (*pipe etc*) atascar; (*view*) tapar; (*hinder*) estorbar; (*progress*) dificultar.

obtain *vt* obtener.

obvious *a* obvio, -a, evidente.

obviously *adv* evidentemente; **o.!** ¡claro!

occasion ocasión *f*; (*event*) acontecimiento *m*.

occasional *a* eventual.

occasionally *adv* de vez en cuando.

occupant ocupante *mf*; (*tenant*) inquilino, -a *mf*.

occupation (*job, profession*) profesión *f*; (*task*) trabajo *m*.

occupy *vt* (*live in*) habitar en; **to o. one's time in doing sth** dedicar su tiempo a hacer algo; **to keep oneself occupied** mantenerse ocupado, -a.

occur *vi* (*event*) suceder; (*change*) producirse; (*be found*) encontrarse; **it occurred to me that . . .** se me ocurrió que . . .

occurrence acontecimiento *m*.

ocean océano *m*.

o'clock *adv* (**it's) one o'c.** (es) la una; (**it's) two o'c.** (son) las dos.

October octubre *m*.

octopus pulpo *m*.

odd 1 *a* (*strange*) raro, -a; (*occasional*) esporádico, -a; (*extra*) adicional; (*not even*) impar; (*unpaired*) desparejado, -a; **the o. customer** algún que otro cliente; **o. job** trabajillo *m*; **to be the o. man out** estar de más; **an o. sock** un calcetín suelto. **2** *adv* y pico; **twenty o. people** veinte y pico *o* y tantas personas.

oddly *adv* extrañamente.

odds *npl* (*chances*) probabilidades *fpl*; (*in betting*) puntos *mpl* de ventaja; **the o. are that . . .** lo más probable es que . . . (+ *subjunctive*); **at o. with sb** reñido, -a con algn; **o. and ends** (*small things*) cositas *fpl*.

odor olor *m*; (*fragrance*) perfume *m*.

of *prep* de; **a friend of mine** un amigo mío; **there are four of us** somos cuatro; **two of them** dos de ellos; **that's very kind of you** es usted muy amable.

off 1 *prep* de; **she fell o. her horse** se cayó del caballo; **a house o. the road** una casa apartada de la carretera; **I'm o. wine** he perdido el gusto al vino. **2** *adv* (*absent*) fuera; **I have a day o.** tengo un día libre; **to be o. sick** estar de baja por enfermedad. ▪ **his arrival is three days o.** faltan tres días para su llegada; **six miles o.** a seis millas. ▪ **I'm o. to New York** me voy a Nueva York; **she ran o.** se fue corriendo. ▪ **ten percent o.** un descuento del diez por ciento. ▪ **with his shoes o.** descalzo. ▪ **on and o.** de vez en cuando. **3** *a* **to be o.** (*meat, fish*) estar pasado, -a; (*milk*) estar agrio, -a; (*gas etc*) estar apagado, -a; (*water*) estar cortado, -a; (*cancelled*) estar cancelado, -a; **on the o. chance** por si acaso; **the o. season** la temporada baja; **you're better o. like that** así estás mejor.

offend vt ofender.

offense delito m; (insult) ofensa f; **to take o. at sth** ofenderse por algo.

offensive a (insulting) ofensivo, -a; (repulsive) repugnante.

offer 1 vt ofrecer; (propose) proponer; (provide) proporcionar; **to o. to do a job** ofrecerse para hacer un trabajo. **2** n oferta f; (proposal) propuesta f; **on o.** de oferta.

offhand 1 a (abrupt) brusco,-a. **2** adv de improviso.

office (room) despacho m; (building) oficina f; (position) cargo m.

officer oficial mf; **(police) o.** agente mf de policía.

official 1 a oficial. **2** n funcionario, -a mf.

officially adv oficialmente.

often adv a menudo; **every so o.** de vez en cuando.

oh interj ¡oh!

oil 1 n aceite m; (crude) petróleo m. **2** vt engrasar.

oil can aceitera f.

oil change cambio m de aceite.

ointment pomada f.

OK, okay 1 interj ¡vale! **2** a bien; **is it OK if . . . ?** ¿está bien si . . . ?

old a viejo,-a; (previous) antiguo, -a; **an o. man** un anciano; **o. age** vejez f; **how o. are you?** ¿cuántos años tienes?; **she's five years o.** tiene cinco años.

old-fashioned a (outdated) a la antigua; (unfashionable) anticuado,-a.

olive (tree) olivo m; (fruit) aceituna f, oliva f.

Olympic a olímpico,-a; **O. Games** Juegos mpl Olímpicos.

omelet tortilla f; **Spanish o.** tortilla española or de patatas.

on 1 prep (position) sobre, encima de, en; **it's on the table** está encima de or sobre la mesa; **on page four** en la página cuatro; **a town on the coast** un pueblo en la costa; **on the right** a la derecha; **on the way** en el

camino. ▪ (time) **on April 3rd** el tres de abril; **on a sunny day** un día de sol; **on Monday** el lunes; **on the following day** al día siguiente; **on his arrival** a su llegada; **on time** a tiempo. ▪ (means) **on the radio** en la radio; **to play sth on the piano** tocar algo al piano; **on TV** en la tele; **on the phone** al teléfono; **on foot** a pie; **on the train/plane** en tren/avión. ▪ (about) sobre; **a lecture on numismatics** una conferencia sobre numismática. **2** a **to be on** (TV, radio, light) estar encendido,-a; (engine) estar en marcha; (tablecloth) estar puesto; **she had a coat on** llevaba un abrigo puesto; **that film was on last week** pusieron esa película la semana pasada. **3** adv **have you anything on tonight?** ¿tienes algún plan para esta noche?; **he talks on and on** habla sin parar; **to work on** seguir trabajando.

once 1 adv (one time) una vez; (formerly) en otro tiempo; **o. a week** una vez por semana; **o. in a while** de vez en cuando; **o. more** una vez más; **at o.** en seguida; **don't speak all at o.** no habléis todos a la vez. **2** conj una vez que.

one 1 a un, una; **he'll come back o. day** un día volverá. **2** dem pron **any o.** cualquiera; **that o.** ése, ésa; (distant) aquél, aquélla; **the blue ones** los azules, las azules; **the o. on the table** el or la que está encima de la mesa; **the ones that, the ones who** los or las que; **this o.** éste, ésta. **3** indef pron uno,-a mf; **give me o.** dame uno; **o. by o.** uno tras otro; **o. never knows** nunca se sabe; **to cut o.'s finger** cortarse el dedo; **o. another** el uno al otro; **they love o. another** se quieren. **4** n (digit) uno m; **a hundred and o.** ciento uno.

oneself pron uno,-a mismo,-a mf; (reflexive) sí mismo,-a mf; **to talk to o.** hablar para sí; **by o.** solo,-a.

one-way a (ticket) de ida; (street) de dirección única.

onion cebolla f.

onlooker espectador,-a mf.

only 1 adv solamente, sólo; **he has o. just left** acaba de marcharse hace un momento; **o. yesterday** ayer mismo. **2** a único,-a. **3** conj pero.

onto prep see **on**.

onward(s) adv en adelante; **from this time o.** de ahora en adelante.

opaque a opaco,-a.

open 1 a abierto,-a; **wide o.** abierto de par en par; **in the o. air** al aire libre; **o. ticket** billete abierto. **2** vt abrir; (exhibition etc) inaugurar; (negotiations, conversation) entablar. **3** vi abrirse. **4** n **in the o.** al aire libre; fig **to bring into the o.** hacer público.

• **open out 1** vt desplegar. **2** vi (flowers) abrirse; (view) extenderse.

• **open up 1** vt (market etc) abrir; (possibilities) crear. **2** vi abrirse.

opening (act) apertura f; (beginning) comienzo m; (aperture) abertura f; (gap) brecha f; (in market) oportunidad f.

openly adv abiertamente.

openness (frankness) franqueza f.

opera ópera f.

operate 1 vi (function) funcionar; (act) actuar; (surgeon) operar. **2** vt (switch on) accionar; (control) manejar; (business) dirigir.

operating system sistema m operativo.

operation (of machine) funcionamiento m; (surgical) operación f.

operator (of machine) operario,-a mf; (telephone) operador,-a mf.

opinion opinión f; **in my o.** en mi opinión.

opponent adversario,-a mf.

opportunity oportunidad f; (prospect) perspectiva f.

oppose vt oponerse a.

opposed a opuesto,-a; **to be o. to sth** estar en contra de algo.

opposing a adversario,-a.

opposite 1 a (facing) de enfrente; (page) contiguo,-a; (contrary) contrario,-a; **in the o. direction** en dirección contraria. **2** n lo contrario m; **quite the o.!** ¡al contrario! **3** prep enfrente de. **4** adv enfrente.

opposition oposición f; **in o. to** en contra de.

opt vi **to o. for** optar por; **to o. to do sth** optar por hacer algo.

optician óptico,-a mf.

optimist optimista mf.

optimistic a optimista.

option opción f; **I have no o.** no tengo más remedio.

optional a optativo,-a.

or conj o; (before a word beginning with a stressed o or ho) u; (with negative) ni; **he can't read or write** no sabe leer ni escribir.

oral 1 a oral. **2** n examen m oral.

orange 1 n naranja f. **2** a de color naranja.

orange juice zumo m de naranja.

orbit órbita f.

orchard huerto m.

orchestra orquesta f.

ordeal mala experiencia.

order 1 n (sequence, command) orden m; (commission) pedido m; **to put in o.** ordenar; **is your passport in o.?** ¿tienes el pasaporte en regla?; **'out of o.'** 'averiado'; **to be on o.** estar pedido; **in o. that** para que (+ subjunctive), a fin de que (+ subjunctive); **in o. to** para (+ infinitive), a fin de (+ infinitive). **2** vt (command) ordenar; (goods) encargar; **to o. sb to do sth** mandar a algn hacer algo; **to o. a dish** pedir un plato.

ordinary 1 a normal; (average) corriente. **2** n **out of the o.** fuera de lo común.

ore mineral m.

organ órgano m.

organic a orgánico,-a.

organization organización f.

organize vt organizar.

organizer organizador,-a mf.

Oriental a & n oriental (mf).

origin origen m.

original 1 a original; (first) pri-

mero,-a; (*novel*) original. **2** *n* original *m*.

originality originalidad *f*.

originally *adv* (*at first*) en un principio.

ornament adorno *m*.

orphan huérfano,-a *mf*.

orphanage orfanato *m*.

ostrich avestruz *f*.

other 1 *a* otro,-a; **the o. one** el otro,
la otra. **2** *pron* otro,-a *mf*; **many
others** otros muchos; **the others**
los otros, los demás; **we see each
o. quite often** nos vemos con bastante frecuencia.

otherwise *adv* (*if not*) si no; (*differently*) de otra manera; (*in other
respects*) por lo demás.

ought *v aux* deber; **I thought I o. to
tell you** creí que debía decírtelo;
she o. to do it debería hacerlo; **you
o. to see the exhibition** deberías
ver la exposición. ▪ (*expectation*)
he o. to pass the exam seguramente aprobará el examen; **that o.
to do** con eso bastará.

ounce onza *f*.

our *poss a* nuestro,-a.

ours *poss pron* (el) nuestro, (la)
nuestra, (los) nuestros, (las) nues-
tras; **a friend of o.** un amigo
nuestro.

ourselves *pers pron pl* (*reflexive*)
nos; (*emphatic*) nosotros mismos,
nosotras mismas; **by o.** a solas.

out 1 *adv* (*outside, away*) fuera; **o.
there** ahí fuera; **to go o.** salir.
2 *prep* **o. of** (*place*) fuera de;
(*cause, motive*) por; (*made from*)
de; (*short of, without*) sin; **move o.
of the way!** ¡quítate de en medio!;
he jumped o. the window saltó
por la ventana; **o. of danger** fuera
de peligro; **forty o. of fifty** cuarenta de cada cincuenta. **3** *a* **to be
o.** (*unfashionable*) estar pasado,-a
de moda; (*not lit*) estar apagado,-a;
(*eliminated from game*) quedar
eliminado; **the sun is o.** ha salido
el sol; **she's o.** (*not in*) ha salido.

outbreak (*of war*) comienzo *m*; (*of*

disease) brote *m*; (*of violence*) ola *f*.

outburst (*of anger*) arrebato *m*.

outcome resultado *m*.

outdated *a* anticuado,-a.

outdo* *vt* exceder; **to o. sb** superar
a algn.

outdoor *a* al aire libre; (*clothes*)
de calle.

outdoors *adv* al aire libre.

outer *a* exterior.

outer space espacio *m* sideral.

outfit (*kit, equipment*) equipo *m*;
(*set of clothes*) conjunto *m*.

outing excursión *f*.

outlet (*for goods*) mercado *m*.

outline (*draft*) bosquejo *m*; (*outer
line*) contorno *m*; (*silhouette*) perfil
m; (*sketch*) boceto *m*.

outlook (*point of view*) punto *m* de
vista; (*prospect*) perspectiva *f*.

outnumber *vt* exceder en número.

out-of-doors *adv* al aire libre.

output producción *f*; (*of machine*)
rendimiento *m*.

outrage 1 *n* ultraje *m*; **it's an o.!** ¡es
un escándalo! **2** *vt* **to be outraged
by sth** indignarse por algo.

outrageous *a* (*behavior*) escandaloso,-a; (*clothes*) extravagante.

outright *adv* (*completely*) por completo; (*directly*) directamente.

outside 1 *prep* fuera de; (*beyond*)
más allá de; (*other than*) aparte
de. **2** *a* (*exterior*) exterior, externo,
-a. **3** *adv* (a)fuera. **4** *n* exterior *m*;
on the o. por fuera.

outskirts *npl* afueras *fpl*.

outstanding *a* (*exceptional*) des-
tacado,-a; (*unpaid, unresolved*)
pendiente.

outward *a* (*appearance*) externo,
-a; **the o. journey** el viaje de ida.

outward(s) *adv* hacia (a)fuera.

oval 1 *a* ovalado,-a. **2** *n* óvalo *m*.

oven horno *m*.

over 1 *prep* (*above*) encima de;
(*across*) al otro lado de; (*during*)
durante; (*more than*) más de; **the
bridge o. the river** el puente que
cruza el río; **all o. Spain** por toda

España; **it's all o. the carpet** está por toda la alfombra; **o. the phone** por teléfono; **men o. twenty-five** hombres mayores de veinticinco años. **2** adv (more) más; (again) otra vez; (in excess) de más; **o. there** allá; **all o.** por todas partes; **o. and o. (again)** una y otra vez; **there are still some o.** todavía quedan algunos. **3** a (finished) acabado,-a; **it's (all) o.** se acabó; **the danger is o.** ha pasado el peligro.

overall 1 a total. **2** adv (on the whole) en conjunto. **3** n guardapolvo m; **overalls** mono m sing.

overboard adv por la borda.

overcharge vt (charge too much) cobrar de más.

overcoat abrigo m.

overcome* vt (conquer) vencer; (overwhelm) abrumar; (surmount) superar.

overdo* vt (carry too far) exagerar; (in cooking) cocer or asar demasiado.

overdraft crédito m al descubierto.

overdue a (rent, train etc) atrasado,-a.

overeat vi comer en exceso.

overexcited a sobreexcitado,-a.

overflow vi (river) desbordarse; (cup etc) derramarse.

overhead a (por) encima de la cabeza.

overhear vt oír por casualidad.

overheat vi recalentarse.

overjoyed a rebosante de alegría.

overlap vi superponerse.

overleaf adv al dorso.

overload vt sobrecargar.

overlook vt (fail to notice) pasar por alto; (ignore) no hacer caso de; (have a view of) tener vista a.

overnight 1 adv por la noche; **we stayed there o.** pasamos la noche allí. **2** a (journey) de noche.

overpass (bridge) paso m elevado.

overrated a sobrestimado,-a.

overseas 1 adv en ultramar; **to live o.** vivir en el extranjero. **2** a de ul-

tramar; (visitor) extranjero,-a; (trade) exterior.

oversight descuido m.

oversleep vi quedarse dormido, -a.

overspend vi gastar demasiado.

overtake* vt adelantar.

overtime horas fpl extra.

overturn vti volcar.

overweight a to be o. ser gordo,-a.

overwhelm vt (defeat) aplastar; (overpower) abrumar.

overwhelming a (desire) irresistible.

overwork vi trabajar demasiado.

owe vt deber.

owing a o. to debido a.

owl búho m.

own 1 a propio,-a; **it's his o. fault** es culpa suya. **2** pron **my o., your o., his o.** lo mío, lo tuyo, lo suyo etc; **to get one's o. back** tomarse la revancha; **on one's o.** (without help) uno,-a mismo,-a; (alone) solo,-a. **3** vt poseer.

• **own up** vi to o. up (to) confesar.

owner propietario,-a mf.

oxygen oxígeno m.

oyster ostra f.

P

pace (step) paso m; (speed) ritmo m.

Pacific the P. (Ocean) el (océano) Pacífico.

pacifier (of baby) chupete m.

pack 1 n paquete m; (rucksack) mochila f; (of cards) baraja f; (of hounds) jauría f. **2** vt (goods) embalar; (in suitcase) poner; (fill) atestar; (press down) (snow) apretar; **to p. one's bags** hacer las maletas; fig marcharse. **3** vi (baggage) hacer las maletas.

• **pack away** vt (tidy away) guardar.

• **pack up** fam **1** vt (give up) dejar. **2** vi (stop working) terminar; (machine etc) estropearse.

package (*parcel, software*) paquete *m*.

package tour viaje *m* todo incluido.

packaging embalaje *m*.

packed *a* (*place*) atestado,-a.

packed lunch almuerzo *m* (para tomar fuera).

packet paquete *m*.

packing embalaje *m*.

pad 1 *n* almohadilla *f*; (*of paper*) bloc *m*. **2** *vt* (*chair*) rellenar.

padded *a* (*cell*) acolchado,-a.

paddle[1] (*oar*) pala *f*.

paddle[2] *vi* chapotear.

padlock candado *m*.

page[1] página *f*.

page[2] (*at club etc*) botones *m inv*.

pain dolor *m*; (*grief*) sufrimiento *m*; **to take pains over sth** esmerarse en algo.

painful *a* doloroso,-a.

painkiller analgésico *m*.

paint 1 *n* pintura *f*. **2** *vt* pintar; **to p. sth white** pintar algo de blanco.

paintbrush pincel *m*; (*for walls*) brocha *f*.

painter pintor,-a *mf*.

painting cuadro *m*; (*activity*) pintura *f*.

paint stripper quitapinturas *mpl inv*.

pair (*of gloves, shoes*) par *m*; (*of people, cards*) pareja *f*.

pajamas *npl* pijama *m*.

Pakistani *a* & *n* paquistaní (*mf*).

pal *fam* amigo,-a *mf*.

palace palacio *m*.

palate paladar *m*.

pale (*skin*) pálido,-a; (*color*) claro,-a.

Palestinian *a* & *n* palestino,-a (*mf*).

palette paleta *f*.

palm (*of hand*) palma *f*; (*tree*) palmera *f*; **p. leaf** palma *f*.

pamphlet folleto *m*.

pan (*saucepan*) cazuela *f*.

pancake crepe *f*.

pane cristal *m*, vidrio *m*.

panel (*of wall*) panel *m*; (*of instruments*) tablero *m*; (*jury*) jurado *m*.

panic pánico *m*; **to get into a p.** ponerse histérico,-a.

pant *vi* jadear.

panties *npl* bragas *fpl*.

pantomime (*play*) función *f* musical navideña.

pantry despensa *f*.

pants *npl* (*underpants*) (*ladies'*) bragas *fpl*; (*men's*) calzoncillos *mpl*; (*trousers*) pantalón *m*.

pantyhose panties *mpl*.

paper papel *m*; (*newspaper*) periódico *m*; (*exam*) examen *m*; (*essay*) trabajo *m* (escrito).

paperback libro *m* en rústica.

paperclip clip *m*.

paper knife cortapapeles *mpl inv*.

parachute paracaídas *m inv*.

parade desfile *m*.

paradise paraíso *m*.

paraffin parafina *f*.

paragraph párrafo *m*.

Paraguayan *a* & *n* paraguayo,-a (*mf*).

parallel *a* paralelo,-a (**to, with** a).

paralyze *vt* paralizar.

parasite parásito *m*.

parasol sombrilla *f*.

parcel paquete *m*.

pardon 1 *n* perdón *m*; **I beg your p.** (Vd.) perdone; (**I beg your**) **p.?** ¿cómo (dice)? **2** *vt* perdonar; **p. me!** ¡Vd. perdone!

parents *npl* padres *mpl*.

parish parroquia *f*.

park 1 *n* parque *m*. **2** *vt* (*car*) aparcar, *Am* parquear.

parking aparcamiento *m*; **'no p.'** 'prohibido aparcar'.

parking light luz *f* de estacionamiento.

parking lot aparcamiento *m*.

parking meter parquímetro *m*.

parking space aparcamiento *m*.

parking ticket multa *f* de aparcamiento.

parliament parlamento *m*.

parrot loro m.

parsley perejil m.

parsnip chirivía f.

part 1 n parte f; (piece) trozo m; (of machine, engine) pieza f; (in play etc) papel m; **for the most p.** en la mayor parte; **to take p. in sth** participar en algo; **in these parts** por estos lugares. **2** (partly) en parte. **3** vi separarse; (say goodbye) despedirse.
• **part with** vi separarse de.

partial a parcial; **to be p. to sth** ser aficionado,-a a algo.

participant participante mf.

participate vi participar (**in** en).

participation participación f.

participle participio m.

particle board madera f aglomerada.

particular 1 a (special) particular; (fussy) exigente; **in this p. case** en este caso concreto. **2** npl **particulars** pormenores mpl; **to take down sb's particulars** tomar nota de los datos personales de algn.

particularly adv particularmente.

parting (in hair) raya f.

partition (wall) tabique m.

partly adv en parte.

partner compañero,-a mf; (in dancing, tennis) pareja f; (in business) socio,-a mf.

partnership (in business) sociedad f.

partridge perdiz f.

part-time 1 a (work etc) de media jornada. **2** adv a tiempo parcial.

party (celebration) fiesta f; (group) grupo m; (political) partido m.

pass 1 n (of mountain) desfiladero m; (permit) permiso m; (in football etc) pase m. **2** vt pasar; (overtake) adelantar; (exam, law) aprobar. **3** vi pasar; (car) adelantar; (people) cruzarse; (in football etc) hacer un pase; (in exam) aprobar; **we passed on the stairs** nos cruzamos en la escalera.
• **pass away** vi pasar a mejor vida.

• **pass by 1** vt pasar de largo. **2** vi pasar cerca; **if you're ever passing by** si alguna vez pasas por aquí.

• **pass off 1** vt **to p. oneself off as sth** hacerse pasar por algo. **2** vi (happen) transcurrir.

• **pass on** vt (hand on) transmitir. **2** vi (die) pasar a mejor vida.

• **pass out** vi (faint) desmayarse.

• **pass over** vt (disregard) pasar por alto.

• **pass through** vi estar de paso.

• **pass up** vt (opportunity) renunciar a; (offer) rechazar.

passable a (road) transitable; (acceptable) pasable.

passage (hallway) pasillo m; (in music, text) pasaje m.

passageway (interior) pasillo m; (exterior) pasaje m.

passenger pasajero,-a mf.

passer-by transeúnte mf.

passing mark (on an exam) aprobado m.

passion pasión f.

passionate a apasionado,-a.

passive a pasivo,-a.

passport pasaporte m.

past 1 n pasado m; **in the p.** antiguamente. **2** a pasado,-a; (former) anterior; **in the p. weeks** en las últimas semanas. **3** adv por delante; **to run p.** pasar corriendo. **4** prep (beyond) más allá de; (more than) más de; **it's five p. ten** son las diez y cinco.

pasta pasta f.

paste 1 n pasta f; (glue) engrudo m. **2** vt (stick) pegar.

pasteurized a pasteurizado,-a.

pastime pasatiempo m.

pastry (dough) pasta f; (cake) pastel m.

pasture pasto m.

pat vt acariciar.

patch (of material) parche m; (of color) mancha f; **to go through a bad p.** pasar por una mala racha.

• **patch up** vt (garment) poner un

parche en; **to p. up a quarrel** hacer las paces (**with** con).

path sendero *m*; (*route*) camino *m*.

pathetic *a* patético,-a; (*hopeless*) malísimo,-a.

pathway sendero *m*.

patience paciencia *f*; **to lose one's p. with sb** perder la paciencia con algn.

patient 1 *a* paciente. **2** *n* paciente *mf*.

patiently *adv* con paciencia.

patio patio *m*.

patriotic *a* (*person*) patriota; (*speech, act*) patriótico,-a.

patrol 1 *n* patrulla *f*. **2** *vt* patrullar por.

pattern (*in sewing*) patrón; (*design*) dibujo *m*.

pause 1 *n* pausa *f*; (*in conversation*) silencio *m*. **2** *vi* hacer una pausa.

paved *a* pavimentado,-a.

pavement acera *f*; (*road surface*) calzada *f*.

pavilion pabellón *m*.

paving stone losa *f*.

paw (*foot*) pata *f*; (*of cat*) garra *f*.

pawn in chess) peón *m*.

pay 1 *n* (*wages*) paga *f*. **2** *vt** pagar; (*attention*) prestar; (*visit*) hacer; (*be profitable for*) compensar; **to be or get paid** cobrar; **to p. sb a compliment** halagar a algn. **3** *vi* pagar; (*be profitable*) ser rentable; **to p. for sth** pagar (por) algo.

• **pay back** *vt* reembolsar.

• **pay in** *vt* (*money*) ingresar.

• **pay off** *vt* (*debt*) liquidar.

• **pay out** *vt* (*spend*) gastar (**on** en).

• **pay up 1** *vt* (*bill*) liquidar, saldar. **2** *vi* pagar.

payable *a* pagadero,-a.

paycheck sueldo *m*.

payment pago *m*.

payphone teléfono *m* público.

pay slip nómina *f*.

pea guisante *m*.

peace paz *f*; (*calm*) tranquilidad *f*; **at or in p.** en paz; **p. and quiet** tranquilidad.

peaceful *a* (*non-violent*) pacífico, -a; (*calm*) tranquilo,-a.

peach melocotón *m*.

peacock pavo *m* real.

peak (*of mountain*) pico *m*; (*summit*) cima *f*; **p. hours** horas *fpl* punta.

peaky *a fam* (*ill*) pálido,-a.

peanut cacahuete *m*.

pear pera *f*.

pearl perla *f*.

pebble guijarro *m*; (*small*) china *f*.

pecan (*nut*) pacana *f*.

peck *vt* (*bird*) picotear.

peckish *a* **to feel p.** empezar a tener hambre.

peculiar *a* (*odd*) extraño,-a; (*particular*) característico,-a.

peculiarity (*characteristic*) característica *f*.

pedal 1 *n* pedal *m*. **2** *vi* pedalear.

pedestrian peatón,-ona *mf*.

pedestrian crossing paso *m* de peatones.

peek 1 *n* ojeada *f*. **2** *vi* **to p. at sth** mirar algo a hurtadillas.

peel 1 *n* piel *f*; (*of orange, lemon*) cáscara *f*. **2** *vt* (*fruit*) pelar. **3** *vi* (*paint*) desconcharse; (*skin*) pelarse.

• **peel off** *vt* (*skin of fruit*) pelar; (*clothes*) quitarse.

peeler potato p. pelapatatas *m inv*.

peep 1 *n* (*glance*) ojeada *f*; (*furtive look*) mirada furtiva. **2** *vi* **to p. at sth** echar una ojeada a algo.

peer *vi* mirar detenidamente.

peg clavija *f*; (*for coat, hat*) colgador *m*.

pen[1] pluma *f*.

pen[2] (*for animals*) corral *m*.

penalty (*punishment*) pena *f*; (*in sport*) castigo *m*; (*in soccer*) penalti *m*.

pencil lápiz *m*.

pencil case estuche *m* de lápices.

pencil sharpener sacapuntas *m inv*.

pendulum péndulo *m*.

penetrate *vt* (*break through*,

grasp) penetrar; (*forest, territory*) adentrarse en.

penguin pingüino *m*.

penicillin penicilina *f*.

peninsula península *f*.

penknife navaja *f*.

penniless *a* sin dinero.

penny (*pl* **pennies**) centavo *m*.

pen pal amigo,-a *mf* por carta.

pension pensión *f*; **retirement p.** jubilación *f*.

pensioner jubilado,-a *mf*.

people *npl* gente *f sing*; (*individuals*) personas *fpl*; (*nation*) pueblo *m*; **old p.'s home** asilo *m* de ancianos; **p. say that . . .** se dice que . . .

pepper (*spice*) pimienta *f*; (*fruit*) pimiento *m*.

peppermint hierbabuena *f*; (*sweet*) pastilla *f* de menta.

per *prep* por; **5 times p. week** 5 veces a la semana; **p. day/annum** al or por día/año; **p. capita** or **person** per cápita.

percent *npl* por ciento.

percentage porcentaje *m*.

perch 1 *n* (*for bird*) percha *f*. **2** *vi* (*bird*) posarse (**on** en).

percolator cafetera *f* de filtro.

perfect 1 *a* perfecto,-a; **p. tense** tiempo perfecto. **2** *vt* perfeccionar.

perfectly *adv* perfectamente; (*absolutely*) completamente.

perfection perfección *f*.

perform 1 *vt* (*task*) realizar; (*piece of music*) interpretar; (*play*) representar. **2** *vi* (*machine*) funcionar; (*musician*) tocar; (*actor*) actuar.

performance (*of task*) realización *f*; (*of piece of music*) interpretación *f*; (*of play*) representación *f*; (*in sport*) actuación *f*; (*of machine etc*) rendimiento *m*.

performer (*singer*) intérprete *mf*; (*actor*) actor *m*, actriz *f*.

perfume perfume *m*.

perhaps *adv* tal vez, quizá(s).

peril (*danger*) peligro *m*.

period período *m*; (*stage*) etapa *f*;

(*at school*) clase *f*; (*full stop*) punto *m*; (*menstruation*) regla *f*.

periodical 1 *n* revista *f*. **2** *a* periódico,-a

peripheral periférico *m*.

perk extra *m*.

• **perk up** *vi* animarse.

perm 1 *n* permanente *f*. **2** *vt* **to have one's hair permed** hacerse la permanente.

permanent *a* permanente; (*address, job*) fijo,-a.

permanently *adv* permanentemente.

permission permiso *m*.

permit 1 *n* permiso *m*. **2** *vt* **to p. sb to do sth** permitir a algn hacer algo.

perpendicular *a* perpendicular.

persecute *vt* perseguir.

persecution persecución *f*.

perseverance perseverancia *f*.

persevere *vi* perseverar.

persist *vi* empeñarse (**in** en).

persistent *a* (*person*) perseverante; (*continual*) constante.

person persona *f*; **in p.** en persona.

personal *a* (*private*) personal; (*friend*) íntimo,-a; *pej* (*comment etc*) indiscreto,-a; **he will make a p. appearance** estará aquí en persona.

personality personalidad *f*.

personally *adv* (*for my part*) personalmente; (*in person*) en persona.

personnel personal *m*.

persuade *vt* persuadir; **to p. sb to do sth** persuadir a algn para que haga algo.

persuasion persuasión *f*.

Peruvian *a* & *n* peruano,-a (*mf*).

pessimist pesimista *mf*.

pessimistic *a* pesimista.

pest (*animal, insect*) plaga *f*; *fam* (*person*) pelma *mf*; (*thing*) lata *f*.

pester *vt* molestar.

pet 1 *n* animal *m* doméstico. **2** *a* (*favorite*) preferido,-a.

petal pétalo *m*.

petition petición f.
petroleum petróleo m.
petticoat enaguas fpl.
petty a (trivial) insignificante; (small-minded) mezquino,-a.
petty cash dinero m para gastos pequeños.
pharmacist farmacéutico,-a mf.
pharmacy farmacia f.
phase 1 n fase f. **2** vt **to p. sth in/out** introducir/retirar algo progresivamente.
PhD Doctor,-a mf en Filosofía.
pheasant faisán m.
phenomenal a fenomenal.
phenomenon (pl **phenomena**) fenómeno m.
philosopher filósofo,-a mf.
philosophical a filosófico,-a.
philosophy filosofía f.
phlegm flema f.
phone 1 n teléfono m. **2** vt llamar por teléfono a.
phone book guía f telefónica.
phone booth cabina f telefónica.
phone call llamada f (telefónica).
phone card tarjeta f telefónica.
phone number número m de teléfono.
phonetic a fonético,-a.
photo foto f.
photocopier fotocopiadora f.
photocopy 1 n fotocopia f. **2** vt fotocopiar.
photograph 1 n fotografía f. **2** vt fotografiar.
photographer fotógrafo,-a mf.
photography fotografía f.
phrase frase f.
phrasebook libro m de frases.
physical a físico,-a.
physically adv físicamente; **p. handicapped** minusválido,-a.
physics física f.
pianist pianista mf.
piano piano m.
pick 1 n (tool) pico m; **take your p.** (choice) elige el que quieras. **2** vt (choose) escoger; (team) seleccionar; (flowers, fruit) coger; (lock)

forzar. **to p. one's nose** hurgarse la nariz.
• **pick on** vt (persecute) meterse con.
• **pick out** vt (choose) elegir; (identify) identificar.
• **pick up 1** vt (object on floor) recoger; (telephone) descolgar; (collect) recoger; (shopping, person) buscar; (acquire) conseguir; (learn) aprender; **to p. up speed** ganar velocidad. **2** vi (improve) mejorarse.
pickax piqueta f.
pickle vt (food) conservar en adobo or escabeche; **pickled onions** cebollas fpl en vinagre.
pickpocket carterista mf.
picnic comida f de campo, picnic m.
picture 1 n (painting) cuadro m; (drawing) dibujo m; (portrait) retrato m; (photo) foto f; (on TV) imagen f; (at cinema) película f. **2** vt (imagine) imaginarse.
picture frame marco m.
picturesque a pintoresco,-a.
pie (fruit) (big) tarta f; (small) pastel m; (meat etc) empanada f; (pasty) empanadilla f.
piece pedazo m; (of paper) trozo; (part) pieza f; (coin) moneda f; **a p. of news** una noticia; **to break sth into pieces** hacer algo pedazos.
pier embarcadero m, muelle m.
pierce vt perforar.
piercing a (sound etc) penetrante.
pig cerdo m.
pigeon paloma f.
pigeonhole casilla f.
piggyback to give sb a p. llevar a algn a cuestas.
pigtail trenza f.
pile 1 n montón m. **2** vt amontonar.
• **pile up 1** vt (things) amontonar; (riches, debts) acumular. **2** vi amontonarse.
piles sing (illness) hemorroides fpl.
pile-up choque m en cadena.
pill píldora f; **to be on the p.** es-

tar tomando la píldora (anti-conceptiva).

pillar pilar m, columna f.

pillar box buzón m.

pillow almohada f.

pillowcase funda f de almohada.

pilot piloto m.

pimple espinilla f.

pin 1 n alfiler m. **2** vt (onto board) clavar con chinchetas.

• **pin up** vt clavar con chinchetas.

pinafore (apron) delantal m.

pinball flipper m.

pincers npl (tool) tenazas fpl.

pinch 1 n (nip) pellizco m; **a p. of salt** una pizca de sal. **2** vt pellizcar; fam (steal) birlar.

pincushion acerico m.

pine (tree) pino m.

pineapple piña f.

pink a rosa inv.

pinkie dedo m meñique.

pint pinta f (0,47 litro); **a p. of beer** una cerveza.

pip (seed) pepita f.

pipe tubería f; (for smoking) pipa f.

pirate pirata m.

pistachio pistacho m.

pistol pistola f.

pit hoyo m; (large) hoya f; (coal mine) mina f de carbón; (of fruit) hueso m.

pitch 1 vt (throw) lanzar; (tent) armar. **2** n (for sport) campo m; (throw) lanzamiento m.

pitch-black, pitch-dark a negro,-a como boca de lobo.

pity 1 n (compassion) compasión f; (shame) lástima f; **what a p.!** ¡qué pena! **2** vt compadecerse de.

pizza pizza f.

placard pancarta f.

place 1 n sitio m, lugar m; (seat) sitio m; (on bus) asiento m; (position on scale) posición f; (house) casa f; (building) lugar m; **to take p.** tener lugar; **to take sb's p.** sustituir a algn; **in the first p.** en primer lugar; **we're going to his p.** vamos a

su casa. **2** vt poner, colocar; (face, person) recordar.

placemat tapete m individual.

place setting cubierto m.

plague peste f.

plain 1 a (clear) claro,-a; (simple) sencillo,-a; (unattractive) poco atractivo,-a; **the p. truth** la verdad lisa y llana. **2** n (land) llanura f.

plainly adv claramente; (simply) sencillamente; **to speak p.** hablar con franqueza.

plait 1 n trenza f. **2** vt trenzar.

plan plan m. **2** vt (for future) planear; (economy) planificar; (intend) pensar; **to p. on doing sth** tener la intención de hacer algo.

• **plan for** vt (disaster) prevenirse contra.

plane[1] avión m.

plane[2] (tool) cepillo m.

plane[3] **p. (tree)** plátano m.

planet planeta m.

plank tabla f.

plant[1] **1** n planta f. **2** vt (flowers) plantar; (bomb) colocar.

plant[2] (factory) planta f (industrial).

plaster yeso m; (for broken limb) escayola f.

plaster cast (for broken arm) escayola f.

plastic 1 n plástico m. **2** a (cup, bag) de plástico.

plastic surgery cirugía f plástica.

plate plato m; (sheet) placa f.

platform plataforma f; (at meeting) tribuna f; (at station) andén m.

play 1 vt (game) jugar a; (team) jugar contra; (instrument, tune) tocar; (part) hacer (el papel) de; **to p. a record** poner un disco; fig **to p. a part in sth** participar en algo. **2** vi jugar (**with** con). **3** n obra f de teatro.

• **play back** vt (tape) volver a poner.

• **play down** vt quitar importancia a.

player jugador,-a *mf*; (*in play*) (*man*) actor *m*; (*woman*) actriz *f*.

playground (*in school*) patio *m* de recreo; (*recreation ground*) parque *m* infantil.

playgroup jardín *m* de infancia.

playing card carta *f*.

playing field campo *m* de deportes.

playtime recreo *m*.

pleasant *a* agradable.

pleasantly *adv* agradablemente.

please 1 *adv* por favor; '**p. do not smoke**' 'se ruega no fumar'. **2** *vt* (*give pleasure to*) complacer. **3** *vi* **do as you p.** haz lo que quieras.

pleased *a* (*happy*) contento,-a; (*satisfied*) satisfecho,-a; **p. to meet you!** ¡encantado,-a!.

pleasing *a* (*pleasant*) agradable.

pleasure placer *m*; **with p.** con mucho gusto.

pleat pliegue *m*.

pleated *a* plisado,-a.

plentiful *a* abundante.

plenty p. of potatoes muchas patatas; **p. of time** tiempo de sobra.

pliers *npl* alicates *mpl*, tenazas *fpl*.

plot¹ **1** *n* (*conspiracy*) complot *m*; (*story*) argumento *m*. **2** *vi* conspirar.

plot² (*ground*) terreno *m*; (*for building*) solar *m*.

plow 1 *n* arado *m*. **2** *vt* arar.

pluck *vt* (*flowers*) coger; (*chicken*) desplumar.

plug 1 *n* (*in bath etc*) tapón *m*; (*electric*) enchufe *m*; **2/3 pin p.** clavija bipolar/tripolar. **2** *vt* (*hole*) tapar.

• **plug in 1** *vt* enchufar. **2** *vi* enchufarse.

plum (*fruit*) ciruela *f*.

plumber fontanero,-a *mf*.

plumbing (*system*) fontanería *f*.

plump *a* (*person*) rechoncho,-a; (*baby*) rellenito,-a.

plunge 1 *vt* (*immerse*) sumergir; (*thrust*) arrojar. **2** *vi* (*dive*) zambullirse; (*fall*) caer.

plural *a* & *n* plural (*m*); **in the p.** en plural.

plus *prep* más; **three p. four makes seven** tres más cuatro hacen siete.

p.m. (*from midday to early evening*) de la tarde; (*at night*) de la noche.

pneumatic *a* neumático,-a.

pneumatic drill martillo *m* neumático.

PO Box apartado *m* (de Correos).

poach *vt* (*egg*) escalfar.

pocket bolsillo *m*.

pocketbook bolso *m*.

pocketful a p. of un bolsillo de.

pocket money dinero *m* de bolsillo.

poem poema *m*.

poet poeta *mf*.

poetic *a* poético,-a.

poetry poesía *f*.

point 1 *n* (*sharp end*) punta *f*; (*place*) punto *m*; (*score*) tanto *m*; (*moment*) **at that p.** en aquel momento; **to be on the p. of doing sth** estar a punto de hacer algo; **there's no p. in going** no merece la pena ir; **six p. three** seis coma tres; **up to a p.** hasta cierto punto; **power p.** toma *f* de corriente; **points** (*on railway*) agujas *fpl*. **2** *vt* (*way etc*) indicar; **to p. a gun at sb** apuntar a algn con una pistola. **3** *vi* **to p. at sth/sb** (*with finger*) señalar algo/a algn con el dedo.

• **point out** *vt* indicar; (*mention*) hacer resaltar.

pointed *a* (*sharp*) puntiagudo,-a.

pointless *a* sin sentido.

poison 1 *n* veneno *m*. **2** *vt* envenenar.

poisonous *a* (*plant, snake*) venenoso,-a; (*gas*) tóxico,-a.

poke *vt* (*fire*) atizar; (*with finger*) dar con la punta del dedo a; (*with stick*) dar con la punta del bastón a; **to p. one's head out** asomar la cabeza.

• **poke about** or **around** *vi* fisgonear or hurgar en.

poker (*for fire*) atizador *m*.
polar *a* polar.
polar bear oso *m* polar.
Pole polaco,-a *mf*.
pole[1] palo *m*.
pole[2] (*north, south*) polo *m*.
police *npl* policía *f sing*.
police car coche *m* patrulla.
policeman policía *m*.
police station comisaría *f*.
policewoman (mujer *f*) policía *f*.
policy política *f*; (*insurance*) póliza *f* (de seguros).
polio poliomielitis *f*.
polish 1 *vt* pulir; (*furniture*) encerar; (*shoes*) limpiar. **2** *n* (*for furniture*) cera *f*; (*for shoes*) betún *m*; (*for nails*) esmalte *m*.
• **polish off** *vt* (*food*) zamparse.
• **polish up** *vt fig* perfeccionar.
Polish 1 *a* polaco,-a. **2** *n* (*language*) polaco *m*.
polite *a* educado,-a.
politely *adv* educadamente.
politeness educación *f*.
political *a* político,-a.
politician político,-a *mf*.
politics política *f*.
poll votación *f*; (*survey*) encuesta *f*; **to go to the polls** acudir a las urnas.
pollen polen *m*.
polling station colegio *m* electoral.
pollute *vt* contaminar.
pollution contaminación *f*.
polo p. neck sweater jersey *m* de cuello vuelto.
polyester poliéster *m*.
polytechnic politécnico *m*.
polythene polietileno *m*.
pomegranate granada *f*.
pond estanque *m*.
pony poney *m*.
ponytail cola *f* de caballo.
poodle caniche *m*.
pool (*of water, oil etc*) charco *m*; **swimming p.** piscina *f*.
pooped *a fam* hecho,-a polvo.
poor 1 *a* pobre; (*quality*) malo,-a. **2** *npl* **the p.** los pobres.

poorly 1 (*badly*) mal. **2** *a* (*ill*) enfermo,-a.
pop 1 *vt* (*burst*) hacer reventar. **2** *vi* (*burst*) reventar; *fam* **I'm just popping over to Ian's** voy un momento a casa de Ian. **3** *n* (*drink*) gaseosa *f*; *fam* (*father*) papá *m*; (*music*) música *f* pop.
• **pop in** *vi fam* entrar un momento.
popcorn palomitas *fpl*.
Pope the P. el Papa.
poppy amapola *f*.
popsicle polo *m*.
pop singer cantante *mf* pop.
popular *a* popular; (*fashionable*) de moda.
populated *a* **thinly p.** poco poblado.
population población *f*.
porch (*of house*) porche *m*; (*veranda*) terraza *f*.
pork carne *f* de cerdo.
porridge gachas *fpl* de avena.
port (*harbor, of computer*) puerto *m*.
portable *a & n* portátil (*m*).
porter (*in hotel etc*) portero,-a *mf*.
porthole portilla *f*.
portion (*part, piece*) parte *f*; (*of food*) ración *f*.
portrait retrato *m*.
Portuguese 1 *a* portugués,-esa. **2** *n* (*person*) portugués,-esa *mf*; (*language*) portugués *m*.
pose 1 *vt* (*problem*) plantear; (*threat*) representar. **2** *vi* (*for painting*) posar; **to p. as** hacerse pasar por.
posh *a* elegante; (*person*) presumido,-a; (*accent*) de clase alta.
position posición *f*; (*location*) situación *f*; (*rank*) rango *m*; **to be in a p. to do sth** estar en condiciones de hacer algo.
positive *a* positivo,-a; (*sign*) favorable; (*sure*) seguro,-a.
possess *vt* poseer.
possessions *npl* bienes *mpl*.
possessive *a* posesivo,-a.

possibility posibilidad *f.*
possible *a* posible; **as much as p.** todo lo posible; **as often as p.** cuanto más mejor; **as soon as p.** cuanto antes.
possibly *adv* posiblemente; (*perhaps*) quizás; **I can't p. come** no puedo venir de ninguna manera.
post¹ (*wooden*) poste *m.*
post² (*job*) puesto *m.*
• **post up** *vt* (*notice*) fijar.
postage franqueo *m.*
postage stamp sello *m* (de correos).
postal *a* postal.
postal order giro *m* postal.
postcard (tarjeta *f*) postal *f.*
poster póster *m*; (*advertising*) cartel *m.*
postgraduate posgraduado,-a *mf.*
postman cartero *m.*
postmark matasellos *m inv.*
post office oficina *f* de correos; **where is the p.?** ¿dónde está correos?
postpone *vt* aplazar.
postponement aplazamiento *m.*
pot (*for cooking*) olla *f*; (*for flowers*) maceta *f.*
potato (*pl* **potatoes**) patata *f.*
potential 1 *a* potencial. **2** *n* potencial *m.*
potter alfarero,-a *mf.*
pottery (*craft, place*) alfarería *f*; (*objects*) cerámica *f.*
potty orinal *m.*
pouch bolsa *f* pequeña; (*of animal*) bolsa *f* abdominal.
poultry (*live*) aves *fpl* de corral; (*food*) pollos *mpl.*
pounce *vi* **to p. on** abalanzarse encima de.
pound¹ (*weight*) libra *f.*
pound² (*for dogs*) perrera *f*; (*for cars*) depósito *m* de coches.
pour 1 *vt* verter; **to p. sb a drink** servirle una copa a algn. **2** *vi* **it's pouring with rain** está lloviendo a cántaros.
• **pour away** *vt* (*liquid*) vaciar.

• **pour in** *vi* (*water*) entrar a raudales; (*applications*) llegar sin parar.
• **pour out 1** *vt* verter. **2** *vi* (*liquid, people*) salir a raudales.
poverty pobreza *f.*
powder 1 *n* polvo *m.* **2** *vt* **to p. one's nose** empolvarse la cara.
powdered *a* (*milk*) en polvo.
power fuerza *f*; (*energy*) energía *f*; (*ability, authority*) poder *m*; (*nation*) potencia *f*; **to be in p.** estar en el poder.
powerful *a* (*influential*) poderoso,-a; (*engine, machine*) potente.
power point enchufe *m.*
power station central *f* eléctrica.
practical *a* práctico,-a.
practical joke broma *f* pesada.
practically (*almost*) casi.
practice 1 *n* (*exercise*) práctica *f*; (*in sport*) entrenamiento *m*; (*rehearsal*) ensayo *m*; (*habit*) costumbre *f*; (*way of doing sth*) práctica *f*; **to be out of p.** no estar en forma; **in p.** en la práctica. **2** *vt* practicar; (*principle*) poner en práctica; (*profession*) ejercer. **3** *vi* practicar; (*in sport*) entrenar; (*rehearse*) ensayar; (*doctor*) practicar; (*lawyer*) ejercer.
praise 1 *n* alabanza *f.* **2** *vt* alabar.
prank travesura *f*; (*joke*) broma *f.*
prawn gamba *f.*
pray *vi* rezar.
prayer oración *f.*
precaution precaución *f.*
precede *vt* preceder.
preceding *a* precedente.
precious *a* precioso,-a.
precise *a* preciso,-a; (*meticulous*) meticuloso,-a.
precocious *a* precoz.
predecessor antecesor,-a *mf.*
predicament apuro *m*, aprieto *m.*
predict *vt* predecir.
predictable *a* previsible.
prediction pronóstico *m.*
preface prefacio *m.*
prefer *vt* preferir; **I p. coffee to tea** prefiero el café al té.

preferable a preferible (**to** a).
preferably adv preferentemente.
preference preferencia f.
prefix prefijo m.
pregnancy embarazo m.
pregnant a embarazada.
prehistoric(al) a prehistórico, -a.
prejudice (bias) prejuicio m.
preliminary a preliminar.
premises npl local m; **on the p.** en el local.
premium prima f.
preparation preparación f; (plan) preparativo m.
prepare 1 vt preparar; **to p. to do sth** prepararse para hacer algo. **2** vi prepararse (**for** para).
prepared a (ready) preparado,-a; **to be p. to do sth** (willing) estar dispuesto,-a a hacer algo.
preposition preposición f.
prescribe vt (medicine) recetar.
prescription (medical) receta f.
presence presencia f; (attendance) asistencia f.
present¹ 1 a (in attendance) presente; (current) actual; **p. tense** (tiempo m) presente m. **2** n (time) presente m; **at p.** actualmente.
present² 1 vt (opportunity) ofrecer; (problems) plantear; (prize) entregar; (introduce) (person, program) presentar; **to p. sb with sth** obsequiar a algn con algo. **2** n (gift) regalo m.
presentation presentación f; **p. ceremony** ceremonia f de entrega.
presenter animador,-a mf.
presently adv (soon) dentro de poco; ahora.
preservation conservación f.
preservative conservante m.
preserve 1 vt (keep) mantener. **2** n conserva f.
presidency presidencia f.
president presidente,-a mf.
presidential a presidencial.
press 1 vt apretar; (button) pulsar; (iron) planchar; (urge) presionar; **to p. sb to do sth** presionar a algn

para que haga algo. **2** vi (push) apretar; **to p. (down) on sth** hacer presión sobre algo. **3** n (newspapers) prensa f.
• **press on** vi seguir adelante.
press conference rueda f de prensa.
pressure presión f; **to bring p. (to bear) on sb** ejercer presión sobre algn.
pressure cooker olla f a presión.
pressure gauge manómetro m.
presume vt suponer.
pretend vti fingir.
pretext pretexto m; **on the p. of** so pretexto de.
pretty 1 a (thing) bonito,-a; (person) guapo,-a. **2** adv bastante; **p. much the same** más o menos lo mismo.
prevent vt impedir; (accident) evitar; **to p. sb from doing sth** impedir a algn hacer algo.
prevention prevención f.
previous a anterior.
previously adv previamente.
prey presa f; fig víctima f.
price precio m.
price list lista f de precios.
prick vt picar; **to p. one's finger** pincharse el dedo.
prickly a espinoso,-a; (touchy) enojadizo,-a.
pride n orgullo m; (arrogance) soberbia f; **to take p. in sth** enorgullecerse de algo. **2** vt **to p. oneself on** enorgullecerse de.
priest sacerdote m, cura m.
primarily adv ante todo.
primary a **p. education/school** enseñanza f/escuela f primaria.
Prime Minister primer,-a ministro,-a mf.
prime number número m primo.
primitive a primitivo,-a.
primrose primavera f.
prince príncipe m; **P. Charming** Príncipe Azul.
princess princesa f.
principal 1 a principal. **2** n (of college etc) director,-a mf.

principle principio *m*; **on p.** por principio.

print 1 *vt* (*publish*) publicar; (*write*) escribir con letra de imprenta; **printed matter** impresos *mpl*. **2** *n* letra *f*; (*of hand, foot*) huella *f*; (*of photo*) copia *f*; **out of p.** agotado,-a.

• **print out** *vt* imprimir.

printer (*person*) impresor,-a *mf*; (*machine*) impresora *f*.

printout impresión *f*.

prior *a* anterior; **without p. warning** sin previo aviso.

priority prioridad *f*.

prison prisión *f*.

prisoner preso,-a *mf*; **to hold sb p.** detener a algn.

privacy intimidad *f*.

private 1 *a* privado,-a; (*individual*) particular; (*personal*) personal; (*letter*) confidencial. **2** *n* (*soldier*) soldado *m* raso.

privately *adv* en privado; (*personally*) personalmente.

prize premio *m*.

prize-giving distribución *f* de premios.

prizewinner premiado,-a *mf*.

probable *a* probable.

probably *adv* probablemente.

problem problema *m*.

proceed *vi* proceder, seguir; **to p. to do sth** ponerse a hacer algo.

process 1 *n* proceso *m*; **in the p. of** en vías de. **2** *vt* procesar.

processed cheese queso *m* tratado.

procession *n* desfile *m*; (*religious*) procesión *f*.

processor procesador *m*.

produce 1 *vt* producir; (*manufacture*) fabricar; (*give birth to*) dar a luz a; (*show*) enseñar; (*bring out*) sacar. **2** *n* productos *mpl*.

producer productor,-a *mf*; (*manufacturer*) fabricante *mf*.

product producto *m*.

production producción *f*; (*manufacture*) fabricación *f*.

production line cadena *f* de montaje.

profession profesión *f*.

professional 1 *a* profesional; (*polished*) de gran calidad. **2** *n* profesional *mf*.

professor catedrático,-a *mf*.

profit 1 *n* beneficio *m*; **to make a p. on** sacar beneficios de. **2** *vi* **to p. from** aprovecharse de.

profitable *a* rentable; (*worthwhile*) provechoso,-a.

program 1 *n* programa *m*; (*plan*) plan *m*. **2** *vti* programar.

progress 1 *n* progreso *m*; **to make p.** hacer progresos; **in p.** en curso. **2** *vi* avanzar; (*develop*) desarrollarse; (*medically*) mejorar.

prohibit *vt* prohibir; **to p. sb from doing sth** prohibir a algn hacer algo.

project proyecto *m*; (*at school*) trabajo *m*.

projector proyector *m*.

prolong *vt* prolongar.

promenade (*at seaside*) paseo *m* marítimo.

prominent *a* (*important*) importante; (*famous*) eminente.

promise 1 *n* promesa *f*; **to show p.** ser prometedor,-a. **2** *vti* prometer.

promising *a* prometedor,-a.

promote *vt* ascender; (*product*) promocionar.

promotion (*in rank*) ascenso *m*; (*of product*) promoción *f*.

prompt 1 *a* (*quick*) rápido,-a; (*punctual*) puntual. **2** *adv* **at 2 o'clock p.** a las 2 en punto.

prone *a* **to be p. to do sth** ser propenso,-a a hacer algo.

pronoun pronombre *m*.

pronounce *vt* pronunciar.

pronunciation pronunciación *f*.

proof prueba *f*.

propeller hélice *f*.

proper *a* adecuado,-a; (*real*) auténtico,-a; **p. noun** nombre propio.

properly (*suitably, correctly, decently*) correctamente.

property (*possession*) propiedad *f*; **personal p.** bienes *mpl*.

proportion proporción *f*; (*part, quantity*) parte *f*.
proposal propuesta *f*; **p. of marriage** propuesta de matrimonio.
propose 1 *vt* proponer; (*suggest*) sugerir. **2** *vi* (*ask to marry*) declararse.
props *npl* (*in theater*) accesorios *mpl*.
prose prosa *f*; (*translation*) traducción *f* inversa.
prospect (*outlook*) perspectiva *f*; (*hope*) esperanza *f*.
prosperous *a* próspero,-a.
protect *vt* **to p. sb from sth** proteger a algn de algo.
protection protección *f*.
protective *a* protector,-a.
protest 1 *n* protesta *f*. **2** *vi* protestar.
Protestant *a & n* protestante (*mf*).
protester manifestante *mf*.
proud *a* orgulloso,-a; (*arrogant*) soberbio,-a.
proudly *adv* con orgullo; (*arrogantly*) con soberbia.
prove *vt* demostrar; **it proved to be disastrous** resultó ser desastroso,-a.
proverb refrán *m*, proverbio *m*.
provide *vt* proporcionar; (*supplies*) suministrar.
provided *conj* **p. (that)** con tal de que.
province provincia *f*.
provincial *a* provincial; *pej* provinciano,-a.
provoke *vt* provocar.
prowl *vi* merodear; **to p. about** *or* **around** rondar.
prowler merodeador *m*.
prune[1] ciruela *f* pasa.
prune[2] (*roses etc*) podar.
psychiatrist psiquiatra *mf*.
psychological *a* psicológico,-a.
psychologist psicólogo,-a *mf*.
pub *n* bar *m*.
public 1 *a* público,-a; **p. holiday** fiesta *f* nacional. **2 the p.** el público; **in p.** en público.
publication publicación *f*.
publicity publicidad *f*.

publish *vt* publicar, editar.
publisher editor,-a *mf*.
publishing (*business*) industria *f* editorial.
pudding pudín *m*; (*dessert*) postre *m*.
puddle charco *m*.
puff 1 *n* (*of smoke*) bocanada *f*. **2** *vi* (*person*) jadear; **to p. on one's pipe** chupar la pipa.
pull 1 *n* **to give sth a p.** (*tug*) dar un tirón a algo. **2** *vt* (*tug*) dar un tirón a; (*drag*) tirar de; **to p. a muscle** sufrir un tirón en un músculo; **to p. the trigger** apretar el gatillo; **to p. sth to pieces** hacer pedazos algo.
• **pull apart** *vt* desmontar.
• **pull down** *vt* (*building*) derribar.
• **pull in 1** *vt* (*crowds*) atraer. **2** *vi* **to p. in(to the station)** llegar a la estación.
• **pull out 1** *vt* (*withdraw*) retirar. **2** *vi* (*car*) **to p. out to overtake** salirse para adelantar.
• **pull over** *vi* hacerse a un lado.
• **pull through** *vi* reponerse.
• **pull up 1** *vt* (*uproot*) desarraigar; (*draw close*) acercar. **2** *vi* (*stop*) pararse.
pullover jersey *m*.
pulse (*in body*) pulso *m*.
pump 1 *n* bomba *f*. **2** *vt* bombear.
• **pump up** *vt* (*tire*) inflar.
pumpkin calabaza *f*.
punch[1] **1** *n* (*for making holes*) perforadora *f*. **2** *vt* (*ticket*) picar.
punch[2] **1** *n* (*blow*) puñetazo *m*. **2** *vt* (*with fist*) dar un puñetazo a.
punctual *a* puntual.
punctuation puntuación *f*.
puncture 1 *n* pinchazo *m*. **2** *vt* (*tire*) pinchar.
punish *vt* castigar.
punishment castigo *m*.
pupil[1] (*at school*) alumno,-a *mf*.
pupil[2] (*in eye*) pupila *f*.
puppet títere *m*.
puppy cachorro,-a *mf* (de perro).
purchase 1 *n* compra *f*. **2** *vt* comprar.

purchasing power poder *m* adquisitivo.
pure *a* puro,-a.
purely *adv* simplemente.
purple *a* morado,-a.
purpose propósito *m*; **on p.** a propósito.
purposely *adv* adrede.
purse (*bag*) bolso *m*.
pursue *vt* (*criminal*) perseguir; (*person*) seguir.
push 1 *n* empujón *m*; **to give sb a p.** dar un empujón a algn. **2** *vt* empujar; (*button*) pulsar; **to p. one's finger into a hole** meter el dedo en un agujero. **3** *vi* empujar.
• **push aside** *vt* (*object*) apartar.
• **push in** *vi* colarse.
• **push off** *vi fam* **p. off!** ¡lárgate!
• **push on** *vi* (*continue*) seguir adelante.
• **push through** *vt* (*crowd*) abrirse paso entre; (*law*) hacer aceptar (a la fuerza).
pushed *a* **to be p. for time/money** estar justo,-a de tiempo/dinero.
puss, pussy mino *m*.
put* *vt* poner; (*place*) colocar; (*insert*) meter; (*express*) expresar; (*invest*) (*money*) invertir; **to p. a stop to sth** poner término a algo; **to p. a question to sb** hacer una pregunta a algn.
• **put across** *vt* (*idea etc*) comunicar.
• **put aside** *vt* (*money*) ahorrar; (*time*) reservar.
• **put away** *vt* (*tidy up*) recoger; (*save money*) ahorrar.
• **put back** *vt* (*postpone*) aplazar.
• **put by** *vt* (*money*) ahorrar.
• **put down** *vt* (*set down*) dejar; (*criticize*) criticar; (*write down*) apuntar.
• **put forward** *vt* (*theory*) exponer; (*proposal*) hacer.
• **put in** *vt* (*install*) instalar; (*complaint, request*) presentar; (*time*) pasar.
• **put off** *vt* (*postpone*) aplazar; (*switch off*) (*radio, light*) apa-

gar; **to p. sb off (doing) sth** (*dissuade*) disuadir a algn de (hacer) algo.
• **put on** *vt* (*clothes*) poner(se); (*switch on*) (*radio*) poner; (*light*) encender; **to p. on weight** engordar.
• **put out** *vt* (*switch off, extinguish*) apagar; (*place outside*) sacar; (*extend*) (*arm*) extender; (*hand*) tender; (*annoy*) molestar; (*inconvenience*) incordiar.
• **put through** *vt* (*on telephone*) **p. me through to Pat, please** póngame con Pat, por favor.
• **put together** *vt* (*assemble*) montar.
• **put up** *vt* (*raise*) levantar; (*picture*) colocar; (*curtains*) colgar; (*tent*) armar; (*prices*) subir; (*accommodate*) alojar; **to p. up a fight** ofrecer resistencia.
• **put up with** *vt* aguantar.
putty masilla *f*.
puzzle 1 *n* rompecabezas *m inv*; (*mystery*) misterio *m*. **2** *vt* dejar perplejo,-a.
puzzling *a* extraño,-a.
pylon torre *f* (de conducción eléctrica).
pyramid pirámide *f*.

Q

qualification (*diploma etc*) título *m*.
qualified *a* capacitado,-a; **q. teacher** profesor titulado.
qualify *vi* (*in competition*) quedar clasificado,-a; **to q. as** (*doctor etc*) sacar el título de.
quality (*excellence*) calidad *f*; (*attribute*) cualidad *f*.
quantity cantidad *f*.
quarrel 1 *n* (*argument*) riña *f*, pelea *f*. **2** *vi* (*argue*) reñir.
quarreling disputas *fpl*.
quarry cantera *f*.
quart cuarto *m* de galón (*0,94 litros*).

quarter cuarto m; (coin) cuarto m (de dólar); (district) barrio m; **it's a q. to three, it's a q. of three** son las tres menos cuarto.

quartz cuarzo m; **q. watch** reloj m de cuarzo.

queen reina f.

queer a (strange) extraño,-a.

quench vt apagar.

query (question) pregunta f.

question 1 n pregunta f; (problem, issue) asunto m; **to ask sb a q.** hacer una pregunta a algn; **out of the q.** imposible; **that's out of the q.** ¡ni hablar! 2 vt (interrogate) interrogar; (query) poner en duda.

question mark signo m de interrogación.

questionnaire cuestionario m.

quibble vi poner pegas (with a).

quiche quiche f.

quick a (fast) rápido,-a; **be q.!** ¡date prisa!

quickly adv deprisa.

quiet a (silent) silencioso,-a; (calm, not crowded) tranquilo,-a.

quietly adv (silently) silenciosamente; (calmly) tranquilamente; **he spoke q.** habló en voz baja.

quit* 1 vt (leave) dejar; **q. making that noise!** ¡deja de hacer ese ruido! 2 vi (go) irse; (resign) dimitir.

quite adv (entirely) totalmente; (rather) bastante; **q. a few** bastantes; **q. often** con bastante frecuencia; **q. (so)!** ¡exacto!

quiz q. show concurso m.

quotation cita f; (commercial) cotización f.

quotation marks npl comillas fpl.

quote 1 vt (cite) citar; **to q. a price** dar un presupuesto. 2 n cita f; (commercial) presupuesto m.

R

rabbi rabino m.

rabbit conejo,-a mf.

rabies rabia f.

race¹ 1 n (in sport) carrera f. 2 vt (car, horse) hacer correr; **I'll r. you!** ¡te echo una carrera! 3 vi (go quickly) correr.

race² (people) raza f.

racehorse caballo m de carreras.

racial a racial.

racing carreras fpl.

racing bike (motorbike) moto f de carreras; (bicycle) bicicleta f de carreras.

racing car coche m de carreras.

racing driver piloto mf de carreras.

racism racismo m.

racist a & n racista (mf).

rack (shelf) estante m; (for clothes) percha f; **luggage r.** portaequipajes m inv; **roof r.** baca f.

racket¹ (din) jaleo m.

racket² (for tennis etc) raqueta f.

radar radar m.

radiator radiador m.

radio radio f; **on the r.** en or por la radio; **r. station** emisora f (de radio).

radioactive a radiactivo,-a.

radish rábano m.

radius radio m.

raffle rifa f.

raft balsa f.

rag n (torn piece) harapo m; (for cleaning) trapo m; **rags** (clothes) trapos mpl.

rage 1 n (fury) cólera f. 2 vi (person) estar furioso,-a.

ragged a (clothes) hecho,-a jirones; (person) harapiento,-a.

raid 1 n (by police) redada f; (robbery etc) atraco m. 2 vt (police) hacer una redada (en); (rob) asaltar.

rail barra f; (railing) barandilla f; (on railroad) carril m; **by r.** (send sth) por ferrocarril; (travel) en tren; (car) vagón m.

railings npl verja f.

railroad ferrocarril m.

railroad station estación f de ferrocarril.

railroad track vía f férrea.

railway line vía f férrea.
rain 1 n lluvia f; **in the r.** bajo la lluvia. **2** vi llover; **it's raining** llueve.
rainbow arco m iris.
raincoat impermeable m.
rainy a lluvioso,-a.
raise 1 n aumento m (de sueldo). **2** vt levantar; (voice) subir; (increase) aumentar; (money, help) reunir; (issue, question) plantear; (crops, children) criar.
raisin pasa f.
rake 1 n (garden tool) rastrillo m. **2** vt (leaves) rastrillar.
rally (political) mitin m.
• **rally around** vi (help out) echar una mano.
ram 1 n (sheep) carnero m. **2** vt (drive into place) hincar; (crash into) chocar con.
ramble (walk) caminata f.
ramp rampa f.
ran pt of **run**.
ranch rancho m.
random 1 n **at r.** al azar. **2** a fortuito,-a; **r. selection** selección f hecha al azar.
range 1 n (of mountains) cordillera f; (of products) gama f; (of missile) alcance m; (stove) cocina f de carbón. **2** vi (extend) extenderse (**to** hasta); **prices r. from five to twenty dollars** los precios oscilan entre cinco y veinte dólares.
rank (position in army) graduación f; (in society) rango m; (taxi) **r.** parada f de taxis.
ransom rescate m.
rape 1 n violación f. **2** vt violar.
rapid a rápido,-a.
rapidly adv rápidamente.
rapist violador,-a mf.
rare a poco común; (steak) poco hecho,-a.
rarely adv raras veces.
rascal granuja mf.
rash[1] (on skin) sarpullido m.
rash[2] a (reckless) impetuoso,-a; (words, actions) precipitado,-a.
rashly adv a la ligera.
raspberry frambuesa f.

rat rata f.
rate 1 n tasa f; **at any r.** (anyway) en cualquier caso; (of interest, exchange) tipo m; **at the r. of** (speed) a la velocidad de; (quantity) a razón de. **2** vt (estimate) estimar; (evaluate) tasar; (consider) considerar.
rather adv (quite) más bien, bastante; (more accurately) mejor dicho; **r. than** (instead of) en vez de; (more than) más que; **she would r. stay here** prefiere quedarse aquí.
ratio razón f.
ration 1 n (allowance) ración f; **rations** víveres mpl. **2** vt racionar.
rational a racional.
rationing racionamiento m.
rattle 1 n (toy) sonajero m; (instrument) carraca f. **2** vt (keys etc) hacer sonar. **3** vi sonar; (metal) repiquetear; (glass) tintinear; (window, shelves) vibrar.
ravenous a **I'm r.** tengo un hambre que no veo.
raw a (uncooked) crudo,-a; **r. material** materia prima; **r. flesh** carne viva.
ray rayo m.
razor (for shaving) maquinilla f de afeitar.
razor blade hoja f de afeitar.
reach 1 vt (arrive at) llegar a; (contact) localizar. **2** vi alcanzar. **3** n (range) alcance m; **out of r.** fuera del alcance; **within r.** al alcance.
• **reach out** vi (with hand) extender la mano.
react vi reaccionar.
reaction reacción f.
reactor reactor m.
read* vt leer; (decipher) descifrar.
• **read about** vt leer.
• **read out** vt leer en voz alta.
• **read up on** vt estudiar.
reader lector,-a mf; (book) libro m de lectura.
readily adv (easily) fácilmente; (willingly) de buena gana.
reading lectura f; fig interpretación f.
ready a (prepared) listo,-a; (will-

ing) dispuesto,-a; **r. to** (*about to*) a punto de; **r. cash** dinero *m* en efectivo.

ready-cooked *a* precocinado,-a.

ready-made *a* confeccionado,-a; (*food*) preparado,-a.

real *a* verdadero,-a; (*genuine*) auténtico,-a.

real estate bienes *mpl* inmuebles.

real estate agent agente *m* inmobiliario.

realistic *a* realista.

reality realidad *f.*

realize *vt* (*become aware of*) darse cuenta de; **don't you r. that . . . ?** ¿no te das cuenta de que . . . ?

really *adv* (*truly*) verdaderamente; **r.?** ¿de veras?

rear¹ **1** *n* (*back part*) parte *f* de atrás. **2** *a* trasero,-a; **r. entrance** puerta *f* de atrás.

rear² **1** *vt* (*breed, raise*) criar. **2** *vi* **to r. up** (*horse*) encabritarse.

rearrange *vt* (*furniture*) colocar de otra manera; (*set new date*) fijar otra fecha para.

reason **1** *n* motivo *m*; **for no r.** sin razón. **2** *vi* (*argue, work out*) razonar.

reasonable *a* (*fair*) razonable; (*sensible*) sensato,-a.

reasonably *adv* (*fairly, quite*) bastante.

reasoning razonamiento *m.*

reassure *vt* (*comfort*) tranquilizar; (*restore confidence in*) dar confianza a.

reassuring *a* consolador,-a.

rebel **1** *a & n* rebelde (*mf*). **2** *vi* rebelarse (**against** contra).

rebellion rebelión *f.*

rebound **1** *n* (*of ball*) rebote *m.* **2** *vi* (*ball*) rebotar.

rebuild *vt* reconstruir.

recall *vt* (*remember*) recordar.

receipt (*paper*) recibo *m*; **receipts** (*takings*) recaudación *f sing.*

receive *vt* recibir.

receiver (*of phone*) auricular *m*; (*radio*) receptor *m.*

recent *a* reciente; **in r. years** en los últimos años.

recently *adv* recientemente.

reception (*party, of TV pictures etc*) recepción *f*; (*welcome*) acogida *f*; **r. (desk)** recepción *f.*

receptionist recepcionista *mf.*

recharge *vt* (*battery*) recargar.

recipe receta *f.*

recite *vti* recitar.

reckless *a* (*unwise*) imprudente.

reckon *vt* (*calculate*) calcular; *fam* (*think*) creer.

• **reckon on** *vt* contar con.

• **reckon with** *vt* (*take into account*) contar con.

reclaim *vt* (*recover*) recuperar; (*demand back*) reclamar; (*marshland etc*) convertir.

recognize *vt* reconocer.

recollect *vt* recordar.

recollection recuerdo *m.*

recommend *vt* recomendar.

recommendation recomendación *f.*

record **1** *n* (*of music etc*) disco *m*; (*in sport etc*) récord *m*; (*document*) documento *m*; (*case history*) historial médico; **public records** archivos *mpl.* **2** *vt* (*relate*) hacer constar; (*note down*) apuntar; (*record, voice*) grabar.

recorder (*musical instrument*) flauta *f*; **(tape) r.** magnetófono *m*; **(video) r.** vídeo *m.*

recording grabación *f.*

record player tocadiscos *m inv.*

recover **1** *vt* (*items, time*) recuperar; (*consciousness*) recobrar. **2** *vi* (*from illness etc*) reponerse; (*economy*) recuperarse.

recruit recluta *m.*

rectangle rectángulo *m.*

rectangular *a* rectangular.

recycle *vt* reciclar.

red **1** *a* rojo,-a; **r. light** semáforo en rojo; **r. wine** vino tinto; **to go r.** ponerse colorado,-a; **to have r. hair** ser pelirrojo,-a. **2** *n* (*color*) rojo *m*; **to be in the r.** estar en números rojos.

red-handed *a* **to catch sb r.** coger a algn con las manos en la masa.

redhead pelirrojo,-a *mf.*

red-hot *a* al rojo vivo.

redirect vt (forward) remitir a la nueva dirección.

redo* vt (exercise, house) rehacer.

reduce vt reducir.

reduction (decrease) reducción f; (cut in price) descuento m.

redundancy despido m.

redundant a to be made r. perder el empleo; to make sb r. despedir a algn.

reed (plant) caña f.

reef arrecife m.

reel (spool) bobina f, carrete m.

refectory refectorio m.

refer 1 vt to r. a matter to a tribunal remitir un asunto a un tribunal. 2 vi (allude) referirse (to a).

referee 1 n árbitro,-a mf. 2 vt arbitrar.

reference referencia f; (character report) informe m; with r. to referente a, con referencia a.

refill 1 n (replacement) recambio m; (another drink) otra copa f. 2 vt rellenar.

reflect 1 vt (light, attitude) reflejar; to be reflected reflejarse. 2 vi (think) reflexionar.

reflection (indication, mirror image) reflejo m.

reflex reflejo m.

reform 1 n reforma f. 2 vt reformar.

refrain vi abstenerse (from de).

refresh vt refrescar.

refresher course cursillo m de reciclaje.

refreshing a refrescante.

refreshment refresco m.

refrigerator nevera f.

refuge refugio m; to take r. refugiarse.

refugee refugiado,-a mf.

refund 1 n reembolso m. 2 vt reembolsar.

refusal negativa f.

refuse 1 vt (reject) rechazar; to r. sb sth negar algo a algn; to r. to do sth negarse a hacer algo. 2 vi negarse.

regain vt recuperar.

regard 1 n (concern) consideración f; with r. to, as regards (con) respecto a; give him my regards dale

recuerdos de mi parte. 2 vt (consider) considerar.

regarding prep (con) respecto a.

regardless 1 prep r. of a pesar de; r. of the outcome pase lo que pase. 2 adv a toda costa.

regiment regimiento m.

region región f, zona f; in the r. of aproximadamente.

regional a regional.

register 1 n registro m. 2 vt (record) registrar; (letter) certificar. 3 vi (enter one's name) inscribirse; (at univeristy) matricularse.

registration inscripción f; (at university) matrícula f.

regret 1 n (remorse) remordimiento m; (sadness) pesar m. 2 vt arrepentirse de, lamentar.

regular 1 a regular; (usual) normal; (frequent) frecuente.

regularly adv con regularidad.

regulation 1 n (control) regulación f; (rule) regla f. 2 a reglamentario,-a.

rehearsal ensayo m.

rehearse vti ensayar.

reign 1 n reinado m. 2 vi reinar.

reins (for horse) riendas fpl.

reindeer reno m.

reinforce vt (strengthen) reforzar.

reinforcements npl refuerzos mpl.

reinstate vt (to job) reincorporar.

reject vt rechazar.

rejection rechazo m.

rejoice vi regocijarse (at, over de).

relate 1 vt (connect) relacionar; (tell) contar. 2 vi relacionarse (to con).

related a (linked) relacionado,-a (to con); to be r. to sb ser pariente de algn.

relation (link) relación f; (family) pariente,-a mf; in or with r. to (con) respecto a.

relationship (link) relación f; (between people) relaciones fpl.

relative 1 n pariente,-a mf. 2 a relativo,-a.

relatively adv relativamente.

relax 1 vi relajarse; **r.!** ¡cálmate! **2** vt (calm) relajar; (loosen) aflojar.
relaxation (rest) relajación f.
relaxed a relajado,-a.
release 1 n (setting free) liberación f; (of product) puesta f en venta; (of film) estreno m; (press release) comunicado m. **2** vt (set free) poner en libertad; (let go) soltar; (product, record) poner a la venta; (film) estrenar.
relevant a pertinente (**to** a); **it is not r.** no viene al caso.
reliable a (person) de fiar; (thing) fiable.
reliability (of person) formalidad f; (of thing) fiabilidad f.
relief alivio m; (aid) auxilio m; (in art, geography) relieve m.
relieve vt aliviar; (substitute) relevar.
religion religión f.
religious a religioso,-a.
relish (seasoning) condimento m.
reload vt (gun, camera) recargar.
reluctance desgana f.
reluctant a reacio,-a; **to be r. to do sth** estar poco dispuesto,-a a hacer algo.
reluctantly adv de mala gana.
• **rely on** vi confiar en.
remain vi (stay) permanecer, quedarse; (be left) quedar.
remaining a restante.
remark 1 n comentario m. **2** vt comentar.
remarkable a (extraordinary) extraordinario,-a.
remarkably adv extraordinariamente.
remedial a **r. classes** clases fpl para niños atrasados en los estudios.
remember 1 vt (recall) acordarse de. **2** vi acordarse.
remind vt recordar; **r. me to do it** recuérdame que lo haga.
reminder aviso m.
remorse remordimiento m.
remote a (far away) remoto,-a; (isolated) aislado,-a.

remote control mando m a distancia.
removal (moving house) mudanza f; (getting rid of) eliminación f.
removal man hombre m de la mudanza.
removal van camión m de mudanzas.
remove vt quitar.
renew vt (contract etc) renovar; (talks etc) reanudar.
rent 1 n (of building, car, TV) alquiler m. **2** vt alquilar.
• **rent out** vt alquilar.
rental (of house etc) alquiler m.
rental car coche m de alquiler.
reorganize vt reorganizar.
repair 1 n reparación f; **in good/ bad r.** en buen/mal estado. **2** vt arreglar; (car) reparar; (clothes) remendar.
repairman técnico m.
repay vt devolver; (debt) liquidar.
repayment pago m.
repeat 1 vt repetir. **2** n (repetition) repetición f; (on TV) reposición f.
repeated a repetido,-a.
repeatedly adv repetidas veces.
repel vt (fight off) repeler.
repetition repetición f.
repetitive a repetitivo,-a.
replace vt (put back) volver a poner en su sitio; (substitute) sustituir.
replacement (person) sustituto, -a mf; (part) pieza f de recambio.
replica réplica f.
reply 1 n respuesta f. **2** vi responder.
report 1 n informe m; (piece of news) noticia f; (in newspaper, on TV etc) reportaje m; (rumor) rumor m; **school r.** informe escolar. **2** vt (tell police, authorities about) denunciar; (journalist) hacer un reportaje sobre; **it is reported that . . .** se dice que . . . **3** vi (committee etc) hacer un informe; (journalist) hacer un reportaje; (to work etc) presentarse.

reported a r. speech estilo indirecto.

reportedly adv según se dice.

reporter periodista mf.

represent vt representar.

representative representante mf.

reptile reptil m.

republic república f.

reputable a (company etc) acreditado,-a; (person, products) de toda confianza.

reputation reputación f.

request 1 n petición f. 2 vt pedir.

require vt (need) necesitar; (demand) exigir.

required a necesario,-a.

rescue 1 n rescate m. 2 vt rescatar.

research 1 n investigación f. 2 vti investigar.

researcher investigador,-a mf.

resemblance semejanza f.

resemble vt parecerse a.

reservation reserva f.

reserve 1 n reserva f; (in sport) suplente mf; **to keep sth in r.** guardar algo de reserva. 2 vt reservar.

reserved a reservado,-a.

residence (home) residencia f; (address) domicilio m.

resident a & n residente (mf).

residential a residencial.

resign 1 vt **to r. oneself to sth** resignarse a algo. 2 vi dimitir.

resignation (from a job) dimisión f.

resist vt (not yield to) resistir; (oppose) oponerse a; **I couldn't r. telling her** no pude resistir a la tentación de decírselo.

resistance resistencia f.

resit vt (in exam) volver a presentarse a.

resort (recourse) recurso m; (place) lugar m de vacaciones; **as a last r.** como último recurso; **tourist r.** centro m turístico.

• **resort to** vt recurrir a.

resource recurso m.

respect 1 n (reference) respeto m; **in that r.** a ese respecto; **with r. to** con referencia a. 2 vt respetar.

respectable a respetable; (clothes) decente.

respond vi responder (to a).

response (reply) respuesta f; (reaction) reacción f.

responsibility responsabilidad f.

responsible a responsable (for de).

rest¹ 1 n (break) descanso m; (peace) tranquilidad f. 2 vt (lean) apoyar. 3 vi descansar.

rest² the r. (remainder) el resto; **the r. of the day** el resto del día; **the r. of the girls** las demás chicas.

restaurant restaurante m.

restful a relajante.

restless a inquieto,-a.

restore vt (give back) devolver; (repair) restaurar.

restrict vt restringir.

restricted a restringido,-a.

restricted area zona f restringida.

restriction restricción f.

restroom aseos mpl.

result resultado m; **as a r. of** como consecuencia de.

resume 1 vt (journey, work, conversation) reanudar; (control) reasumir. 2 vi recomenzar.

résumé resumen m.

retail 1 n r. price precio m de venta al público. 2 vt vender al por menor. 3 adv al por menor.

retailer detallista mf.

retain vt conservar.

retire vi (stop working) jubilarse; (withdraw) retirarse; **to r. for the night** irse a la cama.

retired a jubilado,-a.

retirement jubilación f.

return 1 n (coming or going back) regreso m; (giving back) devolución f; (profit) beneficio m; **r. ticket** billete m de ida y vuelta. 2 vt (give back) devolver. 3 vi (come or go back) regresar.

returnable a (bottle) retornable.

reveal vt (make known) revelar; (show) dejar ver.

revenge venganza *f*; **to take r. on sb for sth** vengarse de algo en algn.

reverse 1 *a* inverso,-a. 2 *n* **quite the r.** todo lo contrario; **r.** (*gear*) marcha *f* atrás. 3 *vt* **to r. the charges** poner una conferencia a cobro revertido. 4 *vi* (*in car*) dar marcha atrás; **to r. in/out** entrar/ salir marcha atrás.

review 1 *n* (*in press*) crítica *f*. 2 *vt* (*book etc*) hacer una crítica de.

revise *vt* (*look over*) revisar; (*at school*) repasar.

revision revisión *f*; (*at school*) repaso *m*.

revive 1 *vt* (*sick person*) reanimar. 2 *vi* (*interest, hopes*) renacer; (*sick person*) volver en sí.

revolt rebelión *f*.

revolting *a* repugnante.

revolution revolución *f*.

revolutionary *a* & *n* revolucionario,-a (*mf*).

revolve *vi* girar; *fig* **to r. around** girar en torno a.

revolver revólver *m*.

revolving *a* giratorio,-a.

revolving door puerta *f* giratoria.

reward 1 *n* recompensa *f*. 2 *vt* recompensar.

rewind* 1 *vt* (*tape*) rebobinar. 2 *vi* rebobinarse.

rheumatism reúma *m*.

rhinoceros rinoceronte *m*.

rhubarb ruibarbo *m*.

rhyme 1 *n* rima *f*; (*poem*) poema *m*. 2 *vi* rimar.

rhythm ritmo *m*.

rib costilla *f*.

ribbon cinta *f*; (*in hair etc*) lazo *m*.

rice arroz *m*.

rich 1 *a* rico,-a. 2 *npl* **the r.** los ricos.

riches *npl* riquezas *fpl*.

rid *vt* **to get r. of sth** deshacerse de algo.

riddle (*puzzle*) adivinanza *f*; (*mystery*) enigma *m*.

ride 1 *n* paseo *m*; **a short bus r.** un corto trayecto en autobús; **horse r.** paseo a caballo. 2 *vt** (*bicycle, horse*) montar en; **can you r. a bike?** ¿sabes montar en bici? 3 *vi** (*on horse*) montar a caballo; (*travel*) (*on bus, train etc*) viajar.

rider (*of horse*) (*man*) jinete *m*, (*woman*) amazona *f*; (*of bicycle*) ciclista *mf*; (*of motorbike*) motociclista *mf*.

ridiculous *a* ridículo,-a.

riding equitación *f*.

rifle rifle *m*.

rig (oil) **r.** (*onshore*) torre *f* de perforación; (*offshore*) plataforma *f* petrolífera.

right 1 *a* (*not left*) derecho,-a; (*correct*) correcto,-a; (*suitable*) adecuado,-a; (*proper*) apropiado,-a; (*exact*) (*time*) exacto,-a; **all r.** de acuerdo; **r.?** ¿vale?; **that's r.** eso es; **isn't that r.?** ¿no es verdad?; **the r. word** la palabra justa; **to be r.** tener razón; **the r. time** (*appropriate time*) el momento oportuno; **r. angle** ángulo recto. 2 *n* (*right side*) derecha *f*; (*right hand*) mano *f* derecha; (*in politics*) **the R.** la derecha; (*lawful claim*) derecho *m*; **r. and wrong** el bien y el mal. 3 *adv* (*correctly*) bien; (*to the right*) a la derecha; **r. away** en seguida; **to turn r.** girar a la derecha; **go r. on** sigue recto; **r. at the top** en todo lo alto; **r. in the middle** justo en medio; **r. to the end** hasta el final.

right hand *a* derecho,-a.

right-handed *a* (*person*) que usa la mano derecha, diestro, -a.

rightly *adv* debidamente; **and r. so** y con razón.

rigid *a* rígido,-a.

rim (*edge*) borde *m*.

rind (*of fruit, cheese*) corteza *f*.

ring¹ 1 *n* (*of doorbell, alarm clock*) timbre *m*; (*of phone*) llamada *f*. 2 *vt** (*bell*) tocar; (*on phone*) llamar por teléfono. 3 *vi** (*bell, phone etc*) sonar.

ring² 1 *n* sortija *f*; (*wedding ring*) anillo *m*; (*metal hoop*) aro *m*; (*circle*) círculo *m*; (*group of people*) corro *m*; (*in boxing*) cuadrilátero *m*; (*for bullfights*) ruedo *m*. 2 *vt* (*surround*) rodear.

• ring out *vi* (*bell etc*) resonar.

rinse vt aclarar; (the dishes) enjuagar.
• **rinse out** vt enjuagar.
riot 1 n disturbio m; **r. police** policía f antidisturbios. **2** vi amotinarse.
rip 1 n (tear) rasgón m. **2** vt rasgar. **3** vi rasgarse.
• **rip off** vt fam **to r. sb off** timar a algn.
• **rip up** vt hacer pedacitos.
ripe a maduro,-a.
ripen vti madurar.
rip-off fam timo m.
rise 1 n (of slope, hill) cuesta f; (in prices, temperature) subida f; (of wages) aumento m; **to give r. to** ocasionar. **2** vi* (prices, temperature) subir; (wages) aumentar; (from bed) levantarse; (stand up) levantarse; (city, building) erguirse.
• **rise by** vi (years) pasar.
risk 1 n riesgo m; **at r.** en peligro; **to take risks** arriesgarse. **2** vt arriesgar; **I'll r. it** correré el riesgo.
risky a arriesgado,-a.
rival 1 a & n rival (mf). **2** vt rivalizar con.
river río m.
road carretera f; (street) calle f; (way) camino m; (accident) accidente m de tráfico; **r. safety** seguridad f vial.
roadside borde m de la carretera.
roadway calzada f.
roadworks npl obras fpl.
roam 1 vt vagar por. **2** vi vagar.
roar 1 n (of lion) rugido m; (of bull, sea, wind) bramido m. **2** vi (lion, crowd) rugir; (bull, sea, wind) bramar.
roast 1 a (meat) asado,-a; **r. beef** rosbif m. **2** n asado m. **3** vt (meat) asar; (coffee, nuts) tostar. **4** vi asarse.
rob vt robar; (bank) atracar.
robber ladrón,-a mf; **bank r.** atracador,-a mf.
robbery robo m.
robe (ceremonial) toga f; bata f.
robin petirrojo m.

robot robot m.
rock 1 n roca f; (stone) piedra f; (music) música f rock. **2** vt (chair) mecer; (baby) acunar; (shake) sacudir. **3** vi (move back and forth) mecerse; (shake) vibrar.
rocket 1 n cohete m. **2** vi (prices) dispararse.
rocking chair mecedora f.
rod (of metal) barra f; (stick) vara f; **fishing r.** caña f de pescar.
rogue granuja m.
role, rôle papel m; **to play a r.** desempeñar un papel.
roll 1 n rollo m; (bread) **r.** bollo m; (of drum) redoble m. **2** vt hacer rodar. **3** vi (ball) rodar; (animal) revolcarse.
• **roll by** vi (years) pasar.
• **roll down** vt (blinds) bajar; (sleeves) bajarse; (hill) bajar rodando.
• **roll over** vi dar una vuelta.
• **roll up** vt (paper etc) enrollar; (blinds) subir; **to r. up one's sleeves** (ar)remangarse.
roller rodillo m; **rollers** (for hair) rulos mpl.
roller skate patín m de ruedas.
rolling pin rodillo m (de cocina).
rolling stock material m rodante.
Roman a & n romano,-a (mf).
Roman Catholic a & n católico,-a (mf) (romano,-a).
romance (love affair) aventura f amorosa.
romantic a & n romántico,-a (mf).
roof tejado m; (of car) techo m.
roof rack baca f.
room habitación f; (space) espacio m; **single r.** habitación individual; **make r. for me** hazme sitio.
roommate compañero,-a mf de habitación.
roomy a amplio,-a.
root raíz f; **to take r.** echar raíces.
• **root for** vt **to r. for a team** animar a un equipo.
• **root out** or **up** vt arrancar de raíz.
rope (small) cuerda f; (big) soga f.

• **rope off** *vt* acordonar.

rose rosa *f*; **r. bush** rosal *m*.

rot *vi* pudrirse.

rotten *a* (*decayed*) podrido,-a; *fam* (*very bad*) malísimo,-a; (*health*) enfermo,-a; **I feel r.** me encuentro fatal.

rough *a* (*surface, skin*) áspero,-a; (*terrain*) accidentado,-a; (*road*) desigual; (*sea*) agitado,-a; (*rude*) grosero,-a; (*violent*) violento, -a; (*approximate*) aproximado,-a; (*plan etc*) preliminar; **r. draft** borrador *m*; **r. sketch** esbozo *m*.

roughly *adv* (*crudely*) toscamente; (*not gently*) bruscamente; (*approximately*) aproximadamente.

round 1 *a* redondo,-a. **2** *n* (*of drinks*) ronda *f*; (*at golf*) partido *m*; (*at cards*) partida *f*; (*in boxing*) round *m*; (*in a competition*) eliminatoria *f*; **rounds** (*doctor's*) visita *f* sing. **3** *adv* **all year r.** durante todo el año; **to invite sb r.** invitar a algn a casa. **4** *prep* (*place etc*) alrededor de; **r. here** por aquí; **r. the corner** a la vuelta de la esquina.

• **round up** *vt* (*cattle*) acorralar; (*people*) reunir.

roundabout 1 *n* (*merry-go-round*) tiovivo *m*; (*on road*) glorieta *f*. **2** *a* indirecto,-a.

round trip viaje *m* de ida y vuelta.

route ruta *f*; (*of bus*) línea *f*.

routine rutina *f*.

row¹ fila *f*; **three times in a r.** tres veces seguidas.

row² *vi* (*in a boat*) remar.

row³ **1** *n* (*quarrel*) bronca *f*; (*noise*) jaleo *m*. **2** *vi* pelearse.

rowboat bote *m* de remos.

royal *a* real. **2** *npl* **the Royals** los miembros de la Familia Real.

royalty (*royal persons*) miembro(s) *m(pl)* de la Familia Real; **royalties** derechos *mpl* de autor.

rub 1 *vt* frotar; (*hard*) restregar; (*massage*) friccionar. **2** *vi* rozar (*against* contra).

• **rub down** *vt* frotar; (*horse*) almohazar; (*surface*) raspar.

• **rub in** *vt* (*cream etc*) frotar con.

• **rub off** *vt* (*erase*) borrar.

• **rub out** *vt* borrar.

rubber (*substance*) caucho *m*; (*eraser*) goma *f* (de borrar).

rubble escombros *mpl*.

ruby rubí *m*.

rucksack mochila *f*.

rudder timón *m*.

rude *a* (*impolite*) maleducado,-a; (*foul-mouthed*) grosero,-a.

rudeness (*impoliteness*) falta *f* de educación; (*offensiveness*) grosería *f*.

rug alfombra *f*.

rugby rugby *m*.

ruin 1 *n* ruina *f*; **in ruins** en ruinas. **2** *vt* arruinar; (*spoil*) estropear.

rule 1 *n* regla *f*; (*of monarch*) reinado *m*; **as a r.** por regla general. **2** *vti* (*govern*) gobernar; (*monarch*) reinar.

• **rule out** *vt* descartar.

ruler (*monarch*) soberano,-a *mf*; (*for measuring*) regla *f*.

rum ron *m*.

Rumanian 1 *a* rumano,-a. **2** *n* (*person*) rumano,-a *mf*; (*language*) rumano *m*.

rummage sale mercadillo *m* de caridad.

rumor rumor *m*.

run 1 *n* (*act of running, in stocking*) carrera *f*; (*trip*) vuelta *f*; **on the r.** fugado,-a; **to go for a r.** hacer footing; (*in car*) dar un paseo; **in the long r.** a largo plazo; **ski r.** pista *f* de esquí. **2** *vt** correr; (*business*) llevar; (*company*) dirigir; (*organize*) organizar; **to r. errands** hacer recados; **to r. a program** pasar un programa. **3** *vi** (*person, river*) correr; (*color*) desteñirse; (*operate*) funcionar; (*film, play*) estar en cartel; **your nose is running** tienes catarro; **trains r. every two hours** hay trenes cada dos horas; **we're running low on milk** nos queda poca leche.

• **run across** *vt* (*meet*) tropezar con.

- **run away** *vi* fugarse.
- **run down** *vt* (*stairs*) bajar corriendo; (*knock down*) atropellar.
- **run in** *vi* entrar corriendo.
- **run into** *vt* (*room etc*) entrar corriendo en; (*people, problems*) tropezar con; (*crash into*) chocar contra.
- **run off** *vi* escaparse.
- **run out** *vi* (*exit*) salir corriendo; (*finish*) agotarse; (*contract*) vencer; **to r. out of** quedarse sin.
- **run over** *vt* (*knock down*) atropellar.

runaway *a* (*vehicle*) incontrolado, -a; (*inflation*) galopante; (*success*) clamoroso,-a.

rung (*of ladder*) peldaño *m*.

runner corredor,-a *mf*.

runner-up subcampeón,-ona *mf*.

running 1 *n* atletismo *m*; (*management*) dirección *f*. **2 a r. water** agua *f* corriente; **three weeks r.** tres semanas seguidas.

runny *a* (*nose*) que moquea.

runway pista *f* (de aterrizaje y despegue).

rush 1 *n* (*hurry*) prisa *f*; (*hustle and bustle*) ajetreo *m*; **there's no r.** no corre prisa. **2** *vt* (*go hastily*) hacer de prisa; **to r. sb to hospital** llevar a algn urgentemente al hospital. **3** *vi* (*go quickly*) precipitarse.

- **rush around** *vi* correr de un lado a otro.
- **rush off** *vi* irse corriendo.

rush hour hora *f* punta.

Russian 1 *a* ruso,-a. **2** *n* (*person*) ruso,-a *mf*; (*language*) ruso *m*.

rust 1 *n* herrumbre *f*. **2** *vi* oxidarse.

rusty *a* oxidado,-a.

rye centeno *m*; **r. bread** pan *m* de centeno.

S

sack 1 *n* (*bag*) saco *m*. **2** *vt* (*employee*) despedir a.

sacrifice 1 *n* sacrificio *m*. **2** *vt* sacrificar.

sad *a* triste.

sadden *vt* entristecer.

saddle *n* (*for horse*) silla *f* (de montar).

sadly *adv* tristemente.

sadness tristeza *f*.

safe 1 *a* (*unharmed*) ileso,-a; (*out of danger*) a salvo; (*not dangerous*) inocuo,-a; (*secure, sure*) seguro,-a; **s. and sound** sano,-a y salvo,-a. **2** *n* (*for money etc*) caja *f* fuerte.

safely *adv* con toda seguridad; **to arrive s.** llegar sin accidentes.

safety seguridad *f*.

safety belt cinturón *m* de seguridad.

safety pin imperdible *m*.

sag *vi* (*roof*) hundirse.

said 1 *pt & pp of* **say**. **2** *a* dicho,-a.

sail 1 *n* (*canvas*) vela *f*; (*trip*) paseo *m* en barco; **to set s.** zarpar. **2** *vt* (*ship*) gobernar. **3** *vi* ir en barco; (*set sail*) zarpar.

sailboard tabla *f* de windsurf.

sailboat barco *m* de vela.

sailing navegación *f*; (*yachting*) vela *f*.

sailor marinero *m*.

saint *n* santo,-a *mf*; (*before all masculine names except those beginning* **Do** *or* **To**) San; (*before feminine names*) Santa.

sake *n* **for the s. of** por (el bien de); **for your own s.** por tu propio bien.

salad ensalada *f*.

salad bowl ensaladera *f*.

salad dressing aliño *m*.

salary salario *m*.

sale venta *f*; (*at low prices*) rebajas *fpl*; **for** *or* **on s.** en venta.

sale price *a* (*article*) a precio rebajado.

salesclerk dependiente,-a *mf*.

salesman vendedor *m*; (*in shop*) dependiente *m*; (*commercial representative*) representante *m*.

saleswoman vendedora *f*; (*in shop*) dependienta *f*; (*commercial representative*) representante *f*.

saliva saliva *f*.

salmon salmón *m*.

salt 1 *n* sal *f*; **bath salts** sales de baño. **2** *vt* (*add salt to*) echar sal a.
salt cellar salero *m*.
salty *a* salado,-a.
same 1 *a* mismo,-a; **at the s. time** al mismo tiempo; **the two cars are the s.** los dos coches son iguales. **2** *pron* el mismo, la misma, lo mismo; **all the s., just the s.** aun así; **it's all the s. to me** (a mí) me da igual.
sample 1 *n* muestra *f*. **2** *vt* (*wines*) catar; (*dish*) probar.
sand arena *f*.
sandal sandalia *f*.
sand castle castillo *m* de arena.
sandpaper papel *m* de lija.
sandwich (*roll*) bocadillo *m*; (*sliced bread*) sandwich *m*.
sandy *a* (*earth, beach*) arenoso,-a; (*hair*) rubio rojizo.
sanitary s. napkin compresa *f*.
Santa Claus Papá Noel *m*.
sardine sardina *f*.
sat *pt* & *pp* of **sit**.
satchel cartera *f* (de colegial).
satellite satélite *m*; **s. dish** antena *f* parabólica.
satin satén *m*.
satisfaction satisfacción *f*.
satisfactory *a* satisfactorio,-a.
satisfy *vt* satisfacer; (*fulfill*) cumplir con.
satisfying *a* satisfactorio,-a.
saturate *vt* saturar (**with** de).
Saturday sábado *m*.
sauce salsa *f*.
saucepan cacerola *f*; (*large*) olla *f*.
saucer platillo *m*.
Saudi Arabian *a* & *n* saudita (*mf*), saudí (*m*).
sauna sauna *f*.
sausage (*frankfurter*) salchicha *f*; (*cured*) salchichón *m*; (*spicy*) chorizo *m*.
save 1 *vt* (*rescue*) rescatar; (*put by, computer file*) guardar; (*money*) ahorrar; (*food*) almacenar; **it saved him a lot of trouble** le evitó muchos problemas. **2** *n* (*in soccer*) parada *f*.

savings *npl* ahorros *mpl*.
savings account cuenta *f* de ahorros.
savings bank caja *f* de ahorros.
saw[1] **1** *n* (*tool*) sierra *f*. **2** *vti** serrar.
• **saw off** *vt* serrar.
saw[2] *pt* see.
saxophone saxofón *m*.
say* *vt* decir; **it is said that . . .** se dice que . . . ; **that is to s.** es decir; **what does the sign s.?** ¿qué pone en el letrero?; **shall we s. Friday then?** ¿quedamos el viernes, pues?
saying refrán *m*.
scab (*on cut*) costra *f*.
scaffolding andamio *m*.
scald *vt* escaldar.
scale[1] (*of fish, on skin*) escama *f*; (*in boiler*) incrustaciones *fpl*.
scale[2] escala *f*; (*extent*) alcance *m*.
scales *npl* (**pair of**) **s.** (*shop, kitchen*) balanza *f sing*; (*bathroom*) báscula *f sing*.
scan (*text, graphics*) escanear.
scandal escándalo *m*; (*gossip*) chismes *mpl*.
Scandinavian *a* & *n* escandinavo,-a (*mf*).
scanner escáner *m*.
scar cicatriz *f*.
scarce *a* escaso,-a.
scarcely *adv* apenas.
scarcity escasez *f*.
scare *vt* asustar.
• **scare away** or **off** *vt* ahuyentar.
scarecrow espantapájaros *m inv*.
scarf (*pl* **scarves** or **scarfs**) (*long, woolen*) bufanda *f*; (*square*) pañuelo *m*.
scarlet *a* **s. fever** escarlatina *f*.
scary *a* espantoso,-a; (*film*) de terror.
scatter 1 *vt* (*papers etc*) esparcir; (*disperse*) dispersar. **2** *vi* dispersarse.
scene (*in theater etc*) escena *f*; (*place*) lugar *m*; **to make a s.** (*fuss*) montar un espectáculo.
scenery (*landscape*) paisaje *m*; (*in theater*) decorado *m*.

scent (*smell*) olor *m*; (*perfume*) perfume *m*.

schedule 1 *n* (*plan, agenda*) programa *m*; (*timetable*) horario *m*; **on s.** a la hora (prevista); **to be behind s.** llevar retraso. 2 *vt* (*plan*) programar.

scheduled *a* previsto,-a; **s. flight** vuelo *m* regular.

scheme (*plan*) plan *m*; (*project*) proyecto *m*; (*trick*) ardid *m*.

scholarship (*grant*) beca *f*.

school (*primary*) escuela *f*; (*secondary*) colegio *m*; (*university*) universidad *f*; **s. year** año *m* escolar.

schoolboy alumno *m*.

schoolgirl alumna *f*.

schoolmate compañero,-a *mf* de clase.

schoolteacher profesor,-a *mf*; (*primary school*) maestro,-a *mf*.

science ciencia *f*; (*school subject*) ciencias *fpl*.

science fiction ciencia-ficción *f*.

scientific *a* científico,-a.

scientist científico,-a *mf*.

scissors *npl* tijeras *fpl*.

scold *vt* regañar, reñir.

scone bollo *m*.

scoop (*in press*) exclusiva *f*.

scooter (*child's*) patinete *m*; (*adult's*) Vespa® *f*.

scope (*range*) alcance *m*; (*freedom*) libertad *f*.

scorch *vt* (*burn*) quemar; (*singe*) chamuscar.

score 1 (*in sport*) tanteo *m*; (*cards, golf*) puntuación *f*; (*result*) resultado *m*; (*twenty*) veintena *f*; (*music*) partitura *f*. 2 *vt* (*goal*) marcar; (*points*) conseguir. 3 *vi* (*in sport*) marcar un tanto; (*soccer*) marcar un gol; (*keep the score*) llevar el marcador.

scorn desprecio *m*.

Scot escocés,-esa *mf*.

Scotch 1 *a* **S. tape**® cinta *f* adhesiva, celo® *m*. 2 *n* (*whiskey*) whisky *m* escocés.

Scots *a* escocés,-esa.

Scotsman escocés *m*.

Scotswoman escocesa *f*.

scoundrel canalla *m*.

scout boy **s.** boy *m* scout; (*talent*) **s.** cazatalentos *m inv*.

scramble *vt* **scrambled eggs** huevos *mpl* revueltos.

scrap¹ 1 *n* (*small piece*) pedazo *m*; **scraps** (*of food*) sobras *fpl*. 2 *vt* (*discard*) desechar; (*idea*) descartar.

scrap² 1 *n* (*fight*) pelea *f*. 2 *vi* pelearse (**with** con).

scrapbook álbum *m* de recortes.

scrape 1 *vt* (*paint, wood*) raspar; (*graze*) arañarse. 2 *vi* (*rub*) rozar. 3 *n* (*trouble*) lío *m*.

• **scrape through** *vti* (*exam*) aprobar por los pelos.

scrap metal chatarra *f*.

scrap paper papel *m* de borrador.

scratch 1 *n* (*on skin, paintwork*) arañazo *m*; **to be up to s.** dar la talla; **to start from s.** partir de cero. 2 *vt* (*with nail, claw*) arañar; (*paintwork*) rayar; (*to relieve itching*) rascarse.

scream 1 *n* chillido *m*. 2 *vt* (*insults etc*) gritar. 3 *vi* **to s. at sb** chillar a algn.

screen (*movable partition*) biombo *m*; (*cinema, TV, computer*) pantalla *f*.

screw 1 *n* tornillo *m*. 2 *vt* atornillar; **to s. sth down** *or* **in** *or* **on** fijar algo con tornillos.

screwdriver destornillador *m*.

scribble *vt* (*message etc*) garabatear.

script (*of film*) guión *m*; (*in exam*) examen *m*.

scrub *vt* frotar.

scrub brush estregadera *f*.

scrum (*in rugby*) melée *f*; **s. half** medio *m* melée.

scuba diving submarinismo *m*.

sculptor escultor *m*.

sculpture escultura *f*.

sea mar *mf*; **by the s.** a orillas del mar; **out at s.** en alta mar; **to go by s.** ir en barco.

seafood mariscos *mpl*.

seafront paseo *m* marítimo.

seagull gaviota *f*.

seal¹ (*animal*) foca *f*.

seal² **1** *n* (*official stamp*) sello *m*; (*airtight closure*) cierre *m* hermético. **2** *vt* (*with official stamp*) sellar; (*with wax*) lacrar; (*close*) cerrar.

• **seal off** *vt* (*area*) acordonar.

seam (*in cloth*) costura *f*.

search **1** *vt* (*files etc*) buscar en; (*building, suitcase*) registrar; (*person*) cachear. **2** *vi* buscar; **to s. through** registrar. **3** *n* búsqueda *f*; (*of building etc*) registro *m*; (*of person*) cacheo *m*; **in s. of** en busca de.

seashell concha *f* marina.

seashore (*beach*) playa *f*.

seasick *a* **to get s.** marearse.

seasickness mareo *m*.

seaside playa *f*.

season¹ (*of year*) estación *f*; (*for sport etc*) temporada *f*; **high/low s.** temporada *f* alta/baja.

season² *vt* (*food*) sazonar.

seasoning condimento *m*.

season ticket abono *m*.

seat **1** *n* asiento *m*; (*place*) plaza *f*; (*in cinema, theater*) localidad *f*; (*in government*) escaño *m*; **to take a s.** sentarse. **2** *vt* (*guests etc*) sentar; (*accommodate*) tener cabida para.

seating asientos *mpl*.

seaweed alga *f* (marina).

second¹ **1** *a* segundo,-a; **every s. day** cada dos días. **2** *n* (*in series*) segundo,-a *mf*; (*gear*) segunda *f*; **the s. of October** el dos de octubre. **3** *adv* **to come s.** terminar en segundo lugar.

second² (*time*) segundo *m*.

secondary *a* secundario,-a.

second-class **1** *a* de segunda clase. **2** *adv* **to travel s.** viajar en segunda.

second hand *a* & *adv* de segunda mano.

secondly *adv* en segundo lugar.

secret *a* secreto,-a; **in s.** en secreto.

secretary secretario,-a *mf*.

section sección *f*.

secure **1** *a* seguro,-a; (*window, door*) bien cerrado,-a; (*ladder etc*) firme. **2** *vt* (*fix*) sujetar; (*window, door*) cerrar bien; (*obtain*) obtener.

securely *adv* (*firmly*) firmemente.

security seguridad *f*; (*financial guarantee*) fianza *f*.

sedation sedación *f*.

sedative *a* & *n* sedante (*m*).

see* *vti* ver; **let's s.** a ver; **s. you (later)/soon!** ¡hasta luego/pronto!; **to s. sb home** acompañar a algn a casa.

• **see about** *vt* (*deal with*) ocuparse de.

• **see off** *vt* (*say goodbye to*) despedirse de.

• **see out** *vt* (*show out*) acompañar hasta la puerta.

• **see to** *vt* (*deal with*) ocuparse de.

seed semilla *f*; (*of fruit*) pepita *f*.

seeing *conj* **s. that** dado que.

seek* **1** *vt* (*look for*) buscar; (*ask for*) solicitar. **2** *vi* buscar; **to s. to do sth** procurar hacer algo.

seem *vi* parecer; **I s. to remember his name was Colin** creo recordar que su nombre era Colin; **it seems to me that** me parece que; **so it seems** eso parece.

seesaw balancín *m*.

segment segmento *m*; (*of orange*) gajo *m*.

seize *vt* (*grab*) agarrar; **to s. an opportunity** aprovechar una ocasión; **to s. power** hacerse con el poder.

seldom *adv* rara vez, raramente.

select *vt* (*thing*) escoger; (*team*) seleccionar.

selection (*people or things chosen*) selección *f*; (*range*) surtido *m*.

self-assurance confianza *f* en uno mismo.

self-assured *a* seguro,-a de uno mismo,-a.

self-confidence confianza *f* en uno mismo,-a.

self-confident *a* seguro,-a de uno mismo,-a.

self-conscious *a* cohibido,-a.

self-control autocontrol *m*.

self-defense autodefensa f.
self-employed a (worker) autónomo,-a.
selfish a egoísta.
self-respect amor m propio.
self-service 1 n (in shop etc) autoservicio m. 2 a de autoservicio.
sell* 1 vt vender. 2 vi venderse.
• **sell out** vi 'sold out' (theater) 'agotadas las localidades'.
seller vendedor,-a mf.
semester semestre m.
semi- prefix semi-.
semicircle semicírculo m.
semicolon punto y coma m.
semiconductor semiconductor m.
semidetached casa f adosada.
semifinal semifinal f.
semolina sémola f.
senate senado m.
senator senador,-a mf.
send* 1 vt enviar; (cause to become) volver. 2 vi to s. for sb mandar llamar a algn.
• **send away** 1 vt (dismiss) despedir. 2 vi to s. away for sth escribir pidiendo algo.
• **send back** vt (goods etc) devolver.
• **send in** vt (application etc) mandar; (troops) enviar.
• **send off** vt (letter etc) enviar; (player) expulsar.
• **send on** vt (luggage) (ahead) facturar.
• **send out** vt (person) echar; (invitations) enviar.
• **send up** vt hacer subir; (make fun of) burlarse de.
sender remitente mf.
senior 1 a (in age) mayor; (in rank) superior; (with longer service) más antiguo,-a; **William Armstrong S.** William Armstrong padre. 2 n (at school) estudiante mf del último curso; **she's three years my s.** (in age) me lleva tres años.
sensation sensación f.
sensational a (marvelous) sensacional.
sense 1 n (faculty) sentido m; (of

word) significado m; (meaning) sentido m; **s. of direction/humor** sentido m de la orientación/del humor; **common s.** sentido m común; **it doesn't make s.** no tiene sentido; **to come to one's senses** recobrar el juicio. 2 vt sentir.
senseless a (absurd) absurdo,-a.
sensible a (wise) sensato,-a; (choice) acertado,-a; (clothes, shoes) práctico,-a.
sensitive a sensible; (touchy) susceptible; (skin) delicado,-a.
sentence 1 n frase f; (legal) sentencia f; **life s.** cadena f perpetua. 2 vt (judge) sentenciar.
separate 1 vt separar (from de). 2 vi separarse. 3 a separado,-a; (different) distinto,-a.
separately adv por separado.
September se(p)tiembre m.
sequence (order) orden m; (series) sucesión f.
sergeant sargento m; (of police) cabo m.
serial (on TV etc) serial m; (soap opera) telenovela f.
series inv serie f.
serious a serio,-a; (causing concern) grave; **I am s.** hablo en serio.
seriously adv (in earnest) en serio; (dangerously, severely) gravemente.
servant (domestic) criado,-a mf.
serve vt servir; (customer) atender; **it serves him right** bien merecido lo tiene.
• **serve out, serve up** vt servir.
server (for computers) servidor m.
service 1 n servicio m; (maintenance) mantenimiento m; **s. (charge) included** servicio incluido. 2 vt (car, machine) revisar.
service area área m de servicio.
service station estación f de servicio.
session sesión f.
set¹* 1 vt (put, place) poner, colocar; (time, price) fijar; (record) establecer; (mechanism etc) ajustar; **to s. one's watch** poner el reloj en hora; **to s. the table** poner la mesa;

to s. sb free poner en libertad a algn. **2** vi (sun, moon) ponerse; (jelly, jam) cuajar; **to s. to** (begin) ponerse a. **3** n (stage) (for film) plató m; (in theater) escenario m; (scenery) decorado m; **shampoo and s.** lavado y marcado m. **4** a (task, idea) fijo,-a; (date, time) señalado,-a; (ready) listo,-a; **s. phrase** frase f hecha; **to be s. on doing sth** estar empeñado,-a en hacer algo.

• **set about** vt (begin) empezar.

• **set aside** vt (time, money) reservar.

• **set back** vt (delay) retrasar.

• **set down** vt (luggage etc) dejar (en el suelo).

• **set off 1** vi (depart) salir. **2** vt (bomb) hacer estallar; (burglar alarm) hacer sonar.

• **set out 1** vi (depart) salir; **to s. out for . . .** partir hacia . . . ; **to s. out to do sth** proponerse hacer algo. **2** vt (arrange) disponer; (present) presentar.

• **set up 1** vt (tent, stall) montar; (business etc) establecer. **2** vi establecerse.

set² (series) serie f; (of golf clubs, keys etc) juego m; (of tools) estuche m; (of people) grupo m; (in math) conjunto m; (tennis) set m; **TV s.** televisor m; **chess s.** juego m de ajedrez.

setback revés m, contratiempo m.

settee sofá m.

setting (background) marco m.

settle 1 vt (decide on) acordar; (date, price) fijar; (of bill) pagar; (account) saldar. **2** vi (bird, insect) posarse; (put down roots) afincarse; **to s. into an armchair** acomodarse en un sillón.

• **settle down** vi (put down roots) instalarse; (marry) casarse; (child) calmarse; (situation) normalizarse.

• **settle with** vt (pay debt to) ajustar cuentas con.

settlement (agreement) acuerdo m; (colony) asentamiento m.

settler colono m.

seven a & n siete (m) inv.

seventeen a & n diecisiete (m) inv.

seventh a & n séptimo,-a (mf).

seventieth a & n septuagésimo,-a (mf).

seventy a & n setenta (m) inv; **in the seventies** en los (años) setenta.

several 1 a varios,-as. **2** pron algunos,-as.

severe a severo,-a; (climate, blow) duro,-a; (illness, loss) grave.

severity severidad f.

sew* vti coser.

• **sew on** vt coser.

• **sew up** vt (mend) remendar.

sewer alcantarilla f.

sewing costura f.

sewing machine máquina f de coser.

sex sexo m; **s. education** educación f sexual; **to have s. with sb** tener relaciones sexuales con algn.

sexual a sexual.

sexy a sexy.

sh! int ¡chitón!, ¡chh!

shabby a (garment) raído,-a; (unkempt) desaseado,-a.

shade (shadow) sombra f; (lampshade) pantalla f; (of color) matiz m; **in the s.** a la sombra.

shadow sombra f.

shady a (place) a la sombra.

shake* 1 vt sacudir; (bottle) agitar; **the news shook him** la noticia le conmocionó; **to s. hands with sb** estrechar la mano a algn; **to s. one's head** negar con la cabeza. **2** vi (person, building) temblar.

shall v aux (used to form future tense) (first person only) **I s.** (or **I'll**) **buy it** lo compraré; **I s. not** (or **I shan't**) **say anything** no diré nada. ▪ (used to form questions) (usually first person) **s. I close the door?** ¿cierro la puerta?; **s. we go?** ¿nos vamos?

shallow a poco profundo,-a.

shame vergüenza f; (pity) pena; **what a s. !** ¡qué lástima!

shameful a vergonzoso,-a.

shampoo 1 n champú m. **2** vt (one's hair) lavarse.

shape forma f; **to take s.** tomar forma; **in good/bad s.** (condition) en buen/mal estado; **to be in good s.** (health) estar en forma.

share 1 n (portion) parte f; (financial) acción f. **2** vt (divide) dividir; (have in common) compartir.
• **share in** vt participar en.
• **share out** vt repartir.

shareholder accionista mf.

shark (fish) tiburón m.

sharp 1 a (razor, pencil, knife) afilado,-a; (needle) puntiagudo, -a; (bend) cerrado,-a; (pain, cry) agudo,-a. **2** adv **at 2 o'clock s.** a las dos en punto.

sharpen vt (knife) afilar; (pencil) sacar punta a.

sharpener sacapuntas m.

sharply adv (abruptly) bruscamente.

shatter 1 vt hacer añicos. **2** vi hacerse añicos.

shave 1 n afeitado m; **to have a s.** afeitarse. **2** vt (person) afeitar. **3** vi afeitarse.

shaver (electric) s. máquina f de afeitar.

shaving brush brocha f de afeitar.

shaving cream crema f de afeitar.

shawl chal m.

she pers pron ella.

shed[1] (in garden) cobertizo m; (workmen's storage) barraca f.

shed[2] vt (blood, tears) derramar.

sheep inv oveja f.

sheepskin piel f de carnero.

sheet (on bed) sábana f; (of paper) hoja f; (of tin, glass, plastic) lámina f; (of ice) capa f.

shelf (pl **shelves**) (on bookcase) estante m; **shelves** estantería f.

shell 1 n (of egg, nut) cáscara f; (of tortoise etc) caparazón m; (of snail etc) concha f; (from gun) obús m. **2** vt (peas) desvainar; (with guns) bombardear.

shellfish inv marisco m; mariscos mpl.

shelter 1 n (protection) abrigo m; **to take s.** refugiarse (**from** de); **bus s.** marquesina f. **2** vt proteger. **3** vi refugiarse.

shelving estanterías fpl.

shepherd pastor m.

sheriff sheriff m.

sherry jerez m.

shield 1 n escudo m; (of policeman) placa f. **2** vt proteger (**from** de).

shift 1 n (change) cambio m; (period of work, group of workers) turno m; **(gear) s.** cambio m de velocidades. **2** vt (change) cambiar; (move) cambiar de sitio. **3** vi (move) mover; (change place) cambiar de sitio.

shin espinilla f.

shine* 1 vi brillar. **2** vt (lamp) dirigir; (pt & pp **shined**) (polish) sacar brillo a; (shoes) limpiar. **3** n brillo m.

shiny a brillante.

ship barco m.

shipping barcos mpl.

shipwreck 1 n naufragio m. **2** vt **to be shipwrecked** naufragar.

shipyard astillero m.

shirt camisa f.

shiver 1 vi (with cold) tiritar; (with fear) temblar. **2** n escalofrío m.

shock 1 n (jolt) choque m; (scare) susto m; (in medical sense) shock m. **2** vt (upset) escandalizar.

shock absorber amortiguador m.

shocking a (causing horror) espantoso,-a; (disgraceful) escandaloso,-a.

shoe zapato m; **shoes** calzado m sing.

shoelace cordón m (de zapatos).

shoe polish betún m.

shoot 1 n (on plant) brote m; (of vine) sarmiento m. **2** vt* (fire on) pegar un tiro a; (wound) herir (de bala); (kill) matar; (execute) fusilar; (film) rodar, filmar; (with still camera) fotografiar. **3** vi* (with gun) disparar (**at sb** sobre, a algn).
• **shoot down** vt (aircraft) derribar.

• **shoot up** vi (prices) dispararse.

shooting 1 n (shots) tiros mpl; (murder) asesinato m; (hunting) caza f; (of film) rodaje m. **2** a (pain) punzante.

shooting star estrella f fugaz.

shop 1 n tienda f; (large store) almacén m. **2** vi hacer compras; **to go shopping** ir de compras.

shop assistant dependiente,-a mf.

shopkeeper tendero,-a mf.

shopping (purchases) compras fpl.

shopping bag bolsa f de la compra.

shopping basket cesta f de la compra.

shopping center centro m comercial.

shop window escaparate m.

shore (of sea, lake) orilla f; (coast) costa f.

short 1 a corto,-a; (not tall) bajo,-a; **in a s. while** dentro de un rato; **in the s. term** a corto plazo; **'Bob' is s. for 'Robert'** 'Bob' es el diminutivo de 'Robert'; **to be s. of food** andar escaso,-a de comida. **2** adv **to cut s.** (vacation) interrumpir; (meeting) suspender; **we're running s. of coffee** se nos está acabando el café.

shortage escasez f.

short cut atajo m.

shorten vt (skirt, visit) acortar.

shorthand typist taquimecanógrafo,-a mf.

shortly adv (soon) dentro de poco; **s. after** poco después.

shorts npl **a pair of s.** un pantalón corto; (underpants) unos calzoncillos mpl.

short-sighted a (person) miope.

short-term a a corto plazo.

shot¹ (act, sound) disparo m; (sport) tiro m (a puerta); (photography) foto f; (in film) toma f.

shot² pt & pp of **shoot.**

shotgun escopeta f.

should v aux (duty) deber; **all employees s. wear helmets** todos los empleados deben llevar casco; **he s. have been an architect** debería haber sido arquitecto. ▪ (probability) deber de; **he s. have finished by now** ya debe de haber acabado. ▪ (conditional use) **if anything strange s. happen** si pasara algo raro; **I s. like to ask a question** quisiera hacer una pregunta.

shoulder hombro m; (beside road) arcén m.

shoulder bag bolso m (de bandolera).

shout 1 n grito m. **2** vti gritar; **to s. at sb** gritar a algn.

shouting gritos mpl.

shove 1 n empujón m. **2** vt empujar. **3** vi empujar; (jostle) dar empellones.

shovel 1 n pala f. **2** vt mover con pala.

show 1 vt* (ticket etc) mostrar; (painting etc) exponer; (film) poner; (latest plans etc) presentar; (teach) enseñar; (temperature, way etc) indicar; **to s. sb to the door** acompañar a algn hasta la puerta. **2** vi (be visible) notarse; **what's showing?** (at cinema) ¿qué ponen? **3** n (entertainment) espectáculo m; **on s.** expuesto,-a; **boat s.** salón m náutico; **motor s.** salón m del automóvil.

• **show off 1** vt (flaunt) hacer alarde de. **2** vi farolear.

• **show up 1** vt (embarrass) dejar en evidencia. **2** vi (arrive) aparecer.

shower (rain) chaparrón m; (bath) ducha f; **to have a s.** ducharse.

showing (cinema performance) sesión f.

show-off farolero,-a mf.

shrimp camarón m.

shrink* **1** vt encoger. **2** vi encoger(se).

shrub arbusto m.

shrug vt **to s. one's shoulders** encogerse de hombros.

shudder vi (person) estremecerse.

shuffle vt (cards) barajar.

shut 1 *vt** cerrar. **2** *vi** cerrarse. **3** *a* cerrado,-a.

• **shut down 1** *vt* (*factory*) cerrar. **2** *vi* (*factory*) cerrar.

• **shut off** *vti* (*gas, water etc*) cortar.

• **shut out** *vt* (*lock out*) dejar fuera a.

• **shut up 1** *vt* (*close*) cerrar; (*imprison*) encerrar. **2** *vi* (*keep quiet*) callarse.

shutter (*on window*) postigo *m*.

shuttle (*plane*) puente *m* aéreo; (**space**) **s.** transbordador *m* espacial.

shy *a* (*timid*) tímido,-a; (*reserved*) reservado,-a.

shyness timidez *f*.

sick *a* (*ill*) enfermo,-a; *fam* (*fed up*) harto,-a; **s. leave** baja *f* por enfermedad; **to feel s.** (*about to vomit*) tener ganas de devolver; **to be s.** devolver.

sickness (*illness*) enfermedad *f*; (*nausea*) náuseas *fpl*.

side *n* lado *m*; (*of coin etc*) cara *f*; (*of hill*) ladera *f*; (*edge*) borde *m*; (*of lake, river*) orilla *f*; (*team*) equipo *m*; (*in politics*) partido *m*; **by the s. of** junto a; **by my s.** a mi lado; **s. by s.** juntos; **she's on our s.** está de nuestro lado; **to take sides with sb** ponerse de parte de algn.

sideboard aparador *m*.

sidelight piloto *m*.

sidewalk acera *f*.

sideways *adv* de lado.

sieve colador *m*; (*coarse*) criba *f*.

sift *vt* tamizar.

sigh 1 *vi* suspirar. **2** *n* suspiro *m*.

sight (*faculty*) vista *f*; (*spectacle*) espectáculo *m*; **at first s.** a primera vista; **to catch s. of** divisar; **to lose s. of sth/sb** perder algo/a algn de vista; **within s.** a la vista.

sightseeing to go s. hacer turismo.

sign 1 *n* (*signal*) señal *f*; (*trace*) rastro *m*; (*notice*) anuncio *m*; (*board*) letrero *m*. **2** *vti* (*letter etc*) firmar.

• **sign on** *vi* (*worker*) firmar un contrato; (*unemployed person*) apuntarse al paro.

• **sign up** *vi* (*soldier*) alistarse; (*worker*) firmar un contrato.

signal 1 *n* señal *f*. **2** *vt* (*direction etc*) indicar.

signature firma *f*.

significant *a* (*important*) importante.

significantly *adv* (*markedly*) sensiblemente.

signpost poste *m* indicador.

silence 1 *n* silencio *m*. **2** *vt* acallar.

silent *a* silencioso,-a; (*film*) mudo, -a; **to remain s.** guardar silencio.

silently *adv* silenciosamente.

silk seda *f*.

sill (*of window*) alféizar *m*.

silly *a* (*stupid*) tonto,-a; (*ridiculous*) ridículo,-a.

silver 1 *n* (*metal*) plata *f*; (*tableware*) vajilla *f* de plata. **2** *a* de plata; **s. paper** papel *m* de plata.

silver-plated *a* plateado,-a.

silverware vajilla *f* de plata.

similar *a* semejante (**to** a); **to be s.** parecerse.

similarity semejanza *f*.

simple *a* sencillo,-a.

simplify *vt* simplificar.

simply *adv* (*only*) simplemente; (*just, merely*) meramente.

simultaneous *a* simultáneo,-a.

simultaneously *adv* simultáneamente.

sin pecado *m*.

since 1 *adv* (*ever*) **s.** desde entonces. **2** *prep* desde; **she has been living here s. 1975** vive aquí desde 1975. **3** *conj* (*time*) desde que; **how long is it s. you last saw him?** ¿cuánto tiempo hace (desde) que lo viste por última vez? ▪ (*because, as*) ya que.

sincere *a* sincero,-a.

sincerely *adv* sinceramente; **Yours s.** (*in letter*) (le saluda) atentamente.

sincerity sinceridad *f*.

sing* *vti* cantar.

singer cantante *mf*.

single 1 *a* solo,-a; (*unmarried*) soltero,-a; **s. bed/room** cama *f*/habitación *f* individual. **2** *n* (*record*) single *m*.

• **single out** *vt* (*choose*) escoger.

singular 1 *a* (*noun form etc*) singular. **2** *n* singular *m*.

singularly *adv* excepcionalmente.

sinister *a* siniestro,-a.

sink¹ (*in kitchen*) fregadero *m*.

sink²* *vi* (*ship*) hundirse.

• **sink in** *vi* (*penetrate*) penetrar; *fig* causar impresión.

sip *vt* beber a sorbos.

sir señor *m*; (*title*) sir.

siren sirena *f*.

sister hermana *f*.

sister-in-law cuñada *f*.

sit* 1 *vt* (*child etc*) sentar (**in**, **on** en); (*exam*) presentarse a. **2** *vi* (*action*) sentarse; (*be seated*) estar sentado,-a.

• **sit around** *vi* holgazanear.

• **sit down** *vi* sentarse.

• **sit up** *vi* incorporarse.

site (*area*) lugar *m*; **building s.** solar *m*; (*under construction*) obra *f*.

sitting room sala *f* de estar.

situated *a* **to be s.** estar situado,-a.

situation situación *f*.

six *a* & *n* seis (*m*) *inv*.

sixteen *a* & *n* dieciséis (*m*) *inv*.

sixth 1 *a* sexto,-a. **2** *n* (*in series*) sexto,-a *mf*; (*fraction*) sexto *m*.

sixtieth *a* & *n* sexagésimo,-a (*mf*).

sixty *a* & *n* sesenta (*m*) *inv*.

size tamaño *m*; (*of garment*) talla *f*; (*of shoes*) número *m*; (*of person*) estatura *f*.

skate 1 *n* patín *m*. **2** *vi* patinar.

skateboard monopatín *m*.

skater patinador,-a *mf*.

skating patinaje *m*.

skating rink pista *f* de patinaje.

skeleton esqueleto *m*.

sketch 1 *n* (*preliminary drawing*) bosquejo *m*; (*on TV etc*) sketch *m*. **2** *vt* (*preliminary drawing*) bosquejar.

skewer pincho *m*, broqueta *f*.

ski 1 *n* esquí *m*. **2** *vi* esquiar; **to go skiing** ir a esquiar.

skid 1 *n* patinazo *m*. **2** *vi* patinar.

skier esquiador,-a *mf*.

skiing esquí *m*.

skillful *a* hábil.

ski lift telesquí *m*; (*with seats*) telesilla *f*.

skill (*ability*) habilidad *f*; (*technique*) técnica *f*.

skilled (*worker*) cualificado,-a.

skim milk leche *f* desnatada.

skin piel *f*; (*of face*) cutis *m*; (*complexion*) tez *f*; (*of fruit*) piel *f*.

skin-diving submarinismo *m*.

skinny *a* flaco,-a.

skip¹ *vi* (*jump*) saltar, brincar; (*with rope*) saltar a la comba. **2** *vt* (*omit*) saltarse.

skip² (*container*) contenedor *m*.

skirt falda *f*.

skull calavera *f*; (*cranium*) cráneo *m*.

sky cielo *m*; **s. blue** azul *m* celeste.

skyscraper rascacielos *m inv*.

slack *a* (*not taut*) flojo,-a; **business is s.** hay poco negocio.

slacken *vt* (*rope*) aflojar; (*speed*) reducir.

slacks *npl* pantalones *mpl*.

slam 1 *n* (*of door*) portazo *m*. **2** *vt* (*bang*) cerrar de golpe; **to s. the door** dar un portazo. **3** *vi* cerrarse de golpe.

slang jerga *f* popular.

slant 1 *n* inclinación *f*. **2** *vi* inclinarse.

slap 1 *n* palmada *f*; (*in face*) bofetada *f*. **2** *vt* pegar con la mano; (*hit in face*) dar una bofetada a; **to s. sb on the back** dar a algn una palmada en la espalda.

slate pizarra *f*.

slaughter 1 *n* (*of animals*) matanza *f*; (*of people*) carnicería *f*. **2** *vt* (*animals*) matar; (*people*) masacrar.

slave esclavo,-a *mf*.

slavery esclavitud *f*.

sleep 1 *n* sueño *m*. **2** *vi** dormir; **to go to s.** dormirse.

• **sleep in** *vi* (*oversleep*) quedarse dormido,-a.

sleeper (*on train*) (*coach*) coche-cama *m*; (*berth*) litera *f*.

sleeping bag saco *m* de dormir.

sleeping car coche-cama *m*.

sleeping pill somnífero *m*.

sleepy *a* **to be** or **feel s.** tener sueño.

sleet 1 *n* aguanieve *f*. 2 *vi* **it's sleeting** cae aguanieve.

sleeve (*of garment*) manga *f*; (*of record*) funda *f*.

sleigh trineo *m*.

slept *pt* & *pp* of **sleep.**

slice 1 *n* (*of bread*) rebanada *f*; (*of cake*) trozo *m*; (*of meat*) loncha *f*. 2 *vt* (*food*) cortar en rodajas.

slide 1 *n* (*in playground*) tobogán *m*; (*photographic*) diapositiva *f*. **s. projector** proyector *m* de diapositivas. 2 *vt** (*throw*) deslizar; (*furniture*) correr. 3 *vi** deslizarse; (*slip*) resbalar.

sliding *a* (*door, window*) corredizo,-a.

slight *a* (*small*) pequeño,-a; (*trivial*) leve; **not in the slightest** en absoluto.

slightly *adv* (*a little*) ligeramente.

slim 1 *a* (*person*) delgado,-a; (*slender*) esbelto,-a. 2 *vi* adelgazar.

sling 1 *n* (*for arm*) cabestrillo *m*. 2 *vt** (*throw*) tirar.

slip 1 *n* (*mistake*) error *m*; (*moral*) desliz *m*; (*under skirt*) combinación *f*; (*of paper*) papelito *m*. 2 *vi* (*slide*) resbalar. 3 *vt* **to s. sth into sth** meter algo en algo; **to s. sth to sb** dar algo a algn con disimulo.

• **slip away** *vi* (*person*) escabullirse.

• **slip off** *vt* (*clothes*) quitarse rápidamente.

• **slip on** *vt* (*clothes*) ponerse rápidamente.

• **slip out** *vi* (*leave*) salir.

• **slip up** *vi* (*make a mistake*) equivocarse.

slipper zapatilla *f*.

slippery *a* resbaladizo,-a.

slit (*opening*) hendidura *f*; (*cut*) raja *f*.

slogan (e)slogan *m*, lema *m*.

slope 1 *n* (*incline*) cuesta *f*; (*of mountain*) ladera *f*; (*of roof*) vertiente *f*. 2 *vi* inclinarse.

sloping *a* inclinado,-a.

slot (*for coin*) ranura *f*; (*opening*) rendija *f*.

slot machine (*for gambling*) (máquina *f*) tragaperras *f inv*; (*vending machine*) distribuidor *m* automático.

slow 1 *a* lento,-a; (*clock*) atrasado, -a; (*stupid*) torpe; **in s. motion** a cámara lenta; **to be s. to do sth** tardar en hacer algo. 2 *adv* despacio.

• **slow down** or **up** *vi* ir más despacio; (*in car*) reducir la velocidad.

slowly *adv* despacio.

slug (*animal*) babosa *f*.

slums barrios bajos *mpl*.

sly *a* (*cunning*) astuto,-a.

smack 1 *n* (*slap*) bofetada *f*. 2 *vt* (*slap*) dar una bofetada a; (*hit*) golpear.

small *a* pequeño,-a; (*in height*) bajo,-a; **s. change** cambio *m*.

smallpox viruela *f*.

smart *a* (*elegant*) elegante; (*clever*) listo,-a.

smash *vt* (*break*) romper; (*shatter*) hacer pedazos. 3 *vi* (*break*) romperse; (*shatter*) hacerse pedazos.

• **smash into** *vt* (*vehicle*) estrellarse contra.

smashing *a fam* estupendo,-a.

smell 1 *n* (*sense*) olfato *m*; (*odor*) olor *m*. 2 *vt** oler *f*. 2 *vi** oler (*of a*); (*stink*) apestar; **it smells good/like lavender** huele bien/a lavanda.

smile 1 *n* sonrisa *f*. 2 *vi* sonreír.

smock (*blouse*) blusón *m*.

smoke 1 *n* humo *m*. 2 *vi* fumar; (*chimney etc*) echar humo. 3 *vt* (*tobacco*) fumar; **to s. a pipe** fumar en pipa.

smoker (*person*) fumador,-a *mf*; (*compartment*) vagón *m* de fumadores.

smooth a (surface) liso,-a; (skin) suave; (beer, wine) suave; (flight) tranquilo,-a.
• **smooth out** vt (creases) alisar.
• **smooth over** vt to s. things over limar asperezas.
smoothly adv sobre ruedas.
smuggle vt pasar de contrabando.
smuggler contrabandista mf.
smuggling contrabando m.
snack bocado m.
snack bar cafetería f.
snail caracol m.
snake (big) serpiente f; (small) culebra f.
snap 1 n (photo) (foto f) instantánea f. **2** vt (branch etc) partir (en dos). **3** vi (break) romperse.
• **snap off** vt (branch etc) arrancar.
snapshot (foto f) instantánea f.
snatch 1 vt (grab) arrebatar. **2** vi to s. at intentar agarrar.
sneakers npl zapatillas fpl de deporte.
sneer vi to s. at hacer un gesto de desprecio a.
sneeze 1 n estornudo m. **2** vi estornudar.
sniff vt (flower etc) oler.
snip vt cortar a tijeretazos.
snooker billar m ruso.
snore 1 n ronquido m. **2** vi roncar.
snoring ronquidos mpl.
snow 1 n nieve f. **2** vi nevar; **it's snowing** está nevando.
snowball bola f de nieve.
snowdrift ventisquero m.
snowflake copo m de nieve.
snowman hombre m de nieve.
snowplow quitanieves m inv.
snowstorm nevada f.
so 1 adv (to such an extent) tanto; **he was so tired that . . .** estaba tan cansado que . . . ; **so long!** ¡hasta luego! ▪ (degree) tanto; **we loved her so (much)** la queríamos tanto; **so many books** tantos libros. ▪ (thus, in this way) así; **and so on, and so forth** y así sucesivamente; **if so** en este caso; **I think/hope so** creo/espero que sí; ▪ (also) **I'm**

going to Spain—so am I voy a España—yo también. **2** conj (expresses result) así que; **so you like England, do you?** así que te gusta Inglaterra, ¿no?. ▪ (expresses purpose) para que; **I'll put the key here so (that) everyone can see it** pongo la llave aquí para que todos la vean.
soak 1 vt (washing, food) remojar. **2** vi (washing, food) estar en remojo.
• **soak up** vt absorber.
soaked through a (person) empapado,-a.
soaking a (object) empapado,-a; (person) calado,-a hasta los huesos.
soap jabón m.
soap flakes jabón m en escamas.
soap powder jabón m en polvo.
soapy a jabonoso,-a.
sob 1 n sollozo m. **2** vi sollozar.
sober a (not drunk, moderate) sobrio,-a.
soccer fútbol m.
soccer player futbolista mf.
social a social; **s. climber** arribista mf; **s. security** seguridad f social; **s. welfare** seguro m social; **s. work** asistencia f social; **s. worker** asistente,-a mf social.
socialist a & n socialista (mf).
society sociedad f.
sock calcetín m.
socket (for electricity) enchufe m.
soda s. water soda f; (fizzy drink) gaseosa f.
sofa sofá m; **s. bed** sofá m cama.
soft a (not hard) blando,-a m; (skin, color, hair, light, music) suave; (drink) no alcohólico,-a; **s. drinks** refrescos mpl.
softly adv (gently) suavemente; (quietly) silenciosamente.
software software m; **s. package** paquete m.
soil (earth) tierra f.
soldier soldado m.
sole[1] (of foot) planta f; (of shoe, sock) suela f.

sole[2] (*fish*) lenguado *m*.

solemn *a* solemne.

solicitor abogado,-a *mf*.

solid 1 *a* (*not liquid*) sólido,-a; (*firm*) firme; (*not hollow, pure*) (*metal*) macizo,-a; (*reliable*) formal. **2** *n* sólido *m*.

solution solución *f*.

solve *vt* resolver.

some 1 *a* (*with plural nouns*) unos,-as, algunos,-as; (*several*) varios,-as; (*a few*) unos,-as cuantos,-as; **there were s. roses** había unas rosas. ▪ (*with singular nouns*) algún, alguna; (*a little*) un poco de; **there's s. wine left** queda un poco de vino. ▪ (*certain*) cierto,-a; **to s. extent** hasta cierto punto. ▪ (*unspecified*) algún, alguna; **s. day** algún día; **s. other time** otro día. ▪ (*quite a lot of*) bastante; **it's s. distance away** queda bastante lejos. **2** *pron* algunos,-as, unos,-as. ▪ (*a few*) unos,-as cuantos,-as. ▪ (*a little*) un poco.

somebody *pron* alguien; **s. else** otro,-a.

somehow *adv* (*in some way*) de alguna forma; (*for some reason*) por alguna razón.

someone *pron* & *n* = **somebody**.

someplace *adv* = **somewhere**.

somersault (*by acrobat etc*) voltereta *f*.

something *pron* & *n* algo; **is s. the matter?** ¿le pasa algo?; **s. else** otra cosa; **s. of the kind** algo por el estilo.

sometime *adv* algún día.

sometimes *adv* a veces.

somewhat *adv* un tanto.

somewhere *adv* (*in some place*) en alguna parte; (*to some place*) a alguna parte.

son hijo *m*.

song canción *f*; (*of bird*) canto *m*.

son-in-law yerno *m*.

soon *adv* (*within a short time*) dentro de poco; (*quickly*) rápidamente; (*early*) pronto; **s. after-**

wards poco después; **as s. as** en cuanto; **as s. as possible** cuanto antes; **I would just as s. stay at home** prefiero quedarme en casa; **I would (just) as s. read as watch TV** tanto me da leer como ver la tele.

soot hollín *m*.

soothe *vt* (*calm*) tranquilizar; (*pain*) aliviar.

sore 1 *a* (*aching*) dolorido,-a; (*painful*) doloroso,-a; *fam* (*angry*) enfadado,-a; **to have a s. throat** tener dolor de garganta. **2** *n* llaga *f*.

sorrow pena *f*.

sorry 1 *a* **I feel very s. for her** me da mucha pena; (*to express sympathy*) sentir (algo); **I'm s. I'm late** siento llegar tarde. **2** *interj* (*apology*) ¡perdón!; (*for repetition*) ¿cómo?

sort 1 *n* (*kind*) clase *f*, tipo *m*; (*brand*) marca *f*; **it's a s. of teapot** es una especie de tetera. **2** *vt* (*classify*) clasificar.

• **sort out** *vt* (*classify*) clasificar; (*put in order*) ordenar; (*problem*) solucionar.

soul alma *f*.

sound[1] **1** *n* sonido *m*; (*noise*) ruido *m*; **I don't like the s. of it** no me gusta nada la idea. **2** *vt* (*bell, trumpet*) tocar. **3** *vi* (*trumpet, bell, alarm*) sonar; (*give an impression*) parecer; **it sounds interesting** parece interesante.

sound[2] **1** *a* (*healthy*) sano,-a; (*in good condition*) en buen estado; (*safe, dependable*) seguro,-a. **2** *adv* **to be s. asleep** estar profundamente dormido,-a.

soundproof *a* insonorizado,-a.

soup sopa *f*; (*thin, clear*) caldo *m*.

sour *a* (*fruit, wine*) agrio,-a; (*milk*) cortado,-a.

source fuente *f*.

south 1 *n* sur *m*; **in the s. of England** en el sur de Inglaterra. **2** *a* del sur. **3** *adv* (*location*) al sur; (*direction*) hacia el sur.

southbound *a* (con) dirección sur.

southeast *n* & *a* sudeste (*m*).

southern *a* del sur.

southerner sureño,-a *mf*.

southward *a* & *adv* hacia el sur.

southwest *n* & *a* suroeste (*m*).

souvenir recuerdo *m*.

sow* *vt* sembrar.

space 1 *n* espacio *m*; (*room*) sitio *m*. **2** *vt* (*also* **s. out**) espaciar.

space age era *f* espacial.

spaceship nave *f* espacial.

space shuttle transbordador *m* espacial.

spacious *a* espacioso,-a.

spade[1] (*for digging*) pala *f*.

spade[2] (*in cards*) (*international pack*) pica *f*; (*Spanish pack*) espada *f*.

spaghetti espaguetis *mpl*.

Spaniard español,-a *mf*.

Spanish 1 *a* español,-a. **2** *n* (*language*) español *m*, castellano *m*; **the S.** los españoles.

spank *vt* zurrar.

spanking cachete *m*.

spare 1 *vt* (*do without*) prescindir de; **can you s. me 10?** ¿me puedes dejar 10?; **I can't s. the time** no tengo tiempo; **there's none to s.** no sobra nada; **s. me the details** ahórrate los detalles. **2** *a* (*left over*) sobrante; (*surplus*) de sobra; **a s. moment** un momento libre; **s. part** (pieza *f* de) recambio *m*; **s. room** cuarto *m* de los invitados; **s. wheel** rueda *f* de recambio. **3** *n* (*for car etc*) (pieza *f* de) recambio *m*.

spark chispa *f*.

sparkle *vi* (*diamond, glass*) destellar; (*eyes*) brillar.

sparkling a s. wine vino *m* espumoso.

spark plug bujía *f*.

sparrow gorrión *m*.

speak* 1 *vt* (*utter*) decir; (*language*) hablar. **2** *vi* hablar; **to s. to sb** hablar con algn; **speaking!** ¡al habla!; **who's speaking, please?** ¿de parte de quién?

• **speak up** *vi* hablar más fuerte.

speaker (*in dialog*) interlocutor,-a

mf; (*lecturer*) conferenciante *mf*; (*of language*) hablante *mf*; (*loudspeaker*) altavoz *m*; **(public) s.** orador,-a *mf*.

spear lanza *f*.

special *a* especial.

specialist especialista *mf*.

speciality especialidad *f*.

specialize *vi* especializarse (**in** en).

specially *adv* (*specifically*) especialmente; (*on purpose*) a propósito.

specialty especialidad *f*.

species *inv* especie *f*.

specific *a* específico,-a; (*precise*) preciso,-a; **to be s.** concretar.

specimen (*sample*) muestra *f*; (*example*) ejemplar *m*.

spectacular *a* espectacular.

spectator espectador,-a *mf*.

speech (*faculty*) habla *f*; (*address*) discurso *m*; **to give a s.** pronunciar un discurso.

speed 1 *n* velocidad *f*; (*rapidity*) rapidez *f*. **2** *vi** (*exceed speed limit*) conducir con exceso de velocidad.

• **speed up 1** *vt* acelerar. **2** *vi* (*person*) darse prisa.

speedboat lancha *f* rápida.

speed limit velocidad *f* máxima.

speedometer velocímetro *m*.

spell[1]* *vt* (*write*) escribir; (*letter by letter*) deletrear; **how is that spelled?** ¿cómo se escribe eso?

spell[2] (*magical*) hechizo *m*.

spell[3] (*period*) período *m*; (*short period*) rato *m*; **cold s.** ola *f* de frío.

spelling ortografía *f*.

spend* *vt* (*money*) gastar (**on** en); (*time*) pasar.

sphere esfera *f*.

spice 1 *n* especia *f*. **2** *vt* (*food*) sazonar.

spicy *a* sazonado,-a; (*hot*) picante.

spider araña *f*; **s.'s web** telaraña *f*.

spike (*sharp point*) punta *f*.

spill[1]* **1** *vt* (*liquid*) derramar. **2** *vi* (*liquid*) derramarse.

• **spill over** *vi* desbordarse.

spin* vt (wheel etc) hacer girar; (washing) centrifugar.

spinach espinacas fpl.

spine (of back) columna f vertebral.

spiral espiral f.

spire aguja f.

spirits (alcoholic drinks) licores mpl.

spit¹* vti escupir.

spit² (for cooking) asador m.

spite in s. of a pesar de; **in s. of the fact that** a pesar de que.

spiteful a (remark) malévolo,-a.

splash 1 vt (spray) salpicar. **2** vi **to s. (about)** (in water) chapotear.

splendid a espléndido,-a.

splinter (wood) astilla f.

split 1 n (crack) grieta f; (tear) desgarrón m. **2** vt* (crack) hender; (cut) partir; (tear) rajar; (divide) dividir.

• **split up 1** vt (break up) partir; (divide up) dividir; (share out) repartir. **2** vi (couple) separarse.

spoil* vt (ruin) estropear; (child) mimar.

spoke¹ pt of **speak**.

spoke² (of wheel) radio m.

spokesman portavoz mf.

sponge 1 n esponja f. **2** vt (wash) lavar con esponja.

• **sponge down** vt lavar con esponja.

sponge cake bizcocho m.

spontaneous a espontáneo,-a.

spool bobina f.

spoon cuchara f; (small) cucharita f.

spoonful cucharada f.

sport deporte m.

sportsman deportista m.

sportswoman deportista f.

spot 1 n (dot) punto m; (on fabric) lunar m; (stain) mancha f; (pimple) grano m; (place) sitio m; **to decide sth on the s.** decidir algo en el acto. **2** vt (notice) notar; (see) ver.

spotless a (very clean) impecable.

spotlight foco m.

spotted a (speckled) moteado,-a.

spout (of jug) pico m; (of teapot) pitorro m.

sprain 1 n esguince m. **2** vt **to s. one's ankle** torcerse el tobillo.

spray 1 n (aerosol) spray m. **2** vt (insecticide, perfume) pulverizar.

spray can aerosol m.

spread 1 n (for bread) pasta f; **cheese s.** queso para untar. **2** vt* (unfold) desplegar; (lay out) extender; (butter etc) untar; (news) difundir; (rumor) hacer correr; (panic) sembrar. **3** vi* (stretch out) extenderse; (news) difundirse; (rumor) correr; (disease, fire) propagarse.

spreadsheet hoja f de cálculo.

spring¹ (season) primavera f.

spring² 1 n (of water) fuente f; (of watch etc) resorte m. **2** vi* (jump) saltar.

springboard trampolín m.

spring onion cebolleta f.

springtime primavera f.

sprinkle vt (with water) rociar (**with** de); (with sugar) espolvorear (**with** de).

sprinkler (for water) aspersor m.

sprout (Brussels) sprouts coles fpl de Bruselas.

spur espuela f.

spurt vi (liquid) chorrear.

spy 1 n espía mf. **2** vi espiar (**on** a).

spying espionaje m.

square 1 n cuadrado m; (in town) plaza f. **2** a cuadrado,-a; **a s. meal** una buena comida.

squash¹ 1 vt (crush) aplastar.

squash² (sport) squash m.

squat vi (crouch) agacharse.

squeak vi (hinge, wheel) chirriar; (shoes) crujir.

squeal 1 n chillido m. **2** vi (animal, person) chillar.

squeeze 1 vt apretar; (lemon etc) exprimir; **to s. paste out of a tube** sacar pasta de un tubo apretando. **2** vi to **s. in** apretujarse.

• **squeeze up** vi (on bench etc) correrse.

squint 1 n bizquera f; **to have a s.**

ser bizco,-a. **2** vi ser bizco,-a; **to s. at sth** (with eyes half-closed) mirar algo con los ojos entrecerrados.

squirrel ardilla f.

squirt 1 vt lanzar a chorro. **2** vi **to s. out** salir a chorros.

stab vt apuñalar.

stable¹ a estable.

stable² (for horses) cuadra f.

stack 1 n (pile) montón m; fam **stacks of . . .** un montón de . . . **2** vt (pile up) amontonar.

stadium estadio m.

staff (personnel) personal m; (of army) estado m mayor.

staffroom sala f de profesores.

stag venado m.

stage 1 n (platform) plataforma f; (in theater) escenario m; (of development, journey, rocket) etapa f; **in stages** por etapas. **2** vt (play) poner en escena.

stagger 1 vi tambalearse. **2** vt (hours, work) escalonar.

stain 1 n mancha f. **2** vt manchar.

stained glass window vidriera f de colores.

stainless a (steel) inoxidable.

stair peldaño m; **stairs** escalera f sing.

staircase escalera f.

stake (stick) estaca f.

stale a (food) pasado,-a; (bread) duro,-a.

stalk (of plant) tallo m; (of fruit) rabo m.

stall 1 n (in market) puesto m; (in theater) **stalls** platea f sing. **2** vi (of engine) calarse.

stammer 1 n tartamudeo m. **2** vi tartamudear.

stamp 1 n (postage stamp) sello m, Am estampilla f; (with foot) patada f. **2** vt (with postage stamp) poner el sello a; **self-addressed stamped envelope** sobre m franqueado; **to s. one's feet** patear.

• **stamp out** vt (racism etc) acabar con.

stamp collecting filatelia f.

stand 1 n (of lamp, sculpture) pie m; (market stall) puesto m; (at exhibition) stand m; (in stadium) tribuna f; **newspaper s.** quiosco m de prensa. **2** vt* (place) poner, colocar; (tolerate) aguantar. **3** vi (be upright) estar de pie; (get up) levantarse; (be situated) encontrarse; (remain unchanged) permanecer.

• **stand around** vi estar sin hacer nada; (wait) esperar.

• **stand aside** vi apartarse.

• **stand back** vi (allow sb to pass) abrir paso.

• **stand by 1** vi (do nothing) quedarse sin hacer nada; (be ready) estar listo,-a. **2** vt (person) apoyar.

• **stand down** vi fig retirarse.

• **stand for** vt (mean) significar; (tolerate) aguantar.

• **stand in** vi sustituir (**for** -).

• **stand out** vi (mountain etc, fig person) destacar(se).

• **stand up** vi (get up) ponerse de pie; fig **to s. up for sb** defender a algn; fig **to s. up to sb** hacer frente a algn.

standard 1 n (level) nivel m; (criterion) criterio m; (norm) estándar m inv; **s. of living** nivel de vida. **2** a normal.

standby a **s. ticket** billete m sin reserva.

standing a (not sitting) de pie.

standpoint punto m de vista.

standstill at a s. (car, traffic) parado,-a; (industry) paralizado, -a; **to come to a s.** (car, traffic) pararse; (industry) paralizarse.

stank pt of **stink**.

staple 1 n (fastener) grapa f. **2** vt grapar.

stapler grapadora f.

star 1 n estrella f. **2** vt (film) tener como protagonista. **3** vi (in film) protagonizar.

stare 1 n mirada f fija. **2** vi mirar fijamente; **to s. at sb** mirar fijamente a algn.

start 1 n (beginning) principio m; (of race) salida f; (advantage) ventaja f. **2** vt (begin) empezar, comen-

zar; **to s. doing sth** empezar a hacer algo. **3** vi (begin) empezar,
comenzar; (engine) arrancar; (take
fright) asustarse; **starting from
Monday** a partir del lunes.
• **start off** vi (leave) salir.
• **start on** vi empezar.
• **start up 1** vt (engine) arrancar.
2 vi (car) arrancar.
starter (in car) motor m de arran-
que; (food) entrada f.
startle vt asustar.
starvation hambre m.
starve vi pasar hambre; **to s. to
death** morirse de hambre.
starving a **I'm s.!** estoy muerto,-a
de hambre.
state 1 n estado m; **The States** (los)
Estados Unidos. **2** vt declarar.
statement declaración f; (financial) estado m de cuenta; **monthly
s.** balance m mensual.
statesman estadista m.
station estación f.
stationary a (not moving) inmóvil.
stationery (paper) papel m de
escribir; (pens, ink etc) artículos
mpl de escritorio.
stationmaster jefe m de estación.
station wagon camioneta f.
statistic estadística f.
statue estatua f.
stay 1 n estancia f. **2** vi (remain)
quedarse; (reside temporarily) alojarse; **she's staying with us for a
few days** ha venido a pasar unos
días con nosotros.
• **stay away** vi (not attend) no asistir; **s. away from her** no te acerques
a ella.
• **stay in** vi quedarse en casa.
• **stay out** vi **to s. out all night** no
volver a casa en toda la noche.
• **stay out of** vt (not interfere in) no
meterse en.
• **stay up** vi (not go to bed) no acostarse; (fence etc) mantenerse en
pie.
steadily adv (improve) constantemente; (walk) con paso seguro;
(gaze) fijamente; (rain, work) sin
parar.

steady a firme; (prices) estable;
(demand, speed) constante.
steak bistec m.
steal* vt robar.
steam 1 n vapor m. **2** vt (food) cocer
al vapor.
• **steam up** vi (window etc) empañarse.
steamroller apisonadora f.
steel acero m; **s. industry** industria
f siderúrgica.
steep a (hill etc) empinado,-a;
(price, increase) excesivo,-a.
steeple aguja f.
steer vt dirigir; (car) conducir;
(ship) gobernar.
steering wheel volante m.
stem (of plant) tallo m; (of glass)
pie m.
stenographer taquígrafo m.
step 1 n paso m; (measure) medida
f; (stair) peldaño m; **s. by s.** poco a
poco; **steps** (outdoor) escalinata f;
(indoor) escalera f. **2** vi dar un
paso.
• **step aside** vi apartarse.
• **step back** vi retroceder.
• **step down** vi fig renunciar; (resign) dimitir.
• **step forward** vi (volunteer)
ofrecerse.
• **step in** vi fig intervenir.
• **step into/out of** vt (car etc) entrar en/salir de.
stepbrother hermanastro m.
stepdaughter hijastra f.
stepfather padrastro m.
stepladder escalera f de tijera.
stepmother madrastra f.
stepsister hermanastra f.
stepson hijastro m.
stereo 1 n estéreo m. **2** a estereo-
(fónico,-a).
sterilize vt esterilizar.
stew estofado m, cocido m.
steward (on plane) auxiliar m de
vuelo.
stewardess (on plane) azafata f.
stick¹ palo m; (walking stick) bastón m.
stick²* **1** vt meter; (with glue etc)
pegar; **he stuck his head out of the**

window asomó la cabeza por la ventana. **2** *vi* (*become attached*) pegarse; (*window, drawer*) atrancarse.
• **stick down** *vt* (*stamp*) pegar.
• **stick on** *vt* (*stamp*) pegar.
• **stick out 1** *vi* (*project*) sobresalir; (*be noticeable*) resaltar. **2** *vt* (*tongue*) sacar.
• **stick to** *vt* (*principles*) atenerse a.
• **stick up** *vt* (*poster*) fijar.
• **stick up for** *vt* defender.
sticker (*label*) etiqueta *f* adhesiva; (*with slogan*) pegatina *f*.
sticking plaster tirita *f*, curita *f*.
sticky *a* pegajoso,-a; (*label*) engomado,-a.
stiff *a* rígido,-a; (*joint*) entumecido,-a; **to have a s. neck** tener tortícolis.
stifle 1 *vt* sofocar. **2** *vi* sofocarse.
stifling *a* sofocante.
still 1 *adv* (*up to this time*) todavía, aún; (*nonetheless*) no obstante; (*however*) sin embargo; (*with comparative*) (*even*) aún; **s. colder** aún más frío. **2** *a* (*calm*) tranquilo,-a; (*motionless*) inmóvil.
sting* 1 *n* picadura *f*. **2** *vt** picar.
stink* *vi* apestar (**of** a).
• **stink out** *vt* (*room*) apestar.
stir *vt* (*liquid*) remover.
• **stir up** *vt* (*memories, curiosity*) despertar.
stirrup estribo *m*.
stitch puntada *f*; (*in knitting*) punto *m*; (*for surgery etc*) punto *m* (de sutura).
stock 1 *n* (*goods*) existencias *fpl*; (*selection*) surtido *m*; (*broth*) caldo *m*; **out of s.** agotado,-a; **to have sth in s.** tener existencias de algo; **stocks and shares** acciones *fpl*. **2** *vt* (*have in stock*) tener existencias de.
• **stock up** *vi* abastecerse (**on, with** de).
Stock Exchange Bolsa *f* (de valores).
stocking media *f*; **a pair of stockings** unas medias.

Stock Market Bolsa *f*.
stomach estómago *m*; **s. upset** trastorno *m* gástrico.
stone piedra *f*.
stool taburete *m*.
stop 1 *n* (*stock*) parada *f*; (*break*) pausa *f*; **to come to a s.** pararse; **to put a s. to sth** poner fin a algo. **2** *vt* parar; (*gas, water supply*) cortar; (*prevent*) evitar; **to s. sb from doing sth** impedir a algn hacer algo; **to s. doing sth** dejar de hacer algo. **3** *vi* (*person, moving vehicle*) pararse; (*cease*) terminar; (*stay*) pararse.
• **stop by** *vi* pasarse; **I'll s. by at the office** me pasaré por la oficina.
• **stop off** *vi* pararse un rato.
• **stop up** *vt* (*hole*) tapar.
stop-off parada *f*; (*flying*) escala *f*.
stopover parada *f*.
stopwatch cronómetro *m*.
store 1 *n* (*stock*) provisión *f*; (*warehouse*) almacén *m*; (*shop*) tienda *f*; **department s.** gran almacén *m*. **2** *vt* (*furniture, computer data*) almacenar; (*keep*) guardar; **to s. (up)** acumular.
storeroom despensa *f*.
stork cigüeña *f*.
storm tormenta *f*; (*with wind*) vendaval *m*.
stormy *a* (*weather*) tormentoso,-a.
story[1] (*tale*) historia *f*; (*account*) relato *m*; (*article*) artículo *m*; (*plot*) trama *f*; **tall s.** cuento *m* chino.
story[2] piso *m*.
stove (*for heating*) estufa *f*; (*cooker*) cocina *f*; (*oven*) horno *m*.
straight 1 *a* (*not bent*) recto,-a; (*hair*) liso,-a; (*honest*) honrado, -a; (*answer*) sincero,-a; (*drink*) solo, -a. **2** *adv* (*in a straight line*) en línea recta; (*directly*) directamente; (*frankly*) francamente; **keep s. ahead** sigue todo recto; **s. away** en seguida.
straighten *vt* (*tie, picture*) poner bien; (*hair*) alisar.
straightforward *a* (*easy*) sencillo, -a.
strain 1 *vt* (*eyes, voice*) forzar;

(*heart*) cansar; (*liquid*) filtrar; (*vegetables, tea*) colar. **2** *n* tensión *f*; (*effort*) esfuerzo *m*; (*exhaustion*) agotamiento *m*.

strainer colador *m*.

strange *a* (*unknown*) desconocido, -a; (*unfamiliar*) nuevo,-a; (*odd*) extraño,-a.

stranger (*unknown person*) desconocido,-a *mf*; (*outsider*) forastero, -a *mf*.

strangle *vt* estrangular.

strap (*on bag*) correa *f*; (*on dress*) tirante *m*.

straw paja *f*; (*for drinking*) pajita *f*.

strawberry fresa *f*; (*large*) fresón *m*.

streak (*line*) raya *f*; (*in hair*) reflejo *m*; **s. of lightning** rayo *m*.

stream (*brook*) arroyo *m*; (*current*) corriente *f*; (*flow*) flujo *m*.

street calle *f*; **the man in the s.** el hombre de la calle.

streetcar tranvía *m*.

street lamp farol *m*.

street map *or* **plan** (plano *m*) callejero *m*.

strength fuerza *f*; (*of rope etc*) resistencia *f*; (*of emotion, color*) intensidad *f*.

strengthen *vt* reforzar; (*intensify*) intensificar.

stress **1** *n* estrés *m*; (*emphasis*) hincapié *m*; (*on word*) acento *m*. **2** *vt* (*emphasize*) subrayar; (*word*) acentuar.

stressful *a* estresante.

stretch 1 *vt* (*elastic*) estirar; (*arm, hand*) alargar. **2** *vi* estirarse. **3** *n* (*of land*) extensión *f*; (*of time*) intervalo *m*.

• **stretch out 1** *vt* (*arm, hand*) alargar; (*legs*) estirar. **2** *vi* (*countryside, years etc*) extenderse.

stretcher camilla *f*.

strict *a* estricto,-a.

strictly *adv* (*categorically*) terminantemente; (*precisely*) estrictamente; **s. speaking** en sentido estricto.

strictness severidad *f*.

stride 1 *n* zancada *f*. **2** *vi** **to s. (along)** andar a zancadas.

strike* **1** *vt* (*hit*) golpear; (*collide with*) chocar contra; (*match*) encender; (*impress*) impresionar; **the clock struck three** el reloj dio las tres; **it strikes me . . .** me parece . . . **2** *vi** (*workers*) declararse en huelga. **3** *n* (*by workers*) huelga *f*; **on s.** en huelga; **to go (out) on s.** declararse en huelga; **to call a s.** convocar una huelga.

• **strike up** *vt* (*friendship*) trabar; (*conversation*) entablar; (*tune*) empezar a tocar.

striker (*worker*) huelguista *mf*.

striking *a* (*eye-catching*) llamativo,-a; (*impressive*) impresionante.

string (*cord, of guitar*) cuerda *f*.

strip¹ *vi* (*undress*) desnudarse.

strip² tira *f*; (*of metal*) cinta *f*, lámina *f*.

• **strip off** *vi* (*undress*) desnudarse.

stripe raya *f*.

striped *a* a rayas.

stroke 1 *n* (*blow*) golpe *m*; (*in swimming*) brazada *f*; (*illness*) apoplejía *f*; **a s. of luck** un golpe de suerte. **2** *vt* acariciar.

stroll 1 *vi* dar un paseo; **he strolled across the square** cruzó la plaza a paso lento. **2** *n* paseo *m*.

stroller (*for baby*) cochecito *m*.

strong *a* fuerte; (*durable*) sólido, -a.

structure estructura *f*; (*building*) edificio *m*.

struggle 1 *vi* luchar. **2** *n* lucha *f*; (*physical fight*) pelea *f*.

stub (*of cigarette*) colilla *f*; (*of check*) matriz *f*.

stubborn *a* testarudo,-a.

stubbornness testarudez *f*.

stuck 1 *pt* & *pp* of **stick**². **2** *a* (*caught, jammed*) atrancado; **I'm s.** (*unable to carry on*) no puedo seguir.

stud (*on clothing*) tachón *m*.

student estudiante *mf*.

studio (*TV etc*) estudio *m*; (*artist's*) taller *m*; **s. apartment** estudio.

study 1 *vti* estudiar; **to s. to be a doctor** estudiar para médico. **2** *n* estudio *m*.

stuff 1 *vt* (*container*) llenar (**with** de); (*in cooking*) rellenar (**with** con or de); (*cram*) atiborrar (**with** de). **2** *n* (*material*) material *m*; (*things*) cosas *fpl*, trastos *mpl*.

stuffed up *a* (*nose*) tapado,-a.

stuffing relleno *m*.

stuffy *a* (*room*) mal ventilado,-a; (*atmosphere*) cargado,-a.

stumble *vi* tropezar; *fig* **to s. across** or **on** tropezar or dar con.

stump (*of tree*) tocón *m*.

stun *vt* aturdir; (*news etc*) sorprender.

stunned *a* (*amazed*) estupefacto, -a.

stupid *a* estúpido,-a.

stupidity estupidez *f*.

sturdy *a* robusto,-a.

stutter 1 *vi* tartamudear. **2** *n* tartamudeo *m*.

sty (*pen*) pocilga *f*.

style estilo *m*; (*of dress*) modelo *m*; (*fashion*) moda *f*.

stylish *a* con estilo.

subject 1 *n* (*citizen*) súbdito *m*; (*topic*) tema *m*; (*at school*) asignatura *f*; (*of sentence*) sujeto *m*. **2** *vt* someter.

subjunctive subjuntivo *m*.

submarine 1 *n* submarino *m*. **2** *n*. submarino,-a.

subscribe *vi* suscribirse (**to** a).

subscriber abonado,-a *mf*.

subscription (*to magazine*) suscripción *f*, abono *m*.

subside *vi* (*land*) hundirse; (*floodwater*) bajar.

substance sustancia *f*.

substantial *a* (*sum, loss*) importante; (*meal*) abundante.

substitute 1 *vt* sustituir. **2** *n* (*person*) suplente *mf*; (*thing*) sucedáneo *m*.

subtitle subtítulo *m*.

subtle *a* sutil.

subtract *vt* restar.

subtraction resta *f*.

suburb barrio *m* periférico; **the suburbs** las afueras.

suburban *a* suburbano,-a.

subway (*underground railway*) metro *m*.

succeed *vi* (*person*) tener éxito; **to s. in doing sth** conseguir hacer algo.

success éxito *m*.

successful *a* de éxito; (*business*) próspero,-a; **to be s. in doing sth** lograr hacer algo.

successfully *adv* con éxito.

such 1 *a* (*of that sort*) tal, semejante; **artists s. as Monet** artistas como Monet. ■ (*so much, so great*) tanto,-a; **he's always in s. a hurry** siempre anda con tanta prisa; **s. a lot of books** tantos libros. **2** *adv* (*so very*) tan; **it's s. a long time** hace tanto tiempo; **she's s. a clever woman** es una mujer tan inteligente.

suck 1 *vt* (*liquid*) sorber, chupar; (*at breast*) mamar. **2** *vi* (*baby*) mamar.

• **suck up** *vt* (*with straw*) aspirar.

sudden *a* (*hurried*) repentino,-a; (*unexpected*) imprevisto,-a; **all of a s.** de repente.

suddenly *adv* de repente.

suds *npl* espuma *f* de jabón.

suede ante *m*; (*for gloves*) cabritilla *f*.

suffer *vti* sufrir; **to s. from** sufrir de.

suffering (*affliction*) sufrimiento *m*; (*pain, torment*) dolor *m*.

sufficient *a* suficiente, bastante.

sufficiently *adv* suficientemente, bastante.

suffix sufijo *m*.

suffocate 1 *vt* asfixiar. **2** *vi* asfixiarse.

sugar 1 *n* azúcar *m* & *f*. **2** *vt* azucarar.

sugar bowl azucarero *m*.

suggest *vt* (*propose*) sugerir; (*advise*) aconsejar; (*indicate, imply*) indicar.

suggestion (*proposal*) sugerencia *f*.

suicide suicidio *m*.

suit 1 *n* traje *m* de chaqueta; (*in cards*) palo *m*. **2** *vt* (*be convenient for*) convenir a; (*be right, appropriate for*) ir bien a; **red really suits you** el rojo te favorece mucho; **s. yourself!** ¡como quieras!

suitable *a* (*convenient*) conveniente; (*appropriate*) adecuado, -a; **the most s. woman for the job** la mujer más indicada para el puesto.

suitcase maleta *f*.

suite (*of furniture*) tresillo *m*; (*of hotel rooms, music*) suite *f*.

sulk *vi* enfurruñarse.

sultana (*raisin*) pasa *f* (de Esmirna).

sum (*arithmetic problem, amount*) suma *f*; (*total amount*) total *m*; (*of money*) importe *m*.

• **sum up** *vt* resumir.

summarize *vt* resumir.

summary resumen *m*.

summer 1 *n* verano *m*. **2** *a* (*vacation etc*) de verano; (*resort*) de veraneo.

summertime verano *m*.

sun sol *m*.

sunbathe *vi* tomar el sol.

sunburn quemadura *f* de sol.

sunburnt *a* (*burnt*) quemado,-a por el sol; (*tanned*) bronceado,-a.

sundae helado *m* de fruta y nueces.

Sunday domingo *m*.

sunglasses *npl* gafas *fpl* de sol.

sunlamp lámpara *f* solar.

sunlight (luz *f* del) sol *m*.

sunny *a* (*day*) de sol; **it is s.** hace sol.

sunrise salida *f* del sol.

sunroof (*on car*) techo *m* corredizo.

sunset puesta *f* del sol.

sunshade sombrilla *f*.

sunshine (luz *f* del) sol *m*.

sunstroke insolación *f*.

suntan bronceado *m*; **s. oil** (aceite

m) bronceador *m*; **s. lotion** leche *f* bronceadora.

suntanned *a* bronceado,-a.

super *a fam* fenomenal.

superb *a* espléndido,-a.

superficial *a* superficial.

superior *a* superior.

superiority superioridad *f*.

supermarket supermercado *m*.

superstition superstición *f*.

superstitious *a* supersticioso,-a.

supervise *vt* supervisar; (*watch over*) vigilar.

supervisor supervisor,-a *mf*.

supper cena *f*; **to have s.** cenar.

supple *a* flexible.

supply 1 *n* (*provision*) suministro *m*; (*delivery*) provisión *f*; **supplies** (*food*) víveres *mpl*. **2** *vt* (*provide*) suministrar; (*with provisions*) aprovisionar; (*information*) facilitar.

support 1 *n* soporte *m*; (*moral*) apoyo *m*. **2** *vt* (*weight etc*) sostener; (*back*) apoyar; (*team*) ser (hincha) de; (*family*) mantener.

supporter (*political*) partidario, -a *mf*; (*in sport*) hincha *mf*.

suppose *vt* suponer; (*presume*) creer; **I s. not/so** supongo que no/ sí; **you're not supposed to smoke in here** no está permitido fumar aquí dentro; **you're supposed to be in bed** deberías estar acostado, -a ya.

sure *a* seguro,-a; **I'm s. (that) . . .** estoy seguro,-a de que . . . ; **make s. that it's ready** asegúrate de que esté listo.

surely *adv* (*without a doubt*) seguramente; **s. not!** ¡no puede ser!

surface superficie *f*; **s. area** área *f* de la superficie; **by s. mail** por vía terrestre *or* marítima.

surfboard tabla *f* de surf.

surfing surf *m*, surfing *m*.

surgeon cirujano,-a *mf*.

surgery (*operation*) cirugía *f*; **s. hours** horas *fpl* de consulta.

surname apellido *m*.

surprise 1 *n* sorpresa *f*; **to take sb**

by s. coger desprevenido,-a a algn. **2** *a* (*visit*) inesperado,-a; **s. attack** ataque *m* sorpresa. **3** *vt* sorprender.

surprised *a* sorprendido,-a; **I should not be s. if it rained** no me extrañaría que lloviera.

surprising *a* sorprendente.

surprisingly *adv* de modo sorprendente.

surrender *vi* (*give in*) rendirse.

surround *vt* rodear.

surrounding *a* circundante.

surroundings *npl* alrededores *mpl*.

survey (*of trends etc*) encuesta *f*.

surveyor agrimensor,-a *mf*.

survive 1 *vi* sobrevivir. **2** *vt* sobrevivir a.

survivor superviviente *mf*.

suspect 1 *n* sospechoso,-a *mf*. **2** *vt* (*person*) sospechar (**of** de); (*think likely*) imaginar.

suspend *vt* suspender; (*pupil*) expulsar por un tiempo.

suspenders *npl* tirantes *mpl*.

suspense suspense *m*.

suspension suspensión *f*.

suspicion sospecha *f*; (*mistrust*) recelo *m*; (*doubt*) duda *f*; (*trace*) pizca *f*.

suspicious *a* (*arousing suspicion*) sospechoso,-a; (*distrustful*) receloso, -a; **to be s. of sb** desconfiar de algn.

swallow[1] *vt* (*drink, food*) tragar.

swallow[2] (*bird*) golondrina *f*.

• **swallow down** *vt* tragarse.

swamp ciénaga *f*.

swan cisne m.

swap 1 *n* intercambio *m*. **2** *vt* cambiar.

swarm enjambre *m*.

sway *vi* (*swing*) balancearse; (*totter*) tambalearse.

swear* **1** *vt* (*vow*) jurar. **2** *vi* (*curse*) decir palabrotas.

swearword palabrota *f*.

sweat 1 *n* sudor *m*. **2** *vi* sudar.

sweater suéter *m*.

sweatshirt sudadera *f*.

Swede (*person*) sueco,-a *mf*.

Swedish 1 *a* sueco,-a. **2** *n* (*language*) sueco *m*.

sweep* *vti* barrer.

• **sweep away** *vt* (*dust*) barrer; (*storm*) arrastrar.

• **sweep out** *vt* (*room*) barrer.

• **sweep up** *vi* barrer.

sweet 1 *a* dulce; (*sugary*) azucarado,-a; (*pleasant*) agradable; (*person, animal*) encantador,-a. **2** *n* (*candy*) caramelo *m*; (*chocolate*) bombón *m*; (*dessert*) postre *m*.

sweetcorn maíz *m* dulce.

sweeten *vt* (*tea etc*) azucarar.

sweetly *adv* dulcemente.

sweet shop confitería *f*.

swell* **(up)** *vi* (*part of body*) hincharse.

swelling hinchazón *f*.

swerve *vi* (*car*) dar un viraje brusco.

swim* **1** *vi* nadar; **to go swimming** ir a nadar. **2** *vt* (*the Mississippi*) pasar a nado. **3** *n* baño *m*; **to go for a s.** ir a darse un baño.

swimmer nadador,-a *mf*.

swimming natación *f*.

swimming pool piscina *f*.

swimming trunks bañador *m*.

swimsuit bañador *m*.

swing 1 *n* (*for playing*) columpio *m*. **2** *vi** (*move back and forth*) balancearse; (*arms, legs*) menearse; (*on swing*) columpiarse. **3** *vt* (*arms, legs*) menear.

Swiss 1 *a* suizo,-a. **2** *n inv* (*person*) suizo,-a *mf*; **the S.** *pl* los suizos.

switch 1 *n* (*for light etc*) interruptor *m*. **2** *vt* (*jobs, direction*) cambiar de.

• **switch off** *vt* apagar.

• **switch on** *vt* encender.

• **switch over** *vi* cambiar(**to** a).

swollen *a* (*ankle, face*) hinchado, -a.

swop *vt* = **swap.**

sword espada *f*.

syllable sílaba *f*.

syllabus programa *m* de estudios.

symbol símbolo *m*.

symbolic a simbólico,-a.
symmetry simetría f.
sympathetic a (showing pity) compasivo,-a; (understanding) comprensivo,-a; (kind) amable.
sympathize vi (show pity) compadecerse (**with** de); (understand) comprender.
sympathy (pity) compasión f; (condolences) pésame m; (understanding) comprensión f; **to express one's s.** dar el pésame.
symphony sinfonía f.
symptom síntoma m.
synagogue sinagoga f.
synonym sinónimo m.
syringe jeringuilla f.
syrup jarabe m, almíbar m.
system sistema m.

T

ta interj fam gracias.
tab (flap) lengüeta f.
table mesa f; **to lay** or **set the t.** poner la mesa.
tablecloth mantel m.
tablemat salvamanteles m inv.
tablespoon cuchara m de servir.
tablespoonful cucharada f.
tablet (pill) pastilla f.
tack (small nail) tachuela f.
tackle vt (task) emprender; (problem) abordar; (grapple with) agarrar; (in sport) placar; (in soccer) entrar a.
tacky a fam (shoddy) cutre.
tact tacto m.
tactful a diplomático,-a.
tactic táctica f; **tactics** táctica f sing.
taffy caramelo m duro.
tag (label) etiqueta f.
tail cola f.
tailor sastre m.
take* vt tomar; (bus etc) coger; (accept) aceptar; (win) ganar; (prize) llevarse; (eat, drink) tomar; (accompany) llevar; (endure) aguantar; (consider) considerar; (require) requerir; **she's taking (a degree in) law** estudia derecho; **to t. an exam (in . . .)** examinarse (de . . .); **it takes an hour to get there** se tarda una hora en ir hasta allí; **it takes courage** se necesita valor.

• **take after** vt parecerse a.
• **take along** llevar (consigo).
• **take apart** vt (machine) desmontar.
• **take away** vt (carry off) llevarse; (in math) restar (**from** de); **to t. sth away from sb** quitarle algo a algn.
• **take back** vt (give back) devolver; (receive back) recuperar; (withdraw) retirar.
• **take down** vt (lower) bajar; (write) apuntar.
• **take in** vt (include) abarcar; (understand) entender; (deceive) engañar.
• **take off 1** vt quitar; (lead or carry away) llevarse; (deduct) descontar; **he took off his jacket** se quitó la chaqueta. **2** vi (plane) despegar.
• **take on** vt (undertake) encargarse de; (acquire) tomar; (employ) contratar.
• **take out 1** vt sacar; **he's taking me out to dinner** me ha invitado a cenar fuera; (insurance) sacarse; (stain, tooth) quitar. **2** n (food) comida f para llevar; (restaurant) restaurante m de comida para llevar. **3** a (food) para llevar.
• **take over 1** vt (office, post) tomar posesión de. **2** vi **to t. over from sb** relevar a algn.
• **take up** vt (occupy) ocupar; **I've taken up the guitar** he empezado a tocar la guitarra.
takeoff (of plane) despegue m.
takings npl (of shop, business) recaudación f sing.
tale cuento m; **to tell tales** contar chismes.
talent talento m.
talented a dotado,-a.
talk 1 vi hablar; (chat) charlar; (gossip) chismorrear. **2** vt hablar; **to t. nonsense** decir tonterías. **3** n (conversation) conversación f;

(*words*) palabras *fpl*; (*gossip*) chismes *mpl*; (*lecture*) charla *f*; **there's t. of . . .** se habla de . . .
• **talk into** *vt* **to t. sb into sth** convencer a algn para que haga algo.
• **talk out of** *vt* **to t. sb out of sth** disuadir a algn de que haga algo.
• **talk over** *vt* discutir.

talkative *a* hablador,-a.

tall *a* alto,-a; **a tree ten meters t.** un árbol de diez metros (de alto); **how t. are you?** ¿cuánto mides?

tambourine pandereta *f*.

tame 1 *a* (*animal*) domado,-a; (*by nature*) manso,-a. **2** *vt* domar.

tampon tampón *m*.

tan 1 *n* (*of skin*) bronceado *m*. **2** *vt* (*skin*) broncear. **3** *vi* ponerse moreno,-a.

tangerine clementina *f*.

tangled *a* enredado,-a.

tank (*container*) depósito *m*; (*with gun*) tanque *m*.

tanker (*ship*) tanque *m*; (*for oil*) petrolero *m*.

tap¹ 1 *vt* (*knock*) golpear suavemente; (*with hand*) dar una palmadita a. **2** *vi* **to t. at the door** llamar suavemente a la puerta. **3** *n* golpecito *m*.

tap² (*for water*) grifo *m*.

tape 1 *n* cinta *f*; **sticky t.** cinta *f* adhesiva. **2** *vt* pegar (con cinta adhesiva); (*record*) grabar (en cinta).

tape measure cinta *f* métrica.

tape recorder magnetófono *m*, cassette *m*.

tar alquitrán *m*.

target (*object aimed at*) blanco *m*; (*purpose*) meta *f*.

tarpaulin lona *f*.

tart (*to eat*) tarta *f*.

tartan tartán *m*.

task tarea *f*.

taste 1 *n* (*sense*) gusto *m*; (*flavor*) sabor *m*; (*liking*) afición *f*; **it has a burnt t.** sabe a quemado; **in bad t.** de mal gusto; **to have (good) t.** tener (buen) gusto. **2** *vt* (*sample*) probar. **3** *vi* **to t. of sth** saber a algo.

tasty *a* sabroso,-a.

tattered *a* hecho,-a jirones.

tattoo 1 *vt* tatuar. **2** *n* (*mark*) tatuaje *m*.

tax 1 *n* impuesto *m*. **2** *vt* gravar.

taxable *a* imponible.

taxi taxi *m*.

taxi driver taxista *mf*.

taxi rank parada *f* de taxis.

taxpayer contribuyente *mf*.

tea *n* (*meal*) merienda *f*.

tea bag bolsita *f* de té.

tea break descanso *m*.

teach* 1 *vt* enseñar; (*subject*) dar clases de; **to t. sb (how) to do sth** enseñar a algn a hacer algo. **2** *vi* ser profesor,-a.

teacher profesor,-a *mf*.

teaching enseñanza *f*.

teacup taza *f* de té.

team equipo *m*.
• **team up to t. up with sb** juntarse con algn.

teapot tetera *f*.

tear¹ lágrima *f*; **to be in tears** estar llorando.

tear² 1 *vt** rasgar; **to t. sth out of sb's hands** arrancarle algo de las manos a algn. **2** *vi* (*cloth*) rasgarse. **3** *n* desgarrón *m*.
• **tear off** *vt* arrancar.
• **tear out** *vt* arrancar.
• **tear up** *vt* hacer pedazos.

tease *vt* tomar el pelo a.

tea service *or* **set** juego *m* de té.

teaspoon cucharilla *f*.

teaspoonful cucharadita *f*.

teat (*of bottle*) tetina *f*.

teatime hora *f* del té.

tea towel paño *m* (de cocina).

technical *a* técnico,-a.

technician técnico,-a *mf*.

technique técnica *f*.

technology tecnología *f*.

teddy bear oso *m* de felpa.

teenager quinceañero,-a *mf*.

tee-shirt camiseta *f*.

teeth *npl see* **tooth**.

telegram telegrama *m*.

telephone teléfono *m*; **to speak to sb on the t.** hablar por teléfono con algn. **2** *vt* telefonear a, llamar por teléfono a.

telephone booth cabina f (telefónica).

telephone call llamada f telefónica.

telephone directory guía f telefónica.

telephone number número m de teléfono.

telescope telescopio m.

televise vt televisar.

television televisión f; **t. (set)** televisor m; **on t.** en la televisión.

tell* 1 vt decir; (relate) contar; (inform) comunicar; (order) mandar; (distinguish) distinguir; **to t. sb about sth** contarle algo a algn; **to t. sb to do sth** decir a algn que haga algo. 2 vi **who can I t.?** (know) ¿quién sabe?

· **tell off** vt reñir.

teller (cashier) cajero,-a mf.

telltale chivato,-a m.

temper (mood) humor m; **to keep one's t.** no perder la calma; **to lose one's t.** perder los estribos.

temperature temperatura f; **to have a t.** tener fiebre.

temple (building) templo m.

temporary a provisional; (setback, improvement) momentáneo,-a; (teacher) sustituto,-a.

tempt vt tentar; **to t. sb to do sth** incitar a algn a hacer algo.

temptation tentación f.

tempting a tentador,-a.

ten a & n diez (m) inv.

tenant (of house) inquilino,-a mf.

tend vi (be inclined) tender, tener tendencia (**to** a).

tendency tendencia f.

tender a (affectionate) cariñoso,-a; (meat) tierno,-a.

tennis tenis m.

tennis court pista f de tenis.

tense¹ a tenso,-a.

tense² n (of verb) tiempo m.

tension tensión f.

tent tienda f de campaña.

tenth a & n décimo,-a (mf).

term (period) período m; (of study) trimestre m; (word) término m; **terms** (conditions) condiciones fpl;

to be on good/bad terms with sb tener buenas/malas relaciones con algn.

terminal terminal f; (for computer) terminal m.

terrace (of houses) hilera f de casas; (patio) terraza f.

terraced houses casas fpl (de estilo uniforme) en hilera.

terrible a terrible; **I feel t.** me encuentro fatal.

terribly adv terriblemente.

terrific a fenomenal.

terrify vt aterrorizar.

terrifying a aterrador,-a.

territory territorio m.

terror terror m.

terrorist a & n terrorista (mf).

terrorize vt aterrorizar.

test 1 vt probar; (analyze) analizar. 2 n (of product) prueba f; (in school) examen m; (of blood) análisis m.

test tube probeta f.

text texto m.

textbook libro m de texto.

textile 1 n tejido m. 2 a textil.

Thai a & n tailandés,-esa (mf).

than conj que; (with numbers) de; **he's older t. me** es mayor que yo; **more interesting t. we thought** más interesante de lo que creíamos; **more t. once** más de una vez; **more t. ten people** más de diez personas.

thank vt agradecer; **t. you** gracias.

thankful a agradecido,-a.

thanks npl gracias fpl; **no, t.** no, gracias; **t. to** gracias a.

thanksgiving T. Day Día m de Acción de Gracias.

that 1 dem a (pl **those**) (masculine) ese; (feminine) esa; (further away) (masculine) aquel; (feminine) aquella; **at t. time** en aquella época; **t. book** ese or aquel libro; **t. one** ése, aquél. 2 dem pron (pl **those**) ése m, ésa f; (further away) aquél m, aquélla f; (indefinite) eso; (remote) aquello; **after t.** después de eso; **like t.** así; **don't talk like t.** no hables así; **t.'s right** eso es; **t.'s**

where I live allí vivo yo; **what's t.?** ¿qué es eso?; **who's t.?** ¿quién es?; **all those I saw** todos los que vi; **there are those who say that . . .** hay quien dice que . . . **3** *rel pron* que; **all t. you said** todo lo que dijiste; **the letter t. I sent you** la carta que te envié; **the car t. they came in** el coche en el que vinieron; **the moment t. you arrived** el momento en que llegaste. **4** *conj* que; **come here so t. I can see you** ven aquí para que te vea; **he said (t.) he would come** dijo que vendría. **5** *adv* así de, tan; **that much** tanto,-a; **cut off t. much** córteme un trozo así de grande; **t. old** tan viejo; **we haven't got t. much money** no tenemos tanto dinero.

thaw 1 *vt* (*snow*) derretir; (*food, freezer*) descongelar. **2** *vi* descongelarse; (*snow*) derretirse. **3** *n* deshielo *m*.

the *def art* el, la; *pl* los, las; **at** or **to t.** al, a la; *pl* a los, a las; **of** or **from t.** del, de la; *pl* de los, de las; **the voice of the people** la voz del pueblo; **George t. Sixth** Jorge Sexto.

theater teatro *m*.

theft robo *m*.

their *poss a* su; (*pl*) sus.

theirs *poss pron* (el) suyo, (la) suya; *pl* (los) suyos, (las) suyas.

them *pers pron pl* (*direct object*) los, las; (*indirect object*) les; **I know t.** los or las conozco; **I shall tell t. so** se lo diré (a ellos or ellas); **it's t.!** ¡son ellos!; **speak to t.** hábleles. ▪ (*with preposition*) ellos, ellas; **walk in front of t.** camine delante de ellos; **with t.** con ellos.

themselves *pers pron pl* (*as subject*) ellos mismos, ellas mismas; (*as direct or indirect object*) se; (*after a preposition*) sí mismos, sí mismas; **they did it by t.** lo hicieron ellos solos.

then 1 *adv* (*at that time, in that case*) entonces; (*next, afterwards*) luego; **since t.** desde entonces; **till**

t. hasta entonces; **go t.** pues vete. **2** *conj* entonces.

theory teoría *f*.

there *adv* (*indicating place*) allí, allá; (*nearer speaker*) ahí; **is Peter t.?** ¿está Peter?; **that man t.** aquel hombre; **t. is, t. are** hay; **t. were six of us** éramos seis.

therefore *adv* por lo tanto.

thermometer termómetro *m*.

Thermos® T. (**flask**) termo *m*.

thermostat termostato *m*.

these *dem a pl* estos,-as. **2** *dem pron pl* éstos,-as; *see* **this.**

they *pron* ellos, ellas; **t. are dancing** están bailando; **t. alone** ellos solos. ▪ (*indefinite*) **t. say that . . .** se dice que . . .

thick *a* (*book, slice, material*) grueso,-a; (*wood, vegetation*) espeso,-a; **a wall two meters t.** un muro de dos metros de espesor.

thicken 1 *vt* espesar. **2** *vi* espesarse.

thickness (*of wall etc*) espesor *m*; (*of wire, lips*) grueso *m*; (*of liquid, forest*) espesura *f*.

thief (*pl* **thieves**) ladrón,-ona *mf*.

thigh muslo *m*.

thimble dedal *m*.

thin 1 *a* delgado,-a; (*hair, vegetation*) ralo,-a; (*liquid*) claro,-a; **a t. slice** una loncha fina. **2** *vt* **to t.** (**down**) (*paint*) diluir.

thing cosa *f*; **my things** (*clothing*) mi ropa *f sing*; (*possessions*) mis cosas.

think* **1** *vt* pensar, creer; **I t. so/not** creo que sí/no; **I thought as much** ya me lo imaginaba. **2** *vi* pensar (*of, about* en); **what do you t.?** ¿a tí qué te parece?

• **think over** *vt* reflexionar; **we'll have to t. it over** lo tendremos que pensar.

• **think up** *vt* idear.

thinly *adv* ligeramente.

third 1 *a* tercero,-a; (*before masculine singular noun*) tercer; **on the t. of March** el tres de marzo. **2** *n* (*in series*) tercero,-a *mf*; (*fraction*) tercera parte.

thirdly adv en tercer lugar.

thirst sed f.

thirsty a to be t. tener sed.

thirteen a & n trece (m).

thirty a & n treinta (m).

this 1 dem a (pl these) (masculine) este; (feminine) esta; **t. book/ these books** este libro/estos libros; **t. one** éste, ésta. 2 (pl these) dem pron (indefinite) esto; **t. is different** esto es distinto; **it was like t.** fue así; **t. is where we met** fue aquí donde nos conocimos; **it should have come before t.** debería haber llegado ya; (introduction) **t. is Mr Álvarez** le presento al Sr. Álvarez; (on the phone) **t. is Julia (speaking)** soy Julia. ▪ (specific person or thing) éste m, ésta f; **I prefer these to those** me gustan más éstos que aquéllos. 3 adv **he got t. far** llegó hasta aquí; **t. small/big** así de pequeño/grande.

thorn espina f.

thorough a (careful) minucioso, -a; (work) concienzudo,-a; (knowledge) profundo,-a; **to carry out a t. inquiry into a matter** investigar a fondo un asunto.

thoroughly adv (carefully) a fondo; (wholly) completamente.

those 1 dem a esos,-as; (remote) aquellos,-as. 2 dem pron ésos,-as; (remote) aquéllos,-as; (with rel) los, las; see that 1 & 2.

though 1 conj aunque; **as t.** como si; **it looks as t. he's gone** parece que se ha ido. 2 adv sin embargo.

thought 1 pt & pp of think. 2 (act of thinking) pensamiento m; (reflection) reflexión f.

thoughtful a (considerate) atento,-a.

thoughtless a (person) desconsiderado,-a; (action) irreflexivo,-a.

thousand a & n mil (m) inv; **thousands of people** miles de personas.

thread 1 n hilo m. 2 vt (needle) enhebrar.

threat amenaza f.

threaten vt amenazar; **to t. to do sth** amenazar con hacer algo.

threatening a amenazador,-a.

three a & n tres (m) inv.

threw pt of throw.

thrill (excitement) emoción f.

thrilled a emocionado,-a; **I'm t. about the trip** estoy muy ilusionado,-a con el viaje.

thriller (book) novela f de suspense; (film) película f de suspense.

thrilling a emocionante.

thriving a próspero,-a.

throat garganta f.

throne trono m.

through 1 prep (place) a través de, por; **to look t. the window** mirar por la ventana. ▪ (time) a lo largo de; **all t. his life** durante toda su vida. ▪ (by means of) por, mediante. ▪ (because of) a or por causa de; **t. ignorance** por ignorancia. 2 a **a t. train** un tren directo. 3 adv (from one side to the other) de un lado a otro; **to let sb t.** dejar pasar a algn; **to get t. to sb** comunicar con algn; **I'm t. with him** he terminado con él.

throughout 1 prep por todo,-a; **t. the year** durante todo el año. 2 adv (place) en todas partes; (time) todo el tiempo.

throw* vt tirar; (to the ground) derribar; (party) dar.

• **throw away** vt (trash, money) tirar; (money) malgastar; (opportunity) perder.

• **throw out** vt (trash) tirar; (person) echar.

• **throw up** vti devolver.

thud ruido m sordo.

thug (lout) gamberro m; (criminal) criminal m.

thumb pulgar m.

thumbtack chincheta f.

thunder 1 n trueno m. 2 vi tronar.

thunderstorm tormenta f.

Thursday jueves m.

tick (mark) marca f de visto bueno.

• **tick off** vt (mark) marcar.

ticket (*for bus etc*) billete *m* ; (*for theater*) entrada *f* ; (*for lottery*) décimo *m* ; (*receipt*) recibo *m* .

ticket collector revisor,-a *mf* .

ticket office taquilla *f* .

tickle *vt* hacer cosquillas a.

ticklish *a* **to be t.** (*person*) tener cosquillas.

tide marea *f* .

tidily *adv* (*to put away*) ordenadamente.

tidy **1** *a* (*room, habits*) ordenado,-a; (*appearance*) arreglado,-a. **2** *vt* arreglar. **3** *vi* **to t. (up)** ordenar las cosas.

tie **1** *vt* (*shoelaces etc*) atar; **to t. a knot** hacer un nudo. **2** *n* (*around neck*) corbata *f* ; (*match*) partido *m* ; (*draw*) empate *m* .

• **tie up** *vt* (*parcel, dog*) atar.

tiger tigre *m* .

tight **1** *a* apretado,-a; (*clothing*) ajustado,-a; (*seal*) hermético,-a; **my shoes are too t.** me aprietan los zapatos. **2** *adv* estrechamente; (*seal*) herméticamente; **hold t.** agárrate fuerte; **shut t.** bien cerrado,-a.

tighten *vt* (*screw*) apretar; (*rope*) tensar.

tights *npl* (*thin*) panties *mpl* ; (*thick*) leotardos *mpl* .

tile **1** *n* (*of roof*) teja *f* ; (*glazed*) azulejo *m* ; (*for floor*) baldosa *f* . **2** *vt* (*roof*) tejar; (*wall*) alicatar; (*floor*) embaldosar.

till¹ (*for cash*) caja *f* .

till² **1** *prep* hasta; **from morning t. night** de la mañana a la noche; **t. then** hasta entonces. **2** *conj* hasta que.

tilt **1** *vi* **to t. over** volcarse; **to t. (up)** inclinarse. **2** *vt* inclinar.

timber madera *f* (de construcción).

time **1** *n* tiempo *m* ; (*era*) época *f* ; (*point in time*) momento *m* ; (*time of day*) hora *f* ; (*occasion*) vez *f* ; **all the t.** todo el tiempo; **for some t. (past)** desde hace algún tiempo; **I haven't seen him for a long t.** hace mucho (tiempo) que no lo veo; **in a**

short t. en poco tiempo; **in t.** a tiempo; **in three weeks' t.** dentro de tres semanas. **(at) any t. (you like)** cuando quiera; **at no t.** en ningún momento; **at that t.** (en aquel) entonces; **at the same t.** al mismo tiempo; **at times** a veces; **from t. to t.** de vez en cuando; **he may turn up at any t.** puede llegar en cualquier momento; **on t.** puntualmente; **what's the t.?** ¿qué hora es?; **t. of the year** época *f* del año; **to have a good/bad t.** pasarlo bien/mal; **four at a t.** cuatro a la vez; **next t.** la próxima vez; **three times four** tres (multiplicado) por cuatro; **four times as big** cuatro veces más grande. **2** *vt* (*speech*) calcular la duración de; (*race*) cronometrar; (*choose the time of*) escoger el momento oportuno para.

timer (*device*) temporizador *m* .

timetable horario *m* .

timid *a* tímido,-a.

timing (*timeliness*) oportunidad *f* ; (*coordination*) coordinación *f* ; (*in race*) cronometraje *m* .

tin (*metal*) estaño *m* ; (*container*) lata *f* .

tinfoil papel *m* de estaño.

tinned *a* enlatado,-a; **t. food** conservas *fpl* .

tin-opener abrelatas *m inv* .

tiny *a* diminuto,-a.

tip¹ (*end*) punta *f* ; (*of cigarette*) colilla *f* .

tip² **1** *n* (*gratuity*) propina *f* ; (*advice*) consejo *m* . **2** *vt* dar una propina a.

tip³ **1** *vt* inclinar. **2** *vi* **to t. (up)** ladearse; (*cart*) bascular.

• **tip over** **1** *vt* volcar. **2** *vi* volcarse.

tipped cigarette cigarrillo *m* con filtro.

tiptoe **on t.** de puntillas.

tire¹ (*of vehicle*) neumático *m* .

tire² **1** *vt* cansar. **2** *vi* cansarse.

• **tire out** *vt* agotar.

tired *a* cansado,-a; **t. out** rendido, -a; **to be t. of sth** estar harto,-a de algo.

tiredness cansancio *m*.

tiring *a* agotador,-a.

tissue (*handkerchief*) Kleenex® *m*.

title título *m*.

to 1 *prep* (*with place*) a; (*towards*) hacia; **he went to France/Japan** fue a Francia/al Japón; **I'm going to Mary's** voy a casa de Mary; **it is thirty miles to New York** Nueva York está a treinta millas; **the train to Madrid** el tren de Madrid; **to the east** hacia el este; **to the right** a la derecha. ▪ (*time*) **ten (minutes) to six** las seis menos diez. ▪ (*with indirect object*) a; **he gave it to his cousin** se lo dio a su primo. ▪ (*towards*) **he was very kind to me** se portó muy bien conmigo. ▪ (*with infinitive*) **to buy/to come** comprar/venir; (*in order to*) para; (*with verbs of motion*) a; **he did it to help me** lo hizo para ayudarme; **he stopped to talk** se detuvo a hablar; **difficult to do** difícil de hacer; **ready to listen** dispuesto,-a a escuchar; **the first to complain** el primero en quejarse; **this is the time to do it** éste es el momento de hacerlo; **to have a great deal to do** tener mucho que hacer.

toad sapo *m*.

toadstool hongo *m* (venenoso).

toast 1 *n* **slice of t.** tostada *f*. **2** *vt* tostar.

toaster tostador *m* (de pan).

tobacco tabaco *m*.

tobacconist t.'s (shop) estanco *m*.

toboggan tobogán *m*.

today *adv* hoy.

toddler niño,-a *mf* pequeño,- a.

toe dedo *m* del pie.

toenail uña *f* del dedo del pie.

toffee caramelo *m*.

together *adv* junto,-a, juntos,-as; **all t.** todos juntos; **t. with** junto con.

toilet wáter *m*; (*public*) servicios *mpl*.

toilet paper *or* **tissue** papel *m* higiénico.

toiletries *npl* artículos *mpl* de aseo.

toilet roll rollo *m* de papel higiénico.

toilet water (*perfume*) agua *f* de colonia.

token (*for telephone*) ficha *f*; **book t.** vale *m* para comprar libros.

told *pt* & *pp* of **tell**.

tolerant *a* tolerante.

tolerate *vt* tolerar.

toll (*for road*) peaje *m*.

toll-free number teléfono *m* gratuito.

tomato (*pl* tomatoes) tomate *m*.

tomb tumba *f*.

tomorrow *adv* mañana; **the day after t.** pasado mañana; **t. night** mañana por la noche.

ton tonelada *f*; *fam* **tons of** montones de.

tone tono *m*.

tongs *npl* (*for sugar, hair*) tenacillas *fpl*; (**fire**) **t.** tenazas *fpl*.

tongue lengua *f*.

tonic (*drink*) tónica *f*.

tonight *adv* esta noche.

tonsil amígdala *f*.

tonsillitis amigdalitis *f*.

too *adv* (*also*) también; (*excessively*) demasiado; **t. much/many** demasiado,-a, demasiados,-as; **ten pounds t. much** diez libras de más; **t. much money** demasiado dinero; **t. old** demasiado viejo.

took *pt* of **take**.

tool (*utensil*) herramienta *f*.

tooth (*pl* teeth) diente *m*.

toothache dolor *m* de muelas.

toothbrush cepillo *m* de dientes.

toothpaste pasta *f* dentífrica.

toothpick mondadientes *m inv*.

top¹ 1 *n* (*upper part*) parte *f* de arriba; (*of hill*) cumbre *f*; (*of tree*) copa *f*; (*surface*) superficie *f*; (*of list etc*) cabeza *f*; (*of bottle etc*) tapón *m*; (*best*) lo mejor; **on t. of** encima de. **2** *a* (*part*) superior, de arriba; (*best*) mejor; **the t. floor** el último piso.

• **top up** *vt* llenar hasta el tope.

top² (*toy*) peonza *f*.

topic tema *m*.

torch (*burning*) antorcha *f*.

torment *vt* atormentar.

tornado tornado *m*.

tortoise tortuga *f* de tierra.

tortoiseshell 1 *a* de carey. **2** *n* carey *m*.

torture 1 *vt* torturar; (*cause anguish*) atormentar. **2** *n* tortura *f*; (*anguish*) tormento *m*.

toss 1 *vt* (*ball*) tirar; (*throw about*) sacudir; **to t. a coin** echar a cara o cruz. **2** *vi* **to t. about** agitarse; (*in sport*) **to t. (up)** sortear.

total total *m*; (*in check*) importe *m*.

totally *adv* totalmente.

touch 1 *vt* tocar; (*lightly*) rozar; (*emotionally*) conmover. **2** *vi* tocarse; (*lightly*) rozarse. **3** *n* toque *m*; (*light contact*) roce *m*; (*sense of touch*) tacto *m*; **in t. with sb** en contacto con algn.

• **touch down** *vi* (*plane*) aterrizar.

touchy *a* (*person*) susceptible.

tough *a* (*material, competitor etc*) fuerte; (*test, criminal, meat*) duro, -a; (*punishment*) severo,-a; (*problem*) difícil.

tour 1 *n* (*journey*) viaje *m*; (*of palace etc*) visita *f*; (*of city*) recorrido *m* turístico; (*of theatrical company, team*) gira *f*; **on t.** de gira. **2** *vt* (*country*) viajar por; (*building*) visitar. **3** *vi* estar de viaje.

tourism turismo *m*.

tourist turista *mf*; **t. class** clase *f* turista.

tourist office oficina *f* de información turística.

tournament torneo *m*.

tow *vt* remolcar.

towards *prep* hacia; **our duty t. others** nuestro deber para con los demás.

towel toalla *f*.

tower torre *f*.

tower block torre *f*.

town ciudad *f*; (*small*) pueblo *m*; **to go into t.** ir al centro.

town council ayuntamiento *m*.

town hall ayuntamiento *m*.

tow truck grúa *f*.

toy juguete *m*.

toyshop juguetería *f*.

trace 1 *n* (*sign*) indicio *m*, vestigio *m*. **2** *vt* (*drawing*) calcar; (*locate*) seguir la pista de.

tracing paper papel *m* de calco.

track (*mark*) huellas *fpl*; (*pathway*) camino *m*; (*for running*) pista *f*; (*of railroad*) vía *f*; (*on record*) canción *f*; **to be on the right t.** ir por buen camino; **to be on the wrong t.** haberse equivocado.

tracksuit chandal *m*.

tractor tractor *m*.

trade 1 *n* (*job*) oficio *m*; (*sector*) industria *f*; (*commerce*) comercio *m*. **2** *vi* comerciar (**in** en). **3** *vt* **to t. sth for sth** trocar algo por algo.

trademark marca *f* de fábrica; **registered t.** marca registrada.

trade union sindicato *m*.

trading comercio *m*.

tradition tradición *f*.

traditional *a* tradicional.

traffic *n* tráfico *m*.

traffic jam atasco *m*.

traffic lights *npl* semáforo *m sing*.

traffic sign señal *f* de tráfico.

tragedy tragedia *f*.

tragic *a* trágico,-a.

trail 1 *vt* **to t. sth (along)** (*drag*) arrastrar algo. **2** *vi* (*drag*) arrastrarse; **to t. (along)** (*linger*) rezagarse. **3** *n* senda *f*; (*bigger*) pista *f* (*of smoke*) estela *f*.

trailer (*behind vehicle*) remolque *m*; (*caravan*) caravana *f*.

train¹ *n* tren *m*; **to go by t.** ir en tren.

train² **1** *vt* (*in sport*) entrenar; (*animal*) amaestrar; (*teach*) formar. **2** *vi* entrenarse; (*be taught*) prepararse.

trained *a* (*skilled*) cualificado,-a.

trainers *npl* (*shoes*) zapatillas *fpl* de deporte.

training entrenamiento *m*; (*instruction*) formación *f*.

traitor traidor,-a *mf*.
tram tranvía *m*.
tramp (*person*) vagabundo,-a *mf*.
tranquillizer tranquilizante *m*.
transfer 1 *vt* trasladar; (*funds*) transferir; **a transferred charge call** una conferencia a cobro revertido. 2 *n* traslado *m*; (*of funds*) transferencia *f*; (*picture, design*) calcomanía *f*.
transfusion transfusión *f* (de sangre).
transistor transistor *m*.
transitive *a* transitivo,-a.
translate *vt* traducir.
translation traducción *f*.
translator traductor,-a *mf*.
transparent *a* transparente.
transplant trasplante *m*.
transport 1 *vt* transportar. 2 *n* transporte *m*.
trap 1 *n* trampa *f*. 2 *vt* (*animal, fugitive*) atrapar; **to t. sb into doing sth** lograr con ardides que algn haga algo.
trap door trampilla *f*.
trash (*inferior goods*) bazofia *f*; (*household waste*) basura *f*; **fam** (*worthless thing*) birria *f*; **fam** (*nonsense*) tonterías *fpl*.
trash can cubo *m* de la basura.
trash dump vertedero *m*.
trashy *a fam* (*book, film*) sin valor.
travel 1 *vi* viajar; (*vehicle, electric current*) ir; **to t. through** recorrer. 2 *vt* recorrer. 3 *n* viajar *m*.
travel agency agencia *f* de viajes.
travel sickness mareo *m*.
traveler viajero,-a *mf*.
traveler's check cheque *m* de viaje.
traveling 1 *a* (*salesman*) ambulante. 2 *n* los viajes *mpl*; **I'm fond of t.** me gusta viajar.
tray (*for food*) bandeja *f*.
treacherous *a* (*dangerous*) peligroso,-a.
tread* *vi* pisar.
• **tread on** *vt* pisar.
treasure tesoro *m*.
treat 1 *n* (*present*) regalo *m*. 2 *vt* tratar; (*regard*) considerar; **he**

treated them to dinner les invitó a cenar.
treatment (*of person*) trato *m*; (*of subject, patient*) tratamiento *m*.
treble 1 *vt* triplicar. 2 *vi* triplicarse.
tree árbol *m*.
tremble *vi* temblar.
trench (*ditch*) zanja *f*; (*for troops*) trinchera *f*.
trial (*in court*) juicio *m*.
triangle triángulo *m*.
triangular *a* triangular.
tribe tribu *f*.
trick 1 *n* (*ruse*) ardid *m*; (*dishonest*) engaño *m*; (*practical joke*) broma *f*; (*of magic, knack*) truco *m*; **to play a t. on sb** gastarle una broma a algn. 2 *vt* engañar.
trickle 1 *vi* (*water*) gotear. 2 *n* hilo *m*.
tricky *a* (*situation*) delicado,-a; (*problem*) difícil.
tricycle triciclo *m*.
trigger (*of gun*) gatillo *m*.
trim (*cut*) recortar; (*expenses*) disminuir.
trip 1 *n* (*journey*) viaje *m*; (*excursion*) excursión *f*. 2 *vi* **to t. (up)** (*stumble*) tropezar (**over** con).
triple 1 *vt* triplicar. 2 *vi* triplicarse.
triumph 1 *n* triunfo *m*. 2 *vi* triunfar.
trivial *a* trivial.
trolley carro *m*.
trombone trombón *m*.
troops tropas *fpl*.
trophy trofeo *m*.
tropical *a* tropical.
trot 1 *vi* trotar. 2 *n* trote *m*.
trouble 1 *n* (*misfortune*) desgracia *f*; (*problems*) problemas *mpl*; (*effort*) esfuerzo *m*; **to be in t.** estar en un apuro; **it's not worth the t.** no merece la pena; **to take the t. to do sth** molestarse en hacer algo; **to have liver t.** tener problemas de hígado. 2 *vt* (*distress*) afligir; (*worry*) preocupar; (*bother*) molestar.
trousers *npl* pantalón *m sing*, pantalones *mpl*.
trout trucha *f*.

truant to play t. hacer novillos.

truck camión *m*.

true *a* verdadero,-a; (*faithful*) fiel; **to come t.** cumplirse; **it's not t.** no es verdad; **it's t. that . . .** es verdad que . . .

trump (*in cards*) triunfo *m*.

trumpet trompeta *f*.

trunk (*of tree, body*) tronco *m*; (*of elephant*) trompa *f*; (*case*) baúl *m*; (*of car*) maletero *m*.

trunks *npl* (**swimming**) **t.** bañador *m sing*.

trust 1 *n* confianza *f*. **2** *vt* (*rely upon*) fiarse de; **to t. sb with sth** confiar algo a algn.

truth verdad *f*.

try 1 *vt* (*attempt*) intentar; (*test*) probar. **2** *vi* intentar; **to t. to do sth** tratar de *or* intentar hacer algo. **3** *n* (*attempt*) tentativa *f*; (*in rugby*) ensayo *m*.

• **try on** *vt* (*dress*) probarse.

• **try out** *vt* probar.

T-shirt camiseta *f*.

tub (*container*) tina *f*; (*bath*) bañera *f*.

tube tubo *m*; (*in body*) conducto *m*.

tuck *vt* **to t. in the bedclothes** remeter la ropa de la cama; **to t. one's shirt into one's trousers** meterse la camisa por dentro (de los pantalones).

Tuesday martes *m*.

tuft (*of hair*) mechón *m*; (*of wool etc*) copo *m*.

tug 1 *vt* (*pull at*) tirar de; (*haul along*) arrastrar; (*boat*) remolcar. **2** *n* (*boat*) remolcador *m*.

tugboat remolcador *m*.

tuition instrucción *f*; **private t.** clases *fpl* particulares; **t. fees** tasas *fpl*.

tulip tulipán *m*.

tumble 1 *vi* (*person*) caerse. **2** *n* caída *f*.

tumble dryer secadora *f*.

tumbler (*glass*) vaso *m*.

tummy *fam* estómago *m*; (*belly*) barriga *f*.

tuna atún *m*.

tune 1 *n* (*melody*) melodía *f*; **in/out**

of t. afinado/desafinado; **to sing out of t.** desafinar. **2** *vt* (*instrument*) afinar; (*engine*) poner a punto.

• **tune in to** *vt* (*on radio etc*) sintonizar.

tuning (*of instrument*) afinación *f*.

Tunisian *a & n* tunecino,-a (*mf*).

tunnel túnel *m*.

turban turbante *m*.

turkey pavo *m*.

Turkish 1 *a* turco,-a. **2** *n* (*language*) turco *m*.

turn 1 *vt* (*revolve*) girar; (*page, head, gaze*) volver; (*change*) transformar (**into** en); **he's turned forty** ha cumplido los cuarenta. **2** *vi* (*revolve*) girar; (*change direction*) torcer; (*turn round*) volverse; (*become*) volverse; **to t. to sb** (*for help*) acudir a algn. **3** *n* (*of wheel*) vuelta *f*; (*in road*) curva *f*; (*in game, line*) turno *m*; **it's your t.** te toca a ti; **to take it in turns to do sth** turnarse para hacer algo.

• **turn around** *vi* (*of person*) volverse.

• **turn away 1** *vt* (*person*) rechazar. **2** *vi* volver la cabeza; (*move away*) alejarse.

• **turn back 1** *vt* (*person*) hacer retroceder. **2** *vi* volverse.

• **turn down** *vt* (*gas, radio etc*) bajar; (*reject*) rechazar.

• **turn into 1** *vt* convertir en. **2** *vi* convertirse en.

• **turn off** *vt* (*light, TV, radio, engine*) apagar; (*water, gas*) cortar; (*faucet*) cerrar.

• **turn on** *vt* (*light, TV, radio, engine*) encender; (*water, gas*) abrir la llave de; (*faucet*) abrir.

• **turn out 1** *vt* (*extinguish*) apagar. **2** *vi* **it turns out that . . .** resulta que . . . ; **things have turned out well** las cosas han salido bien.

• **turn over 1** *vt* (*turn upside down*) poner al revés; (*page*) dar la vuelta a. **2** *vi* volverse.

• **turn round 1** *vt* volver. **2** *vi* (*rotate*) girar.

• **turn up 1** vt (collar) levantar; (TV, volume) subir; (light) aumentar la intensidad de. **2** vi (arrive) presentarse.

turning (in road) salida f.

turnip nabo m.

turnup (of trousers) vuelta f.

turtle tortuga f.

turtleneck a t. sweater un jersey de cuello alto.

tusk colmillo m.

tutor (at university) tutor,-a mf; **private t.** profesor,-a mf particular.

TV TV.

tweezers npl pinzas fpl.

twelfth a & n duodécimo,-a (mf).

twelve a & n doce (m) inv; **t. o'clock** las doce.

twentieth a & n vigésimo,-a (mf).

twenty a & n veinte (m) inv.

twice adv dos veces; **he's t. as old as I am** tiene el doble de años que yo; **t. as big** el doble de grande.

twig ramita f.

twilight crepúsculo m.

twin n mellizo,-a mf; **identical twins** gemelos mpl (idénticos); **t. beds** camas fpl gemelas.

twine bramante m.

twist 1 vt torcer; **to t. one's ankle** torcerse el tobillo. **2** n (movement) torsión f; (in road) vuelta f.

• **twist off** (lid) desenroscar.

two a & n dos (m) inv.

two-way a (street) de dos direcciones.

type 1 n (kind) tipo m; (print) caracteres mpl. **2** vti escribir a máquina.

typewriter máquina f de escribir.

typewritten a escrito,-a a máquina.

typical a típico,-a.

typing mecanografía f.

typist mecanógrafo,-a mf.

U

UFO abbr of **unidentified flying object** OVNI m.

ugliness fealdad f.

ugly a feo,-a; (situation) desagradable.

ulcer (sore) llaga f; (internal) úlcera f.

umbrella paraguas m inv.

umpire árbitro m.

unable to be u. to do sth no poder hacer algo.

unacceptable a inaceptable.

unaccustomed a **he's u. to this climate** no está acostumbrado a este clima.

unanimous a unánime.

unanimously adv unánimemente.

unattractive a (idea, appearance) poco atractivo,-a.

unavailable a no disponible; **Mr Smith is u. today** Mr Smith no le puede atender hoy.

unavoidable a inevitable; (accident) imprevisible.

unavoidably adv inevitablemente.

unaware 1 a **to be u. of sth** ignorar algo. **2** adv (without knowing) inconscientemente; **it caught me u.** me cogió desprevenido.

unbearable a insoportable.

unbelievable a increíble.

unbreakable a irrompible.

unbutton vt desabrochar.

uncertain a (not certain) incierto, -a; (doubtful) dudoso,-a; (hesitant) indeciso,-a.

uncertainty incertidumbre f.

unchanged a igual.

uncle tío m.

unclear a poco claro,-a.

uncomfortable a incómodo,-a.

uncommon a (rare) poco común.

unconnected a no relacionado,-a.

unconscious a inconsciente (**of** de).

unconvincing a poco convincente.

uncooperative a poco cooperativo,-a.

uncork *vt* (*bottle*) descorchar.

uncover *vt* destapar; (*discover*) descubrir.

undamaged *a* (*article etc*) sin desperfectos.

undecided *a* (*person*) indeciso,-a.

undeniable *a* innegable.

under 1 *prep* debajo de; (*less than*) menos de; **u. the circumstances** dadas las circunstancias; **u. there** allí debajo. **2** *adv* debajo.

under- *prefix* (*below*) sub-, infra-; (*insufficiently*) insuficientemente.

undercharge *vt* cobrar menos de lo debido.

underclothes *npl* ropa *f sing* interior.

underdone *a* poco hecho,-a.

underestimate *vt* subestimar.

undergo* *vt* experimentar; (*change*) sufrir; (*test etc*) pasar por.

undergraduate estudiante *mf* universitario,-a.

underground *a* subterráneo,-a.

underline *vt* subrayar.

underneath 1 *prep* debajo de. **2** *adv* debajo. **3** *n* parte *f* inferior.

underpants *npl* calzoncillos *mpl*.

underpass paso *n* subterráneo.

undershirt camiseta *f*.

understand* *vti* entender.

understandable *a* comprensible.

understanding 1 *n* (*intellectual grasp*) comprensión *f*; (*agreement*) acuerdo *m*. **2** *a* comprensivo,-a.

understood 1 *pt & pp of* **understand. 2** *a* (*agreed on*) convenido,-a.

undertake* *vt* (*responsibility*) asumir; (*task, job*) encargarse de; (*promise*) comprometerse a.

undertaker empresario,-a *mf* de pompas fúnebres.

undertaker's funeraria *f*.

undertaking (*task*) empresa *f*.

underwater 1 *a* submarino,-a. **2** *adv* bajo el agua.

underwear *inv* ropa *f* interior.

undo* *vt* deshacer; (*button*) desabrochar.

undone *a* (*knot etc*) deshecho,-a;

to come u. (*shoelace*) desatarse; (*button, blouse*) desabrocharse; (*necklace etc*) soltarse.

undoubtedly *adv* indudablemente.

undress 1 *vt* desnudar. **2** *vi* desnudarse.

uneasy *a* (*worried*) preocupado,-a; (*disturbing*) inquietante; (*uncomfortable*) incómodo,-a.

unemployed 1 *a* **to be u.** estar en paro. **2** *npl* **the u.** los parados.

unemployment paro *m*.

uneven *a* (*not level*) desigual; (*bumpy*) accidentado,-a; (*variable*) irregular.

uneventful *a* sin acontecimientos.

unexpected *a* (*unhoped for*) inesperado,-a; (*event*) imprevisto,-a.

unexpectedly *adv* inesperadamente.

unfair *a* injusto,-a.

unfairly *adv* injustamente.

unfairness injusticia *f*.

unfaithful *a* (*friend*) desleal; (*husband, wife*) infiel.

unfamiliar *a* (*unknown*) desconocido,-a; **to be u. with sth** no conocer bien algo.

unfashionable *a* pasado,-a de moda; (*ideas etc*) poco popular.

unfasten *vt* (*knot*) desatar; (*clothing, belt*) desabrochar.

unfavorable, desfavorable.

unfinished *a* inacabado,-a.

unfit *a* (*food, building*) inadecuado,-a; (*person*) no apto,-a (**for** para); (*incompetent*) incompetente; (*physically*) incapacitado, -a; **to be u.** no estar en forma.

unfold *vt* (*sheet*) desdoblar; (*newspaper*) abrir.

unforgettable *a* inolvidable.

unforgivable *a* imperdonable.

unfortunate *a* (*person, event*) desgraciado,-a; **how u.!** ¡qué mala suerte!

unfortunately *adv* desgraciadamente.

unfriendly *a* antipático,-a.

unfurnished *a* sin amueblar.

ungrateful a (*unthankful*) desagradecido,-a.

unhappiness tristeza f.

unhappy a triste.

unharmed a ileso,-a, indemne.

unhealthy a (*ill*) enfermizo,-a; (*unwholesome*) malsano,-a.

unhelpful a (*advice*) inútil; (*person*) poco servicial.

unhook vt (*from hook*) descolgar; (*clothing*) desabrochar.

unhurt a ileso,-a.

unhygienic a antihigiénico,-a.

uniform a & n uniforme (m).

unimportant a poco importante.

uninhabited a despoblado,-a.

uninjured a ileso,-a.

unintentional a involuntario,-a.

uninteresting a poco interesante.

union 1 n unión f; (*organization*) sindicato m. 2 a sindical.

unique a único,-a.

unit unidad f; (*piece of furniture*) módulo m; (*team*) equipo m; **kitchen u.** mueble m de cocina.

unite 1 vt unir. 2 vi unirse.

universal a universal.

universe universo m.

university 1 n universidad f. 2 a universitario,-a.

unjust a injusto,-a.

unkind a (*not nice*) poco amable; (*cruel*) despiadado,-a.

unknown a desconocido,-a.

unleaded a (*gasoline*) sin plomo.

unless conj a menos que + subj, a no ser que + subj.

unlike prep a diferencia de.

unlikely a (*improbable*) poco probable.

unlimited a ilimitado,-a.

unload vti descargar.

unlock vt abrir (con llave).

unlucky a (*unfortunate*) desgraciado,-a; **to be u.** (*person*) tener mala suerte; (*thing*) traer mala suerte.

unmade a (*bed*) deshecho,-a.

unmarried a soltero,-a.

unnecessary a innecesario,-a.

unnoticed a desapercibido,-a; **to let sth pass u.** pasar algo por alto.

unoccupied a (*house*) desocupado,-a; (*seat*) libre.

unpack 1 vt (*boxes*) desembalar; (*suitcase*) deshacer. 2 vi deshacer la(s) maleta(s).

unpaid a (*bill, debt*) impagado, -a; (*work*) no retribuido,-a.

unpleasant a (*not nice*) desagradable; (*unfriendly*) antipático,-a (**to** con).

unplug vt desenchufar.

unpopular a impopular; **to make oneself u.** ganarse la antipatía de algn.

unpredictable a imprevisible.

unprepared a (*speech etc*) improvisado,-a; (*person*) desprevenido,-a.

unreasonable a poco razonable; (*demands*) desmedido,-a.

unrecognizable a irreconocible.

unrelated a (*not connected*) no relacionado,-a.

unreliable a (*person*) de poca confianza; (*information*) que no es de fiar; (*machine*) poco fiable.

unrest (*social etc*) malestar m.

unroll vt desenrollar.

unsafe a (*activity, journey*) peligroso,-a; (*building, car, machine*) inseguro,-a; **to feel u.** sentirse expuesto,-a.

unsatisfactory a insatisfactorio, -a.

unscrew vt destornillar.

unskilled a (*worker*) no cualificado,-a.

unstable a inestable.

unsteadily adv (*to walk*) con paso inseguro.

unsteady a (*not firm*) inestable; (*table, chair*) cojo,-a; (*hand, voice*) tembloroso,-a.

unsuccessful a (*person, negotiation*) fracasado,-a; (*attempt, effort*) vano,-a; (*candidate*) derrotado,-a; **to be u. at sth** no tener éxito con algo.

unsuccessfully adv sin éxito.

unsuitable a (*person*) no apto,-a; (*thing*) inadecuado,-a.

unsuited a (*person*) no apto,-a; (*thing*) impropio,-a (**to** para).

unsure *a* poco seguro,-a; **to be u. of sth** no estar seguro,-a de algo.

untangle *vt* desenmarañar.

untidy *a* (*room, person*) desordenado,-a; (*hair*) despeinado,-a; (*appearance*) desaseado,-a.

untie *vt* desatar.

until 1 *conj* hasta que; **u. she gets back** hasta que vuelva. **2** *prep* hasta; **u. now** hasta ahora; **not u. Monday** hasta el lunes no.

untrue *a* (*false*) falso,-a.

unused *a* (*car*) sin usar; (*stamp*) sin matar.

unusual *a* (*rare*) poco común; (*exceptional*) excepcional.

unusually *adv* excepcionalmente.

unwell *a* **to be u.** estar malo,-a.

unwilling *a* **to be u. to do sth** no estar dispuesto a hacer algo.

unwillingly *adv* de mala gana.

unworthy *a* indigno,-a.

unwrap *vt* (*gift*) desenvolver; (*package*) deshacer.

unzip *vt* bajar la cremallera de.

up 1 *prep* (*movement*) **to climb up the mountain** escalar la montaña; **to walk up the street** ir calle arriba. ▪ (*position*) en lo alto de; **further up the street** más adelante (en la misma calle). **2** *adv* (*upwards*) arriba; **further up** hacia arriba; **from ten pounds up** de diez libras para arriba; **right up (to the top)** hasta arriba (del todo); **to go** *or* **come up** subir; **to walk up and down** ir de un lado a otro. ▪ (*towards*) hacia; **to come** *or* **go up to sb** acercarse a algn. ▪ (*increased*) **bread is up** el pan ha subido. ▪ (*wrong*) **what's up (with you?)** ¿qué pasa (contigo)?; **something must be up** debe pasar algo. ▪ **up to** (*as far as, until*) hasta; **I can spend up to $5** puedo gastar un máximo de cinco dólares; **up to here** hasta aquí; **up to now** hasta ahora. ▪ **to be up to** (*depend on*) depender de; (*be capable of*) estar a la altura de; **he's up to something** está tramando algo. **3** *a* (*out of bed*)

levantado,-a; (*finished*) terminado,-a; **time's up** (ya) es la hora. **4** *vt* (*increase*) aumentar. **5** *n* **ups and downs** altibajos *mpl*.

uphill *adv* cuesta arriba.

upon *prep* sobre.

upper *a* superior.

upright 1 *a* (*vertical*) vertical; (*honest*) honrado,-a. **2** *adv* derecho.

uproar tumulto *m*.

upset 1 *vt** (*shock*) trastornar; (*worry*) preocupar; (*displease*) disgustar; (*spoil*) desbaratar; (*make ill*) sentar mal a. **2** *a* (*shocked*) alterado,-a; (*displeased*) disgustado,-a; **to have an u. stomach** sentirse mal del estómago.

upside down al revés.

upstairs 1 *adv* arriba. **2** *n* piso *m* de arriba.

up to date *a* (*current*) al día; (*modern*) moderno,-a. **to be u. with sth** estar al tanto de algo.

upward(s) *adv* hacia arriba; **from ten (years) u.** a partir de los diez años.

urge *vt* (*incite*) incitar; (*press*) instar; (*plead*) exhortar; (*advocate*) preconizar; **to u. that sth should be done** insistir en que se haga algo.

urgency urgencia *f*.

urgent *a* urgente; (*need, tone*) apremiante.

urgently *adv* urgentemente.

Uruguayan *a* & *n* uruguayo,-a (*mf*).

us *pers pron* (*as object*) nos; (*after prep, 'to be'*) nosotros,-as; **she wouldn't believe it was us** no creía que fuéramos nosotros; **let's forget it** olvidémoslo.

use 1 *vt* utilizar; (*consume*) consumir; **what is it used for?** ¿para qué sirve? **2** *n* uso *m*; **'not in u.'** 'no funciona'; **to be of u.** servir; **to make (good) u. of sth** aprovechar algo; **it's no u.** es inútil; **it's no u. crying** no sirve de nada llorar.

▪ **use up** *vt* acabar; (*food*) consumir; (*gas*) agotar; (*money*) gastar.

used[1] a (second-hand) usado,-a.

used[2] 1 v aux where did you u. to live? ¿dónde vivías (antes)?; I u. to play the piano solía tocar el piano; I u. not to like it antes no me gustaba. 2 to be u. to sth estar acostumbrado,-a a algo.

useful a útil; (practical) práctico, -a; to come in u. venir bien.

usefulness utilidad f.

useless a inútil.

user usuario,-a mf.

usual a corriente; as u. como siempre.

usually adv normalmente.

utensil utensilio m; kitchen utensils batería f sing de cocina.

utility utilidad f.

utter[1] vt (words) pronunciar; (cry, threat) lanzar.

utter[2] a total.

utterly adv completamente.

U-turn cambio m de sentido.

V

vacancy (job) vacante f; (room) habitación f libre.

vacant a (empty) vacío,-a; (room, seat) libre.

vacation vacaciones fpl; on v. de vacaciones.

vacationer summer v. veraneante mf.

vaccinate vt vacunar.

vaccination vacuna f.

vaccine vacuna f.

vacuum 1 vt limpiar con aspiradora. 2 n vacío m.

vacuum cleaner aspiradora f.

vague a (imprecise) vago,-a; (indistinct) borroso,-a.

vaguely adv vagamente.

vain a in v. en vano.

valid a válido,-a.

valley valle m.

valuable 1 a valioso,-a. 2 npl valuables objetos mpl de valor.

value valor m; to get good v. for money sacarle jugo al dinero.

van furgoneta f.

vandal gamberro,-a mf.

vandalize vt destrozar.

vanilla vainilla f.

vanish vi desaparecer.

varied a variado,-a.

variety (diversity) variedad f; (assortment) surtido m; for a v. of reasons por razones diversas.

variety show espectáculo m de variedades.

various a diversos,-as.

varnish 1 n barniz m. 2 vt barnizar.

vary vti variar.

vase florero m.

Vaseline® vaselina f.

vast a vasto,-a.

VAT abbr of value added tax IVA m.

VCR abbr of video cassette recorder (grabador m de) vídeo m.

veal ternera f.

vegetable verdura f.

vegetarian a & n vegetariano,-a (mf).

vegetation vegetación f.

vehicle vehículo m.

veil velo m.

vein vena f.

velvet terciopelo m.

vending machine máquina f expendedora.

venetian blind persiana f graduable.

Venezuelan a & n venezolano,-a (mf).

ventilation ventilación f.

verb verbo m.

verdict veredicto m; (opinion) opinión f.

verge (of road) arcén m.

verse (stanza) estrofa f; (poetry) versos mpl; (of song) copla f.

version versión f.

vertical a vertical.

very adv muy; v. much muchísimo; at the v. latest como máximo; the v. first/last el primero/último de todos; at this v. moment en este mismo momento.

vest (undershirt) camiseta f; chaleco m.

vet veterinario,-a *mf*.
via *prep* por.
vibrate *vi* vibrar (**with** de).
vibration vibración *f*.
vicar párroco *m*.
vice¹ vicio *m*.
vice² (*tool*) torno *m* de banco.
vicious *a* (*violent*) violento,-a; (*malicious*) malintencionado,-a; (*cruel*) cruel.
victim víctima *f*.
victory victoria *f*.
video vídeo *m*; **v. (cassette)** videocasete *m*; **v. (cassette recorder)** vídeo *m*.
video camera videocámara *f*.
video game videojuego *m*.
video tape cinta *f* de vídeo.
view (*sight*) vista *f*; (*opinion*) opinión *f*; **to come into v.** aparecer; **in v. of the fact that . . .** dado que . . .
viewer (*of TV*) televidente *mf*.
viewpoint punto *m* de vista.
villa (*country house*) casa *f* de campo.
village (*small*) aldea *f*; (*larger*) pueblo *m*.
villager aldeano,-a *mf*.
vinegar vinagre *m*.
vineyard viñedo *m*.
violence violencia *f*.
violent *a* violento,-a.
violently *adv* violentamente.
violin violín *m*.
virus virus *m inv*.
visa visado *m*, *Am* visa *f*.
visible *a* visible.
visit 1 *vt* visitar. 2 *n* visita *f*; **to pay sb a v.** hacerle una visita a algn.
visiting hours *npl* horas *fpl* de visita.
visitor (*guest*) invitado,-a *mf*; (*tourist*) turista *mf*.
vital *a* (*essential*) fundamental.
vitally *adv* **it's v. important** es de vital importancia.
vitamin vitamina *f*.
vivid *a* (*color*) vivo,-a; (*description*) gráfico,-a.
vocabulary vocabulario *m*.
vodka vodka *m & f*.

voice voz *f*; **at the top of one's v.** a voz en grito.
volcano (*pl volcanoes*) volcán *m*.
volume volumen *m*.
voluntary *a* voluntario,-a.
volunteer 1 *n* voluntario,-a *mf*. 2 *vi* ofrecerse (**for** para).
vomit *vti* vomitar.
vote 1 *n* voto *m*; (*voting*) votación *f*. 2 *vti* votar.
voter votante *mf*.
voucher vale *m*.
vowel vocal *f*.
voyage viaje *m*; (*crossing*) travesía *f*.
vulgar *a* (*coarse*) ordinario,-a; (*in poor taste*) de mal gusto.

W

wad (*of paper*) taco *m*; (*of cotton wool*) bolita *f*; (*of money*) fajo *m*.
waddle *vi* andar como los patos.
wade *vi* caminar por el agua.
wading pool piscina *f* para niños.
wafer barquillo *m*.
wag 1 *vt* menear. 2 *vi* (*tail*) menearse.
wage earner asalariado,-a *mf*.
wages *npl* salario *m sing*.
wagon camión *m*; (*of train*) vagón *m*.
waist cintura *f*.
wait 1 *n* espera *f*; (*delay*) demora *f*. 2 *vi* esperar; **to keep sb waiting** hacer esperar a algn.
• **wait behind** *vi* quedarse.
• **wait up** *vi* **to w. up for sb** esperar a algn levantado,-a.
waiter camarero *m*.
waiting 'no w.' 'prohibido aparcar'.
waiting room sala *f* de espera.
waitress camarera *f*.
wake* 1 *vt* **to w. sb (up)** despertar a algn. 2 *vi* **to w. (up)** despertar(se).
walk 1 *n* (*long*) caminata *m*; (*short*) paseo *m*; **it's an hour's w.** está a una hora de camino; **to go for a w.** dar un paseo. 2 *vt* (*dog*) pasear. 3 *vi*

andar; (to a specific place) ir andando.
- **walk away** vi alejarse.
- **walk in** vi entrar.
- **walk out** vi salir.

walker paseante mf; (in sport) marchador,-a mf.

walking (hiking) excursionismo m.

walking stick bastón m.

Walkman® (pl **Walkmans**) Walkman® m.

wall (exterior) muro m; (interior) pared f.

wallet cartera f.

wallpaper 1 n papel m pintado. **2** vt empapelar.

walnut nuez f.

walrus morsa f.

wander vi (aimlessly) vagar.
- **wander about** vi deambular.

want vt querer; (desire) desear; (need) necesitar; **to w. to do sth** querer hacer algo; **you're wanted on the phone** te llaman al teléfono.

war guerra f; **to be at w.** estar en guerra (**with** con).

ward (of hospital) sala f.

warden (of residence) guardián, -ana mf; **game w.** guarda m de coto.

wardrobe armario m (ropero).

warehouse almacén m.

warm 1 a caliente; (water) tibio,-a; **a w. day** un día de calor; **I am w.** tengo calor; **it is (very) w. today** hoy hace (mucho) calor. **2** vt calentar.
- **warm up 1** vt calentar; (soup) (re)calentar. **2** vi calentarse; (food) (re)calentarse; (person) entrar en calor.

warmth calor m.

warn vt advertir (**about** sobre; **against** contra); **he warned me not to go** me advirtió que no fuera; **to w. sb that . . .** advertir a algn que . . .

warning (of danger) advertencia f; (notice) aviso m.

warning light piloto m.

warship buque m de guerra.

wart verruga f.

was pt of **be**.

wash 1 n **to have a w.** lavarse. **2** vt lavar; (dishes) fregar; **to w. one's hair** lavarse el pelo. **3** vi (have a wash) lavarse.
- **wash away** vt (of sea) llevarse; (traces) borrar.
- **wash off** vi quitarse lavando.
- **wash out 1** vt (stain) quitar lavando. **2** vi quitarse lavando.
- **wash up** vi lavarse rápidamente.

washable a lavable.

washbasin lavabo m.

washcloth manopla f.

washing (action) lavado m; (of clothes) colada f; (dirty) w. ropa f sucia; **to do the w.** hacer la colada.

washing machine lavadora f.

washroom servicios mpl.

wasp avispa f.

waste 1 n (unnecessary use) desperdicio m; (of resources, effort, money) derroche m; (of time) pérdida f; (trash) basura f; **radioactive w.** desechos radioactivos. **2** vt (squander) desperdiciar; (resources) derrochar; (time, chance) perder.

wastebin cubo m de la basura.

waste ground (in town) descampado m.

wastepaper papeles mpl usados.

wastepaper basket papelera f.

watch 1 n reloj m. **2** vt (observe) observar; (keep an eye on) vigilar; (be careful of) tener cuidado con. **3** vi (look) mirar.
- **watch out** vi **w. out!** ¡cuidado!
- **watch out for** vt tener cuidado con; (wait for) esperar.

watchstrap correa f (de reloj).

water 1 n agua f. **2** vt (plants) regar.
- **water down** vt (drink) aguar.

watercolor acuarela f.

watercress berro m.

waterfall cascada f; (very big) catarata f.

watering can regadera *f.*

watermelon sandía *f.*

waterproof *a* (*material*) impermeable; (*watch*) sumergible.

water-skiing esquí *m* acuático.

watertight *a* hermético,-a.

wave 1 *n* (*at sea*) ola *f*; (*in hair, radio*) onda *f*. **2** *vt* agitar; (*brandish*) blandir. **3** *vi* agitar el brazo; **she waved (to me)** (*greeting*) me saludó con la mano; (*goodbye*) se despidió (de mí) con la mano.

wavelength longitud *f* de onda.

wavy *a* ondulado,-a.

wax 1 *n* cera *f*. **2** *vt* encerar.

way *n* (*route, road*) camino *m*; (*distance*) distancia *f*; (*means, manner*) manera *f*; **on the w.** en el camino; **on the w. here** de camino para aquí; **which is the w. to the station?** ¿por dónde se va a la estación?; **w. in** entrada *f*; **w. out** salida *f*; **on the w. back** en el viaje de regreso; **on the w. up/down** en la subida/bajada; **(get) out of the w.!** ¡quítate de en medio!; **you're in the w.** estás estorbando; **come this w.** venga por aquí; **which w. did he go?** ¿por dónde se fue?; **that w.** por allá; **a long w. off** lejos; **do it this w.** hazlo así; **which w. did you do it?** ¿cómo lo hiciste?; **no w.!** ¡ni hablar!

we *pers pron* nosotros,-as.

weak *a* débil; (*team, piece of work, tea*) flojo,-a.

weaken 1 *vt* debilitar; (*argument*) quitar fuerza a. **2** *vi* debilitarse; (*concede ground*) ceder.

weakness debilidad *f*; (*character flaw*) punto *m* flaco.

wealth riqueza *f.*

wealthy *a* rico,-a.

weapon arma *f.*

wear 1 *vt** (*clothes*) llevar (puesto, -a); (*shoes*) calzar; **he wears glasses** lleva gafas. **he was wearing a jacket** llevaba chaqueta. **2** *n* (*deterioration*) desgaste *m*; **normal w. and tear** desgaste *m* natural.

• **wear off** *vi* (*effect, pain*) pasar.

• **wear out 1** *vt* gastar; *fig* (*exhaust*) agotar. **2** *vi* gastarse.

weary *a* (*tired*) cansado,-a.

weasel comadreja *f.*

weather tiempo *m*; **the w. is fine** hace buen tiempo; **to feel under the w.** no encontrarse bien.

weather forecast parte *m* meteorológico.

weave* *vt* tejer; (*intertwine*) entretejer.

web (*of spider*) telaraña *f.*

wedding boda *f.*

wedding ring alianza *f.*

wedge 1 *n* cuña *f*; (*for table leg*) calce *m*. **2** *vt* calzar.

Wednesday miércoles *m.*

weed mala hierba *f.*

week semana *f*; **a w. (ago) today/yesterday** hoy hace/ayer hizo una semana; **a w. today** de aquí a ocho días.

weekday día *m* laborable.

weekend fin *m* de semana; **at** or **on the w.** el fin de semana.

weekly 1 *a* semanal. **2** *adv* semanalmente. **3** *n* (*magazine*) semanario *m.*

weep* *vi* llorar.

weigh *vti* pesar.

weight peso *m*; **to lose w.** adelgazar; **to put on w.** engordar.

weird *a* raro,-a.

welcome 1 *a* (*person*) bienvenido,-a; (*news*) grato,-a; (*change*) oportuno,-a; **to make sb w.** acoger a algn calurosamente; **you're w.!** ¡no hay de qué! **2** *n* (*greeting*) bienvenida *f*. **3** *vt* acoger; (*more formally*) darle la bienvenida a; (*news*) acoger con agrado; (*decision*) aplaudir.

weld *vt* soldar.

welfare (*social security*) seguridad *f* social.

well¹ (*for water*) pozo *m.*

well² **1** *a* (*healthy*) bien; **he's w.** está bien (de salud); **to get w.** reponerse; **all is w.** todo va bien. **2** *adv* (*properly*) bien; **w. done!** ¡muy bien!; **as w.** también; **as w. as**

así como; **children as w. as adults** tanto niños como adultos. **3** *interj* (*surprise*) ¡vaya!; **w., as I was saying** pues (bien), como iba diciendo.

well-behaved *a* (*child*) formal; (*dog*) manso.

wellingtons *npl* botas *fpl* de goma.

well-informed *a* bien informado,-a.

well-known *a* (bien) conocido,-a.

well-mannered *a* educado,-a.

well-off *a* acomodado,-a.

Welsh 1 *a* galés,-esa. **2** *n* (*language*) galés *m*; **the W.** pl los galeses.

Welshman galés *m*.

Welshwoman galesa *f*.

went *pt of* **go**.

were *pt of* **be**.

west 1 *n* oeste *m*; **in** or **to the W.** al oeste. **2** *a* occidental. **3** *adv* al oeste.

westbound *a* (con) dirección oeste.

western 1 *a* del oeste, occidental. **2** *n* (*film*) western *m*.

westward *a* hacia el oeste.

westwards *adv* hacia el oeste.

wet 1 *a* mojado,-a; (*slightly*) húmedo,-a; (*rainy*) lluvioso,-a; '**w. paint**' 'recién pintado'. **2** *vt** mojar.

whale ballena *f*.

wharf (*pl* **wharves**) muelle *m*.

what 1 *a* (*in questions*) qué; **ask her w. color she likes** pregúntale qué color le gusta. **2** *pron* (*in questions*) qué; **w. are you talking about?** ¿de qué estás hablando?; **he asked me w. I thought** me preguntó lo que pensaba; **I didn't know w. to say** no sabía qué decir; **w. about your father?** ¿y tu padre (qué)?; **w. about going tomorrow?** ¿qué te parece si vamos mañana?; **w. did you do that for?** ¿por qué hiciste eso?; **w. (did you say)?** ¿cómo?; **w. is it?** (*definition*) ¿qué es?; **what's the matter?** ¿qué pasa?; **w.'s it called?** ¿cómo se llama?; **w.'s this for?** ¿para qué sirve esto? **3** *interj* **w. a goal!** ¡qué golazo!

whatever 1 *a* **w. day you want** cualquier día que quieras; **of w. color** no importa de qué color; **nothing w.** nada en absoluto; **with no interest w.** sin interés alguno. **2** *pron* (*anything, all that*) (todo) lo que; **do w. you like** haz lo que quieras; **don't tell him w. you do** no se te ocurra decírselo; **w. (else) you find** cualquier (otra) cosa que encuentres.

wheat trigo *m*.

wheel 1 *n* rueda *f*. **2** *vt* (*bicycle*) empujar.

wheelbarrow carretilla *f*.

wheelchair silla *f* de ruedas.

when 1 *adv* cuando; (*in questions*) cuándo; **w. did he arrive?** ¿cuándo llegó?; **tell me w. to go** dime cuándo he de irme; **the days w. I work** los días en que trabajo. **2** *conj* cuando; **I'll tell you w. she comes** te lo diré cuando llegue.

whenever *conj* (*when*) cuando; (*every time*) siempre que.

where *adv* (*in questions*) dónde; (*direction*) adónde; (*at, in which*) donde; (*direction*) adonde; **w. are you going?** ¿adónde vas?; **w. do you come from?** ¿de dónde es usted?; **tell me w. you went** dime adónde fuiste.

whereabouts 1 *adv* **w. do you live?** ¿por dónde vives? **2** *n* paradero *m*.

whereas *conj* (*but, while*) mientras que.

wherever *conj* dondequiera que; **I'll find him w. he is** le encontraré dondequiera que esté; **sit w. you like** siéntate donde quieras.

whether *conj* (*if*) si; **I don't know w. it is true** no sé si es verdad; **I doubt w. he'll win** dudo que gane.

which 1 *a* qué; **w. color do you prefer?** ¿qué color prefieres?; **w. one?** ¿cuál?; **w. way?** ¿por dónde?; **tell me w. dress you like** dime qué vestido te gusta. **2** *pron* (*in questions*) cuál, cuáles; **w. of you did it?** ¿quién de vosotros lo hizo? ▪ (*relative*) que; (*after preposition*) que, el/la que, los/las que; **here are the**

books (w.) I have read aquí están los libros que he leído; **the accident (w.) I told you about** el accidente de que te hablé; **the car in w. he was traveling** el coche en (el) que viajaba; **this is the one (w.) I like** éste es el que me gusta; **I played three sets, all of w. I lost** jugué tres sets, todos los cuales perdí. ■ *(referring to a clause)* lo cual; **he won, w. made me very happy** ganó, lo cual me alegró mucho.

whichever 1 *a* el/la que, cualquiera que; **I'll take w. books you don't want** tomaré los libros que no quieras; **w. system you choose** cualquiera que sea el sistema que elijas. **2** *pron* el que, la que.

while 1 *conj (time)* mientras; *(although)* aunque; *(where-as)* mientras que; **he fell asleep w. driving** se durmió mientras conducía. **2** *n (length of time)* rato *m*; **in a little w.** dentro de poco.

whim capricho *m*.

whine *vi (child)* lloriquear; *(complain)* quejarse.

whip 1 *n (for punishment)* látigo *m*. **2** *vt (as punishment)* azotar; *(cream etc)* batir.

whirl *vi* **to w. (round)** girar con rapidez; *(leaves etc)* arremolinarse.

whisk 1 *n (for cream)* batidor *m*; *(electric)* batidora *f.* **2** *vt (cream etc)* batir.

whiskers *(of cat)* bigotes *mpl.*

whiskey whisky *m.*

whisper 1 *n* susurro *m*. **2** *vt* decir en voz baja. **3** *vi* susurrar.

whistle 1 *n (instrument)* pito *m*; *(sound)* silbido *m*. **2** *vt (tune)* silbar. **3** *vi (person, kettle, wind)* silbar; *(train)* pitar.

white 1 *a* blanco,-a; **to go w.** *(face)* palidecer; *(hair)* encanecer; **w. coffee** café *m* con leche. **2** *n (color, of eye)* blanco *m*; *(of egg)* clara *f.*

whitewash *vt (wall)* blanquear.

whiz(z) *vi (sound)* silbar; **to w. past** pasar volando.

who *pron (in questions) sing* quién;

pl quiénes; **w. are they?** ¿quiénes son?; **w. is it?** ¿quién es?; **I don't know w. did it** no sé quién lo hizo. ■ *rel (defining)* que; *(nondefining)* quien, quienes, el/la cual, los/las cuales; **those w. don't know** los que no saben; **Elena's mother, w. is very rich . . .** la madre de Elena, la cual es muy rica . . .

whoever *pron* quienquiera que; **give it to w. you like** dáselo a quien quieras; **w. you are** quienquiera que seas.

whole 1 *a (entire)* entero,-a; *(in one piece)* intacto,-a; **a w. week** una semana entera; **he took the w. lot** se los llevó todos. **2** *n* **the w. of New York** todo Nueva York; **on the w.** en general.

wholemeal *a* integral.

wholesale *adv* al por mayor.

wholesaler mayorista *mf.*

whom *pron (question)* a quién. ■ *(after preposition)* **of** or **from w.?** ¿de quién? ■ *rel* a quien, a quienes; **those w. I have seen** aquéllos a quienes he visto. ■ *rel (after preposition)* quien, quienes, el/la cual, los/las cuales; **my brothers, both of w. are miners** mis hermanos, que son mineros los dos.

whooping cough tos *f* ferina.

whose 1 *pron* de quién, de quiénes; **w. are these gloves?** ¿de quién son estos guantes? ■ *rel* cuyo(s), cuya(s); **the man w. children we saw** el hombre a cuyos hijos vimos. **2** *a* **w. car/house is this?** ¿de quién es este coche/esta casa?

why *adv* por qué; *(for what purpose)* para qué; **w. did you do that?** ¿por qué hiciste eso?; **w. not go to bed?** ¿por qué no te acuestas?; **I don't know w. he did it** no sé por qué lo hizo; **there's no reason w. you shouldn't go** no hay motivo para que no vayas.

wick mecha *f.*

wicked *a* malvado,-a; *(awful)* malísimo,-a.

wicker 1 *n* mimbre *f.* **2** *a* de mimbre.

wide 1 a (road, trousers) ancho,-a; (area, knowledge, support, range) amplio,-a; **it is ten meters w.** tiene diez metros de ancho. **2** adv **w. awake** completamente despierto,-a; **w. open** abierto,-a de par en par.

widely adv (to travel etc) extensamente.

widen 1 vt ensanchar; (interests) ampliar. **2** vi ensancharse.

widespread a (unrest, belief) general; (damage) extenso,-a.

widow viuda f.

widower viudo m.

width anchura f.

wife (pl wives) esposa f.

wig peluca f.

wild a (animal, tribe) salvaje; (plant) silvestre; (temperament, behavior) alocado,-a; (appearance) desordenado,-a; (passions etc) desenfrenado,-a.

wilderness desierto m.

will¹ 1 n voluntad f; (testament) testamento m; **good/ill w.** buena/mala voluntad; **of my own free w.** por mi propia voluntad; **to make one's w.** hacer testamento. **2** vt **fate willed that . . .** el destino quiso que . . .

will² v aux **they w. come** vendrán; **w. he be there? — yes, he w.** ¿estará allí? — sí, (estará). **you w. or you'll tell him, won't you?** se lo dirás, ¿verdad? **you w. be here at eleven!** ¡debes estar aquí a las once!; **be quiet, w. you! — no, I won't!** ¿quiere callarse? — no quiero; **will you have a drink? — yes, I w.** ¿quiere tomar algo? — sí, por favor.

willing a (obliging) complaciente; **to be w. to do sth** estar dispuesto, -a a hacer algo.

willingly adv de buena gana.

willingness buena voluntad f.

willow w. (tree) sauce m.

win 1 n victoria f. **2** vt* ganar; (prize) llevarse; (victory) conseguir. **3** vi* ganar.

wind¹ viento m; (in stomach) gases mpl.

wind*² 1 vt (onto a reel) enrollar; (clock) dar cuerda a. **2** vi (road, river) serpentear.

• **wind back** vt (film, tape) rebobinar.

• **wind on** vt (film, tape) avanzar.

windmill molino m (de viento).

window ventana f; (of vehicle, of ticket office etc) ventanilla f; **(shop) w.** escaparate m.

window box jardinera f.

window cleaner limpiacristales mf inv.

windowpane cristal m.

windowsill alféizar m.

windshield parabrisas m inv; **w. wiper** limpiaparabrisas m inv.

windsurfing windsurfing m.

windy a **it is very w. today** hoy hace mucho viento.

wine vino m; **w. list** lista f de vinos.

wineglass copa f (para vino).

wing ala f.

wink 1 guiño m. **2** vi (person) guiñar el ojo.

winner ganador,-a mf.

winning a (person, team) ganador,-a; (number) premiado,-a.

winnings npl ganancias fpl.

winter 1 n invierno m. **2** a de invierno.

wipe vt limpiar; **to w. one's feet/ nose** limpiarse los pies/la nariz.

• **wipe away** vt (tear) enjugar.

• **wipe off** vt quitar frotando.

• **wipe out** vt (erase) borrar.

• **wipe up** vi secar los platos.

wiper (in vehicle) limpiaparabrisas m.

wire alambre m; (electric) cable m.

wire mesh/netting tela f metálica.

wiring (of house) instalación f eléctrica.

wise a sabio,-a; **a w. man** un sabio; **it would be w. to keep quiet** sería prudente callarse.

wish 1 n (desire) deseo m (for de); **give your mother my best wishes**

salude a su madre de mi parte; **with best wishes, Peter** (at end of letter) saludos de Peter. 2 vt (want) desear; **I w. I could stay longer me** gustaría poder quedarme más tiempo; **I w. you had told me!** ¡ojalá me lo hubieras dicho!; **to w. for sth** desear algo.

witch bruja f.

with prep con; **the man w. the glasses** el hombre de las gafas; **w. no hat** sin sombrero; **he went w. me/you** fue conmigo/contigo; **he's w. Ford** trabaja para Ford; **to fill a vase w. water** llenar un jarrón de agua; **it is made w. butter** está hecho con mantequilla.

withdraw* 1 vt retirar; (statement) retractarse de; **to w. money from the bank** sacar dinero del banco. 2 vi retirarse; (drop out) renunciar.

wither vi marchitarse.

within prep (inside) dentro de; **w. five kilometers of the town** a menos de cinco kilómetros de la ciudad; **w. the hour** dentro de una hora; **w. the next five years** durante los cinco próximos años.

without prep sin; **w. a coat** sin abrigo; **he did it w. my knowing** lo hizo sin que lo supiera yo.

witness 1 n (person) testigo mf. 2 vt (see) presenciar.

wobbly a poco firme; (table, chair) cojo,-a.

wolf (pl wolves) lobo m.

woman (pl women) mujer f; **old w.** vieja f.

wonder 1 n no w. he hasn't come con razón no ha venido. 2 vt (ask oneself) preguntarse; **I w. why** ¿por qué será? 3 vi **it makes you w.** te da qué pensar.

wonderful a maravilloso,-a.

won't = will not.

wood (forest) bosque m; (material) madera f; (for fire) leña f.

wooden a de madera.

woodwork (craft) carpintería f.

wool lana f.

woolen 1 a de lana. 2 npl **woolens** géneros mpl de lana.

word palabra f; **in other words . . .** es decir . . . ; **I'd like a w. with you** quiero hablar contigo un momento; **words** (of song) letra f.

wording expresión f; **I changed the w. slightly** cambié algunas palabras.

word processing procesamiento m de textos.

word processor procesador m de textos.

wore pt of wear.

work 1 n trabajo m; **his w. in the field of physics** su labor en el campo de la física; **out of w.** parado,-a; **a piece of w.** un trabajo; **a w. of art** una obra de arte; **works** (factory) fábrica f. 2 vt (drive) hacer trabajar; (machine) manejar; (mechanism) accionar. 3 vi trabajar (on, at en); (machine) funcionar; (drug) surtir efecto; (system) funcionar.

• **work out** 1 vt (plan) idear; (problem) solucionar; (solution) encontrar; (amount) calcular. 2 vi (train) hacer ejercicio; **it works out to 5 each** sale a 5 cada uno.

worked up a **to get worked up** excitarse.

worker trabajador,-a mf; (manual) obrero,-a mf.

working a (population, capital) activo,-a; **w. class** clase obrera; **it is in w. order** funciona.

workman (manual) obrero m.

workout entrenamiento m.

workshop taller m.

workstation estación f de trabajo.

world 1 n mundo m; **all over the w.** en todo el mundo. 2 a (record, war) mundial; **w. champion** campeón, -ona mf mundial; **The W. Cup** el Mundial m.

worm lombriz f.

worn a gastado,-a.

worn-out a (thing) gastado,-a; (person) agotado,-a.

worry 1 vt preocupar. 2 vi preocu-

parse (**about** por); **don't w.** no te
preocupes. **3** *n* inquietud *f*; **my
main w.** mi principal preocupación.
worrying *a* preocupante.
worse *a & adv* peor; **to get w.** empeorar; **w. than ever** peor que
nunca.
worsen *vti* empeorar.
worship *vt* adorar.
worst 1 *a & adv* peor; **the w. part
about it is that . . .** lo peor es que
. . . **2** *n* (*person*) el/la peor, los/las
peores.
worth 1 *a* a house w. $50,000 una
casa que vale 50,000 dólares; **a
book w. reading** un libro que merece la pena leer; **how much is it
w.?** ¿cuánto vale?; **it's w. your
while, it's w. it** vale la pena. **2** *n* valor *m*; **five dollars' w. of gas** gasolina por valor de 5 dólares.
worthy *a* (*deserving*) digno,-a (**of**
de).
would *v aux* (*conditional*) **I w. go if
I had time** iría si tuviera tiempo;
he w. have won but for that habría
ganado si no hubiera sido por eso.
▪ (*willingness*) **w. you do me a favor?** ¿quiere hacerme un favor? **w.
you like a cigarette?** ¿quiere un
cigarrillo?; **the car wouldn't start**
el coche no arrancaba. ▪ (*custom*)
we w. go for walks solíamos dar
paseos.
wound 1 *n* herida *f*. **2** *vt* herir.
wrap *vt* envolver.
▪ **wrap up 1** *vt* envolver. **2** *vi* **w. up
well!** ¡abrígate!
wrapper (*of sweet*) envoltorio *m*.
wrapping paper papel *m* de envolver.
wreath (*pl* **wreaths**) (*of flowers*) corona *f*.
wreck 1 *n* (*sinking*) naufragio *m*;
(*ship*) barco *m* naufragado; (*of car,
plane*) restos *mpl*. **2** *vt* (*car, machine*) destrozar; (*holiday*) estropear.
wrench (*tool*) llave.

wrestle *vi* luchar.
wrestler luchador,-a *mf*.
wrestling lucha *f*.
wring* *vt* (*clothes*) escurrir.
wrinkle arruga *f*.
wrist muñeca *f*.
wristwatch reloj *m* de pulsera.
write* *vti* escribir (**about** sobre); **to
w. sb** escribira.
▪ **write back** *vi* contestar.
▪ **write down** *vt* poner por escrito;
(*note*) apuntar.
▪ **write off for** *vt* pedir por escrito.
▪ **write out** *vt* (*check*) extender;
(*recipe*) escribir.
write-protected *a* protegido,-a
contra escritura.
writer (*by profession*) escritor,-a
mf; (*of book, letter*) autor,-a *mf*.
writing (*script*) escritura *f*; (*handwriting*) letra *f*; **in w.** por escrito.
writing paper papel *m* de escribir.
wrong 1 *a* (*erroneous*) incorrecto,
-a; (*unsuitable*) inadecuado,-a;
(*time*) inoportuno,-a; (*not right*)
(*person*) equivocado,-a; (*immoral
etc*) malo,-a; **my watch is w.** mi reloj anda mal; **to go the w. way** equivocarse de camino; **I was w. about
that boy** me equivoqué con ese
chico; **to be w.** no tener razón;
what's w. with smoking? ¿qué
tiene de malo fumar? **what's w.
with you?** ¿qué te pasa? **2** *adv* mal;
to get it w. equivocarse; **to go w.**
(*plan*) salir mal. **3** *n* (*evil, bad action*) mal *m*; **you were w.** to hit him
hiciste mal en pegarle; **to be in the
w.** tener la culpa.
wrongly *adv* (*incorrectly*) incorrec-
tamente.

X

Xmas *abbr of* **Christmas** Navidad *f*.
X-ray 1 *n* (*picture*) radiografía *f*; **to
have an X.** hacerse una radiogra-
fía. **2** *vt* radiografiar.

Y

yacht yate *m*.
yard¹ (*measure*) yarda *f* (*aprox 0,914 metros*).
yard² patio *m*.; jardín *m*.; (*of school*) patio *m* (de recreo).
yarn hilo *m*.
yawn 1 *vi* bostezar. **2** *n* bostezo *m*.
year año *m*.; (*at school*) curso *m*.; **I'm ten years old** tengo diez años.
yearly *a* anual.
yeast levadura *f*.
yell 1 *vi* gritar (**at** a). **2** *n* grito *m*.
yellow *a & n* amarillo,-a (*m*).
yes *adv* sí.
yesterday *adv* ayer; **the day before y.** anteayer; **y. morning** ayer por la mañana.
yet 1 *adv* **not y.** todavía no; **as y.** hasta ahora; **I haven't eaten y.** no he comido todavía. ▪ (*in questions*) ya; **has he arrived y.?** ¿ha venido ya? **2** *conj* (*nevertheless*) sin embargo.
yogurt yogur *m*.
yolk yema *f*.
you *pers pron* (*subject*) (*familiar use*) (*sing*) tú; (*pl*) vosotros,-as; (*polite use*) (*sing*) usted; (*pl*) ustedes; **how are y.?** ¿cómo estás?, ¿cómo estáis? ▪ (*object*) (*familiar use*) (*sing*) (*before verb*) te; (*after preposition*) ti; (*pl*) (*before verb*) os; (*after preposition*) vosotros,-as; **I saw y.** te vi, os vi; **with y.** contigo, con vosotros,-as. ▪ (*object*) (*polite use*) (*sing*) (*before verb*) le; (*after preposition*) usted; (*pl*) (*before verb*) les; (*after preposition*) ustedes; **I saw y.** le vi, les vi; **with y.** con usted, con ustedes. ▪ (*subject*) (*impers use*) **y. never know** nunca se sabe.
young 1 *a* joven; (*brother etc*) pequeño,-a. **2** *n* **the y.** los jóvenes *mpl*.; (*animals*) las crías *fpl*.
youngster muchacho,-a *mf*.
your *poss adj* (*familiar use*) (*re-*

ferring to one person) tu, tus; (*referring to more than one person*) vuestro,-a, vuestros,-as. ▪ (*polite use*) su, sus. ▪ (*impers use*) **the house is on y. right** la casa queda a la derecha; **they clean y. shoes for you** te limpian los zapatos.
yours *poss pron* (*familiar use*) (*referring to one person*) el tuyo, la tuya, los tuyos, las tuyas; (*referring to more than one person*) el vuestro, la vuestra, los vuestros, las vuestras; **the house is y.** la casa es tuya. ▪ (*polite use*) el suyo, la suya; (*pl*) los suyos, las suyas; **the house is y.** la casa es suya.
yourself (*pl* **yourselves**) **1** *pers pron* (*familiar use*) *sing* tú mismo,-a; *pl* vosotros,-as mismos, -as; **by y.** (tú) solo; **by yourselves** vosotros,-as solos,-as. ▪ (*polite use*) *sing* usted mismo,-a; *pl* ustedes mismos,-as; **by y.** (usted) solo,-a; **by yourselves** (ustedes) solos,-as. **2** *reflexive pron* **did you wash y.?** (*familiar use*) *sing* ¿te lavaste?; *pl* ¿os lavasteis?; (*polite use*) *sing* ¿se lavó?, *pl* ¿se lavaron?
youth juventud *f*.; (*young man*) joven *m*.
youth club club *m* juvenil.
Yugoslav *a & n* yugoslavo,-a (*mf*).

Z

zebra cebra *f*.
zero cero *m*.
zigzag 1 *n* zigzag *m*. **2** *vi* zigzaguear.
zip *n* **z. (fastener)** cremallera *f*.
▪ **zip up** *vt* subir la cremallera de.
ZIP code código *m* postal.
zipper cremallera *f*.
zit *fam* (*pimple*) espinilla *f*.
zone zona *f*.
zoo zoo *m*.
zucchini calabacín *m*.